SURREALISM, POLITICS AND CULTURE

Published by
Ashgate Publishing Limited
Gower House
Croft Road
Aldershot
Hants GU11 3HR
England

Ashgate Publishing Company
Suite 420
101 Cherry Street
Burlington, VT 05401-4405
USA

Ashgate website: http://www.ashgate.com

British Library Cataloguing in Publication Data
Surrealism, politics and culture. - (Studies in European cultural transition)
1.Surrealism - History 2.Surrealism - Political aspects
3.Politics and culture
I.Spiteri, Raymond II.LaCoss, Donald
700.4'1163

Library of Congress Cataloging-in-Publication Data
Surrealism, politics and culture / edited by Raymond Spiteri and Donald LaCoss.
p. cm -- (Studies in European cultural transition)
Includes bibliographical references and index.
ISBN 0-7546-0989-8 (alk. paper)
1. Surrealism--Europe 2. Arts, European--20th century. 3. Arts--Europe--Political aspects. I. Spiteri, Raymond. II. LaCoss, Donald. III. Series.

NX542 .S865 2003
700'.41163--dc21

2002032609

ISBN 0 7546 0989 8

This book is printed on acid-free paper
Typeset by MHL Production Services Ltd, Coventry
Printed and bound in Great Britain by MPG Books, Bodmin, Cornwall

Surrealism, Politics and Culture

Edited by
Raymond Spiteri and Donald LaCoss

Studies in European Cultural Transition

Volume Sixteen

General Editors: Martin Stannard and Greg Walker

ASHGATE

Contents

General Editors' Preface

The European dimension of research in the humanities has come into sharp focus over recent years, producing scholarship which ranges across disciplines and national boundaries. This series provides a major channel for this work and unites the fields of cultural studies and traditional scholarship. It will publish in the areas of European history and literature, art history, archaeology, language and translation studies, political, cultural and gay studies, music, psychology, sociology and philosophy. The emphasis is explicitly European and interdisciplinary, concentrating attention on the relativity of cultural perspectives, with a particular interest in issues of cultural transition.

Martin Stannard
Greg Walker
University of Leicester

List of Illustrations

Schoenborn and Samuel A. Marx

Fig. 20. Joan Miró, *Still Life with Old Shoe*, Paris, 24 January–29 May 1937. Oil on canvas, 81.3 × 116.8 cm. The Museum of Modern Art, New York. Gift of James Thrall Soby

Fig. 21. Joan Miró, *Painting*, 1933. Oil on canvas, 174 × 196.2 cm. The Museum of Modern Art, New York. Loula D. Lasker Bequest (by exchange)

Fig. 22. Joan Miró, Preparatory sketch for *Still Life with Old Shoe*, 1937. Pencil on newspaper, 7.5 × 12.7 cm. Fundació Joan Miró, Barcelona

Fig. 23. Joan Miró, *The Family*, 1924. Black and red chalk on emery paper, 74.1 × 104 cm. The Museum of Modern Art, New York. Gift of Mr and Mrs Jan Mitchell

Fig. 24. Joan Miró, *Femme*, October 1934. Pastel on velours paper, 107 × 72 cm. Private collection, New York

Fig. 25. Balthus Klossowski, *Still Life*, 1937. Oil on wood, 81 × 99 cm. Wadsworth Atheneum, Hartford, Connecticut. The Ella Gallup Sumner and Mary Catlin Sumner Fund

Fig. 26. Joan Miró, *Table with Glove*, 1921. Oil on canvas, 116.8 × 89.5 cm. The Museum of Modern Art, New York. Gift of Armand G. Erpf

Fig. 27. Joan Miró, *Help Spain* [*Aidez l'Espagne*], 1937, from *Cahiers d'Art*, vol. 12, nos 4–5. Pochoir printed in color, composition 24.8 × 19.4 cm. The Museum of Modern Art. Gift of Pierre Matisse

Fig. 28. Joan Miró, *The Reaper (Catalan Peasant in Revolt)*, 1937. Oil on celotex panels, 550 × 365 cm. Work disappeared

Fig. 29. Joan Miró, Preparatory drawing for *Help Spain*, 1937. Pencil on pasteboard, 11.5 × 9.5 cm. Fundació Joan Miró, Barcelona

Fig. 30. Joan Miró, Study related to *The Tilled Field*, 1923–24. Paper, 19.1 × 16.5 cm. Fundació Joan Miró, Barcelona

Fig. 31. Carles Fontseré, *Libertat!* Poster for the FAI, 1936. Biblioteca Nacional, Madrid

Fig. 32. Jacint Bofarull, *Obrer! Camperol! Unitat per la victoria!* Poster for the FAI/CNT, 1936. Biblioteca Nacional, Madrid

Fig. 33. Salvador Dalí, *Le Mythe tragique de l'Angélus de Millet, Interprétation 'paranoïque-critique'* (Paris: Jean Jacques Pauvert, 1963), front cover

Fig. 34. Postcard reproduced in Salvador Dalí, 'Posició moral del surrealisme', *Hèlix*, no. 10 (22 March 1930), p. 6

Fig. 35. Acme News Agency, Untitled photograph of Salvador Dalí and Gala

List of Contributors

Jonathan P. Eburne teaches in the English Department at the University of Tennessee. He received his PhD in Comparative Literature from the University of Pennsylvania. He has published articles on Surrealism, Marcel Duchamp, Raymond Chandler, and William Burroughs, and his current book project is entitled *Surrealism and the Art of Crime*.

Elena Filipovic is a doctoral candidate in Art History at Princeton University completing a study on Marcel Duchamp and the museum-archive. Recent publications include *Duchamp on Display*, to accompany the exhibition she curated for the Zabriskie Gallery, as well as contributions to *Puppen, Korper, Automaten* (Cologne: Octagon, 1999), *Artpress* and *Frieze*.

Robin Adèle Greeley is Assistant Professor of Latin American Art History at the University of Connecticut. She is author of the forthcoming book, *Organizing Pessimism: Surrealism, Politics and the Spanish Civil War*. She is currently working on a second book, concerning gender and Mexican cultural nationalism, 1920–1970.

Donald LaCoss is currently preparing a manuscript on revolutionary defeatism and anarchism in French surrealism from 1934 to 1945. He works with the Chicago surrealist group and teaches history in western Wisconsin.

Robert S. Lubar is Professor of Fine Arts at New York University's Institute of Fine Arts. His forthcoming book, *Divided Landscapes: Painting and Politics in Spain, 1898–1936*, will be published by Yale University Press.

Amy Lyford is Assistant Professor of Art History at Occidental College in Los Angeles. Her publications include essays on Lee Miller's photography (*History of Photography*, 1994), and surrealism's 'aesthetics of dismemberment' (*Cultural Critique*, 2000). She is currently completing a book entitled *Body Parts: Surrealism and the Reconstruction of Masculinity*.

Alyce Mahon is Lecturer in History of Art and Fellow of Trinity College at the University of Cambridge. Her PhD dissertation, 'Surrealism and the Politics of Eros in Post-war France, 1944–68' (Courtauld Institute, 1999), has led to published essays on André Masson, Hans Bellmer, Unica Zürn, Pierre Klossowski and Jean-Jacques Lebel, and an essay on the surrealist exhibition in *Surrealism: Desire Unbound* (Tate, 2001). Forthcoming publications include *Pierre Klossowksi: Decadence of the Nude* (Blackdog Press, 2002) and *Eroticism and Art* (Oxford University Press, 2003).

Jordana Mendelson teaches at the University of Illinois, Urbana-Champaign. She has published widely on early twentieth-century Spanish art, especially photography, film and print media. Her current research focuses on the Surrealists and their collection, appropriation, and creation of postcards. She guest edited 'From Albums to the Academy: Postcards and Art History,' *Visual Resources* (2001).

Theresa Papanikolas received her PhD in Art History from the University of Delaware. Her work on the cultural politics of Dada and Surrealism includes *Anarchism Between the Wars: The Cultural Politics of Paris Dada*, under consideration by Cambridge University Press. Currently, she is an editor in the publications department at the Museum of Fine Arts, Houston.

E. San Juan, Jr. is a fellow of the Center for the Humanities, and visiting Professor of English, Wesleyan University. His recent books are *Beyond Postcolonial Theory* (Palgrave), *From Exile To Diaspora* (Westview), *After Postcolonialism* (Rowman & Littlefield) and *Racism and Cultural Studies* (Duke University Press). Two forthcoming works are *Spinoza and the Terror of Racism* (Sheffield Hallam University Press) and *Passages From/To the Multitude: Alternative Routes in Cultural Studies*. He helps edit several journals, among them *Nature Society and Thought*, *Left Curve*, *Amerasia*, and *Working Papers in Cultural Studies, Race and Ethnicity*.

Robert Short teaches at the University of East Anglia. He is the author of numerous articles on Surrealism and its environs. His books include *Surrealism: Permanent Revelation* (with Roger Cardinal; Studio Vista, 1970); *Dada and Surrealism* (Chartwell Books, 1980) and *Hans Bellmer* (with Peter Webb; Quartet, 1985). Forthcoming is *The Age of Gold: Surrealist Cinema* (Creation Books). Under contract with Yale University Press is *Surrealism and Its Adversaries*. Robert Short makes collages and has been a filmmaker and instigator of happenings.

Raymond Spiteri is Assistant Professor of Art History at the University of North Dakota. He received his PhD from the University of Western Australia and is currently working on a study of the Breton-Bataille polemic.

Amanda Stansell is a doctoral candidate in the department of English at the University of Wisconsin, Madison. She is currently completing her dissertation, 'The Surrealists' Legacy: "Collage Politics," Anti-Colonialism and Anti-Fascism in 1930's Experimental Fiction', which examines novels by Samuel Beckett, Stevie Smith, Virginia Woolf and Gertrude Stein in the context of interwar aesthetic and political discourses.

M. Stone-Richards is Visiting Assistant Professor in English and Comparative Literature, Stonehill College. He has taught in art history and comparative literature at Northwestern University. Working between philosophical poetics and modern/contemporary art cultural studies, he has most recently published on Guy Debord (*Pleine Marge*, no. 34, 2001), the problem of place in Surrealist experience (*Equinoxe: Revue internationale d'études française* no. 22, Fall 2002) and 'Depression and the Logic of Separation', *Journal of Visual Culture*, vol. 2, no. 1, April 2003. His current research encompasses Debord, Chantal Akerman, Marina Abramovic and the Haitian poet Rene Belance.

Acknowledgments

A project like this requires much unacknowledged work from all involved. At the outset neither Don nor myself knew what to expect, and we were pleasantly surprised by the overwhelming positive response to the initial call for papers and the ongoing support from colleagues in the field. In particular I would like to thank Robert Short and Robert Lubar for their generous aid. Thanks also to all the contributors for their patience with my pedantic editorial questions. I trust the volume is better for my persistence. I would also like to thank Erika Gaffney, our editor at Ashgate, for guiding this project to completion.

This project assumed form during my tenure as an Honorary Research Fellow at the School of Architecture and Fine Arts at the University of Western Australia in 1999–2001. I would like to thank Patrick Beale, Clarissa Ball, Richard Read, Simon Anderson and Elizabeth Oliver at the SAFA for their support and advice. Thanks also to David Bromfield for deepening my interest in Surrealism, and Stephanie Green for all her encouragement.

Finally I would like to thank Melissa McDougall for her enduring love and friendship.

Raymond Spiteri

I deeply thank Susan Crutchfield; Franklin and Penelope Rosemont; Julie Herrada, curator of the University of Michigan's Labadie Collection; and especially Raymond Spiteri, whose contagious vision and enthusiasm made this project possible.

Donald LaCoss

List of Abbreviations

AEAR	Association des écrivains et artistes révolutionnaires
AER	Association des écrivains révolutionnaires
CFLN	Comité français de libération nationale
CGT	Confédération générale du travail
CNT	Confederación Nacional del Trabajo
CTM	Confederación de Trabajadores Mexicanos
FAI	Federación Anarquista Ibérica
FIARI	Fédération internationale de l'art révolutionnaire indépendant
LRS	*La Révolution surréaliste*
LSASDLR	*Le Surréalisme au service de la révolution*
PCF	Parti communiste français
POI	Parti Ouvrier International
POUM	Partido Obrero de Unificación Marxista
RAPP	Association of Proletarian Writers
UIER	Union internationale des écrivains révolutionnaires

Introduction

Revolution by Night: Surrealism, Politics and Culture

Raymond Spiteri and Donald LaCoss

We begin with an example of what is perhaps the Surrealists' first significant intervention into the intricate nexus of culture and politics: the Saint-Pol-Roux banquet of 2 July 1925. What began as a cultured dinner party in Montparnasse organized by the *Mercure de France* to honour the ageing Symbolist poet, Saint-Pol-Roux, ended with Surrealists being arrested, condemned by the press, and threatened with violent right-wing reprisals. This event and the ensuing controversy not only alienated the Surrealists from other guests at the banquet and reinforced Surrealism's oppositional stance against the European cultural mainstream, but it also marked 'Surrealism's final break with all conformist elements of the time', and signalled Surrealism's decisive turn towards Communism.[1]

Saint-Pol-Roux was one of the few living poets the Surrealists held in high regard (admired primarily for his earliest work), and it was out of gratitude for this support that the poet had invited the Surrealists to attend his tribute.[2] The Surrealists, however, decided to use the opportunity to agitate. On the day of the banquet, the newspaper of the Parti communiste français (PCF) *Humanité* and the socialist journal *Clarté* published a collective declaration written by Henri Barbusse and signed by 17 Surrealists.[3] The statement was an outraged response to a militaristic statement that had appeared throughout the nation that had been signed by members of the French literary, artistic, academic and scientific

1 André Breton, *Conversation: The Autobiography of Surrealism with André Parinaud and Others*, trans. Mark Polizzotti (New York: Marlowe, 1993), p. 89.

2 The Surrealists had published an 'Hommage à Saint-Pol-Roux' in May 1925. See *Tracts surréalistes et déclarations collectives, 1922–1939*, vol. 1, ed. José Pierre (Paris: Le Terrain vague, 1980), pp. 41–49.

3 'Les Travailleurs intellectuels aux côté du prolétariat contre la guerre du Maroc', *Humanité*, 2 July 1925. The declaration was signed by 57 individuals associated with the reviews *Clarté*, *Philosophies*, *Humanité* and *La Révolution surréaliste*. The Surrealists who signed were Aragon, Boiffard, Breton, Crevel, Desnos, Eluard, Gerard, Leiris, Lübeck, Malkine, Masson, Morise, Noll, Péret, Soupault, Tual and Vitrac. Alexandre and Artaud added their signatures when the declaration was republished in *Clarté*, no. 76 (15 July 1925). This version, entitled 'Appel aux travailleurs intellectuels: oui ou non, condamnez-vous la guerre?', is reprinted in *Tracts surréalistes*, pp. 51–53.

community in support of Franco-Spanish colonial intervention against the indigenous Riff fighters in Morocco.[4]

Later that day the Surrealists collected from the printers copies of their latest collective tract, an open letter to the French ambassador to Japan, Paul Claudel.[5] Printed on red paper stock, the letter was a reply to an interview that the ultra-Catholic poet-turned-diplomat had given to an Italian Fascist newspaper (later reprinted in *Comœdia*) wherein Claudel bragged of his place in the French cultural firmament, and vaunted his patriotic activity during the war when he travelled to South America to purchase wheat, preserved meat and lard for the French army. Claudel also sized up the Dada and Surrealist movements with a haughty judicial eye, pronouncing that they had nothing to offer European civilization other than 'pederasty'.[6] Even before the interview, Claudel represented everything the Surrealists despised – he was a conservative poet who had advanced a Catholic interpretation of Rimbaud's life and writings, and loyally served the interests of the French ruling class as ambassador – so his comments provided the Surrealists with the chance to denounce him as a dangerous fraud. The Surrealists' retort stated categorically that patriotism and the purchase of 'large quantities of lard' for the 'upkeep of a nation of pigs and dogs' was incompatible with poetry; in fact, 'treason and all that can undermine the security of State' was far more poetic than anything that Claudel could produce. As for Claudel's homophobic comments regarding Surrealism, the authors of the open letter simply said that, to the mind of 'a pedant and a swine' who proudly supported the 'infamous sanctimoniousness' of a Western civilization, the comparison of Surrealism to pederasty was apt because of the swirling haze of 'confusion it introduces into the minds of those who do not take part in it'.[7] The Surrealists decided to distribute the tract at the banquet that night, leaving a copy under each place setting to greet the guests when they arrived.

The Claudel tract set the evening's tone. The majority of the guests – a cross-section of the Parisian literary world – did not know how to respond to the letter or the presence of its authors. To further compound matters, the Surrealists had

---

4 Ibid.

5 Collective tract with 28 signatures, 'Lettre ouverte à M. Paul Claudel, ambassadeur de France au Japon', rpd in *Tracts surréalistes*, pp. 49–50. Claudel's interview with Aldo Sorani for *Secolo* appeared as 'Une interview de Paul Claudel à Florence' in *Comœdia* (24 June 1925), p. 3. Marguerite Bonnet has noted that *Le Journal littéraire* printed the letter on 4 July 1925, along with a sharp article called 'Sur une lettre à M. Paul Claudel' that singled out the signatories who were German, Russian and *apatride* and went on to 'expose' the 'hand of Moscow' pulling the Surrealists' puppet strings. See Bonnet's commentary in *Tracts surréalistes*, p. 392.

6 Claudel cited ibid., p. 49.

7 One can only imagine what Claudel would have said had he known of the centrality of sodomy to both Hellenism and Christianity, as we have learned in the 75 years since these remarks were made.

other grievances with Madame Rachilde (*née* Marguerite Eymery) and Aurélien-Marie Lugné-Poe (a former Symbolist dramatist and anarchist sympathizer who had worked for French military counter-intelligence during World War I), both of whom were seated at the table of honour. Rachilde had recently stated that it was not possible for a French woman to marry a German, a comment she repeated at the banquet. This comment was ill-received by the Surrealists; Breton reminded Rachilde that his friend Max Ernst, a German national, was present at the banquet, and then proceeded to insult her. Saint-Pol-Roux looked on helplessly as the room erupted: the Surrealists exchanged blows with other guests amid shouts of 'Long Live Germany!', 'Victory to the Riff!', 'Hail the workers' paradise!', and 'Hurrah for China!'; Philippe Soupault knocked over plates on the tables while swinging from the chandelier; and the passing crowd attempted to lynch Michel Leiris after he began shouting seditious comments from a window overlooking boulevard Montparnasse. Leiris was arrested and beaten severely while in police custody for his efforts.[8]

It is no exaggeration to say that the events around the Saint-Pol-Roux banquet mark an important turning point in the history of the Surrealist movement. This was not just an aesthetic spat between generations of writers over poetic style; rather, this was subversion of a social, political and cultural nature. The Surrealists' proto-Guevaraist hopes that the Moroccan War would undermine European society, their condemnation of Claudel as a reactionary and apologist for values that they found despicable, the anti-French fury of the Saint-Pol-Roux fracas – all of this was more than a tiff over how to paint or what kind of poems to read. It was nothing less than an assault on 'civilization' itself, an assault that elicited a strong political reaction: *Action française* led the offensive, suggesting that the press greet the Surrealists' works with a conspiracy of silence, and even campaigned for their expulsion from France.[9] Clearly, the concerns of Surrealist activity exceeded the bounds of cultural field, and after 2 July 1925, Surrealism could no longer be considered simply another avant-garde artistic or literary 'ism'.[10]

---

8 This account is based on a number of sources: Maurice Nadeau, *The History of Surrealism*, trans. Richard Howard (Harmondsworth: Penguin, 1973), pp. 122–25; Breton, *Conversations*, pp. 87–89; 'Déclaration des surréalistes à propos du banquet Saint-Pol-Roux', *Tracts surréalistes*, pp. 53–54 and Marguerite Bonnet's commentary, pp. 396–97, which cites contemporary newspaper accounts of the riot.

9 For a detailed analysis of the reaction in the press to the Saint-Pol-Roux banquet see Elyette Guiol-Benassaya, *La Presse face au Surréalisme de 1925 à 1938* (Paris: CNRS, 1982).

10 Surrealism was not unique in divining a link between creative endeavour and politics. The relation between culture and politics had been a concern of the avant-garde since Symbolism of the late nineteenth century, and more recently in the programmes of Futurism, Dada and the Russian avant-garde. Nor was Surrealism the first movement to systematically seek to establish a political position, which was also characteristic of Italian Futurism and the Russian avant-garde, but the longevity of Surrealism has allowed more nuanced articulation of the relation between culture and politics.

By 1925, the Surrealists were making it clear that not only was a revolution needed, but if it was going to succeed, its effects could not be limited to art schools or creative writing workshops. The conventions of consensual reality maintained by the patriarchal, white, Christian establishment in Western Europe had robbed people of their ability to imagine alternatives and wild possibilities by denigrating perception, desire, instinct and intuition. As Théodore Fraenkel said about the Surrealists' revolutionary agenda in 1936, their target was both capitalism and the middle classes, since 'in the bourgeoisie everything is false because it only allows for a disfigured life – narrow, painful, horrible'; it is 'mean and heartless', it 'lacks intelligence' and 'envisages nothing but what is given, the scientific', thereby polluting ethics, education and expression with toxic myths of family values, religion, fatherland, war and colonialism.[11] Herbert Marcuse has identified 'the surrealistic effort' as one that asserts that there are forces operating in the world '[with] which we refuse to come to grips. We are subject not only to the causality of reason, as explored in the natural sciences and in common sense, but also to "irrational," surreal or subreal (in terms of accepted rationality) forces'. In tackling this cultural repression, Surrealism provides 'more than a mere enlargement of our perception, imagination, reason'; it is also a project for the 'restructuring and redirection of the mental faculties [...] to undo the mutilation of our faculties by the established society and its requirements'.[12]

There could be no better support for Fraenkel's and Marcuse's observations than the mechanized carnage of the European war of 1914 or the rationalized murder at Auschwitz and Hiroshima during World War II. To prevent further calamities, the poisonously narrow and limiting conditions of life under the bourgeoisie needed to be dismantled by braiding together the complexities of individual revolt and the many-headed beast of collective rebellion – social realities had to be recovered in all their intensity and transformed into deeper, higher and *more real* levels of reality by delivering the means of production (material and mental) into the hands of the most exploited peoples. In the late 1880s, it was the anarchists and revolutionary syndicalists of Italy, Spain, France, Germany, Russia and the US who had pointed the way towards a catastrophic strategy that would break with the tired, rotten and terrifying historical traditions and institutions of the urban-industrial capitalist juggernaut; after October 1917, one would be guided by the red star that had risen over the Soviet Union. To European observers, Lenin had reinvented everyday life in Russia, thus affiliation with Communism seemed to be the necessary first step to the Surrealist revolution, and those who were uncomfortable with this more

11 See Appendix I of this volume, Théodore Fraenkel, 'Notes in the Hand of Léon Pierre-Quint Being the Record of a Conversation', pp. 337–340.

12 Letter from Herbert Marcuse to Franklin Rosemont (12 October 1972), rpd as 'Letters to Chicago Surrealists', in *Arsenal: Surrealist Subversion*, no. 4 (1989), p. 40.

explicit political position soon distanced themselves from the movement. But that does not mean that the Surrealists' revolutionary ambitions were strictly confined to participation in the PCF. In the 1920s, the Surrealists explored Leninist-Marxism because of 'what was then understood to be the triumph of the Russian Revolution and the dawning of a Workers' State', and when the USSR revealed itself to be a place 'where the most servile kind of obedience is expected, where the most basic of human rights are rejected, and where all social life orbits around the policeman and the state executioner', the Surrealists became strident anti-Stalinists.[13] By the end of the Spanish Civil War, they found themselves more openly aligned with Trotskyists and anarchists; after World War II, when it was immediately apparent that Stalinist state-capitalism and American Marshall Plan market expansion were as threatening to humanity as fascism had been in the 1930s, the Surrealists collaborated with anarcho-communists, anti-imperialists, internationalists and other movements committed to radical freedom.

* * *

All too frequently, previous discussions of the politics of Surrealism have been devoted to the brief period during which the Surrealists were card-carrying members of the PCF (for a few months in 1927, though the period is often incorrectly said to span the years between 1925 and 1933), with occasionally some brief mention of the Surrealist recruitment of Trotsky in 1938. The majority of these histories claim that Surrealist interest in politics faded after 1935, and that the movement itself faded into obscurity during the mid-1940s, eclipsed by the accomplishments of the postwar existentialist *literati* and the rise of Abstract Expressionism in New York.[14] However, this is simply not the case: since 1919, the Surrealists have responded to the partitioning of lived experience with a double strategy: the first stage unmasked the depth of alienation inherent in modern society, and the second move reintegrated splintered life by a fusion of the conscious and unconscious mind. Consequently, the interior realities of the individual were given the same value as the collective forms of the social. One could dispel alienation by restlessly exposing, disassembling, and

---

13 André Breton, 'La Claire tour', *Le Libertaire* (11 January 1952), p. 3.

14 The pattern is established in 1944 by Nadeau, *Histoire du surréalisme* (Paris: Seuil, 1944); Robert Short, 'The Politics of Surrealism, 1920–36', *Journal of Contemporary History* I:3 (September 1966), pp. 3–25, rpd as Chapter 1 here; Helena Lewis, *The Politics of Surrealism* (New York: Paragon House, 1988); Alan Rose, *Surrealism and Communism: The Early Years* (New York: Peter Lang, 1991). Needless to say, the French reception of Surrealism has been more complex; see in particular the invaluable study by Carole Reynaud Paligot, *Parcours politique des Surréalistes, 1919–1969* (Paris: CNRS, 1995). The writings of Louis Janover and Michael Löwy are also valuable here.

rebuilding morality, knowledge, aspiration and desire; Surrealist politics sought to maximize the disruptive forces unleashed by the quest to recover the lost potential of human experience, encouraging a heightened awareness of how the centuries of repressive ideology had whittled away at absolute human liberty. Armed with Rimbaud's 'derangement of the senses', Marx's 'emancipation of the senses', and Freud's dissection of bourgeois sensibility, the Surrealists launched a campaign of personal and political deconstruction that would restore free play between internal and external reality, subjectivity and objectivity, representation and perception, and dream and action.

One can see this easily in the fact that no Anglo-American scholar has followed through on the implicit terms of political engagement from the first pages of the first *Manifesto of Surrealism*. The definition of Surrealism as 'psychic automatism in its pure state' has overshadowed a full consideration of the *Manifesto*, but it is clear that the practice of automatism embodied an experience of freedom that contained profound ethical import for the Surrealists.[15] Indeed, automatism was the means to actualize an experience of freedom, a way of asserting what Breton describes as 'our complete *nonconformism*'.[16] Breton based his argument in the *Manifesto* on a critique of the model of human agency that prevailed in bourgeois society. The basic flaw with this model was that it limited the scope of human behaviour to acts that conformed to an arbitrary model of rational action and which encouraged a thoroughly pragmatic approach to life. Yet rationality foreclosed the possibility of imaginative engagement with the full compass of human experience. Unlike the child, for whom the imagination 'knows no bounds', in the adult the imagination was 'allowed to be exercised only in strict accordance with the laws of an arbitrary utility'.[17] In this way the imaginative liberty of childhood was subordinated to the arbitrary authority of culture.

Breton affirmed the 'unsparing quality' of the imagination as an alternative to this impoverished existence, particularly the imagination's fanatical access to freedom, and hence its potential as an agency for human emancipation:

> The mere word 'freedom' is the only one that still excites me. I deem it capable of indefinitely sustaining the old human fanaticism. [...] To reduce the imagination to a state of slavery – even though it would mean the elimination of what is commonly called happiness – is to betray all sense of absolute justice within oneself. Imagination alone offers me some intimation of what can be, and this is enough to remove to some slight degree the terrible injunction; enough, too, to allow me to devote

---

15 André Breton, *Manifestoes of Surrealism*, trans. Richard Seaver and Helen R. Lane (Ann Arbor: University of Michigan Press, 1972), p. 26. On the ethical significance of the *Manifesto*, see Jacqueline Chénieux-Gendron, *Surrealism*, trans. Vivian Folkenflik (New York: Columbia University Press, 1990), p. 116.

16 Ibid., p. 47.

17 Ibid., p. 4.

> myself to it without fear of making a mistake (as though it were possible to make a bigger mistake).[18]

Breton identified the 'reign of logic' as the principal means employed to suppress the imagination's innate rebelliousness. The influence of positivist philosophy and analytic reason had banished all forms of magical thinking from contemporary life; humanity, having lost any sense of its own purpose, consequently found itself incapable of accepting responsibility for its own destiny. As a result, 'experience has found itself increasingly circumscribed', leaning 'for support on what is most immediately expedient', 'protected by the sentinels of common sense', and 'any kind of search for truth which is not in conformance with accepted practice' was now forbidden.[19]

As another example of academic myopia, one can turn to another early, central Surrealist text, *Nadja*. At various points throughout, Breton expresses his tenacious refusal to compromise in terms that many political activists inspired by the Russian Revolution would have been quick to countersign. 'The idea of freedom, acquired here on earth at the price of a thousand – and the most difficult – renunciations, must be enjoyed as unrestrictedly as possible as it is granted, without pragmatic considerations of any sort', Breton exclaimed. 'This is because human emancipation – conceived finally in its simplest revolutionary form, which is no less that human emancipation in *every respect*, by which I mean, *according to the means at each person's disposal* – remains the only cause worth serving'.[20] This statement, made very early in Surrealism's history, remained a guiding principle throughout its activities to the present day. Yet, despite the persistence of vision in this iron-clad assertion, the revolutionary political ambitions of Surrealism have been concealed by time and recuperated by the movement's enemies, replacing the Surrealist's ambitions for radical change and their obstinate love of freedom with expensive paintings hanging in museums and poems taught in literature classes.

Given the hostility of political groups to Surrealism, the Surrealists were often forced to locate the practice of their politics in creative endeavour: in other words, politics was inscribed into the texture of the work, into its construction and articulation. In retrospect it is easy to describe these attempts to found a Surrealist politics as naive or misguided, but this is to underestimate their

---

18 Ibid., pp. 4–5.

19 Ibid., p. 10.

20 André Breton, *Nadja*, trans. Richard Howard (New York: Grove, 1960), pp. 142–43. Translation modified. This dimension of Surrealism did not escape the attention of Walter Benjamin, who not only credits Surrealism with the first 'radical concept of freedom' since Bakunin, but cites this passage in his magnificent essay of 1929, 'Surrealism: The Last Snapshot of the European Intelligentsia', in *One Way Street and Other Writings*, trans. Edmund Jephcott and Kingsley Shorter (London: Verso, 1985), p. 236.

significance within the ongoing evolution of the movement. The Surrealists repeatedly sought out arenas in which to enact the question of political commitment, arenas that were otherwise neglected, simplified or dismissed by existing political conventions. Further problems are evident when one finds statements made by the Surrealists themselves about the impossibility of working within the political conventions of their time. For instance, in 1960, the astute Surrealist theorist Nora Mitrani explained:

> [...] if it is a matter of political and social revolution as defined by the Marxists, let us say that it falls far short of what surrealism wants. This type of revolution is not enough, and it will never be enough. [...] This promotion of the masses is in fact a betrayal: class consciousness is replaced by the struggle for security and by bureaucratic types of organized irresponsibility. [...] In this mass civilization, humankind has struck a miserable bargain: it has exchanged its independence and the mind's freedom for a higher standard of living and consumption of 'token appearances' [the management of leisure and vacation time], and even on this level, by the way, there is much more to do and gain. But for surrealism, such a bargain is pitiful, and no bargain in the world can satisfy us.[21]

For our part, we found it useful to rewrite the terms of the discussion of politics as it concerns Surrealism. From our historical vantage point, we have found clues in a generation of political theorists that have re-examined the foundation of the political in an attempt to uncover new possibilities of political philosophy following the supposed failure of Marxism to provide a viable theory of radically democratic transformation of society. In particular, the critique of totalitarianism undertaken by Claude Lefort has provided vital insight into the failure of past revolutionary movements and the persistent urgency for social change.[22] Lefort

---

21 Nora Mitrani, *BIEF: Jonction surréaliste*, no. 12 (April 1960), rpd as 'In Defense of Surrealism' in Penelope Rosemont, ed., *Surrealist Women: An International Anthology* (Austin: University of Texas Press, 1999), p. 294. As Chicago Surrealist Franklin Rosemont recently summed it up, 'the Surrealist Movement remains "at the service of the revolution," but it is important to recognize that, for us, revolution is also in the service of Surrealism'. Franklin Rosemont, 'Surrealism, the Chicago Idea', in *The Forecast is Hot! Tracts & Other Collective Declarations of the Surrealist Movement in the United States, 1966–1976* (Chicago: Black Swan Press, 1997), p. xxi.

22 Socialisme ou barbarie (1949–65) was formed by Greek economist Cornelius Castoriadis, Claude Lefort, and other activists from the few hundred supporters in the 'Chaulieu-Montal tendency' of the Parti communiste internationale. Socialisme ou barbarie's intense interest in point-of-production council communism as a means of circumventing the bureaucratization of revolutionary parties was a crucial influence on the events of May 1968; in later life, both eschewed Marxism altogether. See 'An Interview with Claude Lefort', *Telos*, no. 30 (Winter 1976–77), pp. 173–92; Cornelius Castoriadis, *Political and Social Writings, vol. 1: 1946–1955*, ed. David Ames (Minneapolis: University of Minnesota Press, 1988); Marcel van der Linden, 'Socialisme ou Barbarie: A French Revolutionary Group, 1949–1965', *Left History* V:1 (1998), pp. 7–37.

has developed a crucial distinction between 'politics' [*la politique*] and 'the political' [*le politique*] that we think is helpful for articulating the role of politics in Surrealism. Lefort distinguishes between 'politics' as the particular institutional forms of political organization and activity in a society, and 'the political' as the movement that constitutes the social space of a particular society:

> The political is thus revealed [...] in the double movement whereby the mode of institution of society appears and is obscured. It appears in the sense that the process whereby society is ordered and unified across its divisions becomes visible. It is obscured in the sense that the locus of politics (the locus in which parties compete and in which a general agency of power takes shape and is reproduced) become defined as particular, while the principle which generates the overall configuration is concealed.[23]

Unlike political science, which seeks to objectify and legitimize existing social forms, Lefort returns to a political philosophy based on the question: 'what is the nature of the difference between forms of society?' Politics emerge in a social space as 'space of intelligibility articulated in accordance with a specific mode of distinguishing between the real and the imaginary, the true and the false, the just and the unjust, the permissible and the forbidden, the normal and the pathological'.[24]

The significance of this insight is that the politics of Surrealism was animated precisely by the tension that Lefort identified existing between 'politics' and 'the political', and from this model one can see how we regard the Saint-Pol-Roux banquet brawl as an informative example of Surrealism's encounters with politics and culture. On the one hand, the Surrealists attempted to engage in 'politics': they issued tracts and statements on current political crises, sought out radical political groups that appeared sympathetic to their goals and objectives, and even constituted groups such as Contre-Attaque (1935–36) with the deliberate aim of participating in political action. On the other hand, Surrealism was unwilling to forsake 'the political', which for Surrealism may best be described as an experience of freedom grounded in the imaginative possibilities revealed through creative endeavour. It is this experience that constituted the link between the artistic or literary plane and the social plane, between culture and politics in Surrealism. As Breton noted in the *Second Manifesto of Surrealism*: 'The problem of social action [...] is only one of the forms of a more general problem which Surrealism set out to deal with, and this is *the problem of human expression in all its forms*'.[25]

The undercurrents and contexts of the Saint-Pol-Roux banquet scandal are also emblematic of the themes explored by the contributors to this volume. It

---

23 Claude Lefort, 'The Question of Democracy', in *Democracy and Political Theory*, trans. David Macey (Minneapolis: University of Minnesota Press, 1988), p. 11.

24 Ibid., pp. 11–12.

25 Breton, *Manifestoes*, p. 151.

demonstrates the proximity within Surrealism of the themes of politics and culture, the Surrealist belief that creative endeavour required a radical kind of liberty inseparable from a broadly conceived political revolution. If the experience of freedom realized in creative endeavour enabled the Surrealist to approach the political, it is equally necessary to recognize the anarchic character of this experience and its problematical relation to the existing practice of politics in modern societies.

* * *

The essays that we have chosen to include in *Surrealism, Politics and Culture* draw on literary, art historical, and historical studies to explore the complex encounter between culture and politics within the Surrealist enterprise in its full flower. It is important to emphasize to the reader that this anthology does not attempt to present a simple chronicle of the 'politics of Surrealism', nor a study of Surrealism with allusions to the contextual role of politics; rather, it addresses the contested ground between culture and politics within Surrealism and subsequent historical accounts of the movement. Our goal is two-fold: our first ambition is to delineate the role of radical politics in shaping the historical trajectory of Surrealism by incorporating the new perspectives provided by the latest considerations of social history, gender studies, postcolonial and race studies – approaches further modulated by the theoretical, methodological and disciplinary focus of each contributor. The second is to consider the continuing relevance of Surrealism, the relation between contemporary intellectual concerns and the historical actuality of the Surrealist enterprise. We feel that Surrealism frames the historical horizon of current intellectual debates (particularly those debates informed by or opposed to post-1968 French theoretical models), and that it is impossible to understand the use of contemporary French thought by cultural critics all over the world without an understanding of the history that shaped its development in France, a history in which Surrealism played an integral role – sometimes contentious, sometimes complementary. *Surrealism, Politics and Culture* excavates this terrain.

Another important feature of *Surrealism, Politics and Culture* is a self-reflexive awareness of the relation between accounts of Surrealism and the history of the Surrealist movement. The contemporary studies are framed by a key essay that established the initial parameters of the study of Surrealism in the English-speaking world; thus the collection opens with Robert Short's ground-breaking 1966 essay, 'The Politics of Surrealism, 1920–36', which represents the first serious attempt to trace the Surrealist movement's various encounters with politics.[26] Short's essay was published at an important transitional moment

26 Originally published in *Journal of Contemporary History* I:3 (September 1966), pp. 3–25.

in the history of Surrealism: on the one hand, its publication was contemporary with the death of André Breton and the controversial dissolution of the 'historical' Surrealist movement in France.[27] But on the other hand, Short's piece coincided with the renewed political activism of the late 1960s, particularly the entry of New Left 'political critique' within academia that sought alternative understandings and application of the socialist experiment. Paradoxically, the construction of Surrealism as a legitimate object of historical investigation also represented a fundamental shift in the nature Surrealism's politics: as an object of academic discourse 'Surrealism' withdrew from the world of immediate political engagement. Indeed, the compass of the Surrealist enterprise has been sorely truncated in most academic accounts of the movement, which attempt to reduce Surrealism to an artistic or literary movement – more often than not, at the expense of Surrealism's politics.[28] It is in this context that the essays in this collection need to be read.

The gray area between the end of Dada and the beginning of Surrealism has generated much interest and speculation. The relationship is not simply one of historical supersession; too many of Dada's personnel, innovations, and influences followed other trajectories to make that easy connection, and aspects of early Surrealism belie a strict Dadaist inheritance. Theresa Papanikolas has

---

27 Jean Schuster has been the most insistent in explaining the events surrounding the French Surrealists Group's self-dissolution; see Jean Schuster, *Archives 57–68. Batailles pour le surréalisme* (Paris: Losfeld, 1969). In response, see Eric Losfeld, *Procès à 'Coupure'. Tribunal correctionnel de Paris, 17e Chambre, affaire Losfeld-Schuster, audience du 29 juin 1971* (Paris: Losfeld, 1972). Alain Joubert, *Le Mouvement des surréalistes ou le fin mot de l'histoire: mort d'un groupe – naissance d'un mythe* (Paris: Maurice Nadeau, 2001). Also, many factions of the international Surrealist movement refused to follow the lead of the French group, such as the Prague and Chicago Surrealists.

28 For a Surrealist critique of the North American reception of Surrealism see Guy Ducornet, *Le Punching-Ball et la vache à lait: La critique universitaire nordeaméricaine face au Surréalisme* (Angers, France: Deleatur, 1992), condensed and updated as *Le Parasites du Surréalisme: La Critique universitaire américaine versus André Breton* (Soignies: Talus, 2002). The lack of scholarship on Surrealism that addresses these issues has two explanations. The first is that, quite frankly, there are many who insist that configurations of revolutionary possibility are no longer operative in contemporary society, that Marxism's 'failure' is evident in the collapse of the Soviet Union in 1989, that excavating such discourse is about as relevant as unearthing evidence of some long-forgotten medieval Central European Christian heretical sect. The second is the methodological difficulty that such a study of Surrealism presents for academics: Surrealism's attempted union between social and cultural revolution continually evades direct articulation, since the Surrealists rejected the assimilation of art to propaganda characteristic of socialist realism. Therefore, in order to explore the tensions between the political and cultural orientation of the Surrealist project, scholars have found it necessary to track where and how politics enters the movement's work as an unanswered question that exists at the limits of representation.

located one such current in her study of anarchism during the time before the Surrealists moved towards the PCF (see Chapter 2). The tension between the freedom allowed to the individual and the individual's responsibility to the freedom of the collective has always made anarchism one of the most innovative and restless political positions and, even though French anarchism had been badly maligned after World War I because of the syndicalists' participation in the *union sacrée*'s war effort, Surrealism had always found itself drawn towards its principles. Papanikolas disentangles Surrealism from Dada and reassesses automatism with an eye on anarchism. In so doing she brings to light some previously obscure information about the politics of Tristan Tzara, the Barrès show trial, and the St Julien-Le-Pauvre expedition, and argues convincingly that even Surrealists' wild enthusiasm for the possibilities of the 1917 Bolshevik Revolution could not fully eclipse its inherent anarchist sympathies. After World War II Surrealism openly embraced a number of anarchist and anti-statist internationalist positions, but as can be inferred from Papanikolas's work, this was merely a return of the repressed. Hopefully, her work will inspire others to investigate the constant rhythm of anarchism that ran throughout Surrealist politics in the 1920s and 1930s.

In the 75 years since *Nadja* was published, critics and scholars have offered up all manner of 'meanings' for Breton's pioneering text. Raymond Spiteri's contribution to this field concerns itself with the parallels of Breton's encounter with Nadja and his early relationship with the PCF (see Chapter 3). Through this formulation, the Surrealists' temporary enrollment in the PCF appears as little more than a practical application of the movement's fundamental principles of rebellion and liberation, a position that they arrived at through sustained creative experimentation. What is especially intriguing in Spiteri's gloss on *Nadja* is his understanding of how the photographic reproductions used in the text functioned as descriptive (anti-)illustrations of narrative events and their disjunctions. By splitting the seams that stitch the images to the text, Spiteri opens a space where one can follow the Surrealists' course between allegiance to the marvellous and the implementation of Party-sanctioned revolutionary action, a dance done under the eyes of Nadja, a woman whose alternating presence and absence functions in the text as a sign of marvellous possibility and the material limits of actual existence.

The inclusion of Amy Lyford's 'Advertising Surrealist Masculinities: André Kertész in Paris' deserves comment (Chapter 4). The photography of Kertész is not usually associated with Surrealism – although his *Distortions* series was published in *Minotaure* in 1934 – and indeed Kertész was never a member of the Surrealist movement. However, Lyford uses Kertész's auxiliary position to the movement to access new currents in Surrealism. In this case, Lyford approaches Kertész as a way of raising important questions about the politics of gender, particularly masculinity, during the interwar period and its relationship to Surrealism. In focusing on Kertész, Lyford reveals a double for Surrealism marked by both proximity and distance. Kertész shared a fascination together with the Surrealists with the unfashionable side of Parisian life, yet his work is marked by a sense of alienation and distance figured through the masculine body in crisis. This provides an interesting foil to Surrealist iconography, which more often that not displaces any sense of masculine anxiety upon the female body. Lyford's continuing research into masculinity during the 1920s promises to add considerably to our understanding of avant-garde culture during the interwar years.

Jonathan P. Eburne's 'Surrealism Noir' focuses on the sensational crime of the Papin sisters (see Chapter 5); his objective is to explore how the Surrealists employed emerging theories of paranoia to view criminal behaviour as an expression of political revolt. In the wake of the Aragon affair and the continuing hostility of the PCF towards Surrealism, the Surrealists' response to the crime the Papin sisters committed represents the emergence of a 'noir' sensibility (as in the critical label of 'film noir') that employed the paranoiac construction of reality to consider the role of a hyper-attenuated style – the construction and articulation of formal elements in an image – as an implicit critique of conventional reality. Although the Surrealist interest in the Papin affair occurred during a period when the Surrealists temporarily withdrew from direct engagement in 'politics', it nonetheless demonstrates their underlying concern with the 'political', in that they considered the murder as a protest against an unfree society, albeit manifested in the inarticulate language of violence. More significantly, the political is manifested on a stylistic level, in the construction and articulation of formal elements that constitute the image, a route that Eburne takes with the help of René Crevel. In this way Eburne opens a new space for the understanding of the political sphere by suggesting a rich concordance between symptom and style.

It has been common practice to ascribe Surrealist anti-colonial activities to a fascination with the exotic lives, customs and material culture of non-European peoples. But Amanda Stansell follows a different track, turning her attention instead to unravelling notions of race and racism inherent in the colonial practices of interwar France in order to give Surrealism's anti-colonialist positions a deeper reach (see Chapter 6). French theories of race were assembled from the worst distortions of science and rationalism, distortions that were used to excuse colonial predation in Africa, Asia and the Caribbean. In linking the Surrealists' attack on rationalism to their critiques of racist politics and practices, Stansell traces the points of contact between constructions of European identity and the unspoken lies of white privilege; in recasting Surrealist anti-colonialism in this light, she reveals the Surrealists as precursors to those today who seek to dismantle social hierarchies built on the ethnic myths of 'whiteness'. Stansell accomplishes this through a re-examination of *Nègritude* and primitivism in the Surrealist context, and in so doing presents a complex and nuanced picture of Surrealist racial politics that emerges as an alternative to the standard 'colour-blind' policies of the radical left. Stansell finds that, though sometimes simplistic, the Surrealists' insistence upon the fundamental 'otherness' of the Other lays the groundwork for actions informed by the irreconcilability of difference. By paying attention to the implications of this immutable difference, the Surrealists attacked white supremacism at its root.

The relation between artistic endeavour and political events is the theme of Robert Lubar's 'Painting and Politics: Miró's *Still Life With Old Shoe* and the Spanish Republic' (Chapter 7), which discusses Miró's response to the ideological crisis on the left in France and Spain engendered by the tragedy of the Spanish Civil War. Among the artists associated with the French Surrealist movement, Miró had steadfastly maintained his distance from the political position of the movement. However, Lubar sees an encounter with politics disclosed in the formal construction of the work as a tension between antagonistic modes of pictorial representation. He considers *Still Life With Old Shoe* in the context of other artistic responses to the Spanish Civil War (particularly the Spanish Pavilion of the 1937 *Exposition Internationale*) to argue that in Miró's case politics was mediated and worked through as pictorial form. By situating Miró's work within the nexus of political and historical events, Lubar locates a complex response to these events that speaks directly to the debates on the artist's position in revolutionary and bourgeois societies. In this way social life 'in*forms*' a work that refuses didactic political content by unearthing the moral implications of specific visual practices.

Like Eburne, Jordana Mendelson's 'Of Politics, Postcards and Pornography: Salvador Dalí's *Le Mythe tragique de l'Angélus de Millet*' (Chapter 8) explores the connection between Lacan's early theories on paranoia and Surrealism, yet this time in the context of Dalí's fascination with Millet's *The Angelus*. Mendelson draws our attention to the influence of popular, rural archetypes on Dalí's work during the 1930s and examines the role of postcards as an example of Dalí's engagement with notions of national identity circulating in popular culture, around which Dalí elaborates a complex myth that oscillates between paranoid obsessions and political critique. By locating Dalí's obsessions in the historical context of the 1930s, Mendelson articulates the relation between Dalí's fascination with Millet's *The Angelus* and the emergence of totalitarian politics – a relation that Dalí would later deny. Dalí's interest in rural archetypes and mythology also paralleled the interest of Georges Bataille in the psychology of fascism, an ambivalent fascination that often alarmed other Surrealists. Moreover, by situating Dalí's iconography in the politically charged context of the 1930s, Mendelson's essay touches upon the concerns that motivated the rejection of figuration by critics like Clement Greenberg, for figuration was contaminated by its proximity to both mass culture and the didactic politics of Socialist Realism.

In Chapter 9, 'Surrealism in 1938: The Exhibition at War', Elena Filipovic reconsiders the political significance of the Surrealist display in the 1938

Exposition Internationale du Surréalisme. This exhibition is often regarded as proof of Surrealism's withdrawal from political engagement, yet by considering the *Exposition Internationale* in the context of other contemporary exhibitions, particularly the *Grosse Deutsche Kunstausstellung* and the *Entartete Kunst* exhibitions in Nazi Germany, Filipovic is able to uncover a political strategy implicit in the theatricality of Surrealist display. Surrealism not only rejected the ostensibly 'neutral' space of the art museum that underwrote Nazi and modernist aesthetics of display, but also revealed the ideologically charged nature of display, attempting to rethink the question of its ethical, ideological and political form.

Jacqueline Chénieux-Gendron has described Surrealism's interest in Trotskyist Marxism as 'a meeting of opinions, not minds'.[29] The elusive qualities of the Surrealist-Trotskyist connection, however, does not justify the lack of carefully detailed histories of the Breton-Trotsky collaboration or the activities of the FIARI on the eve of World War II.[30] In her spirited essay (Chapter 10), Robin Greeley meditates upon a photograph of a 1938 conversation between Breton, Trotsky and Diego Rivera and calls for future scholarship on the Breton and Trotsky alliance to recognize the importance of the lingering trauma of the Spanish Civil War and the influence of Cárdenismo. Amid a combustible mix of class, racial and ethnic tensions, Mexico's socialist president Lázaro Cárdenas instituted new agrarian reform policies and challenged the powerful petro-capitalists of the US and Britain by nationalizing the oil industry. Greeley believes this to be an important context to the formation of the revolutionary consciousness described in the *For An Independent Revolutionary Art* manifesto, and in this respect, she sees Surrealist cultural analysis, Mexican labour union militancy, and Trotsky's horror of socialist realism as part of the secret history of the Fourth International.

One of the most succinct cultural definitions of the maroon – a fiercely defiant slave who rose up against the criminal authority of the plantation and escaped into the wilderness – is as 'living proof of the existence of a slave consciousness that refused to be limited by the whites' conception or manipulation of it'.[31] Aimé Césaire's explorations of marronage provide E. San Juan, Jr. with a language for understanding how Surrealism served the cause of anti-imperialism and anti-colonialism where Soviet Marxism would not (see

29 Chénieux-Gendron, *Surrealism*, p. 154.

30 A significant exception here is Carole Reynaud Paligot, who has pushed beyond the anecdotal by incorporating accounts of Benjamin Péret's ordeals in Spain and Mexico to show Surrealism's interest in adapting Trotsky's thought. See *Parcours politique des surréalistes*, pp. 123–25.

31 See the 'Introduction: Maroons and Their Communities' in Richard Price, ed., *Maroon Societies: Rebel Slave Communities in the Americas* (Garden City, NY: Anchor Press, 1973), p. 2.

Chapter 11). Césaire's unique dialectical vision blends poetry and politics in urgent ways that are still relevant, and his Surrealist creations stand as compelling exercises in turning the insidious forces of colonial assimilation back against themselves in order to detoxify consciousnesses polluted by European political, religious, economic and cultural domination. San Juan captures the implications of Césaire's politico-aesthetics in a way that informs many of the other investigations in this collection, namely Surrealism's hunt for a political alternative to communism's persistent failures to provide a significant means of individual and collective freedom. Césaire's case is all the more poignant, however, since the context – the legacy of slavery and colonialism – is one that throws even the most subtle machinery of exploitation in high relief.

At first sight the connection between Surrealism's interest in emancipatory politics and the sadistic manipulation of the female body in the work of Hans Bellmer may seem tenuous. Yet recent accounts of Bellmer's work have focused on its relation to the rise of National Socialism in Germany during the 1930s, particularly the way his depiction of the female body deconstructs the fascist ideal of the healthy body.[32] While in Chapter 12 Alyce Mahon agrees that Bellmer's work must be understood in the historical context of Nazi Germany and the postwar *épuration*, she also draws on Lyotard's characterization of Bellmer's art as 'the organic body of political economy' to explore the radical significance of libidinal *jouissance* in Bellmer's treatment of the female figure. She argues that Bellmer's libidinal politics is based on an 'anagrammatic' approach to the female form that not only subverted the totalitarian body politic, but was consistent with the Surrealist belief in desire as political, in which the monstrous feminine threatened socio-political crisis in the established order. Indeed, one implication of Mahon's discussion of Bellmer is not only to question the validity of the charges of misogyny often levelled at Surrealism, but highlight the need to reconsider the gender politics of the movement.

In Chapter 13, 'Attacks of the Fantastic', Donald LaCoss focuses on the appeal of Charles Fourier's utopian socialism for Surrealism after World War II. Although Surrealist interest in utopian socialism and revolutionary Romanticism was not limited to the work of Fourier, his writings exercised an enduring influence on Surrealist political thought from the late 1930s to the uprising of May 1968. According to LaCoss, the Surrealists' research into utopianism was part of an effort to refine and deepen its commitment to social transformation, constituting a key element of the movement's political trajectory during the Cold War period. Their promotion of utopianism was integral to the form and content of the movement's postwar radical politics. Fourier's visionary presence

---

32 See, for instance, Hal Foster, *Compulsive Beauty* (Cambridge: MIT Press, 1993), pp. 101–22; Therese Lichenstein, *Behind Closed Doors: The Art of Hans Bellmer* (Berkeley: University of California Press, 2001).

was at least as significant a centre of gravity for Surrealist theory and practice as Ann Radcliffe, Alfred Jarry and Lenin.

It may seem provocative to conclude this anthology with an essay that claims to pose preliminary questions, but M. Stone-Richards's 'Failure and Community: Preliminary Questions on the Political in the Culture of Surrealism' represents an ambitious and elegant attempt to rearticulate the role of the political in Surrealism (Chapter 14). Stone-Richards avoids much of the perfidy that passes for scholarship on Surrealism in the Anglo-American academy by focusing on the French reception of Surrealism after World War II – notably the extraordinary writings of Maurice Blanchot – which acts as a prism through which to refract the potent legacy of Surrealism. Stone-Richards begins by focusing on Blanchot's response to Jean-Luc Nancy's *La Communauté désœuvrée* – itself part of an ongoing attempt to rethink questions of community and the political in the wake of Marxism's failure – in which Blanchot, refusing any opposition between Bataille and Breton, says that the exigency of community was first posed by the Surrealists. Developing on this insight he then considers the relation between the ethical and the political in Surrealism by examining the meaning of failure in Surrealism: the preoccupation with anguish and boredom, the time of what is always to come, the *informe*, the indeterminate. He also draws on Jules Monnerot's *La Poésie et le sacré* (1945) – an important account of the Surrealist experience of poetry that has been largely overlooked in the English-speaking world, and which provides a compelling alternative to Maurice Nadeau's better known *Histoire du surréalisme* (1944) – to identify certain critical capacities in Surrealism that extricate it from crude accounts of Surrealism and politics, leaving it constantly in a mode of temporality intimately linked to the capacities of the group. In this way Stone-Richards locates the enduring legacy of the political in Surrealism in terms of *sensus communis* and exemplary validity.

The final document in this anthology is an English translation of Léon Pierre-Quint's notes of a 1936 conversation with Théodore Fraenkel on the subject of the political position of Surrealism. Fraenkel had participated in the activities of Paris Dada, but abandoned Dada in favour of medicine. Nonetheless he remained close to Surrealism, and his thoughts on the political trajectory of Surrealism during the interwar years provide a valuable insight into the nexus of politics and culture.

Although this anthology cannot claim to be comprehensive, it does provide a cross-section of recent research on the complex encounter between Surrealism and politics. In so doing we hope not only to demonstrate the central importance of the political for an adequate understanding of the history and legacy of Surrealism, but also to encourage further research on the question of Surrealism, politics and culture.

Chapter 1

The Politics of Surrealism, 1920–36*

Robert Short

> 'Transformer le monde', a dit Marx;
> 'Changer la vie', a dit Rimbaud; ces deux mots d'ordre pour nous n'en font qu'un.
>
> *André Breton*

Including as it did at one time or another writers and artists of the calibre of Louis Aragon, André Breton, Paul Eluard, René Char, Michel Leiris, René Crevel, Robert Desnos, Antonin Artaud, Raymond Queneau, Tristan Tzara, Pierre Naville, Max Ernst, André Masson and Alberto Giacometti, to mention just a handful of the hundred or so who joined its ranks, the Surrealist group probably exercised a greater influence on the intellectual climate of the interwar period in France than any other comparable movement. As such the political history of the Surrealists, who participated collectively in many of the organizations of the revolutionary left, deserves attention.

Not that the Surrealists ever had a decisive effect on the course of political events, or made any original contribution to political theory. The interest in the movement's political history lies in its tenacious efforts, set forth in some highly articulate polemical writing, to associate its intellectual, artistic and moral preoccupations with the aims and methods of international Communism. The issues at stake may be reduced to three: the reconciliation of a generalized spirit of revolt with revolutionary action; the reconciliation of the idea of a 'spiritual revolution' and its accompanying insistence on ethical 'purity' with the practical necessities of political effectiveness; and the reconciliation of an independent revolutionary art with the demands for propaganda and didacticism made by the Communist Party. An examination of them will show how the evolution of the theory of Surrealism, an enterprise which was initially and essentially poetic, led the movement to call for the transformation of society; and an account of Surrealism's ventures into politics and of the repeated setbacks these met with, will suggest some of the reasons why the Surrealists failed to translate their metaphysical and spiritual ambitions into social terms,

---

* Originally published in the *Journal of Contemporary History* I:2 (September 1966), pp. 3–25. Reprinted with permission.

and, more specifically, why they failed to find a permanent place within the Communist movement.

While in the narrow sense, according to the definition in Breton's *Manifesto* of 1924, Surrealism appeared to be no more than a new poetics, a linguistic experiment and a novel method of 'forcing inspiration', in the broad sense it implied an ethics, a philosophy and a politics. Bringing together Rimbaud's 'Lettre du Voyant', Hegel's dialectical method, and Freud's analysis of the unconscious, the Surrealists began by making a drastic revaluation of the poetic image. They believed that the series of images which they brought to light by using automatic techniques represented the 'real process of thought'. They devoted themselves to the exploitation of the untapped resources of the unconscious, hitherto ignored or suppressed by a culture obsessed by technological progress and material comforts. For the Surrealists, poetry was not a cultivated form of escapism; it was an instrument of discovery. Insofar as the source of poetic inspiration was the unconscious mind, a faculty which, like Descartes's reason, was common to all men, they believed that poetry could be 'made by all' and not just by the technically accomplished *littérateur*. It had ceased to be a 'means of expression' and had become 'an activity of mind'.

From the moment poetry was conceived as a spiritual activity accessible to all men, it ceased to be a purely aesthetic matter and became an ethical one. In Paul Eluard's words: 'Toute véritable morale est poétique, la poésie tendant au règne de l'homme, de tous les hommes, au règne de notre justice'. Surrealism thus affirmed the ethical basis of all expression and the 'Communism' of poetry. At the same time, poetry's roots in the unconscious meant that it was the expression not only of primal mental activity but of man's deepest desires as well, for the unconscious was also the seat of the instincts and the libido. As such, poetry could not remain at the abstract level of 'fine art'. As the expression of desire, it involved choices and demands which sought satisfaction in the real world. Far from being a compensation for an inadequate and unworthy reality, poetry represented that towards which reality should progress. The Surrealists were confident that once the mind had a vision of what was possible, the will would struggle to achieve it, and that the 'interpretation' of man and of the world would inevitably be accompanied by their transformation. The poet would lead the struggle to raise man's spiritual and social state up to the level of his dreams. In so far as the disparity between that which existed and that which was desired was the result of alterable social conditions rather than of an immutable human condition, the Surrealists came to demand a radical social upheaval: a revolution.

This, very schematically, was the chain of reasoning that linked the Surrealist conception of art to an attitude of revolt against society and towards political commitment. This sequence of ideas was reflected in the intellectual evolution of the group in the seven years following World War I.

* * *

The word 'revolution' punctuated the writings of the Surrealists with great regularity between 1922 and 1925 but it had not yet acquired political connotations. As a document from April 1925 stated:

> The immediate sense and purpose of the Surrealist revolution is not so much to change anything in the physical and manifest order of things as to create an agitation in men's minds.[1]

At this stage, they believed in a 'revolution' in experience to be brought about by the mind and the imagination once the fetters of rationalism and habit had been struck off. Aragon challenged his audience in Madrid: 'Do you believe, yes or no, in the infinite powers of thought? We will prevail against all odds'. Ignoring social and political forces, the Surrealists claimed to be able to set off their revolution unaided, since it was not something rendered inevitable by the laws of social evolution so much as something ardently desired which, if willed with sufficient passion, was bound to occur. Their first task was to rejuvenate language, the instrument and substance of thought and hence the key to their 'subjective idealist' revolution. Putting to advantage their earlier apprenticeship among the Dadaists in the art of provocation and scandal, the Surrealists turned on the regime whose conventions had crippled and stunted language. They denounced the wretchedness of everyday life, the cults of family and fatherland, the necessity to work, masochistic Christianity, and the whole system of values which had permitted the war in which they themselves had unwillingly sacrificed their youth. As André Breton put it: 'We were possessed by a will to total subversion'. They extolled all forms of anti-social behaviour – crime, drug-addiction, suicide, insanity – as so many expressions of human freedom and revolt. They preferred the criminal to the political militant since crime seemed to be a self-sufficient act implying no fresh determinations. As an indispensable preliminary to the reconquest of liberty, they called for a crime on an international scale: a second 'Terror' or a new wave of barbarian invasions from the East. But these remained poetic symbols of menace. The Surrealists refused as yet to serve any real revolutionary cause because they conceived liberty as an absolute and commitment would have imposed intolerable limitations on their *disponibilité*. 'Je meurs si je m'attache', said Breton.

The distance that separated the Surrealists from young Communist intellectuals was revealed in a controversy between Aragon and the editors of *Clarté,* Marcel Fourrier and Jean Bernier, over *Un Cadavre,* a tract published by the Surrealists on the death of Anatole France. The Clartéists had approved the general spirit of this lampoon but objected to Aragon's use of the phrase

---

1 Maurice Nadeau, *Histoire du surréalisme*, vol. 2, *Documents Surréalistes* (Paris: Seuil, 1948), p. 44.

'Moscou la gâteuse' (doddering Moscow) in his comment on a telegram of condolence sent by the Kremlin to the French nation on its loss. Aragon replied to the Clartéists:

> If you find me antagonistic to the political spirit [...] it is because, as you cannot fail to see, I have always valued and continue to value the spirit of revolt far more highly than any politics [...]. As for the Russian Revolution, you'll forgive me for shrugging my shoulders. Measured by the yardstick of ideas, it is nothing more than a trivial ministerial crisis.[2]

Other Surrealists shared Aragon's contempt for communism. Eluard called it 'a mediocre regime which, just like capitalism, depends on the crude and repulsive order of physical labour'. The group did not yet see revolutionary politics as the means of satisfying their grievances against the world; Breton told Jacques Baron: 'We just don't bother ourselves with politics'.

It was not until the summer of 1925 that the Surrealists began to reassess their resources and what they meant by 'revolution'. The public had remained cheerfully immune to threats of the Terror and an Oriental scourge however vividly these horrors were evoked in the columns of *La Révolution surréaliste*. Breton realized that the social order was not going to yield before mere invective whose extravagant violence rendered it ridiculous. If their revolution was not to deteriorate into an impotent nonconformism it had to be given some tangible content, if necessary social content, and join forces with other revolutionary intellectuals. Critics like Marcel Arland had been quick to pigeonhole the Surrealists' revolt as a symptom of a '*nouveau mal de siècle*' or to identify the group as a latterday generation of 'poètes maudits'. To avoid this forcible assimilation into a literary avant-garde which they despised, no better means was to hand than affiliations with proletarian politics. The press furore aroused by the Surrealists' behaviour at the banquet in honour of the poet Saint-Pol-Roux, where they had shouted overtly political slogans for the first time, proved that this was the way to make the public take notice of their protest.

* * *

The outbreak of hostilities between the French army under Pétain and the Riffs in Morocco precipitated the Surrealists into politics. It was 'le grand choc' which suddenly clarified a highly ambiguous intellectual position. Their admiration for 'Oriental' and particularly for primitive peoples, their hatred of militarism and of the 'professional patriots', the academic intellectuals who celebrated France's civilizing role abroad – all directed their sympathies towards Abd-el-Krim. Nineteen of the group put their signatures to Henri Barbusse's protest: 'Appel aux Travailleurs Intellectuels. Oui ou non condamnez-vous la guerre?', which appeared in *L'Humanité* on 2 July 1925.

---

2 *Clarté,* 1 December 1924.

For Breton, the first step towards conversion to Communism was reading Trotsky's biography of Lenin. He set about convincing his friends, anticipating their objections that the Russian Revolution hardly satisfied the exigencies of Surrealism by insisting that it was not yet over or complete and that on the moral plane there was no incompatibility between the ideas of Lenin and their own. It was necessary, he said, to abandon the myths of revolution for the reality. Communism might represent a minimum programme, but it was the only force in existence capable of bringing about the social revolution which in turn was the necessary condition of 'une revolution dans les esprits'. The autumn of 1925 saw the political conversion of the group *en masse*. Michel Leiris admitted that the individual by himself, however passionate and profound his sense of revolt, was impotent when it came to social action. Aragon was soon writing with the conviction and facility of a lifelong Marxist. In articles such as 'Le Prolétariat de l'esprit', he showed how capital could turn ideas themselves into commodities.[3] The Surrealists seem to have undergone a kind of intoxication with Communism; the hyperbole and naive enthusiasm of their early political writings, their panegyrics on the Cheka and the Ogpu, cast doubt on the permanence and seriousness of their conversion. Breton appeared one morning at the Café Cyrano with a workman's cap over his long curls to demonstrate his solidarity with the proletariat. André Masson, recalling the atmosphere of the group's meetings, admits: 'When I was present at these things I kept saying to myself: "But I'm dreaming. I must be dreaming" '.[4]

The passage towards politics was eased by the instruction and encouragement the Surrealists received from the young editors of *Clarté*. But the national movement that Barbusse had founded in 1919 was now only a shadow of its former self. *Clarté* had long been suffering from shortage of funds, loss of readers, and repeated changes of policy as its successive editors struggled to determine the role that a Communist cultural review independent of the Communist Party could usefully play in a period of prolonged anticipation of the revolution. Despite some misgivings, the Clartéists decided to collaborate with Breton's group, many of whom were brilliant and already notable writers, in the hope of saving their review. *Clarté* was to adopt an editorial policy very close to that already undertaken in part, though for less consciously political motives, in *La Révolution surréaliste*: 'the systematic denunciation of bourgeois thought'. On their side, the Surrealists saw in *Clarté* a useful half-way house on their road towards commitment and one which, unlike membership of the PCF, did not deprive them of their independence.

The *Clarté* 'alliance', made up of the Surrealists, the *Clarté* writers, and the 'Philosophers' (Georges Politzer, Pierre Morhange, Henri Lefebvre, Norbert

3 *Clarté,* 30 November 1925.

4 Georges Charbonnier, *Entretiens avec André Masson* (Paris: René Julliard, 1958), p. 108.

Guterman and Georges Friedman) formed a distinct new generation of Communist adherents. They differed greatly from the original postwar intellectual sympathizers with the October Revolution, such as Barbusse, Romain Rolland, Anatole France, Marcel Martinet and Paul Vaillant-Couturier. They were emphatically not humanitarians, pacifists, or 'men of good will'. Both the Surrealists and the 'Philosophers' came to communism in the course of an independent spiritual quest. The 'Philosophers', who were pioneer existentialists, rebelled against the idea of an irreducible dualism between the human and the absolute which had been taught them by their Sorbonne professors. They retorted: 'Our thought is earthbound and concrete. It is no longer Thought with a capital T'.[5] One way of making their thought concrete seemed to be to make it political. As for the Surrealists, Communism served to give some positive justification to an idealistic revolt which had been turning in a vacuum, propelled only by the energy and passion it consumed. A curious feature common to these novice fellow-travellers was their lack of confidence in the revolutionary will of the French proletariat. They wrote of the 'sickening passivity' of the working class and its contentment with a few wretched improvements in its standard of living. As Marcel Martinet pointed out, it was grotesque for self-styled Marxists to express contempt for the one and only instrument of the social revolution. The reason was that this second generation had not digested the materialism in the Marxist equation. They had come to Communism, as one of their number, Roger Vailland, admitted, to save their souls.[6] Nevertheless, it seemed at first that the *Clarté* alliance would earn the blessing of the PCF. Its inaugural manifesto, 'La Révolution d'abord et toujours', was welcomed by Albert Treint in *L'Humanité* (21 September 1925), where the presence of several Clartéists on the staff guaranteed an initial friendly reception. Lunacharsky, the Soviet Commissar for Education, gave his approval:

> The Surrealists have rightly understood that the task of all revolutionary intellectuals under a capitalist regime is to denounce bourgeois values. Their efforts deserve to be encouraged.[7]

On 19 October, the alliance proved its courage by republishing on its own responsibility a text titled 'Aux soldats et aux marins', which called on the troops in Morocco to fraternize with the Riffs and which had earned its original authors arrest and imprisonment. From September 1925 until the following March, writers from the alliance such as Péret, Victor Crastre and Marcel Noll dominated the cultural pages of *L'Humanité*.

---

5 Henri Lefebvre, 'La Pensée et l'esprit', *L'Esprit*, May 1926.

6 Marcel Martinet, 'Contre le Courant', *Europe*, 15 May 1926; Roger Vailland, *Drôle de Jeu* (Paris: Buchet-Chastel, 1961), p. 21.

7 Quoted by Clement Vautel in *Le Journal*, 1 January 1928.

The break-up of the alliance began in the spring of 1926 after *La Guerre Civile*, the projected review in which the groups hoped to pool their resources and set forth their revolutionary position, failed to appear. No real cohesion or ideological agreement had been forthcoming. The contributions of each to the reviews of the others always seemed incongruous. As Marcel Fourrier put it: 'To tell the truth, a lot went on between individuals but practically nothing collectively'. Determined to preserve the autonomy of Surrealism, Breton had refused to accept the replacement of *La Révolution surréaliste* by the new review. Differences of temperament and formation had also played their part, the imaginative effervescence of the Surrealists never finding harmony with the stolid seriousness of the journalists.

In January 1927, five of the Surrealists: Breton, Aragon, Eluard, Péret and Pierre Unik, applied for membership of the PCF. In 'Au Grand Jour', the five explained that they wanted to give final proof of the sincerity of their communist convictions which were still an object of distrust within the party, and to dispel the ambiguities of their fellow-traveller status. They had long believed that the Hegelian dialectic was the key to the resolution of conflicts in the real world and that Hegelianism found its own historical resolution in Marxism. This logic, they said, brought them face to face with the Communist Party to which, as Surrealists, they had no alternative to offer.[8] They felt bound to lend their full support to the party whose leaders were harassed and imprisoned by Chiappe and Tardieu, the party which Sarraut had identified as 'the vanguard of an Asian movement against Europe'.

* * *

The welcome offered by the PCF to the Surrealists was not a warm one. Breton was summoned five times before its Control Commission and asked to explain why he still needed to call himself a Surrealist now that he had become a Communist. The contents of *La Révolution surréaliste* caused consternation and moral outrage among his interrogators. Despite Breton's promise to change the review's equivocal title and to make other concessions, the persecution of the five did not cease after they had been allocated to their respective party cells. They all beat a hasty retreat when Breton, who found himself posted among the gas-workers in the rue Lafayette, was asked to make a statistical report on the state of that industry in Italy. 'I couldn't do it', he confessed.[9]

It is ironical that it was precisely those characteristics in the communist party of the later 1920s which had impressed the Surrealists that caused the PCF to give them the cold shoulder. The party's 'gauchisme', for instance, which led it to refuse any kind of cooperation with the socialist leaders and which the

8 Maurice Nadeau, *Histoire du surréalisme*, pp. 97–109.
9 André Breton, *Second manifeste du surréalisme* (Paris: Kra, 1930).

Surrealists admired as fine revolutionary intransigence, or the noisy invective of a Jacques Doriot singing the 'Carmagnole' in front of Ministers of State – all these went hand in hand with 'ouvrièrisme', an instinctive hostility to intellectuals whom the workers' party held responsible for its own troubled birth. The party had been completely 'bolshevized'. It was now unquestioningly obedient to orders from Moscow and about to enter its notorious 'third period'. Under the shady direction of the Barbé-Célor faction, it showed less interest in militancy than in the imposition of strict internal discipline and the stifling of all criticism and ideological argument.

Whatever the intellectual shortcomings of the party may have been, the Communists had ample grounds for being suspicious of the Surrealists, whose record of ideological vicissitudes in the previous three years was hardly a recommendation for reliability – and the Communists had not forgotten Aragon's quip about 'doddering Moscow'. Nor could they ignore the comfortable bourgeois origins of the majority of the Surrealists. In general the Communists believed that Surrealist writing and art had no appeal to the masses and that their social activity suffered for the sake of their premature artistic experiments. Anticipating charges later made by Sartre, Pierre Naville, himself a former Surrealist, argued that Surrealist speculation about the mind at a time when it was conditioned by innumerable social factors all of which would be changed by the revolution, suggested that they believed in some form of spiritual liberation anterior to and independent of the abolition of bourgeois conditions of life.[10] Ilya Ehrenburg affirmed quite simply that the Surrealists used their vaunted revolutionary activities as a cloak for immorality; but the proletariat was not deceived.[11]

The Surrealists themselves never made it very clear what functions they could fulfil once they were admitted to the party. They complained that the communists would not use the talents they had to offer, yet it is difficult to see what purpose these talents could have served apart from a purely Surrealist one – and the five stressed the fact that they were joining the party as ordinary individuals and not as Surrealists. They did not conceal their ignorance of economics and Breton behaved as if he had been insulted when he was asked to compile the Italian gas industry report. They were unwilling to take on the journalistic work offered by the party press. Breton had told Marcel Fourrier quite bluntly: 'Literary work is dirty work such as we have never undertaken in any circumstances'. The only task they were prepared to accept, and which they claimed was their special duty, was the defence of the 'moral truth' of the revolutionary cause. To quote Maxime Alexandre: 'In politics, it is our duty to

10 Pierre Naville, *La Révolution et les Intellectuels. Que Peuvent faire les Surréalistes?* (Paris, 1926), pp. 29–31.

11 Ilya Ehrenburg, *Vus par un écrivain de l'URSS* (Paris: Gallimard, 1934), pp. 55, 64.

watch over the moral implications of the revolution with all the energy we can summon up'. To a political party concerned first and foremost with the mobilization of the working class and the day-to-day problems of running a mass movement, a proposition of this kind was totally unacceptable. It was clear that such a moral guardianship was more likely to devote its energies to finding fault with the party itself than with its enemies.

The Surrealists' entry into the PCF thus remained a gesture only and one that was not repeated. Relations with the party were not broken off, however. For the next six years, writes Jacques Fauvet, 'un équilibre qui tourne parfois en équilibrisme s'instaure entre eux et le parti'.[12] The Surrealists were waiting patiently, said Breton in the *Second Manifesto* of 1930, for the better days when the militants would recognize their own.

* * *

From 1927 to 1933, Surrealist political activity, apart from attendance at strike meetings, demonstrations on behalf of Sacco and Vanzetti, and the physical 'correction' of slanderers of the Soviet Union, took the form of pamphleteering – in the pages of *La Révolution surréaliste*, in its successor *Le Surréalisme au service de la révolution*, in numerous tracts and in books such as Aragon's *Traité du Style* (1928), René Crevel's *Le Claveçin de Diderot* (1932), and Benjamin Péret's *Je ne mange pas de ce pain-là* (1934). The Surrealists denounced each successive ministry of the Third Republic, saving their most savage insults for Poincaré, Paul-Boncour and Tardieu. They claimed to be unable to distinguish between the condition of Italy under Mussolini and of France 'where the cop is king'. They vilified the army and reactionary ex-servicemen's organizations. They condemned colonialism and racial discrimination, and helped in the preparation of the PCF's riposte to the Colonial Exhibition of 1931. But in the early 1930s, their campaign against the church and religion eclipsed all the rest. As Crevel put it: 'For a revolutionary intellectual of bourgeois origin, there can be no revolutionary activity without anti-religious activity'.[13] They praised the splendid example set by Russia, where hundreds of churches were dynamited or turned into workers' clubs. From fascism, bourgeois mores, capital punishment, the press, lunatic asylums, to professional sport, the objects of Surrealist polemics paralleled those in the communist party but in range extended far beyond them, finding targets in every section of the superstructure.

Surrealist pamphleteering was predominantly destructive because Surrealist politics remained what they had been from the beginning: the politics of protest. Satire and insult were its main weapons. It proceeded by contradiction and not by argument. It was haphazard and undisciplined, shifting its ground from one

---

12 Jacques Fauvet, *Histoire du Parti Communiste Français,* vol. 1 (Paris: Fayard, 1964), p. 100.

13 René Crevel, *Les Pieds dans le Plat* (Paris: Sagittaire, 1933), p. 277.

phrase to the next. Its tone was invariably violent and tended to swing feverishly between the outraged and the outrageous. It expressed unmistakably the political views of poets – of idealists impatient beyond all endurance at the failure of the real to emulate the imaginable. It reflected an Olympian view of the problems of society: indifferent to all that lay between the poetic image and the Absolute, pitiless towards human weakness, and inexorable in its condemnation of compromise. The technique of Surrealist political writing was also that of poets. When it adopted the verse form, it did not become satire pure and simple, nor did it deteriorate into 'poésie de circonstance'. Its sources were in automatism rather than in dialectical materialism.

A striking series of contrasts may be drawn between Communist propaganda and the Surrealist literature of protest. While the former was addressed to those who might one day make the revolution, the latter was written for its potential victims. The Surrealists' aim was to demoralize their readers and to provoke a class-betrayal on the model of their own. As René Crevel wrote of his most recent book: 'I don't care to see *Etes-Vous Fous?* as anything more than a modest contribution to public demoralization'. While the Communists interpreted contemporary events in the light of the inevitable economic collapse of capitalism, the Surrealists exposed the moral and cultural symptoms of the same *débâcle*. Communist theory explained the substructure of the social system and the Surrealists denounced and ridiculed the decrepit superstructure. They sought not so much to convince as to move, not so much to argue the cause of a particular programme as to arouse the feeling of revolt and to prompt the demand that *something* must be done. While the Communists instructed the proletariat in the strategy of revolution, the Surrealists were trying to bring about the emotional climate in which the revolution might break out.

Spasmodic demonstrations and pamphleteering did not solve the fundamental problem of effectiveness. As Communists outside the Party, the Surrealists' only *raison d'être* could be that the dissemination of their ideas in some way hastened the advent of the revolution. Yet their scanty finances compelled them to publish their works in limited editions which were bought mainly by bibliophiles. The average circulation of their reviews was only 2000, and the quality of their audience as dubious as its size was small. By 1930 there was no escaping the truth of Aragon's warning: 'The snobs are here'.[14] Certain elements in Surrealism – its taste for scandal, for blasphemy, for the bizarre and the erotic – attracted the anarchistic and bohemian set among the aristocracy and bourgeoisie. This unwanted public sought to detach the artistic aspects of Surrealism from their moral and implicitly revolutionary base.

---

14 Louis Aragon, 'Introduction à 1930', *La Révolution surréaliste*, 15 December 1929.

To these threats to neutralize their revolt, the Surrealists replied by enforcing a rigid self-discipline and by eliminating everything in their works that could provide an excuse for misinterpretation. Breton decided to purge the group of those adherents who were seeking to exploit for their own ends the artistic techniques that Surrealism had discovered and those whose revolt was sentimental, anarchistic or a pretence. In February 1929 an ultimatum in the form of a circular letter was sent out to 70 members of the group asking them what form of collective enterprise they were prepared to collaborate in. Many of the addressees did not reply. Some, like Antonin Artaud, who had already been expelled, thought that the social revolution was irrelevant to the problems which Surrealism had originally made its own and that the human condition was incapable of improvement by social means. Others, like Philippe Soupault, refused to submit to a Surrealist discipline after having joined the group with the express intention of escaping that imposed on them by their families in their youth. By the end of 1929, Joan Miró, Robert Desnos, Roger Vitrac, André Masson, Michel Leiris and Raymond Queneau among many others had been banished or had left the group of their own accord.

The extreme bitterness of these internal disputes reflected the habits of a PCF cell rather than of a literary group. Votes of confidence and interrogations of members were universal characteristics of revolutionary organizations such as the Surrealists aspired to become. At the Bar du Château reunion in March, in their reception of the young *Grand Jeu* group, Breton and Aragon adopted inquisitorial techniques, and a sectarian vocabulary and ritual identical with those of which they had themselves been the victims at the hands of the PCF Control Commission only two years before.

Breton's efforts to make Surrealism an effective revolutionary force while maintaining its independence by steering a course between the Scylla of assimilation into the art world and the Charybdis of absorption by the communist party, caused casualties on the left of the group as well as on the right. The most serious defections occurred in 1932 when Aragon, Luis Buñuel, Georges Sadoul, Maxime Alexandre and Pierre Unik left the group for the party. Under the influence of Mayakovsky and Elsa Triolet, whom he had met in 1928, and of his experiences in Russia at the Kharkov Conference of Revolutionary Writers in 1930, Aragon had rejoined the PCF; he became editor of *La Lutte Antireligieuse*, and was encouraged by Maurice Thorez to undertake progressively more responsible work for the party. He was also subject to increasing moral pressure to break with the Surrealists. On 5 January 1932, *L'Humanité* announced the founding of the 'Association des Ecrivains Révolutionnaires' (AER), which would be open only to intellectuals who were already party members. Such regulations might have been deliberately calculated to disunite the Surrealists, some of whom were practising PCF members and some not.

Matters came to a head when Aragon was prosecuted for sedition on account of his most unsurrealistic propaganda poem 'Front Rouge'. The Surrealists rallied to his defence and distributed a petition which soon gathered over 200 signatures, including those of many prominent poets, novelists, painters and musicians. The terms of one paragraph of this petition suggested that the Surrealists expected all poetry, no matter how subversive its implications, to be immune from legal proceedings. Romain Rolland, André Gide, Jules Romains and Roger Martin du Gard refused to sign the petition, believing that the Surrealists were trying to shirk their responsibilities now that they were threatened with serious retaliation from the regime. Breton was in fact restating a point made in the *Manifesto* of 1924, that the Surrealist poet was a mere 'recording machine' of the voice of his unconscious for the utterances of which he could not be held legally or morally liable. Though this may have been true of much Surrealist writing, it was clearly irrelevant in the case of 'Front Rouge', which was a very deliberately composed *poème de circonstance* and as such an example of a genre abominated by the Surrealists. As the affair progressed, it became less a matter of defending Aragon from prosecution than of defending the Surrealist conception of poetry against those who, in Breton's opinion, were prepared to sacrifice the integrity of art to the needs of propaganda. The contradiction in Breton's pamphlet, *Misère de la Poésie*, lay in its attempt to exculpate 'Front Rouge' in the name of an idea of poetry of which this particular work was the very negation. Though Breton may have succeeded in extricating Aragon from the grip of the law, he drove him straight into the arms of the Communists. Breton's public critique of the party's policy towards artists, a critique he had long restrained himself from making despite constant provocation from Léon Moussinac and Jean Fréville in *L'Humanité*, forced Aragon to make the choice about which he had been hesitating for the previous 12 months. On 10 March, a note appeared in *L'Humanité*, in the name of the AER, announcing Aragon's disavowal of all connections with the Surrealists and his denunciation of their position as 'objectively counter-revolutionary'.

The 'Aragon affair' revealed a disagreement between Communist and Surrealist ideas about the writer's role in the revolutionary struggle that had grown deeper as the era of comparative tolerance towards intellectuals, fostered by Trotsky and Lunacharsky, was superseded in the USSR by that of domination by RAPP, the Association of Proletarian Writers, and of the imposition of the dogma of 'socialist realism' in 1934. Since 1928 Breton had argued that there could be no such thing as a 'proletarian art' under a capitalist regime, and that the culture which developed after the revolution would be classless rather than proletarian – the first 'human' culture. The twentieth-century artist, he affirmed, whether in Russia or the capitalist West, was subject to a determinism imposed by the necessary evolution of art in the recent past as well as to the laws of economic determinism. Both were equally ineluctable and it was from its 'situation' in their framework that the artist's work derived its authenticity.[15] As an example of what he meant by 'une culture résolument libératrice', Breton traced out an artistic tradition which went back through Picasso, Lautréamont, Rimbaud, Borel, Courbet and Sade, the work of all of whom was at once an attack on the absurdities of the existing social order and a vision of a new world. He claimed that art would lose its authenticity if it was made to serve immediately political ends and adopted an alien subject matter. The revolutionary artist had to preserve his freedom *as* an artist. If not he was likely to be lost not only as an artist but as a revolutionary. By the very fact that art strove to be totally human it was bound to be subversive in a society that was intrinsically inhuman.[16]

Ultimately, the differences between Breton on one side and Aragon and the communists on the other were about the nature of communication. For Breton, a writer's 'meaning' lay in the words he wrote and the intention behind them; their subversive value was latent within them. For Aragon, meaning lay solely in the interpretation made by the reader or by the majority of society at any given time. Once Aragon became convinced of the ineffectiveness of Surrealist protest, he was driven to seek a uniquely social remedy. If words were vain, it was necessary to change the reader or society as a whole. Aragon concluded that unswerving service to the revolution was the writer's first duty not merely for the sake of his ideals as a man but for the sake of the validity of his writing.

* * *

The mid-1930s, which saw a whole new generation of French intellectuals flocking towards the PCF and its 'front organizations' in recognition of its stand against fascism and its recently adopted 'Popular Front' strategy, coincided with the growing disillusionment of the Surrealists. They had joined the AER, now re-christened the Association des écrivains et artistes révolutionnaires (AEAR), when it was partially liberalized by Vaillant-Couturier following Stalin's dissolution of the sectarian RAPP, on which it had been modelled. Breton and his friends edited tracts, helped to judge a workers' poetry competition, and did their share of routine work in the organization. But harmony was short-lived. Breton found himself voting regularly with the minority at committee meetings. He was called to answer for articles in the Surrealist review, and it was one of these, a letter from Ferdinand Alquié deriding the puritanism of Soviet society, that led to the expulsion of all the Surrealists, save Crevel and Tzara, from both the Association and the PCF in July 1933.

By now the Surrealists had given up their pretence of the 1920s that the Russian Revolution had not yet said its last word. They were no longer reluctant

---

15 André Breton, 'Reply to Enquiry about Proletarian Literature', *Monde*, 8 September 1929.

16 André Breton, *La Position Politique du Surréalisme* (Paris: Sagittaire, 1935).

to voice their disappointment with the social pattern that was emerging in the Soviet Union. The suicides of Essenin and Mayakovsky were evidence that the atmosphere in Russia was profoundly uncongenial to poetry and spiritually barren because, as the Surrealists put it, the problem of material necessity had been allowed to ride roughshod over human necessity. They were appalled by the communists' obsession with material productivity and by the premium they put on the virtues of industry. Before the picture of Russia presented by Soviet propaganda, Breton found it difficult to avoid the reaction: 'Ce n'est que cela!'[17]

The Communists' reversal in May 1934 of the 'class against class' strategy with which they had persevered for the previous six years further alienated the Surrealists, who saw the decision to cooperate with the socialist leaders in the Popular Front as a treacherous concession to the bourgeois democratic system. Another blow was the Stalin-Laval pact of mutual assistance in the spring of 1935. This *volte-face*, after years of propaganda about imperialist war-mongering against the workers' fatherland, meant that French Communists were virtually ordered to put an end to their attacks on the national military build-up and jettison the watchword of 'revolutionary defeatism' which had first attracted the Surrealists to Communism at the time of the Moroccan War. It seemed to them that the aims of the International were being sacrificed for the sake of the security of the Russian state, and that the latter was behaving with the selfish cynicism of any bourgeois regime.

* * *

The Surrealists' final repudiation of Stalinist communism came in the summer of 1935 and was occasioned by a cultural rather than a political issue. Breton was deprived of his right to speak at the International Congress of Writers for the Defence of Culture (as a punishment for boxing the ears of the visiting Russian delegate, Ilya Ehrenburg). René Crevel committed suicide on the eve of the Congress after vain efforts to get this right restored to Breton. In the pamphlet *Du Temps que les Surréalistes avaient raison*, the group gave free rein to their long pent-up anger about the Congress, the recent Pact, socialist realism, the Stalinist personality cult, and Communist Party intolerance. The pamphlet ended with the words: 'Ce régime, ce chef, nous ne pouvons que leur signifier formellement notre défiance'.

The break did not mean that the Surrealists ceased to participate in politics. (The group is still politically active to this day.) In the later 1930s, they were prominent anti-fascists, sent some of their number to serve the Republic in Spain, formed two ephemeral revolutionary organizations: Contre-Attaque and the Fédération internationale de l'art révolutionnaire indépendant (FIARI), and

17 André Breton, *Les Vases Communicants* (Paris, 1932), p. 169.

established close relations with the Trotskyists. Nevertheless from 1935 onwards it was clear that they had failed to achieve the three reconciliations referred to at the beginning of this chapter. They could no longer associate the cause of 'spiritual revolution' with that of international Communism, the only credible agent of social revolution. The group's artistic and political activities were definitively separated. Lacking their own review after 1933, they had begun to contribute to fine art magazines such as *Minotaure* or to friendly literary periodicals, while the only outlets for their politics were sporadic tracts drawn up in response to particular events. As the notoriety of the movement became international and as one exhibition of Surrealist painting succeeded another, the plea that it was essentially different from other avant-garde 'isms' became increasingly difficult to sustain. Ideological rigour in the group had relaxed to such a degree that even Salvador Dalí, who did not hide his fondness for Hitler and Franco, was tolerated until the eve of the war. Except in rare instances, political action arose from individual rather than collective initiatives. The Surrealists' main preoccupation was now the defence of art's independence against the only political movement they had believed in. The intellectual unity which Breton had struggled to maintain for so long was shattered. Not only had the Surrealists to reconcile themselves to a division of labour between those whose watchword was 'change life' and those who worked to 'transform the world'; they had to face the fact that, in the political circumstances of the time, these two forces were working in diametrically opposite directions.

Although it was ostensibly the particular character that Communism assumed under Stalin that accounted for these setbacks, there were many other factors that would have prevented any lasting association between the Surrealists and the militants. The Surrealist argument, for instance, that the common roots of both Surrealism and Marxism in the Hegelian dialectic would make them readily conciliable was highly dubious. On the philosophical plane, the Surrealists grossly distorted their original ideas in order to make them acceptable to the Marxists. Jules Monnerot writes of the unfortunate efforts they made to fit themselves into 'a sort of pseudo-Hegelian orthopedic apparatus'.[18] It was these efforts which explain the misuse or excessive use of Marxist jargon in Surrealist works. They recited the rubrics of Marxism-Leninism like a catechism. They swallowed down the bitter pill of materialist determinism even though, as taught by contemporary communists, it involved a dualism of the kind which it was the avowed aim of Surrealism to surmount. The sincere will to believe was not sufficient to bring faith. Surrealist Marxism was condemned either to remain superficial or to distort Surrealism more profoundly. To quote Breton: 'Personally, the violence that I had to inflict on myself did not enable me to toe the line for very long'.[19]

18 Jules Monnerot, *La Poésie Moderne et le Sacré* (Paris, 1945), p. 76.
19 André Breton, *Entretiens* (Paris, 1952), pp. 69–70.

The Surrealist conception of the mechanism of revolution was different from that of the Marxists. In order to justify Surrealist artistic and psychological speculation in the name of revolutionary utility, Breton was compelled to stress the relative independence of the superstructure and to play down the effects of materialist determinism. He made extensive use of Engels's letter to Joseph Bloch to this effect. Only if the superstructure was independent to some degree could the Surrealists demand that art *should* be free. For this demand presupposed that art *could* be free. If their position was compatible with the ideas of Marx and Engels, it was not so with those of Lenin, who rejected the possibility of any kind of liberation within the terms of the existing substructure since such a hypothesis would make its overthrow less urgent. Breton claimed, on the contrary, that greater awareness of the unused and stifled potentialities of man would make the demand for revolution still more urgent. Psychological awareness would fortify social awareness. Changing the picture which men had of the laws governing the world would make still more necessary the transformation of the substructure. The existing social order, far from being an insuperable barrier beyond which, if it was finally broken down, lay a land where all man's problems would be solved, was for the Surrealists no more than a fragile screen standing between man and the real problems which he had yet to face. Furthermore, unless the business of the 'interpretation of man' went on simultaneously with that of the 'transformation of the world', there was every likelihood that the social order finally emerging from the revolution would not be very different from the one that had been destroyed.

There was a crucial difference between the ends envisaged by Surrealists and by Marxists. If both saw the revolution as the prelude to the founding of a world based on the desires of men, their ideas about the content of these desires were not the same. For the Marxists they were material while for the Surrealists they were primarily subjective and spiritual. The resulting human 'goods' in the view of the latter would be individual rather than social. The joys of 'la poésie faite par tous' would be experienced in privacy even when they were accessible to all. As André Masson remarked: 'What is Surrealism if not the collective experience of individualism?'

The Surrealists set little store by the economic effects of the revolution and by the remedying of social injustice. They were more deeply offended by the stupidity and presumption of the ruling classes than moved by the suffering of the victims of exploitation. The *idea* of social injustice repelled them far more than its real effects. Paul Eluard once confessed:

> For my part I don't love the wretched, not in the least. I don't feel any love for the man I come across begging at the entrance to the Metro. It revolts me, I think it absurd and disgraceful that things can be so. But I feel no pity, no love.[20]

---

20 Jean Duval, 'Avec Paul Eluard', *Europe*, November–December 1962.

In *Nadja*, Breton declared that it was not the misery of the workers that disposed him in their favour but the vigour of their protest against it.

The Surrealist revolution was conceived, in effect, on a different plane of experience from that of the Marxists. A new 'October' was envisaged as the prelude to the 'changing of life' rather than as an organic element in it. Only the ambiguous definitions of the word 'revolution' permitted the prolonged Surrealist misunderstanding that there was real common ground between their aims and those of the Marxists. Their own Marxism could never be more than a 'placage', a flimsy façade tacked on to a philosophy that was different in kind. Their attempt to unite the two meant either the tortured readjustment of Surrealist ideas or the forcible addition to Marxism of ideas that had no place in it. Both alternatives were tried and found impracticable.

If the Marxism of the Surrealists was a 'placage', then their joining the Communist Party, as Pierre Drieu La Rochelle had been the first to warn them,[21] was a coincidence rather than an intellectual and moral necessity. The stalwarts of the PCF Central Committee had more reason to be suspicious of the Surrealists' adherence than that of other intellectuals, since the former had a private revolutionary purpose while the latter, on the whole, did not. The Surrealists' role, ostensibly artistic but refusing to be qualified as such, apparently not political but demanding to be considered as such, made negotiations fruitless. The communists did not want adherents who already identified themselves either as writers or as revolutionaries, but only individuals who were prepared to serve as the party required them. Unlike other fellow-travellers, the Surrealists were conspicuously resistant to what David Caute calls 'the law of compensations', according to which intellectuals who began to support the communists on one issue usually came to support them on all points. The Surrealists, as we have seen, jealously maintained their right to freedom of criticism within the party and outside it.

Their stress on the maintenance of the moral rigour of the revolutionary ideal is perhaps the key to their relations with the Communists. Such moral rigour was meant to meet a need not only in the Communist cause but in Surrealism itself, and its exercise was to be in two directions rather than one. First, and most obviously, the Surrealists claimed to watch over the ideals represented by the Communist revolution. Secondly, and no less important, the Communist revolution was required to act as a guarantor of the real effectiveness of Surrealism. It is for this latter reason that the political history of Surrealism leaves the impression that the Surrealists were using Communism for their own ends. Communism was their shield against absorption by the Paris literary and artistic world, against a decline into dilettantism and bohemia. It seems that,

---

21 Pierre Drieu La Rochelle, 'Troisième Lettre aux Surréalistes', *Les Derniers Jours*, 8 July 1927.

rather than looking forward to the prospects of sustained commitment within the party or its subsidiary organizations, the Surrealists were always looking back over their shoulders to see the effects of their step on their own group and its situation in the cultural scene. Communism was at the furthest remove from aestheticism; it set the seal on an intellectual revolt which the bourgeoisie persisted in not taking seriously. It is noticeable that questions of political principle were invariably raised by André Breton at moments when the group seemed to be on the point of yielding to the temptations of artistic irresponsibility, individualism and gratuitousness. At these moments the degree of political commitment of its members was taken as the test of their integrity as Surrealists. Communism was thus the touchstone by which to judge the health of Surrealism. It offered a means of maintaining discipline and cohesion in the group which would have been most difficult if Surrealism had remained completely un-political. But Communism could be a touchstone only so long as the Surrealists were outside the party, hence the perpetual game of advance and retreat which was endemic to the group's relations with Communism. Breton's movement derived its very existence from the tension, in constant need of readjustment, between the world of art and the party of the proletariat.

It may be that the term 'politics' when applied to Surrealism is a misnomer. The Surrealists seldom advanced beyond the stage of political *agitation*, since they rejected or were incapable of the sustained application which commitment demanded. Breton was the first to confess, to Pierre Naville, this lack of concentration:

> You know the degree to which we are the slaves of impatience. The slightest delay in the achievement of something which we've regarded once and for all as inevitable affects us far more than some other much more serious defeat.

Time and time again they took up a political cause with fire and enthusiasm, pursued it for a while and then let it drop, leaving to others the spadework which could alone lead to any real achievement. The very diversity of the action which they defended as serving the revolution makes one suspect its relative importance. They frequently maintained that, under the existing regime, all kinds of behaviour – interrupting meetings, raiding newspaper offices, insulting priests and soldiers – was of revolutionary value. They never showed satisfactorily, however, that this kind of action possessed an effectiveness equal to that of the militants whom they refused to join. It seems that they committed themselves to little tasks in order to avoid commitment to bigger ones.

Perseverance in any single line of political action would ultimately have been contrary to the very spirit of Surrealism. In the simplest terms: action, which was relative and contingent, was bound to betray the Surreal, which was absolute. Prolonged action belittled or infringed the global nature of Surrealist desires. Agitation, on the other hand, by virtue of its ephemeral character and constant susceptibility to change (it could be taken up and abandoned at will), seemed to escape these limitations. It did not contradict what Julien Gracq calls Breton's 'manie cavalière et intriguante de s'absenter'.[22] It provided a compromise, however disappointing in its final results, in answer to the cruel dichotomy between an end which promised every release (the revolution) and the means which demanded every discipline (militant Communism).

Despite all their declarations to the contrary, it still remains uncertain whether the Surrealists ever chose definitely between the alternative means of saving the human spirit: rescuing it from the world of reality (a metaphysical or 'religious' solution), or creating a new reality in which it could flourish (a social and political solution). In the *Second Manifesto*, Breton referred to 'the supreme irony which applies to everything including political regimes'. Apparently the Surrealists, even in the period of their greatest political activity, never lost their original pessimism or their awareness of the eternal gap between the aspirations of man and his achievements. Such intrinsic pessimism did not stop them believing in the necessity to struggle for reform, but it did make them strangers to the single-minded optimism that was the strength of the Communist militants.

If these are some of the explanations of the failure of Surrealist attempts at active participation in politics, they do not invalidate the fundamental aims of the Surrealist adventure or detract from its unique interest. The Surrealists' demands for a society based on the psychological needs and desires of mankind rather than imposed by the dictates of utility, logic and mindless economic determination, are still profoundly relevant. So too are their efforts to overcome the divorce between the artist and society and to improve the spiritual quality of life. The Surrealists, says André Masson, had to *dream* politically or cease to be. But they were unable at the same time to *act* politically. Perhaps it is unjust to blame them for this failure. As Victor Crastre writes, and his remarks about Breton may be applied to the Surrealists as a whole:

> The debate between politics and mysticism is an eternal one: the pure revolutionary and the creator of new social forms are never the same man ... The man who combined the two vocations would be a sort of monster (of perfection). From this point of view what might be considered as Breton's failure has been on the contrary the condition of his salvation.[23]

---

22 Julien Gracq, *André Breton* (Paris, 1948), p. 202.

23 Victor Crastre, 'André Breton et la Liberté', in Marc Eigeldinger, *Essais et Témoignages à André Breton* (Neuchâtel, 1950).

Chapter 2

Towards a New Construction: Breton's Break with Dada and the Formation of Surrealism

*Theresa Papanikolas**

In 1919 – months before Tristan Tzara brought Dadaism to Paris – André Breton and Philippe Soupault applied automatic writing to literature and composed the series of narratives known as *Les Champs magnétiques*.[1] Three years later, Breton explained that the 'autonomous' creation of this text captured the state of semi-wakefulness ideal for releasing unconscious 'poetic elements':

> In 1919 my attention was fixed on the [...] partial phrases which, [...] while falling asleep, became perceptible to my mind without my being able to discover [what] might have predetermined them. These phrases [...] appeared to me as poetic elements of the first order. At first I confined myself to jotting them down. It was only later that Soupault and I dreamed of reproducing the state in which they were formed.[2]

By this time, Breton had become interested not only in automatic writing, but in all ways of accessing the unconscious, and it is therefore fitting that he would emphasize his somnambulance when describing how *Les Champs magnétiques* 'spontaneously' issued from his and Soupault's pens. Indeed, he continued to claim this book was 'not Dada at all', but 'the first Surrealist work'.[3]

In establishing a Surrealist pedigree for *Les Champs magnétiques*, Breton situated himself and Soupault within a 'proto-Surrealist' lineage that included the Italian metaphysical painter Giorgio de Chirico, the symbolist Comte de Lautréamont, and the Marquis de Sade, thereby sealing that pre-Dada text's Surrealist critical fate. Since then, his lead has been followed by many scholars,

* I am grateful to Patricia Leighten for her help on all phases of this essay. I would also like to thank Linda Henderson, William Homer and Jodi Hauptman for their additional suggestions.

1 Excerpts from *Les Champs magnétiques* were first published in *Littérature*, no. 8 (1919), pp. 4–10, no. 9 (1919), pp. 2–7 and no. 10 (December 1919), pp. 9–16. All translations are mine unless otherwise indicated.

2 André Breton, 'Entrée les médiums', *Littérature*, n.s., no. 6 (1922), p. 2.

3 André Breton, *Entretiens avec André Parinaud* (Paris: Nouvelle Revue Française, 1952), p. 56.

who argue that the existence of this early example of automatism proves that Breton and his colleagues had 'discovered' Surrealism long before their brief collaboration with Tzara, and that Dada therefore had little to do with Surrealism's genesis. Marguerite Bonnet, for example, traces Surrealism's origin to Breton's youthful study of Symbolist poetry and identifies Surrealism's mature expression in *Les Champs magnétiques*; indeed, she concludes, Surrealism was fully formed long before Breton ever met Tzara, and Dada, 'drowning in spectacle', was only a 'momentary diversion'.[4] Robert Short, moreover, argues that Tzara's 'nihilism' offered Breton and his colleagues little more than a 'schematized and radicalized [...] picture of Dada', which was ultimately unable to alter the 'salient principles of Surrealism [already established] prior to the advent of Dada in Paris'.[5]

Other interpretations, however, have challenged Breton's revisionism in order to preserve the 'Dadaist' history of both Surrealism and *Les Champs magnétiques*. Its co-author Soupault, for example, sounded more Dadaist than Surrealist when he described automatism not as a gateway to new poetic styles but as a 'liberation' of poetry from 'systems' and from the 'apparatus of logic'.[6] Michel Sanouillet, moreover, has traced the inspiration for *Les Champs magnétiques* to automatic poetry published by Tzara and Picabia in the early 1919 issues of *Dada* and *391*, and, on the basis of this precedent and others, he concludes that 'Surrealism was the French form of Dada'.[7]

Yet to view Surrealism merely as a continuation of Dada overlooks the substantial differences between the two movements; likewise, to deny Dada's influence ignores its significant role in Surrealism's early history. Indeed, though all of these approaches rightly point out that Paris Dada was never an ideologically unified bloc, none has offered a satisfactory critical examination of the infighting that plagued the *Littérature* poets' tense collaboration with Tzara. The source of the conflict was the critical position of Tzara's revolutionary Dadaism, which was inspired by anarchist theories debated in Zurich Dada circles and aimed at undermining society at the cultural level.

Particularly relevant for Tzara was the egoist philosophy of Max Stirner, who defined society exclusively in terms of the egoist self and thus inspired a

---

4 Marguerite Bonnet, *André Breton: Naissance de l'aventure surréaliste* (1975; rpd, Paris: José Corti, 1988), pp. 402–3, and ch. 6, 'Passage de dada', pp. 198–258.

5 Robert Short, 'Paris Dada and Surrealism', *Journal of European Studies* IX (1979), pp. 76, 80.

6 Philippe Soupault, 'Essai sur la poésie', 1950, cited in Michel Sanouillet, *Dada à Paris*, 3rd edn (Paris: Flammarion, 1993), p. 135.

7 Sanouillet, *Dada à Paris* (Paris: Pauvert, 1965), pp. 130, 420. Other writers substantiate Sanouillet's view. William Rubin, for example, uses a formalist approach to conflate Dada and Surrealist art on the basis of their anthropomorphism and use of the marvellous. See William Rubin, *Dada, Surrealism and their Heritage*, rev. edn (London: Thames and Hudson, 1978).

radically individualist strain of anarchism in which the rebellious pursuit of intellectual 'ownness' contained the key to liberating individuals from dogmas.[8] This form of anarchism, known as anarchoindividualism, emerged in the early twentieth century on the *illégaliste* fringe of the broader anarchist movement, and it developed after World War I as an alternative both to Bolshevism and to anarchocommunism. Though rooted philosophically in the individualist component that existed, in some form or another, in all anarchist theory, anarchoindividualism transformed Stirner's extreme egoism into a non-collective and anti-revolutionary version of anarchism. Anarchoindividualist theorists such as Pierre Chardon and Emile Armand were particularly influenced by Stirner's preference for individual rebellion over organized revolution, and, rejecting violent insurrection in favour of intellectual development, they debated the transformative potential of the unfettered intellect and ultimately located 'revolution' specifically in creative freedom and formal innovation. After World War I, their revolutionary position was elaborated by a second anarchoindividualist faction consisting of writers such as Florent Fels, Marcel Sauvage and André du Bief who, influenced by the aristocratic philosophy of Friedrich Nietzsche, sought to mobilize artistic and poetic 'supermen' into a harmonious coalition of unique, heroic beings.

Tzara had also formulated an interpretation of anarchoindividualism predicated on Stirnerian rebellion, but he located cerebral revolt in the 'destruction' of artistic systems, and, in doing so, placed his Dadaism at ideological loggerheads with other post-WWI avant-garde groups. These groups operated in a politically-charged cultural climate dominated by periodicals such as Paul Dermée's, Amédée Ozenfant's and Charles-Edouard Jeanneret's *L'Esprit nouveau*, Nicolas Beauduin's *La Vie des lettres* and Marcello-Fabri's *La Revue de l'époque*, many of whose contributors paralleled Tzara in exploring intellectual autonomy as a powerful weapon for social change but generally resisted wholesale cultural 'destruction' in favour of 'constructing' a new order in the aftermath of the war. Even Fels's Nietzschean anarchoindividualism can be understood in light of this postwar 'call to order', for he favoured the 'constructive' intellectual elitism implicit in Nietzsche's theories over the vague egalitarianism that could be deduced from Stirner's egoism.[9]

---

8 For Stirner's philosophy, see Max Stirner, *Der Einzige und sein Eigenthum* (1845), trans. Stephen T. Byington as *The Ego and His Own* (New York: Boni and Liveright, 1918).

9 The above discussion of postwar Parisian cultural politics is a synopsis of ideas I developed in *The Cultural Politics of Paris Dada, 1914–1922* (PhD diss., University of Delaware, 1999), where I examined Zurich and Paris Dada both in relation to anarchism and in dialogue with other politicized groups. My interpretation of the call-to-order runs counter to the argument presented by Kenneth Silver in *Esprit de Corps: The Art of the Parisian Avant-Garde and the First World War* (Princeton: Princeton

That these plans for social transformation ran counter to Tzara's Dadaism not only brought about the decline of Paris Dada but also catalyzed the development of Surrealism; indeed, this conflict forced Breton to redefine his individualism, his Dadaism and his anarchism. In 1921, Breton sponsored a series of cultural critiques known as the 'Great Dada Season', and in doing so he began to drift away from Dada destruction to formulate an alternative to the constructive political models debated in postwar milieux. From that revision of Dada to the publication of the first *Manifesto of Surrealism*, Breton and his colleagues developed a new theory of cerebral revolt in which 'revolution' and 'construction' merged in the poetic liberation of the unconscious. Indeed, Breton's uneasy association with Dada, as well as the *Littérature* poets' interest in 'psychological automatism' formed the basis for his revision of Dadaist anarchoindividualism into a plausible anarchist model for social change.

Dada debuted in Paris on 23 January 1920, before an audience that included the angry André Salmon, who felt unfairly lured into a pointless literary trap, and the incensed Fels, who ordered the performers to 'go back to Zurich'.[10] For Tzara, this performance enacted Dadaist revolution, for its spontaneous evolution operated independently of aesthetic laws, and its ephemeral existence negated all possibility of systematization. While Tzara remained satisfied to watch Dada unfold in such spectacular unpredictability, Breton became sceptical that Dada's cultivation of chaos limited it to the provocation of scandal for its own sake. Thus he was disappointed, according to Sanouillet, to discover that Dada had left him ill-equipped ideologically to settle a dispute between anarchist intellectuals and socialist leaders at the Club du Faubourg performance less than a month later. And, when Dada proved too esoteric for its working-class audience at the Université Populaire du Faubourg Saint-Antoine, he

University Press, 1989). Silver has located an avant-garde 'new spirit' in postwar Cubist and other modernist groups, which, he claims, offered a rational alternative to the emotional excess of fin-de-siècle painting and paralleled official efforts to rebuild France after the destructive chaos of the war. Recognizing an affinity between this aesthetic 'construction' and postwar 'reconstruction', Silver argues for the necessary capitulation of the largely internationalist avant-garde to the strident propaganda of the bellicose French right wing, which lay ancestral claim to Latin classicism in order to justify forming an anti-German nationalist front. I have found, however, that the constructive rhetoric and classical aesthetic that Silver identifies as 'nationalist' also entered into anti-nationalist debates, where postwar artists and intellectuals – likewise deeply concerned with 'constructing' a new society – responded to numerous anarchist and individualist theories to reconcile creative individualism and social responsibility. For a sampling of postwar criticism, see Christopher Green, *Cubism and Its Enemies: Modern Movements and Reaction in French Art, 1916–1923* (New Haven and London: Yale University Press, 1987).

10 For a more detailed description of the Première Vendredi de *Littérature*, see Sanouillet, *Dada à Paris* (1993), pp. 150–54.

realized that Tzara's emphasis on revolution indeed carried little critical weight in contemporary political debates.[11]

In fact, Breton had never been comfortable with the idea of wholesale destruction, and even though he did convince Tzara to transfer Dada to Paris, he expressed fear over 'becoming disqualified' by Tzara's unyielding 'passion to destroy'.[12] Indeed, Breton's years as a Dadaist were shaped by an increasing awareness that poetic liberation must evolve into new and original creation, and by 1922, he had ended his association with Dada to articulate its limitations in the manifesto 'After Dada':

> I deplored the stereotyped character our gestures were assuming, and wrote as follows: 'After all there is more at stake than our carefree existence and our good humor of the moment. [. . .] It seems to me that the sanction of a series of utterly futile "dada" acts is in danger of gravely compromising [our] attempt at liberation [. . .]. Ideas which may be counted among the best are at the mercy of their too hasty vulgarization.'[13]

Thus, while Breton admired Tzara's revolutionary pursuit of spontaneity, he considered Dadaist destruction to be limited by its repetitiveness and obsession with instant gratification. In his view, 'The anarchic nature of [Dada's] protest, its love of scandal for scandal's sake, in short, its whole offensive thrust' could never 'free us [. . .] from that hideous cage in which we struggled', and Tzara, though he 'walked for a time with defiance in his eye', ultimately remained unable to 'stage a veritable coup d'état'.[14] Thus, Breton concluded, Dada had become so enslaved by its own pursuit of scandal that it had compromised the intellectual liberty necessary for true revolutionary creation.

---

11 The Club du Faubourg was a revolutionary club that followed the politics of its leader, Léo Poldès. On the evening in question, the Dadaists – Breton, Aragon, Ribemont-Dessaignes and Tzara – were scheduled to appear midway through the programme, following a discussion of a 'debate on beauty', a talk on Henri Barbusse and Dostoyevski by the pacifist writer Paul Perret, and a general debate on the nature of pacifism. Pandemonium ensued upon the distribution of *Bulletin Dada* and later, when Breton read Tzara's *Dada Manifesto 1918*. The Université populaire demonstration repeated the Club du Faubourg programme. For a more detailed account of both demonstrations, see Sanouillet, *Dada à Paris* (1993), pp. 163–67.

12 André Breton to Tristan Tzara, 17 October 1919, cited in Short, 'Paris Dada and Surrealism', p. 86.

13 André Breton, 'Après Dada', *Comœdia* (March 1922), rpd in Robert Motherwell, ed., *The Dada Painters and Poets*, trans. Ralph Manheim, 2nd edn (Cambridge and London: The Belknap Press of the Harvard University Press, 1989), p. 205.

14 André Breton, 'Characteristics of the Modern Evolution and What it Consists Of'', a lecture originally delivered in Barcelona in 1922, rpd in André Breton, *The Lost Steps*, trans. Mark Polizzotti (Lincoln: The University of Nebraska Press, 1996), pp. 122–23.

Breton also remained unconvinced that the constructive rhetoric being 'bandied about [...] in [...] *La Vie des lettres*' offered a suitable alternative to Dada's 'utterly futile [...] acts'.[15] In his view, these postwar debates centred on the 'classical' nature of the 'modern spirit', and they perpetuated a 'rigid return to tradition' that, like Dada, possessed the cult-like potential to descend into dogma.[16] 'Pardon me for thinking that, unlike ivy, I die when I become attached', he wrote, putting distance between himself and all postwar cultural circles. 'Should I worry', he added, 'that my words might damage the cult of friendship that [...] leads straight to the cult of patriotism?'[17] Instead, he theorized his own 'return to tradition', which emphasized 'provocation' as the key to real anti-authoritarian construction.

> A truth will always benefit from adopting an outrageous means of expression. [...] I [do not] desire to impose my point of view [...] indeed, I hold it only as long as I have not yet managed to make others share it. It is at this price I [hope] to maintain a certain aristocracy of thought, which is the only means by which [I] might perhaps be induced to 'return to tradition' – given that this tradition, if there is one [...] proves in its choices to be infinitely less rigid and stubborn than the swine who speak in its name.[18]

Thus, though Breton perceived limitations in Dada destruction, he continued to maintain that 'provocation' was a necessary alternative to the contemporary 'return to tradition'. Though his criticism of both viewpoints was published after he had sealed his anti-Dadaist fate, Breton had begun to explore his provocative alternative while still operating nominally under the Dada banner. In the series of 'visits', 'trials' and 'commemorations' that comprised the 'Great Dada Season', he developed his own version of individual liberation that would address the problems of both the 'stereotyped character' of Tzara's Dadaism and the 'external artifice' of postwar 'construction' by acknowledging and exploring the responsibility implied in the rejection of social constructs.[19]

The season began on 14 April with a visit to the Church of Saint-Julien-le-Pauvre, planned as the first of several visits to 'chosen places, in particular to those which really have no reason to exist'.[20] The Dadaists claimed to have chosen this church because its spacious courtyard was an ideal setting for the delivery of manifestoes and because it offered an alternative venue to the concert

---

15 Ibid., p. 112.

16 Ibid., p. 112.

17 André Breton, 'Lâchez tout', *Littérature*, n.s., no. 2 (1922), trans. as 'Leave Everything' in *The Lost Steps*, p. 78.

18 Breton, 'Characteristics', p. 111.

19 Sanouillet, *Dada à Paris* (1993), p. 251.

20 Ibid., p. 255. Other visits were planned but never made to the Parc Buttes-Chaumont, the Gare Saint-Lazare, and the Ourcq Canal. See Breton, *Conversations*, p. 52.

halls on whose stages Dada had operated in the past.[21] Encoded in the Dadaists' practical explanation, however, was veiled social commentary, for not only was their non-religious use of a consecrated spot implicitly anticlerical, they also drew attention to that spot's own anticlericized – and even touristy – contemporary function as a stop on the Friends of Paris Society's tours to various monuments around the city.[22] By designing their 'visit' as a parody of these tours, the Dadaists highlighted the evolution of Saint-Julien-le-Pauvre from pilgrimage site to tourist destination, and, in doing so, they exposed religion as a socially constructed belief system ultimately rendered meaningless by the obsolete 'sacred' monuments that commemorated it. Indeed, the Dadaists proclaimed, 'It is wrong to insist [on such institutions as] the picturesque (*lycée* Janson de Sailly), historical interest (Mont Blanc) and sentimental value (the morgue) [...]. To take part in this first visit is to take into account human progress'.[23]

The exposure of belief systems as meaningless institutional constructs was only the first step in true human progress, however, for to reject them outright, as Tzara had, would be to deny their apparent necessity in society and, inevitably, to run the risk of constructing a new set of institutions to replace them. This, for Breton, had been the downfall of the writer and politician Maurice Barrès, whom the Dadaists placed on mock 'trial' on 13 May 1921.[24] Indeed, if the visit to Saint-Julien-le-Pauvre had questioned the authority of public institutions by exposing the emptiness of their monuments, the Barrès trial emphasized the integrity necessary when replacing public authority with personal moral codes. Barrès's early novels, *L'Ennemi des lois* (1893) and the trilogy *Le Culte du moi* (1910), reflected the Stirnerian egoism that had dominated the prewar anarchoindividualist movement, and they profoundly influenced Breton's generation in their celebration of individual genius.[25] Yet even as Barrès was writing the third volume of *Le Culte du moi*, he had begun to question his youthful anarchoindividualism and to recognize the self as a mere component of a larger, national whole.[26] From then on, personal identity and

21 Sanouillet, *Dada à Paris*, pp. 242–43.

22 Ibid., pp. 255–56.

23 Cited in ibid., p. 255.

24 The Barrès trial was documented in *Littérature* no. 20 (1921), pp. 1–24. Further documentation was planned for no. 21, but now exists only in galley proofs. Sanouillet has reproduced them in *Dada à Paris* (1993), pp. 632–46. See also *L'Affaire Barrès*, ed. Marguerite Bonnet (Paris: José Corti, 1987), an annotated version of the published and unpublished documents from the trial, as well as Frederik Busi, 'Dada and the "Trial" of Maurice Barrès', *Boston University Journal* XXIII:2 (1975), pp. 63–71.

25 For Barrès's political views, see C. Stewart Doty, *From Cultural Rebellion to Counter-Revolution: The Politics of Maurice Barrès* (Athens: Ohio University Press, 1976) and Robert Soucy, *Fascism in France: The Case of Maurice Barrès* (Berkeley: University of California Press, 1972).

26 Doty, *Politics of Maurice Barrès*, p. 22.

national identity were indistinguishable for Barrès, and he aligned himself with a succession of nationalist and even racist ideologies such as Boulangism, nationalist socialism, the Action Française and the parliamentary right wing.[27]

Like Barrès, Breton recognized that extreme individualism had the potential to degenerate into dogmatic elitism; yet he considered Barrès's nationalist solution to be the criminal equivalent of 'the thefts and the crimes of the week'.[28] 'Right away' he wrote, 'we decided to broaden the debate and form a tribunal',[29] and, on 7 May 1921, he joined forces with Pierre Daval, Théodore Fraenkel, Georges Ribemont-Dessaignes and Louis Aragon in 'formally' charging Barrès with an 'attack on the security of the spirit', thus applying Dada's ironic posture to the more serious moral issue of preserving commitment to one's beliefs.[30] Echoing previous Dada demonstrations, the trial was well-publicized and 'performed' at the Salle des Sociétés Savantes; but it offered a clear (though still hilarious) replacement for Dada chaos by aping the solemnity and pompousness of traditional judicial procedure. The ailing Barrès, held back from the trial by his remote location in the South of France, was present in effigy as a department store mannequin, and his accusers, judges and lawyers appropriated the proper attire of barristers by donning white blouses and wigs.[31]

Barrès's transformation from egoist writer to bellicose defender of blood and soil would seem reason enough for his accusation at the hands of the anti-nationalist Dadaists. The debate, however, went beyond his problematic politics to encompass the moral implications of his dramatic change in beliefs.[32] As Breton explained years later, the purpose of the trial was to explore Barrès's

27 For Barrès's Boulangism, see ibid., p. 64. Soucy argues that Barrès' views were proto-fascist, even in his socialist phase. See Soucy, *The Case of Maurice Barrès*, pp. 15–21.

28 André Breton, 'L'Affaire Barrès', *Littérature*, no. 20 (1921), p. 1.

29 Ibid.

30 Ibid.

31 Busi, 'Maurice Barrès', p. 68.

32 Sanouillet, who views Barrès's shifting politics as an abrupt change rather than the gradual progression that it was, discusses the trial in these terms. See Sanouillet, *Dada à Paris* (1993), pp. 265ff. It bears mentioning that the Dadaists were neither unanimous nor consistent in their opinions of Barrès. Soupault (who questioned the verdict) and Aragon (who, in true illégaliste fashion, wished to defend Barrès in the name of the 'right to crime') took his part in both the discussions leading up to the trial and the actual trial itself. Moreover, the Dadaists often solicited Barrès's support. In 1919, for example, Breton had asked him to write a preface for Jacques Vaché's *Lettres du guerre*, and in 1920 he sent him a copy of *Les Champs magnétiques*. That same year, Soupault sent Barrès some poems and, in early 1921 Breton admitted his enduring esteem for *La Culte du moi* in a letter to Jacques Doucet. By placing him on mock trial, however, the Dadaists indicated that their early admiration had ended in disillusionment. See Bonnet, 'Introduction', *L'Affaire Barrès*, pp. 14–15.

responsibility for the authoritarianism that resulted when his will-to-power replaced his disengagement as the foundation of his individualism:

> The problem was to determine [how] a man could be held accountable if his will to power led him to champion conformist values that diametrically opposed the ideas of his youth. [...] If there was a betrayal, what were the stakes? And what recourse did one have against them? Above and beyond the Barrès case, these questions were to agitate Surrealism for quite some time.[33]

Indeed, in developing a conformist philosophy that was ultimately antithetical to individualism, Barrès proved to the Dadaists that he could not be trusted to 'place [his] present activity under the control of [his] future activity' and thus to 'accord one the same relative importance as the other'.[34] Breton pointed this out in the 'Acte d'accusation' published in conjunction with the trial:

> The meaning of a life does not only look at what has been experienced. [...] psychological rule and [...] moral rule [...] still permit us to make an example of this life. It contributes [...] to the formation of other individualities. [...] Not only has Barrès found himself invested in a mandate that he has not carried out, but the particularly brilliant situation in which he places himself, joined to the action that [...] carries on the works whose re-edition he continually authorizes [...] shed doubt on the value of all revolutionary agitation.[35]

In contradicting his youthful philosophy, Barrès revealed his total disregard for its inevitable impact on the future, and, in endorsing his early works even after he disavowed their original message, he succeeded in stripping all of his ideas of any ideological weight.

Barrès's simultaneous support for and denial of his early political ideas left him, in Breton's opinion, with nothing credible to say. From the chameleon-like Barrès, Breton immediately turned on the equally contradictory Tzara, whose refusal to take responsibility for his own revolutionary statements placed Dadaism in peril of meeting a similar fate.[36] For his part, Tzara was opposed to the trial: not wishing to force Dada into a judicial model, he reluctantly agreed to participate as a witness.[37] He took the stand only to have his interrogator (Breton) force him to defend his anarchoindividualism and what Breton wished to expose as an apparent lack of ideological focus; in doing so he unwittingly became a stooge in Breton's new individualist agenda of 'forming [...] other

33 Breton, *Conversations*, p. 53.

34 Breton, 'Acte d'accusation', pp. 4–5.

35 Ibid.

36 Bonnet also detects Breton's growing disillusionment with Dadaism in his critique of Barrès. See Bonnet, 'Introduction', *L'Affaire Barrès*, p. 19.

37 Dachy, *The Dada Movement* (Paris: Rizzoli, 1990), p. 141.

individualities' through 'psychological and moral rule'.[38] This was Tzara's first public confrontation with Breton, and he fought desperately to retain his Dadaist persona even as his revolutionary Dadaism came under attack:

> Breton: What [does your antipathy] matter if you never place yourself on the social plane?
> Tzara: Are you saying that [you consider] the social plane [to be] the State, the country, the people or the army? In that case, as I am myself the State, the country, the people and the army, my disposition is only to give you great pleasure.
> B: Do you hope someday to attack the security of the spirit?
> T: [...] I only change opinions and all the delays in these changes make me a little more devoted to planning on disappearing. I am not saying that I would not become nationalist, but I am persuaded that all my friends know that it is in a different spirit than the base demagoguery of the accused.[39]

After the blow dealt by the Barrès trial, Tzara bombarded Paris with an onslaught of his own Dada events, including the debut of his 'opera' *Le cœur à gaz* (19 June 1921), the impromptu disruption of the Futurist *Concert bruitiste* (17 June), and the unjuried and riotously spectacular 'Dada Salon' exhibition.[40] Breton, for his part, definitively abandoned Dada, which, he continued to maintain, inevitably compromised individualism. 'To give one's life for an idea, Dada or [otherwise]', he explained, 'would only [...] prove in favour of a great intellectual misery', and he countered Dada's principled destruction with a new anarchoindividualist theory of social change.[41] This new theory was Surrealism, and it stemmed not only from Breton's rejection of the Dadaist destructive 'dogma' but also from his continuing belief that 'literary activity' offered the best way to 'satisfy one's will to power'; after all, he explained, 'ink and paper alone know how to keep the imagination awake'.[42] Indeed, literature, no longer

---

38 Breton, 'Acte d'accusation', pp. 4–5.

39 'Les Témoins: Tristan Tzara', *Littérature*, no. 20 (1921), pp. 10–11.

40 For these events, see Sanouillet, *Dada à Paris* (1965), pp. 275–76 and the exhibition catalogue, *Salon Dada: Exposition internationale* (Paris: Galerie Montaigne, 1921).

41 André Breton, 'Lâchez tout' in André Breton, *Les Pas perdus* (Paris: Gallimard, 1924, rpd Paris: Gallimard, 1969), p. 110.

42 André Breton, 'Les Chants de Maldoror', *La Nouvelle revue française* (1 June 1920), rpd in *Les Pas perdus*, p. 69. The politics of this early phase of Surrealism has long perplexed scholars. Jack Spector argues that Surrealism was initially collectivism that culminated in Breton's review of Trotsky's biography of Lenin (*La Révolution surréaliste*, October 1925). See *Surrealist Art and Writing, 1919–1939: The Gold of Time* (Cambridge: Cambridge University Press, 1997), p. 75. Helena Lewis, in *The Politics of Surrealism* (New York: Paragon House, 1988), focuses mainly on the Surrealists' alignment with Marxism after 1925, describing early Surrealism as a 'revolution of ideas' without tracing it to a politics. Similarly, Robert Short argues that Surrealism originated in the idea that liberty was 'absolute' though undefined. See Robert Short, 'The Politics

a Dadaist casualty, became revolutionary terrain for Breton, capable of liberating any individual from the constraints of the material world and unleashing the 'higher' reality contained in the 'irrepressible personal imagination'.[43]

In Breton's view, the liberating potential of poetry would only become apparent once the mind was released from all predetermined rituals. To this end, he took automatic writing beyond its largely 'literary' application in *Les Champs magnétiques* to explore it fully as a vehicle for transcending rationalism and for creating spontaneously according to 'an otherwise imbecilic formality'.[44] Breton explained that this 'Surrealist' mental plane reflected 'a certain psychic automatism that corresponds [...] to the state of the dream'.[45] Thus, from 1922 until the publication of the *Manifesto of Surrealism* in 1924, Breton, Aragon and Eluard, together with Benjamin Péret and Robert Desnos, conjured with the irrational mental images revealed both in automatic writing and during periods of semiconsciousness. These uncensored images from the interior psychological realm, were, Breton explained, 'of a fairly rare sort, and all I could think of was to incorporate [them] into my material for poetic construction'.[46]

Of course, the Dadaists had also explored the unconscious as a means of liberation, but whereas their focus was on the chance breakdown of all existing and potential systems, the Surrealists were interested in the spontaneous discovery of a new catalyst for creation. Moreover, in contrast to Dada's strong commitment to destruction, as well to the constructive intellectual elitism envisioned by Fels and other Nietzschean anarchoindividualists, Surrealism balanced anarchism's revolutionary and constructive natures by envisioning a modality of 'poetic' creation that would result from the subordination of rationalism to the unregulated unconscious, thereby definitively obviating the rigid authority of cultural systems. In this way, poetry lost its elite status, became redefined as an unprivileged representative of the impersonal

---

of Surrealism: 1920–36', *Journal of Contemporary History* I:3 (1966), p. 6. Walter Benjamin comes close to linking early Surrealism with anarchism when he discusses the activities of the movement in terms of individualist revolt. See Walter Benjamin, 'Surrealism: Last Snapshot of the European Intelligentsia', in *One Way Street and Other Writings*, trans. Edmund Jephcott and Kingsley Shorter (London: Verso Classics, 1979). Michael Löwy, in 'Walter Benjamin and Surrealism: The Story of a Revolutionary Spell', *Radical Philosophy*, no. 81 (1996), argues that Benjamin identifies Surrealism as 'revolutionary libertarianism'.

43 André Breton, 'Pour Dada', *La Nouvelle revue française* 25 (August 1920), p. 202. Bonnet has also recognized Breton's divergence from Dadaism, which she uses to strengthen her argument that Surrealism developed independently of Dada. See Bonnet, *André Breton*, particularly ch. 6.

44 André Breton, 'Entrée des médiums', pp. 1–2.

45 Ibid.

46 André Breton, 'Manifesto of Surrealism' (1924), rpd in André Breton, *Manifestoes of Surrealism*, trans. Richard Seaver and Helen R. Lane (Ann Arbor: University of Michigan Press, 1972), pp. 21–22.

component in the imagination, and was documented in the dream texts, automatic images and interviews with hypnotized Surrealists that appeared, unedited, in the second series of *Littérature*.[47] Though this anti-poetic and even collaborative aspect of Surrealism evolved into a form of collectivism that reached its high point in the mid-1920s with Breton's review of Trotsky's biography of Lenin and the expulsion of Surrealist individualists like Antonin Artaud, its initial genesis was rooted in Breton's subversion of what he recognized as a dogmatic strain in postwar anarchoindividualism, and psychic automatism was therefore conceived as a new version of anarchoindividualism in which dogma became obsolete. In other words, the original Surrealists conjured with psychic automatism not only as a conduit for spontaneous expression but also as an arena for anarchist revolt.

The initial anarchist nature of the Surrealists' revolution was articulated by Artaud, who showed how their refusal to 'recognize [...] thought' could be transformed into insurrection on the interior, unconscious plane.[48] Likening rationalism to a 'beast that thinks' Artaud warned that a 'lack of the self' would unleash this 'glassy-eyed' monster, and, using unmistakably anarchist revolutionary language, he called for a counterattack:

> [the Surrealist] passes judgement on the self through the interior, and before [such personal] thought the world does not weigh so heavily. [...]
>
> In the name of interior liberty [...] [the Surrealist] snubs you, your world abandoned to desiccating reason, to the bogged-down mimeticism of the centuries, and who built your houses of words and established your repertoires of precepts [...] all the better for the Surrealist world to explode, the only one worth uprooting us.[49]

In explaining the individualist basis for Surrealism, Artaud revealed that movement's initial opposition to all forms of organized politics – even Marxism. This was also the point of Louis Aragon's article, 'Libre à vous', which proclaimed that 'one cannot know how to have liberty in any act that turns itself against liberty', but condemned society's definition of 'liberty' as inherently homogenous, disturbingly generalized and, ultimately, authoritarian:

> Morality, liberty are in your vocabulary. But one looks in vain for you to draw definitions from them. It is [because] there is no morality other than the morality of Terror, freedom other than implacable dominating freedom [...]. There will be chains for the enemies of liberty. Man is free, but not men. There is no limit to all the liberty of the one, but there

47 See especially André Breton 'Récit des trois Rêves', *Littérature* n.s., no. 1 (1922), pp. 5–7 and 'Entrée des médiums'.

48 Antonin Artaud, 'L'Activité du bureau des recherches surréalistes', *La Révolution surréaliste*, no. 3 (1925), p. 31.

49 Ibid.

> is no liberty for all. *All* is an empty notion, a clumsy abstraction. Here ends the social history of humanity.[50]

Implicit in all of this is that real human liberation can only exist independently of such unifying social codes. Indeed, 'social constraints have done their time', Aragon elsewhere proclaimed:

> The idea of prison, the idea of barracks [...] [are] common currency today [...] what makes [them] so vile is how calmly [some people] have dealt with their difficulties through diverse moral and physical abdications (honesty, malady, patriotism).[51]

Moreover, though Aragon became active in the Communist Party during the 1930s, in the mid-1920s he was openly critical of the bureaucratic nature of the Russian Revolution. When the quasi-communist cultural review *Clarté* accused him of 'political thoughtlessness', he issued a rebuttal revealing the anarchoindividualist basis for his anti-communism. Denouncing all organized political and revolutionary movements, he wrote to *Clarté*'s editor, Jean Bernier:

> it pleased you to raise up like a prank a phrase that testified a little to the taste I have for the Bolshevik government, and with it all communism. But you know well enough that 'thoughtlessness' is not my strength, and that it is not up to [you] nor to a party to ask me to know or to ignore something. If you find me closed to the political spirit and, even better: violently hostile to this dishonourable pragmatic attitude [...] you cannot doubt that I have always placed [...] the spirit of revolt well outside of all politics. [...] The Russian Revolution [...] on the scale of ideas, was [...] a vague ministerial crisis. [...] You should treat a little less casually those who have sacrificed their existence to the things of the mind.[52]

The early issues of the magazine *La Révolution surréaliste* gave further voice to Surrealist anarchoindividualism by juxtaposing Surrealist texts with articles on society and politics that were completely anti-authoritarian both in rhetoric and scope. In 'The Last Strike', for example, Breton aligned Surrealism with contemporary revolutionary politics when he complained that 'all those who proclaim the sacred character of labour and exalt it all the more, the more physical it is' have created a 'schism between "manual" and "intellectual" labourers'. The only ones, he went on to explain, who stood to profit from this unfortunate rift were the members of that 'unscrupulous race [...] which exploits both sides', and he offered hope of eliminating the conflict by encouraging 'manual' labourers to respect the revolutionary commitment of their 'intellectual' counterparts:

---

50 Louis Aragon, 'Libre à vous!', *La Révolution surréaliste*, no. 2 (1925), p. 13.

51 Aragon, 'Ouvrez les prisons, Licenciez l'armée: Il n'y a pas de crimes de droit commun', *La Révolution surréaliste*, no. 2 (1925), p. 18.

52 Louis Aragon to *Clarté*, rpd as 'Communisme ou Révolution', *La Révolution surréaliste*, no. 2 (1925), p. 32.

> Certainly I do not deny that the first had some reason to complain to the second. [...] [But] It is no less true that a distinction imposes itself here, which threatens that revolutionary ferment will remain inactive in our era. Thus I think along with all liberated human beings that Revolution – even in its abuses – remains the highest [...] expression that a love of the Good [and] a realization of the unity of the universal and individual wills can offer. [...] Do not let [the revolutionary leaders] ask us to take up their cause [...] still less to make their demands succeed.[53]

Not only did Breton admonish against placing intellectuals in the 'service' of revolution, he also asked that they be allowed to operate unthreatened within leftist circles. Indeed, equating intellectuals with anarchists, he explained that the only way to protect 'those [...] dedicated to [...] the triumph of the mind [...] from the powerful in this world' was to '*repeal* [...] *the indefensible laws aimed at anarchist leaders*'.[54]

The continuing anarchoindividualist basis for Surrealism is revealed in the individualist rhetoric and emphasis on individual freedom characteristic of such manifestoes as *Surrealism and Revolution* (1925):

> With regard to a false interpretation of our enterprise, stupidly circulated among the public, [...] we declare as follows: [...]
> 1. We have nothing to do with literature. [...]
> 2. Surrealism is not a new means of expression, [...] nor even a metaphysic of poetry. It is a means of total liberation of the mind. [...]
> 3. We are determined to make a revolution.
> 4. We have joined the word *surrealism* to the word *revolution* solely to show the disinterested, detached and even entirely desperate character of this revolution. [...]
> 8. We are specialists in Revolt. There is no means of action which we are not capable of employing.
> 9. We say in particular to the Western world: *Surrealism* exists [...] and it is determined to break apart its fetters, even if it must be by material hammers![55]

Thus Surrealism – at least in its early phase – was dominated by the study of the liberating potential of the individual unconscious, and it emerged from anarchist rhetoric and ideas to transform that exploration into real revolutionary goals. This anarchoindividualism – and, by extension, Surrealism – originated not so much in the automatist *Les Champs magnétiques*, but in the *Littérature* group's response both to Dada's revolutionary destruction and to the constructive alternatives being debated in postwar cultural circles. Indeed, these debates forced Breton, along with Aragon, Eluard, Péret and Desnos to

---

53 André Breton, 'La Dernière grève', *La Révolution surréaliste* no. 2 (1925), pp. 1–3.

54 Ibid., p. 3.

55 Louis Aragon et al., *Surrealism and Revolution*, trans. in Helena Lewis, *The Politics of Surrealism*, p. 28.

distance themselves from Dada, and, in the Barrès trial, to address the issue of responsibility in cultural politics by exposing the potential for well-meaning anarchist intellectuals to fall victim to contradiction and ultimately foster polarity. In their experiments with psychic automatism, Breton and his group attempted to liquidate the dogmatism into which both the Dadaists and postwar anarchoindividualists had, in their view, descended. In doing so, they merged destruction and construction into a new theory of anarchoindividualism that recognized the necessity both of the revolutionary act and of the liberated creativity that it would inevitably facilitate.

Chapter 3

Surrealism and the Political Physiognomy of the Marvellous*

Raymond Spiteri

In his perspicacious essay of 1929, 'Surrealism: The Last Snapshot of the European Intelligentsia', Walter Benjamin identified the political import of Surrealism in what he called 'profane illumination'. He located an instance of this illumination in the Surrealist experience of the marvellous, exemplified in the urban narratives of André Breton's *Nadja* (1928) and Louis Aragon's *Paysan de Paris* (1926). According to Benjamin, Breton 'can boast an extraordinary discovery' in *Nadja*:

> He was the first to perceive the revolutionary energies that appear in the 'outmoded,' in the first iron constructions, the first factory buildings, the earliest photos, the objects that have begun to be extinct, grand pianos, the dresses of five years ago, fashionable restaurants when the vogue has begun to ebb from them. The relation of these things to revolution – no one can have a more exact concept of it than these authors. [...] Breton and Nadja are the lovers who convert everything that we have experienced on mournful railway journeys (railways are beginning to age), on Godforsaken Sunday afternoons in the proletarian quarters of great cities, in the first glance through rain-blurred windows of a new apartment, into revolutionary experience, if not action.[1]

Benjamin distinguished here between revolutionary *experience* and revolutionary *action*, fully aware the Surrealists continued to hesitate in the face of the discipline of political militancy.[2] Although this distinction echoed previous

---

* This chapter is based on section two of my thesis, *'Battant comme une porte': Painting and the Cultural Politics of Surrealism, 1924–1929* (unpublished PhD thesis, University of Western Australia, 1999). I would like to thank David Bromfied, Stephanie Green, Robert Short, Robert Lubar and Donald LaCoss for their comments on earlier drafts.

1 Walter Benjamin, 'Surrealism: The Last Snapshot of the European Intelligentsia', in *One Way Street and Other Writings*, trans. Edmund Jephcott and Kingsley Shorter (London: Verso, 1985), p. 229.

2 Benjamin criticized the Surrealists for their lack of revolutionary discipline, noting that they subordinated the 'methodical and disciplinary preparation for the revolution entirely to a praxis oscillating between fitness exercises and celebration in advance'. Ibid, p. 236.

critiques of Surrealism's political position – notably that of Pierre Naville, a former editor of *La Révolution surréaliste*, who posed a stark choice between anarchistic revolt and communist revolution in *La Révolution et les intellectuels: Qu'est-ce que faire les surréalistes?* (1926) – Benjamin differed in that he did not simply advocate joining the Communist Party as the only solution.[3]

When Benjamin returned to this theme at the close of his essay, he located the articulation between political action and the experience of the marvellous in what he called the 'image-realm [*Bildraum*]'. Surrealism's political lesson was 'to discover in the realm of political action a realm reserved one hundred percent for images'.[4] His description deserves to be quoted at length:

> [...] in all cases where an action puts forth its own image and exists, absorbing and consuming it, where nearness looks with its own eyes, the long sought image-realm is opened, the world of universal and integral actualities, where the 'best room' is missing – the realm [...] in which political materialism and physical nature share the inner man, the psyche, the individual, or whatever else we wish to throw to them, with dialectical justice, so that no limb remains unrent. Nevertheless – indeed, precisely after such dialectical annihilation – this will be a realm of images and, more concretely, of bodies. For it must in the end be admitted: metaphysical materialism [...] cannot lead without rupture to anthropological materialism. There is a residue. The collective is a body, too. And the *physis* that is being organized for it in technology can, through all its political and factual reality, only be produced in that image-realm to which profane illumination initiates us. Only when in technology body and image-realm so interpenetrate that all revolutionary tension becomes bodily collective innervation, all bodily innervation of the collective becomes revolutionary discharge, has reality transcended itself to the extent demanded by the *Communist Manifesto*.[5]

Benjamin advances a materialist account of the imagination in this passage. The image-realm is opened at a moment of political and cultural crisis in which hegemonic articulations – that is, the traditional oppositions between action and contemplation, individual and collective, mind and body, technology and nature, etc. – collapse and the conceptual constellations of technological society are rearticulated through the space of images and bodies. Significantly, the image-realm performs a double function: it not only constitutes the collective as a political agent, but it also furnishes the matrix through which the collective articulates its political struggle and challenges the hegemony of official culture.[6]

---

3 Pierre Naville, *La Révolution et les intellectuels: Qu'est-ce que faire les surréalistes?* (Paris: Gallimard, 1927), rpd in an augmented edition as *La Révolution et les intellectuels* (Paris: Gallimard, 1975).

4 Benjamin, 'Surrealism', p. 238.

5 Ibid., p. 239.

6 The image plays a central role in the development of Benjamin's writings during the 1930s. The image-realm of the Surrealism essay is eclipsed by his notion of the

Benjamin's essay was published during February and March of 1929, at a time when the outcome of the Surrealists' attempted rapprochement with the Parti communiste français (PCF) was far from certain. Indeed, his discussion of the image-realm helps illuminate the vexed question of Surrealism's relation to revolutionary politics. Simply charting encounters between members of the Surrealist movement and revolutionary movements only leads to a list of ineffectual meetings or frustrated encounters; meanwhile, the reasons why the Surrealists persistently courted the PCF for near on a decade still remain obscure.[7] Clearly, an adequate account of the relation between the cultural and political dimensions of the Surrealist enterprise is needed, one that will go beyond a chronicle of events to discuss the misunderstanding and bad faith of the participants, and, more importantly, to analyze how the political tension implicit in the Surrealists' position in the social space animates and conditions the work of artists and writers associated with the movement.

This essay discusses Breton's *Nadja* in the context of two 'failed' encounters that delineate Surrealism's ambivalent position in the social space, suspended between the fields of politics and culture.[8] The first encounter is Breton's brief liaison with Nadja, which he would later recount in the book *Nadja*; the second is Breton's attempt to embrace political action and join the PCF. Considered together, these two encounters illustrate the nexus of culture and politics in *Nadja*. Success here is tempered by failure; and a close reading of *Nadja* discloses the profound ambivalence Surrealism harboured towards political action, the interval between words and deeds, image and action. This interval is

---

'dialectical image' in the mid-1930s, which in turn is eclipsed by the 'Messianic cessation of happening' in the 'Theses on the Philosophy of History'. For a discussion of this aspect of Benjamin's writings see the excellent study by Sigrid Weigel, *Body- and Image-Space: Re-reading Walter Benjamin*, trans. Georgina Paul with Rachel McNicholl and Jeremy Gaines (London and New York: Routledge, 1996).

7 On Surrealism and politics see Robert Short, 'The Politics of Surrealism, 1920–36', *Journal of Contemporary History* I:3, pp. 3–25; Helena Lewis, *The Politics of Surrealism* (New York: Paragon House, 1988); Marguerite Bonnet, 'Trotsky et Breton', in Léon Trotsky, *Lénine* (Paris: Presses universitaires de France, 1970), pp. 253–76; Alan Rose, *Surrealism and Communism: The Early Years* (New York: Peter Lang, 1991); Louis Janover, *Surréalisme, art et politique* (Paris: Editions Galilée, 1980); Jean-Pierre Morel, *Le Roman insupportable: L'Internationale littéraire et la France (1920–1932)* (Paris: Gallimard, 1985). The Surrealists' attempt to establish a rapprochement with revolutionary political groups also had a profound effect on the internal membership of the Surrealist movement, fuelling the 'dissident' Surrealism of the late 1920s that has become the subject of many recent commentaries on Surrealism.

8 On the notion of social fields see Pierre Bourdieu, *Language and Symbolic Power*, ed. and intro. John B. Thompson, trans. Gino Raymond and Matthew Adamson (Cambridge: Polity Press, 1991), and *The Field of Cultural Production: Essays on Art and Literature*, ed. and intro. Randal Johnson (Cambridge: Polity Press, 1993). Although Bourdieu's writings have informed the present argument, it is beyond the scope of this essay to discuss his work in any detail.

open to a double reading: traditionally, it has been interpreted as a sign of failure, of the persistent gulf between Surrealism and political action; but, as I shall argue in this essay, it can also be considered as a sign of success, as a manifestation of the 'political' in Surrealism. Here attention must focus on the construction of *Nadja*, particularly the deployment of photographic illustrations, which provides a concrete example of Benjamin's 'image-realm' in which 'action puts forth its own image' and 'no limb remains unrent'.

* * *

Breton's first encounter with Nadja occurred on the late-afternoon of 4 October 1926. He had just purchased Trotsky's latest book from the Humanité bookshop, and was strolling aimlessly on the rue Lafayette in the tenth arrondissement of Paris, when he met a woman in the Place Franz Liszt. Her name was Nadja, because, as she would later explain, 'in Russian it's the beginning of the word hope, and because it's only the beginning'.[9] Nadja appeared to Breton as a living incarnation of the marvellous, possessing an extraordinarily poetic relationship to her environment. Although Breton's encounter with her was ultimately unsuccessful – in essence it lasted no more than ten days – it would be recorded in the book *Nadja*. The implications of this book are broader than an event of personal significance: *Nadja* was Breton's first substantial exposition of what he would later define as 'objective chance'. All the themes of the movement converge within its pages: banal events are presented side by side with the most extraordinary coincidence; the mood oscillates between enthusiasm and lassitude, and self-analysis jostles with statements of political commitment.

Breton described his ambition in *Nadja* to write a book that would be left ajar, 'battant comme une porte'.[10] This image is not just a suggestive metaphor, but a literal description of Breton's *modus operandi*. The narrative demands to be scrutinized in light of this image, interrogating the fragmentary evidence to form a coherent picture of the Surrealist movement during the 1920s. Although Breton initially met Nadja in October 1926, he did not begin writing his account of their relationship until August 1927.[11] These dates bracket another significant event in Surrealism's history. In January 1927, following a series of meetings to decide the appropriate course of action, Aragon, Breton, Paul Eluard, Benjamin

9 André Breton, *Nadja*, trans. Richard Howard (New York: Grove Press, 1960), p. 66. *Nadja* was first published in Paris by Editions Gallimard, under the imprint of the NRF, in 1928.

10 André Breton, *Nadja*, in *Œuvres complètes* I, ed. Marguerite Bonnet, Philippe Bernier, Etienne-Alain Hubert and José Pierre (Paris: Gallimard, 1988). The phrase occurs twice, first on p. 651 and then on p. 751.

11 Mark Polizzotti, *Revolution of the Mind: The Life of André Breton* (London: Bloomsbury, 1996), pp. 285–91.

Péret, and Pierre Unik joined the PCF. Although the other Surrealists were accepted, the party hierarchy subjected Breton's revolutionary credentials to close examination. As a result of this incommodious welcome, and continuing suspicion from his fellow comrades, Breton's tenure as a PCF militant was short-lived, and he soon withdrew from active participation in the PCF.

The significance of the image 'battant comme une porte' becomes apparent when *Nadja* is considered in this context. *Nadja* was an attempt to 'work through' the events of the past year, and these events animate the formal construction of the narrative. The book is not simply an account of Breton's encounter with Nadja – although this is the principal thread of the narrative – but an attempt to traverse the impasse that confronted Surrealism in 1927. A door left ajar is as likely to slam shut as to swing open, so this image succinctly encapsulated the tension implicit in the Surrealists' position in the social space. It locates *Nadja* at the nexus of the cultural and political forces animating Surrealism, describing the point where imagination discovers its double in the quotidian to challenge the hierarchy of values that separate aesthetic from practical objects.[12] Breton was careful to secure the text's proximity to the quotidian, incorporating numerous photographs – ostensibly as a substitute for description.[13] The illustrations introduce a documentary counterpoint to the narrative, establishing a complex articulation between description and event, the marvellous and the quotidian. Yet concern with the proximity of art and life obscures another important aspect of *Nadja*: the proximity of culture and politics. Indeed, considered *in situ*, the illustrations describe Surrealism's trajectory across the social space, plotting its course across the fields of culture and politics.

* * *

The Surrealists discussed joining the PCF in a meeting held on 23 November 1926, some six weeks after Breton's encounter with Nadja. The principal

---

12 For a discussion of the distinction between aesthetic and utilitarian objects see Martin Heidegger, 'The Origins of the Work of Art' in *Poetry, Language, Thought*, trans. Albert Hofstadter (New York: Harper and Row, 1971), pp. 17–87. Heidegger develops his argument as an implicit critique of Kant's description of the judgement of beauty as 'purposefulness without purpose', yet he nonetheless maintained the separation between art and practical life. For a critique of this distinction see Jacques Derrida, 'Restitutions', in *The Truth in Painting*, trans. Geoff Bennington and Ian McLeod (Chicago: University of Chicago Press, 1987), pp. 255–382; Pierre Bourdieu, *Distinction: A Social Critique of the Judgement of Taste*, trans. Richard Nice (London: Routledge and Kegan Paul, 1984), pp. 485–500.

13 Breton revised *Nadja* in 1963, adding a preface, in which he described the 'antilittéraire' character of the book's illustrations as a substitute for description. See 'Avant-dépêché', in Breton, *Œuvres* vol. 1, p. 645.

question on the agenda was whether it should be incumbent on the Surrealists, either individually or collectively, to join the PCF. Although the majority of the participants agreed in principle that it was not only necessary to translate Surrealism into some form of political action, but that joining the PCF was the logical course of action, two members were expelled for their lack of conviction. Philippe Soupault was dismissed after he failed to convince a subsequent meeting that, in the light of his literary and journalistic ambitions, his profession of political commitment was genuinely sincere; Antonin Artaud departed because he was not willing to affirm Surrealism's current political position in favour of Communism.[14]

Surprisingly, the decision to join the PCF occurred under the sign of the marvellous. The opening address to the 23 November meeting – read by Roland Tual but in all likelihood written by Breton – noted the convergence of revolutionary action and the marvellous:

> It is necessary to consider the revolutionary origin of our idealism, which is in perfect accord with revolutionary ideology, in the correct sense of the word. The noted intercession of the marvellous is of the same order as revolutionary action which has communism as its goal. I ask that we examine if the action of Surrealism is no longer valuable except on a political plane, that is to say practical. It will be necessary to examine rigorously if Surrealism is a spiritual state which can have consequences without its members participating in communist action – action tending to realize an order of things which is also a part of Surrealism. Today's meeting is taking place because the individual activity of many among us is clearly insufficient, as much from a communist perspective as Surrealist.[15]

Two points are significant here. First, the criticism of individual activity as 'clearly insufficient' recalled Pierre Naville's criticism of Surrealism in *La Révolution et les intellectuels*. Second, Surrealism was to enter the PCF through the portal of the marvellous: the 'intercession of the marvellous' was equated with 'revolutionary action which has communism as its goal'. It is difficult not to hear Breton's encounter with Nadja echoed here.

Breton had earlier responded to *La Révolution et les intellectuels* in *Légitime défense*, published about two weeks before his encounter with Nadja. Whereas Naville had posed a stark choice between two options – metaphysics or materialism, anarchism or Communism – and argued that the Surrealists should join the PCF, Breton sought to disarm Naville's critique by questioning the validity of the categories he used to criticize Surrealism. According to Breton, Naville's opposition between the 'interior reality' of the mind and the

14 On Soupault see *Adhérer au Parti communiste? Septembre–décembre 1926*, ed. Marguerite Bonnet, Archives du Surréalisme, vol. 3 (Paris: Gallimard, 1992), pp. 56–57, 70 and 82; on Artaud see ibid., p. 21.

15 Ibid., pp. 19–20.

'world of facts' was a 'wholly artificial opposition that does not bear up under scrutiny':

> In the realm of facts, as far as we're concerned there can be no doubt: there is not one of us who does not hope for the passage of power from the hands of the bourgeoisie to those of the proletariat. In the meantime, we deem it absolutely necessary that inner life should pursue its experiments, and this, of course, without external control, not even Marxist. Doesn't Surrealism, moreover, tend to posit these two states as essentially one and the same, refuting their supposed irreconcilability by every means possible – beginning with the most primitive of all, the use of which we would otherwise be hard put to defend: I mean the appeal to the marvellous.[16]

Whereas Naville presented Surrealism with a choice between two possible courses of action, Breton called on the marvellous to defuse this antinomy. The reality of the mind was no less valid than that of facts; moreover, this opposition was resolved in the experience of the marvellous, where the image constituted an articulation between the subjective reality of the mind and material facts. The 'appeal to the marvellous' was an appeal to the revolutionary dimension of Surrealist experience – what Benjamin later called 'profane illumination'.[17] This goes to the heart of Surrealism's difficult relation to politics, since the marvellous would never completely shed its mystical guise. Benjamin, however, attempted to defrock Surrealism at this point by introducing the notion of the image-realm as the matrix for the revolutionary rearticulation of experience. In what way did Breton's encounter with Nadja answer this appeal?

Surprisingly, Breton presents his initial encounter with Nadja under the sign of revolutionary politics. After stopping at the Humanité bookshop and buying Trotsky's latest book, Breton began walking towards the Opéra:

> The offices and workshops were beginning to empty out [. . .] and already there were more people in the street now. I unconsciously watched their faces, their clothes, their way of walking. No, it was not yet these who would be ready to create the Revolution.[18]

Then, crossing the Place Franz Liszt, he saw Nadja:

> Suddenly, perhaps ten feet away, I saw a young poorly dressed woman walking towards me, she had noticed me too, or perhaps had been watching me for several moments. She carried her head high, unlike

16 Breton, 'In Self-Defence', in *Break of Day*, trans. Mark Polizzotti and Mary Ann Caws (Lincoln and London: University of Nebraska Press, 1999), p. 34.

17 Benjamin, 'Surrealism', p. 227. On Benjamin and Surrealism see Susan Buck-Morss, *The Dialectics of Seeing: Walter Benjamin and the Arcades Project* (Cambridge: MIT, 1989); Margaret Cohen, *Profane Illumination: Walter Benjamin and the Paris of Surrealist Revolution* (Berkeley and Los Angeles: University of California Press, 1993).

18 Breton, *Nadja*, pp. 63–64.

> every one else on the sidewalk. [...] Without a moment's hesitation, I spoke to this unknown woman, though I must admit that I expected the worst.[19]

Breton's attention was drawn by the contrast between Nadja, who 'carried her head high', and the crowd of office workers, who were not 'ready to create the Revolution'. The figure of Nadja appeared, in other words, as an alternative to both the work-a-day routines of office workers and the PCF. Breton's encounter with Nadja embodied precisely the 'appeal to the marvellous' that he had called for in *Légitime défense*. However, despite choosing her name because it was part of the Russian word for hope, Nadja did not possess any explicit revolutionary sympathies (Breton would chide her for describing employees as 'good people' during their first meeting).[20]

In this way Breton's encounter with Nadja assumes a pivotal role in the unfolding of Surrealism's political position: in the wake of this encounter, Breton revised the position he had adopted in *Légitime défense* to advocate joining the PCF, basing his decision on the convergence between the 'intercession of the marvellous' and 'revolutionary action which has Communism as its goal'. His encounter with Nadja disclosed the equivocal character and limits of Surrealism's 'appeal to the marvellous', exposing the 'clearly insufficient' scope of individual action, and the gulf between 'the realm of facts' and 'the experiment of the inner life'. Yet this is not to claim a direct causal link between Breton's encounter with Nadja and his subsequent decision to join the PCF. In all likelihood Breton would have joined the PCF even if he had never met Nadja, since *Légitime défense* failed to satisfy the political ambitions of the Surrealists. The point, however, is that it is difficult to isolate the two events; the unsuccessful character of Breton's encounter with Nadja functioned as a catalyst, giving renewed urgency to the question of joining the PCF. Indeed, the full significance of Breton's failed encounters with Nadja and the PCF only emerged in retrospect – in Breton's attempt to recount his experience through the construction of the narrative *Nadja*.

* * *

In the *Second Manifesto of Surrealism* Breton gave an account of what occurred when he applied to join the PCF in January 1927. Unlike 'so many undesirable characters', Breton claimed he was 'unable to cross the threshold of the French Communist Party headquarters, freely and unnoticed':

> In the course of three interrogations, each of which lasted several hours, I had to defend Surrealism from the puerile accusations that it was

19 Ibid., p. 64.
20 Ibid., p. 68.

> essentially a political movement with a strong anticommunist and counterrevolutionary orientation. [...] How is it possible not to be extremely concerned about such a noticeable decline in the ideological level of a party which not long ago had sprung so brilliantly armed from two of the greatest minds of the nineteenth century! [...] I was asked to make a report on the Italian situation to this special committee of the 'gas cell,' which made it clear to me that I was to stick strictly to the statistical facts (steel production, etc.) *and above all not to get involved with ideology*. I couldn't do it.[21]

In 1952 Breton gave a more detailed account of this experience. He had to justify his activity as a Surrealist and his commitment to the communist cause. Although Breton's explanations quickly satisfied his interrogators, there always came the moment when a copy of *La Révolution surréaliste* would be exhibited and his position would again be scrutinized. In particular, he recalls the provocative role played by the review's illustrations, specifically the reproductions of Picasso's work:

> Before the illustrations, they got excited trying to outdo each other, seeing who could be the most caustic: [they asked] in what way should we look at this, can I say what this represents, [do] I have time to waste with these petit-bourgeois stupidities, [do] I consider this compatible with the Revolution, etc.[22]

André Masson gave another account of Breton's experience in the PCF, this time regarding the welcome he received from his comrades after he was assigned to the local branch, the gas workers' cell of the tenth arrondissement. The director of the cell refused to address him as 'comrade', then accused him of frequenting the Jockey nightclub with Jean Cocteau and directing a review entitled *La Révolution surréaliste*.[23] To prove his revolutionary credentials Breton took copies of *La Révolution surréaliste* along to the next meeting of the cell; returning to the Café Cyrano after the meeting, he turned to Masson and said:

> My friend, over there, they don't much like what you do, and it's because of you that things went badly. I showed the review and, you know, above all else they looked at the illustrations. I would have thought Picasso and Chirico would annoy them! Not at all, it's you. For example, they discovered *The Armour* [...] and turning towards his comrades, the director of the cell said: 'Monsieur Breton pretends that all his friends, who collaborate on his review, are revolutionaries! Look at this [...] is it

---

21 Breton, *Manifestoes of Surrealism*, trans. Richard Seaver and Helen R. Lane (Ann Arbor: University of Michigan Press, 1972), pp. 142–43.

22 Breton, *Entretiens 1913–1952 avec André Parinaud* (Paris: Gallimard, 1952), p. 127.

23 Ironically, Breton despised Cocteau for his right-wing politics, aestheticism and aristocratic homosexuality.

revolutionary? It's sadistic and sick'. And Breton added, 'The others were of the same mind and I don't know if I will be able to keep it up'.[24]

Masson described *The Armour* as a 'very surrealist painting' that was 'highly admired' by the Surrealists, particularly Breton. It was reproduced in the July 1925 issue of *La Révolution surréaliste* (fig. 1) – the first edited by Breton – which also included reproductions of Picasso's *Les Demoiselles d'Avignon* (fig. 2) and *The Three Dancers*, Miró's *The Hunter*, and Ernst's *Pietà or Revolution by Night*. What apparently appalled Breton's comrades was the violent fragmentation of the female figure: her breast is detached from her torso, and her head and limbs dissolve into a swirl of curvilinear lines. Whereas Picasso frequently distorted the female figure in his work, he did not attack the integrity of the body to the same degree as Masson. Yet Masson derived the fragmentation of the figure's body from his interpretation of Cubism, which suggested an analogy between spatial fragmentation and the cursive flow of automatism.[25] Indeed, it was not a literal imitation of reality, but conceptual: an interplay of the mind's 'inner reality' and the 'world of facts' that typified the marvellous. Breton's comrades interpreted this fragmentation literally, as performed on an actual body, and were unable to engage with the work on a conceptual or stylistic level.[26]

According to these accounts, the aspect of Surrealism which placed Breton outside the PCF was the avant-garde painting supported by the movement. Although the PCF considered itself the guardian of the revolutionary spirit, it was nonetheless blind to the revolutionary significance of the types of creative endeavour championed by the Surrealists. It maintained a conservative, if not reactionary, attitude towards the underlying structure of human experience explored by Surrealism. This attitude attacked Surrealism at the very point where it sought to distinguish itself from the aesthetic avant-garde. Whereas Breton and the Surrealists had arrived at an ethics of rebellion through creative endeavour, and believed that political action was an extension of creative endeavour, the PCF did not share this conviction; in creative endeavour they only saw the disingenuous signs of bourgeois decadence.[27]

---

24 Masson, *Entretiens avec Georges Charbonnier* (Paris: René Julliard, 1958), pp. 113–14. *The Armour* was reproduced in *La Révolution surréaliste*, no. 4 (July 1925), p. 22.

25 The affinity between Masson's work and Cubism was implied in Max Morise, 'Les yeux enchantés', *La Révolution surréaliste*, no. 1 (December 1924), pp. 26–27. See also Christopher Green, *Cubism and its Enemies: Modern Movements and Reaction in French Art, 1916–1928* (New Haven: Yale University Press, 1987).

26 Two further points are relevant here. First, as Pierre Bourdieu has noted in *Distinction* there is a marked correlation between class and aesthetic taste. Second, although Breton's comrades may have interpreted the fragmentation of the woman's body literally, there is an undeniable correlation between gender and violence in Surrealism.

27 Cf. the suppression of the avant-garde in the Soviet Union under Stalin.

Breton's brief tenure as a militant revolutionary culminated in *Au grand jour*, a series of five open letters published in May 1927. These letters were addressed to various factions and individuals in the Surrealist and communist movements, and were written and signed by the five Surrealists who had joined the PCF (Aragon, Breton, Eluard, Péret and Unik).[28] Breton withdrew from active participation in the PCF after May 1927 and now directed his activity towards 'cultural' pursuits.[29]

* * *

Breton had always intended to record his encounter with Nadja in some form, but was unable to work consistently on *Nadja* until August 1927.[30] Although he had kept detailed notes of their relationship, which enabled him to give the text an aura of verisimilitude, he wrote the first two parts only with difficulty.[31] *Nadja* also included 44 photographic illustrations of places or objects mentioned in the narrative. These illustrations introduce another dimension to the book. In contrast to photography employed as a Surrealist technique, where distortion and manipulation of the image estranged it from conventional appearances, the illustrations in *Nadja* were remarkably faithful to appearances.[32] They simply recorded people, objects or places mentioned in the text; their function was to ground the verisimilitude of the text in the quotidian.

When Breton revised *Nadja* in 1962, he added a preface, 'Avant-dire (dépêche retardée)', which identified 'two overriding antiliterary principles' in the book: photographic illustrations in the place of description, and the scientific

---

28 The five letters were addressed to Paul Nougé and Camille Goemans (editors of the Belgian review *Correspondances*), Marcel Fourrier (an editor of *Clarté*), Pierre Naville (former Surrealist and currently an editor of *Clarté*), and published under the rubrics 'Aux surréalistes non communiste', and 'Aux communistes'. The authors not only sought to justify their decision to join the PCF, but defended themselves against the apparent incomprehension that had greeted them within the PCF. 'Au Grand jour' is included in Breton, *Œuvres*, vol. 1, pp. 928–42.

29 In June 1927 Editions Gallimard published a deluxe limited edition of Breton's *Introduction au discours sur le peu de réalité*, which was originally written and published in 1924. On the dating of this text see Breton, *Œuvres*, vol. 2, p. 1439.

30 According to the Romanian poet and diplomat Marko Ristic, who visited Breton on 23 December 1926, Breton was already planning to write a book in December 1926, but was yet to discover 'le ton' he was seeking: 'Breton n'a pas devant moi fait allusion à Nadja, mais le livre qu'il me disait vouloir écrire sans en avoir encore trouvé *le ton* devait vraisemblablement être *Nadja*'. Marko Ristic, 'La Nuit du tournesol', *Nouvelle revue française* XXIX:172 (April 1967), p. 703.

31 Mark Polizzotti, *Revolution of the Mind*, pp. 281–85; Breton, *Entretiens*, p. 145.

32 On the role of distortion and framing in Surrealist photography, see Rosalind Krauss, 'The Photographic Conditions of Surrealism', in *The Originality of the Avant-Garde and Other Modernist Myths* (Cambridge: MIT Press, 1985), pp. 87–118.

tone of a medical report.[33] Although both principles attest to the degree of objectivity Breton sought to impart to his subjective experience, *Nadja* was not simply 'antiliterary': rather, it employed an innovative 'literary' technique to establish its verisimilitude, one that surpassed existing literary conventions by permeating its pages with the quotidian. The photographic illustrations incorporated fragments of 'reality' into the text; these fragments did not shed their referential dimension, nor were they subordinated to the stylistic unity of the novel. Indeed, like *papiers collés*, they punctuate the text with heterogeneous fragments, incorporating little pieces of the 'real' into the narrative's textual economy, thereby binding it to the external world. As a substitute for description the illustrations were left to speak for themselves: they place the reader immediately before objects, subordinating the diachrony of the narrative to the synchrony of visual images.[34]

Breton's encounter with Nadja lasted only ten days – from 4 to 13 October.[35] An element of ambivalence characterized their relationship: Breton did not love Nadja unreservedly, and his image of her oscillated between the poetic possibility of the marvellous and the sordid reality of her actual existence.[36] Intimacy only exacerbated the conflict between Breton's fantasy of Nadja, marvellously emancipated from practical concerns, and the woman living in Paris, paying rent, forced to earn a living. These pragmatic concerns marooned the possibility of Nadja's marvellous existence on the shoals of social reality, and although Breton perceived the marvellous in Nadja's behaviour, in the eyes of society she was ready to be unscrupulously exploited.

Breton maintained occasional contact with Nadja until February 1927. In early March she was interned in a mental asylum because she had committed certain 'eccentricities' in the hallway of her hotel.[37] Nadja's internment raised – and continues to raise – a number of difficult issues for Surrealism. Although

---

33 Breton identified 'deux principaux impératifs "antilittéraire" auxquels cet ouvrage obéit': 'l'abondante illustration photographique a pour objet d'éliminer toute description – celle-ci frappée d'inanité dans le *Manifeste du surréalisme* –, le ton adopté pour le récit se calque sur celui de l'observation médicale, entre toutes neuro-psychiatrique, qui tend à garder trace de tout ce qu'examen et interrogatoire peuvent livrer, sans s'embarrasser en le rapportant de moindre apprêt quant au style'. Breton, *Œuvres*, vol. 1, p. 645.

34 Although the stylistic novelty of *Nadja* served to establish its status beyond art, it simultaneously established a new definition of avant-garde practice, which other agents in the cultural field could then co-opt.

35 On the chronology of Breton's and Nadja's relationship, see below, n. 37.

36 Breton, *Nadja*, pp. 89–90.

37 Ibid., p. 136. For a discussion of the events between 13 October 1926 and Nadja's internment on 21 March 1927, see Marguerite Bonnet, 'Notice', in Breton, *Œuvres*, vol. 1, pp. 1510–13. According to Bonnet, the hotel owner called the police after Nadja, greatly distressed and suffering from visual and olfactory hallucinations, called for aid.

Breton aided Nadja financially, he proved unable to provide the modicum of support necessary to maintain her mental stability. Had he failed her? These questions remain impossible to answer; silence has condemned her to haunt the text, little more than a name.[38]

The conflict between Nadja's marvellous possibility and the limitations of her actual existence emphasized the political ambivalence of their encounter. For all her visionary power, intuition and freedom, Nadja was still subject to the economic and social constraint of society, which made her life increasingly difficult, and ultimately impossible. To what degree was the failure of their encounter due to the inability of the marvellous to reconcile the 'world of facts' and 'inner reality of the mind'? This question not only cast doubt on the validity of Breton's 'appeal to the marvellous' in *Légitime défense*, but it exposed the limitation of the Surrealist belief in the marvellous at this particular historical juncture. Moreover, the intertwined chronology of events in 1926 and 1927 – the incommodious welcome Breton received from his comrades in the 'gas cell' must have occurred within weeks, if not days, of Nadja's internment – could not but exert a reciprocal influence on Breton's understanding of Surrealism.

Nadja – and, by extension, the marvellous – acts as an incantatory limit-figure whose function was to articulate the disparate fragments of experience into a semblance of a whole. Within Breton's narrative Nadja embodies the aporia of the marvellous. It is no coincidence that this occurs across the body of a woman, for as it is often noted, the feminine functions as an ideological projection in the masculine universe of Surrealism; yet the corollary here is that

38 *Nadja* is often considered symptomatic of the problematical status of women in the Surrealist movement. Whitney Chadwick has criticized the 'lack of equality' between Breton and Nadja, which is characteristic of the conflict in Surrealism between 'a nineteenth-century image of woman as passive, dependant, and defined through her relationship to an active male presence, and a more contemporary demand for female autonomy and independence'. Nadja's internment highlighted Breton's inability to support Nadja on an emotional or psychological level: ultimately, he was 'unwilling or unable to assume responsibility for her care', nor to 'resolve the complex issues that [arose] from his relationship with her'. (*Women Artists and the Surrealist Movement*, London, Thames and Hudson, 1985, p. 34.) Chadwick's critique remains partial and incomplete. It attempts to gather evidence of Surrealist misogyny, yet Nadja dwells less in the text on the level of content than on a formal level. She is nowhere more present than in her absence – as a lacuna or blind spot in the text. She emerges at the point where representation falters, as the traumatic kernel that the text seeks to envelope. In this context Nadja does not *represent* the idea of woman as muse, she is an actual person encountered on the streets of Paris; yet the modality of this encounter is that of a missed or failed encounter. Her absence conditions the text; as the elusive figure of Breton's desire, she haunts the text rather than inhabits it. Nadja, for the reader, exists through Breton, who gives consistency to her as the focus of his desire; yet simultaneously, his desire veils and distances her. For a fascinating discussion of the constitutive role of silence in *Nadja*, see M. Stone-Richards, 'Encirclements: Silence in the Construction of *Nadja*', in *Modernism/Modernity* VIII:1 (2001), pp. 127–57.

Nadja also functions as a point of maximum stress in the narrative – and by extension in the enterprise of Surrealism – through which the irreconcilable aspects of Breton's project are articulated. It is at this level that Breton's encounter was always already a failed encounter, since a successful encounter would, if not render his project obsolete, at least profoundly transform his relation to any potential audience.

* * *

Breton responded to these setbacks by writing an account of his encounter with Nadja, in which he sought to 'work through' his disappointment with the turn of events. Consequently, *Nadja* represents a unique record of Surrealism's travails, one that contributed to a reorientation of Surrealism.[39] These encounters not only inform the composition of *Nadja*, but they animate the use of photographic illustrations in the text. Three illustrations executed by J.-A. Boiffard stand out here: *I Will Take the Hôtel des Grands Hommes as my Point of Departure* (fig. 3), *The Humanité Bookshop* (fig. 4), and *The Illuminated Mazda Billboard on the Grands Boulevards* (fig. 5). On close scrutiny these illustrations appear to be interrelated: thematically, they relate to the theme of a new departure; iconographically, they employ a similar repertoire of motifs. Furthermore, each illustration occupies a significant position in the structure of the original 1928 edition of *Nadja*: each one is the first illustration to appear in one of the book's three parts.[40] One way to understand this formal and iconographic concordance is in terms of Surrealism's ambivalent position in the social space. Indeed, the illustrations in question seem to trace Surrealism's trajectory across the social space, suspended between the fields of culture and politics.[41]

39 On the role of *Nadja* in the reorientation of Surrealism see Raymond Spiteri, *'Battant comme une porte': Painting and the Cultural Politics of Surrealism, 1924–1929*, unpublished PhD thesis, University of Western Australia, 1999.

40 *Nadja* is divided into three parts. Breton wrote the initial two parts while staying at the Manoir d'Ango during August 1927, and the third part during December 1927, after he met Suzanne Muzard. The first part functions as a prologue to the encounter with Nadja (which is the subject of the second part), describing a series of chance events and encounters which established his 'difference' from other men. The second part describes Breton's encounter with Nadja, initially as a series of nine journal entries, then as two digressions on the significance of the encounter and its denouement. The third part, written three months later, discusses the interval between the composition of the second and third section, Breton's disappointment with the illustrations, his encounter with an unnamed woman (Suzanne Muzard), and a brief meditation on beauty.

41 The argument here is based on the order of images in the original French edition of *Nadja*, published by Editions Gallimard in 1928. When Breton revised *Nadja* in 1962–63 he supplemented the original 44 illustrations with a number of extra photographs and reorganized the order of the illustrations in relation to the text. Similarly, subsequent

Breton's relation to the field of culture is evident in the illustration of the Hôtel des Grands Hommes, which he took as his 'departure point'.[42] The illustration displays a striking resemblance to Giorgio de Chirico's *The Enigma of Day* (fig. 6), a painting which Breton owned at the time. The position, pose and gesture of the statue of Jean-Jacques Rousseau in Boiffard's photograph recalls the statue in *The Enigma of Day*, suggesting Breton and Boiffard were alluding to the painting.[43] The illustration also contains a number of other elements reminiscent of *The Enigma of Day*. A woman appears seated at one of the windows (directly below the letters 'mes' of the word 'hommes'), which recalls the figures in the background of de Chirico's painting, while the waiting horse and cart echo the removal van in the painting. Both elements create an atmosphere of anticipation in the image – precisely the quality Breton had celebrated in de Chirico's work in *Le Surréalisme et la peinture*.[44] The parallels in the composition and iconography of the two images suggest a convergence between creative endeavour and the quotidian: that Breton's encounter with Nadja would actually realize the promise of de Chirico's painting.[45]

If the *Hôtel des Grands Hommes* indicates Breton's relation to culture, then the illustration of *The Humanité Bookshop* indicates his relation to politics. The Humanité bookshop is the first specific place mentioned in the second part of

---

paperback editions of *Nadja* (including Richard Howard's English translation) as well as the text of *Nadja* in Breton's *Œuvres complètes*, do not respect the original order of images in the 1928 edition. The book's structure produces a complex web of meaning and associations between images, the narrative and the text. Jean Arrouye has discussed some effects of the organization of the illustrations in his article 'La photographie dans "Nadja" ', *Mélusine*, no. 4, pp. 123–51.

42 This phrase is part of the illustration's title and later appears in the text. See Breton, *Nadja* (1928), pp. 17 and 26.

43 This parallel also accounts for one weakness in the photograph: although it echoed de Chirico's composition, the statue seems to be located too far to the right; consequently, its gesture seems ineffectual, failing to work in relation to the other elements in the image. However, a comparison of Boiffard's photograph to other photographs of the statue discloses that Boiffard composed the photograph to accentuate the statue's gesture. The statue was not situated directly in front of the Hotel, but somewhat to the left (opposite the point where the Hôtel des Grands Hommes meets the neighbouring building). If the statue had been placed further left in Boiffard's image, the statue's hand would no longer project forward from its body. Thus the attempt to echo the composition of *The Enigma of Day* and juxtapose the statue's gesture with the façade of the hotel dictated the statue's position in the photograph.

44 See Breton, *Surrealism and Painting*, trans. Simon Watson Taylor (London: Macdonald, 1972), pp. 17–19.

45 The hotel's name emblazoned on the railing of the fifth floor balcony recalls the inscription in the pediment of the Pantheon: 'Aux grands hommes la patrie reconnaissante'. Whereas the Pantheon was a memorial devoted to the official acknowledgment of great men, the Hôtel des Grands Hommes was a cheap hotel where Breton had lived around 1920: the official recognition of the first building contrasts ironically to the anonymity of the second.

Nadja, which narrates Breton's liaison with Nadja. Significantly, this illustration depicts the actual branch of the PCF Breton joined in January 1927: it is dominated by a sign proclaiming 'On signe ici' [Sign up here], which points towards an open door; in the foreground, a man, wearing the cloth cap of the working class, leaves his cart to enter the office, suggesting a worker about to join the revolution.[46] These motifs also recall the statue and cart standing before the hotel door in the *Hôtel des Grands Hommes* (and by extension *The Enigma of Day*).

When this illustration is considered in relation to the events of 1926–27, it appears curiously overdetermined. In the context of the narrative it precedes Breton's initial encounter with Nadja, only emphasizing a marginal event – Breton's purchase of Trotsky's latest book.[47] However, it places the encounter under the sign of Communist politics, and indeed anticipates Breton's membership of the PCF by three months. In this way it establishes an ambivalent link between culture and politics: Breton initially hesitates on the threshold of the PCF, and it is only after the failure of his encounter with Nadja that he decides to cross this threshold and join the PCF. Yet Breton would fare no better in the PCF than with Nadja, and both encounters ultimately ended in disappointment. The photograph was executed in full knowledge of these two failed encounters, since it was taken a full year after the events it illustrates. This cleavage between the original event and its subsequent description delineates the 'cultural politics' of the text, producing an ambivalent link between Communism and the marvellous.

The Illuminated Mazda Billboard also included a handcart, thus echoing the other two illustrations. Similarly, it was related to the theme of departure, yet this time it was Nadja's departure from Breton's life. The billboard represented a symbolic portrait of Nadja, who associated herself with the Mazda light bulb, ram's horns, and the mythical figure of Melusina.[48] As a symbolic portrait of Nadja it represented Breton's desire for the marvellous and the imagination's

46 Did Breton pose for this photograph? The figure's posture resembles Breton, and he has similar lips, ears and expression.

47 According to Bonnet, Breton purchased either *Europe et Amérique* or *Où va l'Angleterre?* See her commentary in Breton, *Œuvres*, vol. 1, p. 1542, n. 2. Trotsky represents an ambivalent figure during the late 1920s, since he had been expelled from the Soviet Union and his influence was viewed with suspicion in the PCF. On the purge of Trotskyists from the PCF see Robert Wohl, *French Communism in the Making, 1914–1924* (Stanford: Stanford University Press, 1966). In 1938 Breton would collaborate with Trotsky on the manifesto '*For An Independent Revolutionary Art*'.

48 'Nadja has also represented herself many times with the features of Melusina [...]. She enjoyed imagining herself as a butterfly whose body consisted of a Mazda (Nadja) bulb towards which rose a charmed snake (and now I am invariably disturbed when I pass the luminous Mazda sign on the main boulevards, covering almost the entire façade of the former Théâtre du Vaudeville where, in fact, two rams do confront one another in a rainbow light)'. Breton, *Nadja*, pp. 129–30.

ability to transform the quotidian through a convergence of subjective and objective elements. The ladder also suggested a passage between the sidewalk and the image. The position of *The Illuminated Mazda Billboard* is also noteworthy: it is the penultimate illustration in the book, appearing almost 40 pages after the corresponding reference in the text, and after four other illustrations.[49] It was reproduced facing the description of the changed appearance of the Boulevard Bonne-Nouvelle, 'the façades of the cinemas repainted'.[50] In this context it represented a temporal horizon in the narrative, the symbolic effacement of Nadja's empirical presence and her transformation into a protagonist in the narrative *Nadja*; it also prefigured the entrance of a new woman in Breton's life.

The three illustrations plot Surrealism's ambivalent position in the social space. The allusions to de Chirico's *The Enigma of Day* in *Hôtel des Grands Hommes* not only established a link between de Chirico's work and the illustrations in *Nadja*, but suggested that Breton's encounter with Nadja, and by extension Surrealism, effected a convergence between creative endeavour and the quotidian; conversely, *The Humanité Bookshop* established a link between Surrealism and Communism, as if creative endeavour led ineluctably to the possibility of political action. What, then, does *The Illuminated Mazda Billboard* represent? It is tempting to conclude that it represents a synthesis of the first and second illustrations, a resolution of creative endeavour and political action in the quotidian, but this conclusion would be premature. Here Benjamin's discussion of the image-realm is illuminating; for what is *The Illuminated Mazda Billboard* if not an example of this image-realm in which 'action puts forth its own image' and 'no limb remains unrent'?

The juxtaposition of *The Illuminated Mazda Billboard* with Breton's description of the Boulevard Bonne-Nouvelle underlines the proximity of *Nadja* to Benjamin's revolutionary image-realm. The illustration is placed in the midst of Breton's comments on his disappointment with the illustrations for *Nadja*, which he described as 'quite inadequate'. However, a digression on the Sacco-Vanzetti riots suddenly interrupts his description of the Boulevard Bonne-Nouvelle:

49 Most illustrations were located close to the relevant reference in the text.

50 Breton, *Nadja* (1928), p. 202. *The Illuminated Mazda Billboard* appeared opposite a passage that commented on Breton's disappointment with the photographs that illustrate the book: 'I have begun by going back to look at several of the places to which this narrative happens to lead; I wanted [...] to provide a photographic image of them taken at the special angle from which I myself had looked at them. On this occasion, I realized that most of the places more or less resisted my venture, so that, as I see it, the illustrated part of *Nadja* is quite inadequate.' (Ibid., pp. 151–52.) Although the illustrations apparently resisted Breton's attempt to restage the marvellous, and in this sense they demonstrate the limits of the Surrealist project, they nonetheless perform a unique function in the text: they constitute brief hiatuses in the rhythm of the narrative, arresting its temporal flow in a wealth of incidental detail.

> While the Boulevard Bonne-Nouvelle, after having, unfortunately during my absence from Paris in the course of the magnificent days of riot called 'Sacco-Vanzetti', seemed to come up to my expectations, after even revealing itself as one of the major strategic points I am looking for in matters of chaos, points which I persist in believing obscurely provided for me, as for anyone who chooses to yield to inexplicable entreaties, provided the most absolute sense of love or revolution are at stake and that this, naturally, involved the negation of everything else; while the Boulevard Bonne-Nouvelle, the façades of its movie-theaters repainted, has subsequently become immobilized for me, as if the Porte Saint-Denis had just closed [...].[51]

This revealing passage not only embodies one of the major impasses of Surrealism, but demonstrates the tension between the cultural and political dimensions of the Surrealist enterprise. In discussing the role of illustrations in *Nadja* Breton was addressing the cultural significance of the book, yet this significance was poised on the threshold of the political. The mere mention of the Boulevard Bonne-Nouvelle opened a convoluted parenthesis on the revolution; Breton's measured prose returned only after he had stated his political philosophy.[52]

The Sacco-Vanzetti riots erupted after Nicolas Sacco and Bartolomeo Vanzetti were executed in the United States. Their case became an international symbol of proletarian opposition to capitalism because the court appeared unduly influenced by the anarchist political beliefs of the accused. International agitation culminated in a series of riots that broke out in major cities across the world immediately after their execution. *L'Humanité* celebrated the heroism of the Paris workers, who staged a major demonstration after the execution – the headline for the 24 August 1927 edition indicated the communist line: 'Paris workers master the street!'[53] *L'Humanité* provided detailed coverage of the evening's events and underlined the PCF's role in the unfolding of the demonstration.[54]

Breton accepted the Sacco-Vanzetti riots as an article of revolutionary faith, yet ironically these riots also indicate his distance from direct political action.

51 Breton, *Nadja*, pp. 152–54. Translation modified.

52 Note the repeated use of subordinate clauses in the passage.

53 'Paris ouvrier maître du pavé! Montmartre et le Centre en état de siège. La foule ouvrière en deuil impose silence aux "boites" où l'on s'amuse. Violentes bagarres: carrefours Montmartre, Rougemont, Poissonnière, portes St-Denis et St-Martin, place Blanche, gare de l'Est, etc. Des blessés, des arrestations par centaines'. *L'Humanité*, 24 August 1927, p. 1.

54 The Sacco-Vanzetti riots coincided with the appointment of Jean Chiappe as the *Préfet de police* of Paris and prompted him to adopt a repressive attitude towards the PCF. This in turn would affect the Surrealists' relation to the PCF, since the atmosphere of police repression effectively transformed the PCF into an illegal organization, with little time to accommodate avant-garde intellectuals. On Chiappe see Lucien Zimmer, *Un Septennant policier: Dessous et secrets de la police républicainne* (Paris: Fayard, 1967), pp. 24–33.

The reason for Breton's absence from Paris during August 1927 was his preoccupation with writing *Nadja*. He had retreated to the Manoir d'Ango in Varengeville-sur-Mer on the Normandy coast, where he slowly wrote the first two parts of *Nadja*.[55] Although the riots represented a contingent event, Breton's response to them in *Nadja* is telling: the juxtaposition of *The Illuminated Mazda Billboard* with his description of the Boulevard Bonne-Nouvelle and the Sacco-Vanzetti riots opens a place for the appearance of another politics – the politics of the marvellous – that operates in the interval between event, image and text. This strategy goes to the heart of the constitutive role of silence, interval and failure in the construction of *Nadja*, in which silence acts as an unsurpassable limit around which the narrative unfolds.[56] Breton does not attempt to articulate an explicit political strategy in *Nadja*, since his efforts to align Surrealism with Communism have already resulted in an impasse; rather he incorporates the encounter with politics as one coordinate in the construction of *Nadja*.

* * *

Nadja thus represents a perspicuous demonstration of the political and cultural nexus of Surrealism.[57] The image of a door ajar, 'battant comme une porte', not

---

55 On the progress of Breton's writing of *Nadja* see Mark Polizzotti, *Revolution of the Mind*, pp. 281–91.

56 I am unable to develop the full implications of this reading in the present context. On the role of silence in *Nadja* see Stone-Richards, 'Encirclements'. Maurice Blanchot has a fascinating discussion of the encounter in 'Tomorrow at Stake' in *The Infinite Conversation*, trans. Susan Hanson (Minneapolis: University of Minnesota Press, 1993), pp. 407–21. The relation between Blanchot's and Benjamin's reading of Surrealism is a topic worthy of further investigation.

57 One problem with the neologism 'cultural politics' is that it conflates two distinct social fields (i.e. the fields of *culture* and *politics*) without providing an adequate theoretical articulation of their interaction. It is difficult to point to a set of social practices or institutions that could constitute an enduring form of 'cultural politics'. At best, cultural politics appears to describe a state of institutional indeterminacy, a situation in which the outcome remains uncertain; by contrast, it is not difficult to identify the institutional form assumed by cultural or political endeavour. It is important to distinguish between the tradition of *ideologiekritik* – the critique of the ideological forms of 'false-consciousness' – and the interaction between culture and politics as distinct positions in the social space. Whereas the former addresses the ideas and categories that structure perception and behaviour in society, the latter describes a series of actual encounters between agents of the political and cultural fields. The difference between these two senses of cultural politics is one of degree: ideology acts to inhibit behaviour, representing historical social relations as natural ones. The second case is active, representing a mode of praxis: it describes actual instances of social agents challenging hegemonic authority; agents not only reject fundamental hegemonic beliefs (i.e. ideology), but they articulate social antagonisms through their actions. In the 'Theses on Feuerbach' Marx articulated these two aspects of cultural politics in the contrast between 'contemplation' and 'human sensuous activity' – an opposition that reappears in

only accurately describes the ambivalent character of *Nadja* – simultaneously aesthetically significant and politically charged – but also articulates the limits of Surrealism's political ambitions. Although the experience of the marvellous harboured a moment of illumination that overcame the opposition between imagination and action, this illumination was not sufficient to transform latent possibility into the manifest actuality of revolutionary action.[58]

In the context of interwar France, Surrealism rarely managed to escape the orbit of culture, and any political effect it may have had largely resulted from its position in the cultural field as an avant-garde movement – a predicament that severely restricted the political impact of *Nadja* on any audience. This is a matter of historical record. France – despite the best efforts of the extreme left and right – was not facing a revolutionary situation during the interwar years: the apparatus of government functioned efficiently, resolving class antagonism through the letter of the law.[59] Yet not only did the Surrealists steadfastly

---

the theory-praxis dialectic. See 'Theses on Feuerbach', in *The Marx-Engels Reader*, ed. Robert C. Tucker, 2nd edn (New York: Norton, 1978), pp. 143–45. The second dimension of cultural politics is often developed in post-Marxism. In particular, see Ernesto Laclau and Chantel Mouffe, *Hegemony and Socialist Strategy: Towards a Radical Democratic Politics* (London: Verso, 1985); Slavoj Žižek, *The Sublime Object of Ideology* (London: Verso, 1989), and *For They Do Not Know What They Do: Enjoyment as a Political Factor* (London: Verso, 1991). On the notion of social fields see Bourdieu, *Language and Symbolic Power* and *The Field of Cultural Production*.

58 An insight by Slavoj Žižek is valuable here. In *For They Do Not Know What They Do* he draws on the work of Ernesto Laclau and Claude Lefort to differentiate two modalities of the political: 'politics' and the 'Political'. In the first case 'politics' refers to the social sub-system of politics, the institutional apparatus of government existing in a hegemonic society. In this context political activity does not fundamentally challenge the interests of the dominant class, since it is simply an expression of these interests articulated through hegemonic discourse. By contrast, the 'Political' refers to a situation in which hegemonic discourse falters, allowing social and political antagonisms to emerge as irreconcilable conflicts within the social space. This is a revolutionary situation: the legitimacy of the existing political institutions is suddenly open to question, vested interests are exposed, grievances voiced. (See Slavoj Žižek, *For They Do Not Know What They Do*, pp. 186 ff. particularly, pp. 193–95.) In this context the structure of the social space becomes fluid and the notion of a 'cultural politics' assumes substance: in the openness of a revolutionary situation possibility can suddenly become transformed into actuality. The classic example of the way all actions become politicized during a revolutionary situation is the excesses perpetrated during the Reign of Terror after the 1789 French Revolution. For an interesting discussion of the political role of culture during the French Revolution see Lynn Hunt, *Politics, Culture, and Class in the French Revolution* (Berkeley and Los Angeles: University of California Press, 1984).

59 This is not to deny the existence of potentially revolutionary political crises in France during the interwar period, such as the currency crisis of 1926, the Sacco-Vanzetti riots, or the street fighting of 6 February 1934; but while these events challenged the legitimacy of parliamentary democracy, and indeed had significant implications for the government of the time, they did not undermine the actual political institutions of the Third Republic, which continued to function effectively until the Occupation in 1940.

maintain their orientation towards emancipatory politics, which displayed their belief in the convergence of cultural endeavour and revolutionary action, but this orientation framed and influenced their tactics as agents in the cultural field. The appeal to the marvellous was symptomatic of the problematical status of Surrealism as a mode of political action. The marvellous was nothing other than the resonance of creative endeavour in the quotidian, yet it could only be represented as an estrangement of the quotidian, a sudden shift in perspective that disrupted the normal circulation of signs. Consequently, the Surrealist image underwent a process of aesthetic or metaphoric displacement that divorced it from contemporary historical experience. For Surrealism to succeed on a cultural level it had to dress politics in metaphor; yet for it to succeed politically, it had to strip culture of its metaphoric veils. Surrealism never overcame this impasse, which inscribed its political position as an over-determined subtext in Surrealist productions;[60] hence the fugitive, provisional character of Surrealist political manifestations. Although cultural endeavour *could* have political repercussions under certain conditions, in Surrealism's case these repercussions were *not* an actuality, and they consequently assumed the form of a series of missed or failed encounters.[61] Surrealism remained stranded beyond art, yet before politics.

60 This is not to say that Surrealist productions were necessarily non-political, only that their political content resided in the inarticulate form of Surrealist works. This form occasionally refracted the latent political anxieties in French society. The scandal caused by the exhibition of *L'Age d'Or* in 1930 was one example of this process. This film became the focus of political antagonism between opposed factions in the political field and in this way transcended the limits of a cultural manifestation to participate in the political field.

61 This insight is implicit in recent accounts of Surrealism, particularly those indebted to psychoanalytical theories of the uncanny: repetition, the insistence of the Real, is the failed encounter *par excellence*; it points to the fundamental trauma that can only be recuperated through repetition. However, repetition is not a purely psychic event; it also has a social and political dimension. It represents a horizon of possibility, but, given the contingency of the historical process, this horizon is always subject to change. Hal Foster develops some of the implications of this reading in *Compulsive Beauty*. Cf. Slavoj Žižek, *Tarrying With the Negative: Kant, Hegel, and the Critique of Ideology* (Durham: Duke University Press, 1993), pp. 157–61.

Chapter 4

Advertising Surrealist Masculinities: André Kertész in Paris

Amy Lyford

Walking in Paris can be an unsettling experience. Louis Aragon recognized this in the 1920s, as did many of his Surrealist friends. To the fresh eye of Aragon's newly-arrived, streetwalking *paysan de Paris*, the city's streets, shop windows and odd little corners had the potential to mobilize Surrealist experiences. Teeming with visual juxtapositions and uncanny associative combinations that one could find along commercial streets and in the passages between boulevards, Paris held the promise of awakening its inhabitants from the numbness that envelops the habitual experiences of everyday life.

Aragon's *paysan* stared into dusty shop windows bursting with medical supplies, ageing corsets, neatly-tailored suits worn by headless mannequins, rows and rows of shoes, canes and stockings. And Eugène Atget, one of the Surrealists' favourite urban guides in the 1920s, revealed the world of modern commerce as something strange by fixing the viewer's attention on the strangeness of the shop window's bodily displays (fig. 7). The Surrealists' recovery of Atget as an honorary member of their collective might thus appear to be a natural result of the group's interest in the city as an object ripe for cultural analysis. As it had been for generations of artists, Paris was a potential site of revolutionary experience and activity for the Surrealists. But in the 1920s, it was not only Atget's but André Kertész's photographs of the city that seized the world laid bare by Aragon's wandering peasant. His images of men in and around the city's streets enabled one to see things that one might otherwise have overlooked or outright avoided while walking in Paris (fig. 8). Kertész's images proposed a way of understanding the city that embodied a Surrealist approach to visual experience. It was Kertész's achievement (even though he did not adhere to the formally-recognized social and political structures of the Surrealist groups) to have created photographs of the city's male inhabitants whose fragmented forms encapsulate a crucial component of Surrealist aesthetics. These were photographs that reflected Surrealism's interest in the way the war's trauma was being rapidly overlaid by the progressive notion of a 'return to order'. Echoing the prominent photography critic Pierre MacOrlan's 1928 claim that photography had the power to depict a culture's 'social fantastic', Kertész's photographs press their viewers to see what might otherwise be missed. For

MacOrlan, and as we shall see in the work of André Kertész, it was 'through the intermediary of photography that one is still able to seize the fantastic forms of life that require, at least, a second of immobility in order to be perceived'.[1] Kertész's Paris photographs of the 1920s capture 'outmoded' male bodies that, because of their visibly fragmented forms, stand out against the healthy, robust figures so key to the reordering of postwar French society. Strong and active young men would rebuild the nation, not the tattered remnants of wartime often pictured by Kertész. Whereas André Breton laid claim to the importance of the image of a 'man cut in two by a window' in his 1924 Surrealist manifesto, Kertész's traumatic male types subtly contest the embodied rhetoric of regeneration that permeated the discourse of France's return to order.[2] Kertész aligned himself visually with the Surrealists, insisting on representing masculinity as fragmented and vulnerable. His photographs envision a world in which damaged men inhabit the city, not those pristine physical specimens who came to Paris to compete in the 1924 Olympics. Kertész's images describe the traumatized male body as a sign of modern French culture, yet they do so in ways that advertise a side of postwar experience that intersects with Surrealist aims and methods, a fact that has been largely ignored in discussions of either Surrealism or the work of André Kertész.[3]

* * *

Cultural destabilization was one of Surrealism's primary goals in the years after World War I; in France, programmes for national reconstruction made attractive targets for Surrealist cultural critique. This 'return to order' marked a national effort to rebuild not only the state and its institutions, but also the individual combatant and the social structures of which he was a part. For those invested in the process of rebuilding the nation, it was key that the new, postwar society would not differ much from the old, particularly in terms of relations between the sexes.[4] Many hoped that men and women alike would return to

---

1 Unless otherwise indicated, all translations are my own. Pierre MacOrlan, 'La Photographie et le Fantastique Social', *Les Annales politiques et littéraires* (1 November 1928), p. 414.

2 André Breton, 'Manifesto of Surrealism', in *Manifestes du surréalisme* (Paris: Gallimard, 1963), pp. 31–32. For an account of what I take to be Surrealism's articulation of the traumatized male body as a foundational image within Surrealist practice, see my essay 'The Aesthetics of Dismemberment: Surrealism and the Musée du Val-de-Grâce in 1917', *Cultural Critique*, no. 46 (Fall 2000), pp. 45–78.

3 Kertész's 'Surrealism' is usually confined to his 1933 series of female distortions in the bulk of the literature on Surrealist photography.

4 Important texts on the return to order in France include Carolyn Dean, *The Self and its Pleasures: Bataille, Lacan and the History of the Decentered Subject* (Ithaca: Cornell, 1992); Briony Fer, David Batchelor and Paul Wood, *Realism, Rationalism,*

their prewar social roles, with women at home and men in the fields or in the factory. Aggressively countering this conservative model of cultural rebirth, Surrealist artists and writers aimed to upend such conventions by dramatizing alternative forms of economic, sexual, psychological and political life. They worked hard, in other words, to produce images that actively critiqued the increasingly rationalized, hierarchical and backward-looking approach to cultural reconstruction.

Surrealist practices, as such, often emphasized disorder, hybridity and the free play of the unconscious as a means of opposing this increasing reliance upon order, technology and rationalized social organization.[5] According to André Breton, Surrealist artists and writers ought to become '[...] simple receptacles [...] modest recording instruments' that would express the 'actual functioning of thought, in the absence of any control exercised by reason, [and] exempt from any aesthetic or moral concern'.[6] By rejecting all sorts of aesthetic and social conventions, Surrealist representations would (it was hoped) create a revolution in the mind of the individual. Only later would that individual's experience spill into the streets as an outgrowth of collective transformation. Crucial material for that change existed in the media of collage, photography and even the game of the exquisite corpse – a collective game that only worked because of its dependence upon the confection of a whole out of disparate parts.[7] Rather than celebrating ideal bodies, Surrealist practices emphasized bodily

---

Surrealism: Art Between the Wars (New Haven and London: Yale University/Open University, 1993); Christopher Green, *Cubism and its Enemies* (New Haven and London: Yale University, 1987); Romy Golan, *Modernity and Nostalgia: Art and Politics in France between the Wars* (New Haven: Yale University, 1995); Mary Louise Roberts, *Civilization without Sexes: Reconstructing Gender in Postwar France, 1917–1927* (Chicago: University of Chicago, 1994); Kenneth Silver, *Esprit de Corps: The Art of the Parisian Avant-Garde and the First World War, 1914–1925* (Princeton: Princeton University Press, 1989); Sidra Stich, ed., *Anxious Visions: Surrealist Art* (Berkeley: University Art Museum and New York: Abbeville, 1990); Daniel Sherman, *The Construction of Memory in Interwar France* (Chicago: University of Chicago, 1999); *La Course au Moderne. France et Allemagne dans l'Europe des Années Vingt 1919–1933* (Paris: Musée d'Histoire Contemporaine/BDIC, 1993).

5 On interwar France and the rationalization of culture, see: Marjorie Beale, *The Modernist Enterprise: French Elites and the Threat of Modernity* (Stanford: Stanford University Press, 1999); Carol S. Eliel, ed., *L'Esprit Nouveau: Purism in Paris, 1918–1925* (Los Angeles: Los Angeles County Museum of Art and New York: Abrams, 2001); Golan, *Modernity and Nostalgia*; Green, *Cubism and Its Enemies*; Silver, *Esprit de Corps*; Nancy J. Troy, *Modernism and the Decorative Arts in France: Art Nouveau to Le Corbusier* (New Haven: Yale University, 1991).

6 André Breton, 'Manifesto of Surrealism', in *Manifestoes of Surrealism*, trans. Richard Seaver and Helen Lane (Ann Arbor: University of Michigan, 1972), p. 26.

7 On the specific ways in which Breton, Aragon and poet Robert Desnos articulated an aesthetics of dismemberment in the 1920s, see Lyford, 'The Aesthetics of Dismemberment', pp. 45–78.

dismemberment in order to critique, or at least question, prevalent ideas about bodily integrity and social progress.

It is at the intersection of France's 'return to order' and Surrealism's efforts to inhibit that return that André Kertész's Paris photographs reside. For his images parallel Surrealist forms of body politics in that they instantaneously ensnare their viewer in a disjointed web of cultural associations. Interestingly, Kertész suggested that his work might be considered Surrealist, even if he didn't adhere to a specific Surrealist programme. Moreover, he not only frequented Le Dôme, but he published his work in magazines sympathetic to Surrealism (including *Variétés*, *Bifur* and *L'Art vivant*) and exhibited his photographs alongside those of Man Ray and Brassaï in the late 1920s.[8] More important than his social and professional habits is the fact that his photographs often appear to question the success of the return to order. By investigating and recording the traumatic experience of the present – a trauma embedded in the mutilated male bodies he often chose to photograph – Kertész's images counter modernity's as ideal of cultural evolution. Rather, in Kertész's hands, modernity's emphasis on technologies of reproduction and consumption function as the backdrop for a darker, more ominous image of postwar culture.[9]

Rather than emphasizing a robust masculinity like that associated with France's rebuilding campaign (fig. 9), Kertész's images document a world in transition. His version of the city is prodded, even shocked into recognition of modernity's impact on human culture. Kertész's photographs borrow the signs of war, industry and advertising in order to publicize the traumatic *effects* of

---

8 Sandra Phillips notes that although Kertész often denied any interest in Surrealism and any relationship with the members of the group, he himself noted that in the case of his 1925 photograph of mannequin legs upside down in a sculptor's studio, 'some would like to call this Surrealist'. Sandra Phillips, *The Photographic Work of André Kertész in France, 1925–1926: A Critical Essay and Catalogue,* Vol. 1 (unpublished PhD dissertation, City University of New York, 1985), p. 357. Phillips goes on to note in Chapters 2 and 4 that although Kertész was neither a member of the Surrealist group nor a close friend of Breton or Aragon, he knew Man Ray, and published his work in journals sympathetic to the movement (*Variétés*, *Bifur*, *L'Art Vivant*, *Arts et Métiers Graphiques*, *Vu*). He also exhibited his work in the important 1928 'Salon of Independent Photography' at the Théâtre des Champs-Elysées in May of that year, alongside photographers such as Man Ray, Berenice Abbott and Atget, a photographer whose images of the city of Paris had earned him a special place in the canon of Surrealist precursors.

9 Atget's images were often reproduced in *La Révolution surréaliste*, and were beloved by both Man Ray and Berenice Abbott who purchased the bulk of Atget's photographs upon his death in 1925. Interestingly, the Salon de la Photographie in 1928 showed a retrospective of Atget's work at the same time that it exhibited the work of Kertész and Man Ray. On this exhibition, see Phillips, *André Kertész in France*. On early twentieth-century interest in Atget's work, see the indispensable publication 'Colloque Atget', *Photographies* (hors-série), March 1986.

industry and consumer culture upon the idealized image of a coherent, unified society being promoted by the state during the 1920s. In Kertész's Paris, the spectacle of the fragmented male body pointed out the underlying realities of postwar progress. Unlike nineteenth-century critiques of modernity in which the female body often served as a point of departure for the consumer's fantasies, desires and fears, Kertész's Paris photographs often represent the male body as a cipher for postwar culture.

An exemplary image in this vein is Kertész's 1928 photograph of a man at a Parisian café (fig. 10). From the number of plates on his small table, this man appears to have been drinking. Slouched at a small café table in a pose that contrasts dramatically with that taken by the muscular young man in the Ovomaltine ad just behind him, the older man's slack figure suggests the failure of social reconstruction by emphasizing the contrast between a weakened and an idealized image of masculinity. By juxtaposing life with advertising – the idealized, if fictional young man versus the reality of an older man's inactivity – Kertész reveals the Paris street as a site of conflict between different forms of manhood while simultaneously underscoring the tension between a fantasy of a return to order and its melancholic, decaying counterpart.[10] Paralleling the juxtapositions that are often at the core of Surrealist images, whether textual or visual, this photograph provokes its viewers to see, perhaps even to identify with, the tensions that existed between different ways of being in the postwar world. The comparison of an ideal, advertised man with a body marked by lassitude and decay pushes us to notice the difference between the two and to objectify that difference as the subject of our own visual experience. The image provokes us to see this difficult cultural clash concretely, in a frozen instant, as proposed by Pierre MacOrlan. By subtly disrupting cultural norms in images such as this one, Kertész publicizes the problematic transformation of postwar cultural experience by focusing our attention on the conflict inherent in that process of social change. Because the image makes it possible to see the difference between the two men, it counters the heroic imagery of the postwar period by giving us a sign of reconstruction's drive to submerge the traces of loss within a sea of productivity.

10 Another version of this image, taken from behind and to the left of a seated café patron (a different man, if one can judge from the neater felt hat and suit, although an equally impressive stack of plates is also in evidence in this version), was published in an auction sales catalogue in 1979. The Ovomaltine poster is just visible at the upper left of the image, and another blurred male body (suited, hatted in almost identical fashion as the seated man) walks into the image at the upper right. Christie's London, *19th and 20th Century Photographs*, 31 October 1979, no. 228.

Surrealism, Publicity and Visual Consumption

Although a few historians of Surrealism have pointed to links between Surrealism and advertising, none has described the specific nature of that relationship, especially in visual terms.[11] If Surrealism proposed itself as a practice that depended on the unconscious for the liberation of the subject through desire, it did so not by rejecting publicity but by appropriating certain of publicity's rhetorical strategies for revolutionary ends. Louis Aragon perceived the poster as a form of expression that had much to teach both artists and poets about the transformation of art and experience in modern French culture. For Aragon, the rhetorical structures associated with advertising were potentially important visual sources. The only question for Surrealism was how best to use the genre's visual effects: 'a poem [...] if it were written on the walls, would it stop the crowd? would they read it? would they hold on to it?' Aragon wondered.[12] By studying and using the techniques of mass culture, Aragon believed that the Surrealists might learn to manipulate those techniques in order to create a Surrealist visual culture – and in this way, then, images could becomes tools to advertise Surrealism.[13]

This approach to advertising as a model for Surrealist practice is echoed in Walter Benjamin's critical approach to the connections between advertising (and its fundamental reliance on repetition), industrial production and the unconscious. 'Publicity', wrote Benjamin in his Arcades project, 'is the ruse

---

11 Among them is Tag Gronberg, 'Beware Beautiful Women: The 1920s Shopwindow Mannequin and the Physiognomy of Effacement', *Art History* 20:3 (September 1997), pp. 375–96. Gronberg not only discusses the Exposition des Arts Décoratifs of 1925, but also the female mannequin's relationship to visual and stylistic modernity, eventually drawing a connection to the 1938 Surrealist exhibition in which Surrealist mannequins reflect a reworking of the rhetoric of contemporary French publicity.

12 Louis Aragon, 'Introduction à 1930', *La Révolution surréaliste*, no. 12 (15 December 1929), p. 60.

13 Louis Aragon notably focused attention, beginning in the early 1920s, on advertising and publicity. Especially interesting in terms of a critique of the commodification of contemporary culture is Aragon's 'Au bout du quai, les Arts Décoratifs!', *La Révolution surréaliste*, no. 5 (15 October 1925), pp. 26–27. An early poem, entitled 'Réclame d'aucun produit', *L'Œuvre Poètique*, Vol. 1, 1917–1920 (Paris: Livre Club Diderot, 1974), emphasizes the relation between the rejection of advertising and violence in Aragon's work. There is also, finally, his most famous work addressing the city as a scene of commercial overload, *Paysan de Paris* (Paris: Gallimard, 1926, 1953). On Paris as a critical site of consumer culture and mass media three texts which suggest the city's role as an image of modernity through consumption are Susan Buck-Morss, 'The City as Dreamworld and Catastrophe', *October*, no. 73 (Summer 1995), pp. 3–26, Susan Buck-Morss, *The Dialectics of Seeing: Walter Benjamin and the Arcades Project* (Cambridge: MIT Press, 1991), and Christina Kiaer, 'Rodchenko in Paris', *October*, no. 75 (Winter 1996), pp. 3–35.

that permits the dream to impose itself on industry'.[14] For Benjamin, Surrealist poetry had begun to mine the possibilities of consumer culture quite successfully: 'The poetry of the Surrealists treats words like the names of commercial firms and their texts are at bottom prospectuses for businesses which have not yet been created. Today the dreams that one believed had been catalogued long ago in the treasury of 'poetic' words hide themselves in the names of firms'.[15] Could advertisements and their visual-rhetorical codes actually be used to teach the viewer to see the world differently from usual?[16] Surrealism's attraction to advertising imagery centred on the possibility of reframing the viewer's experience through visual shock and juxtaposition. Kertész's photographs (in ways Benjamin might have appreciated) play with that form of visual shock as well as the ambiguity of postwar social order in ways that resonate with Aragon's words.

Doing their part for capitalist culture, many theorists and practitioners of publicity in the 1920s developed a visual language that would solicit a customer's attention just long enough for a desire for the product to lodge in the viewer's mind. The most successful advertisement would generate a chain of associations in the individual through powerful visual imagery.[17] The subject's

---

14 Walter Benjamin, Section G [Expositions, publicité, Grandville], in *Paris, Capitale du XIXe Siècle*, trans. Jean Lacoste (Paris: Editions du 'Cerf', 1993), p. 190.

15 Benjamin, *Paris, Capitale du XIX Siecle*, p. 192–93 [G 1a,2].

16 Siegfried Kracauer's understanding of the ways in which images create psychophysical 'correspondances' has been helpful to me as a means of understanding the ways in which strong visual images (films, advertisements, photographs) operate on the psyche of the viewer. See Siegfried Kracauer, *Theory of Film: The Redemption of Physical Reality* (Princeton: Princeton University Press, 1997), pp. 68–69.

17 Marjorie Beale's research on the psychological and medical sources of early twentieth-century French publicity reveals that many publicists and social planners during the 1920s were invested in the construction of visual and rhetorical procedures that would attract the burgeoning Parisian market to an expanding array of products and ideas. Drawing heavily on Hippolyte Bernheim's work on suggestion, many of these early professional publicists espoused techniques which were dependent on visual imagery as a catalyst for the brain's transformation of a suggestion into activity, a concept Bernheim called 'idéo-dynamisme'. In Bernheim's account of the image's role in suggestion, the subject would perceive an image that would then be 'deposited' in the subject's brain. Successive visual stimuli would enter the subject's brain and act dialectically with the others stored there, each image shifting the affect and impact of the others in a process of association. This 'collection' of perceived visual messages would then form a network of visual stimuli that would eventually generate mental and physical action in the perceiving subject. This relationship between perceived visual stimuli and the workings of the subject's mental life was what attracted Surrealism to the workings of publicity in the 1920s. What was at stake in discussions about publicity's visual rhetoric in this postwar period was the image's presumed ability both to captivate and transform the viewing subject. It is not hard to imagine the Surrealists' delighting in the sight of a street plastered high not only with advertisements for Monsavon or the face of Bébé Cadum, for example, but also with images that would create and interact with explicitly Surrealist

consciousness would be captured and then modified by the advertisement. Soon after first contact, the image would create a desire for the displayed object. And key to this unfolding desire was the mobilization of the viewer's sense of sight.[18] Through visual suggestion, an image would ideally provoke physical action, generating not only desire for the product but also a psychological attachment or identification with that object which would develop 'unconsciously'. And the image would work best when influenced by external associations, ones that would mesh with the advertisement to create a desire in the viewing subject:

> The advertisement, when it is simply 'seen' does not have the same value for immediately creating the desire for the purchase, it is even frequently seen by passers-by without their knowledge. Because, publicity, like any thing which falls under the senses, may be perceived in the state of waking, or on the contrary in the state of sleeping – during the hours where the spirit is passive, available for the impressions that are indifferent to it in appearance. – An idea is going to lodge itself in one of the folds of the brain, in one of its mysterious pockets, in the subconscious! – The seed is sown; and external influence will make it germinate. The need for a product or an article will happen unexpectedly one day, and this need, impersonal at first, will make itself more concrete and will take for its object the brand read everywhere. [...][19]

In this 1927 formulation of the rhetoric of publicity published in the high-end advertising and design journal *Arts et Métiers Graphiques*, the image lodges itself in the brain's 'mysterious' folds – the *subconscient* – where it lies awaiting the proper motivation in order to complete its task: the need for a particular commodity.[20] Visual suggestion was characterized by the 'sudden eruption' into consciousness of an image or an idea that became an integral part of the chain of thought, an idea that could in turn provoke physical action. Publicity not only

---

human subjects. Marjorie Beale, *Advertising and the Politics of Public Persuasion in France, 1900–1939* (unpublished PhD dissertation, University of California, Berkeley, 1991), pp. 24–74. These pages deliver a succinct, well-researched account of the relations between psychiatry, philosophy and advertising in the 1920s as it was played out in the debates about the nature of suggestion and psychological analysis in the work of figures such as Bernheim and Henri Bergson. The concept of idéo-dynamisme and its relation to Bernheim's 'doctrine of suggestion' is clearly articulated in Hippolyte Bernheim, *Automatisme et Suggestion* (Paris: Alcan, 1917), pp. 9–14. Beale provides a more concise and nuanced account of advertising's role in the construction of varied accounts of modernity in interwar France in her chapter 'Advertising as Modernism', from *The Modernist Enterprise: French Elites and the Threat of Modernity* (Stanford: Stanford University Press, 1999), pp. 11–47.

18 Walter S. Maas, 'Subconscient et Publicité', *Arts et Métiers Graphiques*, no. 1 (15 September 1927), pp. 56–57.

19 Ibid.

20 Both Kertész and Man Ray published their photographs in this journal during the late 1920s.

generated desire, but it provoked the subject to act on a range of different psychological and emotional experiences.[21]

During the 1920s in France, the advertising establishment joined modern technologies of reproduction with psychology as a way to create a more scientific form of publicity. Borrowing ideas about automatism, hypnosis and visual suggestion from nineteenth-century figures like Pierre Janet, Hippolyte Bernheim and Henri Bergson, ad-men of the 1920s refined new ways to plant the seeds of desire for consumer products in the minds of their audience.[22] Borrowing, too, from commercial culture as a model – in this respect the photographs of Man Ray come to mind – Surrealist artists and writers saw a poetic potential for the advertisement as a form of communication. For advertisements, like many Surrealist images, depended on fragmentation and decontextualization for their visual and rhetorical power.[23]

Kertész's photographs of the Paris streets, particularly those in which advertising is mobilized as a comparative tool for representing social identities, appear to document the process by which a photograph might produce first a visual shock and, potentially, desire in the viewer. Yet Kertész's images do not represent shiny new products hot off the assembly line, but the decay of masculinity in postwar life. And this is a form of cultural dissolution at the heart of André Breton's *Second Manifesto of Surrealism*, a 1929 text in which Breton exhorted his readers to realize that 'everything remains to be done, every means must be worth trying, in order to lay waste to ideas of family, fatherland, [and] religion'.[24] Kertész's images make the implication of Breton's words visible: masculinity's destruction or decay might help to create a desire for a new image of man. But this desire would conform to a Surrealist one – traumatic,

21 Maas, 'Subconscient et Publicité', pp. 55–56. Interestingly in terms of its relevance for a Surrealist appropriation of publicity, Maas suggests that advertising itself was an inherently dialectical one. The subject's response to external stimuli, in his account, would eventually produce an idea in direct opposition to the newly-received one. Although this opposition would likely reject the image implanted in the subject's mind, the triumph over the foreign object would permanently alter the subject. And in this sense, publicity offered itself to Surrealism as a working model for the transformation of the human psyche. On this latter point, see Maas, 'Subconscient et Publicité', p. 57.

22 Marjorie Beale, 'Advertising as Modernism', in *The Modernist Enterprise*, pp. 11–47.

23 Beale, *The Modernist Enterprise*, p. 44. Because advertising itself took fragmentation as a key visual mode during the 1920s, perhaps it is not surprising to find a photographic conversation with advertising on the cover of the July 1925 issue of *La Révolution surréaliste*. Man Ray, a member of Breton's collective, worked a great deal in fashion and advertising production, and indeed it is one of his images, produced for the 1925 Exposition des Art Décoratifs in Paris, that appeared on the cover of *La Révolution surréaliste*, no. 4 (15 July 1925).

24 The emphasis is Breton's. André Breton, 'Second Manifeste du Surréalisme', *La Révolution surréaliste*, no. 12 (15 December 1929), p. 2.

ambiguous, and unsettling – instead of the one proposed by French corporations or government ministers.

The Surrealists believed they could turn the nation's wartime devastation to different ends by borrowing from contemporary publicity. By producing and disseminating images permeated by a language that emphasized dismemberment instead of a seamless process of reconstruction, it seemed possible to develop an advertising campaign for Surrealist culture. Although that campaign ultimately proved unsuccessful at producing anything like social revolution, the particular ways in which Surrealist practices politicized the rhetoric of contemporary advertising nonetheless needs explaining. For it was the Surrealists' aim to destabilize the relations between mass culture and the individual subject in ways that would create an *unconscious* revolution, one to be carried out in the viewer's mind, and which would spread in turn through the belly of modernity. Ultimately, they hoped that the methods used by consumer culture to fabricate social and political consent could be turned against a consumption-driven society. And it was with this aim of loosening the grip of conventional ideas about French society – gender identities included – that proved for a time to be an effective catalyst for mounting attacks on the rhetoric of the return to order.

Picturing Masculinities

Walking along the Seine one day in 1926, André Kertész stopped to take a photograph (fig. 8). What captured his attention was not a *bouquiniste*'s display of books, however. Kertész's eye fell on a pair of men standing along a quai near Saint-Michel, looking down and away at the river beneath them. The man on the left is a *mutilé de guerre*, his somewhat shabbily-dressed figure framed by the crutches he uses to supplement a missing leg. The photograph compares his body with a larger, undamaged man by framing the two figures as if one were the reflection of the other, although only one of them is missing a leg.[25] The *mutilé de guerre*'s successful assimilation into postwar society was expected to occur in French life, yet from Kertész's image one might conclude that the process of assimilation had yet to occur even nine years later. Viewed in the context of postwar cultural reconstruction, Kertész's photograph is important

25 Although this photograph is currently most widely titled 'On the quai near Saint-Michel', it was originally captioned in *Paris Vu par André Kertész* (1934) in a way that identified the amputee as a war veteran: 'Au fil de l'eau, ce robuste ancien combattant regarde défiler les images du 269e de ligne dans le passé et celles du 269e de ligne, dans l'avenir'. Phillips notes that this photograph was cropped so that only the amputee appeared when it was published in *Paris Vu par André Kertész* (Paris, 1934), p. 19. See Phillips, *The Photographic Work of André Kertész*, vol. 1, p. 213. The image of the *mutilé* along the Seine corresponds to Phillips' catalogue number 1926.85, in ibid., vol. 2, 141.

because it registers social experience in embodied terms, serving up male dismemberment as a fact of contemporary Parisian life.

It is one thing to see pictures of the war's dead and wounded in an illustrated magazine, where soldiers' bodies lie twisted in graves miles away from one's study or café table.[26] It is quite another to pass by a man whose traumatized flesh forces one to a realize how that body might be used as a political tool. Kertész's photograph registers the immediacy of such a visual experience by representing the *mutilé de guerre* as both an object of national sacrifice (one might presume his injuries are a result of the war) and the subject of reconstruction (one might read the two-legged man to his right as a symbol of possible rehabilitation). The framing of the shot accomplishes this narrative pairing through visual comparison, suggesting that we read the mens' bodies as a pair. Although these men are not one and the same individual (their clothing and their bodies suggest differences of class as well as bodily integrity), the implications of Kertész's tight framing of their figures is that we *ought* to read them together. The figures' proximity to one another proposes an approach to the male body in which physical trauma is expressed as one possible layer of the truth about the healthy male body. It is as if the photograph has peeled apart different aspects of the lived experience of war in order to make them visible simultaneously, as two sides of the same coin. Kertész's comparison moves back and forth between the two men, pairing the two so that the image appears to document (and secure) the impossibility of forgetting war-induced mutilation.[27]

---

26 Many images of *mutilés de guerre* were published between the war years and the late 1920s, at times accompanied by text which registers the degree to which the memory of war trauma bubbles up into the present some ten years later. One image, in the widely-disseminated illustrated journal *L'Illustration* was accompanied by the following text: 'Try to imagine a heap of unformed skin bearing the traces of deep tears and offering the most hideous sight – the sinister hollowing from bullets, the pulverizing from grenades, the stabbing from bayonets or daggers, the flattening from hatchet blows or pickaxes, facial smashing, nasal or chin disappearance. Such is the condition of these monsters whose lot is worse than death.' Albéric Cahuet, 'Le Château des faces massacrées', *L'Illustration* CLXIX:2 (11 June 1927), p. 626, as quoted and translated by Stich, *Anxious Visions*, p. 27.

27 For intriguing, thorough accounts of the representation of the mutilated soldier in postwar Great Britain, see Seth Koven, 'Remembering and Dismemberment: Crippled Children, Wounded Soldiers, and the Great War in Great Britain', *American Historical Review* (October 1994), pp. 1167–202, and Joanna Bourke, *Dismembering the Male* (Chicago: University of Chicago, 1995). Koven and Bourke have both read postwar efforts to hide, efface or 'forget' male dismemberment as a sign of the mutilated body's ineradicable difference. Through the repetition of images of the disabled soldier in textbooks on the war, Koven reminds us, the figure of the mutilated soldier is now something of a cliché by which we learn to remember and represent the war of 1914–1918. On the reconstruction of the French soldier during World War I, see Sophie Delaporte, *Les Gueules Cassées. Les blessés de la face de la Grande Guerre* (Paris: Editions Noêsis, 1996) and Roxanne Panchasi, 'Reconstructions: Prosthetics and

Here the man without a leg is made visible as a phantom limb for postwar culture – that which was lost or left behind, but remained a nagging presence in its very absence. Kertész depicts this *mutilé* as a trace of the dismemberment that haunts the unified ideal of manhood.[28] Unlike the optimistic image of male power in the American Express advertisement from 1920, Kertész's image presents the male body as a dialectical pair in which trauma and reconstruction are linked together. The back-and-forth movement between the two bodies makes it hard to avoid a crucial fact (that was also of central interest to Surrealism): that the return to order depended structurally on the brutality and violence of a war that the nation wanted to forget.

Kertész's Parisian street photographs are valuable for an understanding of Surrealist visual culture in that they explore the male body's place in France's rhetoric of postwar reconstruction. While representations of the modern woman of the 1920s are now staples of French cultural history, the image of the mutilated or prosthetic man – in many ways the modern woman's counterpart – has not been adequately addressed. Because Kertész's photographs highlight the visibility of male mutilation in postwar France, they not only register male trauma but also suggest that representations of the mutilated male body might have the potential to derail the unimpeded 'progress' of the return to order. Such prosthetic men were new and improved, yes; but their presence also recalled the trauma of war for those who saw them. If the rehabilitated veteran ought to look like that muscled, straining man of the American Express poster from 1920, Kertész's photographs function like echoes of a failed rehabilitation. And in the context of Surrealist Paris, Kertész's dismembered, or mutilated bodies look like cultural ready-mades, waiting on the street, ready to generate a desire for a new Surrealist order.[29]

In contrast to Kertész's layered visual account of trauma's relation to masculine identity along the Seine, his image of a battered prosthetic leg from 1927 objectifies male mutilation in order to suggest masculinity's regeneration (fig. 11). Under Kertész's intimate gaze, this artificial body part seems magically to turn itself into an image of phallic unity – at least momentarily. The chipped prosthetic leg sits unceremoniously atop a mounded blanket, its bulk

---

Rehabilitation of the Male Body in World War I France', *differences* VII:3 (1995), pp. 109–40. For a more detailed study of Surrealism's interest in, and manipulation of, the rhetoric of reconstruction, see Lyford, 'The Aesthetics of Dismemberment'. I attend to these issues of Surrealism's aesthetics of dismemberment in several different contexts in *Body Parts: Surrealism and the Reconstruction of Masculinity* (unpublished PhD dissertation, University of California, Berkeley, 1997).

28 My thanks to Donald LaCoss for lively discussion about this material; it was he that offered the suggestion of this experience of reading the image as a visual equivalent to a 'phantom limb'.

29 Kertész displayed a long-standing interest in making photographs of amputees. There were roughly 15 final prints of different amputees that Kertész made during the 1920s. Phillips, *The Photographic Work of André Kertész*.

demanding attention because of the way that it fills the bed. With its flattened top at rest on a wrinkled pillow and its black shoe nearly touching the bed's frame at bottom, the leg appears as an equivalent of the person who would usually sleep there. Now, however, the prosthetic device stands in for the absent body, foregrounding the body's incompleteness. It is as if the leg's status as a body part is hardly different from the status of the body as a whole. Numbered like a specimen for scientific analysis, or even a product of the assembly line, the prosthetic leg appears to be the thirteenth in a series of (part) bodies, a series implied by the cut of the photographic frame.

There is a subtle difference between this photograph's emphasis on a partial body and the comparison between men in the image taken along the Seine. This leg also mimics the elongated form of a phallus, signifying as both a (simulated) lost leg and as a figure for the body's symbolic loss of cultural authority. Instead of filling in the bodily gaps created by amputation, the battered leg calls forth its absent owner in the viewer's imagination: is he hobbling around the edges of the bed on a stump? Is he hopping? Or must he crawl? This image represents the injured male body as both artificially complete and pitiably lacking because of the way that it functions as both part and whole simultaneously.

Just as rhetoric about reconstruction relied on gendered language in order to demonstrate the need to refurbish a masculinist culture after the war, so these images by Kertész represent the relationship between reconstruction and wartime destruction as an integral one. Indeed, because these images do not settle on a single way to read the brutalized or weakened male body, they reveal a contradiction within the rhetoric of reconstruction: phallic plenitude is dependent on the successful repression of male dismemberment.

What Kertész's photographs of the quai St Michel and that single prosthetic leg show us about 1920s Paris is this: difference *within* masculinity operated visually in relation to the concept of social progress. We read the two men as if they represent a passage from mutilation to regeneration, with a fragmented male body compared to one that suggests masculine totality. Implicit in this movement from part to whole is not only a visualization of the logic of the return to order – from part to whole, from absence to presence – but an unwillingness to settle on either position for the subject. The play with the body's cultural meanings thus exists as Kertész's brand of body politics.

As has been pointed out in recent years by a number of scholars, interwar rhetoric about reconstruction relied on gendered language in order to articulate the need for a new patriarchal culture that would pull France out of physical and moral decay.[30] Kertész's images of the male body show us how important

30 Important accounts of the relationships between fascism, modernism and the avant-garde in France during this period include David Carroll, 'Literary Fascism and the Problem of Gender: The Aesthetics of the Body in Drieu la Rochelle', in *French Literary Fascism: Nationalism, Anti-Semitism, and the Ideology of Culture* (Princeton: Princeton

embodiment was to the work of reconstruction; moreover, they suggest an anxiety about the role and meaning of the male body in that process of cultural evolution. That anxiety welled up not only within the context of thinking about men; it also came forth in terms of the ways that masculinity and femininity were intertwined in the rhetoric of postwar reconstruction.

Kertész's 1928 image of a flower vendor on the Champs-Elysées is exemplary in this respect, as it images a moment of commercial exchange between a legless male flower-seller and a possible female client (fig. 12). Here, however, the photograph reverses traditional ideas about the structure of sexual difference. Briefcase in hand, this self-assured woman strides headlong into the mouth of the *métro*. The vendor's need – physical as well as economic – is expressed rather poignantly in contrast to the woman's brusque self-sufficiency; his proffered posy stands for a conventional set of gender roles that she has no interest in buying. Instead of juxtaposing the amputee with another male body, this image focuses on a man in the midst of confronting a modern woman. The photograph situates his body somewhere between the traditional polarities of sexual difference, acknowledging the fact that a third term – the one he represents – has been wedged between conventional representations of masculinity and femininity. While his torso mimics the gestures of heterosexual courtship, his missing legs attract attention to the inadequacies of his masculine body. Evading his offer, the striding woman's lack of interest in him reads as a threat to his manhood and his ability to make a living.

There is, however, another role available for the male subject in this image, and it is the figure that walks into the image at the upper left. This second man appears as the striding, upright, properly active counterpart to the vendor whose squat, legless form literalizes a deformation of ideal masculinity. Here the modern woman is visible as a problem for those who would like to maintain a conventional definition of masculinity. The publicity-saturated streets of Paris were the places where individuals were forced to grapple with a shifting social landscape, one in which both a mutilated and a prosthetic masculinity were pitted against 'modern woman' as visible indicators of social change. Precisely

---

University Press, 1995), pp. 147–70; Hal Foster, 'Armor Fou', *October*, no. 56 (Spring 1991), pp. 64–97; Andrew Hewitt, *Fascist Modernism: Aesthetics, Politics and the Avant-Garde* (Stanford: Stanford University Press, 1993); Alice Yaeger Kaplan, *Reproductions of Banality: Fascism, Literature and French Intellectual Life* (Minneapolis: University of Minnesota, 1986), and Robert Soucy, *Fascist Intellectual: Drieu la Rochelle* (Berkeley: University of California, 1979). I have proposed an intersection between Surrealist interest in gender play as a political weapon and the ways in which that play also finds its way into fascist approaches to the body in France in the paper '*Le Numéro Barbette*: Photography and the Politics of Embodiment in Interwar France' presented at the symposium *The Modern Woman Revisited*, Stanford University, October 2000, and forthcoming in Whitney Chadwick and Tirza Latimer, eds, *The Modern Woman Revisited* (Rutgers University Press).

because of her widely-commented upon physical appearance – slim, trim and bobbed – the modern woman embodied the changing relationships between the sexes. At a time when many men had literally lost a measure of social authority along with a leg, the streamlined, self-assured *garçonne* demonstrated that the world could no longer be the same. Social and sexual freedom for the modern woman was being won at the cost of the traditional structure of relations between women and men.

By 1934, Kertész's interest in the political valence of the body on the streets of Paris not only structured itself around sexual difference, but also articulated how the mass produced male body appeared increasingly to overpower the flesh-and-blood version (fig. 13). In this image, Kertész interrogates the relations between the sexes within consumer culture (something implicit in the image of the flower vendor's rebuffed exchange with a female customer). This photograph of a Paris street plastered with advertisements for the popular apéritif Dubonnet captures the texture of a culture in which a consumption-driven male body – in this case, a repeating pattern of men drinking set in contrast to the top-hatted smile of a masculinized *bourgeoise* – replicates itself across a city wall. The repeated forms of drinking men in the Dubonnet posters conflate industrially produced men with the real thing. Here Kertész's image reveals its indebtedness to the work of Atget most explicitly, even as Kertész frames the city of Paris around mass culture and advertising instead of the haunting old shopfronts of Atget's disappearing world. On the fast-paced boulevards of Paris exist signs that point to the impact of modern industrial technology and production upon personal and sexual identities. Masculinity is multiplied here – there are several different versions of manhood made visible in this image – and envisioned by Kertész in the context of mass production. Manhood is for sale here, and there are choices to be made.

Sexual difference is also confused in this photograph, as images of masculine and feminine identities also appear to distill sexual difference into gender-identified (if conflated) bodily forms. For example, Kertész's photograph denies us access to the face of the man who strides away at the upper left of the image; yet at the same time, the image supplies us with a range of possible identities for this man that circulate throughout the photograph. Masculinity is shown as separate from the femininity we might presume for the woman in the foreground, a separation pictorially emphasized by the form of the bench she sits on and by the sign just to her left. Although the advertisement attached to the bench visually separates male from female, it simultaneously joins them through the textual slippage from 'Georges' to 'Georgette'. Gender, and by extension a shift from masculine to feminine, accrues within this image as a conglomerate of visual signs that stress visual identification with a legible gender identity ('Georges' as masculine, 'Georgette' as feminine).

Viewed in contrast to the firm set of boundaries between masculinity and femininity encoded into postwar rhetorics of reconstruction (particularly in the case of pro-natalist rhetoric), this photograph represents the competition between the gender-specific forms of consumer culture in ways that propose sexual difference as something more fluid than one might imagine, as something that can move from an attachment to a masculine subject (Georges) to a feminine one (Georgette). The photograph suggests that the body is complicit in its own objectification; the image emphasizes how one might sift through the masses of visual information that crowded Parisian streets as a means of finding an appropriate object with which to identify. Why imagine that there was only one type of man when there were evidently several types of women?

While Kertész's metro-riding young woman dramatizes a new role for women in this cultural shift, his photographs of damaged or prosthetically rehabilitated men reveal that France's social transformation was catalyzed by male mutilation as well. As framed by Kertész, masculinity could not be understood in any totality, nor made sense of within the confines of a single idealized image. Like other kinds of products for consumption, masculinity in the 1920s seemed to entail as many shapes and sizes as did femininity. Difference within gender was documented by Kertész as a byproduct of comparative visual analysis, with vision itself shaping the body as a carrier of social identity. Yet as Kertész's image of the flower vendor at the métro entrance reveals, the process of reintegrating the mutilated male body into a hyper-masculinized postwar French culture was incomplete. The masculine subject that Kertész's photographs present to us seems to be in danger of losing his traditional position of power. A sense of desperation permeates these photographs, and it is both economic, physical and psychic, a desperation which suggests the possible failure of the return to order.

We ought to read Kertész's photographs as part of the terrain that is Surrealism's historical context, as images of a street that appears to be a disturbingly palpable museum filled with objects that each hold within them the power to generate a Surrealist beholder. Kertész's extended visual attention to the bodies of men in postwar Paris is significant in that it appears to have been something more than the representation of a morbid interest in amputees, drunks or men with prosthetic limbs. His photographs offer evidence of the ways in which the body's shifting postwar significance enabled it to function as a physical support for a new way of speaking about modernity and its impact upon French culture. Like any other product to be consumed, masculinity in Paris took many forms. In the end, we ought to read Kertész's photographs as part of Surrealism's terrain because they are images of a conflicted masculinity being worked out in public, on the street, and within mass culture. What he puts his finger on in the image of two men at the Seine, or the single leg in the *Hôtel de Reveil*, is the way in which the image of male dismemberment was both a sign of trauma, and an emerging figure of fascination and desire. Whereas his image of two men at the Seine articulates the differences within masculinity as a process of comparison that highlights narrative time, the act of juxtaposition and the experience of seeing difference at close range, Kertész's own practice as a commercial photographer would soon capture the facts of that fragmented male body quite literally as spectacle (fig. 14). In an intense, and focused image that was shot as one of a series of photographs of a one-legged, African-American dancer named Clayton 'Peg Leg' Bates who performed in Parisian Jazz clubs, the male body's status as a product of trauma to be consumed cannot be made much plainer: shooting from above Bates's legs and torso, Kertész orients our gaze around the join between thigh and wooden limb. He pushes us to look, to see the gap between the two, and the way that the heavy leather belt neatly holds the two together, a pillow for a kneecap, signalling the facts of Bates's mutilation even as Bates's own arms cross neatly over his lap. While this image was not one of those selected for publication in the German magazine *Münchner Illustrierte Presse* in 1929, the photograph did make it into the collection of the well-known Surrealist collector, Julien Levy, as early as 1932.[31] If the logic of Kertész's earlier images of male dismemberment brought the existence of male dismemberment into the light, by 1929 the commercialization of male trauma represented by Bates's popular international success suggests that it was also possible to see the traumatized male body as a commodity form to be exploited rather than avoided or repressed. If photographs such as Kertész's registered the conflicts inherent within the discourse of a return to order, they also possessed the ability to sell alternative forms of embodiment, and potentially alternative forms of desire, to a postwar audience as well. It is here, in the intersection between trauma and reconstruction, between Surrealism and consumer culture, that Kertész's photographs laid the groundwork for a politicization of the male body, even as that body became a vehicle for the spectacularization of trauma. The commercialization of male dismemberment in the form of a dancer who drew crowds because of his body's difference suggests some of the ways that Kertész's photographic concentration on the traumatized male body reflected a dialectic we see within Surrealism itself. If on the one hand such photographs force us to see manhood weakened and fragmented, Clayton 'Peg Leg' Bates's popular appeal suggests that the fragmentation of masculinity had by 1929 become a new commodity form to be exploited. Kertész's photographs of

31 Sandra Phillips reproduces the title page of the article on Clayton 'Peg Leg' Bates and briefly discusses Kertész's commission for this work in her essay 'André Kertész: The Years in Paris', in Sandra S. Phillips, David Travis and Weston Naef eds, *André Kertész, Of Paris and New York* (New York and London: Thames and Hudson/Art Institute of Chicago, 1985), pp. 40–41. She also discusses Bates briefly in *The Photographic Work of André Kertész*. Interestingly for our thinking about Kertész as a Surrealist is the fact that a signed and dated print of this image in the collection of the Art Institute of Chicago was in Julien Levy's collection, a collection which was heavily weighted towards Surrealist photography. For more information on the Levy print, and its possible exhibition at the Levy gallery in the 1930s, see Phillips, *André Kertész, Of Paris and New York*, p. 269.

mutilés document how the gendered body could be used to map, describe and transform the postwar subject into an explicitly Surrealist one in that these images have the potential to 'advertise' not only the existence of, but to create a desire for, the very bodies whose forms remind one of the culture's inability to renew itself. If these photographs register the conflicts inherent within the discourse about a return to order, they also sold alternative forms of embodiment, and potentially desire, to their modern audiences. Thus the weakened or fragmented body laid the groundwork for Kertész's politicization of masculinity, even as it became a vehicle for the commodification of a wounded masculinity. But it was also a form that carried the traces of its violent birth. And those traces might force a moment of recognition that could enable a critique (and not just an acknowledgement), of the ways in which the traumatized male body had come to represent the pleasures of Parisian nightlife and recall the terrors of the trenches. The ambiguity of these photographic fragments, then, is what gives them their Surrealist charge. The alternation between one reading and another, between spectacular entertainment and traumatic recognition, parallels the dialectical process of seeing that permeates Surrealism.

Chapter 5

Surrealism Noir

Jonathan P. Eburne

> Interested in human destinies and their simple and secret causes, I had at first wanted to judge rashly: hatred, hatred of their employers, hatred slowly accumulated in the minds of two animalistic girls. And, one day, the explosion [...] the aggression, the eyes torn out [...] the horror that testified to a stored-up rancour. And yet! no [...] That's not it.
>
> Maurice Coriem, 'Histoire d'un drame passionnel: "Le Crime des Sœurs Papin" ' (1933)[1]

The full-page double portrait of Christine and Léa Papin (fig. 15), printed in the back of the fifth issue of *Le Surréalisme au service de la Révolution* (hereafter *LSASDLR*), is as remarkable an illustration of what would be known as 'the Papin affair' for what it does not show as it is for what it does show. In February 1933, the Papin sisters, cook and housekeeper in a haute-bourgeois household in Le Mans, brutally, almost ritualistically, slaughtered their employers, Mme and Mlle Lancelin. While the victims were still alive, the sisters gouged out their eyes with their bare hands, bludgeoned them to death with a hammer and a pewter jug, and then hacked at their legs with knives. For the local and Parisian press, the murders provided a gory spectacle of domestic terror and class conflict whose clearly anti-bourgeois significance seemed immediately and unmistakably clear: how else to explain the virulence with which the atrocities were committed? However, rather than co-opting the murderers as allegorical political figures, or interpreting their crimes in terms of class conflict, the Surrealists focused instead upon the 'clinical' aspects of the crime, that is, upon the sisters' enigmatic motives and their obvious but undiagnosed insanity.

Indeed, in spite of their page reference to a brief article by Paul Eluard and Benjamin Péret, the twin photographs do not so much illustrate the murder as omit it, or suppress it. And yet, the images nevertheless register the effect of the murders in a way that nevertheless resonates with the impact of a terrible change. This effect is largely the function of a comparison of the photographs, the orientation of two seemingly incompatible images in terms of their temporal references to the murders: 'before' and 'after'. On an immediate level, the juxtaposition plays upon the possibility that the sisters, in their kimonos – the

1 Maurice Coriem, 'Histoire d'un drame passionnel: "Le Crime des sœurs Papin" ', *Scandale*, no. 5 (December 1933), pp. 233–36. All translations are my own unless otherwise noted.

only clothes they wore as they were taken to prison – somehow manifest the crimes' sadistic urges in a language of sartorial and physiognomic signs. However, the comparison also performs a reversal of this physical reading, casting suspicion upon the 'innocent' first picture: are there not signs of murderous urges in this 'before' image? The ironic possibilities of this studio portrait were first exploited by *Détective* magazine, which, a week after the murder, printed it on its front cover with the caption, 'two angels? no! two demons.'[2] However, when the images are placed together in *LSASDLR*, this irony gives way to the simple, terrible fact of the sisters' transformation. Although it is clear what has happened in the time between the photographs – the crime is 'written all over their faces' – the murders are inscribed in no definitive way within the pictorial language of the photographs.

This effect of this photographic juxtaposition thus does more than sensationalize the crime's emotional or psychic burden; rather, its disjunction invokes motive as a question instead of citing any significant physical trait as its answer. The juxtaposition itself shows the disastrous fact that the sisters are the same people without in any way resolving the disparity into a unified image. The blank space between the photographs, in its mute resistance to the formal assimilation of the two images, thus suddenly 'speaks' as an allegory of the murders and the enigma of its cause.[3] Maintaining the breach between the photographs, this space exceeds the formal duality of the images in its exoteric reference to the murders, the unrepresented act between 'before' and 'after' manifest only as a change in the sisters' appearance.

At the same time, though, it is important to note that the second, 'afterward' image is not a straight photograph but a montage. The sisters, separated from each other at the time of their arrest, were never photographed together; the

---

2 *Détective*, no. 244 (9 February 1993), cover. Similarly, Christopher Lane writes in his caption to the double-portrait reprinted in his article, 'The interval between these images designates a transformation, a loss of meaning, and an act of murder. But chronology is deceptive here, as the photographs could easily be reversed with the distress of the "after" incorporated into the apparent calm of the "before". Although more visible, then, the unconscious does not simply register in the aftermath of external violence'. See 'The Delirium of Interpretation: Writing the Papin Affair', *differences* V:2 (1993), p. 24.

3 In their recent overview of the long legacy of French intellectual fascination with the Papin sisters, Rachel Evans and Keith Reader discuss the murder itself as a form of speech. As they write, 'Christine and Léa Papin, from the depths of their cultural deprivation, "said" something when they so horribly murdered their mistresses. That something, if like the Lacanian "real" it remains necessarily unsayable in its totality, continues to have a claim on our attention'. *The Papin Sisters* (Oxford: Oxford University Press, 2001), p. 3. Yet it is important also to note that if the sisters' actions 'spoke' (in an enigmatic language that remains unsayable), then the question of this speech's meaning provided – and continues to provide – a case study for the question of how both language and deadly force figured in bringing about social and ideological change.

second image is a collage made from individual mug shots, pasted together as a mirror image of the studio portrait. Both formally and metaphorically, the manufactured doubling of the images insists all the more forcefully upon the breach between the 'before' and 'after' images; in disavowing the actual separation of the sisters in prison, it further dramatizes the incompatibility of the docile 'before' picture and the decadent 'after' picture, and invokes once again the violence at the root of this transformation. Unlike the Surrealist image of the early 1920s, though, this photomontage invokes such disruptive violence for analytical rather than affective purposes; its aim is no longer to 'disorien[t] us in our own memory by depriving us of a frame of reference', as Breton writes in 1921, but rather to orient.[4] Indeed, by 1933 disorientation and disillusionment were no longer the goal of Surrealist activity, but had instead become conditions of political life under the threat of fascism's 'incomprehensible' rise. At this moment, the Surrealist image offers instead a new 'frame of reference' derived not from logic but, as we shall see, from paranoia, whose challenge to the naive realism at the core of communist modes of resistance provides the epistemological, even ontological, grounds for a new morality of revolt.

In the smouldering political climate of the early 1930s, Breton's 'simplest Surrealist act' of randomly firing a pistol into a crowd was met, in a very literal sense, by its opposite: the mobilization of a crowd which threatened at any moment to fire back. While in Germany such crowds testified to fascism's terrifying rise to power, in Paris, Louis Aragon's 1931 demand for readers of 'Red Front' to 'kill the cops / comrades / kill the cops' exploded the already turbulent relationship between Surrealism and Communism which, since the late 1920s, had been fraught with disagreements over the revolutionary status of Surrealism itself.[5] Particularly at stake in the 'Aragon affair' was the question of whether an avant-garde group defending its interest in bourgeois cultural forms like psychoanalysis and literature possessed any ability to mobilize the proletariat against a reigning capitalist order.[6] And indeed, in the wake of the

---

4 André Breton, preface for Max Ernst's 1921 exhibition catalogue, cited in Dawn Ades, *Photomontage* (London: Thames and Hudson, 1986), p. 115.

5 On the 'Aragon affair' and the history of Surrealism's ties with the French Communist Party, see André Thirion, *Révolutionnaires sans révolution* (Paris: Laffont, 1972); see also C. Reynaud Paligot's more recent *Parcours politique du surréalisme 1919–1969* (Paris: CNRS, 1995), and Helena Lewis, *The Politics of Surrealism* (New York: Paragon House, 1990).

6 Few were more eager to criticize Surrealism's lack of political efficacy than Aragon himself, whose scorn for Breton's defence of 'Red Front' was attacked by Paul Eluard: 'at the exact moment when Breton commented upon the results of the protest we raised against the inculpation of one of his [Aragon's] poems, he did not hesitate to accuse us of being counter-revolutionaries'. Paul Eluard, 'Certificat', in *Tracts Surréalistes et Declarations Collectives 1922–1939*, vol. 1, ed. José Pierre (Paris: Le Terrain Vague, 1980), pp. 229–30.

Aragon affair, the Surrealist movement appeared to retreat from active political engagement following a brief renewal of its communist militancy.[7] As Breton writes in a 1933 letter to Paul Eluard, 'I believe more and more in the necessity of a brilliant rupture with these commies and the resumption of the most intransigent Surrealist activity'.[8] It is difficult, however, to determine precisely what Breton means by this 'intransigence': in spite of any new-found autonomy, the group's flagship journal *Surréalisme au service de la Révolution* foundered after the two issues published simultaneously in May of 1933. Instead, the group began to contribute to the journal *Minotaure*, which, according to Eluard, began to 'succeed' as a properly Surrealist journal with the appearance of its double issue 3–4 in December 1933.[9]

The passage from the overtly Marxist *LSASDLR* to the luxuriously illustrated *Minotaure* reflects Surrealism's political migration from a 'red' period of communist activism into what I wish to call its 'noir' period. Characterized by a renewed interest in formal innovation, mental aberration and automatism, this period's affinity with both the *roman noir* and film noir derives from its use of style and psychoanalysis 'in the service' of realism. That is, its mannered proliferation of stylistic motifs exceeds its own formalism in order to evoke latent forces of terror and social dissolution at work in 'reality'. This change in the group's tenor constitutes neither an 'exasperated'[10] retreat from politics nor, for that matter, a failure of the movement to establish an effective political platform.[11] Instead, this 'noir' period accomplishes what might be considered a

7 This, too, ended in turmoil with Breton's expulsion from the leftist Association of Revolutionary Writers and Artists (AEAR) in July of 1933. On Breton and the AEAR, cf. Gérard Durozoi, *Histoire du mouvement surréaliste* (Paris: Hazan, 1997), and Thirion, *Révolutionnaires sans révolution*; see also Mark Polizzotti, *Revolution of the Mind: The Life of André Breton* (London: Bloomsbury, 1995), also Paligot, *Parcours politique*.

8 Letter from André Breton to Paul Eluard, 11 March 1933, cited in Paligot, p. 95.

9 Eluard considered *Minotaure*, nos 3–4 as representative of the Surrealist 'success' in the journal. Paul Eluard, *Lettres à Gala 1924–1948*, ed. Pierre Dreyfus (Paris: Gallimard, 1984), p. 220.

10 Eluard, in a letter to Salvador Dalí (February–March 1933), writes, 'Tu sais bien que je suis en tout cas d'accord pour la reprise d'une activité surréaliste exaspérée mais on doit tenir compte à côté de cela de toutes les aspirations politiques en majorité parmi nous. Et d'ailleurs elles renforceraient si elles pouvaient se donner libre cours, l'expérimentation surréaliste, elles permettraient parallèlement le libre exercise du surréalisme expérimental. Je suis, provisoirement, pour cette séparation des tâches du surréalisme'. Eluard, *Lettres à Gala*, pp. 202–3.

11 For some, this latter period has seemed a dark one indeed, more concerned with style than with Revolution. Tristan Tzara later claimed (from a resoundingly Stalinist standpoint) that the double issue of *LSASDLR* represented the exhaustion of Surrealism's 'creative phase'; the luxuriousness of *Minotaure* was the symptom of the movement's 'grandeur and decadence', while its attempts at autonomy bore a pretentiousness which revealed that the group had lost its revolutionary dynamism. Tristan

sublation of the group's overt political activities, a dialectical synthesis which 'negates the negation' of their activism in returning to earlier Surrealist interests like automatic writing and the interpretation of dreams. Its political use-value lies in its reassessment of the moral and epistemological bases of Surrealism's political platform, in response to a historical moment rapidly becoming – to cite the title of an article in *Minotaure* 3–4 – an 'Age of Fear'.

Striving less, for the time being, to 'change life' or to 'change the world' than to understand the nature of causality itself, the Surrealists attempted to read the cultural universe of the early 1930s in terms of the forces which threatened it: its dark motives, its ritualized patterns of behaviour, its terrifying outbursts of violence. Indeed, as Gérard Durozoi has suggested, as a whole the 'Surrealist' issue of *Minotaure* 3–4 can be described as articulating a similarly dystopian theme: 'the diverse ways in which behaviour and invention escape the control of attention and reason'.[12] In spite of its 'decadent' interest in stylized forms of representation, then, I wish to argue that Surrealism's noir period is nonetheless driven by serious political concerns insofar as this dystopian theme actually performs analytical work in the service of the group's political philosophy. Increasingly suspicious of the dangers of stylizing *actual* terrorist violence, the Surrealists instead make style itself the terrain for better understanding the 'superior reality' of the historical, unconscious, sexual and social facts whose complex structure conditions lived experience and determines political change.

The methodical nature of this investigation into the nature of causality becomes clear in the role played by Christine and Léa Papin in Surrealist discourse. Spanning the 'divide' between *LSASDLR* and *Minotaure*, the Papin affair sprung forth 'fully armed' into the already well-developed nexus of Surrealist and Lacanian thinking about mental illness and paranoia that had been particularly active since Breton's *Second Manifesto,* from Salvador Dalí's 'The Rotten Ass' (1930) to René Crevel's 'Notes Toward a Psycho-dialectic' (1933). The Papin sisters provide a cross-section of Surrealist thought which registers its reaction to the Aragon affair and the group's struggles with Party Communism. In particular, the murders raise the question of what such an outburst of abject violence reveals about motive, desire and breaches in the basic structure of everyday reality. By addressing how the sisters' ferocity could stem from causes incomprehensible even to the killers themselves, the Surrealists attempt to determine the use-value of the paranoiac imagination as a systematic distortion of reality. On the one hand, this analytical turn is an extension of the group's more general efforts to understand the relationship of the unconscious to

---

Tzara, *Œuvres Complètes*, vol. 5 (Paris: Flammarion, 1982), pp. 393 and 693. At the close of a series of radio broadcasts in the 1940s, Tzara explains how 'under the title of "Grandeur and Decadence of Surrealism", I could, at the return, prepare two new broadcasts which would report on *LSASDLR*, and *Minotaure*'. Ibid. p. 693.

12 Gérard Durozoi, *Histoire du mouvement surréaliste*, p. 244.

historical and political causality. On the other hand, its examination of motive necessarily entails a new theory of representation. As Jacques Lacan argues in the first of his two *Minotaure* articles, paranoia's systematic distortion of reality provides a 'new syntax' that offers a model for better understanding, as well as better expressing, the nature of causality in the first place. The role of formal elements of style in this project, like the role of style in many 'noir' forms – the gothic *roman noir,* Breton's own '*humour noir*', and the film noir of the 1940s and 1950s – is thus not merely 'politicizable', in the sense that its latent political tendencies can be teased out by criticism, but analytical and deliberate in its ability to represent complex structures of social and psychological forces for the sake of political understanding.

* * *

As the crime-scene photographs gruesomely attested, the murder of Mme Lancelin and her daughter by their servants on 2 February 1933 was committed with a ferocity that mystified and fascinated the popular press. Although the photographs were not made public until much later,[13] equivalently graphic eyewitness accounts of the crime scene injected substantially more sensational detail into Parisian newspapers than the usual *faits divers.* What made the violence particularly compelling was not only its symbolic character but the irony of its context as well: exploding the tranquillity of a bourgeois household in the equally tranquil town of Le Mans, the murders were committed by two seemingly docile servants (soon baptized 'the enraged ewes' by *Détective* magazine[14]). The image of bourgeois domesticity rent furiously asunder was exploited even in the earliest descriptions of the murders, inflecting their language with political or mock-political overtones. As the American writer Janet Flanner writes in her *Paris Journal*, brilliantly capturing the tone of contemporary accounts,

> On the third step from the landing, all alone, staring uniquely at the ceiling, lay an eye. On the landing itself the Lancelin ladies lay, at odd angles and with heads like blood puddings. Beneath their provincial petticoats their modest limbs had been knife-notched the way a fancy French baker notches his finer long loaves.[15]

Borrowing its language from the original reports in the local newspaper, *La Sarthe*, Flanner's depiction of the bodies as bourgeois comestibles – blood

---

13 Cf. Paulette Houdoyer, *Le diable dans le peau: l'affaire des sœurs Papin* (Paris: Juliard, 1966). Two crime-scene photographs are reprinted in Francis Dupré, *La 'Solution' du passage à l'acte: le double crime des sœurs Papin* (Toulouse: Erès, 1984).

14 *Détective*, no. 244 (9 February 1933), cover, pp. 3 and 7.

15 Janet Flanner, *Paris Was Yesterday, 1925–1937*, ed. Irving Drutman (New York: Harcourt, Brace, Jovanovitch, 1972), pp. 98–99.

puddings, fine bread – not only invites disgust in evoking their formal similarities to food, but also reflects the degree to which the butchering was treated by the press as a critique, however nominal, of bourgeois life. Indeed, echoing the more overtly politicized language of Parisian journals like *Détective* and the Communist newspaper *Humanité*, Flanner writes of the Papin affair that

> it was not a murder but a revolution. It was only a minor revolution – minor enough to be fought in a front hall by four females, two on a side. The rebels won with horrible handiness. The lamentable Lancelin forces were literally scattered over a distance of ten bloody feet, or from the upper landing halfway down the stairs. The physical were the most chilling details, the conquered the only dull elements [. . .].[16]

Flanner's account, written after the trial in late 1933, represents particularly well the degree to which the murders originally played out, in the 'first wave' of coverage, as a particularly gruesome form of petty class warfare. *Humanité*'s coverage was, in fact, even more literal in its interpretation of the affair, transforming the cynical tone of Flanner's 'minor revolution' into more adamantly political terms. Without in any way questioning the reliability or psychology of the Papins' story, *Humanité* published two short articles on 4 and 5 February under the headlines, 'Christine and Léa Papin Give the Reasons Why They Mortally Beat their Mistresses', and, more straightforwardly, 'The Murderesses of Le Mans Are the Victims of Exploitation and Servitude'. In the latter, the paper derives 'a distinctly social character' from the murders, explaining decisively that 'Poverty, isolation, continual confinement, servitude, doubtlessly working upon a hereditarily bad terrain, produced this double monstrosity'.[17] Though not exactly the revolution Flanner mentions, *Humanité*'s version of the murders sentimentalizes its motives as it portrays Christine and Léa as the crime's real victims.[18]

The Surrealist response to the Papin affair, on the other hand, is remarkable not only for its relative quiescence but also, more significantly, for its rejection, even parody, of the terms set up by the likes of *Humanité* and the bourgeois press alike. Indeed, their response seems directed more toward the press's sentimental Marxism than toward the sisters themselves, insofar as it takes issue with the vulgar reduction of the crime's motive and significance to an emblem of class struggle. In two articles – the first by Eluard and Péret, the second by Jacques Lacan – as well as in two illustrations, the Surrealists address the

16 Ibid., p. 98.

17 *Humanité* (5 February 1933), p. 3.

18 As Evans and Reader point out in their discussion of *Humanité*'s trial reports from later that year, however, the Communist Party newspaper *was* surprisingly attentive to the conditions of gender oppression that were also in play during the sisters' employment as housemaids, a fact that was rarely alluded to at the time. Evans and Reader, *The Papin Sisters*, p. 16.

crime's mysterious causality in an effort to specify the role of the unconscious in an act whose political significance was not even comprehensible to the women who committed it.[19] The articles, like the illustrations, address the murders in a language that is deliberately abstracted from the press's literal reading of the murders. Without ever advocating the Papin sisters' crimes, the Surrealist response to the affair attempts to reconcile the group's earlier attempts to legitimate conscious revolutionary violence, with the methodological necessity of acknowledging the role of unconscious desire in both human action and historical change.

In the May 1933 double issue of *LSASDLR*, Eluard and Péret compile a series of brief 'reviews of the press' that lambaste the bourgeois press's disavowal of class conflict and social tension in recent social and political issues. However, the final segment about the Papin sisters seems an exception, since its language abstracts, rather than attacks, the terms of both the bourgeois press's false liberalism as well as the Communist Party paper's 'real' leftism. When read alongside other accounts of the murders, the article seems remarkable for its *distance* from the press's sudden willingness to politicize the murders as a manifestation of what it all too readily ignores elsewhere. The full review reads:

> The Papin sisters were raised in a convent in Le Mans. Then their mother placed them in a 'bourgeois' house in the same town. For six years, they endured remarks, demands, insults, with perfect submission. Fear, fatigue, and humiliation gave birth slowly to hatred within them, that alcohol, so sweet, that consoles in secrecy because it promises to supplement its violence, sooner or later, with physical force.
>
> When the day came, Léa and Christine Papin repaid the currency of evil in coins of red-hot iron. They literally massacred their mistresses, tearing out their eyes, crushing their heads. They washed themselves carefully and, released, indifferent, went to bed. The thunder had struck, the woods had burnt, the sun had been definitively put out.
>
> Sprung forth fully armed from a canto of Maldoror.[20]

Though it certainly does not ignore the determining role of domestic servitude in the murders, the article's representation of economic conditions is mediated in a way for which Lacan's article will later account theoretically. Eluard and Péret cite emotions – fear, fatigue, humiliation – in place of *Humanité*'s emphatically material list of conditions, 'doubtlessly working upon a hereditarily bad terrain', which 'give this horrible drama a distinctly social character'. Eluard and Péret do not so much ignore the material conditions faced by the Papin sisters, as suggest that their motives are better accounted for in psychological terms. Describing hatred as an alcohol, Eluard and Péret indicate an unreason, an intoxication, behind the crimes, distancing their account from the headline in

19 On the sisters' incomprehension, see Lane, 'The Delirium of Interpretation'.

20 Eluard and Péret, 'Revue de la presse', *LSASDLR*, no. 5 (May 1933), p. 28.

which the sisters lucidly 'give the reasons' for their atrocities. At the same time, the mannered, mythology-laden style of Eluard and Péret's writing further complicate the 'doubtless' causality of the murders. While the notion of paying back evil in coins of red or red-hot iron (*fer rouge*) may sound like a stroke of quasi-communist rhetoric, its inflated metaphorical language satirizes the banal circumstances under which, according to Christine Papin, the murders occurred: the Lancelins, returning home, rebuked the sisters for a blown fuse caused by a hot iron (*un fer à repasser*). Rather than struggling to make sense of the affair as a gruesomely literal, 'eye for an eye' retribution for the evils of class oppression, Eluard and Péret poke subtle fun at the press's belief in the face value of Christine Papin's 'reasoned' account of the murders as an act of reciprocity. In the article's final line, they instead invoke the gratuitous evil of Lautréamont's *Les Chants de Maldoror*, whose 'fully armed' offspring the Papin affair becomes: significantly, the allusion to Athena, or to Sin in Milton's *Paradise Lost,* implies that in spite of their Maldororian 'alienation' from reason, the murders promise a 'sign portentous', a perverse kind of wisdom.

The direct, mythic lineage established here between the Papin affair and Lautréamont's Maldoror has been interpreted as evidence of the Papin sisters' place within the Surrealist pantheon of 'revolutionary' heroes, alongside its other female criminal 'muses' like the anarchist Germaine Berton and the poisoner Violette Nozières. However, the group neither pays explicit, collective homage to the Papins, nor do they rally in 'legitimate defence' of their crimes, as they do for Berton in 1924 and, albeit in a much different way, for Nozières later in 1933.[21] Instead, the Papin murders are significant precisely because they complicate any efforts to legitimate their violence as revolutionary or 'heroic'. As early as 1923, Aragon had begun to define in violent terms the ethical position he would maintain in 'Red Front', that 'if an individual becomes conscious of the monstrous inequality, of the vanity of all speech in the face of the growing strength of a certain faction, I hold this individual to be authorized, moreover, to resort to terrorist means, in particular to murder, in order to safeguard, at the risk of losing everything, that which appears to him – rightly or wrongly – to be precious beyond all worldly things'.[22] By 1932, Aragon had

---

21 Germaine Berton assassinated Marius Plateau, the anti-Semitic royalist and editorial secretary of the right-wing *Action Française*, in 1923; Aragon published two brief tributes to her assassination first in *Littérature* and again in the inaugural issue of *La Révolution surréaliste*, which also contains the well-known gallery of Surrealist portraits surrounding Berton's in the centre. See *La Révolution surréaliste*, no. 1 (December 1924), pp. 12 and 15. Violette Nozières, an 18-year-old woman who poisoned her parents and killed her father, incited the moral outrage of many popular journalists when she 'soiled' her father's memory by claiming that he had been sexually abusing her since she was 12. The Surrealists published a collective homage at the end of 1933, *Violette Nozières*, (Brussels: Nicolas Flamel, 1933), rpd, José Pierre, ed. (Brussels: Terrain Vague, 1991).

22 Louis Aragon, *Littérature*, n.s., no. 9 (February–March 1922), p. 15.

tailored this radical individualism to the collective rigour of the Communist Party; yet its emphasis on consciousness remains crucial to 'Red Front's' incitement to murder, as well as to the Communist Party's own ideological stance. Yet while the Papin affair itself could spring 'fully armed' from *Maldoror*, the Surrealists were critical of Aragon's assumption that this revolutionary consciousness was similarly spontaneous or ready-made.

With characteristic rigour, René Crevel's 'Notes Toward a Psycho-dialectic' (1933) revises this justification of violence as a function of 'visionary' class awareness, instead describing proletarian revolution as a gradual process of increasing consciousness as a subject:

> The best quality of a proletariat is its class consciousness. Thanks to this, it turns from an object into a subject. It is no longer an instrument in a stranger's hand. It is its own instrument. Its eyes urging it, it sees clearly. It looks only to demolish the walls that confine its life, its view for constructing houses made of light.[23]

Though it confirms Communism's moral ground as a function of 'clear vision', Crevel's methodology tempers its concept of awareness with a psychoanalytical notion of subjectivity at odds with party-line communist thinking. Crevel's Marxist depiction of workers as tools emphasizes the passage from object to subject as constitutive of the proletariat's 'clear vision'. Such psychoanalytical models of consciousness were, however, explicitly excluded from communist ideology in the early 1930s. At the 1930 Soviet writer's conference in Kharkov that was so influential to Aragon, the directors rejected Freud, claiming that his work's ultra-individualist character veils and minimizes the significance of class struggle: 'The wave of Freudian enthusiasm which has passed through occidental Europe is a wave of bourgeois reaction against materialism, a wave of decadence'.[24] Fittingly, *Humanité*'s coverage of the Papin murders reflects – to a fault, Eluard and Péret suggest – this predilection against the 'pessimistic' operation of instincts and unconscious drives. Its ideological premise, that the social character of the crime is self-evident, so clearly assumes a wilfulness behind the sisters' 'savagery' that the justification of its extremity requires an outmoded notion of hereditary degeneracy, the biological 'terrain' which

---

23 René Crevel, 'Notes en vue d'une psycho-dialectique', *LSASDLR*, no. 5 (May 1933), p. 52.

24 Statement of the Soviet directors at Kharkov, cited Paligot, p. 80. As Elisabeth Roudineso has explained, the Soviet Union reproached psychoanalysis for its pessimistic insistence upon the instinctive nature of man, of which Freud's theory of the libido was the reflection. In the face of communist ideals of improvement and reconditioning, psychoanalysis, particularly its notion of sexuality, 'seemed dangerous because it was considered "asocial", that is, taking part in an anarchistic order which risked pulling the masses toward debauchery and preventing them from turning towards future happiness'. Elisabeth Roudinesco, *La bataille de cent ans: une histoire de la psychanalyse en France*, vol. 2 (Paris: Fayard, 1994), p. 56.

exacerbated the effects of servitude. In contrast, it is the Papin affair's challenge to the possibility of explaining, or justifying, such violence as something fully conscious that makes it so significant to Surrealist political thought. Indeed, arguing that violence can never be understood or justified without recourse to the unconscious, Crevel advances a theory which explains both political action and psychological motive in terms of a dialectical synthesis between the 'thesis' of consciousness and the 'antithesis' of the unconscious.

In order to articulate the significance of unconscious activity to political thought, Crevel turns to Jacques Lacan's 1932 doctoral thesis, as well as to Dalí's writing on paranoia. Published in the same issue of *LSASDLR* as Eluard and Péret's review of the press, Crevel's article does not actually discuss the Papin affair (for it had not yet been linked to paranoia), but Lacan's paranoiac patient, 'Aimée', in order to show how psychotic crime can provide a means for better understanding political expression. In a passage whose reference to beauty recalls the Maldororian allusion in Eluard and Péret's article, Crevel writes,

> In the case of a sexual or murderous exhibitionism, how do we judge it, unless we go back to the repression that is at its origin? The beauty of certain assaults upon modesty or upon life is that they accuse, with all their violence, the monstrosity of laws and the constraints that make monsters.[25]

Although this passage seems to mimic the 'revolutionary' language used by the press to describe the Papin murders, its apparent straightforwardness is challenged by Crevel's notion of 'exhibitionism': as the physical manifestation of an illness with a 'moral' rather than biological or hereditary origin, this exhibitionism's 'beauty' lies in its ability to represent, or at least indicate, repressed elements of the unconscious. Like Lautréamont's famous definition of beauty as an encounter – 'as beautiful as the fortuitous encounter of an umbrella and a sewing machine upon a dissecting table' – Crevel's understanding of the 'beauty' of paranoiac crime derives from the idea that its traumatic encounter, between the 'interior' structure of unconscious motive and the exterior world, thus 'accuses' an otherwise invisible third element, the (social) forces of repression which both unite and divide them. Such an encounter thus enables the application to political theory of what Crevel calls a 'psycho-dialectic', a model of revolutionary uprising understood as an empowerment made possible by an increasing consciousness of repressed desires and repressive forces, whose dialectical progression can account for the deformations, difficulties and ambivalence through which an object becomes a subject. Paranoia's psychotic exhibitionism is a particularly powerful example of this process because, as Crevel learns from Lacan, the physical manifestations of paranoia are *already* a unique synthesis of conscious and unconscious processes.

25 Crevel, 'Notes Toward a Psycho-dialectic', p. 50.

As Crevel explains, a psychotic criminal can be 'cured' when the unconscious mechanism of her aggression is somehow satisfied.[26] In paranoia, this unconscious mechanism can be described as a desire for self-punishment which, unexpressed and incomprehensible to the conscious subject, morbidly projects itself outward, finding expression as an aggressive 'punishment' of another person who functions as an image of the self. For Lacan, psychoanalysis can cure psychosis by first detecting, and then representing to the subject, these unconscious desires, a process which 'satisfies' them by rendering them conscious. Crevel, though, is more interested in the curative value of the physical illness itself, that is, of 'murderous exhibitionism' as an indirect or 'expressionist' form of representation. As Crevel asks, 'does not the organic illness itself at all satisfy the self-punishing drive? [. . .] For those who have looked for or found the material conditions of illness, this physical illness will be the moral illness's chance for recovery'.[27] Crevel is not actually interested in the nosology of mental patients (and seems misguided in thinking that the organic illness provides any satisfaction for the subject, except insofar as it allows the analyst to diagnose the subject). Rather, he is interested in using Lacan's and Dalí's understanding of paranoia as a psychotic structure which 'systematizes confusion' in order to bolster Marxist dialectical materialism with an acceptable theory of the unconscious.[28]

The 'accusation' performed by murderous exhibitionism thus does not canonize the criminal as a revolutionary figure; rather, insofar as the physical illness represents the moral illness which produces it, Crevel's structuralist notion of behaviour as a representation allows his further ideas about *political* 'illness' and oppression to be a matter of extension. The shift from a moral illness produced in the unconscious by oppressive conditions to a physical illness – outbursts of violence and crime – is authorized not for its conscious intentionality but for the 'curative' value of the manifestation itself. This version of political and psychological causality structured as a 'fortuitous encounter' is particularly useful to Surrealism insofar as it rethinks the causality not only of 'legitimate' revolution but of the most inexplicable, brutal and regressive of events as well. Indeed, if the truth of France's complicity in the spread of fascist totalitarianism would not become consciously, physically manifest until the pro-fascist demonstrations in Paris on 6 February 1934 – prompting the Surrealists into a more active anti-fascist campaign – at the time of the Papin affair, the Surrealists were already interrogating the motives behind France's attempts to repress fascism's rise to power by portraying it as either a temporary fluke or an

26 Lacan's patient Aimée (Marguerite Pantaine) stabbed but did not kill the actress Huguette Duflos. See Elisabeth Roudinesco, *Jacques Lacan*, trans. Barbara Bray (New York: Columbia University Press, 1997), pp. 32–51.

27 Crevel, 'Notes Toward a Psycho-dialectic', p. 51.

28 Salvador Dalí, 'L'âne pourri', *LSASDLR*, no. 1 (1930), p. 9.

utterly alien terror. Yet at the same time, it is fascism's precipitous rise that severely challenges any idea that 'murderous exhibitionism' – acts of terror, whether random or massively organized – can be mobilized in service of revolution as a viable activity. Indeed, Crevel's thinking about the use-value of paranoiac crime would be challenged by the Papin sisters' explosion of the possibility of increased consciousness, or increased comprehensibility, of their motives in the months following their crime.

* * *

When *Minotaure* 3–4 appeared in mid-December 1933, the Papin sisters had been tried and, in Christine's case, sentenced to death. The trial and psychological diagnosis of the sisters as 'sane' and thus 'responsible' did little, however, to answer questions about the motives behind such exaggerated acts of violence. In the meantime, numerous reports had begun to circulate about the sisters' peculiar, almost catatonic, behaviour during the trial, Christine's psychotic outbursts in prison (literally 'sexual and murderous exhibitionism') and the fiasco of their having been found 'perfectly sane' by psychiatric experts. According to article 64 of the Penal Code, as legally sane they were fully punishable and thus subject to the death sentence. Breton had himself railed against the injustice of the penal code article in 1932, calling it 'philosophically incomprehensible';[29] Lacan's article on paranoiac style in *Minotaure* 1 (1933) echoes Breton's outrage in its critique of the penal code and academic psychiatry, explaining that

> we must not misrecognize that the interest in mental illness is born historically from needs that are juridical in origin. These needs appeared at the time of the establishment, formulated on the basis of law, of the bourgeois philosophical conception of man as gifted with an absolute moral liberty and a responsibility proper to the individual. [...] Since then the major question landed practically on the science of psychiatrists has been, artificially, that of an all-or-nothing of mental forfeiture (article 64 of the Penal Code).[30]

Lacan's attention to the historical basis of psychiatry is designed less to critique its ideological tendencies than to dislodge the practice of diagnosis from questions of criminal responsibility or irresponsibility which risked reducing definitions of insanity to a moral choice policed by the state. He is thus committed instead to determining the motives for the crimes committed by the mentally ill – if not to authorize them, then to understand the forces which

---

29 André Breton, 'La médecine mentale devant le Surréalisme', *Œuvres complètes*, vol. 2.

30 Lacan, 'Problème du Style et la conception psychiatrique des formes paranoïaques de l'expérience', *Minotaure*, no. 1 (1933), p. 68.

determine them, and the conditions through which they are reproduced. This abandonment of the ideological foundations of psychiatry is particularly apparent in Lacan's diagnosis of the Papin sisters as paranoid. Lacan extends to this difficult case a methodology sensitive to the crimes' opacity as well as to the difficulty of understanding the complex interaction of social and psychological factors in paranoia.

In a manner which reflects their accordance with Breton's and Lacan's objection to Article 64, several journalists published articles challenging the verdict and diagnosis of the two women. Both the Tharaud brothers, writing for *Paris Soir*, and Maurice Coriem, writing for *Police* magazine as well as for the glossy crime review *Scandale*, express doubt about the ability of psychiatric experts to define and detect madness in an acceptable way, and thus legitimately make 'comprehensible' their ability to determine legal responsibility.[31] However, as Lacan explains in his own reading of the case (by way of the Tharaud reports), mere judgment in favour of insanity is not enough to escape the 'bourgeois philosophical conception' which structures such all-or-nothing decisions. Indeed, the Papin sisters posed an unusual problem for the public and the psychiatric community alike, due precisely to the mysterious extremity of their violence. Not only were they unable to give 'any comprehensible motive, any hatred, any grief' of their own, but, as Lacan contends, the judge, jury, and all but one of the experts testifying to their accountability similarly failed to notice any peculiarities about their behaviour and their past. Yet Lacan, like the Tharauds and Coriem, enumerate several such 'peculiarities': a suspicion of their incestuous lesbianism voiced by several witnesses, and certainly their peculiar attachment to each other; Christine's psychotic, hallucinatory outbursts in prison (even if 'simulated', as she claimed); and especially reports of an alcoholic father who raped their other sister. However 'sociological' these overlooked factors were, they suggest that the material conditions which determined their behaviour were more subtle, more deeply buried in the formation of the unconscious, than the jury and most of the press were willing to notice, even in their willingness to ascribe the crime an anti-bourgeois political meaning. Moreover, the extension of the sisters' persecution fantasies and delirium well into their incarceration suggested that the 'murderous exhibitionism' of the crimes failed to satisfy the unconscious desires which caused them. However, Lacan strives to render comprehensible – to show how the Papins' crimes and their behaviour afterwards manifest – the motives that in this case were unavailable or invisible not only to the legal system but to Christine and Léa

31 See the articles by Jérôme and Jean Tharaud from *Paris-Soir*, 30 September–8 October 1933, rpd. *Littoral*, no. 9 (June 1983). Also Maurice Coriem, 'A-t-on comdamné deux folles?' *Police* (5, 12, 17 and 29 November 1933); and Coriem, 'Histoire d'un drame passionnel: "Le Crime des sœurs Papin",' *Scandale*, no. 5 (December 1933), pp. 233–36.

themselves. For Lacan, the question would be not merely whether 'murderous exhibitionism' provided a means of representing unconscious drives, but of *how* it represented them.

Lacan's diagnosis of the Papin sisters as paranoiac strikes a delicate balance between multiple fields of inquiry: not only does its very definition of paranoia challenge existing psychiatric models of the illness, but it also refines his own explanation of paranoia in terms of style. The article acts as a kind of test case for his doctoral thesis, which was more than slightly influenced by Salvador Dalí and which, in turn, provided clinical support for later articles by Dalí and Crevel that advocate paranoia's artistic and political possibilities. The disciplines – artistic and psychiatric – are not mutually exclusive for Lacan, since paranoia reveals the operation of style, images and signification within subjectivity as well as on the level of culture and artistic production. Indeed, Lacan's work on the Papin sisters builds upon his description of paranoiac lived experience, in the first issue of *Minotaure*, as an 'original syntax', a mode of symbolic expression that is at once intentional and determined by social tensions with an historical actuality. Surrealism is particularly useful to Lacan here because of its rejection of naive realism in favour of an understanding of psychiatric symptoms as viable forms of expression in themselves. The classic symptoms of paranoia described by Freud – interpretive delirium, fantasies of grandeur and persecution, outbursts of murderous aggression – simulate intellectual behaviour without corresponding to reason or logic. Lacan's early contribution to the psychiatric field was his argument that such symptoms are the product neither of a biological or 'constitutional' degeneracy, nor of a retroactive attempt by the reasoning mind to 'explain' its outbursts of dementia. Rather, paranoia organizes itself as a 'coherent structure of immediate noumenal apprehension of oneself and the world'; the illness simulates reason because its delirious interpretation, what Dalí calls its mechanism of 'systematized confusion', occurs at the level of perception. While this may nominally account for the unfortunate ease with which the Papin sisters' insanity went unrecognized, the real usefulness of Lacan's work lies in its ability to model the complicated interaction of conscious will, unconscious desire and social 'conditioning' that produced the gruesome murders as a play of images, whose Maldororian beauty lies not in the act itself, but in the imaginary character of its motives.

Lacan's theory of paranoia hinges upon the notion that paranoiac crime is motivated by an unconscious drive for self-punishment, whose misrecognition by the subject results in its eruption, on a social level, as a murderous aggression toward a person who serves as the subject's ego-image. But this ego-image is not the only instance of representation at work in paranoia, since, as Lacan writes, on every level the unconscious drives bear the imprint of social relations, thus representing their effects in trace form. Even the aggressive drive itself is similarly referential, subject to 'social tensions' in both its formation and its expression, insofar as

> the intentional content that translates it [the aggressive drive] into consciousness cannot manifest itself without a compromise with the social exigencies integrated by the subject, that is, without a camouflage of motives which is precisely all the delirium.
>
> But even this drive is imprinted with a social relativity: it always has the intentionality of a crime, almost constantly that of vengeance, often the sense of a punishment, that is, a sanction issued from social ideas, often finally it identifies itself as the act achieved by morality, it has the carriage of an atonement (self punishment).[32]

Such a play of camouflage and simulacra certainly obfuscates the problem of using paranoia to better understand the relationship between a political subject and the social and material conditions of her life. However, by mapping psychosis as a structure rather than as a linear relationship of cause and effect, Lacan suggests that even if the ultimate causality of the motive cannot be located, determined or represented definitively, the interaction of unconscious desire and 'social relativity' can be witnessed in their distortions and imprints upon each other. Lacan suggests, in fact, that the real effects of social relations upon the subject – so readily misrecognized in the case of the Papin sisters as direct class oppression – become recognizable as motives for the crime only insofar as they become visible as motifs. Indeed, his title 'motifs du crime paranoaïque' suggests that, as the sequel to his earlier article on paranoiac style, the French term *motifs* can signify both causal 'motives' and stylistic 'motifs'. That is, Lacan's study of motive stresses how the structure of psychosis involves simultaneously an interpretation and a representation of 'reality'; within this structure, social and material conditions are manifest not merely as the 'facts' which a subject represents to herself, but as the determining forces which the unconscious must represent to the consciousness.

Christopher Lane has argued that this psychotic structure – which is not political in itself, since the people involved are unaware of its meaning – may be politicized insofar as its 'motifs', its exhibitionism, provide a reminder of 'the fragile supports on which subjectivity is so reliant, and the way each precarious identification fosters an illusion of psychical stability'.[33] However, to limit the political meaning of psychosis to a subversion of subjectivity alone requires, once again, the separation of the social from the psychological that Lacan, like Crevel, strives to eradicate. Rather, the 'fragile supports' rendered apparent by an understanding of psychotic structure include the social as well as the subjective, or, more accurately, the 'syntax' of reality itself as lived experience in the world. As Dalí writes, paranoia's systematized confusion is thus 'corrosive to reality', insofar as it shows lived experience, the noumenal relation of the self and the world, to be, in the words of a later Lacan, *imaginary*, a 'heap

32 Lacan, 'Motifs du Crime Paranoïaque: Le Crime des sœurs Papin', *Minotaure*, nos 3–4 (1933), p. 26.

33 Lane, 'The Delirium of Interpretation', p. 31.

of broken images' fit together by the subject to form a concrete idea of reality. I call this Surrealist understanding of political as well as psychological reality 'noir' because it subjects individual action to a play of images, reflections and haunts, whether mobilized in service of an atmosphere of gothic claustrophobia or of hard-boiled ambivalence. Noir fiction and film dramatize the struggle to make sense of this play of images on the level of its characters, whose moral 'ambiguity' is a result of their own unconsciousness of the constructedness of reality. On the level of narrative, however, the stylistic universe of the story makes possible the analysis it denies its characters, becoming itself a kind of epistemological engine for investigating the structure of 'reality' that makes action possible.

* * *

If the presence of the political in *Minotaure* is similarly deferred or exoteric, I have attempted to show how this deferral represents a theoretical turn in Surrealism's political project, rather than its dissolution or failure. The group's resumption of psychoanalytical and formal experimentation in 1933 actually represents a serious investigation into the constitutive elements of political praxis: motive, causality, and the role of signification in political representation. In much the same way, historical 'noir' and gothic forms rarely seem overtly progressive or avant-garde in their politics; in fact, their proliferation of stylistic motifs (from uncanny landscapes and hauntings to the play of light and shadow upon 'mean streets') often seems to emphasize explicitly conservative fears: the threat of family dissolution, of sexual and racial corruption, and of political usurpation. And yet, even if the terror and 'systematized confusion' of noir fictions uses such fears to reinforce, rather than critique, the existing order or political structure, their 'exhibitionism' nevertheless provides a means for witnessing the otherwise unrepresentable sources of this terror. Indeed, what seems 'progressive' about noir and gothic fictions is precisely their configuration of political, psychological, and historical questions as a problem of representation, or, more accurately, as a problem of style. Similarly, it is Surrealism's efforts to represent otherwise invisible, unconscious forces determining the course of history – just as it had been the group's original claim to 'photograph' the unconscious through automatic writing – that lend its noir period a political use-value. Although, as we have seen, actual photography is central to this function, the stylistic means for 'photographing' unrepresentable phenomena is virulently anti-realist.[34] Instead, the stylistic means for depicting

34 As Edouard Jaguer writes, even the allure of photography for Surrealism lay in its reliance upon a *cliché* (negative) in order to capture the 'hidden face of reality'; see *Les Mystères de la chambre noire: Le surréalisme et la photographie* (Paris: Flammarion, 1982), p. 115.

'the real' itself is best described by Maurice Heine: 'the truth does not return except by the synthesis of style: art's veracity lies in the stylization of a fetish'.[35] Heine's notion of 'truthful' representation as a kind of synthesis, made possible by a fetishistic use of style, thus deliberately subverts what the Surrealists considered to be the 'naive realism' of orthodox Marxist ideology.

The 'synthesis' represented by the stylistic apparatus of noir forms is, in fact, easily fetishized – indeed, the terms 'gothic' and 'noir' tend to connote, above all, an almost baroque proliferation of stylistic motif and all-too-familiar verbal and visual codes. However, such an absorption in formalism obscures the extent to which this style itself operates fetishistically, as a way of symbolizing the traumatic knowledge of an otherwise disavowed 'hidden truth'. Indeed, the formal architecture of noir fictions dramatizes the 'unconscious' irruption of an indeterminate but powerful evil into the realm of everyday life. What the evil *is* remains mysterious, yet its traumatic power suggests that, like the 'moral illness' Crevel discusses, the evil is not only subject to a social relativity, but actually comprises the simultaneously political and psychological nature of causality itself – that is, the inadmissible knowledge that violence, crime and social dissolution are not merely 'external' forces but 'internal' ones as well. Could not the standard noir plot twist be described as the uncanny realization that an evil 'out there', against which the protagonists so gallantly attempt to safeguard themselves, is suddenly revealed to have been in their midst all along?[36]

What unites the numerous historical noir genres, then, is not only the role of formal motif in representing such traumatic effects, but the mobilization of these motifs to configure what Slavoj Žižek calls the 'noir universe'. For their audiences, noir forms offer a certain legibility, a structural consistency whose existence is denied to its protagonists; unlike the naive representation of naturalist realism, the 'clichés' of noir genres are useful, particularly for the Surrealists, for their ability to map lived reality in the 'world gone wrong' of the 1930s precisely in terms of the paranoia it dramatizes. As Žižek writes of the noir universe,

---

35 Maurice Heine, *Documents* II:3 (1930), pp. 175–76.

36 Of course, the various noir genres, subject to distinct historical circumstances, could not appear to represent the effects of this evil more differently: the gothic romances of Horace Walpole and Anne Radcliffe stage this irruption largely in domestic terms, in terms of the architecture from which the name derives: the presence, within the walls of a decaying hereditary castles, of precisely the foreign element the walls were designed to exclude. Similarly, urban gothic novels, from Poe and Eugène Sue to the Fantômas series, borrow the structural disorder of crammed urban centres to represent anti-democratic forces operating at the very core of democratic organization. In later film noir and hard-boiled fiction, the irruption of 'evil' is staged more visually, in terms of the architectural boundaries of filmic or literary composition itself: the way camera angles, dialogue tics, and metonymic association maintain the constant likelihood of ambivalence and betrayal within even the most trusted object of affection.

> The intersubjective, 'public' symbolic space has lost its innocence: narrativization, integration into the symbolic order, into the big Other, opens up a mortal threat, far from leading to any kind of reconciliation. What one should bear in mind here is that this *neutrality* of the symbolic order functions as the ultimate guarantee for the so-called '*sense of reality*': as soon as this neutrality is smeared, 'external reality' itself loses the self-evident character of something present 'out there' and begins to vacillate, i.e., is experienced as delimited by an invisible frame: the paranoia of the *noir* universe is primarily visual, based upon the suspicion that our vision of reality is always already distorted by some invisible frame behind our backs [. . .].[37]

Žižek's description of the vacillation of external reality renders apparent the degree to which the noir universe does not only exist as a structure, but also operates as a function 'corrosive to reality'. However, while for Žižek the noir style and the Cold War-era world it describes are already recognizable as historical forms, for the Surrealists the noir style remains a 'paranoiac' response to contemporary historical and political events within which they were participants as well as observers, 'unconscious' protagonists as well as enlightened analysts. Thus bound within the psychological fabric of the story of the 1930s, the paranoiac knowledge Žižek describes is made available, as an interpretive structure or function, only through the stylistic motifs themselves; for the Surrealists, this meant that such motifs, as elements within the narrative framework of history, were present as material elements as well: the uncanny objects, architectural forms and urban spaces whose fetishistic significance is normally disavowed by the characters which inhabit them.

The role of such 'objective' motifs becomes clear, I believe, in the understated *Homage to the Papin Sisters*, a drawing by the Belgian Surrealists Paul Nougé and René Magritte published in 1934, in the special issue of *Documents 34* entitled 'The Surrealist Intervention' (fig. 16). The simple, naturalistic drawing style of the image seems at once to betray its own immediate legibility: while the domestic setting and class markers are firmly in place, the lone, sweeping housekeeper bears neither a physical nor an allegorical resemblance to the Papin sisters, her face betraying neither a reserve nor a madness which might signify whether the scene occurs after or before a murder. Despite its momentary illegibility, though, the image, and the curious expression of the housekeeper, take on a sudden surplus of meaning in relation to the jug – a pewter jug? – in the background of the drawing. The jug, out of place within the image's narrative of cleanliness and domestic order, seems not to belong on the floor, but instead in the litany of household torture devices used in the Papin affair: pewter jug, kitchen knives, hammer, and the sisters' bare hands. The object in Nougé and Magritte's drawing explodes its order and 'innocence' in a

37 Slavoj Žižek, *Enjoy Your Symptom: Jacques Lacan in Hollywood and Out* (New York: Routledge, 1992), p. 152.

way that does not legitimate the crimes any more than Eluard and Péret's press review does; what it instead achieves is the effect of transforming the housekeeper's curious expression – almost the enigmatic smile of Mona Lisa – from an 'unconscious' absorption to a knowing smile. Does the drawing not suggest, in its homage to the Papin sisters, that *the means for violence are at hand?* Once the object reorders the meaning of the image and injects it with knowledge, this 'paranoiac' knowledge of the non-neutrality of innocent spaces becomes more immanent.

In shifting their efforts from the legitimation of terrorism, to the stylistics of terror, and finally to a strategy for deriving paranoiac knowledge, the Surrealist activity during its relationship with *Minotaure* strives to create an atmosphere which is not so much conducive to 'revolution', as it is conducive to the knowledge represented in the smile of Nougé and Magritte's housekeeper: *the means* – moral as well as material – *are at hand.*[38] By calling Surrealism's period of political and epistemological reassessment both a 'noir' period and a period of negation, I have attempted, first, to show that the group's poetic and political aims in 1933 are not limited to revealing irrational forces at work within exterior reality, but of determining the nature of these forces in a way which reveals their frightening contiguity with existing structures of political and ideological logic. Secondly, I maintain that this noir period *enables* rather than *performs* the group's political work. Indeed, it provides the basis for a new 'morality of revolt' which advocates a massive, collective restructuration of society upon diverse fronts – from mental institutions to literature to family structure to political parties – instead of the merely destructive violence of Aragon's 'Red Front'. In fact, it is my contention that Surrealism's synthesis of political and formal investigation of itself in its noir period in fact permits the 'strong' politics of the group's active anti-fascist militancy and worldwide dissemination, from 1934 ('L'Intervention Surrealiste'), to the group's final attempts, in the name of an allied anti-fascist campaign, to reunite with the Communist Party in 1934 and 1935, and to form 'Contre-Attaque' with Georges Bataille in 1936.

---

38 In her provocative study of Breton's poetically dense 'gothic Marxism', Margaret Cohen discusses how Breton's writing fuses Marx and Freud, or Engels and Freud, to forge a theoretical position which could reveal the unconscious operating in both objective and subjective domains. However, Cohen's assessment of this gothic Marxism's political role is tempered by her belief in its romanticism – that its 'political' effectiveness is a function of the theoretical framework itself. Approaching this question through Althusser's writing on ideology, Cohen argues that Breton's primary mode of political action was, essentially, the 'post-modern' notion of subversion. Surrealist politics, she argues, used psychoanalysis to find 'new sites of resistance', but the result was merely a configuration of lyric behaviour as a social praxis. See *Profane Illumination: Walter Benjamin and the Paris of the Surrealist Revolution* (Berkeley: University of California Press, 1993), pp. 127 and 111.

Chapter 6

Surrealist Racial Politics at the Borders of 'Reason': Whiteness, Primitivism and Négritude

Amanda Stansell

In his 1934 essay 'What is Surrealism?', André Breton cites the 1925 Riff War in Morocco as the primary impetus for the Surrealists' turn to more direct political action. What Breton does not mention is that the Surrealist protest against the Moroccan War was in part an anti-colonialist protest. Indeed the explicit issue of racial politics does not arise in Breton's essay summarizing 15 years of Surrealist work, and most commentators have followed the author's lead: direct discussion of 'race'[1] in Surrealism has generally been avoided.[2] Yet the topic *was* specifically addressed by the Surrealists in other work, particularly in a photocollage by Benjamin Péret, a counter-exhibit, and several manifestos in response to colonialism. Through attention to the ways complex notions of race function in these works, I argue that the Surrealists attempted to galvanize anti-racist and anti-colonialist action.

1 Although race as a biological category is scientifically untenable, race as a social category continues to be an important object of analysis, since notions of race shape public policy, discussions of cultural difference, as well as prejudices. See Kenan Malik, *The Meaning of Race: Race, History, and Culture in Western Society* (New York: New York University Press, 1996).

2 In this chapter, 'Surrealism' refers to Breton's group. The para-Surrealist group surrounding *Documents* has received significant critical attention regarding race and ethnography. See James Clifford, *The Predicament of Culture* (Cambridge: Harvard University Press, 1988); Petrine Archer-Straw, 'The Darker Side of Surrealism', in *Negrophilia: Avant-Garde Paris and Black Culture in the 1920s* (New York: Thames and Hudson, 2000) and Ian Walker, 'Phantom Africa: Photography between Surrealism and Ethnography', in *Cahiers-d'études-Africaines*, no. 37 (1997), pp. 635–55. To my knowledge, the only substantial recent studies on race and Breton's group are Jack Spector, 'The Surrealist Woman and the Colonial Other', in *Surrealist Art and Writing, 1919–1939: The Gold of Time* (Cambridge: Cambridge University Press, 1997) and Jean-Claude Blachère, *Les Totems d'André Breton* (Paris: L'Harmattan, 1996). See Jody Blake, *Le Tumulte Noir: Modernist Art and Popular Entertainment in Jazz-Age Paris, 1900–1930* (University Park: Pennsylvania State University Press, 1999), pp. 111–36, for a discussion of African-American jazz and French Surrealism.

What distinguishes this anti-racism as specifically Surrealist will not become apparent, however, until we examine the context in which it occurred. Important aspects of the Surrealists' anti-racism, as well as its limitations, are linked to their most central theoretical position: the critique of 'reason'. In the Surrealists' attempts to put this idealistic theory into practice, they used inventive aesthetic strategies that challenged fixed categories of race and therefore anticipated current scholarship on 'whiteness'. At the same time, their theoretical critique of reason contributed to the Surrealists' interest in non-Western art and linked them to dominant discourses that uncritically celebrated the 'primitive', an ideology used to justify colonialism.[3] Nevertheless, even this limited viewpoint was at the time politically advantageous, since it precipitated alliances with Caribbean intellectuals and *Négritude* activists who were using a similarly broad critique of Western 'reason' to promote a strong African diasporic cultural identity. Examining the contradictions between the Surrealists' ideals and their practice thus reveals the ways they both challenged and replicated the discourses of their time. The result will be a more nuanced picture of the Surrealists' racial politics.

Several historical factors made 1930s France a place where racial discourses could substantially influence political change. First, the political and economic volatility of France during this time created an atmosphere that encouraged xenophobia in spite of the country's egalitarian tradition. Second, the visibility of colonized peoples and their views was growing. An increased number were living in Paris following World War I, particularly intellectuals studying at French universities who were producing dissident magazines such as *Cri des nègres* and forming political associations such as the *Union des travailleurs nègres*.[4] Finally, although this period is often called the 'apogee' of French colonialism, independence movements by indigenous peoples in Syria, Tunisia, Morocco and Indo-China during the 1920s and 1930s threatened to crack the façade of colonialism as a peaceful *mission civilisatrice*.[5] The French government therefore needed to justify colonialist policies and elicit popular support

3 From the early nineteenth century, the term 'primitive', based on social Darwinism, referred to cultures thought to have 'progressed' less than European ones. Edward Said argues that 'theories of racial types [such as] Gustave LeBon's primitive [...] guided French imperial practices'. See *Culture and Imperialism* (New York: Vintage, 1993), p. 170. Although colonialism, as Nkiru Nzebwu argues, depends on 'power and dominance and need not entail racism', in Europe 'racist narratives provided moral and political justification for [...] colonization'. 'Colonial Racism: Sweeping Out Africa with Mother Europe's Broom', in Susan E. Babbitt and Sue Campbell, eds, *Racism and Philosophy* (Ithaca: Cornell University Press, 1999), pp. 130–32.

4 For more on black activists in Paris during this time, see Phillipe Dewitte, *Les Mouvements nègres en France, 1991–1939* (Paris: L'Harmattan, 1985).

5 See Jean Suret-Canale, *French Colonialism in Tropical Africa, 1900–1945*, trans. Till Gottheiner (New York: Pica Press, 1971), pt 2, and Raoul Girardet, *L'idée coloniale en France de 1871 à 1962* (Paris: Table Ronde, 1972), pt 2.

through grand exhibits of colonial 'success', such as the 1931 International Colonial Exposition in Paris at Vincennes.[6] Over seven million visitors witnessed these exhibits, which deflected attention from colonialism's social and economic realities by presenting indigenous culture (African sculpture, replicas of mosques and pagodas, music and dance) as an exotic escape. Such grandiose displays appear to have been successful; very little public interest in decolonization existed.[7] Striving to unseat the hierarchical notions of racial and cultural difference underlying this propaganda was clearly a necessary task during the 1930s. It was this challenge that the Surrealists explicitly undertook.

Radical Notions of Difference: Juxtaposition and Anti-Whiteness

Both the radical nature of the Surrealists' racial politics and the limitations of their viewpoints are intimately connected with their critique of 'reason', a critique central to the Surrealists' project and present from the first stages of their work. Although what they mean by 'reason' shifts throughout the movement's history (and even within a single text), one important articulation connects reason with conceptual categories. In the 1924 *Manifesto*, Breton writes, 'if objective reason does a frightful job – as indeed it does – of serving him who calls on it, is it not fitting and proper to avoid all contact with these categories?'[8] Here Breton, through a grammatical slippage, seems to be equating reason with unnecessary conceptual categories, since 'these categories' have no prior referent other than as an implied aspect of 'objective reason'. A similar critique of reason is elaborated many times throughout the early Surrealist writings, which frequently propose that the binary oppositions (or 'old antinomies', in the Surrealists' terminology) that seemed foundational to Western thinking are simply false constructions of the rational mind. The *Second Manifesto of Surrealism*, for example, argues that the primary goal of Surrealism is achieving the 'state of mind' in which 'life and death, the real

6 See Thomas August who argues that such propaganda was crucial to the success of colonialism, in *The Selling of Empire: British and French Imperialist Propaganda, 1890–1940* (Westport: Greenwood Press, 1985). For information on the Exposition see Catherine Hodeir and Michel Pierre, *L'Exposition Coloniale* (Brussels: Complexe, 1991); Herman Lebovics, *True France: The Wars Over Cultural Identity, 1900–1945* (Ithaca: Cornell University Press, 1992), ch. 2, and Patricia A. Morton, *Hybrid Modernities: Architecture and Representation at the 1931 Colonial Exposition, Paris* (Cambridge: MIT Press, 2000).

7 Alec G. Hargreaves argues that even anti-colonialists were 'more concerned to humanize the colonial regime than to reject it'. *Colonial Experience in French Fiction: A Study of Pierre Loti, Ernest Psicheri, and Pierre Mille* (London: Macmillan, 1981), p. 9.

8 André Breton, *Manifestoes of Surrealism*, trans. Richard Seaver and Helen R. Lane (Ann Arbor: University of Michigan Press, 1969), p. 8.

and the imagined [...] high and low, cease to be perceived as contradictions'.[9] Such a state of mind was to be achieved through the liberation of the unconscious.

As it is impossible to avoid 'all contact' with conceptual categories, however, the Surrealists' search to enact their theoretical idealism had two repercussions in their practice, with different implications for racial politics. One strategy that emerged from the theory of eliding contradictory categories was the aesthetic practice of juxtaposition, a technique that allows the artist to place two contradictory images or ideas side by side. As Max Ernst wrote in 'Au-delà de la peinture' (1937), 'What is the most noble conquest of collage? It is the irrational'.[10] The Surrealists apparently intended this practice to combine contradictions and avoid rational categories. The result, however, privileges a complex logic that is neither fixed nor entirely ambiguous. Since the materials the artist uses are taken from other contexts, they never lose their associations with those cultural arenas and arc not easily integrated into the artwork; both the former context and the new one remain in play. Conceptual categories therefore appear culturally constructed, yet unfixed, and such fragmentation requires the audience to reconstruct, consciously or unconsciously, the meaning of the artwork. When the Surrealists arranged representations of race and culture in unusual combinations, they challenged the ideologies of colonialism, since many of those ideologies depended on presenting racial categories as fixed and natural. The spectator was encouraged to confront a dialectic of differences without synthesis, rather than to accept or deny a particular 'rational' statement. The well-known Surrealist aesthetic of juxtaposition therefore extends to a politically viable strategy because of the active role it demands of the viewer. Since this action remains on an ideational level, however, the Surrealists' tactics were most potentially effective during the initial stages of political change: agitation for public awareness of colonialism's racist propaganda.

A little-known photocollage by Benjamin Péret, *Collage (untitled)* (1929), juxtaposes cultural clichés to trouble their normative status as part of colonialism's justification (fig. 17). The collage poses two figures, a large white man and a small black woman, in front of a grand display of Western art and architecture. A whip extends from the man's hand to the woman's neck. As Elza Adamowicz persuasively argues in *Surrealist Collage in Text and Image*, Péret's collage is a rewriting of the colonialist narrative, since it intimately links the brutality of colonialism with the 'glories' of Western civilization.[11]

---

9 Breton, *Manifestos*, p. 123.

10 Max Ernst, 'Au-delà de la peinture', *Cahiers d'Art* XII:6–7 (1937), rpd in *Ecritures* (Paris: Gallimard, 1970), p. 264. Translations are my own unless otherwise noted.

11 Elza Adamowicz, *Surrealist Collage in Text and Image* (Cambridge: Cambridge University Press, 1998), pp. 70–72.

What makes Péret's collage a political work of art in Surrealist terms, however, is not any explicit statement or stance, but the fact that its fragments do not easily rest in any new unified meaning. The cultural signs continue to point in two directions. Both the new meaning resulting from the images' combination and the stereotypes to which they refer are simultaneously in play, thereby challenging the very interpretive process that would lead to a rewriting of the colonialist narrative, as well as creating an active (and uncomfortable) role for the spectator. For example, the white male figure, whose pose, physique and sandals link him with body-builders and Greek athletes, is a European physical ideal. The figure's cultural 'reality' is highlighted by Péret's choice to use a photograph only for this part of the collage. At the same time, the figure's expression and exaggeratedly large position within the picture make him an absurd-looking figure; he seems out of place. This idea of 'place', or context, is one of the most important concepts that juxtaposition highlights: How did such a male figure come to be thought of as an ideal? How does he still function as an ideal in other contexts, a direct contradiction with his place in the image as a brutal colonialist? Conversely, the naked female figure would have been recognized as a stereotype of deviant sexuality and perhaps even more specifically as 'the Hottentot Venus', the name given to two black women exhibited in London and Paris during the nineteenth century; variations of this image appeared in numerous contexts, ranging from cartoons to pseudo-scientific publications.[12] In Péret's collage, the figure's small stature and innocent expression question this simplistic association of black women with uncontrollable sexuality, yet the vicious stereotypes to which the figure refers are not erased. In other words, rather than simply presenting new images of race, which could then eventually become fixed stereotypes, Péret keeps hierarchical racial categories in play and thus encourages the spectator to reconsider their complex cultural meanings. Such artwork reaches toward a racial politics that avoids the limitations of both a humanist liberalism based on universal similarity, and a separatist essentialism based on unbridgeable alterity. This dialectic of difference encourages a continually unsettling movement between identity categories, since it foregrounds relationships among groups of people, while acknowledging that cultural constructions have material social effects that cannot be dismissed simply through a representational synthesis.

The Surrealists' presentation of racial difference as socially constructed, yet unfixed, anticipates the work of 'whiteness' critics.[13] The social category of

---

12 On this figure and the black female as an 'icon for deviant sexuality', see Sander Gilman, 'The Hottentot and the Prostitute: Toward an Iconography of Female Sexuality', in *Difference and Pathology: Stereotypes of Sexuality, Race, and Madness* (Ithaca: Cornell University Press, 1985), pp. 76–108.

13 For an overview of this scholarship, see Ruth Frankenberg, ed., *Displacing Whiteness: Essays in Social and Cultural Criticism* (Durham: Duke University Press,

'whiteness' does not simply refer to skin colour, but emphasizes the discursive practices that uphold social hierarchies. One of these practices is the equation of whiteness with humanness:

> For those in power in the West, as long as whiteness is felt to be the human condition, then it alone both defines normality and fully inhabits it [...] white people, unable to see their particularity, cannot take account of other people's.[14]

The normative status of whiteness paradoxically makes it both ubiquitous and unseen. To combat whiteness is therefore to make it visible, and to accomplish this goal, 'whiteness needs to be made strange', as Richard Dyer argues.[15] Some critics connect this process, as the Surrealists did, with a critique of the stable categories that are often used to support racial hierarchies.[16] In Péret's collage, the image of the white male figure performs such a critique since it simultaneously references both the cultural power of the masculine ideal as a white man and its particularity or 'strangeness'.[17]

Although juxtaposition is most commonly connected to visual art collages, the Surrealists also used the technique in the arrangement of the art objects themselves in the exhibit 'La Vérité sur les Colonies' (September 1931–February 1932).[18] Since the Surrealists' role in this exhibit has been controversial, a turn to the historical background is necessary before examining the exhibit itself. 'La Vérité' was a direct response to the 1931 International Colonial Exposition in Paris, which had received little public criticism to balance the admiration it generated; the Surrealists' dissenting voices stood out. In addition to two manifestoes, *Ne visitez pas l'Exposition Coloniale*, and *Premier bilan de l'Exposition Coloniale*, in which the Surrealists demanded an 'immediate evacuation of the colonies',[19] they offered a concrete alternative to

---

1997) and Mike Hill, ed., *Whiteness: A Critical Reader* (New York: New York University Press, 1997). For a postcolonial emphasis see Raka Shome, 'Whiteness and the Politics of Location: Postcolonial Reflections', in Thomas K. Nakayama and Judith N. Martin, eds, *Whiteness: The Communication of Social Identity* (Thousand Oaks: Sage Publications, 1999), pp. 107–28.

14 Richard Dyer, *White* (London: Routledge, 1997), p. 9.

15 Ibid. This formulation is strikingly similar to Clifford's description of the Surrealists' 'ethnographic' mode of operation that 'ma[de] the familiar strange', *The Predicament of Culture*, p. 121.

16 See Ross Chambers, 'The Unexamined', in Hill, ed., *Whiteness*, pp. 197–203.

17 See Franklin Rosemont, 'Notes on Surrealism as a Revolution against Whiteness', in *Race Traitor*, no. 9 (1998), pp. 19–29; for an overview of the Surrealists' work in relation to race and 'whiteness' see 'Surrealists on Whiteness From 1925 to the Present', in ibid., pp. 5–18.

18 See Lebovics, *True France*, pp. 105–10; Hodeir and Pierre, *L'Exposition*, pp. 111–34; and Morton, *Hybrid*, pp. 98–127.

19 André Breton et al., *Ne visitez pas l'Exposition Coloniale* (Paris, 1931), rpd in Maurice Nadeau, *Histoire du surréalisme, suivi de documents surréalistes* (Paris: Seuil,

the Colonial Exposition through a counter-exhibit. According to André Thirion, the Surrealist exhibit was suggested by Alfred Kurella, a German Comintern member who was dismayed at the French Communist Party's (PCF) lack of response to the Colonial Exposition and found that only the Surrealists had 'demonstrated an intelligent hostility' against it.[20] Minutes from a PCF meeting ('Plan du Travail', February 1931) recently uncovered by Janine Mileaf reveal the reason for the Party's tepid response to the Colonial Exposition. In order to avoid recrimination by the French government, the PCF decided to form a separate organization, the Anti-Imperialist League, and to ask the Surrealists to hold the anti-exhibit under its name. If the government did not ban the exhibit, the PCF planned to take credit, which it later did.[21] 'La Vérité', then, can be considered principally a Surrealist exhibit in design and execution. Thirion and Georges Sadoul organized rooms with photos displaying the forced labour of colonized peoples and texts revealing, for example, that 18,000 workers died while working on the Brazzaville-Ocean railroad. Paul Eluard, Yves Tanguy and Louis Aragon planned the inventive art exhibit.[22]

In contrast to the 1931 Exposition Coloniale which used native art to promote an ideal of *la Plus Grande France*,[23] the art exhibit in 'La Vérité sur les Colonies' juxtaposed European cultural objects with art indigenous to colonized countries in order to interrogate assumptions about European cultural hierarchies or 'whiteness' (fig. 18). African masks and statues were placed in the same room with Christian iconographic objects; West Indian music was interspersed with popular French music. Jody Blake argues that the exhibit represented 'the Surrealists' conviction that asserting the artistic integrity of subjugated peoples

---

1964), p. 327. These tracts were distributed near the Exhibition by the Surrealists. For other Surrealist anti-racist texts, see René Crevel, 'The Negress in the Brothel', in Nancy Cunard, ed., *Negro Anthology* (London: Wishart, 1934), rpd (New York: Negro University Press, 1969); Jacques Viot, 'N'Encombrez pas les colonies', in *Le Surréalisme au service de la Révolution*, no. 1 (1930), pp. 43–45, and Paul Eluard, 'La Suppression de l'esclavage', in *La Révolution surréaliste*, no. 3 (1925), p. 19.

20 André Thirion, *Revolutionaries without Revolution*, trans. Joachim Neugroschel (New York: Macmillan, 1975), p. 289. Several of the Surrealists had been PCF members since 1927, but they remained on the margins of the Party.

21 See Janine Mileaf, 'Body to Politics: Surrealist Exhibition of the Tribal and the Modern at the Anti-Imperialist Exhibition and the Galerie Charles Ratton', *Res*, no. 40 (Fall 2001), pp. 239–55.

22 At the time of the exhibit, 'l'affaire Aragon' had begun, but Aragon had not yet broken with the Surrealists. See Helena Lewis, *The Politics of Surrealism* (New York: Paragon, 1988), p. 110.

23 This phrase literally means 'Greater France', but it also implied 'Greatest France'. See Panivong Norindr, '*La Plus Grande France*: French Cultural Identity and Nation Building under Mitterand', in Steven Ungar and Tom Conley, eds, *Identity Papers: Contested Nationhood in Twentieth-Century France* (Minneapolis: University of Minnesota Press, 1996), pp. 233–58.

was one of the strongest arguments against European imperialism'.[24] Jack Spector argues the converse: the exhibit makes 'the ironic point that [both the African and French figures] are all equally cult objects'.[25] Both scholars identify important aspects of the exhibit, yet within their opposed emphases lies the radical nature of the Surrealists' project: the circumscribed ambiguity of the presentation depicted art as culturally constructed, but did not limit the comparison to a single framework of either art or cult objects. Instead, each object encouraged the viewer to rethink their assumptions regarding the other object, a process that called for a shifting reasoning rather than one which used stable oppositional categories. For example, the Surrealists' juxtapositions required the audience to consider the role of cultural conventions in the categorization of 'art' versus 'functional' and 'religious' versus 'superstitious' objects. Through this strategy the Surrealists presented objects which were central to French bourgeois culture, such as Catholic icons and popular music, as unusual; European culture could not be uncritically equated with a broader 'human culture'. At the same time, the objects continued to refer to their original context, hinting that the cultural power of Catholic icons, for example, cannot be removed simply by exhibiting them in another place. Thus the Surrealists critiqued 'whiteness' even when no explicit racial rhetoric or image was present.

Although the attendance at this exhibit was large for an avant-garde art exhibition (around 5000 visitors), the limitations of audience reception must be taken seriously in any attempt to evaluate Surrealism's political potential. The very thing that made their art potentially radical, the requirements it placed on the viewer, was also that which ensured its limited audience. The Surrealists' anti-colonialist texts, however, did reach toward a wider readership, in that they couched their moments of complexity within unambiguous political statements.

The anti-colonialist texts are usually seen as part of the Surrealists' stance against all forms of imperialism. For example, Jack Spector writes that the Surrealists were 'less concerned with racial issues than with Marxist anti-imperialist ones'.[26] Indeed their support for colonized countries stemmed from a general hatred of French nationalism and Western society, as is clear in their 1925 open letter to the French ambassador in Japan, 'we fervently hope that wars and colonial insurrections will annihilate this Western civilization'.[27] In other words, they used the struggles of the colonized to help their own agenda of a broader cultural revolution.

---

24 Blake, *Tumulte Noir*, p. 135.

25 Spector, *Surrealist Art*, p. 179.

26 Ibid., p. 288.

27 Maxime Alexandre et al., 'Open Letter to M. Paul Claudel', in Maurice Nadeau, *The History of Surrealism*, trans. Richard Howard (Cambridge: Belknap Press, 1965), p. 238.

Yet in texts written several years later, the Surrealists went beyond a Marxist critique of imperialism when they explicitly addressed issues of race. In *Ne visitez pas l'Exposition Coloniale*, one of the manifestoes written in direct response to the 1931 International Exposition, the Surrealists undermine assumptions that white Europeans are the norm from which others deviate. In a passage indicting the forced labour that sometimes even killed native workers, the Surrealists write: 'these [colonized] men who are distinguished from us only by our *whiteness* [*notre qualité de* blanc], we who say men of colour, we [who are] men without colour'.[28] When they name themselves and the colonialists 'men without colour', having colour becomes the norm from which white people deviate. Furthermore, the subtleties of the phrase 'notre qualité de *blanc*' connect it very closely to current notions of 'whiteness'. On one level, the word 'qualité' in this kind of construction means a position, distinction or authority, and therefore the phrase translates to 'our status as whites' and speaks of power structures rather than skin colour. Yet the choice to italicize the word 'white' and to use the word 'qualité', which can also mean simply an attribute with no positive connotations, deflates 'the status of whites' by showing such status to be based on something as arbitrary as skin colour. Like the images in Péret's collage, this phrase acknowledges the cultural power of 'whiteness', while at the same time undermining it.

In a later essay, 'Murderous Humanitarianism' (written in 1932 but not published until Nancy Cunard's 1934 *Negro Anthology*), the Surrealists focus even more explicitly on racial issues: 'we placed our energies in the service of revolution [. . .] and defined our attitude towards the colonial problem, and hence towards the colour question'.[29] This manifesto was the first one signed by Caribbeans Jules-Marcel Monnerot and Pierre Yoyotte, who had proclaimed their support for Surrealism in the single 1932 issue of *Légitime défense*, a publication devoted to anti-colonialism and 'the Caribbean question'.[30] 'Murderous Humanitarianism' is consequently an important document of white Surrealists' affiliations with black intellectuals.

28 Breton et al., *Ne visitez*, p. 326, italics original. Among those who signed were Breton, Eluard, Péret, Aragon and Tanguy.

29 André Breton et al., 'Murderous Humanitarianism', in Cunard, ed., *Negro Anthology*, rpd in André Breton, *What Is Surrealism?: Selected Writings*, ed. Franklin Rosemont (New York: Monad, 1978), p. 325. This text was translated by Samuel Beckett and never published in French. The original has been lost.

30 Etienne Léro et al., 'Légitime défense: declaration', in *Légitime défense*, no. 1 (1932), p. 2. Caribbean Surrealism has recently begun to generate significant interest. See Michael Richardson, ed., *Refusal of the Shadow: Surrealism and the Caribbean*, trans. Richardson and Kryzystof Fijalkowski (London: Verso, 1996); Jean-Claude Michel, *The Black Surrealists* (New York: Peter Lang, 2000); and Bernard Lecherbonnier, *Surréalisme et francophonie: la Chair du verbe* (Paris: Publisud, 1992). See Brent Hayes Edwards, 'The Ethnics of Surrealism', in *Transition*, no. 78 (1999), pp. 84–135, for a critique of the priority Richardson gives to European Surrealism.

Perhaps as a result of these affiliations, 'Murderous Humanitarianism' presents a complex picture of the relationship between race and social hierarchies when the voice of the essay shifts between white and black. As in Péret's collage and the anti-colonial exhibit, the Surrealists use a juxtapositional logic that yields several contradictory meanings. The voice is not 'white', since the essay uses the phrase 'the white man and his actions' to represent the object of critique. Yet it is not written exclusively from the perspective of the Caribbean Surrealists, nor is it a 'colourless' voice. Instead the perspective is unstable. This strategy is most apparent in the essay's final sentence:

> [T]he whole object of our romantic exoticism and modern travel lust is of use only in entertaining that class of blasé client sly enough to see an interest in deflecting to his own advantage the torrent of energies which soon – much sooner than he thinks – will close over his head.[31]

The 'our' in this passage refers to three groups simultaneously. It refers to the French, since the essay as a whole criticizes the bourgeoisie for an obsession with a 'mystic Orient'. Yet 'our' is also a specifically black voice, since a referral to the 'degradation' of those blacks who play 'fashionable jazz' precedes this sentence; presumably they would be the ones 'entertaining blasé clients'. Finally, 'our' is the Surrealists – originally a white group, at this moment in transition to being racially mixed – in which case 'romantic exoticism' is a self-critique of their fascination with other cultures and their former self-definition as an extension of romanticism.[32] The reader is encouraged to consider *who* is culturally linked to such an exoticism and why.

This shifting enunciation shuns oppositional critique and works toward what whiteness critic Mike Hill calls 'categorical disintegration'.[33] Hill argues that this process arises from analyzing the interconnected sets of affiliations created by introducing other social categories such as gender and class. Such analysis is particularly applicable to the French Caribbean context where those who had lighter skin and adopted upper-class cultural values were more likely to succeed. In 'Murderous Humanitarianism', the contradictory perspectives implicitly point to the tangled relationships between social categories. The text acknowledges both white and black Surrealists' potential complicity in bourgeois culture, even as they try to undermine that culture. Furthermore, the white Surrealists' disloyalty to whiteness does not involve a simple choice to disassociate themselves from white privilege; they are simultaneously in the margins and at the centre of European society. As befits political manifestoes written by poets, it is only through our close attention to their language that

31 Breton et al., 'Murderous Humanitarianism', p. 327.

32 See the *Second Manifesto of Surrealism*, in which the Surrealists refer to themselves as the 'prehensile tail' of romanticism. Breton, *Manifestos*, p. 153.

33 Hill, *Whiteness*, p. 7.

these texts reveal the insidious complexity of racial categories and point to new ways of thinking.

Reversing the Binary: Affinities with Primitivism

Juxtapositional logic, whether in visual collage, exhibit or text, was only one aspect of the Surrealists' practice connected with their intention to avoid the dualities of objective 'reason'. The other aspect was an emphasis on what they saw as those aspects of life – dream, madness, emotion – that could not be understood from a rationalist perspective. As Michael Löwy notes, a celebration of the irrational does not accurately describe the Surrealists' viewpoint because it 'relates to a rationalist world-view inherited from the philosophy of the Enlightenment, which is the very thing [Breton is] attempting to transcend'.[34] Yet the Surrealists' philosophies and practices regarding what they saw as 'reason' and 'unreason' are uneven. In their theory, the Surrealists wrote about attaining the state of mind where binaries such as dream and reality disappear, yet in fact they often ironically remained firmly within the grip of the 'old antinomies' of 'reason', since they simply reversed the hierarchy of the rational/non-rational binary.

This privileging of the non-rational appears to have motivated the Surrealists' interest in non-Western art and culture. In the early twentieth century, the notion that 'primitive' cultures ignored 'reason' appeared self-evident to many. Prominent ethnologist Lucien Lévy-Bruhl, for example, wrote in *The Primitive Mentality* that indigenous cultures emphasized dreams and 'invisible forces'. In contrast to these discourses that explicitly or implicitly upheld the superiority of European society, the Surrealists glorified non-Western cultures through emphasizing the potential of the non-rational to 'liberate' repressive European society. For example, Breton wrote in 'Situation surréaliste de l'objet' (1935) that Surrealism wanted to 'liberate instinctive impulses, to break down the barrier that civilized man faces, a barrier that primitive people and children do not experience'.[35]

---

34 Micheal Löwy, 'Walter Benjamin and Surrealism: The Story of a Revolutionary Spell', in *Radical Philosophy*, no. 80 (1996), p. 17.

35 Breton, *Manifestos*, p. 273. See Evan Maurer, 'Dada and Surrealism', in William Rubin, ed., *'Primitivism' in 20th Century Art: Affinity of the Tribal and the Modern*, vol. 2 (New York: Museum of Modern Art, 1984), pp. 535–94. See also Caribbean Surrealist Monnerot's *La Poésie moderne et le sacré*, which proposes affinities between Surrealist and Native American thought (Paris: Gallimard, 1945); and Elizabeth Ezra, 'René Crevel's Allegories of Exclusion', which examines René Crevel's work and discourses of primitivism in *The Colonial Unconscious: Race and Culture in Interwar France* (Ithaca: Cornell University Press, 2000).

Yet this attempt to step outside dominant Western culture ironically allied the Surrealists with another set of European ideas – 'primitivism',[36] a perspective on non-Western art. Although primitivism was intended to be commendatory, those who saw art in these terms were limited by the tendency to romanticize the 'innate creativity', or 'emotional nature' of indigenous peoples.[37] The Surrealists often shared these assumptions. Their critical lens did not allow them to see other peoples as equally 'cultured'. Instead the Surrealists interpreted non-Western peoples principally in relation to their own project to criticize European society and in so doing they often ironically revealed their affinities with their object of critique.

Furthermore, if primitivism had at one time appeared 'revolutionary' because of its potential to destabilize Western norms, by the 1930s it had become fashionable. '*L'art nègre*' was a part of high art culture,[38] African and African-American music were being played in nightclubs across Paris, and the term 'primitivism' had been accepted by the discipline of art history. Since primitivism was clearly part of stable institutions, it no longer appeared to have the potential to reveal their limitations. Moreover, primitivism in fact had always relied on the social institution of colonialism and vice versa. The objects celebrated as art were often acquired by colonialist-supported expeditions which looted native peoples' places of worship, and colonialist governments often depended upon the ideology of primitivism to divert attention from atrocities, as in the 1931 International Colonial Exposition.

It is crucial, however, that we examine the Surrealists' primitivism in the broader context of their entire œuvre. Although they were drawn to some aspects of primitivism, they were *also* in violent reaction against the faddish *art nègre* that had taken Paris by storm during the 1920s. The Surrealists had always been extremely critical of the mainstream art world, and the appearance of primitivism in that context apparently allowed them to see, at least to some extent, how flawed their own position had been. In 'Murderous Humanitarianism', for example, the Surrealists criticize the exploitation often involved in the celebration of black culture: '[t]hose blacks who have [...] been compelled to distort in terms of fashionable jazz the natural expression of their joy'.

36 The term was initially associated only with art history and referred to Western perspectives on tribal artifacts; its use dates from between 1897 and 1904. See Rubin, *'Primitivism' in 20th Century Art*, pp. 1–6 for an overview. This topic has been an extremely contentious one for recent scholarship. See Hal Foster, 'The "Primitive" Unconscious of Modern Art', in *October*, no. 34 (1985), pp. 5–70, for a critique of Rubin's use of Western criteria.

37 Charles Harrison, Francis Frascina and Gill Perry, *Primitivism, Cubism, Abstraction: The Early Twentieth Century* (New Haven: Yale University Press, 1993), p. 6.

38 See Jean-Louis Paudrat, 'From Africa', in Rubin, *'Primitivism' in 20th Century Art*, vol. 1, pp. 535–94, for a history of African art in Paris during the first part of the twentieth century.

Furthermore, as we saw above, they identify the typical relation to the 'other' as a part of 'our romantic exoticism', thus taking responsibility for their own role in such exploitation.

Not only were the Surrealists conscious of the political and ethical problems associated with Western ideas of 'the primitive', but primitivism itself consists of heterogeneous ideas with multiple political functions. If we situate the Surrealists' primitivism historically and geographically, we will find that the very ideas that might seem unsatisfactory from a twenty-first century perspective actually precipitated alliances with black intellectuals who contributed significantly to a nascent decolonialism.

One such alliance was with Martinican poet and politician Aimé Césaire, who both influenced Surrealism and was influenced by it. Césaire encountered Surrealism during the mid-1930s while studying in Paris at the prestigious Ecole Normale Supérieure. When Breton and Césaire met in 1941, each felt his work confirmed as well as extended through association with the other: 'There was a complete convergence between my research and Surrealist research; in other words, their research made me stronger in my convictions', Césaire later said.[39] Breton similarly wrote that he felt 'a close communion' at their meeting.[40]

This mutual affinity stemmed in part from each man's interest in the critique of Western 'reason'. In the late 1930s, Césaire and future Senegalese president Léopold Sédar Senghor had initiated the political literary movement *Négritude*, intending to unite peoples of Africa and the African diaspora by emphasizing a common cultural identity in opposition to Western values.[41] Negritude, like Surrealism and primitivism, often simply reversed racial hierarchies. Evidence of this strategy exists even within the neologism '*Négritude*', which invests the derogatory '*nègre*' with positive meanings.[42] Similarly, in order to counter the psychological effects of the French colonialist policy of assimilation which had rewarded black Martinicans for capitulating to white bourgeois culture, the proponents of negritude emphasized attributes such as 'natural intuition' which

39 Aimé Césaire and François Beloux, 'Un Poète politique: Aimé Césaire', *Magazine Littéraire*, no. 34 (1969), p. 28. For recent work in English on Césaire, see Janis L. Pallister, *Aimé Césaire* (New York: Twayne Publishers, 1991) and Gregson Davis, *Aimé Césaire* (Cambridge: Cambridge University Press, 1997). See Robin D.G. Kelley, 'A Poetics of Anticolonialism', in *Monthly Review* LI:6 (1999), pp. 1–21, for an analysis of Césaire's transformation of Surrealist thought to serve the anti-colonialist project.

40 André Breton, 'A Great Black Poet: Aimé Césaire', in *What Is Surrealism?*, p. 232. This piece was later published as the preface to Césaire's *Cahier*.

41 For more information on negritude, see James A. Arnold, *Modernism and Negritude: The Poetry and Poetics of Aimé Césaire* (Cambridge: Harvard University Press, 1981) and Abiola Irele, *The African Experience in Literature and Ideology* (Bloomington: Indiana University Press, 1990).

42 '*Nègre*' as a noun was a racist epithet in Martinique, but was used as an adjective comparable to '*noir*' in France.

they felt were denied by mainstream European culture. In other words, rather than challenging the Western/non-Western binary, they sought to make that distinction itself politically and psychologically useful. Césaire writes in his epic poem, *Cahier d'un retour au pays natal* [*Notebook of a Return to my Native Land*] (1939), in which he coined the term 'Negritude': 'we hate you, you and / your reason, we call upon / the early dementia, the flaming madness / of a tenacious cannibalism [*nous vous haïssons vous et / votre raison, nous nous réclamons de la / démence précoce de la folie flambante / du cannibalisme tenace*]'.[43] Here the colonizer is equated with 'reason', and the colonized with 'madness', thereby exhibiting uncomfortable parallels with European primitivism. In another parallel, negritude's celebration of a pan-African identity echoed European primitivism's elision of cultural differences among non-Western peoples. Indeed these similarities led later critics to denounce the movement for merely replicating Western stereotypes of Africans and cementing existing power structures by supporting a black educated elite. One of the earliest critics was Franz Fanon, who argued in *Peau noire, masques blancs* (1952) that Negritude was part of a dialectic that functioned to maintain white people as the dominant term.[44]

In spite of these limitations, however, Negritude was a necessary early step toward decolonization, particularly in terms of fighting the 'psychological chains of colonization', as Césaire put it. Negritude used what post-colonial theorists now term 'strategic essentialism', the use of stable identity categories in specific historical situations to achieve the sense of self-respect necessary for combating colonialism.[45] In other words, both Negritude and Surrealism were most powerful in the galvanizing stage of political change. Césaire emphasized Surrealism's initiatory role when he said that Breton, 'cut short [...] our hesitations'.[46] Césaire took this energy further by effecting concrete political change after World War II. As the first black mayor of the Martinican capital Fort-de-France and *député* to the French National Assembly, Césaire fought for greater autonomy for Martinique, Guadeloupe, Guyana and Réunion, changing their status from 'colony' to 'department' of France in 1946. His life's work

43 Aimé Césaire, *Cahier d'un retour au pays natal/Return to My Native Land*, trans. Emile Snyders (Paris: Presence Africaine, 1968), pp. 52–55, both original and translation.

44 Criticism of negritude has centred principally on Senghor's more rigid formulation. See Wole Soyinka, *Myth, Literature, and the African World* (Cambridge: Cambridge University Press, 1976), pp. 126–39, and Ezekiel Mphahlele, *The African Image* (London: Faber and Faber, 1962).

45 See Giyatri Chakravorty Spivak, 'Criticism, Feminism and the Institution: An Interview with Giyatri Chakravorty Spivak', in *Thesis Eleven*, nos 10–11 (1984–85), pp. 183–84.

46 Aimé Césaire, 'Entretien avec Aimé Césaire par Jacqueline Leiner', in *Tropiques*, no. 1 [facsimile reproduction] (Paris: Jean-Michel Place, 1978), p. VI.

extended the Surrealists' dream of integrating art and politics, since he put his poetic ideal of a strong black identity into practice by promoting the socio-political concerns of the Martinicans.

Surrealism's incendiary role was again apparent in Port-au-Prince, Haiti, where Breton's series of lectures in December 1945 received an enthusiastic response from both artists and activists. When one of the lectures was printed on the front page of the student Marxist journal *La Ruche* and then censored by the Lescot dictatorship, it incited the Haitian students to strike, leading two days later to the dictatorship's demise and the election of Dumarsais Estimé, the first black (non-mulatto) president since US occupation in 1915.[47] In Breton's account of the event, we see a marked shift in perspective from earlier Surrealism, which had used indigenous art and thought principally in service of the white Surrealists: 'I tried [...] in deference to the spirit animating their history, to align Surrealist aims with the age-old aims of the Haitian peasants'.[48] Breton attempts to aid, rather than set, the Haitians' goals. He thus avoids the hubris of the earlier primitivism, while continuing to invoke it to form coalitions. In a speech to Haitian poets, he says, 'we have found ourselves linked from the beginning with 'primitive' thought, which remains less alien to you than to us'.[49] In this speech and in later texts, Breton seems very aware of the problematic nature of the term primitive and always uses quotation marks as if to signal this understanding. Although Surrealism's role as an instigator is apparent in the events in Haiti, Breton is also aware of its limits, since it necessarily cannot follow through and determine an ideal outcome. He cautions that the revolution was 'controversial' and that one cannot be sure of the 'results'.[50]

Since Breton's visit to Haiti was preceded by Césaire's, the relationship between Surrealism and Césaire functioned inversely as well: black intellectuals were at the forefront of the new directions in Surrealism. The Surrealists' interactions with Haitian and Caribbean people also helped the artists to see the Eurocentric ideologies that had earlier influenced their thought. For example, in the foreword to the 1947 edition of Césaire's *Notebook*, Breton writes, with a tone of humility not often found earlier in Surrealism, that indigenous peoples must set the agenda for decolonization: 'the emancipation of people of colour

---

47 Although the Haitian events are not strictly anti-colonialist, since Haiti received independence from France in 1804, the country had been ruled by a mulatto elite of European heritage and its people continued to fight the psychological effects of a colonial history.

48 André Breton, 'Interview with Jean Duché', in *Le Littéraire* (5 October 1946), reprinted in *What Is Surrealism?*, p. 262.

49 André Breton, 'Speech to Young Haitian Poets', in *What Is Surrealism?*, p. 259.

50 Indeed the outcome was not the permanent revolution hoped for; the army took over the country and overthrew Estimé in 1948.

can only be the work of those people themselves, with all the implications inherent in that'.[51] Surrealism sustained this anti-racist action in the following decades, action which continues to the present day.[52]

An analysis of the Surrealists' links with Césaire and the Haitians challenges contentions that their effective political action ended with their break with Communism in 1935, as some commentators have argued. Robert Short, for example, writes that, 'from 1935 onwards [...] [t]he group's artistic and political activities were definitively separated'.[53] Similarly, Alan Rose argues that 'the political evolution of the Surrealists was linked [...] to the question of their relationship to the French Communist Party'.[54] Yet the Surrealists' anti-colonialist work qualifies such received ideas. While their interest in 'the primitive' often required them to adopt the European worldview against which they fought in other areas, their anti-'whiteness' work exhibited a complex notion of difference and their alliances with colonized peoples made significant contributions. The Surrealists' racial politics require us to revise histories of Surrealism and to continue to investigate the very notion of 'the political'.

---

51 André Breton, 'Aimé Césaire', p. 235.

52 See 'Declaration Concerning the Right of Insubordination in the Algerian War' (1960) in *What Is Surrealism?*, pp. 346–48, and Rosemont, 'Surrealists on Whiteness From 1925 to the Present', pp. 13–18.

53 Robert S. Short, 'The Politics of Surrealism, 1920–1936', in *The Journal of Contemporary History* I:3 (1966), p. 19.

54 Alan Rose, *Surrealism and Communism: The Early Years* (New York: Peter Lang, 1991), p. 283.

Chapter 7

Painting and Politics: Miró's *Still Life with Old Shoe* and the Spanish Republic*

Robert S. Lubar

On the eve of the Spanish Civil War, in July 1936, Miró began a series of 27 mixed-medium paintings on Masonite while summering at his *masia* in Montroig (fig. 19). The figuration of the individual panels is in part derived from drawings for earlier sculptural projects, and from sketches Miró had executed in 1932 for the sets and costumes of Boris Kochno's production of *Jeux d'enfants*, which the Ballets Russes de Monte Carlo performed in April of that year.[1] On rough, resistant grounds, whose texture Miró's biographer has described as 'somewhere between baked earth and hammered, flattened, slightly carbonized straw',[2] Miró built up layers of encrusted matter – telluric deposits of brown and black pigment mixed with sand, casein and tar. With an almost savage intensity, he suppressed all hints of the lyricism he had achieved in the ballet designs, transforming his earlier cast of characters into a *teatrum mundus* of grotesque and anguished figures. Correspondingly, his drawing had become rough and awkward, and his compositions dispersed and fragmented. In several instances, messy blotches of white paint beneath broad sweeps of colour suggest that the surface has been patched, or that an earlier design has been hastily covered, while elsewhere the traditional relationship defining the boundaries between form and contour is violated. At every turn, these raw, even violent,

---

* An early draft of this essay was presented at the Primer Symposi Internacional de Joan Miró, organized by the Fundació Pilar i Joan Miró, Palma de Mallorca, Spain, in May 1993, and at the Museum of Modern Art, New York, in November 1993. I am grateful to Patricia Gray Berman of Wellesley College and to Raymond Spiteri for their insights and editorial suggestions in preparing this essay for publication.

1 For a discussion of Miró's preparatory sketches for the Masonite paintings, see Carolyn Lanchner, '*Peinture-Poésie*, Its Logic and Logistics' in *Joan Miró* (New York: The Museum of Modern Art, 1993), pp. 66–68. On Miró's collaboration with the Ballets Russes de Monte Carlo, see Rosa Maria Malet, 'Jeux d'enfants' in *Miró en escena* (Barcelona: Fundació Joan Miró, 1994–95), pp. 71–116.

2 Jacques Dupin, *Miró* (Barcelona: Ediciones Polígrafa, 1993), p. 204.

works assault the tradition of *belle peinture*. Conceptually related to the artist's earlier efforts to 'assassinate' painting, Miró's 'shattered landscapes'[3] of July 1936 are charged with a defiant air of protest.

Eight years later, Miró looked back on the summer of 1936 as a period of deep spiritual and artistic crisis. 'Looking at the Masonite *Peintures*', he explained, 'you can see that I had already reached a very dangerous impasse from which I saw no possible way out. – The war broke out in July 1936 and made me interrupt my work and close myself into my spirit; the premonitions I had that summer and the need to keep my feet on the ground by using realism took shape in Paris with the still life of the shoe'.[4] Characteristically laconic, Miró discussed the Masonite panels in the same context as the Civil War, yet he was careful to avoid any implication of a direct, causal link between the series and political events. In the letter he merely suggests the proximity of his artistic crisis to the Spanish conflict, pointing to an entirely different work as his testimony to the violence in his homeland: *Still Life with Old Shoe* (fig. 20).

This painting, which carried Miró out of his aesthetic impasse, is, in the artist's words, a 'unique phenomenon'[5] in his artistic career. Executed between 24 January and 29 May 1937, during which time Miró was living in self-imposed exile in Paris, *Still Life with Old Shoe* is perhaps the artist's most complex and enigmatic artistic response to the Civil War. On a flat plane that is both a tabletop and a landscape, Miró assembled the humble protagonists of his drama: a bottle of gin wrapped in paper and cord; a fork driven into an apple; a half loaf of black bread; and the worn old shoe itself, sculpted by years of use. As Miró had forecast to his New York dealer Pierre Matisse four months earlier:

> I don't deny that one day I will plunge in again and set out on the discovery of a *profound* and *objective* reality of things, a reality that is neither superficial nor Surrealistic, but a deep poetic reality, an extrapictorial reality, if you will, in spite of pictorial and realistic appearances. The moving poetry that exists in the humblest things and the radiant spiritual forces that emanate from them.[6]

As these statements suggest, Miró's engagement with the most unassuming, familiar objects of the home at a time of social and political crisis speaks to his long-held belief that popular imagery constitutes the symbolic ground of national unity, continuity and endurance. Like van Gogh's famous *souliers*,

---

3 Ibid., p. 205.

4 Joan Miró, 'Working Notes, 1941–42', in Margit Rowell, ed., *Joan Miró: Selected Writings and Interviews* (Boston: G.K. Hall, 1986), p. 182.

5 Joan Miró, letter to James Thrall Soby dated 3 February 1953, in ibid., p. 232.

6 Joan Miró, letter to Pierre Matisse dated 28 September 1936, in ibid., p. 126. The remark is prefaced by Miró's indication that the Masonites from the summer would be completed by 15 October.

which Miró later remembered,[7] the tattered old shoe evokes a discrete human presence in the material world, just as the recurrent motif of the enlarged foot in Miró's work suggests the Catalan peasant's ancient ties to the land. As Miró once told James Johnson Sweeney: 'We Catalans believe you must always plant your feet firmly on the ground if you want to be able to jump up in the air'.[8] In *Still Life with Old Shoe*, however, any possibility of spiritual ascension is foreclosed by the oppressive and claustrophobic space of the painting. Miró's old shoe emerges as the protagonist of a drama whose most salient feature is its lack of transcendence.

Throughout, *Still Life with Old Shoe* is fraught with contradictions, a field of opposing forces that seems to close in upon the solid objects. Locked within cell-like pockets of space, the still life elements are isolated and disjoined. In contrast to the constellated structure that is a hallmark of Miró's art, in which signs are deployed in a relational network across unmarked grounds,[9] the space of Miró's still life is discontinuous and fragmented. Harsh, acidic colours create the effect of an unnatural, nocturnal conflagration, while the still life elements seem to irradiate an eerie glow from within. Few works in Miró's œuvre prepare us for the violent dissonance of this palette and the peculiar intensity of his use of light.

Clearly, Miró's self-described interest in recording the 'profound and objective reality of things' did not presuppose a return to naturalism in the traditional sense. If he employed the devices of illusionistic representation in *Still Life with Old Shoe* it was to emphasize the materiality and physical presence of objects in space without insisting on a mimetic relationship. At the same time, Miró's illusionism does not constitute a wholesale retreat from the more conceptual space of his earlier work, as epitomized by the *Peinture* series of 1933 (fig. 21). Indeed, the detailed rendering of the objects in *Still Life with Old Shoe* – observe the pitted crust and granular texture of the loaf of black bread – is set off by the artist's tendency to generalize and wilfully distort form elsewhere in the painting. And what about the nature of Miró's 'realism' in relation to the ways in which the subject of the painting appears to shift along a representational divide? If we view the painting as a landscape – the undulating line of the tabletop establishes an irregular horizon – the organic black forms that are distributed throughout the composition suggest ominous storm clouds or

7 Miró told Lluís Permanyer, 'I was very likely thinking about van Gogh's *Still Life with Boots* when I put in the old shoe'. Lluís Permanyer, 'Revelacions de Joan Miró sobre su obra', *Gaceta ilustrada* (23 April 1978), pp. 45–56, in ibid., p. 293.

8 James Johnson Sweeney, 'Joan Miró: Comment and Interview', *Partisan Review* XV:2 (1948), pp. 206–12, in ibid., p. 211.

9 For a recent discussion, see Margit Rowell, 'Joan Miró: Campo-Stella', in *Joan Miró: Campo de Estrellas* (Madrid: Museo Nacional Centro de Arte Reina Sofía, 1993), pp. 14–41.

deep shadows. If the landscape is read as a still life, however, these same forms suddenly resist unitary meanings. On the one hand, they appear to be fragments – residual traces of things – recalling the organic morphology of the *Peintures* of 1933, which were based on preparatory collages of industrial objects. On the other hand, these same shapes suggest tears in the visual field, a disruption in spatial syntax at the structural level that invites interesting comparisons with the technique of photomontage, to which I will return later. Herein lies the profound ambiguity of Miró's realism in *Still Life with Old Shoe*. As he crosses the boundary between still life and landscape, illusionistic representation and formal reduction, Miró brackets and ultimately suspends the terms of each pair in uncertainty. David Lomas refers to Miró's realism as a visionary negation of the real.[10] The artist's visionary imagination, I want to argue, is also a highly mediated form of social protest.

In saying this, I am making a broad interpretative leap from painting to politics, from aesthetics to social life. In what ways can Miró's still life be thought of as the artist's personal *and* political meditation on the tragic events of July 1936 through May 1937? Just how much do we need to know before Miró's still life discloses its relation to the Spanish conflict? The problem is compounded by the fact that Miró did not specifically address the Spanish Civil War in his painting, as did Picasso in *Guernica*.[11] However much Picasso's great mural has been interpreted as a statement of universal human suffering, its title and public display in the Spanish Republican Pavilion of the 1937 Paris World's Fair locate it within a clear social and historical context that continues to be politically charged for Spaniards today. Miró's still life, by comparison, is decidedly reticent. If, beyond the level of its peculiar iconography, it communicates something about social life at a time of crisis, it does so through the agency of form itself, through the terms of aesthetic conflict and contradiction I have identified above. The question to consider, then, is how social life can in*form* a work of art that actively resists – indeed, negates – didactic political content. In asking this question I want to propose that *Still Life with Old Shoe* is a highly mediated aesthetic interrogation that locates the relation of painting to politics within a wider field of cultural production. I will argue that contemporary debates on the social and political status of visual representation constitute the discursive arena in which Miró's tense drama unfolds.

---

10 David Lomas, 'Inscribing Alterity: Transactions of Self and Other in Miró's Self-Portraits', in Joanna Woodall, ed., *Portraiture: Facing the Subject* (Manchester: Manchester University Press, 1977), pp. 167–86.

11 Miró himself compared *Still Life with Old Shoe* to Picasso's painting. But, as he informed Lluís Permanyer, 'I wasn't aware that I was painting my Guernica [...]. What I do remember is that I was fully aware that I was painting something tremendously serious'. Permanyer interview, see note 7.

The critical reception of *Still Life with Old Shoe* sheds considerable light on the social implications of form in Miró's painting.[12] For the American abstract artist George L. Morris, writing in February 1938, Miró's return to a 'realist' mode of figuration was closely aligned with politics, much to the detriment of his work. Positioning the *Peinture* series of 1933 at the summit of Miró's career, Morris remarked:

> No one knows toward what end this development might have led, since the Civil War has obliterated the old creative approaches. [...] The works of these months are confused episodes in a welter of unabsorbed sense-impressions; he must leave Spain for a long contemplation in tranquility and gather up the meaning of the social upheavals that begin to make themselves felt. [...] It is now eight months since Miró recommenced his work in Paris. [...] For four months he works over a painting of his shoes, but he has not yet found the plastic expression to hold the change of viewpoint.[13]

Significantly, Morris's comments appeared in the progressive American journal *Partisan Review* just as Leftist writers and intellectuals were experiencing a profound disillusionment with ideological politics and the possibility of direct social action through art and literature. Numerous authors have charted the process through which the utopian promise of revolutionary politics in the mid-1930s was transferred to the aesthetic sphere by the end of the decade. The collapse of Léon Blum's Popular Front government in 1938; the ominous spectre of fascism in Central Europe and the West's shameful appeasement of Hitler; Stalin's brutal purges of artists and intellectuals in the Soviet Union; the devastating carnage of the Spanish Civil War; and, within the realm of advanced art and literature, relentless campaigns by the French, Spanish and Soviet Communist Parties to enlist art directly in the service of propaganda, were among the decisive events that left Marxists and Socialists alike demoralized.[14] As Leon Trotsky expressed it in a letter to André Breton dated 22 December 1938: 'The

---

12 With the exception of Jacques Dupin's comments, American criticism provides the most illuminating responses to Miró's painting. In 1937, after a brief showing in Paris in the exhibition 'Origines et développement de l'art international indépendant' at the Musée du Jeu de Paume, *Still Life with Old Shoe* was exhibited twice in 1938 at the Pierre Matisse Gallery, and subsequently entered into an American private collection. The painting was acquired by The Museum of Modern Art in 1969. For a complete provenance and exhibition history, see Lilian Tone, 'Catalogue' in Lanchner, *Joan Miró*, pp. 411–12.

13 George L.K. Morris, 'Art Chronicle: Miró and the Spanish Civil War', *Partisan Review* IV:3 (1938), pp. 32–33.

14 For a lucid account of the political and ideological debates that gripped the American Left in the mid–late 1930s, see T.J. Clark, 'Clement Greenberg's Theory of Art', and Fred Orton and Griselda Pollock, '*Avant-Gardes* and Partisans Reviewed', in Francis Frascina, ed., *Pollock and After: The Critical Debate* (New York: Harper and Row, 1985), pp. 47–64 and 167–84.

struggle for revolutionary ideas in art must begin once again with the struggle for artistic *truth* [...]. [T]ruly independent creation cannot but be revolutionary by its very nature, for it cannot but seek an outlet from intolerable social suffocation'.[15] If, however, Trotsky believed that advanced art might by its very nature be the bearer of revolutionary truth in a confused world by setting its sights *above* ideological politics, Morris played the trump card of formal purity against political and social responsibility. His criticism of Miró's 'unabsorbed sense-impressions' directly speaks to the imbrication of aesthetics and politics in *Still Life with Old Shoe* which, in his opinion, had diverted the Catalan artist from his 'true' path as a pure painter.

Morris was not alone in this damning criticism. On the occasion of Miró's first retrospective in 1941, at The Museum of Modern Art, James Johnson Sweeney similarly interpreted Miró's realism as a sign of his entry into the political arena. Noting that Miró had executed *Still Life with Old Shoe* in response to his 'suffering and the consciousness of a separation from his home', Sweeney lamented that Miró's 'decorative spirit' had temporarily yielded to illusionistic representation. In what today appears to be a remarkably impoverished reading of the painting, Sweeney adopted Morris's position. 'If [Miró's] conscience was in the effort', he asserted, 'certainly his heart was not'.[16]

By 1959, however, on the occasion of Miró's second retrospective at the museum, James Thrall Soby seemed less concerned with Miró's formal 'regression', than he was with questions of iconography. 'For the melancholy protest Miró wished to make against Spain's poverty and suffering', Soby asserted, 'a return to the realism of his early career must have seemed necessary'.[17] Soby went on to read the painting as a kind of allegory, in which the apple is 'savagely impaled' by the fork; the loaf of bread is configured in the form of a skull; and the old shoe itself is 'a symbol of need'.[18] Miró in turn both confirmed and denied such associations.[19] He later told Lluís Permanyer, 'I

15 Leon Trotsky to André Breton, 22 December 1938. Significantly, the letter appeared in translation in *Partisan Review* VI:2 (1939), pp. 126–27. On Trotsky's views on artistic independence and his involvement with the Fédération internationale de l'art révolutionnaire indépendant (FIARI), see note 120 below.

16 James Johnson Sweeney, *Joan Miró* (New York: The Museum of Modern Art, 1941), p. 68. For a discussion of the critical reception of Miró at The Museum of Modern Art, see Robert S. Lubar, 'Miró, Dalí and their American Critics in 1941', in *IV Jornades d'Estudis Catalano-Americans* (Barcelona: Generalitat de Catalunya, 1992), pp. 27–32.

17 James Thrall Soby, *Joan Miró* (New York: The Museum of Modern Art, 1959), p. 83.

18 Ibid., pp. 83 and 86.

19 Miró wrote to Soby on 3 February 1953: 'Despite the fact that while working on the painting I was thinking only about solving formal problems and getting back in touch with a reality that I was inevitably led to by current events, I later realized that without my knowing it this picture contained tragic symbols of the period – the

asked my wife to go and buy me an apple. I stuck a fork in it. When I did it, I wasn't thinking about the soldier sticking his bayonet into the enemy's body. I put in the fork because it was a utensil for eating the apple. I didn't intend the crust of bread to be a symbol of hunger'.[20] Characteristically taciturn about his own work, yet impatient with the literal interpretations advanced by his critics, Miró refused to elaborate on the question of art and politics.

How, then, are we to engage the painting in relation to the political events that frame it? Weighing the available evidence, Jacques Dupin rejects an interpretation of the artist's tragic expression as a 'vague testimony to human distress in general'.[21] Although the painting, for Dupin, 'does not illustrate an episode of the Civil War, does not even portray the horrors of war', he insists that 'it expresses all this, the artist's consciousness afflicted by all this even as he contemplates everyday objects'. *Still Life with Old Shoe*, he continues, 'is an appalling witness. [...] The scope of this work is greatly cut down unless the Spanish Civil War that underlies and motivates it is taken into account'.[22]

To read Miró's painting as an existential witness to a collective human tragedy is, of course, to emphasize a symbolically veiled allusion to the Civil War in relation to the artist's psychic alienation. There is no question that Miró's exile in Paris and the safety of his wife and daughter in Spain weighed heavily on his mind. Indeed, he executed a preparatory sketch for the painting – the only surviving study – on the front page of the 22 January 1937 issue of the Parisian daily *Le Jour* (fig. 22), which carried a story about the difficulties encountered by refugees in Madrid seeking asylum in foreign embassies.[23] But whether we see Miró's still life as a specific statement about *his* suffering, or that of the Spanish people in general, we must not forget that it is largely through the agency of style and competing representational codes that Miró stages his protest. This is all the more striking when we consider how Miró reversed the relation of sketch to painting that generally characterizes his working method as a process of distillation from the concrete to the abstract. In the preparatory drawing for *Still Life with Old Shoe*, Miró employed the same descriptive shorthand that he first used to configure the sign for a shoe in *The Family* of 1924 (fig. 23). In the final painting, however, the sign assumes the physical presence of an object in space.

---

tragedy of a miserable crust of bread and an old shoe, an apple pierced by a cruel fork and a bottle that, like a burning house, spread its flames across the entire surface of the canvas'. In Rowell, *Selected Writings and Interviews*, p. 232.

20 Lluís Permanyer, 'Revelacions de Joan Miró sobre su obra', in Rowell, *Selected Writings and Interviews*, p. 293.

21 Dupin, *Miró*, p. 211.

22 Ibid., pp. 210–11.

23 'Les Réfugiés dans les ambassades se verront-ils privés du droit d'asile?', *Le Jour* V:22 (1937). I am grateful to Laura Morowitz for locating this reference for me in Paris.

The interpretation of Miró's 'crisis' – of conscience and of representation – in relation to the Civil War is further complicated by the fact that the first signs of a change in his style, away from formal reduction and toward a renewed interest in modelling, came with a series of pastels in October 1934 (fig. 24).[24] At that time, as Dupin and others have remarked, Miró was deeply disturbed by recent political and social developments in France and Spain: an extreme right-wing demonstration in Paris that had escalated into a riot involving nationalists and Communist workers on 6 February 1934, paving the way for the emergence of the Popular Front government of Léon Blum two years later; increasing syndicalist agitation in Spain that culminated in the ill-fated Asturian Revolution in October of that year; and, closer to home, the temporary suspension of the Catalan Statute of Autonomy and the imprisonment of members of the Generalitat, the autonomous government of Catalonia.[25] As with the Masonite paintings of 1936, Miró's grotesque distortions of form, the tortured anatomies of his figures, and the unnatural lighting and glaring dissonance of his palette challenge the bourgeois tradition of *belle peinture*, but a specific relation to external events remains tenuous.

And yet there is a way in which Miró's art addresses social conflict with a degree of specificity, and, by the spring of 1937, speaks of the Civil War itself. With reference to *Still Life with Old Shoe*, Miró suggested that we look elsewhere to configure the relation of art to politics – not in terms of biography or an external referent, but within the structure of the painting itself. In a letter to James Thrall Soby of 1953, Miró stated unequivocally that his painting is 'entirely devoid of any narrative or literary intentions', and that he had confined

---

24 For a discussion of the pastels, see Dupin, *Miró*, pp. 186–89, who dates the pastels to the summer of 1934; and Lanchner, '*Peinture-Poésie*', p. 61. Both Lanchner and Anne Umland convincingly date the pastels to October of that year. See Anne Umland's authoritative chronology in the same catalogue, p. 331.

25 Catherine Freedberg, following Dupin's earlier dating of the pastels to the summer of 1934, suggests that they 'no doubt were generated in part by the increasingly open hostilities which led to the events of the fall'. Catherine Freedberg, *The Spanish Pavilion at the Paris World's Fair of 1937* (New York: Garland Publishers, 1986), p. 589, n. 57. Following Lanchner and Umland's chronology, a more direct link can now be established. The Asturian uprising was sparked by the entry of the Confederación Española de Derechas Autónomas into the Spanish government. As general strikes erupted throughout Spain and miners assumed control of villages and cities in Asturias, Lluís Companys declared an independent Catalan state. Martial law was imposed, and troops from North Africa were called in to quell the revolution. For a discussion of these events in relation to the increasing polarization of the Spanish left in the years of the *biennio negro*, see Gerald Brenan, *The Spanish Labyrinth: An Account of the Social and Political Background of the Spanish Civil War* (Cambridge and New York: Cambridge University Press, 1990); Raymond Carr, *Modern Spain: 1808–1975* (Oxford and New York: Oxford University Press, 1980); and Gabriel Jackson, *The Spanish Republic and the Civil War, 1931–1936* (Princeton: Princeton University Press, 1965).

himself 'solely to the external and human laws of art'.[26] Whereas Miró's friend Balthus had employed a related iconography of violent assault in an untitled still life of 1937 (fig. 25) – borrowing from Miró such details as the loaf of bread, and substituting a potato for the apple pierced by a fork – he conceived his painting within the traditional terms of allegory: the hammer and broken carafe represent conflict and rupture.[27] In *Still Life with Old Shoe*, however, Miró transferred that content to the gaps and breaks in the visual field; that is to say, he expressed the idea of conflict and rupture formally in relation to a visual structure that simultaneously figures and negates the real. In this reading, it is not politics and social life that *in*form Miró's great painting so much as the artist *per*forms – stages – a tense battle from within his own field of expertise: painting. Following Miró's advice to Sweeney, then, I want to suggest that painting is a form of social praxis for Miró, and with that observation consider how pictorial space can be a powerful metaphor for the space of political action. For as Miró himself insisted, *Still Life with Old Shoe* is an image of conflict that is enacted through the language of form; its meanings are secured in the contested ground of representation at a precise historical juncture.

The events of 1936 definitively polarized the avant-garde in France and Spain, which had entered into a period of political and ideological crisis. At issue was the position of avant-garde art in bourgeois society, the commitment of the artist to revolutionary action, and the actual form that commitment would assume in works of art. Miró, I want to argue, makes over the crisis of aesthetic ideology as form, locating his work in the space *between* aesthetics and politics. If we view Miró's still life as an ideological rather than a literal landscape, the artist's 'tragic realism' no longer emerges as a regression to illusionistic painting, but as a discursive strategy in a debate that pits political against aesthetic action. The symbolic ground of politics, the trace of which is contained in the newspaper fragment of the preparatory sketch, is reconfigured as form through the very activity of painting.[28] To insist that *Still Life with Old Shoe* is

---

26 Miró to James Thrall Soby, as in note 5.

27 Balthus and Miró were on close personal terms at this time and under contract to the Parisian dealer Pierre Loeb. A connection between the two paintings was first made by Sabine Rewald, who notes that Miró painted *Still Life with Old Shoe* on the second floor of the Galerie Pierre, where both he and Balthus exhibited. Sabine Rewald, *Balthus* (New York: The Metropolitan Museum of Art and Harry N. Abrams, Inc., 1984), p. 84. Given the specificity of Miró's iconography in relation to his early work, it is likely that Balthus's still life was a response to Miró's.

28 To the extent that the form of the black 'cloud' in the upper right-hand quadrant may have been suggested by the configuration of the word 'Le' in the masthead of the newspaper, Miró seems to have returned to a working method he first adopted in the *Portrait of Queen Louise of Prussia* of 1929, in which an advertisement for a diesel motor provided the initial point of departure for the image of the queen. Four years later, Miró again used this technique to great effect in the *Peinture* series.

not directly *engagé* does not mean that Miró's painting cannot be understood in relation to politics, and to debates on the status of a political art in France and Spain.[29] *Still Life with Old Shoe* is, in the most profound sense, an ideological and aesthetic battlefield.

* * *

The outbreak of the Civil War on 18 July 1936 seems to have caught Miró by surprise. Writing to Pierre Matisse from Montroig on 15 August, Miró indicated that he had gone to Barcelona 'to find out more about the actual situation'.[30] Among Miró's concerns, the welfare of his wife Pilar and daughter Maria Dolors were foremost on his mind.[31] Sometime before 28 October, Miró returned to Paris in advance of his family.[32] In a letter to Matisse dated 16 November, he expressed concern that his wife had encountered difficulties with her passport. At the same time, the letter suggests that Miró was optimistic that the hostilities would end in the near future: 'I don't know whether I will stay here and wait for the storm to die down or whether I will return to Spain'.[33] However, by March 1937, as Margit Rowell has remarked, Miró was reconciled to the fact that his return to Spain, where he hoped to continue works in progress, would have to be postponed indefinitely.[34] Faced with self-imposed exile in Paris and an

29 To my knowledge, Catherine Freedberg was the first author generally to consider Miró's return to a more traditional mode of figuration in his work of 1936–38 in relation to the artist's 'liberal yet essentially apolitical attitude'. Freedberg discusses Miró's particular aversion to the politicization of culture in France and Spain at the time of the Civil War. Freedberg, *The Spanish Pavilion*, chapter VII. In her unpublished doctoral thesis Elizabeth Higdon likewise draws attention to these issues. She does not, however, examine the Spanish context in any depth, nor does she consider the possibility that Miró's *Still Life with Old Shoe* represents a dialectical critique of both revolutionary and bourgeois culture through a bracketing of aesthetic codes. Instead, Higdon assumes a Freudian model to analyze Miró's expression of psychic torment and despair in his painting, which she interprets as a projection of psychic repression and melancholy in symbolic form. Elizabeth G. Higdon, 'Joan Miró's Self-Portraits: Context and Content' (Bryn Mawr College, PhD dissertation, October 1981), pp. 48–51.

30 Umland, 'Chronology', p. 332.

31 Miró to Pierre Matisse, letters of 16 November 1936, 14 December 1936 and 18 December 1936, in Rowell, *Selected Writings and Interviews*, pp. 130–34.

32 Umland, 'Chronology', p. 332.

33 A month later, following the arrival of Pilar and Maria Dolors in Paris, Miró again seemed optimistic that the hostilities would soon end: 'We are going to remain in Paris until life returns to normal in Catalonia', he informed Matisse. Letters to Pierre Matisse from Paris, 16 November 1936 and 18 December 1936, in Rowell, *Selected Writings and Interviews*, pp. 130–34.

34 Miró to Pierre Matisse, letters of 12 January and 7 March 1937, in ibid., pp. 145–48. As Rowell notes, the letter of 12 January suggests that Miró realized his exile would be prolonged. As late as 7 April 1938, Miró remained optimistic. In a letter to Matisse from Paris, he stated: 'The situation in Spain is very agonizing, but far from

interruption in the rhythm of his work, Miró had already informed Matisse on 12 January:

> [...] I have decided to do something absolutely different; I am going to begin doing *very realistic* still lifes. I was already thinking of doing that, *but later*, and alternating with other things in which I would have attempted to escape reality entirely – and create a new reality, with new figures and fantasmagoric beings, but ones filled with life and reality. [...] We are living through a terrible drama, everything happening in Spain is terrifying in a way you could never imagine. I feel very uprooted here and am nostalgic for my country.[35]

Twelve days later, Miró began *Still Life with Old Shoe*.[36]

In Miró's first clear reference to the painting, a letter to Pierre Matisse dated 12 February 1937, he discussed his personal *and* aesthetic motivations:

> It is somewhat reminiscent of *The Farm* and *Table with Glove* – less anecdotal than the first and more powerful than the second. No sentimentalism. Realism that is far from being photographic, and also far from the realism exploited by some of the Surrealists. Profound and fascinating reality. [...] As I had already suggested to you, this idea has been cooking in my mind for some time. *An inner necessity*, not at all to show off and prove that I can paint, which would be a *pretentious* and *tendentious* society game.[37]

Miró's language in the letter is telling. He talks about the 'inner necessity' that informs his vision, which he carefully qualifies in oppositional terms: neither photographic realism nor the veristic approach maintained by several of the leading Surrealists. But this oddly banal expression also serves an important rhetorical function in that it underscores Miró's refusal to enlist his painting in the direct service of politics and thereby compromise his voice as an independent artist. In this light the terms 'exploited' and 'photographic' are

---

being desperate, we have the firm hope that some event will take place to tip the balance in our favor'. Ibid., p. 159. By 2 January 1939, Miró realized that the situation was hopeless. In an unpublished letter to Matisse, he was preoccupied with the safety of his mother in Montroig. On 16 January 1939, Matisse responded to Miró: 'Hier j'ai lu que les Rebels avaient pris Montroig et j'ai fait des voeux pour les votres aient été [sains chaufs]. On se demande à quel degré d'aberration les français sont tombés pour laisser une pareille chose se produire'. On 26 January 1939, Franco's troops entered Barcelona. Pierre Matisse Archives, New York (courtesy of Anne Umland).

35 Miró to Pierre Matisse, letter of 7 March 1939, in Rowell, *Selected Writings and Interviews*, p. 148.

36 Among the other problems Miró had to negotiate was securing suitable lodgings and a working space in Paris. The Miró family lived in the Hôtel Récamier in January and February 1937, before moving into a studio at 98 Boulevard August Blanqui some time before 7 March. In the interim, Miró had begun painting *Still Life with Old Shoe* on the mezzanine of Pierre Loeb's gallery.

37 Miró to Pierre Matisse, letter of 12 February 1937, in Rowell, *Selected Writings and Interviews*, pp. 146–47.

likely veiled allusions to the Surrealists' decade-long equivocations over the issue of art and revolutionary action, as the French Communist Party relentlessly sought to censure and control the form and content of their work. When further on in the same letter Miró cites actual models for his conception of realism in *Still Life with Old Shoe*, his references are more universal and hermetic: the Spanish naturalist tradition of Velázquez and the visionary imagination of Redon and the Symbolists.[38] Similarly, when Miró discusses *Still Life with Old Shoe* in relation to his early work, specifically citing *Table with Glove* of 1921 (fig. 26) and *The Farm* of 1922, it is to emphasize continuity in his aesthetic approach and thereby discourage political readings. In both paintings, Miró had established a related tension between flatness and surface detail, between spatial compression and illusionistic modelling. Yet it must also be observed that the explosive force of *Still Life with Old Shoe* raises this tension to an unprecedented level, so much so that formal comparisons with the earlier paintings seem tenuous at best.[39] In the end, Miró's reference to *Table with Glove* and *The Farm* defines a symbolic as much as a stylistic association, as *The Farm*, in particular, embodies what Carolyn Lanchner has described as 'the essential nature of his identity',[40] one rooted in the rural experience of the Catalan landscape. In this reading, both *The Farm* and *Still Life with Old Shoe* constitute portrait-landscapes.[41]

---

38 Miró informed Matisse: 'I am going to push this painting to the limit, for I *want* it to hold up against a good still life by Velázquez'. Quoting Redon, he added: ' "My most fertile routine, the one most necessary to my development, is to copy reality directly, attentively reproducing the objects of external nature in their most particular and accidental aspects. After making the effort to do a meticulous copy of a pebble, a blade of grass, a hand or a profile, I then need to let myself go to the representation of an imaginary world. Nature, thus measured out and infused, becomes my source, my leaven, my ferment" [Redon]'. Ibid., p. 147. On the significance of Velázquez as a model for Spanish painting at this time, see Josep Renau's important essay 'Función social del cartel publicitario', published in the April and May 1937 issues of *Nueva Cultura*, in which he declares: 'Velázquez es el pintor más profundamente español, y a través de la ambición cósmica que emana de su arte, el más universal de su época. A través de su verbo espontáneo, la entraña popular española que vibra como condición suprema en toda nuestra plástica realista, se recrea al sentirse reflejada'. In his efforts to create a public popular art, realist in form and anchored in the Spanish tradition, Renau upheld Velázquez as a moral paradigm for contemporary Spanish artists. Josep Renau, *Función social del cartel publicitario* (Valencia: Editorial J. Doménech, 1976).

39 Miró had occasion to reflect upon his early work at this time, as Pierre Loeb had acquired all the paintings that had figured in his first Paris exhibition in 1921, and was preparing to show them again in the late spring of 1937. The exhibition ran from 28 May–15 June 1937. In an unpublished letter to Pierre Matisse dated 6 April 1937, Miró kept his New York dealer apprised of Loeb's plans. Pierre Matisse Archives, New York (courtesy of Anne Umland).

40 Lanchner, '*Peinture-Poésie*', p. 69.

41 For a discussion, see Higdon, 'Joan Miró's Self Portraits'.

If these comments indicate that Miró was deliberately vague about the question of political content in *Still Life with Old Shoe*, there is another reference in the letter to Pierre Matisse which locates a different kind of discourse operating at the surface of Miró's painting in relation to aesthetics, politics and the Spanish Civil War. Commenting on the forthcoming publication of an interview with Georges Duthuit, Miró informed Pierre Matisse: 'I express myself very violently and strike out very hard at the things we are fed up with. You will readily see who and what I am striking out against, and I'm sure that you will share most of my opinions'.

Duthuit's text appeared in the May 1937 issue of *Cahiers d'Art*.[42] It is impossible to establish with certainty the date of the interview, although it clearly occurred before the 12 February letter to Matisse. Miró had returned to Paris by 28 October 1936, where he was to remain. Duthuit's reference to Spain, and Miró's reticence to discuss political events, suggest that the interview was granted in the autumn or winter of 1936. Given the fact that Miró tended to keep Pierre Matisse informed of recent developments in his life and work, it is likely that the interview was conducted sometime in January or early February 1937. In response to Miró's comment 'Our generation lacks heroism and a deeply revolutionary spirit', Duthuit interjected, 'It seems to me that in Spain, however ...'. Miró apparently did not allow Duthuit to complete the sentence, as he quickly retorted, 'I am confining myself exclusively to the realm of painting'. This is not to say, however, that Miró viewed painting as an end in itself, for he emphatically condemned the doctrine of aestheticism. He rhetorically asked Duthuit:

> Have you ever heard of anything more stupid than 'abstraction-abstraction'? And they ask me into their deserted house, as if the marks I put on a canvas did not correspond to a concrete representation of my mind, did not possess a profound reality, were not a part of the real itself.

For Miró, the problem was to engage social life through the rhetoric of form; to use the languages of painting to articulate the artist's position in society.

But exactly how could the formal means of painting communicate that content? Were its languages disinterested, or did they come to the artist already laden with heavy ideological and political baggage? Miró's reference to 'abstraction-abstraction' – by which he means the Abstraction-Création group formed by Herbin, Vantongerloo and Hélion in February 1931 – provides important clues. In a letter dated 15 April 1933, Miró's friend Hélion had invited him to participate in a group exhibition with Arp, Calder, Pevsner and Séligmann: 'Nous avons l'intention d'apporter tous nos soins à ce que cette

42 Georges Duthuit, 'Où allez-vous Miró?', *Cahiers d'Art* XI:8–10 (1936); in Rowell, *Selected Writings and Interviews*, pp. 150–55. As Rowell observes, the 1936 date is misleading, as the interview did not appear until May 1937.

exposition soit la meilleure qu'elle puisse être', Hélion wrote, 'la mieux annoncée et à amener le plus grand nombre possible de ceux que s'intéressent à la peinture libre. [...] C'est une exposition purement et simplement, mais quand tout tourne à la marmelade photographique, elle prendra d'elle-même une allure de protestation'.[43] Miró agreed to participate. A year later, however, he had a change of heart about the group. In a letter to Christian Zervos dated 2 June 1934, he remarked: 'Je viens de répondre à Hélion en m'excusant de ne pas exposer avec eux. Arp et lui le sont fort sympathiques, vous le savez bien, mais [...] en tant que groupe, ça sent trop abstraction création, dont le seul nom me fiche le caffard'.[44] Miró's disdain for the tenets of abstract art are apparent in a letter to Matisse dated 12 October 1934, in which he gives Matisse permission to choose titles for recent works, 'based on the *real things* my works might suggest to you, provided these titles do not evoke some tendency or other, something I want to avoid completely: "composition", for example (which evokes the Abstraction-Création group), or literary titles in the Surrealist manner'.[45] Clearly, the 'freedom' of an art of pure form was anathema to Miró.[46]

So too were academic painting and traditional forms of figuration. Miró wrote to Man Ray on 15 August 1934, asking for a photograph to publish in the special Christmas issue of the Catalan magazine *D'Ací i d'Allà*: 'Il faudrait que ce soit une chose *très réaliste*', he informed his friend, 'une tête par exemple, pour pouvoir l'opposer à la peinture soit-disant réaliste – dans le sens banal du mot – et pouvoir [...] démontrer la faiblesse et l'idiotie de celle-ci'.[47] As his instructions to Man Ray suggest, Miró refused to position himself within narrow aesthetic frames, especially when they were enlisted in the service of dogmatic

43 Umland, 'Chronology', p. 330. I am grateful to Anne Umland for providing me with a transcript of the unpublished text.

44 Excerpted in *Vente à Paris – Drouot-Richelieu*, 19 April 1991, no. 475; cited by Umland, 'Chronology', pp. 355, n. 452. Umland notes that Miró's work was nonetheless included in the exhibition 'Abstract and Concrete: An Exhibition of Abstract Painting and Sculpture, 1934 and 1935', Oxford, England, 15–22 February 1936, although the work was probably lent by a private collector.

45 Letter to Pierre Matisse, in Rowell, *Selected Writings and Interviews*, p. 124. Several months earlier, when a number of Miró's canvases from the *peinture* series of 1933 were exhibited at the Pierre Matisse Gallery as 'compositions', Miró complained. See Miró's letter to Pierre Matisse dated 7 February 1934, in ibid., p. 124.

46 The very day Miró wrote to Zervos, Fernandez, Arp, Sophie Tauber, and Hélion sent a letter to Otto Freundlich informing him of their resignation from the Abstraction-Création group: 'We are giving you notice that yesterday we sent to Herbin our letter of resignation as members of Abstraction-Création, because we do not agree with him on either the way he works in a committee or the line he wants the association to follow'. Cited by Christian Derouet, 'Kandinsky in Paris: 1934–1944', in *Kandinsky in Paris* (New York: The Solomon R. Guggenheim Museum, 1985), p. 44, n. 109.

47 Unpublished. Archives Centre Georges Pompidou, Paris (courtesy of Anne Umland). For Man Ray's views on photographic Surrealism as a confrontation with social reality, see Man Ray, 'Sur le réalisme photographique', *Cahiers d'Art* X:5–6 (1935), p. 120.

theoretical platforms and partisan ideologies. For at stake in the programmes advanced by the Surrealists, the Abstraction-Création group, and especially in the political uses of traditional forms of figuration in the years preceding the outbreak of the Civil War, was nothing less than an interpretation of the artist's position in society. If Miró singled out Abstraction-Création for criticism in 1936 it is because painting had attained an unprecedented level of moral and political urgency in the aftermath of the February 1934 riots, which publicly exposed the ominous spectre of fascism in France. The need to define the social position of contemporary art in relation to the masses occasioned Christian Zervos to ask a diverse group of artists a year later, 'Est-il permis au créateur de conditionner son effort d'après les possibilités spirituelles de la multitude, ou doit-il, au contraire, étendre sa pensée à l'extrême, la rendre multiple, afin qu'elle puisse exercer sur les spectateurs sa force d'attraction et les élever, selon leurs capacités, à une compréhension plus approfondie du monde visible?'[48] In this context, the position advanced by the Abstraction-Création group represented a utopian model of culture predicated on the idea of formal purity as a moral paradigm. Miró's sense of himself as an artist in the world was not compatible with the group's aesthetic idealism.[49] However, the idea of an art in the direct service of politics proved equally problematic. Not without a note of concern over his friend's entry into the debate, Pierre Matisse responded to Miró's comments on the Duthuit interview:

> A que vous me dites de l'article de Zervos m'a fait beaucoup réflexion. Je vois les choses d'un peu loin ici et je me demande si cela est si nécessaire de batailler ainsi, d'autant plus que cela ne servira pas à grand chose. [...] Je vous dis tout cela mon cher Miró parce que ce genre de manifestation est dangereux pour un peintre. L'action d'un peintre est tellement plus puissante dans sa peinture. Regardez Picasso par exemple! Il ne parle jamais, ne donne jamais d'interview mais quelle force sa peinture ne prend-elle pas![50]

* * *

The Duthuit interview did not represent Miró's first public declaration of his 'political' position. In February 1929 André Breton, Louis Aragon and Raymond Queneau had circulated a letter asking their colleagues for a position statement

48 Z[ervos], C[hristian], 'Enquête', *Cahiers d'Art* X:1–4 (1935), pp. 6–7 and 9.

49 Miró's position was by no means unique. As early as 1931, Tériade published a survey in *Cahiers d'Art* in which he asked a number of 'abstract' painters – including Mondrian, Léger, Arp and Kandinsky – to defend their work against the accusation that abstract painting was excessively cerebral and decorative. See 'Enquête', *Cahiers d'Art* VI:1, 3, 4, 7–8 (1931), pp. 41–43, 151–52, 215–16, 350–53.

50 Unpublished letter from Pierre Matisse to Miró, 2 [5?] February 1937. Pierre Matisse Archives, New York (courtesy of Anne Umland).

on the effectiveness of communal versus individual activity. Miró's ambiguous response is indicative of the distance he maintained from the political position of Surrealism, which Breton was to define later that year in the *Second Surrealist Manifesto*. Miró stated:

> There is no doubt that when action is taken, it is always the result of a collective effort. Nevertheless, I am convinced that individuals whose personalities are strong or excessive, unhealthy perhaps, deadly if you like – that is not the question here – these people will never be able to give in to the military-like discipline that communal action necessarily demands.[51]

Over the next six years, Miró observed from a distance the political evolution of Surrealism, as the movement entered into a difficult and ill-fated relationship with the Communist Party. From Louis Aragon's first repudiation of Freudianism and 'all idealist ideologies' following the 1930 Second International Congress of Revolutionary Writers in Kharkov; through the so-called 'Aragon Affair' of 1931; the Party's move to censure Salvador Dalí for his 'amoral' and 'counterrevolutionary' text 'Réverie', which appeared in the December 1931 issue of *Le Surréalisme au service de la révolution*; and the Surrealists' break with the Association des ecrivains et artistes révolutionnaires[52] late in 1933 over the question of a proletarian art and literature – through all this the difficulty in cementing a direct alliance between art and the Party had become apparent. At issue was whether the proletarian revolution and the Surrealist revolution in consciousness were compatible, and precisely what form a revolutionary art would have to assume.[53] With the official adoption of Socialist Realism at the First Congress of Soviet Writers in August–September 1934, the Party insisted upon aesthetic orthodoxy. Still, André Breton believed some form of reconciliation was possible. In his 1934 essay, *Qu'est-ce que c'est le surréalisme?*, he explained:

---

51 Joan Miró, 'Statement', *Le Surréalisme en 1929*, special issue of *Variétés* (June 1929), p. xi, in Rowell, *Selected Writings and Interviews*, p. 108.

52 The AEAR was founded in 1932 as the French section of the Union Internationale des Ecrivains Révolutionnaires (UIER), under the patronage of the Communist International. It fostered a broad-based alliance of leftist artists and writers regardless of political or aesthetic affiliation in an attempt to build a united intellectual and cultural front under the watchful eyes of the Communist Party. The literary mouthpiece of the AEAR was the monthly journal *Commune*, which began publication in 1933.

53 Hal Foster has recently argued that Breton's ' "early Marxian" account of the human subject [came] into tension with the "late Freudian" one', as the Surrealists' investigation of the death drive in works of the 1930s posed a significant challenge to the principles of utopian Marxism and the promise of future liberation. This tension is visible in Breton's increasingly difficult negotiations with the Party, as evidenced by the Dalí scandal, cited above. Hal Foster, *Compulsive Beauty* (Cambridge and London: MIT, 1993), pp. 1–17.

> We hold the liberation of man to be the *sine qua non* condition of the *liberation of the mind*, and we expect the liberation of man to result only from the proletarian revolution. The two problems are essentially distinct, and we deplore their becoming confused [...]. There is good reason, then, to take up a stand against all attempts to weld them together and, more especially, against the urge to abandon all such researches as ours in order to devote ourselves to the poetry and art of propaganda.[54]

By June 1935, at the Congrès International des Ecrivains pour la Défense de la Culture,[55] all hope of reconciliation was shattered. Following the events of February 1934, leftist intellectuals had become acutely aware of the need to forge an alliance with the middle classes in the fight against fascism, a move which the Surrealists interpreted as a setback for international socialism. The Franco-Soviet Pact of May 1935 confirmed their worst fears of political rapprochement, and the Surrealists suspected that the writer's congress had been timed precisely to garner support among intellectuals for the pact.[56] On both the question of a proletarian art and the idea of a broad-based 'defence of culture', the Surrealists registered a loud voice of dissent to what they perceived to be an untenable and contradictory situation.

Although Miró continued to participate in Surrealist group exhibitions, and remained on good terms with Breton through the 1930s,[57] he never joined the French Communist Party.[58] Unlike Dalí, who signed a collective document in December 1932 establishing specific guidelines for the Surrealists' collaboration with the bourgeois press,[59] Miró viewed with suspicion Breton's attempts to maintain political orthodoxy within the movement. Indeed, Miró had been

---

54 André Breton, 'What is Surrealism?', in *What is Surrealism? Selected Writings*, ed. Franklin Rosemont (London: Pluto, 1978), p. 128.

55 The Congress was convened in Paris by Henri Barbusse, with André Gide as President. Among the participants were Louis Aragon, Bertold Brecht, Aldous Huxley, André Malraux and Heinrich Mann.

56 For a discussion of Surrealism and the Party, see Helena Lewis, *The Politics of Surrealism* (New York: Paragon House, 1988); and François Moulignat, 'Les artistes en France, face à la guerre d'Espagne et la montée du fascisme, 1936–1939', in *Thèse de Doctorat de Trosième Cycle* (Paris: Université de Paris I, February 1977).

57 On Miró's relationship with Breton, see Margit Rowell, 'André Breton et Joan Miró', in *André Breton: La Beauté convulsive* (Paris: Musée national d'art moderne/Centre Georges Pompidou, 1991), pp. 179–82.

58 Responding to Georges Raillard's observation that he appeared to have distanced himself from the Communist Party affiliations of Breton and Aragon, Miró stated: 'Je n'ai pas coupé ... Simplement je ne me suis pas inscrit. Ca n'empêche pas que je pensais que tous ensemble, les poètes, les cinéastes, les peintres, pouvaient faire quelque chose en faveur de la révolution'. Georges Raillard, *Joan Miró: Ceci est la couleur de mes rêves* (Paris: Seuil, 1977), p. 176.

59 On Dalí's adherence to the political position of Surrealism, see Rafael Santos Torroella, *Salvador Dalí: Corresponsal de J.V. Foix, 1932–1936* (Barcelona: Editorial Mediterràànea, 1986), pp. 12–17.

rebuked by the Surrealists – notably Dalí – for his collaboration on *Jeux d'enfants*, just as he had been criticized in 1926 for his work with Max Ernst on *Romeo and Juliette*. In a letter to the Catalan art critic Sebastià Gasch, Dalí expressed his contempt for Miró's involvement with spectacular culture: 'What a shame that it involves a ballet, again. By this fact alone, Miró's work, no matter how good, will cease to be subversive, given the abominable significance of this type of artistic amusement'.[60] Gasch responded to Dalí in print,[61] ridiculing the painter's political pretences. Insults were exchanged, occasioning a definitive break between the two men.[62] Miró also seems to have distanced himself from Dalí at this time.[63]

Similarly, within Breton's inner circle the problem of a proletarian art in the service of the revolution had created deep ideological divisions. However much his comments to Miró suggest that he towed the Surrealist party line, it was in fact Dalí who refused to get in line. Following his return from Kharkov, Louis Aragon condemned Dalí's eccentric activities,[64] complicating Breton's already

60 Gasch published excerpts from the letter in 'L'Esperit Nou', *La Publicitat* (15 April 1932). The article is reprinted in ibid., pp. 171–72.

61 Gasch, 'L'Esperit Nou'.

62 The complete events and related documents are discussed by Torroella, *Salvador Dalí: Corresponsal*, pp. 32, 65–67, 71–74; and Joan M. Minguet Batllori, 'Salvador Dalí i Sebastià Gasch: Una amistat truncada', in *Cloenda dels actes commemoratius del centenari Sebastià Gasch* (Barcelona: KRTU, 1999). In a letter of circa 30 June 30–1 July 1932, Dalí communicated his displeasure with Miró's ballet to the poet J.V. Foix: 'it is distressing to see Miró's magnificent intuition used for the most exquisite, artistic and boring spectacle that is, now more than ever, the Ballets Russes'.

63 Some time after Gasch's article appeared, Dalí wrote a somewhat disingenuous letter to Miró which in effect asked him to condemn the critic's dismissal of Surrealism's revolutionary political position ('It is the most rotten kind of art of the literary group', Gasch had written), just as he warned Miró that his collaboration with the Ballets Russes jeopardized their friendship and Miró's standing with the Surrealists: 'Dear Miro, I suppose you shall have already read Gasch's article, where he exposes his appreciation for Surrealism. I hope that after these objections you will break off relations with this personage, who is more compromised than anybody else in Catalonia. He is as dense as a house. The news of the "ballet" has hardly pleased the Surrealists but I don't think there will be grave consequences. I hope you will respond as quickly as possible concerning your views about Gasch, as our friendship and probably that of all our friends is at stake'. Dalí to Miró, undated correspondence of 1932. Archives of the Fundació Pilar i Joan Miró a Mallorca.

64 In addition to the controversy sparked by Dalí's text 'Rêverie', Aragon derided Dalí's artistic production. When Dalí presented a project for his first Surrealist object – a woman's evening pump containing a glass of lukewarm milk that was to be placed in the centre of a semi-soft paste the colour of excrement – Aragon was indignant: 'Finies les excentricités de Dalí! Le lait chaud sera pour les enfants des chômeurs'. For a discussion, see José Pierre, 'Dalí, Hitler, Lénine ... et Breton', in *Salvador Dalí Rétrospective: 1920–1980* (Paris: Musée national d'art moderne/Centre Georges Pompidou, 1979), p. 134. The text in which Dalí discusses the project, 'Objets surréalistes' (1931), is reprinted in Salvador Dalí, *Oui: Methode paranoïaque et autres textes* (Paris: Editions Denoel, 1971), p. 196.

difficult negotiations with the French Communist Party.[65] Three years later, as Breton sought to define unequivocally the political position of Surrealism in response to the rise of fascism, the appearance of Hitlerian imagery in Dalí's work caused great concern. On 15 February 1934 a special meeting was convened at Breton's apartment in which the artist, risking expulsion, had to defend himself against the accusation of 'actes contre-révolutionnaires tendant à la glorification du fascisme hitlérien', an opportunity which Dalí skilfully turned to his advantage.[66] With an unmistakable note of cynicism, Dalí remarked to the poet Josep Vicenç Foix the following August: 'There is nothing more abject than poetry "applied" to propaganda, whether patriotic, marxist, hitlerian, etc.'.[67]

By the summer of 1936, with the Moscow Trials underway and the Civil War advancing rapidly in Spain, the Parisian avant-garde entered into a period of moral crisis. The charge of elitism levelled at abstract art was the subtext of a series of debates on 'Le Réalisme et la Peinture' organized by the Maison de la Culture in Paris[68] in May and June of 1936, and published the following July as *La Querelle du Réalisme*.[69] The debates focused on two key questions: (i) Is the revolutionary

65 For a discussion, see Maurice Nadeau, *The History of Surrealism*, trans. Richard Howard (Harmondsworth, England: Penguin Books, 1973, 1978), pp. 182–98; 208–15; and Lewis, *The Politics of Surrealism*, pp. 77–119.

66 For a discussion of the complete events surrounding this incident, see José Pierre, 'Dalí, Hitler, Lénine ... et Breton', pp. 134–38; and Karin Von Maur, 'Breton et Dalí, à la lumière d'une corréspondance inédite', in *André Breton: La Beauté convulsive*, pp. 196–202.

67 Letter from Dalí to Foix, August 1934; in Santos Torroella, *Salvador Dalí: Corresponsal*, pp. 131–32. A year later, Dalí in turn singled out the members of Abstraction-Création and non-figurative artists in general as 'Sticky and retardian Kantians of scatological sections d'or [who] continue to want to offer us upon the fresh optimism of their shiny paper, the soup of abstract aesthetics ...'. Salvador Dalí, *Conquest of the Irrational* (New York: Julian Levy, 1935).

68 The Association des Maisons de la Culture was founded in 1935 to advance artistic practice within the political and ideological guidelines established by its sister organization, the Association des Ecrivains et Artistes Révolutionnaires. As the parent organization for individual Maisons de la Culture in cities throughout France (by 1936 there were approximately 60), it sponsored a wide range of cultural programmes, including exhibitions, dramatic events, literary and artistic conferences, and the publication of bulletins, magazines and brochures. Louis Aragon served as general secretary of the Association, which promoted the 'politique d'ouverture' of the Parti communiste français working in collaboration with the Front Populaire. For a discussion, see Moulignat, 'Les artistes en France, face à la guerre d'Espagne', pp. 24–31.

69 Transcriptions of the debates were supplemented in the book by a quotation from Daumier, Courbet's text on *The Artist's Studio*, and excerpts from an *enquête* conducted by René Crevel which appeared in the May and June 1935 issues of *Commune* under the title 'Où va la peinture?' Francesca Dal Lago, in 'The Ambiguity of Objectivity: Realism and Politics in French Art of the 1930s' (unpublished Qualifying Paper for the Institute of Fine Arts, New York University, 1994), also notes that the book contained additional excerpts from a lecture by Crevel at the Maison on 9 May 1935, and

art of today to be realistic or non-realistic? and (ii) If realistic, what form(s) would this art assume? As responses by invited artists and writers immediately demonstrated, the term realism itself could be attached to a broad range of aesthetic positions on both the Left and the Right within Naturalist, Expressionist, and Surrealist camps. More importantly, the position of revolutionary art in bourgeois society and its role in a global process of historical and social transformation was at stake. Could an art that did not have its roots in the ascendant class properly be called revolutionary? To what extent could the forms of bourgeois representation be adapted to revolutionary subject matter? Was bourgeois culture the precondition for socialist culture within the dialectical movement of history, or would transformations in social relations give rise to changes in modes of representation? Would painting reflect contemporary social life transparently, or become a site of intervention in which viewers actively participate in the construction of history? And what of the position of works of art espousing a revolutionary political tendency within the dominant modes of production in capitalist society? Was not the functional transformation of the institutional apparatus in which works of art are produced and circulate a necessary consideration? Finally, amidst the hope and optimism that the election of the Front Populaire generated in June 1936, the question of an accessible, high culture for the masses resulted in a sustained debate on the tradition of easel painting versus public (mural) art at the Maison de la Culture. As Anthony Blunt summarized the situation in his review of *La Querelle du Réalisme* in April 1937:

> [...] the most important feature of the whole quarrel is that there is a growing number of artists in France who are no longer prepared to regard painting as a kind of game, but believe that it is, in the phrase of Lurçat, 'an aggressive activity'; who regard the painter as, above all, 'a transformer of energy'; who will not be content to let the painter deal only with still-life and so confine himself to statements about a fruit-to-man relation, but demand that he shall deal rather with the central realities of his period; who believe that 'corn, bread, copulation, revolution, water, space are not small, dirty and unworthy ideas, and that painting has no right to be coy in front of such solid problems.'[70]

---

a report by Léon Moussinac on the debate 'Le Peintre devant le "sujet" ', which had originally been published in *Commune*, no. 21 (1935). As Dal Lago astutely comments, 'the title *La Querelle du Réalisme* is very much a fictional term that does not correspond to a specific event, but refers instead to the widespread discussions surrounding the issue at the time', just as the noun *querelle* conveys the heated atmosphere surrounding the 1936 debates. For a recent reprint of the 1936 edition, see Serge Fauchereau, ed., *La Querelle du Réalisme* (Paris: Editions Cercle d'Art, 1987).

70 Anthony Blunt, 'The "Realism" Quarrel', *Left Review* (London) III (1937), pp. 169–71. I am grateful to Larissa Bailiff for bringing this review to my attention. In a series of articles appearing in this journal, Blunt argued that a true revolutionary art must have its roots in the ascendant class. In contrast, he viewed Dada and Surrealism as the moribund expression of bourgeios society in decline. See his 'Rationalist and Anti-rationalist Art', *Left Review* II:10 (1936), pp. iv–vi.

* * *

As he laboured over *Still Life with Old Shoe*, Miró, like his contemporaries in France and Spain, considered the multivalent implications of realism and figuration in painting. Following the outbreak of the Civil War, Spanish artists were called upon to establish positions on a cultural front that was far from clearly defined. Before the advent of the Second Republic in 1931, the question of the political position of art and artists had rarely been raised.[71] Although the issue gained momentum through the 1930s, especially after 1935, there was no consensus concerning the relation of art to politics – conservative or radical – either among members of the avant-garde or partisans of realism in painting. The ideological landscape surrounding artistic production in Republican Spain remained as complex, uneven and contradictory as the political landscape.[72] Moreover, the geographical landscape was regionally divided. There were numerous institutional channels for avant-garde art in Barcelona, owing to the efforts of organizations like ADLAN (Amics de l'Art Nou) and GATCPAC (Grup d'Arquitectes i Tècnics Catalans per al Progrés de l'Arquitectura Contemporània). In Tenerife, the artists and writers who grouped around the *Gaceta de Arte* maintained close ties with the Surrealists in Paris, while in València, and to a lesser degree Madrid, proponents of a politically-engaged Socialist Realism gained considerable ground.

The outbreak of the Civil War inevitably brought greater immediacy to debates on the form and political tendency of contemporary art, its position in bourgeois society, and its role in the struggle against fascism. Sebastià Gasch lamented that political art had made a strong showing after July 1936, as artists were mobilized by trade unions, political parties, and the Catalan government itself in the wartime effort. Commenting on an aggressive campaign against aestheticism in painting, Gasch decried the predominance of propagandistic art in Barcelona's 1937 Exposició de Primavera:

> There are works that have a revolutionary content but no pictorial value, and there are works that have no argument but are magisterially painted. Well balanced, there are also revolutionary paintings that are at the same time works of art.[73]

Quoting André Gide, who at the Congrès international des écrivains pour la défense de la culture had criticized the theory of art as a mirror of reality, Gasch

71 Jaime Brihuega, *La Vanguardia y la Republica* (Madrid: Ediciones Cátedra, 1982), p. 13. A notable exception is the questionnaire that the *Gaceta Literaria* circulated to artists and writers in 1927 concerning the relation of art to politics.

72 For a discussion, see Brihuega, ibid.; and Valeriano Bozal, *Pintura y escultura españolas del siglo XX (1900–1939)* (Madrid: Espasa Calpe, 1992), pp. 562–662.

73 Sebastià Gasch, 'Notes sobre l'art revolucionari', *Revista de Catalunya* XVI (1938), reprinted in Joan M. Minguet Batllori, ed., *Sebastià Gasch: Escrits d'art i d'avantguarda (1925–1938)* (Barcelona: Edicions del Mall, 1987), pp. 228–33.

continued, 'What a work of art offers by being beautiful in itself is education enough'.[74]

Although Gasch's statements were categorical,[75] they immediately underscore the intensity of the debate surrounding the issue of art and propaganda and the definition of a political art in Spain. At the Deuxième congrès international des écrivains pour la défense de la culture, which convened in València in July 1937,[76] Gide's criticisms were addressed. A 'Collective Communication' was issued in which a humanist conception of revolutionary artistic practice was advanced: 'Abstract art of recent art appears false to us. But we cannot accept as revolutionary, as truthful, a painting that refers to a worker with a raised fist or [...] any other symbol without expressing the most essential nature of reality'. Emphasizing the idea of a free and democratic culture of 'the people', an ideological figure that was intended to efface class divisions in Spanish society, the document vindicated the tradition of bourgeois humanism maintained by the Popular Front and supported by the Soviet Union: 'to win the war is to conquer the category of man, of human dignity'.[77] Nonetheless, a precise definition of 'the people' as a spiritual force or a material presence, as passive voices of rural mystification or as active participants in the transformation of society,[78] was not forthcoming. How might these distinctions be articulated in an art that refused didactic content? At what point does form itself become a sign of revolutionary consciousness? And what relations exist between the political and social functions of painting? Miró's *Still Life with Old Shoe* provides some insights.

74 Ibid. Gide's text, 'Défense de la Culture', had tremendous resonance at the time. It was immediately translated into several languages. For a reprint of the Spanish translation and a discussion, see Manuel Aznar Soler, ed., *I Congreso Internacional de Escritores Para la Defensa de la Cultura (Paris, 1935)* (València, Generalitat Valenciana, 1987), pp. 201–8.

75 Specifically, Gasch seems not to have fully comprehended Gide's adherence to Marxist principles, despite his condemnation of official Soviet cultural policy. For the context of Gide's remarks, see Bozal, *Pintura y escultura españolas del siglo XX*, pp. 631–34.

76 The Congress opened in Valencia on 4 July 1937, before moving on to Madrid and Barcelona. The sessions concluded in Paris on 16–17 July.

77 Miguel Angel Gamonal Torres, ed., *Arte y política en la Guerra Civil española: El Caso republicano* (Granada: Diputación Provincial de Granada, 1987), p. 239. As Carmen Grimau observes, the collective ponencia expressed the moderate position of the Stalinist-backed government in Spain, in opposition to the more doctrinaire insistence on Socialist Realism as the form and content of a proletarian culture within the Soviet Union. To this end, Grimau notes that the ponencia did *not* express the majority opinion at the Congress. Carmen Grimau, *El Cartel Republicano en la Guerra Civil* (Madrid: Ediciones Cátedra, 1979), pp. 100–2.

78 For a discussion of this polemic in relation to the work of Alberto Sánchez, see Bozal, *Pintura y Escultura Españolas del Siglo XX*, pp. 635–37.

In the interview with Duthuit, Miró expressed himself unequivocally on the issue of a political art:

> The people are always the same, in fact, and everywhere – spontaneously – they create marvelous things. [...] The worst thing that could happen would be to put ourselves above the crowd, to flatter it by telling miserable little stories. The present leaders, the bastard products of politics and the arts who claim to be regenerating the world, are going to poison our last sources of renewal. While they talk about nobility and tradition or, on the contrary, about revolution and the proletarian paradise, we see how their little bellies grow and how the fat invades their souls.[79]

As Miró became reconciled to a prolonged exile in Paris, the humble objects of his still life assumed special significance. Rejecting the possibility of a retreat into the realm of fantasy, as he had confided to Pierre Matisse on 7 March 1937,[80] Miró confronted his situation and, in the process, sought to address the nameless victims of the Civil War – the Spanish people – beyond ethnic, class or political distinctions.[81] But Miró, as we have seen, articulated that content through the language of painting, mapping the opposing terms of an ideological and political crisis in French and Spanish art while refusing to declare a partisan position. Miró's work on two related projects, *Aidez l'Espagne* (fig. 27) and the mural *Catalan Peasant in Revolt*, also known as *The Reaper* (fig. 28), sheds considerable light on the political and social implications of his broadly 'humanist' conception of art.

* * *

Some time before 7 March 1937, Miró was asked by Christian Zervos[82] to design a one franc stamp that would be sold to raise money for the Spanish Republican government. Zervos, who had organized the monumental exhibition of Catalan art from the ninth to the fifteenth centuries that was then on view at the Jeu de Paume,[83] had close ties with the Generalitat de Catalunya, and may

---

79 Duthuit, 'Où allez-vous Miró?', see note 42.

80 Miró to Pierre Matisse, letter of 7 March 1937, in Rowell, *Selected Writings and Interviews*, p. 148.

81 As William Rubin writes: 'It seems certain that during the war that racked Spain Miró questioned whether his art, so beyond the comprehension of all but a few of his countrymen, was sufficiently in the service of their humanity. It was not that he was interested in particular causes or serving the ends of political propaganda; but the desire to communicate more readily, an aim that led some artists of his generation to Social Realism, was surely on his mind'. *Miró in the Collection of the Museum of Modern Art* (New York, The Museum of Modern Art, 1973), p. 73.

82 According to Miró's testimony to Lluís Permanyer, 'Revelaciones de Joan Miró sobre su obra', as in note 7.

83 Zervos also wrote the text of the exhibition catalogue, *L'Art de la Catalogne de la seconde moitié du neuvième siècle à la fin du quinzième siècle* (Paris: Editions Cahiers d'Art, 1937). The exhibition ran from March to April 1937.

have served as an intermediary between Miró and the autonomous Catalan government. Miró's preparatory gouache for the stamp was published in the June 1937 issue of the Catalan architectural review *A.C.*,[84] with a text indicating that Miró's anti-fascist stamp was sponsored by the Commissionar's Office on Propaganda. As we shall see, this reference provides an important context for Miró's imagery in relation to the political content of Spanish Civil War posters.

Miró later recalled, 'I painted the figure of a Catalan peasant wearing a barretina because it's a human being I know very well and because he is a person who stems from the earth. This was more genuine than the figure of an intellectual would have been'.[85] Iconographically, the reference to the Spanish conflict is established in the image of the defiant raised fist – the sign for the loyalist salute – and in the predominant red and yellow coloration of the pochoir, a symbolic allusion to the Spanish and Catalan flags. Nowhere, however, does Miró identify the figure specifically as a Catalan militiaman, although the image has been interpreted in this way.[86] Indeed, the stamp is enlisted in the service of a great political cause, yet achieves its aims squarely within the cultural domain. It is printed by an artist, not a government; and its irregular typography underscores the free movement of the artist's hand rather than standardization and obedience to the authority of state.[87]

Moreover, as Miró abandoned his initial, more anecdotal conception for the stamp (fig. 29), he transferred meaning to the very structure of his design. In the preparatory sketch, a figure with a swollen head and a reptilian tongue raises his fist in a threatening gesture before a fantastic bird. Miró relocated this expression of defiance to the tumescent arm of the figure in the final image, fashioning a dual signifier of vital force and collective resistance.[88] Here, as Carolyn Lanchner has observed, the configuration of the peasant's extended arm closely approximates that of a tree in a preparatory sketch for *The Tilled*

84 *A.C.* (June 1937). The journal was the mouthpiece of GATCPAC, with which Josep Lluís Sert, Miró's friend and co-designer of the Spanish Republican Pavilion, was closely associated. I am grateful to Carme Escudero i Anglès of the Fundació Joan Miró, Barcelona, for bringing this reference to my attention.

85 Lluís Permanyer, 'Revelaciones de Joan Miró sobre su obra', as in note 7.

86 Fernando Martín Martín, *El Pabellón Español en la Exposición Universal de París en 1937* (Sevilla: Universidad de Sevilla, 1983), p. 180.

87 As Valeriano Bozal writes: 'El sello de Miró ... [e]s popular, no populista. No respeta esa noción de minimuseo, desprecia los criterios académicos y las concepciones gráficas establecidas. Desde este punto de vista, su figura deforme, su puño creciendo, pudiera resultar grotesca. Las letras de su leyenda ofrecen esas cualidades 'anormalizadas' de la grafía de Miró, forman parte de la imagen. La imagen habla por sí misma. No es la ilustración de una leyenda ni el recuerdo del pasado'. Valeriano Bozal, 'Cinco motivos iconográficos', in *España. Vanguardia artística y realidad social*, p. 64.

88 For a discussion, see Pere Gimferrer, *The Roots of Miró* (Barcelona: Edicions Polígrafa, 1993), pp. 220–22.

Field of 1923–24 (fig. 30), cementing the peasant/landscape metaphor.[89] This association is in turn reinforced in the axial configuration of the design. The sign 'Espagne' to which the figure is joined is positioned on the lower, horizontal register of the image, providing a kind of symbolic ground for the figure. By means of a quasi-calligramatic construction, Miró identifies the sign with the Spanish landscape, the stable physical and symbolic ground of the nation. In contrast, the hand defines a vertical axis of dynamic ascension, for which the sign 'Aidez' is the terminus. Floating in a celestial blue field, 'Aidez' is inscribed within the domain of the spiritual; it speaks simultaneously of transcendence and the annihilation that will result from a failure to comply with the command (here, the 'vous' form of the verb 'aider' puts the indexical shifter to work, interpellating the viewer as the collective subject of the text's address). Finally, the composite sign '1 Fr(anc)', morphologically linked with a brilliant red sun, mediates the space between the horizontal and vertical axes of the composition; its monetary exchange value is both real and symbolic, as *Aidez l'Espagne* defines a wider field of social commerce.

Although the stamp was never issued, Miró prepared two separate editions of a pochoir based on the original design. One edition was accompanied by an inscription which altered its meaning.[90] In the space below the print Miró wrote: 'Dans la lutte actuelle, je vois du côté fasciste les forces périnées, de l'autre côté le peuple dont les immenses ressources créatrices donneront à l'Espagne un élan qui étonnera le monde'.

This is as close as Miró ever came to an overt political declaration during the Civil War, but on this point, too, his language remains curiously open. On the one hand, the inscription forestalls an arbitrary political appropriation of the image; the forces of evil are clearly identified. This is an important inclusion, for as Romy Golan and François Moulignat have shown, both the Left and the Right in France made political use of peasant imagery throughout the 1930s,[91] and Miró's message was specifically directed to the *French* public. But a similar deployment of peasant imagery across political lines also occurred in Spain,[92] a

---

89 Lanchner, '*Peinture-Poésie*', p. 23.

90 According to Jacques Dupin, two editions of the pochoir were published, one of which contained the supplementary text. The second version appeared in *Cahiers d'Art* XII:4–5 (1937). Jacques Dupin, *Miró Engravings, Vol. I: 1928–1960* (New York: Rizzoli, 1989), p. 40.

91 Nevertheless, Romy Golan, *Modernity and Nostalgia: Art and Politics in France Between the Wars* (London and New Haven: Yale University Press, 1995), observes significant differences in the political application of the rural paradigm in French art, with a general emphasis on the actual conditions of rural labour in leftist imagery.

92 For an analysis, see Carmen Grimau, *El Cartel Republicano*; and Josep Termes, *Carteles de la República y de la Guerra Cívil* (Barcelona: Centre d'Estudis d'Història Contemporània, 1978).

situation that, as we shall see, gave rise to a certain degree of ambiguity in the didactic panels of the Republican Pavilion. On the other hand, Miró does not specifically name the Republic at all. The burden for this identification rests entirely on the raised fist, and, by association, on the accompanying text. Indeed, Miró's pochoir tells us precious little about partisan ideologies and political parties under the Republic: Left or Radical Republicans; Marxists or Communists; Socialists or Anarcho-Syndicalists; 'humanist socialism' or the revolutionary dictatorship of the proletariat? And what of regional identities and autonomous politics in Catalonia and the Basque Country? What would it have meant, we might ask, to name the Republic?

At a time of deep economic divisions in Spanish social life, the political boundaries of the Republic were constantly shifting. The early days of the Civil War issued in a social revolution, with particularly dramatic consequences in Catalonia. The state infrastructure collapsed as power passed to armed popular militias under the control of the CNT (Confederación Nacional del Trabajo) and its political action wing, the FAI (Federación Anarquista Ibérica). As local committees and trade unions seized power from the army and government, factories, farms, basic services and some small businesses were collectivized. By the autumn of 1936 a political battle was joined between those who advanced the cause of revolution, and those factions within the government – including the Socialists and Communists – who maintained a policy of moderate reform and social conservatism in order to gain the support of the middle classes in the war effort. Under directives from the Soviet Union, the only foreign government to provide the Republic with military supplies, a campaign was launched to contain revolutionary activity and establish a united Popular Army and an orthodox police force. With the entry of CNT officials into Largo Caballero's government, the main dissenting voices were the POUM (Partido Obrero de Unificación Marxista), and CNT purists and members of the rank and file who believed the leadership had betrayed their cause. By May 1937, after a week of violent confrontations in Barcelona, the power of the CNT and POUM was finally broken. In the aftermath, a more politically centralized Republic emerged, but it had lost any claim to moral authority as the representative of the popular masses. Its unity was fictitious.[93]

Circumstance demanded that Miró support the Republican effort, yet he refused to reify an abstraction by giving it a proper name. His address to 'the people' through the image of a Catalan peasant cuts through the institutional structure of political parties, trade unions and the Republican government itself.

---

93 For a discussion of the early days of the Civil War, see Carr, *Spain 1808–1975*, pp. 656–72; and Jackson, *The Spanish Republic*. On the events of May 1937, see David T. Cattell, *Communism and the Spanish Civil War* (New York: Russell and Russell, 1965); and Burnett Bollotten et al., *The May Days. Barcelona 1937* (London: Freedom Press, 1987).

Given the clear didactic functions that posters were called upon to perform during the Civil War, Miró's position is indicative of his general withdrawal from ideological politics.

From the earliest days of the conflict, organizations like the Comissariat de Propaganda of the Generalitat, the Republican government, and a broad range of political parties and trade unions had issued posters as tools of propaganda and as vehicles for the dissemination of practical information. Just as the institution and/or political party commissioning the poster was clearly identified, discrete iconographies of war and revolution appeared across the political spectrum.[94] In Carles Fontseré's poster for the FAI (fig. 31), for example, the image of a peasant holding a sickle in his raised right hand is deployed as an exhortation to revolution. The black and red colours of the anarchist flag in the background, and the word 'Llibertat!' inscribed across the frontal plane, reinforce the message. In Jacint Bofarull's poster for the FAI/CNT (fig. 32), the anarchist colours again dominate the background, setting into relief the dual image of a monumental peasant/worker. The poster was distributed during a campaign to re-establish discipline among the rank and file of the anarchist movement following the outbreak of political violence in the early days of the war. In both cases, the raised fist signifies a specifically partisan solidarity.

In contrast, Miró's tone in *Aidez l'Espagne* is 'suprapolitical',[95] as he reconfigures the language of revolutionary poster art in Spain. For all his refusal of institutional politics, however, Miró's message remains complicit with Republican ideology. The text that Miró wrote to accompany the pochoir is a declaration against fascism in general at a time when the Republic, as we have seen, sought to contain revolutionary activity. By insisting on a universal human content, Miró's text frames the raised fist as a sign of resistance rather than revolution. In directing the meaning of this powerful image, the text advances the politics of the Frente Popular and the bourgeois myth of national solidarity which the Republic aggressively advanced.[96] Miró's position was consistent. *Aidez L'Espagne* was the immediate catalyst for his next major project, an enormous mural commissioned by the Spanish government for the Republican Pavilion of the 1937 Paris World's Fair.[97] Miró had received the commission some time before 25 April 1937,[98] although he probably did not execute the

94 For a discussion, see Grimau, *El Cartel Republicano*, pp. 93, 147–48 and 185–95.

95 Rubin, *Miró in the Collection of the Museum of Modern Art*, p. 72.

96 Moulignat, 'Les artistes en France, face à la guerre d'Espagne', pp. 112–15.

97 Catherine Freedberg, interview with Josep Lluís Sert, *The Spanish Pavilion*, p. 546, n. 47.

98 Miró informed Pierre Matisse in a letter dated 25 April 1937: 'The Spanish government has just commissioned me to decorate the Spanish pavilion at the 1937 Exposition'. Referring to *Aidez l'Espagne*, he indicated 'The stamp has still not been printed'. In Rowell, *Selected Writings and Interviews*, p. 157.

painting until June–early July;[99] that is, *after* he had completed *Still Life with Old Shoe*. As the complex evolution of the Republican Pavilion and the story of Miró's collaboration have been recounted in depth by Catherine Freedberg and Josefina Alix,[100] I will limit my discussion to a few key points.

From the outset, the Spanish government, working through a host of ministries at home and in France, and in close collaboration with the autonomous governments of Catalonia and the Basque Country, chose to emphasize the cultural achievements of the Republic and its continued commitment to agrarian and pedagogical reform, rather than showcase Spain's industrial and technological accomplishments.[101] Interior exhibits of popular arts and crafts, as well as photomontages detailing the extraordinary measures taken to protect the national cultural patrimony,[102] emphasized the moral authority of the Republic as the legitimate voice of the people, its ability to contain revolutionary insurrection, and its spiritual vitality.[103] An interior photograph of Federico García Lorca with the inscription 'Poète Fusillé à Grenade' left no room to doubt the spiritual annihilation that a fascist victory would represent.[104] Miró's

99 Umland, 'Chronology', p. 333, n. 576. See also Freedberg, *The Spanish Pavilion*, pp. 527–28.

100 Josefina Alix, *Pabellón Español: Exposición Internacional de París 1937* (Madrid: Museo Nacional Centro de Arte Reina Sofía, 1987).

101 This strategy was in keeping with the general tenor of the 1937 fair, which promoted regionalism. As Romy Golan has observed, the Republican Pavilion boasted the largest exhibition of regional arts and crafts at the fair, using rural and popular imagery to advance the idea of a moderate yet progressive republicanism representing the entire Spanish nation. Golan, *Modernity and Nostalgia*, pp. 105–36.

102 On the defence of the cultural patrimony, see Moulignat, 'Les artistes en France, face à la guerre d'Espagne', pp. 33–36.

103 The exhibition of medieval Catalan art that Christian Zervos had organized for the Jeu de Paume reinforced this image of a secure Republican government committed to advancing the ideals of Western civilization in the face of fascism and revolutionary insurrection alike. In the pages of *Cahiers d'Art*, Zervos explicitly stated: 'Les oeuvres réunies dans cette exposition, en même temps qu'elles donnent une idée d'ensemble de l'art catalan des époques romane et gothique, elles infligent un démenti formel à tous ceux qui se sont complaisamment étendus sur les destructions de monuments et d'oeuvres d'art commises par les foules catalanes. L'accusation de vandalisme portée contre elles est sans fondement et l'histoire des destructions est montée de toutes pièces. Au plus fort des combats de rue, le 20 juillet 1936, le gouvernement catalan, sur l'initiative du Conseilleur de la Culture, a fait tout son possible pour sauver de l'exaspération du peuple les édifices religieux que ses ennemis avaient utilisés pour l'attaquer'. Christian Zervos, 'A l'ombre de La Guerre Civil: L'Art catalan du Xe au XVe siècle au musée du Jeu de Paume des Tuileries, Mars–Avril, 1937', *Cahiers d'Art* XII:8–10 (1937), pp. 213–56.

104 At the ground-breaking ceremony of the Republican Pavilion on 27 February 1937, Luís Araquistain, the Spanish Ambassador in Paris, explicitly stated: 'Parece que algunos se han extrañado de que en plena guerra la España Republicana encuentre el tiempo y el estado de ánimo para presentarse a esta manifestación de la Cultura y del Trabajo. Es este, precisamente, lo que la distingue de la minoría facciosa en

Aidez l'Espagne pochoir, which was sold at the Pavilion, underscored this message in its appeal to the 'boundless creative will' of the Spanish people.

The exterior decoration of the Pavilion was no less politically charged. Alberto Sánchez's monumental sculpture, *El pueblo español tiene un camino que conduce a una estrella*, spoke to ideals of resistance and resilience, evoking at once a tree, a rocky formation upon which a dove is perched, and a liberty figure bearing a torch or abstracted sickle.[105] Mounted on a grindstone (Alberto was a baker by trade), the sculpture may be interpreted as a symbol of endurance, although its meaning remains open. Similarly, Julio González's *Montserrat*,[106] the personification of fecundity in the form of a maternal reaper, represented renewal. Positioned at the entrance to the Pavilion, its meaning, like that of Alberto's monument, was framed intertextually in relation to Josep Renau's exterior photomurals, which were periodically changed to chronicle the military course of the war[107] and thereby underscore the human cost of preserving the general principles that the sculptures embodied. In this carefully orchestrated movement between poetic emotion and political information, the entire Pavilion assumed the form of 'un espace symbolique à fonction politique'[108] in which an elaborate *imaginaire*[109] of the Civil War was publicly staged.[110]

---

armas que sólo tiene tiempo y capacidad para destruir la vida y los valores humanos. Para la España Republicana la guerra sólo es un accidente, un mal impuesto y transitorio, que no le impide, de ninguna manera, continuar creando obras espirituales y materiales'. Cited by Alix, *Pabellón Español*, p. 26. The political significance of this message was underscored by none other than Salvador Dalí, who recalled in his autobiography how Lorca's death was exploited for propaganda purposes: 'This was ignoble, for they knew as well as I that Lorca was by essence the most a-political person on earth. Lorca did not die as a symbol of one or another political ideology, he died as the propitiatory victim of that total and integral phenomenon that was the revolutionary confusion in which the Civil War unfolded'. Salvador Dalí, *The Secret Life of Salvador Dalí* (New York: Dial Press, 1942).

105 For a discussion of Alberto's imagery, see Martín Martín, *El Pabellón Español*, pp. 78–80, who likens the monument to a cactus. With the exception of Miriam Basilio, 'Images of the Landscape', no one has commented on the ambiguous configuration of the star/sickle as an appropriated political sign, although the sculpture has been generally interpreted as a female figure.

106 There has been some question in the González literature concerning the circumstances of the commission. Freedberg, *The Spanish Pavilion*, pp. 295–316, proposed that González had in fact begun the sculpture as early as 1934–35, later adapting the theme for the Pavilion. Based on documentary evidence, Alix, *Pabellon Español*, pp. 91–92, has convincingly disputed this assertion.

107 Alix, *Pabellón Español*, p. 40.

108 Moulignat, 'Les artistes en France, face à la guerre d'Espagne', pp. 90–108.

109 Ibid., p. 13.

110 The extent to which the commission of works of art for the Pavilion was programmatic is not entirely clear. However, the available evidence suggests that considerable efforts were made to project a unified political message that would be immediately comprehensible to the public. When Julio González informed José Gaos,

Essential to this operation was the production of a rural myth of popular solidarity, organic unity, and Republican good deeds, to which Miró's *Reaper*, and the sculptures of Alberto and González, jointly contributed. On the second floor of the Pavilion a series of photomurals emphasized economic and social progress under the Republic – its dedication to education, public welfare and especially to agrarian reform. The latter objective was a key issue in the declaration of the Republic, although attempts to legislate land distribution and improve the conditions of rural labour were unsuccessful. In this respect, the photomurals attempted to redeem a failed social policy by inscribing it within the language of myth. If one mural charted the inequitable distribution of land in Spain and the miserable wages earned by day laborers working from dusk until dawn, another presented an organic image of the Catalan nation, complete with a heroic reaper and the majestic silhouette of Montserrat. The contradiction that emerges here between the social reality of the historical present and a static, idealized view of tradition and the past is precisely the condition of Republican ideology itself: a temporally divided space of political and social representations. Indeed, many of the photographic images of regional life in the Pavilion were appropriated from ethnographic archives whose objective was to document an 'eternal' rural subject that was quickly disappearing under the pressures of modernity.[111]

There is a definite symmetry in Miró's collaboration with the Republic in relation to the ideological work the Pavilion performed at this critical moment in the Civil War. On the one hand, the discourse attending the universality and spiritual plenitude of an art of 'the people' was deeply politicized, as the Republican government sought to assure France and the world of its commitment to democratic ideals and thus win economic and military support for its cause.[112] An interior exhibit went so far as to insist that Spain was *not* a Socialist state, and that the right to own private property would be respected by a coalition government in which Communist ministers wielded enormous power by virtue of their control over Soviet arms.[113] On the other hand, the broadly

---

Comisario General Español of the exhibition, that he wished to replace *Montserrat* with a more abstract sculpture, *Mujer Ante el Espejo*, Gaos asked him to reconsider, arguing 'Se trata de una obra poderosa, inteligible para todos y completamente actual'. José Gaos to Julio González, letter of 14 September 1937. Freedberg, *The Spanish Pavilion*, pp. 298–99, as cited by Alix, *Pabellón Español*, p. 92.

111 On the often conservative implications of the ethnographic campaigns that produced these photographic archives, see Jordana Mendelson, 'From Documents to Monuments: The Representation of Spain and the Avant-Garde in the 1930s' (unpublished doctoral dissertation, Yale University, 1999).

112 One of the primary objectives of the Republican government was to persuade France to proceed with arms sales agreements approved prior to the French Non-Intervention Pact of August 1936.

113 According to Alix, *Pabellón Español*, p. 32, Angel Ossorio y Gallardo, who replaced Luís Araquistain as Ambassador in Paris under the government formed by

humanist agenda advanced by the Frente Popular accorded with Miró's refusal of a partisan art. His apocalyptic *Reaper*[114] recuperates a powerful political sign – the Communist sickle – and recodes it as the weapon wielded by a rebellious peasant whose freedom has been threatened. Although Miró's stated referent was the heroic *segador* of Catalan nationalist mythology, and not international Communism,[115] the fact that he later felt the need to make this distinction indicates a certain mobility that registers in the sign.[116] Within the political frame of the Pavilion, Miró's *Reaper* – what it does and does not say – participates in the production of a popular myth of solidarity and collective resistance that is circumscribed by Republican ideology.

From the moment Miró agreed to execute a mural for the Spanish Republican Pavilion, he left the terrain of painting and entered *de facto* into the public domain of politics. Current events demanded that Miró support the Republican effort, although he remained characteristically silent about the political tremors that shook the Republic from the time of its inception. This situation gave rise to a powerful yet ambiguous image. *The Reaper*, measuring over $5\frac{1}{2} \times 3\frac{1}{2}$ meters, impresses by sheer visual and moral force. Yet for all its telluric strength and poetic expression, Miró's sign of resistance is curiously uprooted from the social landscape – a cipher for that nameless figure whose political identity had been evacuated of a clear and stable meaning: the Spanish Republic.

Juan Negrín on 17 May 1937, provided two disclaimers for didactic panels in the Pavilion: 'La pequeña propiedad y los pequeños proprietarios, para nosotros son sagrados. Mr. Uribe, Ministro Comunista de Agricultura'; and a statement by Azaña himself: 'C'est une enorme sottise sinon une malignité de dire que nous nous battons pour le communisme. Nous luttons pour l'indepépendence de l'Espagne et pour la liberté des espagnols'. In 'Images of the Landscape: Surrealism and Politics During the Spanish Civil War' (unpublished Qualifying Paper for the Institute of Fine Arts, New York University, 1994), Miriam Basilio astutely observes that Uribe's political affiliation was deleted from the actual text of the panel, while an explicit 'condemnation of agricultural monopolies and exploitation of rural workers' was added. Negrín's Ministry, it must be remembered, was formed in the aftermath of the bloody confrontations between the government and the CNT/POUM in Barcelona.

114 For a discussion of apocalyptic imagery in Miró's mural, see Juan Larrea, 'Miroir d'Espagne: A propos du "Faucheur" de Miró au Pavillon Espagnol de l'Exposition de 1937', *Cahiers d'Art* XII:4–5 (1937), pp. 157–59.

115 Martín Martín, *El Pabellón Español*, p. 172, claims that the words to the Catalan national anthem, 'Els Segadors', were printed beneath the mural, although he offers no documentary evidence.

116 Miró told an interviewer in 1959: 'Of course I intended [*The Reaper*] as a protest. [. . .] The Catalan peasant is a symbol of the strong, the independent, the resistant. The sickle is *not* a communist symbol. It is the reaper's symbol, the tool of his work, and, when his freedom is threatened, his weapon'. Aline B. Saarinen, 'A Talk with Miró About his Art', *The New York Times*, Section 2 (24 May 1959), p. 17, as cited by Freedberg, *The Spanish Pavilion*, p. 553.

This is not to suggest that Miró retreated to the high ground of culture. But it does underscore the problems inherent in participating in a project fraught with contradictions. Public art makes immediate rhetorical, and often political, demands. Collaboration on the Pavilion meant that Miró's message had to be located within the domain of the Republic's *imaginaire politique*, a compromise which under the circumstances was a matter of individual conscience. As he later commented, 'I participated in the Spanish pavilion *because I felt human solidarity with what it represented*'.[117] Still, the question remains: was there another way in which Miró could make over his refusal of politics as form without performing the work of Republican ideology? Could this refusal be worked through critically as a *private* protest, and, in the process, engage the historical contradictions which propelled Spain into a devastating civil war? *Still Life with Old Shoe* suggests that such a possibility did exist.

By way of conclusion, two remarks will serve to underscore the problematic that is bracketed by these questions. The first represents the voice of intellectual disillusionment. As the West turned its back on the defeated Spanish Republic, and as Hitler and Stalin entered into a non-aggression pact on the eve of World War II, the days of political idealism within culture were drawing to a close. The English critic Herbert Read, an ardent supporter of Surrealism and a vocal opponent of Socialist Realism,[118] pessimistically remarked upon the situation in February 1939:

> In our decadent society [...] art must enter into a monastic phase. [...] Art must now become individualistic, even hermetic. We must renounce as the most puerile delusion the hope that art can ever again perform a social function. [...] This is equally true in Russia and in the West. Art has become nonsense [because] it matters little whether your army is military or industrial; it is still an army and the only art appropriate for an army is the music of a military marching band.[119]

Aligning himself with the short-lived Fédération internationale de l'art révolutionnaire indépendant (FIARI), the organization that Léon Trotsky, André Breton and Diego Rivera had founded in Mexico in 1938,[120] Read participated

117 'Participé en el pabellón español [...] *porque me sentía humanamente solidarizado con lo que representaba*'. Miró, communication to Martín Martín, *El Pabellón Español*, p. 173.

118 See, for example, Read's 'Surrealism – The Dialectic of Art', *Left Review* II:10 (1936), pp. ii–iii, in which the author condemns Socialist Realism and makes a case for the compatibility of Surrealism and Marxism.

119 Herbert Read, 'L'Artiste dans le monde moderne', *Clé*, no. 2 (1939), p. 7, cited by Lewis, *The Politics of Surrealism*, p. 158.

120 According to Lewis, *The Politics of Surrealism*, pp. 146–60, the formation of the FIARI was announced at the end of the manifesto *Pour un art révolutionnaire indépendant* which Breton and Rivera had signed, but which Trotsky largely authored. The central theme of the manifesto was its commitment to an independent artistic practice

in the transfer of political idealism to the aesthetic sphere.[121] The crisis of ideology within the wider culture seemed to justify political renunciation and spiritual retreat; the ivory tower of art was the last outpost in which the avant-garde's shattered hopes for a better world would survive.

The second remark, a statement by Miró, appeared two months later in the April/May issue of *Cahiers d'Art*. In response to George Duthuit's question 'Is the creative act affected by contemporary events, when these events involve no less than the destruction of the forms of that very civilization which the painter or the sculptor was consciously trying to enrich at the beginning of his career?', Miró inverted the terms of Read's argument:

> There is no longer an ivory tower. Retreat and isolation are no longer permissible. But what counts in a work of art is not what so many intellectuals want to find in it. The important thing is how it implicates lived facts and human truth in its upward movement. Pure formal discoveries have absolutely no significance in themselves. One must not confuse the commitments proposed to the artist by professional politicians and other specialists of agitation with the deep necessity that makes him take part in social upheavals, that attaches him and his work to the heart and flesh of his neighbor and makes the need for liberation in all of us a need of his own.[122]

Although Miró would undoubtedly have sympathized with Read's argument that independent art must position itself outside a conflicted political arena, he rejected the notion that painting could no longer perform a social function. Affirming his position as an artist *in* society, Miró believed that painting could still represent the contradictions of a nation and a world in crisis.

---

that would further the cause of the revolution. To this end, the manifesto rejected the doctrine of socialist realism and condemned Stalin's regime as a counter-revolutionary force, just as it maintained its opposition to the doctrine of bourgeois aestheticism and the administration of culture by the fascist regimes. As the manifesto stated, 'Every progressive tendency in art is destroyed by fascism as "degenerate." Every free creation is called "fascist" by the Stalinists. Independent revolutionary art must now gather its forces for the struggle against reactionary persecution'. The manifesto was published in the short-lived journal *Clé* in France, in the *Worker's International News* in England, and in the American literary magazine *Partisan Review*. By the autumn of 1938, when the manifesto appeared, *Partisan Review* had severed its ties to the Communist Party and would subsequently organize the American section of the FIARI.

121 In an illuminating letter to Kandinsky dated 9 November 1938, occasioned by the presence of Otto Dix's antiwar painting *Flanders* at the 'Twentieth Century German Art' exhibition in London, Read unequivocally expressed his position on art and politics: 'Politically and intellectually I am totally opposed to fascism and continually fight against it. But there are political realities and there are aesthetic realities, and it is necessary to preserve the distinction. I mean, that if one strives for the freedom of art, one does not at the same time strive for the politicisation of art'. Christian Derouet, 'Kandinsky in Paris: 1934–1944' in *Kandinsky in Paris*, p. 20.

122 Joan Miró, statement in *Cahiers d'Art* XIV:1–4 (1939), p. 73, in Rowell, *Selected Writings and Interviews*, p. 166.

It is Miró's insistence on the rhetorical dimensions of form in *Still Life with Old Shoe*, in relation to the political and representational codes attending painting at a precise historical moment, which bears the full force of his defiant protest. If the Republican Pavilion performed an elaborate ideological operation in which deep fractures in the social façade were seamlessly mended, Miró's *bodegón* exposed the decomposition that lay just beneath the surface of a united cultural and political front. In contrast to the seamless narratives of the Pavilion's photomurals, Miró divided the space of representation, countering the ideal of Republican unity with a fragmented and discontinuous visual field. Surely, great numbers of people saw *The Reaper* and purchased Miró's pochoir *Aidez l'Espagne*, while *Still Life with Old Shoe* remained a private testimony. But for this very reason, Miró's still life did not have to perform additional tasks. Miró could stage the political crisis within culture as form, exposing the terms of a far-reaching social collapse in the process. In the most profound sense, Miró's painting is a microcosm of the crisis of ideology that ravaged the ill-fated Second Republic. Speaking beyond partisan alliances through the language of painting, on behalf of a suffering nation, Miró's position was prophetic. For the failure to address a volatile social reality in the decades preceding the Civil War sacrificed an entire generation of Miró's countrymen to the political, social and cultural repression of a brutal and anachronistic military dictatorship. Critically negotiating the terrain of aesthetics and ideology, painting and politics, public art and private conscience, Miró's *Still Life with Old Shoe* bears witness to this tragedy.

Chapter 8

Of Politics, Postcards and Pornography: Salvador Dalí's *Le Mythe tragique de l'Angélus de Millet*

*Jordana Mendelson**

Salvador Dalí's *Le Mythe tragique de l'Angélus* [Tragic Myth of *The Angelus*] was published by Jean Jacques Pauvert in 1963.[1] It was based on his writings from the 1930s and according to the artist was completed in 1938, after which it was left in France in 1940, only to be rediscovered and published over 20 years later. Despite the additional illustrations and notes, Dalí claimed that the text was published 'as was'.[2] The first edition of the book was issued in a schoolboy's canvas cover with buckle, making it not only a document of his recent past, but an inquiry into individual and collective childhood memories and myths (fig. 33). It has become one of Dalí's most examined texts, used by scholars and critics alike to decipher the personal iconography in Dalí's paintings, especially the series that he made in the 1930s on the theme of *The Angelus*.[3] It has, more recently,

* This text is a much revised section from my dissertation, *From Documents to Monuments: Representing Spain and the Avant-garde in the 1930s* (Yale University, 1999), which was generously funded by the Jacob K. Javits Fellowship, a Dissertation Research Grant from Program for Cultural Cooperation between Spain's Ministry of Culture and North American Universities, a Fulbright Award, and a Whiting Foundation Fellowship at Yale University.

1 Salvador Dalí, *Le Mythe tragique de l'Angélus de Millet. Interprétation 'paranoïaque-critique'* (Paris: Jean Jacques Pauvert, 1963). English translations of this text, unless otherwise noted, are from Salvador Dalí, *The Tragic Myth of Millet's Angelus Paranoiac-Critical Interpretation including The Myth of William Tell (The Whole Truth about my Expulsion from the Surrealist Group)*, trans. Eleanor R. Morse (St Petersburg, Florida: The Salvador Dalí Museum, 1986).

2 'The manuscript of this book was lost when we left Arcachon a few hours before the German occupation. Having found it again after twenty-two years, I reread it and decided to publish it as it was without even touching a comma'. Dalí, *Tragic Myth of Millet's Angelus*, p. iii. Several drafts of the manuscript are conserved at the Fundació Gala-Salvador Dalí, Figueres, Spain. To my knowledge, they have not been transcribed. I thank the staff of the Fundació for allowing me to consult the manuscripts in 1997.

3 For an iconographic analysis of Dalí's paintings using his texts on *The Angelus*, see Whitney Chadwick, *Myth in Surrealist Painting, 1929–1939* (Ann Arbor: UMI, 1980). Also see Haim Finkelstein, *Salvador Dalí's Art and Writing, 1927–1942:*

attracted serious attention as an example of the artist's engagement with the writings of Sigmund Freud and Jacques Lacan, especially the former's analysis of Leonardo da Vinci and the latter's work on paranoia.[4] It is also one of many books and articles that Dalí wrote and published during his lifetime that take as their subject the intersection of artistic self-fashioning and theoretical inquiry. Like his autobiographies, *The Secret Life* (1942), *Diary of a Genius* (1964), and *Unspeakable Confessions* (1973), Dalí utilizes himself as the subject of his study. His are texts that explore the limits of realism in the face of obvious elaboration. They confront the fallacy of artistic autonomy as they simultaneously claim creative genius. As examples of artistic self-promotion, they are among the most widely read and the most heavily criticized of Dalí's texts.

Perhaps not surprisingly, then, except for rare and recent exceptions, *Le Mythe tragique de l'Angélus* has not been critically situated within the historical context in which it developed.[5] It is my contention that Dalí's theoretical inquiry into paranoia and his choice of Jean-François Millet's *The Angelus* have a political dimension which Dalí negotiates like a cultural critic. In the case of Dalí, his roles as critic and analyst were not co-terminous with that of the distanced observer. As I hope to show, Dalí's work directly engaged the political significance of paranoia and mass (and popular) culture at a time when such an analysis hit a raw nerve with artists and intellectuals working against fascism. Ironically, what were considered delusional creations by Surrealism's 'bad boy' have more in common with the 'serious' writing on fascism by intellectuals like Georges Bataille than scholars have previously acknowledged. In his study of the mechanisms for analyzing and creating works with his 'paranoiac-critical method', Dalí engaged the dangers and pleasures of both high art and mass culture. He confronts his reader with their structural similarities and locates his fascination for both within a broader study of the collective myths of violence, desire and family described by Freud. In addressing the political and historical

---

The Metamorphosis of Narcissus (Cambridge and New York: Cambridge University Press, 1996), pp. 177–226, and Ángel García González, 'El Método paranoico-crítico', in Antonio Bonet Correa, ed., *El Surrealismo* (Madrid: Universidad Menéndez Pelayo and Cátedra, 1983), pp. 173–82.

4 See Naomi Schor, 'Dalí's Freud', *Reading in Detail. Aesthetics and the Feminine* (New York and London: Routledge, 1989), pp. 101–9; and Dawn Ades and Fiona Bradley, *Salvador Dalí: A Mythology* (London: Tate Gallery, 1998). Dalí's reading of Freud goes back to probably the mid-1920s as suggested by Fèlix Fanés, *Salvador Dalí. La Construcción de la imagen 1925–30* (Electa, 1999), p. 223, n. 43.

5 An exception to this is the work of Robert Lubar, especially his recent analysis of Dalí's paintings on *The Angelus* theme in *Dalí. The Salvador Dalí Museum Collection* (Boston: Bulfinch Press, 2000). Romy Golan has convincingly situated Dalí's paranoiac-critical method and his writings and paintings on *The Angelus* in the context of interwar France in her 'Mythes surréalistes et imaginaires telluriques dans la France de l'entre-deux-guerres', *Pleine Marge*, no. 7 (1996), pp. 183–206.

dimensions of Dalí's *Le Mythe tragique de l'Angélus*, my study considers the writings of Dalí's critics, his own writings and paintings about *The Angelus* from the 1930s, and critical theories of folklore and fascism by Freud and Bataille.

Pornography and Postcards

The first book that Dalí published following his departure from France in 1940 and his arrival in the United States was his 1942 *The Secret Life of Salvador Dalí*. He was, by then, well established as a famous figure in the New York art scene. He had appeared on the cover of *Time* magazine and his design for the 1939 New York World's Fair, 'Dream of Venus', brought him even greater notoriety as a showman and fabricator of Surrealist provocations.[6] One of the harshest and most emotional criticisms of *The Secret Life* came from George Orwell, whose 1944 review 'Benefit of Clergy' was itself initially censored, and only appeared two years later in his book *Dickens, Dalí & Others*.[7] Orwell accused the artist of moral and aesthetic perversion, writing: 'you have here a direct, unmistakable assault on sanity and decency [...] some of Dalí's pictures would tend to poison the imagination like a pornographic postcard'.[8] Instead of upholding the expectations that Orwell held for the socially responsible fine artist, he accused Dalí of behaving more like a comic illustrator. Ironically, Orwell had just previously celebrated the cheap appeal of the mechanically reproduced and comically risqué postcards designed by Donald McGill in 1941.[9] The difference between McGill and Dalí, it seems, was that as a fine artist Dalí was supposed to achieve more, and instead embodied the pleasures and perversities of both the elite and the masses in his own behaviour. He revised his autobiography within the framework of his own theories about paranoia and his interest in Freud. He distanced himself from his earlier political and artistic beliefs and made of his past a chaos from which he had been saved by embracing Gala and the moral and religious beliefs of the elitist right.[10] For

6 On Dalí in America, see *Salvador Dalí. Dream of Venus*, exh. cat. (Barcelona: Fundació Gala-Salvador Dalí and Fundació 'la Caixa', 1999), especially the essays by Fèlix Fanés; and Eric M. Zafran, ' "I am not a madman": Salvador Dalí in Hartford' in Dawn Ades, ed., *Dalí's Optical Illusions* (New Haven and London: Yale University Press, 2000), pp. 38–58.

7 P. Vervoort, 'Orwell as Art Critic. "Benefit of Clergy": Opposition to Salvador Dalí' in J.M. Richardson, ed., *Orwell × 8: A Symposium* (Winnipeg: Ronald P. Frye, 1986), p. 67.

8 George Orwell, 'Benefit of Clergy: Some Notes on Salvador Dalí (1944)', in *Dickens, Dalí and Others* (New York: Harcourt, Brace and World, 1946), p. 176.

9 Orwell, 'The Art of Donald McGill', in ibid., pp. 124–39.

10 This interpretation of Dalí's autobiographies was made by David Villaseca in his excellent review, 'In Dalí more than Dalí himself': *Un Diari: 1919–20* and the Real Salvador Dalí Autobiography', *New Formations*, no. 30 (Winter 1996–97), pp. 63–71.

Orwell, Dalí's autobiography was 'a record of fantasy, of the perversion of instinct that has been made possible by the machine age'.[11] Though meant as a barb, Orwell's observation here is astute. Dalí's engagement with mass culture was key to his formulation of the paranoiac-critical method and his *Le Mythe tragique de l'Angélus.*

Despite his disapproval of Dalí, Orwell discouraged the censorship of his perversions and, perhaps unintentionally, made an important link between the postcard aesthetic of the artist's paintings and Dalí's cultural context: 'Short of the dirty postcards that used to be sold in Mediterranean seaport towns, it is doubtful policy to suppress anything, and Dalí's fantasies probably cast useful light on the decay of capitalist civilization [...]. He is a symptom of the world's illness'.[12] As a symptom, Dalí's escapades and his violation of moral and aesthetic purity placed him among the degraded products of the 'machine age'. The 'pornographic postcards' that Orwell recalled, connected Dalí to the tastes and habits of the masses and to the artist's past. Dalí grew up among the 'dirty postcards that used to be sold in Mediterranean seaport towns'.[13] The conditions that Orwell assigned to the artist – perversity, immorality and obscenity – were personal and social characteristics: they recalled all that was associated with Barcelona's mass culture industries.[14] Orwell's description of the sale of dirty postcards as an activity of the past further located Dalí's perversions as outmoded and decadent. For Orwell, then, it was not just a question of morals or aesthetics, but one of geography and chronology too. Dalí committed an act of transgression that for Orwell was 'something disgraceful'.[15]

In 1930, Dalí published two texts that began to outline his interest in paranoia: 'The Rotten Donkey' and 'Moral Position of Surrealism'. It is the second, published in the Catalan avant-garde magazine *Hèlix* (Vilafranca del Penedés, 1929–30), that I want to study in relation to this question of mechanically reproduced images and Dalí's nascent theories on paranoia as a critical and artistic tool. Dalí first presented his paper as a talk at Barcelona's Ateneu, or cultural centre. He delivered a serious inquiry into the mechanisms of desire, violence and mass culture, which at the same time served as a diatribe against traditional Catalan intellectuals. The talk outlined the main objectives of Surrealism and posited paranoia as one of the group's key critical and creative tools. Dalí argued that multiple images, brought on with violent intensity and

11 Orwell, 'Benefit of Clergy', p. 170.

12 Ibid., p. 179.

13 Orwell spent time as a volunteer in Spain during the Civil War. He no doubt is thinking about Barcelona and the port towns along the Catalan coast.

14 See Juan José Lahuerta, 'Gaudí, Dalí: Las Afinidades Electivas', *Decir Anti es Decir Pro: Escenas de la vanguardia en España* (Teruel: Museo de Teruel, 1999), pp. 117–49.

15 Orwell, 'Benefit of Clergy', p. 179.

elaborated from subtle imperceptible details, had the potential to discredit the real. In describing those elements that challenged the reigning orders in art and the state, Dalí focused on two: turn-of-the-century or *modernista* architecture and pornographic postcards.

Central to Dalí's celebration of turn-of-the-century architecture and postcards was his conclusion that both corresponded to a popular unconscious:

> And if I can say today that Art Nouveau, which is exceptionally well represented in Barcelona, comes closest nowadays to what we could truly love, it is a proof precisely of a disgust and complete indifference for art – the same disgust that makes us consider the postcard as the document that is the most alive of modern popular thought, the thought whose profundity is often so acute as to take flight towards psychoanalysis (I am referring in particular to pornographic postcards).[16]

The only visual reference to postcards included in *Hèlix* was a single illustration, the banality of which is seemingly at odds with the revolutionary and pornographic qualities that Dalí exalted. The postcard, of a kind available and collected in Barcelona, shows a young man staring longingly to one side (fig. 34). His eyes wander to a vignette of himself in an amorous embrace with a female lover. Longing and desire are portrayed photographically through the overlay of two different images of reality at once. The viewer assimilates both as part of a single event that, for Dalí, came close to the multiple images brought on by paranoia. As a 'document' of 'modern popular thought', the postcard could only be deciphered using the tools of psychoanalysis. Dalí had already professed his (and the Surrealist's) interest in postcards in an article for the Madrid avant-garde magazine *La Gaceta literaria.* He announced the preparation of a book by André Breton and Paul Éluard, in which the study of postcards 'constitutes a disconcerting, experimental base for the study of modern popular unconscious thought'.[17] Both Breton and Éluard held long-standing interests in postcards.[18] What differentiates Dalí's postcard articles and works of the early 1930s from those of Breton and Éluard is the central and recurring position that they occupy in his pictorial and theoretical investigations.

16 Salvador Dalí, 'Posició moral del surrealisme', *Hèlix*, no. 10 (March 1930), p. 5; trans. in Salvador Dalí, *The Collected Writings of Salvador Dalí*, ed. and trans. Haim Finkelstein (Cambridge: Cambridge University Press, 1998), p. 221. Ian Gibson's translation of this passage differs, in that he writes 'the postcard as the most vital document of modern popular thought, a thought often so profound that it defies psychoanalysis'. Trans. in Ian Gibson, *The Shameful Life of Salvador Dalí* (New York and London: Norton, 1998), p. 306.

17 Ernesto Giménez Caballero, 'Palabras con Salvador Dalí', *La Gaceta literaria*, no. 96 (15 December 1930), p. 3.

18 For Éluard, his collection of and writings about postcards culminated in a multi-page illustrated article in *Minotaure* in 1934. Paul Éluard, 'Les Plus belles cartes postales', *Minotaure*, nos 3–4 (1934), pp. 85–100.

In 1931 Dalí published the first illustrated explanation of his paranoiac-critical method for a Parisian public. 'Communication: Paranoiac Visage' is distinct from his earlier 'Moral Position of Surrealism' in that it focused entirely on the paranoiac potential of postcards. Appearing as a one-page announcement in *Le Surréalisme au service de la révolution*, 'Communication' explained the delusions and interpretations possible from a single mass-produced image. Dalí recounted confusing a postcard of an African tribe for a painting by Pablo Picasso.[19] Taking place during a time in which he was studying Picasso's painting in detail, Dalí explained that his unconscious had modified the image at the moment of perception. A simple change in the image's direction allowed Dalí to realize his confusion, restoring the original image to view. Consulting with Breton, Dalí recounted that the leader of the Surrealists saw in the postcard the profile of the Marquis de Sade, which proved to Dalí the relative instability of any image.

Dalí's use of an image of Africa as his paranoiac object held deep political significance in 1931. As Romy Golan has suggested: 'we may establish in fact a one-to-one correspondence between the system of representation of paranoia as elaborated upon by Dalí and Lacan circa 1931 and the mechanisms of colonialism as they were exposed at precisely that time at the Colonial Exposition': delirium, delusion of grandeur, fusion, doubling and ubiquitous multiplication.[20] Dalí's 'Communication' was, thus, not only a brief on the function of paranoia as a critical tool, it also demonstrated his awareness of the political interests of the Surrealists. Although in *The Secret Life*, he openly criticized Picasso's fascination for African objects, here he seems to work precisely with an image (and an artist) that at the time was highly over-determined. It is as if Dalí were remarking that behind the paintings of his compatriot were colonialist images shared by both the French and the Spanish. The repercussions of Spain's colonial past were also bringing political unrest. The transition from the dictatorship of General Miguel Primo de Rivera to the Second Republic was inextricably linked to the widespread discontent following Spain's colonial defeats in America and Morocco and the military regime that followed. Despite the dictatorship's desire to shore up national and international support with its twin exhibitions of 1929 – the International Exposition in Barcelona and the Ibero-American Exposition in Seville – the collapse of the monarchy and the dictatorship took place before the close of both exhibitions. An open reading of Dalí's use of the postcard of an African tribe in terms of its possible political significance for both French and Spanish audiences is further supported by the tracts issued by the Surrealists in 1931. One protested the Colonial Exposition in Paris, titled 'Ne visitez pas l'exposition coloniale', and the other, 'Au Feu!'

19 Salvador Dalí, 'Communication: Visage Paranoïaque', *LSASDLR*, no. 3 (1931).

20 Romy Golan, 'Triangulating the Surrealist Fetish', *Visual Anthropology Review* X:1 (Spring 1994), p. 62.

celebrated the church burnings in Spain and the establishment of the Second Republic.[21]

Paranoia and *The Tragic Myth of the Angelus*

After experimenting with various images from mass culture, Dalí was shortly overtaken with Jean-François Millet's painting as the primary object of his paranoiac-critical method. In *Le Mythe tragique de l'Angélus*, Dalí explained:

> In June 1932, the image of the *Angelus* by Millet suddenly appeared in my mind without any recent recollection or conscious association to offer an immediate explanation. The image was composed of a very clear visual representation in colors. It was almost instantaneous [...]. the *Angelus* of Millet suddenly became for me the most troubling of pictorial works, the most enigmatic, the most dense, the richest in unconscious thoughts that had ever existed.[22]

In his prologue to *Le Mythe tragique*, published in *Minotaure* in 1933, Dalí did not mention the painting's sudden appearance. More striking is that he did not mention the attack that took place on the painting on 12 August 1932.[23] As he explained in the 1963 edition of his text, 'Dr Jacques Lacan, who was brought in to question the sick man [Georges Pierre-Théophile Guillard], obtained certain declarations from him that we consider "sensational" '.[24] These declarations explained that the attacker wanted to puncture the most famous painting in the Louvre, but hesitated before Leonardo da Vinci's *Mona Lisa*, Watteau's *The Embarkation of Cythera*, and Millet's *The Angelus*. Dalí continued that the choice between the *Mona Lisa* and *The Angelus* was linked by the connection of both paintings to Freud's analysis of the Oedipus complex. They were both, according to Dalí, paintings which took as their unconscious subject universal myths of desire and the fear of castration. The attack on *The Angelus* was triggered, Dalí would argue, by the painting's latent violence, unleashing not only a physical act of aggression, but also the psychic disturbance that Dalí noted in the painting's impact on his own unconscious.

Following the publication of 'The Rotten Donkey' in 1930, Dalí met Jacques Lacan. Reportedly, the two engaged in a conversation which may have mutually influenced their work.[25] In the 1933 issue of *Minotaure*, Lacan's 'The Problem of style and the psychiatric conception of paranoiac forms of experience'

---

21 Helena Lewis, *The Politics of Surrealism* (New York: Paragon House, 1988), pp. 95–96.

22 Dalí, *Tragic Myth of Millet's Angelus*, p. 3.

23 Lubar, *Dalí: The Salvador Dalí Museum Collection*, p. 87.

24 Dalí, *Tragic Myth of Millet's Angelus*, p. 171.

25 For a more detailed account of this meeting, see Patrice Schmitt, 'De la psychose paranoïaque dans ses rapports avec Salvador Dalí', *Salvador Dalí.*

followed Dalí's 'Paranoiac-critical interpretation of the obsessive image. *The Angelus* by Millet. Prologue. New considerations on the paranoiac phenomenon from the Surrealist point of view'. Both agreed that paranoia differed from other psychoses in that the paranoiac deformed reality as it was perceived and expanded on these initial delusions in an episodic, systematic fashion. The extremity of the multiple visions depended on the individual's delusional capacity. In all of the cases of paranoiac delusions – grandeur, persecution and eroticism – the potential for violence was inevitable as the paranoiac accumulated observations of the most detailed minutiae and directed their aggression outside themselves.[26] In their articles for *Minotaure*, Dalí and Lacan brought the conditions of paranoia to bear on art and style.

Lacan's description of the delusions experienced by paranoiacs dovetailed with Dalí's own explanation of double and multiple images from 1930. According to Lacan, 'delirium is found to be very rich in phantasms of cyclical repetition, ubiquitous multiplication, endless periodic recurrence of the same events, doubling and tripling of the same persons and, occasionally, hallucinations or doublings of the subject's own self'.[27] In addition, Lacan pointed to two other symptoms of paranoia related to style. The first was that paranoia, as a non-hierarchical condition, was equally present in the works of 'masters' as it was in folklore. Secondly, Lacan observed that at certain moments of great social tension, paranoiac tendencies were heightened. One might argue that this last condition impacted both the clinical cases of paranoia and the interest in the condition on the part of artists, psychoanalysts and theorists. Apparently, both social tension and paranoia were at high points during the politically unstable 1930s.

The story that Dalí believed to uncover in Millet's painting was grounded in an atavistic tale of peasant eroticism and violence. The looming figure of the mother stood like a praying mantis waiting to devour her mate. The body of their dead son was located by Dalí in front of the couple in the field that they were harvesting. He saw the figures of the couple in natural formations and cultural products throughout the 1930s and retrospectively in his childhood. If his 'Prologue' in *Minotuare* provided the theoretical groundwork for his paranoiac-critical method, his *Le Mythe tragique de l'Angélus* provided the anecdotal evidence that supported his delusions and their translation into paintings from the 1930s onwards. The shapes of the pebbles on the Catalan coast of Cadaqués reminded him of Millet's peasant couple. The landscape of Cap de Creus, near

---

Rétrospective 1920–1980 (Paris: Centre Georges Pompidou, 1979), pp. 262–66; and Elisabeth Roudinesco, *Jacques Lacan & Co.: A History of Psychoanalysis in France 1925–1985* (Chicago: Chicago University Press, 1990).

26 Lacan discussed this in his article 'Motifs du crime paranoïaque: Le Crime des sœurs Papin', *Minotaure*, nos 3–4 (1933), pp. 25–28.

27 Jacques Lacan, 'Le Probleme du style et la conception psychiatrique des formes paranoïaques de l'expérience', *Minotaure*, no. 1 (1933), pp. 68–69; trans. and cited in Finkelstein, *Salvador Dalí: Art and Writing*, p. 197.

Cadaqués, with its porous, monumental, archaic rock formations, was transformed into another simulacrum of the painting. Later, an *Angelus* tea set, discovered while driving in Port de la Selva, brought forth cannibalistic associations of desire. His collection of 'materials on peasant eroticism' escalated over time.[28] As a reference for his study on the painting, Dalí kept a colour postcard of it, which he associated through his paranoiac-critical method with various other documents: colour photographs of cherries, postcards of women praying to St Catherine, photographs of praying mantis and other ephemera. This collection spilled over into his Parisian living quarters and inhabited his paintings, objects, articles and conferences. In one photograph taken in the mid-1930s, Gala and Dalí are shown seated on their sofa with pillows covered with an embroidered *Angelus* sham (fig. 35).

Breaking the line between art and life was a tenet endorsed by the Surrealists. Dalí's accumulation of popular artifacts pushed the limits of such a crossover to a point of excess. It was as if he demonstrated through his collection of *Angelus* ephemera that whatever specific, historical meaning the painting held was radically dislocated upon its entrance, through mass reproduction, into the popular sphere. Paradoxically, upon shedding the original conditions of its production, the painting opened to Dalí's analysis its current uses (and abuses) by painters, writers and the public. In distinction to art historian Robert Herbert, who wrote, 'Nostalgia for the pre-industrial past, which Millet had sensed with dignity and heroism, became adulterated and sentimentalized',[29] Dalí relished the painting's ubiquitous reproduction. It was through its multiple appearances in nature and culture that *The Angelus* revealed to Dalí its 'hidden' significance as a universal myth.

Painting Photographs

Dalí's work on *The Angelus* brought about a slippage between categories of difference (high and low, subject and object, politicized and non-partisan art). His model was undoubtedly Marcel Duchamp's iconoclastic reworking of Leonardo da Vinci's *Mona Lisa* as *LHOOQ*, which Dalí reproduced in his 1963 *Le Mythe tragique*. In the same year, he also published 'Why they attack the Mona Lisa', in which he offered a Freudian analysis of the painting's Oedipal significance, using as his primary example Duchamp's readymade.[30] Both artists

28 Salvador Dalí and André Parinaud, *The Unspeakable Confessions*, trans. Harold J. Salemson (New York: William Morrow, 1976), p. 155.

29 Robert L. Herbert, 'City vs. Country: The Rural Image in French Painting from Millet to Gauguin', *Artforum* (February 1970), p. 50.

30 Salvador Dalí, 'Why they attack the Mona Lisa', *Art News* LXII:1 (March 1963), pp. 36, 63–64.

shared an interest in the appropriation of high art to engage the politics of mass culture. They did this primarily through their shared study of mechanical reproduction and the history of optics.[31] But, unlike Duchamp, whose critical commentary written on the face of the painting played with the meaning of linguistic signs, Dalí called upon the didactic procedures of the paranoiac-critical method to explain why *The Angelus* had brought about 'violent and different kinds of aggressions'.[32] Dalí drew out *The Angelus*'s unexpected scenarios of eroticism, castration and death, whereas Duchamp played with the sexual expectations of Mona Lisa's smile.[33] In addition, while the *Mona Lisa* was stolen from the Louvre and missing during its foray into popular culture, *The Angelus* suffered the damage of its attack in 1932 but was never removed from its museum setting, making its dual status as original and mass-produced derivative always coexistent.[34]

Dalí made *The Angelus*'s appearance in unexpected locations, along with its constant reduplication and transformation, a central theme in his paintings of the 1930s. To begin, the format and technique of many of Dalí's paintings often imitated the look of a postcard. As a writer for *Time* commented in 1936, 'Salvador Dalí, with exquisite drawing and brilliant color, began to paint his nightmares on pieces of panel hardly bigger than postcards'.[35] This observation is not one imposed upon the artist; Dalí himself insisted that creating paintings like handmade photographs was a 'philosophical provocation'.[36] For example, *Atavism at Twilight* (1933–34), the painting that most resembles the composition of *The Angelus*, measures just 14 × 18 centimetres, taking as its model the postcard-sized reproductions of the painting rather than the original (fig. 36). Painted in the saturated colours of a chromolithographic reproduction, *Atavism at Twilight* revealed for Dalí's audience the original painting's latent violence: a pitchfork impales the back of the praying woman, the man's face becomes a skull with a wheelbarrow emerging from it, and the outline of a map of France cuts into the fabric of the man's shirt at the level of his heart. The painting resists being read as exclusively French in that Dalí placed the figures amidst the familiar rock formations of the Cap de Creus.

31 Dawn Ades, 'Dalí's Optical Illusions' in Ades, ed., *Dalí's Optical Illusions*, p. 22.

32 Dalí, 'Why they attack the Mona Lisa', p. 36.

33 For an excellent study on Duchamp, the *Mona Lisa* and mass culture, see Molly Nesbit, 'The Rat's Ass', *October*, no. 56 (Spring 1991), pp. 6–20.

34 *The Angelus* remained in its damaged state until restoration was undertaken in anticipation of the 1976 exhibition of Millet's work. Robert Herbert, 'Catalogue', *Jean-François Millet* (London: Arts Council of Great Britain and Hayward Gallery, 1976), p. 87.

35 'Art', *Time* (14 December 1936), p. 62.

36 Salvador Dalí, 'Derniers modes d'excitation intéllectuelle pour l'été 1934', *Documents* 34 (June 1934), pp. 33–35. Trans. in *Collected Writings of Salvador Dalí*, p. 254.

In other paintings, Dalí created 'paintings within paintings', which address the ubiquitous multiplication of *The Angelus* not only by imitating the trappings of the postcard but by placing miniature-sized replicas within his own versions. In *Gala and the Angelus of Millet Immediately Preceding the Arrival of the Conic Anamorphoses* (1933), Dalí presents Gala looking at a male Lenin-like figure (fig. 37). Her gaze passes through the figure and continues forward to confront the viewer. Above a doorway, which opens onto the scene, appears a copy of *The Angelus*. We see Millet's painting as if it were a mass reproduced image that circulates at will within Dalí's body of work.

Although they engage the dynamics of mechanical reproduction and imitate its guises, Dalí's paintings are just that: meticulously created simulacra. His *Angelus* paintings do not contain multiple images nor do they engage in the optical illusions that characterize some of Dalí's other paranoiac-critical paintings, like *The Endless Enigma* (1938). Instead they take as their subject an aspect of *The Angelus* that Dalí reconstructed as part of his own childhood memories: the unexpected appearance of the painting in daily life. In *The Secret Life*, Dalí told of his early experiences with Millet's couple. Whether true or false, Dalí represents the tale as a formative experience in his thinking about the painting. He wrote of daydreaming in his classroom and making of the cypress trees outside the window a terrifying image of the expectant couple. Upon turning his eyes back to the interior of the school, he explained: 'the corridor leading to the classroom would be lighted, and then through the glass-paneled door I could observe the oil paintings which decorated this corridor: one represented a fox's head [...] the other was a copy of Millet's *Angelus*'.[37] The chain of images that Dalí parades before the reader, each one more incredible than the next, were part of the artist's recreated past: 'All the fantasies and representations of my childhood period again vigorously took possession of my brain'.[38]

In revisiting what he claimed were memories from his childhood, Dalí brought to bear upon his theories of paranoia Freud's conclusion that childhood memories took on mythic importance when converted into 'screen memories'. In *The Psychopathology of Everyday Life*, Freud linked the choice of an adult's childhood memories with a paranoiac's fixation on particular objects and events. He observed that an adult remembered from his childhood the most unimportant of details and events, just as the paranoiac perceived in others and his environment that which was normally overlooked. According to Freud, 'the "childhood memories" of individuals come in general to acquire the significance of "screen memories" and in so doing offer a remarkable analogy with the childhood memories that a nation preserves in its store of legends and

37 Salvador Dalí, *The Secret Life of Salvador Dalí*, trans. Haakon Chevalier (New York: Dial Press, 1942), p. 64.

38 Ibid., p. 219.

myths'.[39] The connection between a paranoiac's false memories and screen memories is significant, for it sheds light on Dalí's choice of symbols of manifest and latent nationalism. He tells a personal narrative of obsession that speaks to a collective experience of identification. The myths that Dalí addressed, like the false memories that he created, were heavily influenced by Freud. So, too, was his definition of the three greatest simulacra, which were not to be found in exact replicas of the past or the present, but in the decayed, heterogeneous matter of excrement, blood and putrefaction.[40] In this, Dalí's work intersects with two different, but related, investigations into heterogeneity, folklore and fascism authored by Freud and Georges Bataille.

Freud and Folklore: Golden Dreams

In 1911 Freud and D.E. Oppenheim wrote an essay entitled 'Dreams in Folklore'. References to the project appeared in *The Interpretation of Dreams* and *Totem and Taboo*, where Freud indicated the potential for mining folklore as a repository of the social unconscious. Writing on the difference between real dreams and those portrayed in folklore, Freud explained:

> Dreams are obliged to conceal things and only surrender their secrets to interpretation; these comic anecdotes, however, which are disguised as dreams, are intended as communications, meant to give pleasure to the person who tells them as well as to the listener. [...] These stories delight in stripping off the veiling symbols.[41]

'Dreams in Folklore', like Dalí's paranoiac-critical method, revealed the hidden, unspoken significance of symbols that society had censored from conscious thought. These dreams adopt an anti-aesthetic language that Freud appreciated: 'we wanted to suggest that one should not be deterred by the often repulsively dirty and indecent nature of this popular material [; ...] behind these ugly façades are concealed mental reactions to impressions of life which are to be taken seriously'.[42] Freud continued, placing excrement as a central, recurring symbol in folklore: 'In dreams in folklore gold is seen in the most unambiguous way to be a symbol of feces'.[43] In folklore, the heterogeneous was converted into the most valued of materials. Dalí similarly fused elements that were most

---

39 Sigmund Freud, *The Psychopathology of Everyday Life* (1901), trans. James Strachey (New York and London: Norton, 1989), p. 68.

40 Salvador Dalí, 'L'Âne pourri', *LSASDLR*, no. 1 (1930). Trans. in *Collected Writings of Salvador Dalí,* p. 225.

41 Sigmund Freud and D.E. Oppenheim, *Dreams in Folklore*, trans. A.M.O. Richards (New York: International Universities Press, 1958), p. 27.

42 Ibid., p. 65.

43 Ibid., p. 65.

valued in society (works of art) with those that were the most devalued (mass reproductions and folklore).

Dalí famously incorporated images of excrement into his paintings. His *Le Jeu lugubre* (1929) received critical attention from both André Breton and Georges Bataille for the stained pants of the painting's protagonist.[44] Years later, Dalí dramatized the impact of this detail upon his audience:

> When Breton discovered my painting, he was shocked by the scatological elements that stained it. This surprised me. I started from shit, which from the psychoanalytical point of view could be interpreted as the happy prediction of the gold that – fortunately! – threatened to pour down on me.[45]

As with his other autobiographies, this passage from *Diary of a Genius* was elaborated to sensationalize Dalí's rupture with Breton.[46] Important here, however, is not Dalí's false memories, but the analogy that he makes between 'shit' and 'gold'. Dalí was not the only one to make this correlation either. Orwell had not only compared *The Secret Life* and Dalí's paintings to pornographic postcards, but he exclaimed: 'If it were possible for a book to give a physical stink off its pages, this one would'.[47]

Dalí grounded his fantasies of monetary conversion in Freudian terms and, like Lacan, he claimed folklore as one of the realms in which the characteristics of paranoia could be located. Important here is the interrelation between visions of prosperity and the most abject of substances, between the homogeneous and heterogeneous. The most irrational of combinations finds its place within an ordered system of relations. For Dalí that system became his paranoiac-critical method. His attention to the necessary presence of excrement, blood and putrefaction within the contained relations of paranoiac-criticism, converted the most banal scenarios into violence. As I hope to demonstrate in the next section, such a formulation resembled Bataille's critical theories of fascism of the 1930s. Indeed, Dalí's investigation into Millet was partner to his fascination with totalitarian leadership. Paranoia and its related symptoms of identification, violence and delusions of grandeur were the ground upon which Dalí simultaneously exalted and unmasked mechanisms of power.

---

44 See Georges Bataille, 'Le Jeu lugubre', *Documents* I:7 (December 1929), pp. 297–302; trans. in Georges Bataille, *Visions of Excess: Selected Writings, 1927–1939*, ed. Allan Stoekl (Minneapolis: University of Minnesota Press, 1991), pp. 24–30.

45 Salvador Dalí, *Diary of a Genius*, trans. Richard Howard (New York: Doubleday, 1965), p. 10.

46 In his study on Dalí, Fèlix Fanés documents the history of the reception of *Le Jeu lugubre* among the Surrealists and clarifies that neither Breton nor Bataille was as scandalized by the painting as Dalí indicates in his autobiographies. Fanés, *Salvador Dalí*, pp. 161–69.

47 Orwell, 'Benefit of Clery', p. 175.

Fascism, Socialist Realism and Paranoia in the 1930s

In several articles and announcements for his future book-length publication on *The Angelus*, Dalí simultaneously defended his 'paranoiac' fascination with Hitler and his ongoing investigations into Millet.[48] Paintings like *The Weaning of Furniture Nutrition* (1934), accompanied by his inflammatory declarations on Hitler, drew the scrutiny of his fellow Surrealists, but Dalí's work on Millet went virtually unnoticed. In 1934 when Breton wrote to Dalí about his inappropriate obsessions, Dalí responded with a multi-page letter in which he defended himself against Breton's accusations.[49] In his last autobiography, *The Unspeakable Confessions*, Dalí continued to claim that 'political or moral criteria [. . .] did not signify in relation to [his] paranoia-critical concepts',[50] despite the fact that his lectures at the time demonstrate a critical knowledge of the workings of what Dalí called 'itlerisme' and its importance as a mass movement.[51] Thus, Dalí's understanding of his obsession with totalitarianism was quite different from that of his peers. He understood his paranoiac-critical method to be the tool with which the irrational could be analyzed, or as he explained in his *Diary of a Genius*: 'Dalí, the absolute rationalist, wanted to know all about the irrational [. . .] to reduce and submit this irrational whose conquest he was making'.[52]

In 1935, Dalí fused his investigations into *The Angelus* with his paranoiac inquiries into the mechanisms of power. He had himself photographed as a Napoleon-like figure dressed in pillow shams of Millet's *The Gleaners* and *The Angelus*. Some of the photographs of the performance accompanied his 'Aerodynamic Apparition of "Beings-Objects" ', published in *Minotaure* (fig. 38). That Dalí should turn to Napoleon during the course of his paranoiac-critical method is not surprising. Emil Kraepelin, in his 1906 *Lessons in Clinical Psychiatry*, had documented the prevalence of Napoleon as a figure emulated by paranoiacs suffering from delusions of grandeur. In addition, as

48 J[ust] C[abot], 'Una estona amb Dalí', *Mirador*, no. 297 (18 October 1934); Salvador Dalí, *The Conquest of the Irrational*, p. 18; and Salvador Dalí, 'The Angelus of Millet', *The New Hope* II:4 (August 1934), pp. 10ff.

49 Ian Gibson provides a summary of these events in the *Shameful Life of Salvador Dalí*, pp. 375–80. For a thorough reading of Dalí's engagement with fascism in relation to his paranoiac-critical method and the writings of Jacques Lacan, see Robin Adèle Greeley, 'Dalí's Fascism; Lacan's Paranoia', *Art History* 24:4 (September 2001) 465–92.

50 Dalí, *Unspeakable Confessions*, p. 112.

51 Ibid., p. 112. Fèlix Fanès has published the manuscript of Dalí's talk in 1934 in Barcelona, 'Per un tribunal terrorista de responsabilitats intelectuals', in which the painter details his work on *The Angelus* and addresses his theories about Hitler. This is a critical document for understanding Dalí's theoretical position at the time. Fanés, *Salvador Dalí*, pp. 255–60.

52 Dalí, *Diary of a Genius*, p. 17.

Haim Finkelstein has argued, Dalí's 'Beings-Objects' offered the final stage in the artist's theories on the object.[53] From his *Surrealist Object Functioning Symbolically* to the 'Beings-Objects', Dalí moved from the activation of the object by the individual to the erosion of the boundary between object and self.[54]

In contrast to his 1935 parody of Napoleonic power dressed in *Angelus* designs, Dalí made a more direct statement against the assignment of partisan meanings to artistic styles. His 1937 article 'I Defy Aragon' explicitly stated his challenge to Socialist Realism. Writing in response to Louis Aragon's complaints against his *Aphrodisiac Jacket*, Dalí criticized what he saw to be the inconsistency and hypocrisy of politically motivated aesthetic decisions. Citing Aragon's enthusiastic support of the changing dictates of the Communist Party following the 1932 Kharkov Congress, Dalí described the party's aesthetic criteria as a mere formula that sought to oversimplify and categorize every level of cultural production. Dalí reminded his readers that in 1935 he had issued one of his clearest accounts of the paranoiac-critical method, *Conquest of the Irrational*, which he 'tied [around] with a red band upon which is written "In the face of Socialist Realism!" I repeat as a slogan: "Conquest of the irrational opposed to socialist realism" '.[55] As an illustration of the kind of arbitrary judgments that Dalí believed socialist realism made, he referred to a news photograph of Greta Garbo as a way to criticize Aragon's judgement: 'If instead of Garbo the photo were of Stalin it would already be "Socialist Realism", or if it were Hitler it would be "National Socialist Realism". All depends on the face which is hidden'.[56] In pointing to the 'hidden face' of ideology, Dalí defended his paranoiac-critical method as the means to reveal what ideology naturalized.[57]

In 1933–34, at the time that Dalí was producing many of his versions of *The Angelus* and elaborating his paranoiac-critical theory, Bataille penned 'The Psychological structure of fascism'. In this text, Bataille wrote: 'social homogeneity is a precarious form, at the mercy of violence and even of internal

---

53 Haim Finkelstein, 'The Incarnation of Desire: Dalí and the Surrealist Object', *Res*, no. 23 (Spring 1993), p. 135.

54 Dalí begins *Secret Life* with similar delusions of grandeur, writing: 'At seven I wanted to be Napoleon. And my ambition has been growing steadily ever since'. Dalí, *Secret Life*, p. 1.

55 Salvador Dalí, 'I Defy Aragon', *Art Front* III:2 (March 1937), p. 8.

56 Ibid., p. 8.

57 Dalí wrote a novel about the decadence of the aristocracy in the context of World War II titled *Hidden Faces* (1944), trans. Haakon Chevalier (New York: William Morrow and Company, 1974). For a discussion of this novel in relation to Dalí's paranoiac-critical method and his literary models, see Fèlix Fanés, 'Mig secret, mig ocult. Salvador Dalí, escriptor', *Els Marges*, no. 42 (1990), pp. 3–17.

dissent'.[58] Locating the foundation of homogeneity in money, Bataille insisted that social cohesion was constantly threatened by the heterogeneous, or 'unproductive expenditure'. The unconscious, dreams, excrement, violence, excess, delirium, and persons, words, or acts with erotic value (i.e. folklore and postcards) all fell within the category of the heterogeneous. Thus, according to Bataille, the circulation of currency, exchange itself, was constantly threatened by its heterogeneous complement: waste. Fascism, drawing upon some of these elements as well as the historical categories of nobility and honour, was likewise heterogeneous. In characterizing the qualities of totalitarian leadership as historical in nature, Bataille introduced the concept of anachronism as a key element in fascism. It is fascism's ability to reappropriate and reconstitute power based on the careful incorporation of the anachronistic that defines its relation to the homogeneous. It is through fascist leadership that those elements seen as irrational or uncontrollable are given vent within a carefully orchestrated system.

In an article titled 'The latest modes of intellectual stimulation for the summer of 1934', Dalí described the place of the anachronistic in his own work:

> Anachronism is the single '*imaginative constant*' capable of perpetual '*traumatic renewal*,' thanks to which it becomes possible to snatch raw and living lumps from that hard and extremely thick thing which is the sentimental fog from which are formed the very cheeks of memory [...]. Far from being the unusable, so-called 'stuffed thing,' considered inoffensive by the intellectual pseudo-experience which ironically disposes of it in the 'storehouse of junk of the ages,' 'anachronism' is, on the contrary, a real and living thing, a thing having flesh and bones.[59]

Dalí envisioned the anachronistic in biological terms as a live, explosive element. Anachronisms, like the symptoms of paranoia, were active, disturbing and intrusive. His *Angelus* paintings of these years introduced the concept of the anachronistic as an iconographic element. Paintings like *The Architectonic Angelus of Millet* of 1933 and *Archeological Reminiscence of Millet's Angelus* of 1935 presented the viewer with monumental phantasms of the peasant pair as architectural embodiments of the past (fig. 39). In the former, Dalí drew from the fluid shapes of *modernista* architecture that he celebrated in his articles of the 1930s. In the latter, he envisioned the pair as solitary archaeological ruins. Both paintings placed these anachronisms in a setting long familiar to viewers as the Catalan coast and the Empurdà plains.

---

58 Georges Bataille, 'The Psychological Structure of Fascism', *La Critique sociale*, no. 10 (November 1933) and no. 11 (March 1934); trans. in Bataille, *Visions of Excess*, p. 138.

59 Dalí, 'Derniers modes d'excitation intéllectuelle pour l'été 1934', *Documents* 34 (June 1934), pp. 33–35; trans. in *Collected Writings of Salvador Dalí*, p. 253.

NOMENCLATURE

Antonin Artaud — hart des os étreints.

André Breton — prête aux dés l'encre tonne.

André Masson — le son des antres.

Benjamin Péret — le nain aime les jambes de mon père.

Francis Gérard — frange d'assises gisantes.

Giorgio de Chirico — orchidées orgues de l'orgie.

Georges Limbour — limbes des orles et des proues.

Georges Malkine — gorge câline de la mort.

Jacques-André Boiffard — boire hanté par les affres.

Jacques Baron — l'arbre aux fleurons de nacre.

Louis Aragon — l'ouragan.

Max Ernst — nerfs à l'est exacerbés.

Mathias Lübeck — luths et rebecs.

Michel Leiris — le risque des échelles irisées.

Max Morise — horizon masqué.

Marcel Noll — mer d'argent anneau salé.

Paul Eluard — ailes sol éludé.

Pierre Naville — île animale pétrie hier.

Pablo Picasso — équipollence des paraboles astrales.

Pierre Reverdy — hydre épie et rêve.

Philippe Soupault — elfe au souffle d'opium.

René Crevel — les ravins du crâne et du réveil.

Robert Desnos — noces de la haine et des bordels.

Raymond Roussel — la rousseur du monde sourit à tes aisselles.

Roger Vitrac — les arcs ivres t'interrogent.

Roland Tual — lente tuerie rôde, ailes tues.

JACQUES-ANDRÉ BOIFFARD

L'ARMURE André Masson.

Fig. 1. André Masson, *The Armour*, 1924. Oil on canvas, 80.6 × 54 cm. Peggy Guggenheim Collection, Solomon R. Guggenheim Foundation, Venice. © 2002 Artists Rights Society (ARS), New York/ADAGP, Paris. Reproduced in *La Révolution surréaliste*, no. 4, July 1925, p. 22. Photograph courtesy Brown University Library

Michel Leiris :

1° Je suis mort. Je vois le ciel poudroyer comme le cône d'air traversé, dans une salle de spectacle, par les rayons d'un projecteur. Plusieurs globes lumineux, d'une blancheur laiteuse, sont alignés au fond du ciel. De chacun d'eux part une longue tige métallique et l'une d'elle perce ma poitrine de part en part, sans que j'éprouve aucune douleur. J'avance vers les globes de lumière en glissant doucement le long de la tige et je tiens par la main d'autres hommes qui montent comme moi vers le ciel, suivant chacun le rail qui les perfore. On n'entend pas d'autre bruit que le crissement de l'acier dans nos poitrines.

2° Je perçois si nettement le rapport entre le déplacement rectiligne d'un corps et une palissade perpendiculaire à la direction de ce mouvement, que je pousse un cri aigu.

3° J'imagine la rotation de la terre dans l'espace, non d'une façon abstraite et schématique, l'axe des pôles et l'équateur rendus tangibles, mais dans sa réalité. Ruguosité de la terre.

4° André Masson et moi évoluons dans l'air comme des gymnasiarques.

Une voix nous crie : « Acrobates mondiaux, allez-vous bientôt descendre tous les deux ? » A ces mots, nous nous renversons par-dessus l'horizon et tombons dans un hémisphère concave.

LES DEMOISELLES D'AVIGNON — *Picasso 1908*

Fig. 2. Pablo Picasso, *Les Demoiselles d'Avignon*, 1906–07. Oil on canvas, 244 × 234 cm. The Museum of Modern Art, New York, acquired through the Lillie P. Bliss Bequest. © 2002 Estate of Pablo Picasso/Artists Rights Society (ARS), New York. Reproduced in *La Révolution surréaliste*, no. 4, July 1925, p. 7. Photograph courtesy Brown University Library

Fig. 3. J.-A. Boiffard, *I Will Take the Hôtel des Grands Hommes as my Point of Departure*. Photograph, 1927. Illustration for *Nadja* (Paris: Gallimard, 1928), pl. 1

Fig. 4. J.-A. Boiffard, *The Humanité Bookshop*. Photograph, 1927. Illustration for *Nadja* (Paris: Gallimard, 1928), pl. 17

Fig. 5. J.-A. Boiffard, *The Illuminated Mazda Billboard on the Grands Boulevards*. Photograph, 1927. Illustration for *Nadja* (Paris: Gallimard, 1928), pl. 43

Fig. 6. Giorgio de Chirico, *The Enigma of Day*, 1914. Oil on canvas, 185.5 × 139.7 cm. Museum of Modern Art, New York, James Thrall Soby Bequest. © 2002 Artists Rights Society (ARS), New York/SIAE, Rome. Photograph © The Museum of Modern Art/Licensed by SCALA/Art Resource, NY

Fig. 7. Eugène Atget, *Avenue des Gobelins*, 1925. Albumen-silver print, 24 × 18 cm. The Museum of Modern Art, New York. Print by Chicago Albumen Works. Abbott-Levy Collection. Partial gift of Shirley C. Burden. Copy Print © 2002 The Museum of Modern Art, New York

Fig. 8. André Kertész, *On the Quai Near St.-Michel*, 1926. Photograph André Kertész. © 2002 Ministère de la Culture, France

Fig. 9. 'Help him to rebuild!', American Express Peace Loan Poster, 1920. Musée d'Histoire Contemporaine, BDIC, Paris

Fig. 10. André Kertész, *At a Cafe*, 1928. Photograph André Kertész. © Ministère de la Culture, France

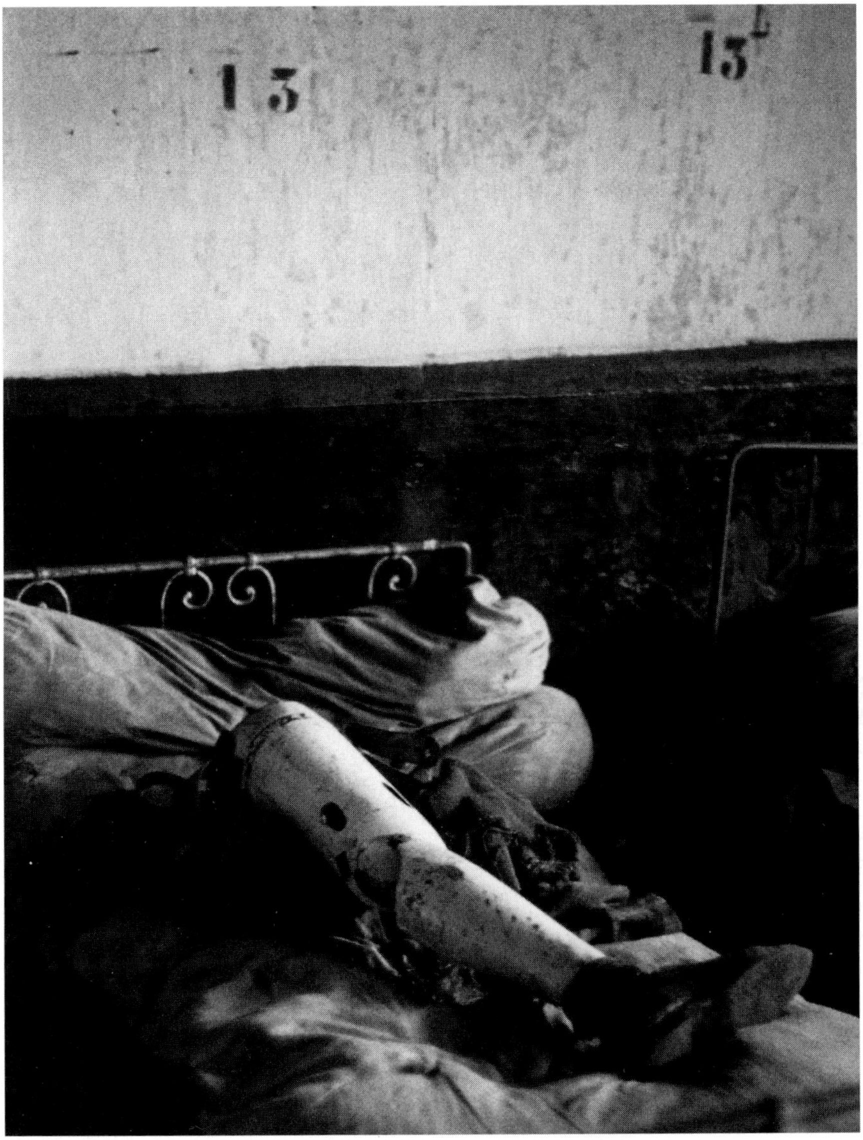

Fig. 11. André Kertész, *Leg (Hôtel de Reveil)*, 1927. Photograph André Kertész.
© Ministère de la Culture, France

Fig. 12. André Kertész, *Muguet Seller, Champs-Elysées*, 1928. Photograph André Kertész. © Ministère de la Culture, France

Fig. 13. André Kertész, *Paris, On the Boulevards*, 1934. Photograph André Kertész. © Ministère de la Culture, France

Fig. 14. André Kertész, *Clayton 'Peg Leg' Bates*, 1929. Photograph André Kertész. © Ministère de la Culture, France

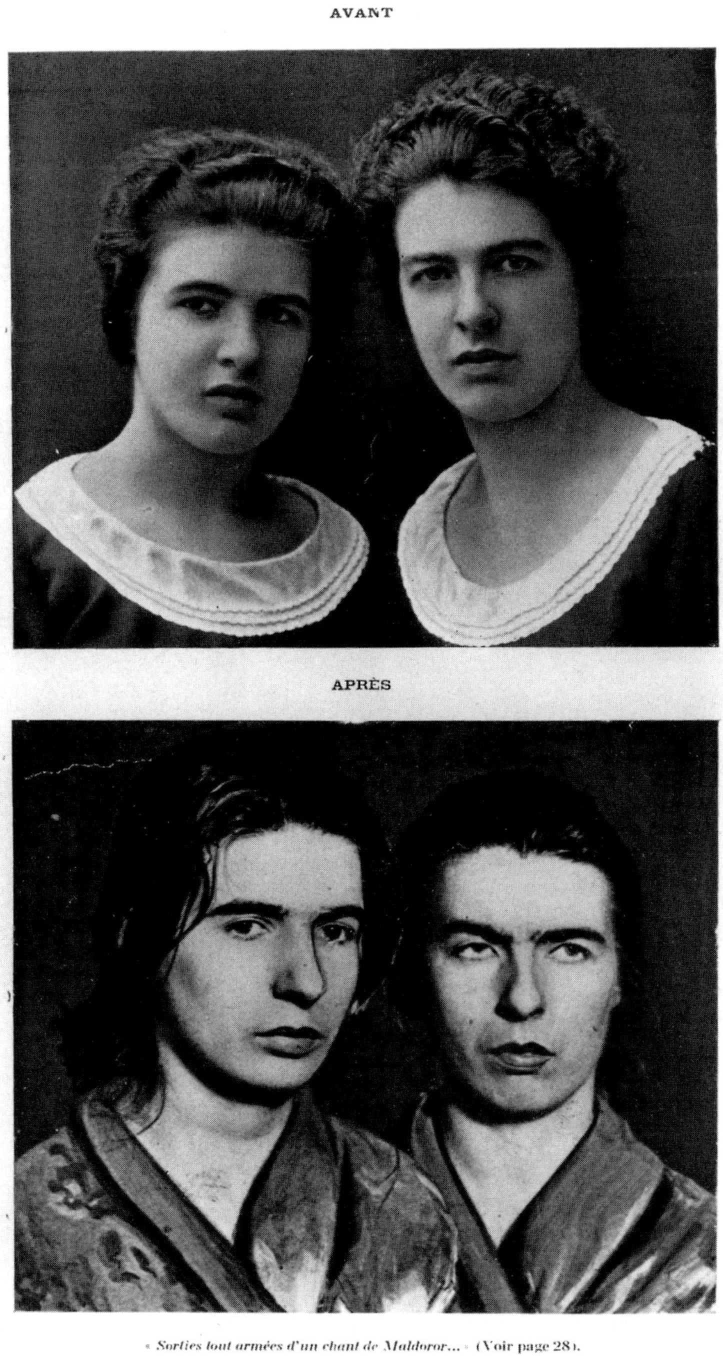

Fig. 15. 'Before, After', Photomontage of Christine and Léa Papin reproduced in *Le Surréalisme au service de la révolution*, no. 5 (July 1933). Image courtesy of the University of Pennsylvania Special Collections

Fig. 16. Paul Nougé and René Magritte, *Homage to the Papin Sisters*, from the special issue of *Documents 34: The Surrealist Intervention* (November 1934). © 2002 Artists Rights Society (ARS), New York/SABAM, Brussels; © 2002 C. Herscovici, Brussels/ Artists Rights Society (ARS), New York

Fig. 17. Benjamin Péret, *Collage (untitled)*, 1929. Frontispiece to Péret, *Œuvres complètes*, vol. 4 (Paris, Losfeld-JoséCorti, 1991)

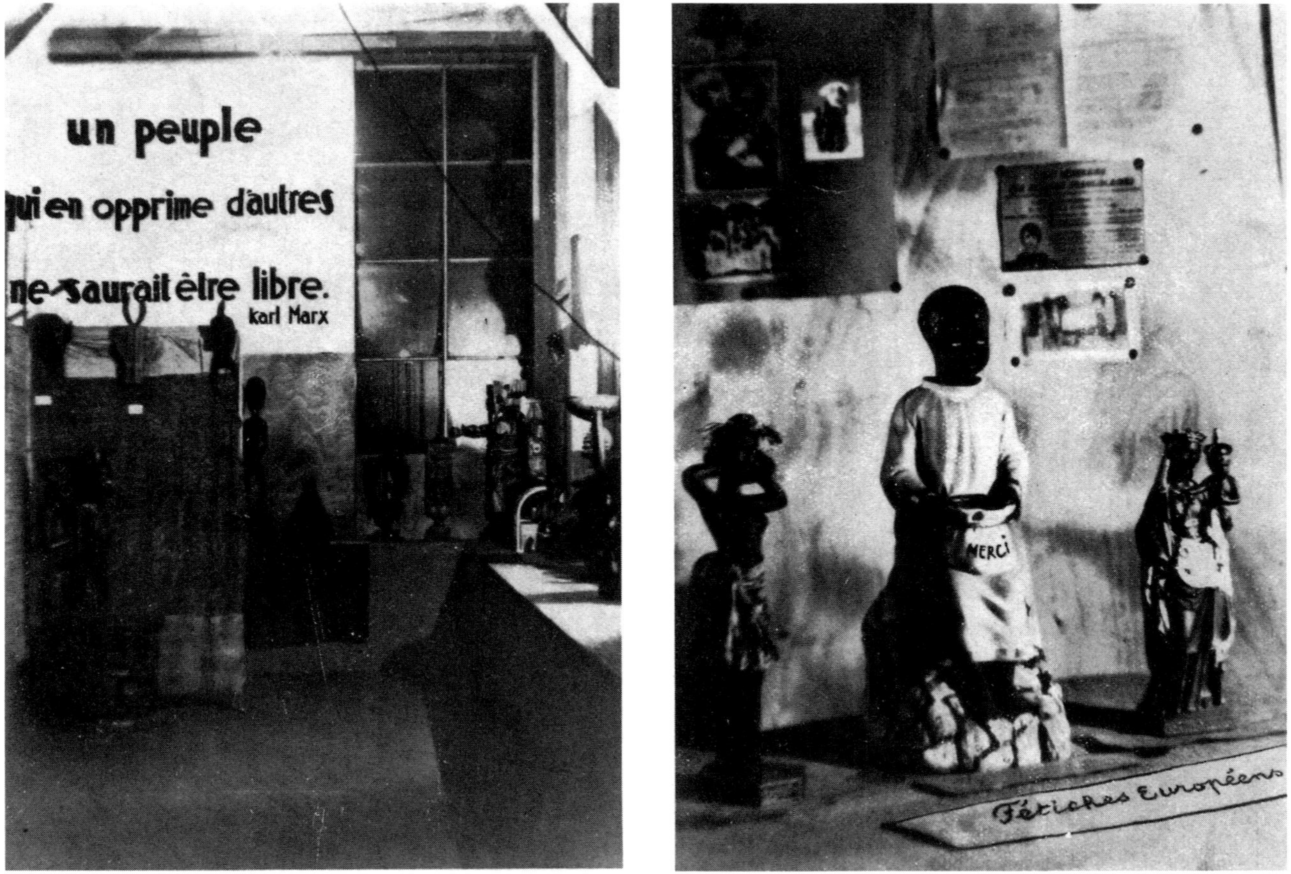

Fig. 18. 'A l'Exposition "La Vérité sur les Colonies" ', 1931. Photograph reproduced in *Le Surréalisme au service de la révolution*, no. 4 (December 1931)

Fig. 19. Joan Miró, *Painting*, summer 1936. Oil, gravel and pebbles on Masonite, 77.6 × 107.2 cm. The Art Institute of Chicago. Gift of Florence May Schoenborn and Samuel A. Marx. © 2002 Successió Miró/Artists Rights Society (ARS), New York/ ADAGP, Paris. Photograph © 1994, The Art Institute of Chicago

Fig. 20. Joan Miró, *Still Life with Old Shoe*, Paris, 24 January–29 May 1937. Oil on canvas, 81.3 × 116.8 cm. The Museum of Modern Art, New York. Gift of James Thrall Soby. © 2002 Successió Miró/Artists Rights Society (ARS), New York/ ADAGP, Paris. Photograph © 1994, The Museum of Modern Art, New York

Fig. 21. Joan Miró, *Painting*, 1933. Oil on canvas, 174 × 196.2 cm. The Museum of Modern Art, New York. Loula D. Lasker Bequest (by exchange). © 2002 Successió Miró/Artists Rights Society (ARS), New York/ADAGP, Paris. Photograph © 1994, The Museum of Modern Art, New York

Fig. 22. Joan Miró, Preparatory sketch for *Still Life with Old Shoe*, 1937. Pencil on newspaper, 7.5 × 12.7 cm. Fundació Joan Miró, Barcelona. © 2002 Successió Miró/Artists Rights Society (ARS), New York/ADAGP, Paris

Fig. 23. Joan Miró, *The Family*, 1924. Black and red chalk on emery paper, 74.1 × 104 cm. The Museum of Modern Art, New York. Gift of Mr and Mrs Jan Mitchell. © 2002 Successió Miró/Artists Rights Society (ARS), New York/ADAGP, Paris. Photograph © 1994, The Museum of Modern Art, New York

Fig. 24. Joan Miró, *Femme*, October 1934. Pastel on velours paper, 107 × 72 cm. Private collection, New York. © 2002 Successió Miró/Artists Rights Society (ARS), New York/ADAGP, Paris

Fig. 25. Balthus Klossowski, *Still Life*, 1937. Oil on wood, 81 × 99 cm. Wadsworth Atheneum, Hartford, Connecticut. The Ella Gallup Sumner and Mary Catlin Sumner Fund. © 2003 Artists Rights Society (ARS), New York/ADAGP, Paris

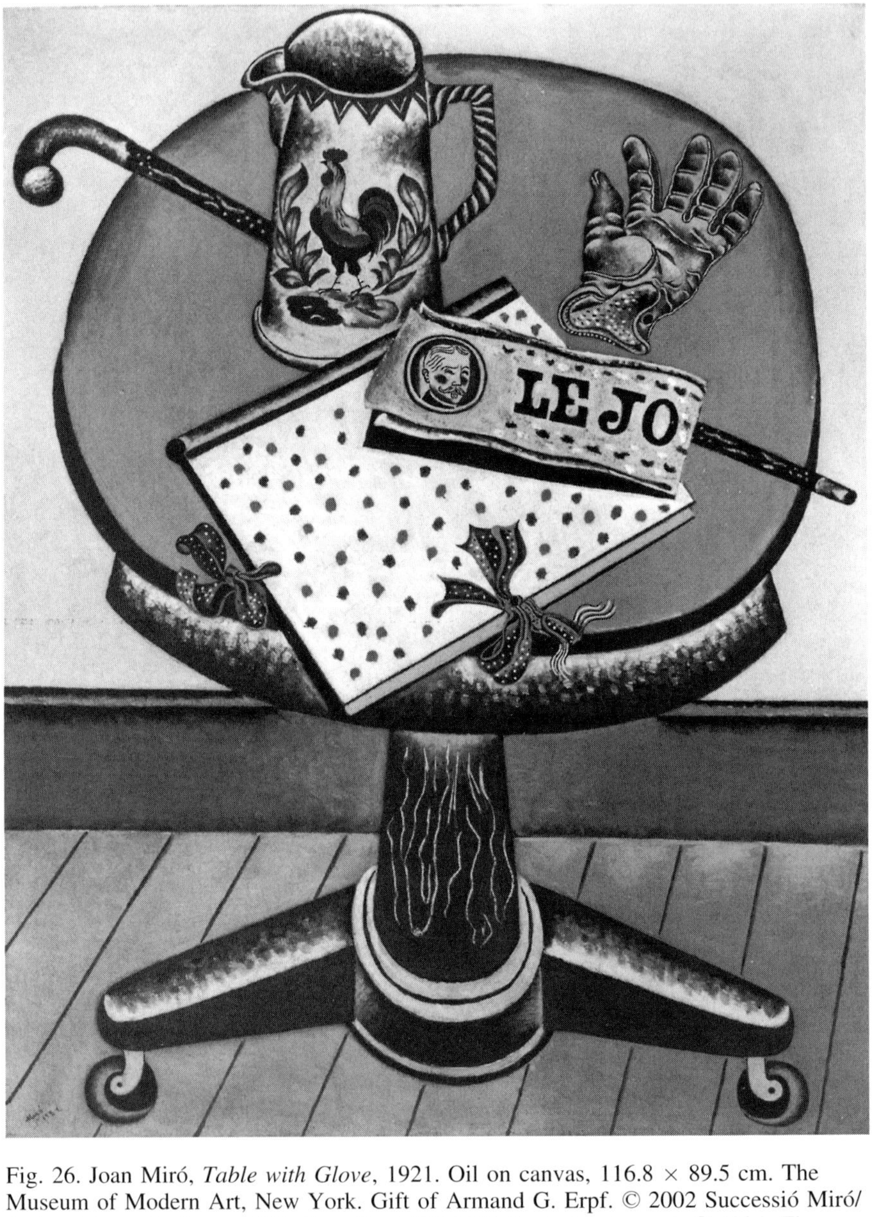

Fig. 26. Joan Miró, *Table with Glove*, 1921. Oil on canvas, 116.8 × 89.5 cm. The Museum of Modern Art, New York. Gift of Armand G. Erpf. © 2002 Successió Miró/ Artists Rights Society (ARS), New York/ADAGP, Paris. Photograph © 1994, The Museum of Modern Art, New York

Fig. 27. Joan Miró, *Help Spain* [*Aidez l'Espagne*], 1937, from *Cahiers d'Art*, vol. 12, nos 4–5. Pochoir printed in color, composition 24.8 × 19.4 cm. The Museum of Modern Art. Gift of Pierre Matisse. © 2002 Successió Miró/Artists Rights Society (ARS), New York/ADAGP, Paris. Photograph © 1994, The Museum of Modern Art, New York

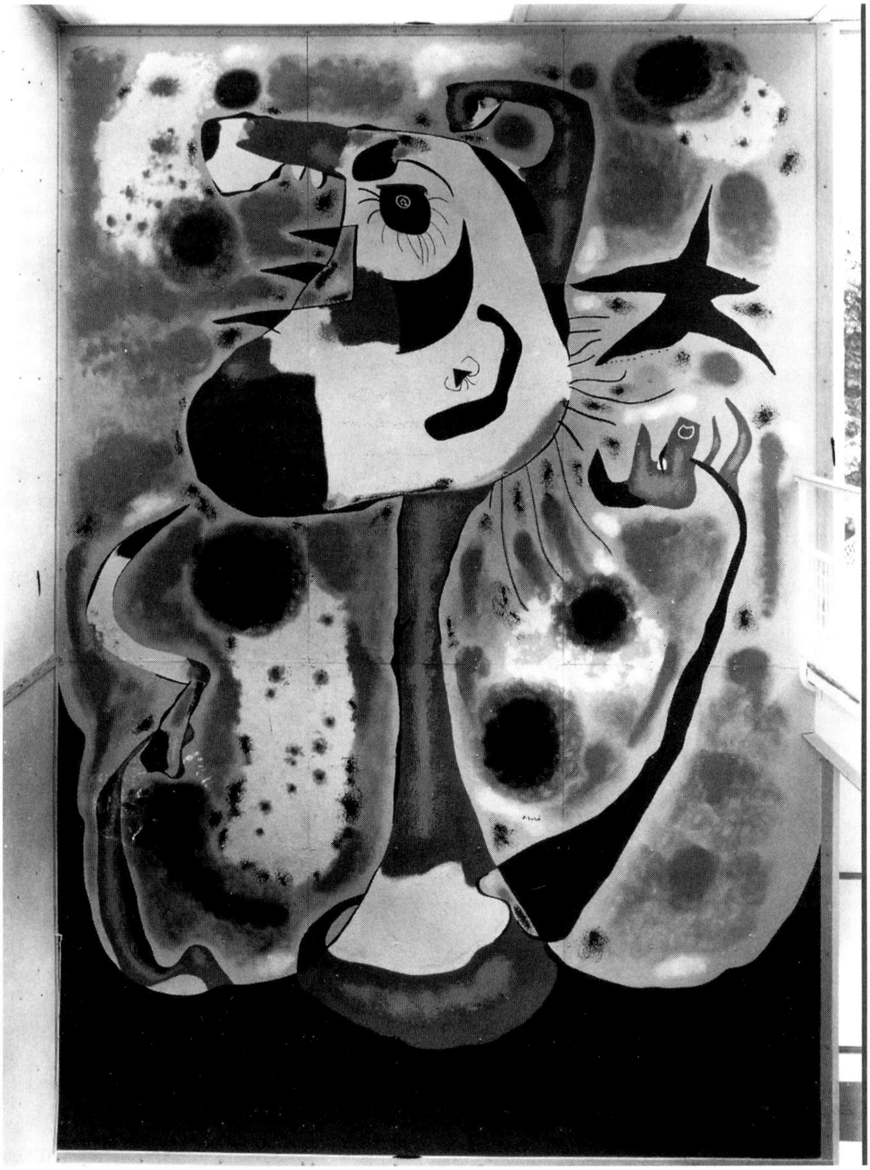

Fig. 28. Joan Miró, *The Reaper (Catalan Peasant in Revolt)*, 1937. Oil on celotex panels, 550 × 365 cm. Work disappeared. © 2002 Successió Miró/Artists Rights Society (ARS), New York/ADAGP, Paris. Photograph François Kollar

Fig. 29. Joan Miró, Preparatory drawing for *Help Spain*, 1937. Pencil on pasteboard, 11.5 × 9.5 cm. Fundació Joan Miró, Barcelona. © 2002 Successió Miró/Artists Rights Society (ARS), New York/ADAGP, Paris. Photograph © F. Catala-Roca

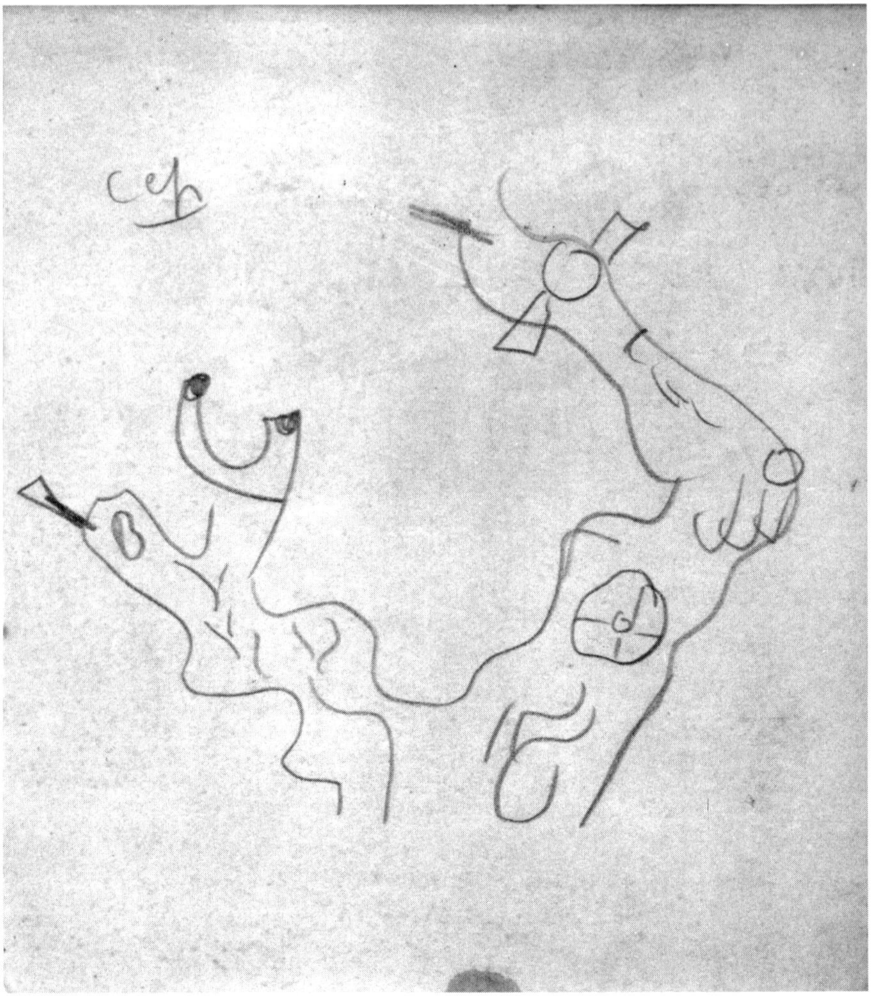

Fig. 30. Joan Miró, Study related to *The Tilled Field*, 1923–24. Paper, 19.1 × 16.5 cm. Fundació Joan Miró, Barcelona. © 2002 Successió Miró/Artists Rights Society (ARS), New York/ADAGP, Paris

Fig. 31. Carles Fontseré, *Libertat!* Poster for the FAI, 1936. Biblioteca Nacional, Madrid

Fig. 32. Jacint Bofarull, *Obrer! Camperol! Unitat per la victoria!* Poster for the FAI/CNT, 1936. Biblioteca Nacional, Madrid

Fig. 33. Salvador Dalí, *Le Mythe tragique de l'Angélus de Millet, Interprétation 'paranoïque-critique'* (Paris: Jean Jacques Pauvert, 1963), front cover

Fig. 34. Postcard reproduced in Salvador Dalí, 'Posició moral del surrealisme', *Hèlix*, no. 10 (22 March 1930), p. 6

Fig. 35. Acme News Agency, Untitled photograph of Salvador Dalí and Gala with pillow shams of Jean-François Millet's *The Angelus*, c. 1934–35. Courtesy Fundació Gala-Salvador Dalí, Figueres. © 2002 CORBIS

Fig. 36. Salvador Dalí, *Atavism at Twilight*, 1933–34. Oil on wood, 14 × 18 cm. Courtesy Kunstmuseum Bern. © 2002 Salvador Dalí, Gala-Salvador Dalí Foundation/ Artists Rights Society (ARS), New York

Fig. 37. Salvador Dalí, *Gala and the Angelus of Millet Immediately Preceding the Arrival of the Conic Anamorphoses*, 1933. Oil on wood, 24.2 × 19.2 cm. Courtesy National Gallery of Canada, Ottawa. © 2002 Salvador Dalí, Gala-Salvador Dalí Foundation/Artists Rights Society (ARS), New York

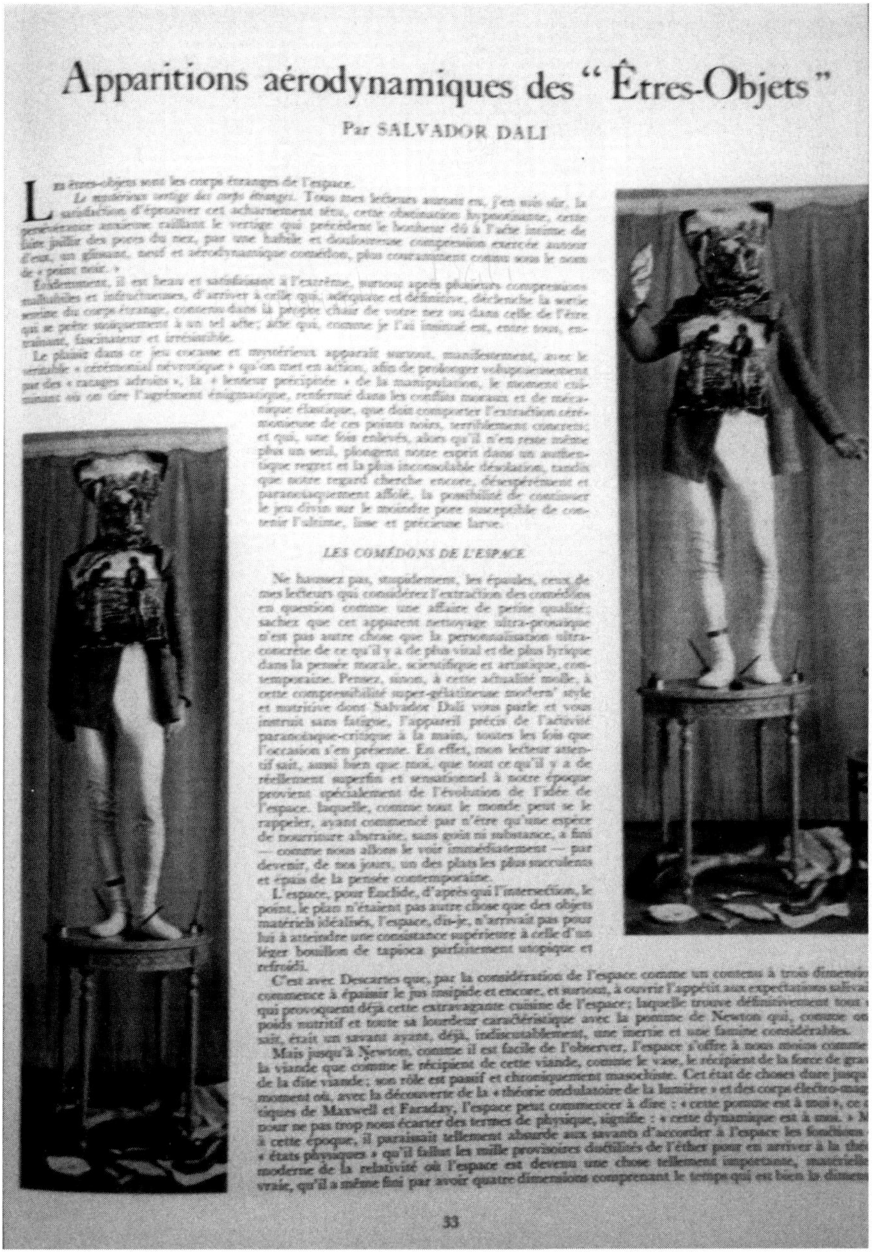
Apparitions aérodynamiques des " Êtres-Objets "

Par SALVADOR DALI

LES COMÉDONS DE L'ESPACE

33

Fig. 38. Salvador Dalí, 'Apparitions aérodynamiques des "Etres-objets" ', *Minotaure*, no. 6 (1935), p. 33

Fig. 39. Salvador Dalí, *The Architectonic Angelus of Millet*, 1933. Oil on canvas, 73 × 61 cm. Courtesy Museo Nacional Centro de Arte Reina Sofia, Madrid. © 2002 Salvador Dalí, Gala-Salvador Dalí Foundation/Artists Rights Society (ARS), New York

Fig. 40. Salvador Dalí, *Café Scene. The Figures at the Table make a Skull – Drawing for the Nightmare in 'Moontide'*, 1941. 13.6 × 12.6 cm. Courtesy Fundació Gala-Salvador Dalí, Figueres. © 2002 Salvador Dalí, Gala-Salvador Dalí Foundation/Artists Rights Society (ARS), New York

Fig. 41. Postcard. Collection Joaquím Gomis, Barcelona. Courtesy Gerard Gomis, Barcelona

Fig. 42. Installation photograph of the *Grosse Deutsche Kunstausstellung* at Hitler's Haus der Deutschen Kunst, Munich 1937. © Landeshauptstadt, Stadtarchiv Munich

Fig. 43. Postcard image of the Dada wall at the *Entartete Kunst*, Munich 1937. Courtesy Akademie der Kunst, Berlin

Fig. 44. Josef Breitenbach, Installation photograph of the 1938 *Exposition Internationale du Surréalisme*, Galerie Beaux Arts, 1938. © The Josef Breitenbach Trust, New York

Fig. 45. Press photograph of spectators viewing work by flashlight at the *Exposition Internationale du Surréalisme*. Courtesy Zabriskie Gallery, New York

Fig. 46. Press photograph of dancer Hélène Vanel preparing for her performance with a group of Surrealist artists (including George Hugnet, Man Ray, Salvador Dalí as seen from behind, and Wolfgang Paalen). Courtesy Bibliothèque Historique de la Ville de Paris, Paris

Fig. 47. Press photograph of Hélène Vanel performing at the *Exposition Internationale du Surréalisme*. Courtesy Wildenstein Archive, Paris

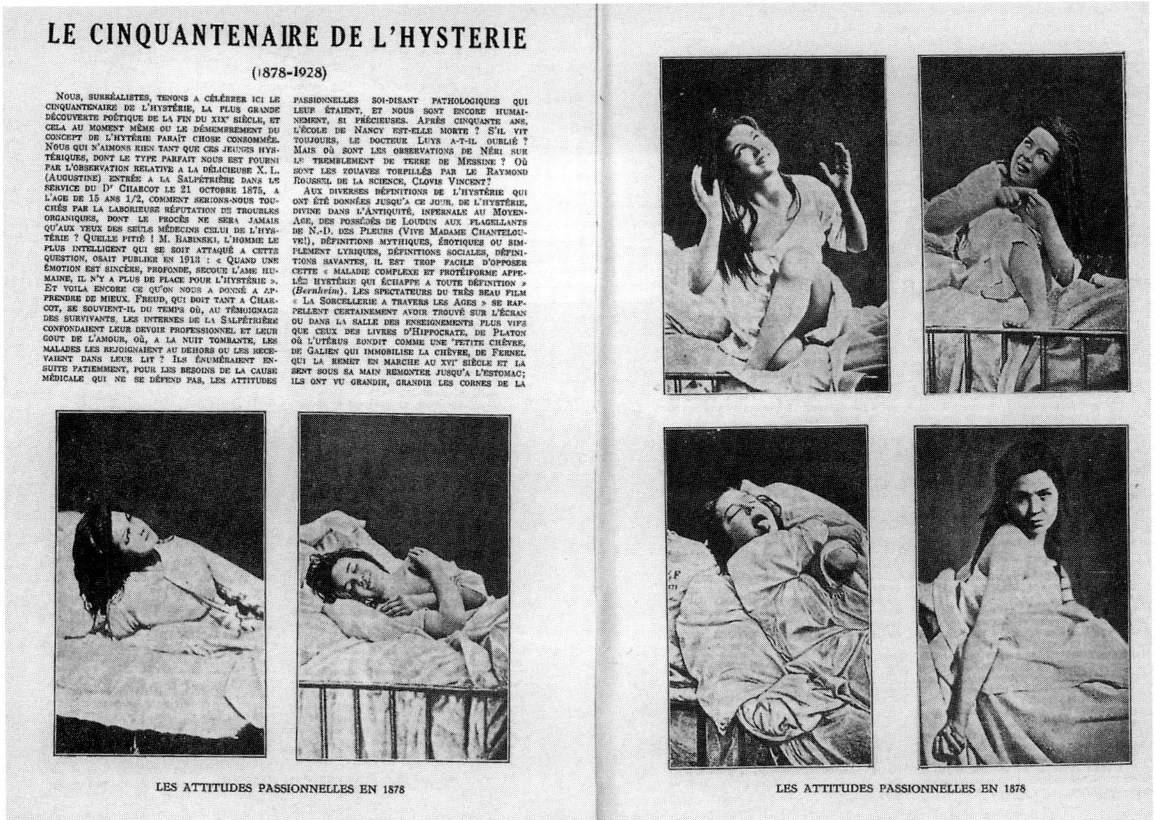

LE CINQUANTENAIRE DE L'HYSTERIE

(1878-1928)

Nous, surréalistes, tenons a célébrer ici le cinquantenaire de l'hystérie, la plus grande découverte poétique de la fin du XIXe siècle, et cela au moment même ou le démembrement du concept de l'hytérie paraît chose consommée. Nous qui n'aimons rien tant que ces jeunes hystériques, dont le type parfait nous est fourni par l'observation relative a la délicieuse X. L. (Augustine) entrée a la Salpétrière dans le service du Dr Charcot le 21 octobre 1875, a l'age de 15 ans 1/2, comment serions-nous touchés par la laborieuse réfutation de troubles organiques, dont le procès ne sera jamais qu'aux yeux des seuls médecins celui de l'hystérie ? Quelle pitié ! M. Babinski, l'homme le plus intelligent qui se soit attaqué a cette question, osait publier en 1913 : « Quand une émotion est sincère, profonde, secoue l'ame humaine, il n'y a plus de place pour l'hystérie ». Et voila encore ce qu'on nous a donné a apprendre de mieux. Freud, qui doit tant a Charcot, se souvient-il du temps où, au témoignage des survivants, les internes de la Salpêtrière confondaient leur devoir professionnel et leur gout de l'amour, où, a la nuit tombante, les malades les rejoignaient au dehors ou les recevaient dans leur lit ? Ils énuméraient ensuite patiemment, pour les besoins de la cause médicale qui ne se défend pas, les attitudes passionnelles soi-disant pathologiques qui leur étaient, et nous sont encore humainement, si précieuses. Après cinquante ans, l'école de Nancy est-elle morte ? S'il vit toujours, le docteur Luys a-t-il oublié ? Mais où sont les observations de Néri sur le tremblement de terre de Messine ? Où sont les zouaves torpillés par le Raymond Roussel de la science, Clovis Vincent?

Aux diverses définitions de l'hystérie qui ont été données jusqu'a ce jour, de l'hystérie, divine dans l'Antiquité, infernale au Moyen-Age, des possédés de Loudun aux flagellants de N.-D. des Pleurs (Vive Madame Chantelouve!), définitions mythiques, érotiques ou simplement lyriques, définitions sociales, définitions savantes, il est trop facile d'opposer cette « maladie complexe et protéiforme appelée hystérie qui échappe a toute définition » (*Bernheim*). Les spectateurs du très beau film « La Sorcellerie a travers les Ages » se rappellent certainement avoir trouvé sur l'écran ou dans la salle des enseignements plus vifs que ceux des livres d'Hippocrate, de Platon où l'utérus bondit comme une petite chèvre, de Galien qui immobilise la chèvre, de Fernel qui la remet en marche au XVIe siècle et la sent sous sa main remonter jusqu'a l'estomac; ils ont vu grandir, grandir les cornes de la

LES ATTITUDES PASSIONNELLES EN 1878

LES ATTITUDES PASSIONNELLES EN 1878

Fig. 48. André Breton and Louis Aragon, Celebration of the 'Fiftieth Anniversary of Hysteria', appearing in *La Revolution surréaliste*, no. 11 (15 March 1928)

Dessin de ISSAIEV.

AU SALON DES SURRÉALISTES

— Tu t'es sûrement trompé, ça doit être le Salon des Arts... déménagés.

Fig. 49. Cartoon rendering of the *Exposition Internationale du Surréalisme*, appearing in *Le Rire* (4 February 1938)

Fig. 50. Fritz Bach, *André Breton, Diego Rivera and Léon Trotsky*, 1938. Photograph. © Aube Breton; photograph by author from *Minotaure*, nos 12–13 (1939)

SOUVENIR DU MEXIQUE

Terre rouge, terre vierge tout imprégnée du plus généreux sang, terre où la vie de l'homme est sans prix, toujours prête comme l'agave à perte de vue qui l'exprime à se consumer dans une fleur de désir et de danger! Du moins reste-t-il au monde un pays où le vent de la libération n'est pas tombé. Ce vent en 1810, en 1910 irrésistiblement a grondé de la voix de toutes les orgues vertes qui s'élancent là-bas sous le ciel d'orage: un des premiers fantasmes du Mexique est fait d'un de ces cactus géants du type candélabre de derrière lequel surgit, les yeux en feu, un homme tenant un fusil. Il n'y a pas à discuter cette image romantique: des siècles d'oppression et de folle misère lui ont conféré à deux reprises une éclatante réalité et, cette réalité, rien ne peut faire qu'elle ne demeure latente, que ne persiste à la couver l'apparent sommeil des étendues désertiques. L'homme armé est toujours là, dans ses loques splendides, comme il peut seul se relever soudainement de l'inconscience et du malheur. Des prochains embroussaillements de la route il se détachera à nouveau, porté par une force inconnue il ira au devant des autres, pour la première fois il se reconnaîtra en eux. Qu'on ne s'arrête pas à ce qu'au bout de telles aventures entraîne apparemment de rigide la formation de toute hiérarchie militaire; peut se parer du titre de général au Mexique quiconque a été ou est encore capable de mouvoir, de sa propre initiative, un certain nombre d'hommes pris individuellement dans les campagnes. Les « généraux » dont je parle, formés pour la plupart à la rude école d'Emiliano Zapata, et dont quelques-uns tiennent le pouvoir, continuent eux-mêmes, il faut le dire, à participer de cette admi-

51

Fig. 51. Page layout from André Breton, 'Souvenir du Mexique', *Minotaure*, nos 12–13 (1939), including two photographs by Manuel Alvarez Bravo, *Flowering Tomb*, 1937, and *Striking Worker, Assassinated*, 1934. © Familia Alvarez Bravo y Urbajtel; photograph by author

Fig. 52. Hannah Höch, *Zerbrochen* (*Broken*), 1925. Collage, rotogravure on Japan paper, 15.2 × 11.4 cm irregular image. The Museum of Fine Arts, Houston. Museum purchase with funds provided by the Brown Foundation Accessions Endowment Fund. © DACS 2003

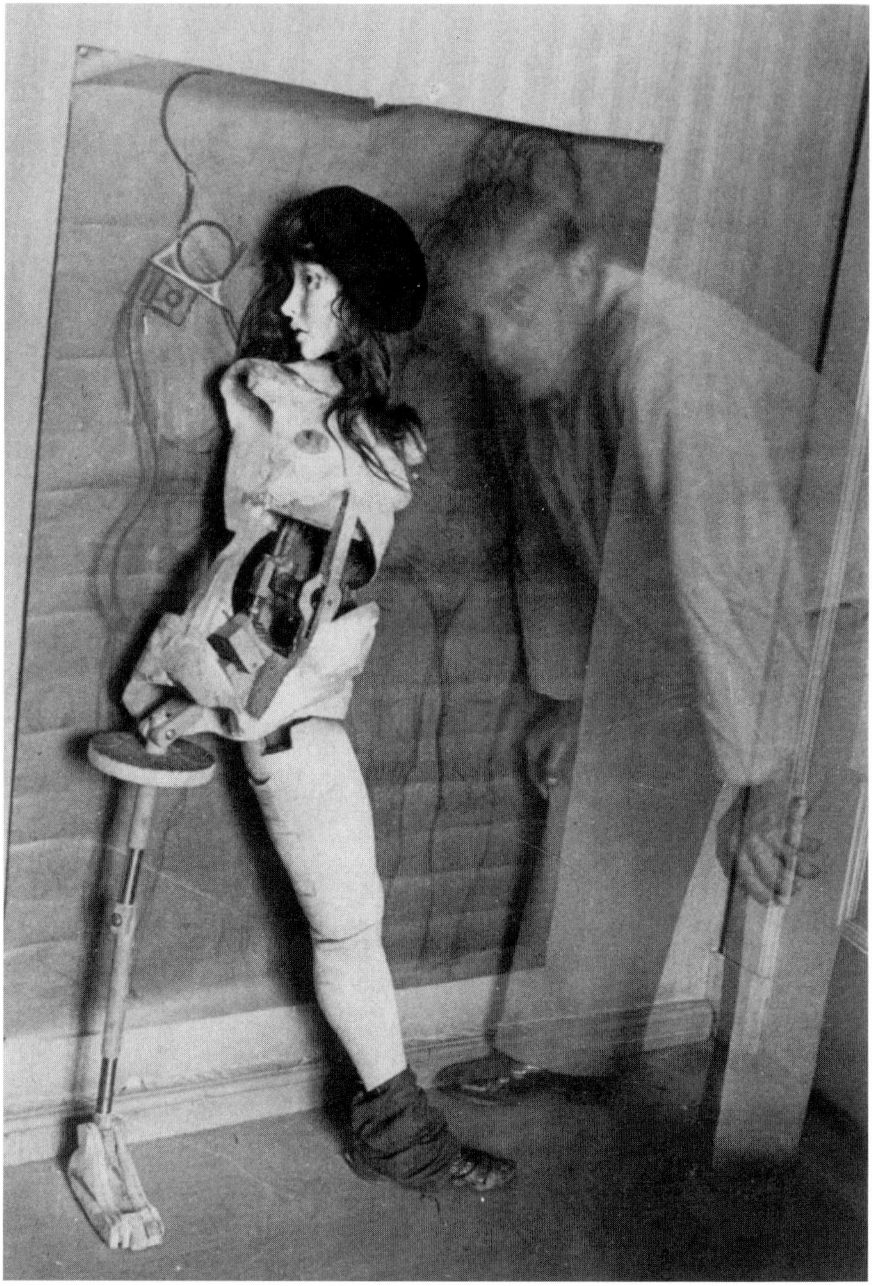

Fig. 53. Hans Bellmer, *La Poupée*, 1934, printed 1936. Vintage gelatin silver print (from the book *La Poupée*), 11.7 × 7.7 cm. Courtesy Ubu Gallery, New York and Galerie Berinson, Berlin. © ADAGP, Paris and DACS, London 2003

Fig. 54. Hans Bellmer, *La Poupée*, 1935. Hand-coloured vintage gelatin silver print, 14.2 × 14 cm. Courtesy Ubu Gallery, New York and Galerie Berinson, Berlin.

Fig. 55. Hans Bellmer, *La Croix gamahuchée*, 1946. Hand-coloured vintage gelatin silver print, signed on recto, 11.7 × 11.9 cm. Private collection. Courtesy Howard Greenberg Gallery, New York; Ubu Gallery, New York and Galerie Berinson, Berlin.

Fig. 56. Hans Bellmer, *Tenir au frais*, 1958. Collaged photographs and gouache, 23.4 × 23.9 cm. Courtesy Ubu Gallery, New York and Galerie Berinson, Berlin. © ADAGP, Paris and DACS, London 2003

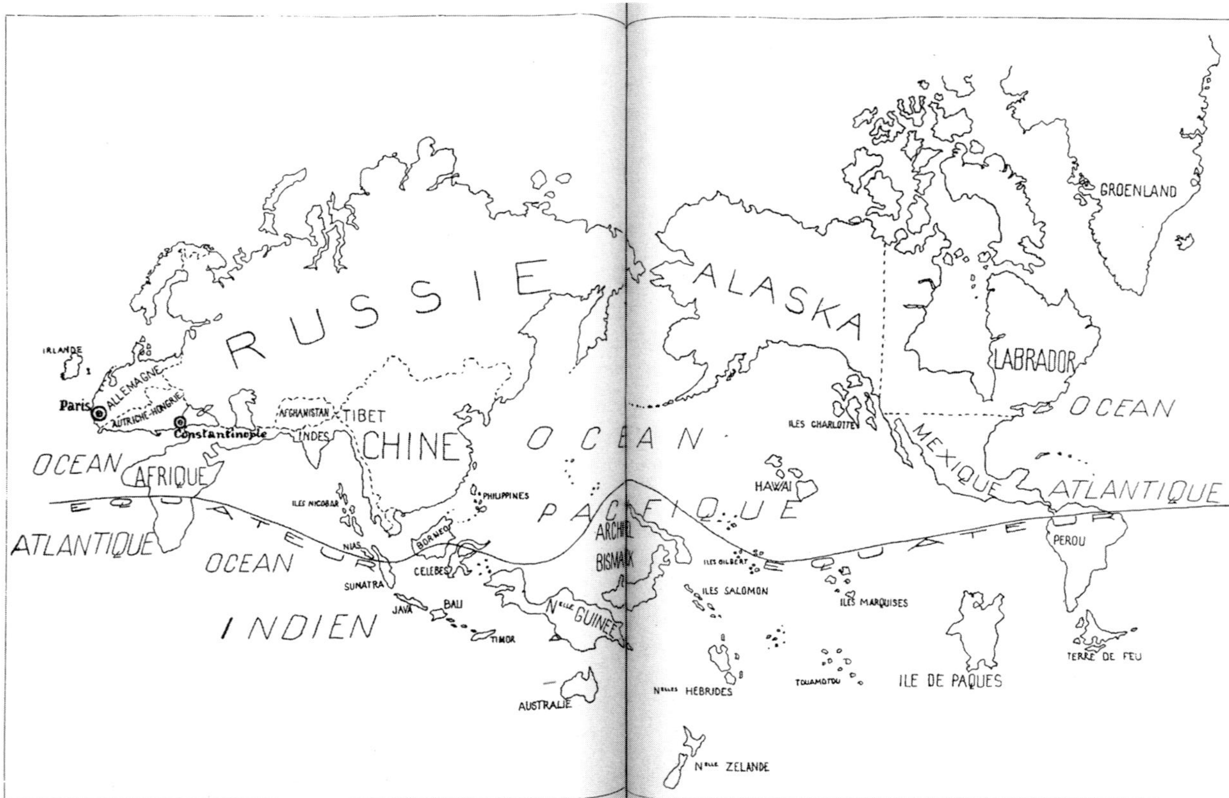

LE MONDE AU TEMPS SURREALISTES

Fig. 57. *Surrealist Map of The World*, from 'Le Surréalisme en 1929', special issue of *Variété*, May 1929

Fig. 58. Max Ernst, plate from *Une semaine de bonté ou les sept éléments capitaux* (Paris: Editions Jeanne Bucher, 1934). © 2003 Artists Rights Society (ARS), New York/ADAGP, Paris

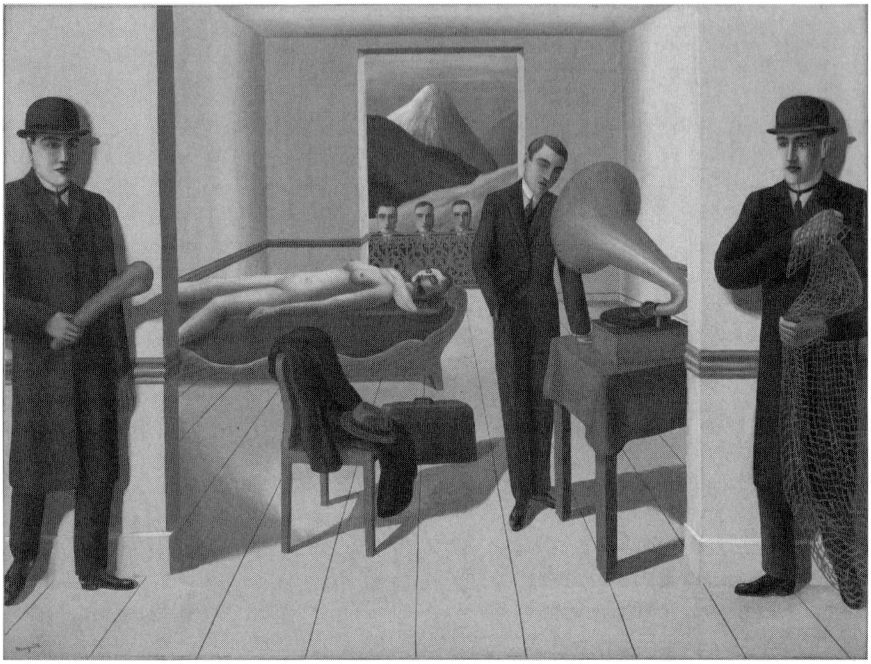

Fig. 59. René Magritte, *The Menaced Assassin* (*L'assassin menacé*), 1926. Oil on canvas, 152 × 195 cm. Museum of Modern Art, Kay Sage Tanguy Fund. © 2003 C. Herscovici, Brussels/Artists Rights Society (ARS), New York. Photograph © The Museum of Modern Art/Licenced by SCALA/Art Resource, NY

Fig. 60. Man Ray, André Breton in front of Giorgio de Chirico's painting, *The Enigma of Day*. © 2003 Man Ray Trust/Artists Rights Society (ARS), New York/ADAGP, Paris

Fig. 61. Giorgio de Chirico, *La Politique*, 1916. Oil on canvas, 33 × 26 cm. Private collection. © 2003 Artists Rights Society (ARS), New York/SIAE, Rome

Fig. 62. Alberto Giacometti, *La Boule suspendue*, 1930–31. Plaster and metal, 61 × 36.2 × 34.3 cm. Illustration from *Le Surréalisme au service de la révolution*, no. 3 (1931). © 2003 Artists Rights Society (ARS), New York/ADAGP, Paris

Fig. 63. Man Ray, *Surrealist Group, Waking Dream Session*, 1924. Photograph.

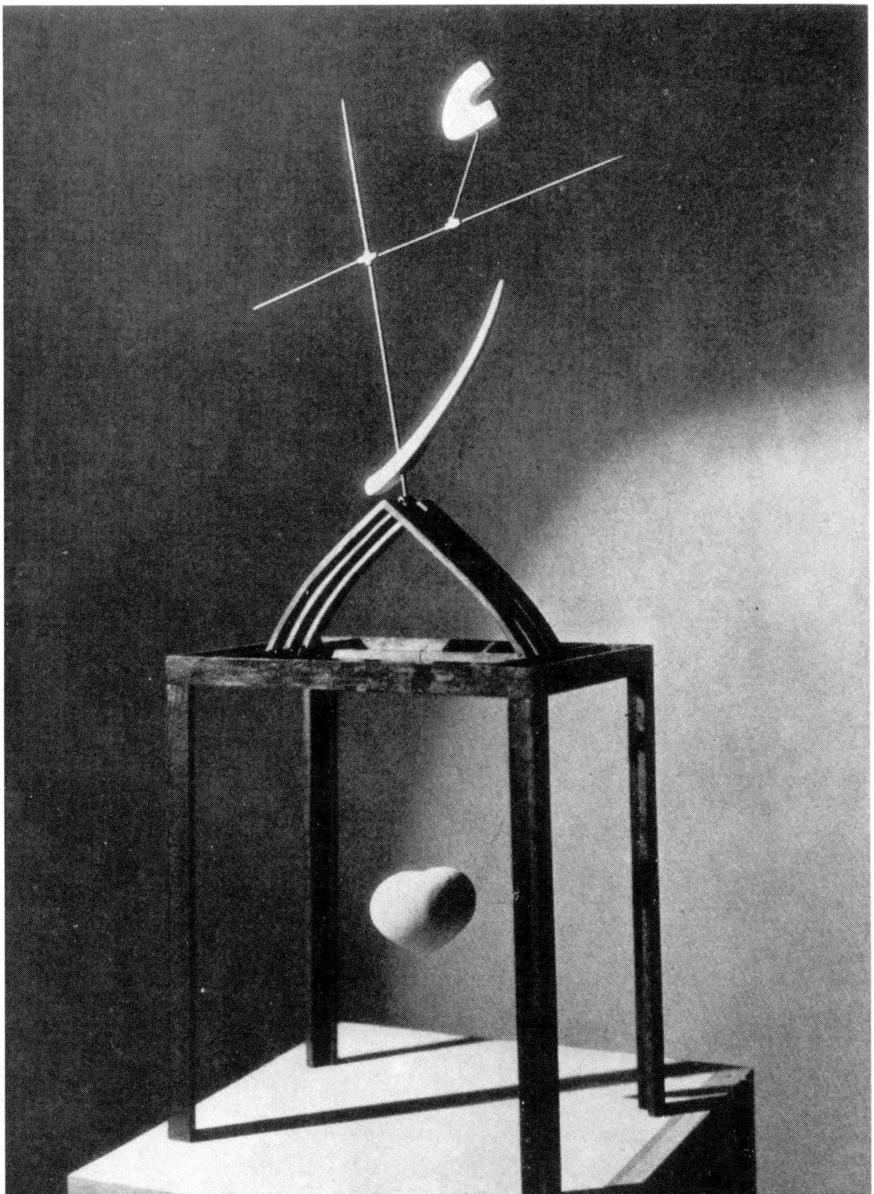

Fig. 64. Alberto Giacometti, *L'heure des traces*, 1930. Wood, plaster and metal. Whereabouts unknown. Illustration from *Le Surréalisme au service de la révolution*, no. 3 (1931). © 2003 Artists Rights Society (ARS), New York/ADAGP, Paris

No 4 — Première année 15 Juillet 1925

LA RÉVOLUTION SURRÉALISTE

ET GUERRE

AU TRAVAIL

SOMMAIRE

Pourquoi je prends la direction de la R. S. : André Breton.

POÈMES : Louis Aragon, Paul Éluard.

RÊVES : Max Morise, Michel Leiris.

TEXTES SURRÉALISTES : Philippe Soupault, Marcel Noll, Georges Malkine.

Les parasites voyagent : Benjamin Péret.

La baie de la faim : Robert Desnos.

Glossaire (*suite*) : Michel Leiris.

Nomenclature : Jacques-André Boiffard.

CHRONIQUES :

Fragments d'une conférence : Louis Aragon.

Le surréalisme et la peinture : André Breton.

Note sur la liberté : Louis Aragon.

Exposition Chirico : Max Morise.

Philosophies, L'étoile au front : Paul Éluard.

Correspondance.

ILLUSTRATIONS :

Giorgio de Chirico, Max Ernst, André Masson, Joan Miro, Pablo Picasso, Man Ray, Pierre Roy, etc.

ABONNEMENT, les 12 Numéros : France : 45 francs Etranger : 55 francs

Dépositaire général : Librairie GALLIMARD 15, Boulevard Raspail, 15 PARIS (VIIe)

LE NUMÉRO : France : 4 francs Étranger : 5 francs

Fig. 65. *Guerre au travail! C'est le parfait mannequin de Giorgio de Chirico, descendant l'escalier de la Bourse.* Front cover of *La Révolution surréaliste*, no. 4, 15 July 1925

Fig. 66. André Breton, *Jacques Vaché*, Collage. © 2003 Artists Rights Society (ARS), New York/ADAGP, Paris

Fig. 67. *L'intérieur de la vue*. Max Ernst, plate from *Une semaine de bonté ou les sept éléments capitaux* (Paris: Editions Jeanne Bucher, 1934). © 2003 Artists Rights Society (ARS), New York/ADAGP, Paris

Dalí's 'Samplers' and Greenberg's Criticism

After leaving Arcachon (and his manuscript for *Le mythe tragique*), Dalí lived in the United States from 1940 to 1948.[60] In 1945, Dalí's major American collector, the businessman A. Reynolds Morse, remarked: 'The fact that Dalí has never come out with any clear-cut statement as to his political leanings means that he and his art are both probably suspected by the party in ascendancy as well as by the party being submerged'.[61] Morse continued with an observation about the impact of the Spanish Civil War and World War II on Dalí's work:

> Dalí will undoubtedly be called a casualty of war, for since he left Spain and his native Catalan background, he has perhaps tended to reminisce rather than to create, [. . .] since he has been in this country he has painted more like a man influenced by Salvador Dalí than like Dalí himself. [. . .] When he sits down to paint he will be likened to an old maid making Dalí samplers.[62]

In a constant replay of his old themes, Dalí exhibited the symptoms of melancholia, a condition that Freud had linked to paranoia through narcissism and identification.[63] Unlike the mourner, who knows what he or she has lost and is able to work through the resultant pain, the melancholic ceases to be interested in the outside world. Though Dalí would never exhibit the abnegation that typically characterizes melancholia, he practised another aspect of melancholia as described by Freud: the conversion of loss into mania.[64] Dalí's relentless production and his return to and reworking of previously elaborated themes might be considered a manifestation of a manic activity that blocked out that loss which remained unconscious but present. In works like his *Ballerina in a Death's-Head* of 1939 and his sketch for the nightmare scene in the film *Moontide* of 1941, Dalí returned to postcards as a model. This time he used popular sources to reveal death within images of prosperity, not just agrarian piety as he had done with the *Angelus* (fig. 40). The double vision of the skull contained within an image of middle-class innocence, such as a café scene or a pair in conversation, was a constant in turn-of-the-century vanitas theme postcards (fig. 41). The replaying of a discourse that had characterized Dalí's first writings on paranoia, especially his speech of 1930, was not limited to Dalí himself. As I argued earlier, Orwell had, unintentionally, repeated the artist's

60 Gibson, *Shameful Life of Salvador Dalí*, pp. 459–99.

61 A. Reynolds Morse, 'The Dream World of Salvador Dalí', *Art in America* XXXIII:3 (July 1945), p. 120.

62 Ibid., p. 114.

63 Editor's note in Sigmund Freud, 'Mourning and Melancholia (1917)', *The Standard Edition of the Complete Psychological Works of Sigmund Freud*, trans. James Strachey, vol. 14 (London: Hogarth Press), p. 241.

64 Freud, 'Mourning and Melancholia', pp. 244–46.

own earlier assertion that pornographic postcards exhibited the popular unconscious more than any other artifact. Only, it was Dalí's works that now, ironically, took the place of turn-of-the-century pop culture.

In the same year as Orwell's review, Clement Greenberg published a two-part article in *The Nation*, in which he too described Dalí's 'desire to sin against decorum, violate the rules, [and] do the disreputable thing' as a 'symptom'.[65] Like Orwell, he also compared Surrealist works to postcards, writing:

> For the sake of hallucinatory vividness the Surrealists have copied the effects of the calendar reproduction, postal card chromotype and magazine illustration. In general they prize the qualities of popular reproduction because of its incongruously prosaic associations and because the reproduction heightens illusionistic effect by erasing paint texture and brushstroke.[66]

Unlike Orwell, who alluded to the postcard's pornographic content, Greenberg focused on the aesthetic perversity of the Surrealists' postcard-style, especially its disavowal of the inherent characteristics of painting. As Greenberg accused: 'The attempt is made to depress [painting] to a popular level instead of raising the level of popularity itself'.[67] In turning toward the model of popular, mass-produced images, Greenberg characterized Surrealism as backward looking, reiterating Orwell's description of Dalí's autobiography as breaking the forward march of the avant-garde. Orwell saw this nostalgic move as recalling the earlier perversions of Barcelona. Similarly, Greenberg associated it with an erasure of present-day difficulties: 'Its very horrors are nostalgic and day-dreamy, having associations with a more pleasant-seeming past'.[68] Greenberg complained that the Surrealists lowered painting from the heights of fine art to the common status of the everyday: he labelled paintings like Dalí's 'a new and interesting kind of [...] document'.[69] With his own work becoming 'a new kind of document', Dalí had come to imitate with precision that which he had all along studied and, in a previous moment, had criticized: the hidden ideological and psychoanalytic content of fine art's relationship to popular culture.

---

65 Clement Greenberg, 'Surrealism', *The Nation* (12 and 19 August 1944). Reprinted in *Perceptions and Judgments 1939–1944*, vol. 1 of *Clement Greenberg: The Collected Essays and Criticism*, ed. John O'Brien (Chicago and London: The University of Chicago Press, 1986), p. 229.

66 Ibid., p. 229.

67 Ibid., p. 225.

68 Ibid., p. 231.

69 Ibid., p. 231.

Chapter 9

Surrealism in 1938: The Exhibition at War

Elena Filipovic

According to many accounts, the *Exposition Internationale du Surréalisme* (International Surrealist Exhibition) of 1938 marks the irremediable withdrawal of Surrealism from political engagement. After publishing enraged manifestoes, after joining and breaking with the French Communist Party, after trying and failing to take to the streets with Georges Bataille, the Surrealist poets and artists turned – so the story goes – to the comfortable, genteel space of the art exhibition. There, they constructed a lavish, frivolous installation that pandered to the same bourgeois class they had so long railed against. In short, at the moment when the most treacherous war in modern history menaced, the revolutionary fervour and vociferous anti-fascism of the movement went into hiding.[1]

To what extent does this narrative of the passage of Surrealism from 'the political street to the artistic salon', as one historian has put it, depend on stable notions of aesthetics and politics?[2] To what degree does it fathom Surrealism's

---

I thank Boris Belay, Vivian Rehberg, Donald LaCoss and Raymond Spiteri for their careful readings and suggestions with early drafts of this essay. I also gratefully acknowledge the Dedalus Foundation whose fellowship supported the research for the larger project from which this essay is a part.

1 If this narrative of Surrealism reproduces the overwhelming opinion of the press and critics in 1938 at the moment of the *succès de scandale* of the *Exposition Internationale du Surréalisme*, it is also carried through in many recent histories of the movement. See in particular: Jack D. Spector, 'The Avant-Garde Object: Form and Fetish in between World War I and World War II', *Res*, no. 12 (Autumn, 1986), p. 139; Susan Rubin Suleiman, 'Between the Street and the Salon', in Lucien Taylor, ed., *Visualizing Theory: Selected Essays from V.A.R., 1990–1994* (New York: Routledge, 1994), pp. 143–58; and Martica Sawin, *Surrealism in Exile* (Cambridge: MIT Press, 1996). And even when the 1938 *Exposition* is not cited as emblematic, for historians such as Maurice Nadeau and Peter Bürger, the mid to late 1930s marks the end of the relevance of the movement's political agitation. Cf. Nadeau, *The History of Surrealism*, trans. Richard Howard (Cambridge: Harvard University Press, 1989), and Bürger, *Theory of the Avant-Garde*, trans. Michael Shaw (Minneapolis: University of Minnesota Press, 1984).

2 Suleiman points to the absence of a 'collective (or for that matter individual) programmatic declaration' to accompany the 1938 *Exposition Internationale du Surréalisme* as the evidence that Surrealists had, by that point, abandoned their ideological concerns. This fact is evoked to support her claim that the movement found

various efforts as politically motivated (even if ultimately impotent) only when they take common or at least explicit forms of ethical and ideological criticality? What if one of the responses of the Surrealist movement to its historical condition in the late 1930s eschewed the most common tactics of organized politics (slogans, declarations, banners), all the better to expose the hidden assumptions and political inscriptions of that armature (the art exhibition) on which authoritative narratives, disciplining systems and so-called normative experiences were built?

A reconsideration of the relationship of politics to Surrealism requires an interrogation of what remains among the least explored aspects of the movement's activity: exhibition practice. The undermining of the social order so central to Surrealism was, in the years before the war, thought through the space of art display and the experience within it. In particular, the first of the movement's 'Exposition Internationale' held in Paris in 1938 extended the movement's developing concern with the ideological potential of the object and its display, attending as pointedly to the situation of the object as to the viewing subject.[3] Of course, for Surrealism, what was at stake in their various exhibitions was not the display of 'Art'. One sees this already in the *Exposition Surréaliste d'objets* (Surrealist Exhibition of Objects) of two years earlier, where the heterogeneous mix of *objets trouvés*, lava formations, mathematical models, Duchampian readymades, African and Oceanic artifacts, Surrealist constructions, and other objects reinterpreted the categories and taxonomies of the art gallery and museum. The exhibition importantly did so through a presentation that mimed as closely as possible – with vitrines, pedestals and an orderly display – some of the gallery-museum's most visible codes and

---

itself in a 'perhaps totally unwilling but nevertheless indubitable movement [...] out of the political street and into the artistic salon'. Literally looking for evidence of the political in the word, however, one might say that she misses the writing on the wall; Suleiman searches the exhibition's accompanying 'dictionary' only to come up disappointed, not once considering the space and installation as possible sites of ideological inscription. Yet, it is precisely in this newly privileged Surrealist arena for expression – the exhibition space itself – that I would argue that the *Exposition* sought to redefine the movement's relationship to the ideological. Suleiman, 'Between the Street and the Salon', pp. 143–58.

3 Several exhibitions of the 1930s testify to the Surrealist concern with the relationship of ideology and exhibiting, notably the group's anti-colonialist counter-exhibition in 1931 and the *Exposition Surréaliste des Objets* in 1936. Indeed, it is hardly insignificant that in 1935, in the midst of fervent efforts to form the radical left-wing revolutionary group *Contre-Attaque*, the Surrealists organized an exhibition of drawings – exhibitions and political convictions were not so far apart for the group. This exhibition was closely followed by a series of international Surrealist exhibitions (with accompanying lectures and journal-production) where the subject of 'art and politics' was consistently treated in Prague, Tenerife and London in 1935–36, thus stressing that the art exhibition should be linked to political consciousness and the critique of authority.

systems.[4] However, the 1938 *Exposition Internationale du Surréalisme* operated differently from prior shows, promoting instead a recoding of the actual space and architecture of the art gallery as it rethought the gallery worthy object – Art – defined by it. The difference was decisive, introducing a perceptual and performative dimension integral to understanding the *Exposition Internationale du Surréalisme* and the later Surrealist exhibitions for which it served as an important model.

Dirty, dark, loud and hysteric, the 1938 *Exposition*'s substitution of interference and disorientation for the traditional orderliness of the exhibition space touched on more than simply aesthetic issues. Without banners, slogans or explicit political declarations, the Surrealists' idiosyncratic installation defined a form of ideological critique that concentrated on the disruptive potential of process, ephemerality, instability and visual frustration against the period's exhibitionary commonplace of stasis, solidity, sanity and visual primacy. However, the failure of scholars to see the prewar show as anything more than an aesthetic or anti-aesthetic event stems at least in part from a failure to adequately treat the spatial and performative dimensions of Surrealism, even as these dimensions arguably fostered the movement's most provocative and ideologically charged work of the period. As the movement's 1938 staging recast the bourgeois eighteenth-century interior of the Parisian gallery in which it was housed, it also pointed to what museological spaces of the day hid: that walls were not neutral, that display strategies were not objective, and that careful taxonomies and rooms *enfilade* held up the fragile foundations of national chauvinism, authoritative rule and art history alike. Moreover, as it dissolved typical modes of display, the *Exposition* worked in direct contestation of the concurrent impulse to organize modern museums and galleries into neat, ordered and 'scientific' structures for the classification and presentation of the Truth of Art and History.[5]

---

4 The question of the *category* is, I think, crucial to this 1936 show, both through Breton's development of new object 'types' (his manuscript notes for the catalogue suggest he moved objects – among them Duchamp's 'readymades' – between categories before he settled on the final version) and the deliberately heterogeneous (but not at all messy) display of the works which refused compartmentalization into their anti-aesthetic taxonomies. On this exhibition and the 1931 anti-colonial Surrealist manifestation, see Janine Mileaf, 'Body to Politics: Surrealist Exhibition of the Tribal and the Modern at the Anti-Imperialist Exhibition and the Galerie Charles Ratton', *Res*, no. 40 (Fall 2001), pp. 239–55.

5 The presentation of the museum as a stable, objective and scientific enterprise was the role of an unusual exhibition entitled *Muséologie* that formed part of the 1937 Paris *Exposition Universelle*. For its vast World's Fair public, the exhibition on modern museology articulated – through charts, graphs, miniaturized museum displays, a 'model' exhibition, informative guidebook, etc. – the aesthetics and organizational practices that made the museum a 'scientific' arbiter of history and taste. What this exhibition on exhibitions did not address, and what in fact its claims for a museum's objectivity helped to mask, was the arbitrariness of the museum's choices, the partialness of the narratives it validated, and, the very real imbrication of politics in display.

The Surrealist effort uncovered the exhibition as a terrain of ideological battle, a museological frame whose purported innocuousness hid contesting meanings and questionable aspirations. This uncovering was all the more relevant – and urgent – given that the show opened at a moment when art exhibitions had become increasingly active implements of terrifying ideological instruction. This situation was embodied in the Third Reich's simultaneous *Grosse Deutsche Kunstausstellung* (Great German Art Exhibition) and the *Entartete Kunst* (Degenerate Art) exhibition of 1937. The Surrealist exhibition opened its doors in the midst of France's near-daily press reportage of the unfolding of these Nazi exhibitions in Munich, and just weeks after the closing of the 1937 Paris World's Fair where Germany's pavilion had displayed the new Nazi museum in maquette form.[6] To evaluate the Surrealist and the Nazi exhibitions in one essay is more than to outline near coincident histories and geographies. The fact that these exhibitions opened in the period after Nazism's rise to power and just before the outbreak of the war is but an external aspect of another tie that binds them: each discursively underscores the exhibition space as a site whose hangings tell a carefully chosen narrative and whose chronologies and taxonomies choreograph objects and viewers alike.[7]

The 1938 *Exposition Internationale du Surréalisme* is perhaps most productively illuminated in contrast to the Nazi exhibitions of 'Great' and 'Degenerate' art, opened in Munich less than six months earlier. However, to discuss these exhibitions together is not to argue for causal connections nor to point to necessary responses or reactions; rather, it is to refute the

6 For the press of both the Right and Left, the connections between these events and the Nazi presence in Paris for the *Exposition Universelle* did not escape comment. French art journals including *Cahiers d'Art*, *La Revue de l'Art*, *Beaux Arts*, *Mercure de France*, and *Peintres et sculptures de la maison de la culture* all published articles in 1937 and 1938 which reflected on the aesthetico-political situation of the Third Reich. Moreover, many French dailies, such as *Le Temps*, also kept a correspondent in Munich, publishing quotidian reports to keep the French abreast of both the *Grosse Deutsche Kunstausstellung* and the *Entartete Kunst* exhibitions as they opened; see *Le Temps* (17–21 July 1937).

7 There are certainly other contemporary exhibits that might usefully be looked at in relation to the Surrealist *Exposition* instead of or in addition to the twin Nazi shows; one might, for instance, think of the exhibition entitled *L'Art Cruel*, an explicitly anti-fascist exhibition of 'realist' depictions of the danger of Fascism, or the various exhibitions of French art sent throughout Nazi Germany as part of the good relations efforts on the part of both governments. However, in these latter examples there is a sense that the exhibition is little more than the mute vehicle for the presentation of works which speak their ideological message for themselves. In the Surrealist exposition, as in the 'Degenerate Art' exhibition (from which a reading of the 'Great German Art' exhibition cannot be extricated), on the other hand, I see a very explicit engagement with the space, architecture, codes and terms of artistic/museal display and a recognition that these, as much as the works themselves, are *on display*. Thus, it seemed to make most sense here to look at the Nazi exhibitions, in particular, in relation to the Surrealist display.

characterization of Surrealism's emphasis on the space of exhibition as a turn to a comfortable, genteel site. For, in the late 1930s, there was, in fact, little safe or genteel about the role or potential of exhibition spaces. The twin Nazi exhibitions forcefully demonstrate the extent of the imbrication of politics in exhibition spaces in prewar Europe. In other words, Surrealism's move from 'street to salon' need not be seen as a move away from politics, but *towards it*.

To look, then, at these disparate shows together is to ask how three extreme examples of late 1930's exhibition practice articulate and contradict the ways in which movements, regimes, governments and publics can be politically engaged. To insist that the *Exposition Internationale du Surréalisme* be read in relation to this larger exhibition context is thus to refuse the accounts of the Surrealist exhibition that have for so long understood it as a merely ludic, aesthetic or even anti-aesthetic event; it is to consider the ways in which its various offerings – hysteric simulation, dirt, acoustics or darkness in an exhibition space – could serve as a riposte to a stable idea of exhibition display and thus, to both modernist and Nazi exhibition practices. And, finally, it is to probe the ways in which the accepted terms of political action may have been defied by Surrealism so as to rethink, precisely, the question of ethical, ideological and political form.

Munich: 18 July 1937

During the summer of 1937, Adolf Hitler celebrated the completion of the Nazi regime's first major architectural undertaking: an art museum. Because the Nazi regime justified itself in its self-proclaimed lineage to classical antiquity, the importance of history and the importance of the museum as that site capable of exhibiting it, codifying it – indeed constructing it – was of no small order. Thus, on that sunny opening day in July, nominated the 'Day of German Art', hundreds of thousands of people gathered into lines bordering the Prinzregentenstrasse in Munich, where columns of Hitler Youth, SS and SA soldiers marched along the city axis leading to the new museum. Following them, maquettes of Germany's past and present architectural projects were carted alongside larger-than-life statues of nude classical figures. The accompanying parade dramatized 2000 years of German history with costumed participants acting out a historical continuum that unfolded centuries of Teutonic culture – in chronological order – right to the doorstep of architect Paul Ludwig Troost's Haus der Deutschen Kunst (House of German Art) and to the opening of its inaugural exhibition, the *Grosse Deutsche Kunstausstellung*.

The parade's spectacular performance of obedience, health and order served as a perfect allegorization of the Third Reich's orchestration of both the representation of history and the body within the new museum. The repeated conflation of Nazi body and the Nazi museum in parade and publicity alike (in some posters, the juxtaposition of Troost's museum and an idealized, nude male torso even offered up the building in the place of that body's most virile organ) was more than fitting: Troost's structure was meant to house a sane and healthy vision of the German body cast in bronze and canvas (the overwhelming majority of the museum's representations were figurative, including no less than ten portraits or busts of Hitler himself). And, as Hitler's preoccupation with the museum indicates, the Nazi museum served as a fundamental crucible for the Reich's civic indoctrination – an indoctrination that implicitly pivoted on the representation of the clean and healthy body.[8]

The exhibition space itself was no less capital to the Nazi enterprise than were the representations within the museum.[9] Hygienic, spare and purged of the dense arrangement typical to the Wunderkammer or Salon, the interior of Troost's museum refused a certain traditional model of the exhibition space: no tapestried walls, baroque hues, texture or ceiling mouldings there.[10] The Haus der Deutschen Kunst, with its antiseptic sparseness and aesthetic of white sobriety, was, in fact, highly indebted to the modern display aesthetics of precisely those museums whose collection policy, curatorial staff and works were most condemned by the Nazi regime.[11] Thus, paradoxically, while Hitler

8 As recent studies have begun to make evident, the museum has always been both an ideologically laden and disciplining site crucial to the formation of modern subjectivity, see especially Tony Bennett, *The Birth of the Museum: History, Theory, Politics* (London: Routledge, 1995); Douglas Crimp, *On the Museum's Ruins* (Cambridge: MIT Press, 1993); and Donald Preziosi's various reflections on the museum including, 'Modernity Again: The Museum as Trompe L'Oeil', in Peter Brunette and David Wills, eds, *Deconstruction and the Visual Arts* (Cambridge: Cambridge University Press, 1994) and 'Brain of the Earth's Body: Museums and the Framing of Modernity', in Paul Duro, ed., *The Rhetoric of the Frame* (Cambridge: Cambridge University Press, 1996).

9 Indeed the two need be seen as intimately connected: the Nazi museum was conceived to hold essentially one and only one exhibition – for, whatever the arrangement, one would only ever see 'Great German Art', and the works, literally created for the museum, had been for the most part painted and sculpted in the four years since the cornerstone for the building had been laid in 1933 at which time Hitler made a call for the creation of appropriate German art for the building.

10 See Barbara Miller Lane's excellent architectural history of this period, *Architecture and Politics in Germany, 1918–1945* (Cambridge: Harvard University Press, 1968).

11 Although the Folkwang museum was precisely one of those museums whose collection was devastated by the Nazi seizure of modern art, its light, neutral-coloured walls, simplified interior aesthetic and display of paintings generously spaced out would become a decisive model for both the official Nazi museum and international museums of modern art. Indeed, Alfred Barr visited German institutions like the Folkwang before the opening of the Museum of Modern Art in 1929 and based the nascent museum's presentational strategies on their example. For an excellent discussion of MoMA's selective appropriations, see Christophe Grunenberg, 'The Politics of Presentation: The Museum of Modern Art, New York', in Marcia Pointon, ed., *Art Apart: Art Institutions and Ideology Across England and North America* (Manchester: Manchester University Press, 1995).

and his agent in cultural policing, Joseph Goebbels, emptied out those German museums committed to the display of 'degenerate' modern art, Troost retained their spare, light-coloured interior spaces as a prototype.

Surfaces were stripped of ornament. Right angles and rational order prevailed. As if to proclaim its utter neutrality as a container, those emblems of the Reich so highly visible inside other public buildings (eagle, swastika, etc.) were almost completely effaced from the Haus der Deutschen Kunst's exhibition galleries (that they were ostentatiously represented in the works on display is another thing). Moreover, the Nazi museum appropriated the rhetoric used also by an architectural modernism that conflated hygiene, social order and masculinity with the whitewash of modernist architecture.[12] Thus, 'clean' white walls were erected as the perfect frame for those spaces that were meant to welcome, teach and discipline a social body into cleanliness – moral, racial, physical and mental.[13] Those walls supported open, monumentally proportioned exhibition spaces whose impressive skylights marked the otherwise unadorned ceilings with industrio-modernist grids – all of which helped celebrate the Nazi museum (and by extension the Nazi regime) as the site and purveyor of visibility, knowledge and rationality (fig. 42). There were no dark corners or cluttered displays, the vast illuminated space choreographed the visitor through an exhibition where he or she could in one long look grasp the art historical dramaturgy that had been laid out.

This dramaturgy was one of order and prosperity, sanity and racial purity. Hitler had lined the walls with a highly nationalistic, *völkish* art to counter the putative degeneracy of international modernism. The same themes were highlighted over and over again: idyllic landscapes filled with happily obedient, healthy Aryan bodies in their most 'natural' role as mother or father, soldier or worker. Nude, erect, muscled and de-sensualized, the 'useful' body was everywhere represented in the painting and sculpture in the museum. Arno Breker's monumental male bronzes, Adolph Ziegler's graceful and beribboned

---

See also the well-documented though less critically engaged, Mary Ann Staniszewski, *The Power of Display: A History of Exhibition Installations at the Museum of Modern Art* (Cambridge: MIT Press, 1998).

12 For a sense of the rhetorical construction that accompanied architectural modernism, see Le Corbusier, *Vers un architecture* (Paris: Editions Crès, 1923), and *L'Art decoratif d'aujourd'hui* (Paris: Editions Grès, 1925). The seminal work on the implications of the white wall is Mark Wigley, *White Walls, Designer Dresses: The Fashioning of Modern Architecture* (Cambridge: MIT, 1996).

13 As Wigley has demonstrated in *White Walls, Designer Dresses*, the 1920s and 1930s whitewashed spaces were far from accidental, blank or silent; so too does the Haus der Deutschen Kunst's whiteness 'speak volumes'. And it speaks all the more loudly for the National Socialists' condemnation of so much that was modernist or avant-garde while at the same time appropriating certain of their aesthetics. See also Lane, *Architecture and Politics in Germany* for an overview of the debates about the use of modernism and classicism in National Socialist architectural aesthetics.

female nudes – these frozen models helped constitute a visual narrative that presented the ideal to strive for, the benchmark against which every other body should be judged. In short, this museum worked as do most others, serving as an active pedagogical tool in the instruction of a civic public, except the Nazi museum offered terrifyingly belligerent directives, including aggressive national chauvinism, unquestioned allegiance to the Führer, and corporeal mobilization for the Party.

Munich: 19 July 1937

Only one day after the opening of the inaugural *Grosse Deutsche Kunstausstellung* show in the Haus der Deutschen Kunst, and just a bit further up the street, an exhibition of art considered degenerate opened in the annex to Munich's Archaeological Institute. The two exhibitions' difference – and relation – was underscored: one was housed in the place of dead history, the other in Hitler's newly-constructed temple to the 'eternal'. Indeed, the two need be thought of together, like twin heads emerging from the same beast. It is no coincidence that the largest of the Third Reich's exhibitions of unacceptable, diseased, mad art opened as a simultaneous pendant to the inaugural exhibition at the Haus der Deutschen Kunst: Munich's *Entartete Kunst* show signalled negatively what the work of art, the body and the museum ought to look like.[14]

Much in the style of Paul Schultz-Naumburg's *Kunst und Rasse* (Art and Race) of 1928, a pseudo-scientific pamphlet of 'evidence' of the infirmity of modern art, the *Entartete Kunst* exhibition and catalogue decried modern art as the very work and representation of mental illness and degeneracy. All the representations displayed in the exhibition constituted anti-models extracted from state museums, the vast number of images depicting the human form – Expressionist Christ figures, Dadaist whores, Cubist Jews – deemed degenerate. These abject representations had no place in the immaculate, healthy space of the Nazi museum. Indeed, Goebbels called the process of gathering the contents for this *Entartete Kunst* show a 'cleansing' of the state museums.[15] The resulting

14 For a discussion of the *Entartete Kunst* exhibition, see the thorough documentation in Stephanie Baron, ed., *'Degenerate Art': The Fate of the Avant-Garde in Nazi Germany* (LACMA, 1991); as well as, Berthold Hinz, ' "Degenerate" and "Authentic": Aspects of Art and Power in the Third Reich', and David Elliot, 'Life and Death Struggle: Painting and Sculpture', in Dawn Ades, Tim Benton et al., eds, *Art and Power: Europe Under the Dictators, 1930–1940* (London: Thames and Hudson, 1995).

15 The Third Reich began its seizure of avant-garde art almost as soon as the fire had been put out in the Reichstag and relatively small-scale precursor exhibitions to the 1937 'Degenerate Art' show had been held beginning as early as in April 1933. Nevertheless, none of the regime's efforts against modern art matched the scale or publicity of the Munich exhibition. For a thorough study of the smaller early versions of

exhibition of rejected modernist art, then, was made to seem the site of infuriating disorder. The works were displayed in cluttered masses (the paintings sometimes even unframed, the sculpture sometimes even directly on the floor) against portable room dividers, a system which only partially covered the windows, plaster casts and debris of the site's other life as annex to the Archaeological Institute. However, the cramped and haphazardly-organized exhibition of unacceptable art cannot simply be accounted for, as has long been the tendency, by noting that the organizers only had a mere two weeks to round up and hang the work. As historian Neil Levi insists, one must consider how the appearance of carelessness was vital to the function of this abject 'counter-exhibition' as propaganda.[16] For, in contrast with the hygienic sanity of the exhibition rooms of the Haus der Deutschen Kunst, the interior of the *Entartete Kunst* show was meant to seem as irrational and ridiculously flimsy as the work in it (fig. 43).

One discerns even in the various manifestations of the counter-exhibition (*Entartete Kunst* travelled throughout Germany) some important purposes of the manifestation: a blatantly ideologically-driven display that ridiculed not only modernist art but also criticized those museums from which the works were seized and damned the methods by which art had been shown. Jimmy Ernst (who, in fact, went to see a painting by his father, the Surrealist Max Ernst) recalled that in Hamburg the exhibition was held in narrow trailers and moving vans so that 'the event was staged in the manner of a sideshow of freaks at a tawdry carnival'.[17] There, a recording of Hitler's speech at the opening ceremonies for the Haus der Deutschen Kunst blared endlessly from loudspeakers in each display trailer. Similarly, quotations from this speech could be found throughout the *Entartete Kunst* exhibition catalogue that had been prepared in time to accompany the travelling show. In short, even if only in acoustic or citational form, Hitler, his model of 'Great' art, and his idea of a proper museum were present wherever the *Entartete Kunst* show travelled, reminding visitors that Germany's former museums (under Weimar), like the World War I-ravaged German body, had been infected, dirtied and pathologized. Moreover, the lesson stressed, museum and body both could fall back into this unhealthy state if Jews, homosexuals, communists or the disabled were allowed to mingle freely with the good German *Völk*.

To most effectively spread its message, entry to the Munich-based *Entartete Kunst* and to the later travelling versions was free, its widespread publicity

---

the 'Degenerate Art' show, see Christoph Zuschlag, *'Entartete Kunst': Ausstellungstrategien im Nazi-Deutschland* (Worms: Wernersche Verlagsgesellschaft, 1995).

16 See the engaging study by Neil Levi, 'Judge for Yourselves! – The Degenerate Art Exhibition as Political Spectacle', *October*, no. 85 (1998), pp. 41–64.

17 Jimmy Ernst, *A Not So Still Life* (New York: St. Martins/Marek Press, 1984) p. 95.

attracting incredible numbers – too many to be adequately held in the relatively small spaces. Thus, even had the organizing officials not imagined exactly how popular the exhibition would be, the experience was calculated to be as unpleasant as possible to the eyes as well as the body. Alongside the unacceptable corporeal types or formal styles, the condemnation of a certain model of the museum was also on exhibit. Thus, not only was the title and artist's name listed (with more or less accuracy) near most of the works in the show, the name of the museum from which the works were taken and the prices these museums had paid for them was almost always also listed. However, as Levi argues, even if the 'Munich Degenerate Art exhibition is largely about art institutions and their administrations [...] the Nazis do not attack the museum as such. They attack museums only insofar as museums are not National Socialist "art temples" '.[18] Thus, the presentation tactics of *Entartete Kunst* could reproduce the avant-garde's slogans, agitational graphics and attempted dissolution of the work of art's cult value (one wall of the Munich show mimed Dadaist typography and exhibition tactics) with little risk of being misunderstood. The Nazi-organized spectacle effectively enacted a hijacking of the avant-garde's message, making exhibition practice itself another example of the insolent, 'degenerate' nature of modernism. And, if the Nazis appropriated the avant-garde's display strategies, they could safely do so because the *Entartete Kunst* was not one but part of a bifurcate exhibition installation – the clean alternative found in the Haus der Deutschen Kunst's *Grosse Deutsche Kunstausstellung* show constituted the vital other part. The two seemingly contradictory exhibitions, in fact, only served to further cement the architecture and space of 'the museum' as a place of authority, regulation, cleanliness and order.

Paris: 17 January 1938

During the first weeks of 1938, in what would be the last collective manifestation of the Surrealist movement before World War II, the group's artist and poet members unsettled the rarefied experience of the exhibition space. The small card invitation for the opening of the *Exposition Internationale du Surréalisme* on the evening of 17 January 1938 hinted at the manoeuvre with its promise of hysteria and coal sacks, flashlights and echoes among the exhibition's attractions. But few of the attendees knew exactly what they would be getting. These were not, after all, things that the frequenters of the Galerie Beaux-Arts and readers of the well-respected *Gazette des Beaux-Arts* were used to finding at Georges Wildenstein's Parisian establishment. For the exhibition history of the Galerie Beaux-Arts read much like the journal after which it was named:

---

18 Levi, 'Judge for Yourselves', p. 56.

conservative, highly nationalist and filled with the *grands maîtres*. The gallery's last show, visitors remembered well, had been the highly-acclaimed exhibition of the work of El Greco. Nevertheless, Wildenstein (who did not seem to be interested in Surrealism *per se*, but only in an exhibition to end a series of surveys of modern art movements), gave Surrealist leader André Breton and fellow poet Paul Eluard *carte blanche* to organize a collective exhibition in his unlikely gallery.[19]

Organizers Breton and Eluard decided right away to appoint Marcel Duchamp to be a kind of exhibition ringmaster. In the choice one finds the roots of the exhibition's foundational paradox: the organizers gave an artist renowned for his detachment from politics and official non-member of the movement a pivotal role in the conception of the show.[20] For this group of artists, poets and intellectuals in revolt against bourgeois values and institutions of authority, order and nationalism, moral codes and rationalist doxa, the exhibitionary frame of the artwork itself was to become, in 1938, an object to be disrupted and challenged. Where the Futurists had called to burn the museum and Dada had insisted that the exhibition be the site for derision and political proclamations, the 1938 *Exposition Internationale du Surréalisme* would undermine the space of display, recasting the art exhibition's typical architecture and stagecraft as it frustrated the structures of subjectivity and representation

19 While the details of the negotiation between the Surrealist group and Galerie Beaux-Arts for the organization of the 1938 exhibition remain a bit foggy, it is evident that Wildenstein's artistic director, Raymond Cogniat, was very involved in the defence and promotion of the Surrealist exhibition, and most likely had a role in convincing Wildenstein to hold the exhibition. This would not be the first time that Wildenstein unwittingly contributed to the history of the avant-garde: in the late 1920s he sponsored Georges Bataille's radical, idiosyncratic *Documents* just long enough to realize that it was not the harmless ethnographic journal he had thought it would be.

20 Even if Duchamp positioned himself as explicitly uninterested in politics and even if the Surrealists knew better than to approach him to sign their various manifestoes and declarations, the artist's sustained critique of art was vital to the Surrealist effort in 1938. Moreover, such a collective recasting of the gallery space seems to have been as important to the Surrealist project as it was to Duchamp. The contributions of the conceptualist-ringmaster bear the marks of some of his most persistent concerns. As he explained when asked about his participation, 'I had been borrowed from the ordinary world by the Surrealists. They liked me a lot; Breton liked me a lot; we were very good together. They had a lot of confidence in the ideas I could bring them, ideas which weren't anti-surrealist, but which weren't always surrealist, either'. Pierre Cabanne, *Dialogues with Marcel Duchamp* (New York: Da Capo Press, 1979), p. 81. Duchamp would go on to participate in the conceptualization of the 1942 *First Papers of Surrealism* show in New York, the 1947 *Exposition Internationale du Surréalisme*, the 1959 *Exposition Internationale du Surréalisme*, both in Paris, and the 1960 Surrealist *Enchanter's Domain* exhibition at the D'Arcy Gallery in New York.

cemented in that institution of looking.[21] And there was perhaps no better candidate to help critically respond to the art institution than Duchamp, who would go on to have a marked role as installation collaborator in all of the later international Surrealist exhibitions.

In his official capacity as the 'generator-arbitrator' of ideas for the show, Duchamp imagined Wildenstein's top lit, cream-coloured, elegantly appointed eighteenth-century interior as a dark 'grotto'. He covered the ornate mouldings, ceiling and bank of lights with what was announced as '1200' suspended coal sacks. He installed an iron brazier in the centre of the main hall and hung works on uprooted department store revolving doors. Not even outspoken worries about the flammable nature of the coal sacks or cautions from an insurance executive could get him to alter the project much (the sacks were filled with crumpled newspaper instead of coal, but soot remained just the same). The ceiling undulated, the walls were blackened, and coal dust would invariably fall onto the finery of the exhibition's guests. As the installation's inaugural act, Duchamp's '1200 coal sacks' insisted on derision (what are coal sacks doing on the ceiling? And why such appeal to seemingly impossible mathematics?) as much as the *poussière* that invariably fell from them would work against clear vision. And in their inversion of interior and exterior, up and down, the sacks initiated the unsettling of the architecture of the gallery that would set in motion the exhibition's larger destabilization. More than an insertion of any particular object, this dust breeder's determination to recast the gallery unleashed in the others, as more than one participant insisted, a watershed of ideas about how to undermine the 'beaux-arts' space.[22]

Meetings were held and the brainstorming continued. Salvador Dalí, Max Ernst, Man Ray, Wolfgang Paalen and others – each taking on a special function – rendered further unrecognizable the Galerie Beaux-Arts and expanded even more fully on the spectacle that would await visitors. The invitation they devised

21 While there remains a striking paucity of commentary on the critical aspects of the collective Surrealist exhibitions in general, the 1938 *Exposition Internationale du Surréalisme* has been treated in lively detail by Ian Dunlop, '1938: The International Surrealist Exhibition', *The Shock of the New: Seven Historic Exhibitions of Modern Art* (London: Weidenfeld and Nicolson, 1972); Bruce Altshuler, 'Snails in a Taxi', *The Avant-Garde in Exhibition: New Art in the Twentieth Century* (New York: Abrams, 1994); Martica Sawin, *Surrealism in Exile: The Beginning of the New York School* (Cambridge: MIT Press, 1995); James Herbert, *Paris 1937: Worlds on Exhibition* (Ithaca: Cornell University Press, 1997), chapter 4; and, most recently and with much valuable documentation, Lewis Kachur, *Displaying the Marvellous: Marcel Duchamp, Salvador Dalí and the Surrealist Exhibitions* (Cambridge: MIT Press, 2001).

22 Among these are the three most thorough descriptions of the event by its participants, Georges Hugnet, 'L'Exposition Internationale du Surréalisme' *Preuves*, no. 91 (September 1958), pp. 38–47; Marcel Jean and Arpad Mezei, *Histoire de la peinture surréaliste* (Paris: Seuil, 1959), pp. 280–89; and Man Ray, *Autoportrait,* trans. Anne Guérin (Paris: Robert Laffort, 1964), pp. 205–6 and 243–44.

promised anything but the ordinary display of art; the image and caption in the centre of the small card did not reproduce a Surrealist painting or a sculpture, but instead announced that a life-sized automaton named 'Enigmarelle' would visit at half-past midnight on the opening night. In true Surrealist form, the group never even arranged for the promised figure to appear. Similarly derisive, the thin *Dictionnaire abrégé du Surréalisme*, which Breton and Eluard published in conjunction with the event, offered poetic and non-sensical 'definition' entries of artists, art works, ideas and themes; although not an official catalogue (it did, however, hold the loose four page pull-out 'list of works'), its existence was prompted by and intimately connected to the Surrealist event. Indeed, it is perhaps little surprise that while the larger exhibition contravened the Enlightenment organization of knowledge and rationalist project of the museum, the show's literary accomplice worked playfully against that other archetypal Enlightenment construction – the encyclopedia/dictionary. Within the *Dictionnaire* one found countless works from the exhibition reproduced, as well as a kind of urban plan that made reference to the decorated corridor of the Galerie Beaux-Arts, entitled the *Ville Surréaliste*. In a gesture that would inspire Situationism's *détournement* of the rationalism of modern city-planning, the Surrealist map in the Surrealist dictionary was useless: it traced a space different from the corridor's indoor metropolis and, needless to say, had little to do with the actual layout of Paris.

Even before entering the gallery, the elegantly clad guests would encounter Salvador Dalí's outrageous *Taxi-Pluvieux* (*Rainy Taxi*) in the outer courtyard. Dalí had filled a rented taxicab with two mannequins, a smartly dressed blonde in the back seat and her chauffeur in the front. The driver wore goggles and a shark's jaw bones on his head. The dame was covered with vegetation, crawling with 200 live Burgundy snails, and drenched from the incessant shower of a water-hose hidden in the lining of the taxi's roof. Extending the parameters of the exhibition space, introducing a work in a perpetual state of change (the mannequin and her strange accoutrements progressively deteriorated to the glee of Dalí who gauged the mutations with each visit), the installation ushered the visitors into the exhibition's manifold transgressions.[23]

Having passed Dalí's work, spectators would enter the gallery's lengthy hallway where the street – Breton's 'strategic point of disorder' and that site so important to the Surrealists as the ground of revolutionary energies, collective action and chance encounter – was brought *intra muros*. The artists had papered the walls with posters, photographs and publications, and hung blue street plaques inscribed with the names of real and imagined streets along the length of the corridor-cum-metropolitan axis. Lining the passage and carefully

23 Daniel Wildenstein, son of the gallery owner and a young man at the time of the *Exposition*, recalled Dalí's interest in the progressive undoing of his Taxicab installation. (Interview with the author, 1996.)

posed beneath the fictive street signs were the inhabitants of this Surrealist city: a convoy of 16 female department store mannequins rented for the exhibition and each 'dressed' in strange and eclectic wares by a different artist-participant.

Somewhere between mass-cultural detritus and works of art (they were produced at the hands of artists such as Joan Miró, Yves Tanguy, Marcel Duchamp and André Masson), the Surrealist mannequins brought together elements of the avant-garde's early experiments with performance and object-making. Conceived for the exhibition, executed on the premises, and existing as Surrealist 'being-objects' only for the duration of the show, the dressed mannequins literally wore their ambiguous artistic status on their sleeves. Indeed, in an exhibition concerned with the nature and function of art object and the art institution, these strange objects pointed to a constellation of questions about the definitions of the work of art, the limits of the museological impulse to possess, and the gallery's role in the commercialization of the art.[24]

The mannequin-filled faux urban landscape opened onto the largest of the gallery's three rooms where the irregular dips of the grotto-like ceiling of coal sacks hovered not far off the floor that Wolfgang Paalen had covered with a thick layer of dead leaves and dirt. From it sprung a pool of water, contrived in a corner of this main hall and surrounded with overgrown vegetation. Within this elaborate cavity, even the visitors' olfactory senses were tampered with: behind a screen, roasting coffee beans sent the invitation's promised *odeurs de Brésil* wafting through the air. As the *Vogue* correspondent described it, 'unrest, claustrophobia, and a feeling of some terrible disaster hung over the rooms'.[25] Indeed, dirty and lugubrious, the space 'destroyed', as Man Ray recalled, 'that clean, clinical atmosphere generally seen in the most modern of exhibitions'[26] (fig. 44).

Added to this, sight – that sense so privileged in the typical art context – was troubled. However, it was more than simply the dust kicked up from Paalen's dirty floors or Duchamp's coal sacks that obscured vision. The interior of the Galerie Beaux-Arts was dotted with only a few faint lights, one emerging from an iron brazier placed in the main hall, and another, in a smaller side room, glowing from within a giant pair of women's underwear. The exhibition was meant to be shrouded in shadowy darkness, the gallery's main lights extinguished. As Marcel Jean recollected, 'Duchamp had thought of installing "magic eyes", so that lights would have gone on automatically as soon as the

---

24 The status of the dressed mannequins at the *Exposition* in relation to art, photography, and commerce is the subject of my 'Abwesende Kunstobjekte: Mannequins und die Exposition Internationale du Surréalisme von 1938', in Pia Müller-Tamm and Katharina Sykora, eds, *Puppen, Körper, Automaten: Phantasmen der Modern* (Cologne: Oktagon, 1999), pp. 200–18.

25 Bettina Wilson, 'Surrealism in Paris', *Vogue* (1 March 1938).

26 Man Ray, *Autoportrait*, p. 243.

spectator had broken an invisible ray when passing in front of the paintings'.[27] But when that proved infeasible, Man Ray in his capacity as 'Master of Lighting', adapted Duchamp's idea by having visitors view the work 'on display' with little more than the dim illumination of pocket flashlights handed out at the entrance. In a gesture that combined a transgression of the museological space (a version of the stealing into the museum at night with a torch in hand to see a work as Breton had advocated in *Nadja*) and a problematizing of vision (a persistent theme in Duchamp's œuvre), the Surrealist Exposition refused the protocol of the gallery-museum's Enlightenment project.[28] The idea that light stood for knowledge, and the commonplace that the museological space was the haven to both was troubled, shaken, refused.

Even if, in the end, Duchamp's proposal remained unachieved and Man Ray's flashlights only employed for the opening night, both illumination systems also reveal an attempt to rethink the typical relationship between the body of a spectator and the artwork in an exhibition space. For, if throughout the exhibition the bourgeois notion of the 'normal' was under attack, Duchamp's refiguring of viewing also reimagined the relationship of bodies to works on display, of the experience of subject and object. This had implications for notions of the normative aesthetic experience, but also for those institutions – gallery, museum, salon, public exhibition space – that defined and indeed depended on these categories and the spectator's relationship to them. Leaning, squinting, almost touching, the viewer at the Surrealist exhibition was to bring his or her body close to the work, refusing the museum-gallery interdiction to stand away, to gaze disinterestedly, and to sacralize the object and the space that separated the viewer from it.

In this half-shadow one might have spied photographs, paintings and graphic works (fig. 45). These were hung on blackened walls or, like parodic statements on the commodification of the work of art, attached to revolving doors that had been uprooted from defunct department stores. Gone were stiff gallery benches; instead, a satin-lined bed occupied each of the four corners of that main hall. For this movement that sought to transgress the boundaries between interior and exterior, between dream and reality, the gallery was a site to be unmoored. Thus

---

27 Marcel Jean and Arpad Mezei, *The History of Surrealist Painting*, trans. Simon Watson Taylor (New York: Grove Press, 1960) pp. 281–82.

28 Breton, *Nadja* (Paris: Gallimard, 1928) p. 150. The perceptual and anti-retinal, so much the *idées fixes* of Duchamp, also importantly influence the attention to modes of 'seeing' in the 1938 Surrealist exhibition. Concerns with the visual and the conditions of perception are behind much of the artist's preoccupation with display, seen in his various exhibition conceptions for the Surrealists and carried through to his final, museum-encrusted optical machine, *Etant donnés: 1. la chute d'eau, 2. la gaz d'eclairage*. For discussions of these, see my *Marcel Duchamp on Display: Optics, Exhibition Installations, Portable Museums*, exh. cat. (New York: Zabriskie Gallery, 2001) and *The Museum Laid Bare/Marcel Duchamp*, unpublished PhD thesis, Princeton University.

gallery corridor and urban *ville*, hall and dirty grotto, art exhibition and department store were dislocated and their differences suggestively blurred.

At the crossroads of these contradictory places, a hired dancer simulated 'hysteria' in successive acts during the exhibition's opening night. Dalí and several other Surrealists choreographed the haptic gestures, high-pitched screams, and erotic gyrations that made up dancer Hélène Vanel's multiple performances, the most spectacular of which was entitled *L'Acte manqué* (fig. 46).[29] With her tattered white nightdress, bared breasts, and live rooster in hand, the dancer writhed in and out of the crowd of exhibition onlookers. She moved between floor, pond and the exhibition's quartet of beds, hissing, screaming and splashing visitors with mud and pond muck. Photographic traces of the rehearsal and the opening night reveal the constructed resemblance between Vanel's bodily distortions and the images of hysteria 'documented' by nineteenth-century neurologist Jean-Martin Charcot (fig. 47). In fact, the convulsive dance offered a live staging of the Surrealist celebration of hysteria that had been published a decade earlier in the pages of *La Revolution surréaliste*. There, Breton and Louis Aragon appropriated photographs from Charcot's 1878 *Iconographie photographique de la Salpétrière*, reproducing the doctor's most famous patient, Augustine, in stop-action poses, writhing and gesticulating in white bedclothes on her clinic bed (fig. 48). The accompanying text denounced bourgeois society and its designation of hysteria as a pathology; instead, the Surrealists hailed the hysteric's 'reciprocal seduction' and capacity to disturb all 'relations between the subject and the moral world', calling hysteria the 'most poetic discovery of the 19th century', a 'supreme mode of expression'.[30]

In mimicking those signature contortions of the hysteric, Vanel's dance was as much about aesthetic subversion and bourgeois derangement as it was a kind of cornerstone in the exhibition's unbuilding of the 'museological' regime.[31]

---

29 Hugnet recounts that when the exhibition team decided to stage a performance piece for the opening night, he and Eluard scouted out professional dancer Hélène Vanel at her studio in Montmartre and Dalí volunteered for the task of rehearsing with her. Hugnet, 'L'exposition internationale', pp. 45–46. Dalí and the other Surrealists, who were for the most part avid readers of psychoanalytic texts, no doubt scripted Vanel's dance title *l'acte manqué* (what, in English, would be translated as a 'Freudian slip') as well as its accompanying moves.

30 André Breton and Louis Aragon, 'La Cinquantenaire de l'hysterie', *La Revolution surréaliste*, no. 11 (15 March 1928).

31 Vanel's Surrealist-organized dance provides an important instance (and rare Surrealist example) of the early avant-garde's experiments with live performance. For a discussion of the Futurist and Dada anticipations of 'performance art', see RoseLee Goldberg, *Performance Art: From Futurism to the Present* (London: Thames and Hudson, 1988). More than simply an exalted heroine, however, the hysteric served as an important performative model for the movement. For, central to the Surrealist project was the approximation of the hysteric's unmitigated access to the unconscious. Curiously, the staging of hysteria at the 1938 exhibition has been largely ignored even in treatments of

Like so many aspects of the Surrealist installation, the performance assaulted the idea of a passive, contemplative public and the codes upon which exhibition viewing typically depended; it shattered the phonic vacuum of the gallery-museum, and sounded the 'purity' of the exhibition space. While Charcot had offered the 'real' nineteenth-century hysteric for edifying observation, his clinic and amphitheatre becoming what the doctor called a *musée pathologique vivant* (museum of living pathology), the Surrealists offered a simulation of hysteria so as to frustrate the gallery-museum, to pathologize its pretence of normalcy and neutrality.[32]

Perhaps for these reasons, the live 'hysteric' served as the perfect cipher for the Surrealist exhibition's provocation against both modernism and its most authority-weighted institutions. Remote from the productivist/rational/utopian concerns of what is now understood as high modernism, the Surrealists violently rejected, in particular, architectural modernism throughout the life of the movement.[33] During the 1930s, Dalí even conflated hysteria with the 'terrifying and edible beauty' of Art Nouveau – that architecture whose asymmetry, undulating curves and 'perversity' offered a corrective, in the Spaniard's view, to the right angles and functionalism of the modernist architecture championed by Le Corbusier.[34] An edifice as hysterical body, womb, psychic envelope or crumbling ruin emerged as the only possible

---

precisely the Surrealist use of the hysteric trope, most recently evidenced in its absence from David Lomas's chapter on hysteria in *The Haunted Self: Surrealism, Psychoanalysis, Subjectivity* (New Haven: Yale University Press, 2000).

32 Charcot's appellation of his clinic as a kind of 'museum' is mentioned in what remains the most illuminating treatment of the question of the image and hysteria: Georges Didi-Huberman, *Invention de l'hysterie: Charcot et l'iconographie de la Salpétrière* (Paris: Macula, 1982).

33 In addition to the body of Surrealist *récits* (from *Nadja* to *Le Paysan de Paris* to *La Liberté ou l'amour!*) that celebrate the irrational, feminine or decrepit aspects of the urban-landscape, attacks on modernism in architecture and city-planning are explicit in a considerable number of Surrealist essays, including: Tristan Tzara, 'D'un certain automatisme du goût', *Minotaure*, nos 3–4 (December 1933); Breton, 'La Situation surréaliste de l'objet' (Speech given in Prague, 1935); collective questionnaire, 'Sur certains possibilités d'embellissement irrational d'une ville', *Le Surréalisme au service de la révolution* (*LSASDLR*) (1933); Roberto Matta, 'Mathématic sensible – Architecture du Temps', *Minotaure*, no. 11 (March 1938); and Dalí's writings (see below).

34 See Dalí, 'L'âne pourri', in *LSASDLR*, no. 1 (1930) p. 12, and translated as 'The Stinking Ass', *This Quarter*, no. 51 (1932); 'De la Beauté terrifiante et comestible de l'architecture modern style', and 'Le phénomène de l'Extase', *Minotaure*, nos 3–4 (December 1933). Years after he had used photographs of Guimard's 'hysteric' metal Métro structures to illustrate his article 'De la Beauté terrifiante', Dalí looked into buying one of those Métro structures, hoping, it seems, to erect the undulating metal forms at the 1938 Surrealist exhibition. But the Engineer in Chief of the Paris Métro authority announced that they were not for sale (letter dated 10 January 1938, housed in the Dalí archive, Figueres, Spain).

counter for Surrealism to the repressive authority of Architecture. Hal Foster underlines the issue:

> Functionalism is about discipline: it breaks down the domestic body into functions and assigns them to antiseptic spaces; the result is often a house type with scant allowance for history, sexuality, the unconscious. Surrealism is about desire: in order to allow it back into architecture it fixes on the outmoded and the ornamental, the very forms tabooed in such functionalism, associated as they became not only with the historical and the fantastic, but with the infantile and the feminine. In effect, against 'the machine for living in,' surrealism presents the house as a hysterical body.[35]

The Surrealist 'house' Foster speaks of is figurative, represented in Ernst's collages of uncanny bourgeois interiors, Aragon's paean to the *passages*, or Dalí's enthusiasm for Guimard-Métro entrances. But, for perhaps the first time, in their temporary occupation of the Galerie Beaux-Arts, the Surrealists collectively worked with (against) real architecture and space. The exhibition space became, in 1938, the 'hysterical body', both against the rationality and functionalism of architecture in general, and against the disciplining, taxonomic impulse of modern museology in particular. Within the walls of the Galerie Beaux-Arts, Vanel as body/object – live, convulsive, ecstatic and seemingly irrational – figured the limits of the social order and, in turn, the limits of the gallery and museum's classificatory, ordering project. Her dance attacked the straitjacket of conventional art display: with each gesticulation Vanel performatively constructed an anti-ideal, offering a body deemed degenerate, uncontrollable and pathological as object of exhibit.

Although Surrealism's unapologetic cult of woman and long interest with hysteria undoubtedly undergirds Vanel's performance at the *Exposition*, the ideological stakes of the use of hysteria in an exhibition space in 1938 should not be underestimated. For precisely at the moment that the Nazis put the museum at the forefront of political aims and the specifically corporeal disciplining of the civic body, the Surrealists offer in counterpoint an installation with an uncontrollable, convulsive body at its centre. The Surrealist performance of hysteria within the exhibition space takes on a distinctive complexity in light of the 'degeneracy' that haunts the Nazi museum. Vanel's performance induced *délire* and passion, not action in the name of State or enterprise. Thus, even if hysteria has been useful to describe the almost libidinal frenzy of the masses pulled by the shamanic power of Hitler, hysteria remained abhorrent to Nazi ideology. It proscribed the aesthetic and architectural frame of order and rationality that tightly organized the masses into political spectacles in Olympics, rallies, parades and armies where the body was subsumed to the utmost control. Fragile, feminine, excessive, uncontrollable, sensual, passionate,

35 Hal Foster, *Compulsive Beauty* (Cambridge: MIT Press, 1993) p. 190.

irrational, the infirm hysteric body could not but be a sharp riposte to any notion of a utilitarian body, including the Soviet social citizen, the Taylorist industrial worker, and particularly, the idealized and armoured Fascist body. In short, the Surrealist exhibition put at its centre what the Nazi museum expelled.

As aural accompaniment to Vanel's performance, phonographs hidden along the walls emitted discordant soundtracks: the recorded cries of insane asylum patients, and the German army's parade march. Newspaper critics reporting on the show repeatedly mentioned the acoustic aspect of the exhibition without much precision, recalling the chaos of sounds, but for the most part failing to name exactly what they heard. Several invoked the hysteric cries, and a few alluded to other sounds, described ambiguously as birds screaming or crowds stamping; but not one of the reporters seemed to have been able – or willing – to name the ominous and timely acoustic reference to a Teutonic militia. Nevertheless, of the few participants who left accounts of the show preparation, Man Ray attested that one part of the exhibition soundtrack was made up of screams of hysterics recorded at an insane asylum and then played over the exhibition's phonograph. And it is from participant Marcel Jean, who recounts the inclusion of loudspeakers blaring the German army's 'pas de parade' at the opening night of the exhibition, that we glean this further detail of the show's acoustics.[36] With these sounds, the artists wanted, as Man Ray explained, 'to cut short any desire the visitor might have had to laugh or joke'.[37] In a moment when the spectre of Nazism loomed high, the ominous acoustics pitted soldierly body against degenerate body, martial discipline against irrational convulsion.

Playful, ludic, chaotic, derailing: the exhibition's various parts operated in a way deeply inimical to order, stability and any possible usefulness of the exhibition to the State or greater authority. The varied elements of the exhibition's *mise-en-scène* worked together to disturb the solemnity that typically imbues the work of art with aura and cult value. Cartesian logic was broken, the traditional way of experiencing an exhibition was refused. No longer a temple to Western rationality, nor a laboratory of contemplation, the art gallery had become the site of psychic disorder, the terrain of desire, anguish and catastrophe. The putative 'ridiculousness' of the staging masked a considerably more serious endeavour: to critique the gallery and museum by rending the typical space of art display and threatening its assumed neutrality.[38] Thus, even the impression of

36 Jean and Mezei, *History of Surrealist Painting*, p. 282.

37 Man Ray, *Autoportrait*, p. 243.

38 The Surrealists were not against collecting or collections, exhibitions or exhibiting as such; what the development of Surrealist exhibitions suggests, however, is that they opposed both a restricted notion of 'Art' and the gallery-museum as embodiment of repressive authority, a veritable bastion of historical memory (re)constructed as strict chronology or ordered taxonomy. Breton's own cabinet of curiosities-like atelier, with its mixing of genres and periods and its refusal of modern museal arrangement, offers an interesting opposition to the museum's ordering impulse. And, in a different

fixity and stability of the architecture of the Galerie Beaux-Arts was shaken in 1938: with the Surrealist exhibition's dark and low sagging, soot-emitting ceiling, the existing structure was covered over; and with its layer of decaying moss and dead leaves, the very floor of the gallery was in ruins underfoot. The gallery and museum's sanctuary-like separation from the outside world was refused: street noises, odours and rank vegetation found themselves within the gallery's walls. Nationalism and the collection and celebration of patrimonial capital was challenged: the *Exposition Internationale du Surréalisme* presented the work of 60 artists from over 14 countries, insisting on a commitment to 'internationalism' that took on a politicized resonance in those prewar years when much of Europe was privileging *la Nation* over the international.[39]

* * *

Despite, or perhaps precisely because of the transgressions enacted within and upon the Beaux-Arts space, the pearl- and monocle-bedecked bourgeois audience that attended the *Exposition* was by turns horrified and amused. They gasped or laughed while critics scurried to make the evening press with their reviews. According to an unlikely agreement, one review after another denounced the exhibition – on grounds that its bizarre environment had been orchestrated too well or not well enough, that the art was too academic or not 'real' art at all, that the Surrealists were hopelessly occult or the latest darlings of a bourgeois public. The artistically-minded said there was not any real art to be seen in the whole of the exhibition, because if there had been, the ridiculous Surrealist *mise-en-scène* would not have been necessary. As François Fosca, writing for the fiercely Right wing *Je Suis Partout* put it, 'If the work of the Surrealists had any real interest, this whole staging wouldn't have been necessary. It is hard to imagine Corot, Delacroix or Degas running around in this way; it is obvious that those artists had talent'.[40] The

way, Duchamp's 'portable museum' the *Boîte-en-valise* – developed at the same time as the artist conceptualizes the Surrealist exhibitions – embodies its own complex response to the museum.

39 The movement, while largely based in Paris before the war and New York during the war, was itself a diverse mix of nationalisms; the effort to announce this exhibition-manifestation as 'international' can be seen, then, as part of a profound Surrealist disagreement with the prejudice and myopia of chauvinism and the potentially dangerous consequences to which it drove nations in the 1930s. In fact, the concept of the international for the Surrealists spans their various exhibitions from 1935 on and was central to the movement's development. Thus, I disagree with the reading that the 'internationalism' of the Surrealist exhibition in 1938 was conceived as an 'ironization' of the 1937 World's Fair as proposed by James Herbert in *Paris 1937*, ch. 4.

40 François Fosca, 'Les Arts: La duperie du Surréalisme', *Je Suis Partout* (28 January 1938). For their valuable help securing press clippings and documentary photographs of the *Exposition*, I wish to thank Adam Boxer of Ubu Gallery above all as well as the late Daniel Wildenstein, James Herbert, Myrtille Hugnet, Lewis Kachur, Martica Sawin and the Yale Beineke Library.

left and right both denounced it; the politically-minded claiming that the exhibition was not political, the staged environment again pointed to as evidence. Rather than a revolutionary event from a group so committed to critical opposition and awakening political consciousness, the exhibition was regarded as a spectacular failure.

Perhaps because so many visitors and critics came with the traditional notion of what an art exhibition should be, few paused to consider the way in which the Surrealist installation and its objects put the institution of art and authority into question. Because the exhibition was, as the *L'Epoque* journalist described it, 'not solely composed of pictorial elements but also a receptacle for unformed or obscene elements', most visitors seem to have found it 'impossible to discuss any of it in terms of aesthetics'.[41] But if critics could not talk about aesthetics because the exhibition evaded or surpassed the aesthetic, neither did they speak of it in other terms. Consequently, no one questioned the fact that, while previous Surrealist exhibitions had been fairly conventional in their approach to display (even if the works themselves were not), this exhibition – at this particular moment in history – looked so different. And, if only one critic of the lot admitted that 'one should salute the real merit of the exhibition: that of being "contre" ', no one articulated the way this 'contre' might have significant ramifications for notions of exhibitions and objects, artists and engagement.[42]

In fact many treated the opening as a fancy dress party. After all, the event was held at the esteemed Galerie Beaux-Arts, a site often frequented by wealthy patrons who came to see exhibitions of established Masters. And so, in the reports appearing the following day, the press complained incessantly about the density of snob aesthetes. That the poets and artists of the Surrealist group, who had long-proclaimed a revolutionary agenda and their contempt for the moneyed class, chose to present their exhibition at Georges Wildenstein's fashionable gallery struck many critics as singularly unfortunate; they regarded it as the sign of the end of the criticality of the avant-garde movement and its downward spiral into irredeemable *embourgeoisement*.

It was no accident, however, that the 1938 exhibition was crammed full of evening gowns and shiny tuxedos. The exhibition invitation's request that the gallery's visitors arrive in 'evening attire', was an impertinent wink. Not a selling out to the bourgeoisie (they would by definition be at any opening *chez* Wildenstein), the Surrealists required that the visitors attend the exhibition in all the pomp and regalia of their class. Indeed, it was decisive to the Surrealist exhibition that Wildenstein's gallery was the sort of place that it was: stately, highly-esteemed, frequented by the bourgeoisie and practically an annex to France's state museums (Wildenstein would go on to be awarded the French Legion of Honour for his cultural contributions). Surrealism's temporary

41 'D'un pinceau à l'autre', *L'Epoque* (1 April 1938) (Seligman Archives, Yale Beineke Library, New Haven).

42 Fermet, 'L'Exposition surréaliste', n.d. (Hugnet Archive, Paris).

transformation of the Galerie Beaux-Arts meant to sully, as participant Georges Hugnet characterized them, 'those walls accustomed to semi-official exhibits'.[43] Of course, the stain was quickly washed away. Nevertheless, for over a month in 1938, the Surrealist exhibition soiled a venerated gallery, its complacent bourgeois clientèle, and its parent institution, the museum.[44]

To look today for the critical value of the *Exposition Internationale du Surréalisme* is to be placed in front of a work that is fundamentally residual, indeed, nonexistent except as an ensemble of traces (photographs, eye-witness descriptions, press reviews). These traces, however, bear witness to a critical reflection on the space of exhibition. To accept this reflection as more than mere nihilistic or playful, it must be said, is to encounter more questions than answers. To refuse to dismiss the show is to ask how the *Exposition* may problematize the definitions of both the work of art and political action, fulfilling neither definition in any neat way. And, it is invariably to face a question about how one can assess the critical value of an enterprise whose various elements (female mannequins, hysteric dancer) may have helped attack certain authorities while more firmly cementing other repressive positions (hysteria as poetic, woman as object).[45] None of these have easy answers. However, to take seriously the *Exposition Internationale du Surréalisme* – problematic as it is – is to open the possibility that such questions be asked.

Serious in their sense of play, or playing at not reproducing the seriousness of art's institutions, one senses something very urgent, something indeed serious, in

43 Hugnet, 'L'exposition internationale', p. 38.

44 The movement faced the double-bind that various responses to art institutions would thereafter often encounter: to critique the museum, the Surrealists entered a space that was as close as possible to it. However, moving from exhibition space to pen in the year after the show, a scathing article entitled 'Le Nationalisme dans l'Art' condemned not only the nationalism in the cultural suppression rampant in Italy, the USSR and Germany, but also the complicity of the Beaux-Arts enterprises in a dangerous and reactionary promotion of French nationalism. The journal, its critics (particularly Waldemar Georges and Raymond Cogniat), and the gallery where the Surrealists had held their exhibition came under attack. Published in the final issue of *Minotaure*, and collectively signed 'La Rédaction', the article denounced the highly chauvinist 'sous-führer' character of the *Beaux-Arts*'s reviews, as well as the journal's publication of advertisements for the auction of art 'coming from museums in Munich'. Their accusation need not say more – as readers of both *Minotaure* and of *Beaux-Arts* would have understood well, to advocate and advertise these auctions in 1939 was to implicitly support the machine of war that was Hitler's Nazi Germany. Cf. 'Le Nationalisme dans l'Art', *Minotaure*, nos 12–13 (May 1939).

45 From the movement's celebration of murderesses, hysterics and patricidal figures, one encounters a masculinist project that imagined the female as both an object of desire *and* an object of transgression of authority. Thus one question that might be asked of this Surrealist event, as of others, is to what extent – and at what cost – was the movement's notion of liberty, transgression and indeed the political, tied to a notion of the feminine.

the 1938 *Exposition Internationale du Surréalisme*. Some of the objects on display pointed to the imminent war, including Paalen's full-size hangman's gallows hewn in wood occupying the corner of the gallery, or an anonymous work composed of a suitcase with a skull, a newspaper headline about gas masks and another proclaiming 'This is Fascist Civilization!' But, it was the *mise-en-scène* which arguably launched the more important and least-understood of the exhibition's critiques of political regimes, attacking as it did that exhibitionary site which had become deeply imbricated in the insidious machinations of Fascism, Nazism and Totalitarianism.[46] Dalí's taxi in the courtyard, the creation of 'streets' in the exhibition corridor, German marching music in the main hall: the immediate outside was brought inside and the inside was brought out. Typical exhibitions pretended that life and politics did not enter their space; the Surrealist exhibition made sure that no one forgot that, in fact, they were not separate at all.

André Breton said of the 1938 Surrealist exhibition that, 'The organizers had concentrated their efforts on creating an atmosphere as remote as possible from that of an "art" gallery'.[47] He names no regimes and points to no particular 'art' exhibitions. A site, an institution, an atmosphere, a public, a way of viewing, a way of representing, an understanding of 'art': all these things ruled by and complicitous with the museological space were under attack. It remains, however, that no other set of exhibitions in the period showed as brazenly the desired manipulation of a public through art and its museological frame as the Nazi regime's 'Great' and 'Degenerate' displays; no other exhibitions offered a more violent picture of the ideological implications of art display; and no other structure embodied the authority, cult of order, and dominant bourgeois ideology of the museum's architectural and discursive framework more effectively than the new Nazi Haus der Deutschen Kunst. As such, Hitler's museum-as-armoured-Nazi-body represents not simply the archetypal architectural incarnation of Nazism, but *an extreme of what an exhibition and museological space could be*.

46 What was becoming more and more undeniable in that sombre period before World War II was that, however different the approved aesthetics of exhibition spaces (and aesthetic policy, for that matter) for the various regimes of the 1930s – Nazi, Fascist or Totalitarian – the exhibition, in each case, was a crucial and much manipulated political tool. Indeed, although they were conceived on a much smaller scale and garnered much less public attention, the Soviet Union was involved in a condemnation of art deemed unacceptable to the State and in fact had begun some years before the Nazis did. For a brief discussion of these Soviet exhibitions, see O.K. Werckmeister, book review for Barron, 'Degenerate Art' and Zuschlag, 'Entartete Kunst', *Art Bulletin* LXXIX:2 (June 1997), pp. 337–41.

47 André Breton, 'Devant le rideau', written on the occasion of the 1947 *Exposition Internationale du Surréalisme* and reprinted in *La Clé des champs* (Paris: Sagittaire, 1953).

The Surrealist movement did not, on the other hand, base their *Exposition* on a utopian vision of what a museum or art exhibition should or could be, in other words, they did not imagine their exhibition as a newer, better way to show art. The failure of Surrealism's idiosyncratic installation to coalesce into a stable and comprehensive whole – its continual oscillation between inside and outside, its refusal to uphold pretences of clarity, knowledge and progress, and its attack on the architectural and discursive order of art exhibitions – offered a construction distinctly at odds with the stability and self-evidence of any museum and gallery display. Thus, whatever the *Exposition Internationale du Surréalisme* may seem to share with the disordered presentation of the *Entartete Kunst*, unlike the latter, the Surrealist show offered no proper alternative of the museum or the body. In contrast with a Nazi museum erected as spectacularly complete, a steeled and totalized image of Classical Hellas modernized, the Surrealists erected an architecture in ruins, an exhibition that violated the idea of the art exhibition.

In the end, the Surrealists' move toward a rethinking of the exhibition space in 1938 caused little more than temporary local derangement. Misunderstood in its day, Surrealism's dirt was easy to sweep up, the blackened gallery walls quickly repainted white. A cartoon from the period epitomizes the problem: the exhibition's public recognized the disorder as nothing more than impotence; for them, the gallery and everything it represented remained unscathed by the Surrealist intervention (fig. 49). But, perhaps this misunderstanding stemmed from a deeper and more problematic relationship of artistic production and politics. For visitors who were disappointed that the Surrealists had not filled the exhibition with anti-fascist banners or explicit signs of their ideological engagement had good reason to lament: hysteric and ridiculously prankish, the Surrealist exhibition *did* leave a certain notion of politics behind. And, perhaps therein lies the 1938 Exposition's ultimate force: its refusal of the traditional forms of organized politics. Or rather, its utter refusal of the space and the idea of the body that were useful to and used by institutional politics, and were, most notably, in the anxious overdetermined months before the war, useful to and used by Hitler. And this may help explain why it was not simply a matter for the Surrealists in 1938 of hanging a banner or two, thereby attesting to the fierceness of their ideological convictions. A riposte to exhibitionary complexes of the 1930s, the 1938 *Exposition Internationale du Surréalisme* revealed white to be a choice, not a silent fact of exhibition walls.[48] Thus, it was not about putting the

48 This effort distinguishes the Surrealist political effort, if one agrees that it can be called that, from other Leftist political gestures that involved art exhibitions. A number of critics who visited the 1938 *Exposition* denounced it because, as they said, there was hardly anything 'cruel' about it. Implicitly, indeed almost in code set out for readers in-the-know, these critics made reference to *L'Art cruel*, an anti-fascist exhibition held in Paris that closed just 11 days before the Surrealist show opened. Among the works presented were explicitly political pieces that were meant to express directly and legibly

gallery's white walls in the 'service of the revolution' – it was a matter of insisting on a consciousness of an exhibition's walls and of the body as impacted by them. All the better to point – if only temporarily, if only impotently – to the imbrication of these walls and these bodies in the politics of power.

the *cruel* threat of Fascism. Thus, for some reporters, the 'failure' of the 1938 Surrealist exhibition – and Surrealism writ large – was based on the movement's seeming negligence to put art in the service of politics at such an urgent moment in history. What these critiques demonstrate, and what descriptions of *L'Art cruel* make clear, however, is the degree to which the cultural politics of the Left depended on traditional museological display in order to convince the public of the cruelty of Fascism through pedagogic means. See especially, Jean Bazin, 'La Peinture: Exposition Surréaliste', *Esprit*, no. 66 (March 1938); Marcel Morel and Jean Bazin, 'Le Faillité du Surréalisme', *Temps Présents*, n.d. (Seligman Archive). Jean Cassou's preface for the *L'Art cruel* exhibition he organized was reprinted with commentary by François Moulignat in 'L'Art Cruel', *Cahiers du Musée Nationale d'Art Moderne*, no. 9 (1992).

Chapter 10

For an Independent Revolutionary Art: Breton, Trotsky and Cárdenas's Mexico

*Robin Adèle Greeley**

I begin with a photograph taken in 1938 of André Breton, Diego Rivera and Léon Trotsky that marks a critical moment in the history of Surrealism (fig. 50). Its basic details are by now well rehearsed: in February 1938, Breton travelled to Mexico to meet Trotsky, then in exile and hunted by Stalin's assassins. He was introduced to the great revolutionary by Rivera, the flamboyant Communist leader of the Mexican Mural Movement, while a friend snapped the picture. Out of the meeting came the famous manifesto 'For An Independent Revolutionary Art', the founding text of the Fédération internationale de l'art révolutionnaire indépendant (FIARI). But the euphoria of vivid intellectual and cultural interchange embodied in the photo ultimately succumbed to the desperation of the period: Breton's efforts to establish the French sector of the FIARI came to naught; Rivera's political vagaries became ever wilder; and Trotsky was murdered less than two years later.

Of the few scholars to address Breton's Mexico visit, most have lauded his efforts to forge a non-Stalinist political path for Surrealism.[1] The interlude evidenced in the famous photograph is often interpreted, however, almost exclusively through textual examination of the manifesto written by Breton and Trotsky, in addition to anecdotal references to their conversations, fishing trips or expeditions to the Mexican countryside.[2] What remains almost entirely

---

* My thanks to Anthony Lee, Raymond Spiteri, Donald LaCoss and Michael Orwicz for their criticism and suggestions. Thanks also to Sarah White for her timely research assistance, and to the University of Connecticut Research Council for research funding.

1 Helena Lewis, *The Politics of Surrealism* (New York: Paragon House, 1988), p. 159. Gérard Roche, 'Breton, Trotsky: une collaboration', *Pleine Marge*, no. 3 (May 1986), pp. 73–93. Arturo Schwarz, *André Breton, Trotsky et l'Anarchie*, trans. Amaryllis Vassilikioti (Paris: Union Générale d'Editions, 1974). Mark Polizzotti, 'When Breton Met Trotsky', *Partisan Review* LXII:3 (Summer 1995), pp. 406–18. Alain Dugrand, *Trotsky, Mexico 1937–1940* (Paris: Documents Payot, 1988).

2 Some of the essays that fall deepest into this trap are Polizzotti, 'When Breton Met Trotsky', and Dugrand, *Trotsky, Mexico 1937–1940.*

uninvestigated, however, is the historical and ideological impact of Trotsky's thinking on Surrealism at this moment, and the related issue of the significance to Surrealism that this encounter occurred in the Mexico of President Lázaro Cárdenas (1934–40). These two issues might be brought together under the following question: what were the effects of Cárdenas's programme of 'Revolutionary Nationalism'[3] on determining Surrealism's encounter with Trotsky's key theory of permanent world revolution? In Mexico – a nation 'formed by conquest and colonization' – issues of class are continually formulated in relation to questions of race and ethnicity, and the concept of a 'modern' nation has been built upon the violent incorporation of whole peoples into social structures they can never call their own.[4] This deeply affected the Mexican search in the late 1930s for a socialist economic and political programme on a national and international scale. It in turn affected how Mexico (especially those Mexican artists most predisposed to Surrealism) responded to Trotsky, and thus the cultural milieu in which Surrealism and Trotskyism came together.

This formulation of the problem puts the entire nature of Surrealism's – and Trotsky's – espoused 'internationalist' focus under particular scrutiny on both political and cultural levels. It raises questions about subsequent Surrealist attitudes – both in Paris and in Mexico – towards other cultures. Was the manifesto, for example, an effective means of judging cultural freedom in Mexico as well as in Europe? Did it elaborate a Marxist policy that could address cultural hegemony and cultural resistance in situations as different as Moscow, Berlin and Mexico City? In addition to the manifesto itself, Breton and Trotsky each produced a number of other essays on Mexico, including Breton's 1939 essay, 'Souvenir du Mexique', Trotsky's 'Nationalized Industry and Workers' Management' on Cárdenas's nationalization of Mexico's oil industry, and his many articles on Mexican trade unions. Taken together, they form a significant body of work that brings the thoughts of the two leaders to bear on Mexico.

Most importantly, the shift in context from Europe to Mexico begins to throw into high relief the essential distinctions between the programmes of Breton and Trotsky. Despite their effort to find a common platform in 'For An Independent Revolutionary Art', one that would combine theory and practice, what begins to emerge instead, both in the manifesto and in other related essays, are the

3 This is the phrase used to describe the ruling ideology of the Mexican State brought about by the Mexican Revolution. Cárdenas retained the Presidency from 1934 to 1940.

4 Jean Franco, *Plotting Women: Gender and Representation in Mexico* (New York: Columbia University Press, 1990), p. xii, and 'Beyond Ethnocentrism: Gender, Power, and the Third-World Intelligentsia', in Cary Nelson and Lawrence Grossberg, eds, *Marxism and the Interpretation of Culture* (Urbana: University of Illinois Press, 1988), p. 504.

fundamental differences in their basic conceptions of imperialist capitalism and how to combat it in order to set up a socialist state.

* * *

'For An Independent Revolutionary Art' is a text marked by its time.[5] In a tone that seeks to gauge the depths of the looming horror of war without falling into helpless despondency, the opening paragraph connects the problem of artistic freedom directly to the impending holocaust of World War II and to Stalin's purges. Thus the terms 'freedom' and 'equality' are not merely linked to economic parity or political democracy, but are also linked to attitudes towards culture. What the manifesto purports to offer, therefore, is a means of judging social freedom by thinking about the conditions of artistic production. On the surface, this produced a landmark collaboration between two of the most powerful and innovative interwar schools of thought on social revolution.

Despite its grand intentions, however, the manifesto obfuscates a history of difficult interactions between Trotskyists and Surrealists that spanned more than a decade. Surrealism's tendentious history with the Communist Party is by now well-documented. Its interactions with Trotskyist groups has been less thoroughly investigated, but stem back to the heated arguments between Breton and Pierre Naville in the mid-1920s. Naville, originally a member of Breton's coterie, left Surrealism for the Communist Party in 1926 after experiencing one of Breton's notorious personal attacks. That year he published a pamphlet, *La Révolution et les intellectuels. Que peuvent-faire les Surréalistes?*, in which he argued that Surrealism and Marxism were incompatible, as the Surrealists were too individualist and bourgeois to contribute to the collective, 'disciplined action of class struggle' necessary to overthrow capitalism.[6] Breton responded in December 1926 with *Légitime défense*, which rebutted not only Naville's attack but also the refusal of the entire Communist Party to take Surrealism seriously.[7]

5 Written by Breton and Trotsky in July 1938, the manifesto was signed by Breton and Rivera perhaps for reasons of distribution or for reception – a manifesto on art would be better received if signed by two artists. Trotsky had also been officially forbidden by the Cárdenas government to write on political subjects, under threat of revoking his hard-won visa. This injunction seems to have been understood rather loosely by Cárdenas himself, however; Trotsky did write on economic policy in Mexico, which for a Marxist writer of course had a directly political dimension. Cárdenas chose to ignore such publications, in large part because of his personal esteem for Trotsky. Trotsky was also able to voice his opinions through other writers such as Octavio Fernández Vilchis, although with less impact than under his own name.

6 Pierre Naville, *La Révolution et les intellectuels. Que peuvent-faire les Surréalistes?* (Paris: n.p., 1926), p. 17.

7 *Légitime défense* was first published in *La Révolution surréaliste*, no. 8 (December 1926), pp. 30–36.

The Naville-Surrealism debates are of particular importance because of Naville's own political trajectory away from the Communist Party: in 1927, he visited the Soviet Union where he saw first hand the battle between Trotsky and Stalin, coming home convinced that Trotsky held the true path to social revolution. Back in France, Naville founded the journal, *La Lutte des Classes*, and became a leading member of the Trotskyist POI (Parti Ouvrier International). Breton hinted later that he would have worked more closely with the Trotskyists, but was kept from doing so by the leaders of the Trotskyist POI.[8] Naville in particular, Breton claimed, was against any collaboration between the two groups.[9] This is no surprise, given the very public overtures made by Breton and the Surrealists towards the French Communist Party during the 1920s, and the slanderous personal attacks against Naville himself in the *Second Manifesto of Surrealism*. Naville later denied Breton's accusation of non-cooperation, pointing out that Breton's story of himself as victim was largely invented.[10] Yet whatever differences between Naville and Breton may have existed at this point seemed substantially to disappear upon Breton's arrival in Mexico; Trotsky wrote to Naville for his opinion on the Surrealist leader, and Naville responded very favourably.[11]

The continual difficulties and internecine squabbling over the next decade between the Surrealists and the Trotskyists make the outward success of Breton's meeting with Trotsky in Mexico all the more surprising. In fact, a close look at these differences of opinion indicates that not only did the Surrealists have very little idea of what Trotsky actually stood for, but the reverse was also true.[12] There is little solid evidence that the Surrealists comprehended Trotsky's role in Soviet leadership – his arguments, for instance, with Lenin over the question of labour unions, his views on the Chinese revolution, or his attitude towards anarchism. And although Trotsky had no doubt heard of Breton and the Surrealists, his knowledge of their work was extremely limited.[13] His mistrust of

8 Breton, *Entretiens, 1913–1952* (Paris: Gallimard 1952), p. 179.

9 Indeed, Breton invited Naville to the Bar du Château meeting in 1929 to discuss the recent expulsion of Trotsky from the Soviet Union, but Naville did not attend. My thanks to Raymond Spiteri for reminding me of this point.

10 Pierre Naville, *Trotsky vivant* (Paris: Lettres Nouvelles, 1962), p. 100. See also Naville, *Le Temps du suréel* (Paris: Galilée, 1977), especially pp. 491–503.

11 Naville, *Trotsky vivant*, pp. 100–1.

12 Although Breton had written essays on Trotsky as early as 1925, these functioned more as poetic elegies to a Communist hero than as analyses of Trotsky's political positions. See André Breton, 'Léon Trotsky's "Lenin" ', *La Révolution surréaliste*, no. 5 (1925), p. 29. See Alan Rose's discussion of this issue, 'For an Independent Revolutionary Art: André Breton's Manifesto With Léon Trotsky', *European Studies Journal* II:1 (1985), pp. 56–57.

13 Upon learning of Breton's intention to visit, Trotsky asked his secretary to obtain a selection of Breton's writing to review.

certain principles fundamental to Surrealism – the theory of objective chance in particular – was in many ways linked to his general incomprehension of modernist literature and the visual arts.[14] For the Surrealists, what was most important by 1938 was that Trotsky was anti-Stalinist, and that his 1924 book, *Literature and Revolution,* advocated freedom of cultural expression as necessary to any true proletarian state. In 'For An Independent Revolutionary Art', Breton would restate Trotsky's famous dictum from *Literature and Revolution* that 'art must, above all, be judged by its own laws, that is to say the laws of art'.

Although Breton had already sided with the Trotskyists on several previous occasions, it was not until Surrealism's definitive rupture with the French Communist Party in 1933 that he and other Surrealists actively pursued connections to Trotskyist groups in France and elsewhere.[15] By January 1937, when he wrote the 'Declaration on the Second Moscow Trial', Breton had clearly come around to supporting Trotsky against Stalin. In the text, he not only decries the Moscow Trials themselves, but also the treachery of Moscow as it aimed bullets at the backs of non-Stalinist Leftists in the Spanish Civil War.[16] The Surrealist leader recapitulates Trotsky's analysis of Moscow as a Bonapartist political regime – one that promises to represent the revolutionary energy of the proletariat but in the end concentrates power in a state bureaucracy 'determined

---

14 Breton speaks of his argument with Trotsky over the theory of objective chance in his 11 November 1938 speech for the PCI, 'Visite à Léon Trotsky', subsequently published in *Quatrième Internationale*, nos 14–15 (November–December 1938) and reprinted in *Cahiers Léon Trotsky*, no. 12 (December 1982), p. 116. This mistrust seems to have been overcome at least partially, as 'For An Independent Art' argues for 'precious chance' as integral to cultural enrichment. Jacqueline Lamba, Breton's wife at the time, notes Trotsky's inability to comprehend modern writers such as Mayakovsky. Lamba interviewed by Schwarz, *André Breton, Trotsky et l'Anarchie*, pp. 209–10.

15 There is evidence of Breton's interest in Trotsky before this period, in his review of Trotsky's biography of Lenin published in *La Révolution surréaliste*, in the Bar du Château meeting of 1929 organized by Breton to discuss Trotsky's expulsion from the Soviet Union, and, importantly, in the *Second Manifesto* where Breton quotes Trotsky from the 1923 text, 'Révolution et culture', on the dangers of expecting a proletarian culture to arise any time soon. Breton utilizes Trotsky here to refute Communist Party charges that Surrealism was merely a 'bourgeois' art form and therefore inherently anti-revolutionary. After years of difficulty, the rupture with the PCF finally occurred over an article published by Fernand Alquié in *Le Surréalisme au service de la révolution* (May 1933) which criticized a Soviet film. Breton signed an *Appel à la lutte* manifesto with several Trotskyists after the February 1934 Stavisky riots, and published 'La Planète sans visa', *Documents 34* (June 1934), pp. 9–10, protesting the French government's decision to expel Trotsky from France.

16 André Breton, *Déclaration d'André Breton à propos du second procès de Moscou* (Paris, 26 January 1937), trans. in André Breton, *What Is Surrealism? Selected Writings*, ed. Franklin Rosemont (New York: Monad, 1978), pp. 168–72.

at all costs to prevent a new revolutionary wave from breaking on the world'.[17] Breton also emphasizes two crucial elements in Trotsky's concept of permanent revolution: the necessary relationship between proletarian revolutions in different countries not only to each other, but also to world revolution; and the notion of a revolutionary vanguard. These were key aspects of Trotsky's doctrine, which sought to foment unceasing revolutionary pressure by the international proletariat on all fronts. He damns the 'Stalinist bureaucracy' for seeking 'to abort the Spanish revolution as it has previously aborted the German revolution and the Chinese revolution', and calls upon his reader to support the 'Catalan and Spanish revolutionary vanguard'.[18] While Breton's willingness to support the 'Catalan revolutionary vanguard' indicates an enthusiasm for anarcho-syndicalist politics that Trotsky adamantly rejected, his concern over the fate of the Spanish Republic attests to his commitment to Trotsky's most dearly held principle of permanent world revolution.[19] In this regard, Breton resolutely resisted Stalin's plan of 'socialism in one country', as did Trotsky. Indeed, in a 1938 letter to Philip Rahv of *Partisan Review*, Trotsky commented warmly upon the similarities between Breton's political trajectory and his own:

> André Breton, the recognized head of Surrealism, is now in Mexico. As you certainly know, in artistic as well as in political matters, he is not only independent of Stalinism, but also absolutely hostile to it. He has sincere sympathies for the Fourth International.[20]

* * *

It was, of course, out of Trotsky's harsh critique of Stalinism's attack on world proletarian organization that he articulated one of his most significant goals: the founding of the Fourth International. That the charter conference of the Fourth

---

17 Ibid., p. 171. See also, Léon Trotsky, 'The Bonapartist Philosophy of the State', (1 May 1939) reprinted in Trotsky, *Writings of Léon Trotsky, 1938–39* (New York: Pathfinder Press, 1974), pp. 318–25.

18 Breton, *Déclaration*, trans. in *What Is Surrealism?*, p. 171.

19 See Murray Bookchin, *The Spanish Anarchists: The Heroic Years, 1868–1936* (New York: Harper and Row, 1977), and John Brademas, *Anarcosindicalismo y Revolución en España (1930–1937)* (Barcelona: Editorial Ariel, 1974) on the role of anarchism, especially anarcho-syndicalism, in 1930s Catalonia. Breton's interest in anarchism was almost as long-standing as Trotsky's rejection of it. For its increased importance to Surrealism after World War II, see José Pierre, *Surréalisme et anarchie: les 'billets surréalistes' du 'Libertaire': 12 octobre 1951–8 janvier 1953* (Paris: Plasma, 1983). Trotsky, vehemently opposed to any collaboration with the anarchists, only accepted an alliance between Trotskyist groups in Spain and the anarchists after the former had been so devastated by Stalinist and fascist attacks as to be on the verge of extinction. See Léon Trotsky, *The Spanish Revolution, 1931–1939* (New York: Pathfinder Press, 1973).

20 Trotsky to Philip Rahv, 12 May 1938, *Œuvres*, vol. 17 (Paris: Institut Léon Trotsky), p. 230. Quoted in Gérard Roche, 'Breton, Trotsky: un collaboration', p. 74, my translation from the French.

International took place in Paris just after Breton returned there from Mexico; that Trotsky concretized its principles from Mexico as he watched Cárdenas nationalize Mexico's all-important oil industry; and that the great Russian revolutionary must have discussed the significance of the new International with Breton as they observed Mexican events unfold during the Spring and Summer of 1938 – all these circumstances form the immediate context in which both the manifesto, 'For An Independent Revolutionary Art', and Breton's essay, 'Souvenir du Mexique', were elaborated.

The Fourth International, founded in Paris on 3 September 1938, marked the culmination of a long struggle to reform the previous International, aiming to rid it of its Stalinist elements in order to return it to its original Leninist path. When it became clear that the Soviet Communist Party was willing to sell out its own proletariat so as to form alliances with the capitalist bureaucracies of Europe, Trotsky realized that reform was no longer possible and that an entirely new organization needed to be built.[21] The new International was to embody the militant working-class vanguard that would form the revolutionary leadership for the proletariat across all nations. It would address what Trotsky saw as a key problem: that, in the twentieth century, 'the crisis of mankind is the crisis of the revolutionary leadership of the proletariat'.[22] Without a revolutionary vanguard with a developed class consciousness and clear understanding of class struggle in relation to a world economy, Trotsky argued, the spontaneous energy of the proletariat would continually be threatened with dissipation and defeat.[23] Trotsky understood the development of world revolution and consequently of such a proletarian vanguard to be, as Ernest Mandel puts it, a 'concrete process arising out of the inner contradictions of world capitalism [...] but a world capitalism structured into specific states, with specific state powers that the working class and its allies had to overthrow'.[24] Thus, the particularities of social and political struggles within any given nation-state had the potential to advance the cause of the proletariat on a world level, but only if the link between national and international were adequately theorized and actively pursued. Against Stalin's concept of 'socialism in one country', Trotsky argued that the

---

21 Ernest Mandel, *Trotsky: A Study in the Dynamic of His Thought* (London: New Left Books, 1979), p. 109.

22 Ibid., p. 115.

23 Ibid. The concrete relationship of this revolutionary vanguard to the proletariat is, of course, one of the most tendentious aspects of Trotsky's thought. For a view opposed to that of Mandel, see Leszek Kolakowski, *Main Currents of Marxism, vol. 3: The Breakdown* (Oxford: Oxford University Press, 1978), especially chapter 5. Kolakowski argues that on this point there was essentially no theoretical difference between Stalin and Trotsky on the issue of the vanguard leadership of the proletariat; the only real difference, according to Kolakowski, was that Stalin managed to retain power while Trotsky did not.

24 Mandel, *Trotsky*, p. 33

connections between the national and the international were crucial: 'the international revolution [...] is a chain – moreover not a continuous one – of national revolutions, each of which nourishes the others with its successes and in turn suffers from their failures'.[25] Exactly how Trotsky understood this would become an issue in his understanding of the Mexican situation.

Although Breton and many others felt that in the late 1930s Republican Spain was the most significant battleground for Trotsky's concept of world revolution, by 1938 it was increasingly clear that the Spanish proletariat had suffered irreparable defeat at the hands of both the fascists and the Communist Party.[26] Mexico, geographically distant from the conflicts engulfing Europe, governed by a socialist president, and a key nation in the American hemisphere, seemingly offered a chance for renewed Fourth International efforts. President Cárdenas was highly sympathetic to Trotsky's ideas, and within Mexico, his presidency was the only administration after that country's own revolution (1910–20) that might potentially have provided an official forum for Trotsky's Fourth International goals.[27] Crucial to the entire situation was the fate of Mexico's oil industry.[28] Heavily infiltrated by foreign investment, but also the locus of

25 Trotsky, quoted in Mandel, *Trotsky*, p. 34.

26 Breton, in a speech given to the Trotskyist International Workers' Party in Paris, December 1936 (almost two years before his trip to Mexico), declared 'Camarade Trotsky, toi qui fus le grand organisateur de l'Armée Rouge, ta place ne serait pas au Mexique. Puisque presque toutes les frontières se sont fermées devant toi, il est du moins une porte qui devrait s'ouvrir tout grande pour te laisser passer et c'est celle de Barcelone'. André Breton, 'Déclaration d'André Breton au Meeting du P.O.I. en Décembre 1936', *Cahiers Léon Trotsky*, no. 9 (January 1982), p. 114. Benjamin Péret, fighting in a POUM brigade in Barcelona, was soon to send back reports on the treacherous annihilation, on the orders of the CPSU, of the non-Stalinist Left in May 1937. See Claude Courtot, *Introduction à la leture de Benjamin Péret* (Paris: La Terrain vague, 1965), pp. 28–32. In 1938, when preparing to visit Mexico, Breton himself was subject to a Stalinist smear campaign designed to ruin his reputation in Mexico and foil any attempts to collaborate with either Cárdenas or Trotsky. Breton specifically names Tristan Tzara, Louis Aragon and a certain 'René Blech', a pseudonym for an unidentified foe. See André Breton, 'Visite à Léon Trotsky', pp. 106–8.

27 Not only did Cárdenas grant Trotsky asylum without hesitation, but he also expressed his view that Trotsky's path remained the true revolutionary one. See Lázaro Cárdenas, *Obras I. Apuntes 1913–1940*, vol. 1 (Nueva Biblioteca Mexicana, Dirección General de Publicaciones, UNAM, 1972) entries for August 1940. Trotsky also commented positively on his respect for Cárdenas. See Trotsky, 'Autour de l'enquête' (letter to Alfred Rosmer) 12 June 1938, *Œuvres*, vol. 18, p. 73. For information on the Mexican Revolution and Mexico's subsequent political development, see Leslie Bethell, ed., *Mexico Since Independence* (Cambridge: Cambridge University Press, 1991).

28 Another key to Cardenismo was, of course, agrarian reform. Despite the historic importance of land reform and the peasantry in determining Mexico's economic and social conditions, however, Trotsky concentrated on Mexico's working class as the locus of revolutionary energy. Trotsky, of course, continually insisted that only the proletariat could foster a true revolution, no matter what country was concerned. See note 34 below.

militant worker unionization, the oil industry became central both to Cárdenas's plan of 'revolutionary nationalism' and to Mexico's role in the international sphere. When Cárdenas nationalized the oil industry on 18 March 1938, the manoeuvre not only fell on the foreign oil companies 'like a bolt of lightning in a blue sky',[29] but also seemed the moment to bring together anti-imperialist, national and proletarian interests.

Until Cárdenas nationalized the oil industry, Mexico's role in global politics had largely followed the nationalist traditions of respect for national sovereignty, non-intervention and self-determination.[30] Under the platform of 'revolutionary nationalism' – a programme consistently claimed by all post-1920 presidencies in Mexico[31] – cross-national worker solidarity was favoured far less than cross-class national cohesion.[32] Beyond its own borders, the government adhered to a policy of negotiated settlements of international disputes and non-partisan condemnation of military aggression, whether it be the US intervention in Nicaragua, the Nazi invasion of Poland, or, more surprisingly, the Soviet campaign against Finland.[33]

After March 1938, however, both the government and the Sindicato de Trabajadores Petroleros de la República Mexicana (the Mexican Oil Workers Union, formed in 1935) found themselves the object of international diplomatic outrage. Oil companies in Britain and the United States were especially vociferous, successfully lobbying for an economic boycott of Mexico. US relations with Mexico – always central to Mexico's foreign policy – worsened, while Britain forced a break in diplomatic ties.[34] The nationalization of the oil industry had thrust the entire country onto an international stage that could not be ignored, and foreign relations became central to governmental strategies both external and domestic. The main point of conflict forcing nationalization was

---

29 The US Ambassador, quoted in Héctor Aguilar Camín and Lorenzo Meyer, *In the Shadow of the Mexican Revolution: Contemporary Mexican History 1910–1989* (Austin: University of Texas, 1993), p. 153.

30 Alan Knight, 'The Rise and Fall of Cardenismo, c. 1930–c. 1946', in Leslie Bethell, ed., *Mexico Since Independence* (Cambridge: Cambridge University Press, 1991), p. 284.

31 Francisco Valdés-Ugalde, 'Nationalism and the Polity in Mexico', unpublished paper delivered at Brown University, 1999. It remains to be seen if the current PAN president Vicente Fox, elected in July 2000 and the first to break the hold of the PRI, will follow this ideology.

32 Under Cárdenas, a superficial glance at this policy might mistake it for the Popular Front ideologies current in other Allied nations of the period. But it has a much longer – and therefore distinct – history based in the Mexican Revolution and in the centuries-long history of colonialism and imperialism suffered by Mexico.

33 Knight, 'The Rise and Fall of Cardenismo', p. 284.

34 The US boycott affected the buying of Mexican silver, plans for a commercial treaty, and the problem of indemnity for the oil fields. Knight, 'The Rise and Fall of Cardenismo', p. 285.

not deed titles to oil-rich land, but rather contract negotiations between the oil companies and the Mexican workers' unions. Those unions understood foreign oil company refusal to accede to labour demands as part and parcel of a long history of colonial and imperialist disregard for Mexico's autonomy. The moment seemed ripe for linking an international class solidarity to a fervently held nationalist economic policy; facing down the concerted efforts of foreign oil companies to topple Cárdenas's decision to nationalize might have provided a crucial focus around which to consolidate real international solidarity among workers' groups.[35]

Yet a confluence of historical and cultural circumstances, along with ideological differences, served to undermine any such solidarity. On an international level, the approach of World War II had a decisive effect. The US, fearing that Mexico would sell oil to Germany and Italy, soon mollified its previous harsh tone in favour of a Mexico–US détente. To avoid forcing its southern neighbour into the arms of the Axis powers, US oil companies concluded an indemnity settlement in 1942, while already in 1940 Cárdenas had authorized US–Mexican military talks. National solidarity with hemispheric opposition to the fascist threat began to predominate over class solidarity, particularly as a new military service law meant that the previous socialist tool of national integration – Cárdenas's rural school system and the national literacy programme – was supplanted by a different one – the military barracks.[36]

On the domestic level, oil also proved crucial in relations between the government and workers' unions. Oil workers argued for a labour-run administration of the newly-nationalized companies, but Cárdenas was unwilling to sacrifice government control of such an important economic asset. Thus the new governing body, PEMEX, was controlled through union–government collaboration. This meant that union leaders confronted a continual difficulty: as historian Alan Knight puts it, 'traitors to their country if they obstructed the running of this new national asset, they were traitors to their class if they

35 Note, for example, Trotsky's call to the British Labour Party to take action against the British government's boycott of Mexico. See Léon Trotsky, 'La parole est au Labour Party', 22 April 1938, *Œuvres*, vol. 17, p. 208. See also Olivia Gall's analysis in *Trotsky en México, y la vida política en el periodo de Cárdenas, 1937–1940* (Mexico D.F.: Ediciones Era, 1991), pp. 228–30. Knight and others note the popular euphoria at Cárdenas's decision to nationalize, and the ingenuity and energy that the Mexican workers demonstrated in running the oil industry. Knight, 'The Rise and Fall of Cardenismo', p. 282; Aguilar Camín and Meyer, *In the Shadow of the Mexican Revolution*, pp. 153–54; R.H.K. Marett, *An Eye-Witness of Mexico* (London, 1939), p. 227; Joe C. Ashby, *Organized Labor and the Mexican Revolution Under Lázaro Cárdenas* (Chapel Hill, 1963), p. 237.

36 President Avila Camacho, Cárdenas's successor, proclaimed the new obligatory military service as providing 'a disciplined education which would benefit the youth of our country in all walks of life'. *Hoy*, 20 September 1940, translated in Knight, 'The Rise and Fall of Cardenismo', p. 287.

scrupulously followed government direction'.[37] Union leaders, the most powerful of whom were Stalinist in orientation, ultimately colluded with Cárdenas in urging the workers to tighten their belts in the interest of both the nation and – so they claimed – their own class. As Trotsky warned in his 1939 essay, 'Nationalized Industry and Workers' Management', this provoked a rift between union leadership and the workers themselves.[38] Trotsky noted that although the Mexican government had made certain concessions toward the proletariat, it was by no means a workers' state free of the heavy pressures of private foreign capital. Ultimately, Trotsky argued, it remained tied – if even reluctantly – to capitalism. Thus the danger in any government–union collaboration lay in the tendency of union leaders to be swayed by the 'apparatus of state capitalism' against the interests of their own constituency, transforming those leaders into 'political agents of the bourgeoisie and of its state'.[39]

* * *

Unlike Trotsky, Breton never wrote directly on the subject of the Mexican proletariat or the nationalization of the oil industry. Nevertheless, it is possible to glean something of his thoughts on these issues from his important essay, 'Souvenir du Mexique', published in 1939 in *Minotaure*. Breton begins the text by evoking a succession of modern Mexico's cataclysmic social struggles – first the War for Independence (1810) and second the Mexican Revolution (begun in 1910) – to make the grandiose claim that 'there is at least one country in the world where the wind of liberation has not fallen'.[40] He alludes to the military generals (including Cárdenas) who continue to follow in the footsteps of the great Mexican revolutionary, Emiliano Zapata, responsible (so Breton writes) for leading the Indian peons and tenant farmers to victory. It is in Mexico, he argues, that the hopes of other betrayed revolutions – those in the Soviet Union, Germany, China and Spain – continued to burn brightly.

Despite these opening allusions to revolutionary class struggles, however, and despite the inclusion in the essay of that famous photograph of Breton, Trotsky and Rivera (fig. 50), it soon becomes clear that Breton's agenda in addressing Mexican culture and society is quite different from Trotsky's. Breton

37 Knight, 'The Rise and Fall of Cardenismo', p. 283.

38 Trotsky, 'Nationalized Industry and Workers' Management', *Writings of Léon Trotsky*. This was especially the case with the CTM (Confederación de Trabajadores Mexicanos), led by the powerful Stalinist Victor Lombardo Toledano. Olivia Gall, based on the tentative date published in the *Fourth International*, mistakenly identifies this essay as having been written in June 1938. Pathfinder Press notes, however, that the original manuscript in the Trotsky Archives, Harvard University, is dated 12 May 1939. Ibid., p. 416, n. 317.

39 Trotsky, 'Nationalized Industry and Workers' Management', p. 328.

40 Breton, 'Souvenir du Mexique', *Minotaure*, nos 12–13 (1939), p. 31.

quickly drops into a poetic prose that conceptualizes historical time in grand sweeps reaching from the country's pre-conquest past to the twentieth century. In typical Surrealist fashion throughout the essay, Breton utilizes a logic of interplay between the familiar and the strange meant here as a corrosive analysis of Western experience and its cultural orders. He privileges Mexican culture over European, locating the contemporary wonders of this Latin American country in what he sees as its archaic culture, the 'Surrealist' nature of which has allowed it to escape the desecrations of Western civilization. In the sections that follow the first, he lyrically describes a walk of discovery through a Guadalajaran town, the unsettling enchantment of Diego Rivera's surrealizing landscape paintings, the chaotic military compound at Monterrey, and the seductive charms of 'Madame Vaudeville', whom he met just as he was leaving Mexico. The text is accompanied throughout by a long series of images – taken from Mexican artists, from Breton's archive of travel images and from Mexican popular culture – which themselves form a complementary 'text' to Breton's written word.

The first section sets the tone for the entire essay. In it, Breton links the art and architecture of Mexico's pre-conquest past to its revolutionary present, finding in Aztec culture an essential key to modern Mexico's power. Breton claims that the Aztec had given contemporary Mexico one of its greatest enticements for the rest of the world: the power to reconcile life and death. Indeed, the photographs he chooses to illustrate the text elaborate upon the theme of violent death as integral to any concept of Mexican life (fig. 51). These images, mostly taken by the photographer Manuel Alvarez Bravo whom Breton had met while in Mexico, repeat this theme through a variety of complex visual strategies. Beginning with the pairing of two images of death – a grave out of which grows a flowering plant, and a murdered worker – we find it repeated throughout the essay in the form of the candied *Día de los Muertos* skulls, children's coffins, bar-room knifings and firing squads. The first two images locate the theme of human mortality within a tradition stemming back to the Aztec, who believed that death was necessary to maintain the cycle of life. Without human sacrifice, so the Aztec assumed, angry gods might not choose to continue the cycle of time within which the cycle of life moved. Flowers in Aztec iconography not only symbolized the concept of rebirth from death, but were also the emblem of the powerful god of war and poetry, Xochipilli. The connection made between death, war and poetry clearly appealed to Breton, who names Xochipilli in the second paragraph. The 'poetry' of death as sacrifice is evoked by comparison in the next image of the assassinated worker, who lies prone on a city street, the lyrically beautiful victim of extreme social violence. This travel into the world of death, a realm irrevocably beyond this one, is echoed but softened on the following page by the horizontal orientation and closed eyes of a dreaming boy. Throughout Alvarez Bravo's images, carefully orchestrated by Breton in relation to each other and to the text, we gain a sense of worlds beyond this one, entered through sleep and dreaming, play and death.[41]

In this way, Breton sets up a quasi-Hegelian dialectic, in which the 'thesis' of life is continually faced with the 'antithesis' of death, resulting in a holistic synthesis of the two that marks a continual life-cycle.[42] But unlike Hegel's insistent rationalism, Breton sees this synthetic totality as emerging as much out of irrational forces as out of rational logic. In fact, it is his observation of the synthesis of the contradictory poles of the rational and irrational in Alvarez Bravo's photographs that attract Breton to them. That Breton hopes to harness the energies of this particular dialectic is evident in his choice of Alvarez Bravo's extremely disquieting image of a murdered striking worker as the title image to his essay. Rather than locating the worker's death purely in relation to the materialist circumstances of trade union politics, as Trotsky would have done, Breton (through Alvarez Bravo) places it evocatively within the much larger sweep of Mexico's long history of anti-imperialist struggle. We are reminded of Aztec resistance to the Spanish conquistadors in 1521, Hidalgo's resistance to European colonization in 1810, Zapata's resistance to the latifundios in 1910, and the Mexican proletariat's resistance to foreign capital in 1938. The camera's close focus on the worker eliminates almost all immediate external information. Apart from the picture's brief title, *After the Strike*, all that we know of the worker's tragedy comes from his own body, and perforce we concentrate on its details: dressed in the short shirtsleeves and pants of an urban worker, right arm flung out and black hair swept gracefully back. The flow of blood down the sides of his face, seeping into the ground in delicate, lace-like patterns, covers his mouth and eyes almost like war-paint. Death here is tragic, but beautifully, defiantly and nobly so.

It is in his use of Alvarez Bravo's imagery that Breton approaches most overtly the subject of the Mexican proletariat and the political situation in 1938 Mexico.[43] Unlike Trotsky in his Mexican essays, however, Breton clearly wants to secure a certain level of conceptual mediation with regard to the 'impress' of the political on culture. And on the other side of the coin, Breton recognizes that the reader of 'Souvenir du Mexique' might be brought to certain political

---

41 Perhaps surprisingly, Breton's interest in death, war and poetry in 'Souvenir du Mexique' might be compared to the concerns of Georges Bataille and the Collège de Sociologie. I thank Raymond Spiteri for bringing up this issue. Nevertheless, there is a sense of Hegelian resolution evident in Breton's thinking that differs from that of Bataille.

42 For an analysis of Surrealism's understanding of Hegel, see Martin Jay, *Marxism and Totality: the Adventures of a Concept from Lukács to Habermas* (Berkeley: University of California, 1984), pp. 285–86.

43 Because of *Minotaure*'s wealthy and relatively conservative audience, publisher Alber Skira refused to allow contributors to discuss their political or ideological views. See José Pierre, 'André Breton et/ou *Minotaure*', in *Regards sur Minotaure: La revue à tête de bête* (Geneva: Musée d'Art et d'Histoire, 1987), p. 95.

insights in ways *only* possible through the signifying procedures peculiar to cultural forms. He relies on the qualities of Alvarez Bravo's photography itself to mediate between an explicit alliance with institutional politics (in this case Trotskyites and Mexican trade unionists) and a position that can maintain a critical attitude towards those same affiliations.

* * *

On almost all levels, Breton's tactics in 'Souvenir du Mexique' differ considerably from Trotsky's address to the Mexican situation. Against the rationalism of Trotsky's matter-of-fact, quasi-scientific political discourse, Breton gives us a prose description highly reminiscent of the more prophetic style of the nineteenth-century Romantic movement.[44] Against Trotsky's insistent focus on the immediate present, Breton gives us an image of Mexico located at once in the past and in the future. Trotsky's materialism opposes Breton's reformulated Hegelian dialectics. The former's interest in the minutiae of trade union politicking in Mexico contrast with Breton's description of the ghosts that haunt colonial mansions and whom – García Márquez style – the current occupants take to be the source of all trouble in the house. The oppositions between the two writers go on and on, leading us to recognize that the differences are not merely stylistic, but reach to more fundamental levels. Breton's manner of writing, in conjunction with his use of visual imagery, is one that allows certain insights while it forbids others, and the same is true of Trotsky's essays; but the insights differ substantially between the two.

Trotsky's agenda in 'Nationalized Industry and Workers' Management', like the majority of his numerous Mexican essays, focuses intently on the nature of the Mexican proletariat in relation to the Cárdenas government, and examines various strategies for creating and maintaining a revolutionary vanguard leadership that would link the Mexican struggle to other international proletarian movements. In this, Trotsky is clearly able to offer day-to-day political strategies that Breton does not even pretend to, and his critique of Mexico as having been stymied in the bourgeois phase of its revolution is largely accepted today.[45] But his insights come at the expense of other areas, the most crucial of which are those of culture and of the agrarian class. Although Trotsky himself recognizes that agrarian reform is 'the main question in Mexico today', he dedicates only

44 Breton identifies Surrealism in the *Second Manifesto of Surrealism* as the 'tail' of the Romantic movement. André Breton, *Manifestoes of Surrealism*, trans. Richard Seaver and Helen R. Lane (Ann Arbor: University of Michigan, 1972), p. 153.

45 See Octavio Fernández Vilchis, '¿Qué es y a dónde va la revolución mexicana?' *Clave*, nos 3–4 (November–December 1939). Fernández echoes Trotsky's own views on the Mexican Revolution.

fragments of a single essay to it.[46] In arguing for the Mexican proletariat as the exclusive locus of revolutionary energies, Trotsky treats the Mexican situation as though it were subject to the 'objective' laws of economics in the same way as Europe or the Soviet Union. He negates the prevailing view that revolution in Mexico was impossible without forging alliances between workers and the peasantry, ignoring the fact that the Mexican peasantry – not the proletariat – was the historically revolutionary class.[47] Trotsky thus falls into the trap (for which Gramsci criticized him) of disregarding national differences in the revolutionary potential of various oppressed groups, and in particular of homogenizing the international working class.[48]

This is the point at which the issue of culture arises. For it is not only political and economic specificities that determine differences, but cultural factors as well. And it is here that Breton clearly has the edge. Unlike Trotsky's persistent view that culture was ultimately a subsidiary issue, Breton and the Surrealists conceptualized it as central both to any understanding of power relationships under capitalism and to any theory of social change. In fact, Surrealism's dedication to cultural theory marks its fundamental opposition to Trotsky's more orthodox Marxism. In this, Surrealism formed part of the current of Western Marxism, in opposition to Trotsky's Marxist-Leninism and its conviction that the 'objective' laws of economics would automatically bring about the fall of capitalism and the rise to power of the proletariat.[49] Along with other Western

46 Trotsky, 'On Mexico's Second Six Year Plan', *Writings of Léon Trotsky*, p. 223. In this regard it is important to note that Trotsky, of course, advocated forced industrialization in the Soviet Union at great cost to the peasantry. Stalin would later take up this policy.

47 Of all classes and periods, it was the peasantry under Emiliano Zapata during the Mexican Revolution that came the closest to instituting real social reform. See John Womack, Jr., 'The Mexican Revolution, 1910–1920', in Leslie Bethell, ed., *Mexico Since Independence*, especially p. 156. Cárdenas, to his great credit, was the post-Revolution president who came closest to fulfilling the Zapatista peasants' goals through his sweeping agrarian reform policies.

48 See Antonio Gramsci, *Selections from the Prison Notebooks*, ed. and trans. Quintin Hoare and Geoffrey Nowell Smith (New York, 1971), p. 237, and Guiseppe Fiori, *Antonio Gramsci: Life of a Revolutionary*, trans. Tom Nairn (New York, 1971), p. 213f, both indicated in Martin Jay, *Marxism and Totality*, p. 163. In this, the Mexican situation might be compared to Gramsci's analysis of the 'southern question' in Italy and his advocation of an alliance between workers and peasants.

49 Western Marxists criticized orthodox Marxism's inability to separate its scientific self-understanding from the inappropriate methods of bourgeois science. Against orthodox Marxism, Western Marxism based itself in a tradition of philosophical critique, stemming back to Kant and German Idealism, that emphasized human action over economic determinism in overcoming oppression. It incorporated influences from other areas, particularly psychoanalysis, in an effort to link a nuanced theoretical practice more closely with a pragmatic politics. As Martin Jay notes, in the Soviet Union orthodox Marxism produced a 'doctrinaire ideology of legitimation by a tyrannical

Marxists such as Antonio Gramsci and Walter Benjamin, the Surrealists argued that a critique of culture in relation to politics was crucial to any revolutionary analysis of capitalist society. Susan Buck-Morss, writing on Benjamin, notes the key lesson he learned from Surrealism: that the cultural contents of history were:

> the source of critical knowledge that alone can place the present into question. Benjamin makes us aware that the transmission of culture (high and low), which is central to this rescue operation, is a political act of the highest import – not because culture in itself has the power to change the given, but because historical memory affects decisively the collective, political will for change.[50]

While Benjamin questioned Surrealism's absolute faith in the transformatory power of aesthetics, both shared a commitment to cultural analysis and artistic production as essential to Marxism that was far from Trotsky's view.[51]

It is easy to see why in 1938 Breton might not have comprehended the wide distinctions between Surrealism's attitude towards Marxism and that of Trotsky. Stalin's persecution of his former co-revolutionary had reached a fever pitch even in Mexico, making it seem that the two were in absolute theoretical opposition as well as being sworn political enemies.[52] Without a concrete understanding of Trotsky's Marxism, it would have been very easy to fall into thinking that an enemy of Stalin must necessarily be a friend and ally, and that differences of opinion with Trotsky's programme were surely minor. Breton seems to have been very reluctant to separate pragmatic politics from theory in this instance; his differences from Trotsky appear only in fits and starts, a subliminal message only tentatively placing into question his admiration of the great Bolshevik leader and his very real sense that only Trotsky could save the world from both Stalin and Hitler.[53] Those differences appear most clearly in 'Souvenir du Mexique', where Breton was least under the scrutiny of Trotsky; there, Breton credits cultural resistance over economic resistance as having allowed Mexico to remain free from the stagnation of

---

regime', for no small part of which Trotsky must be held accountable. Martin Jay, *Marxism and Totality*, p. 2. Kolakowski is the most severe critic of Trotsky's part in setting up the conditions for Stalin's dictatorship. See Kolakowski, *Main Currents of Marxism: The Breakdown*. See also note 42 above. For a counterargument to the distinctions between Western and orthodox Marxism that Jay stakes out, see his assessment of Perry Anderson's *Considerations on Western Marxism* (London, 1976), in his *Marxism and Totality*, pp. 3–4.

50 Susan Buck-Morss, *The Dialectics of Seeing: Walter Benjamin and the Arcades Project* (Cambridge: MIT Press, 1989), pp. x–xi.

51 Trotsky argues in *Literature and Revolution* that 'the Marxian methods are not the same as the artistic'. This view had not fundamentally changed by 1938.

52 See, for example, the rabid anti-Trotsky tone of the pamphlet, *La CTM y Trotsky* (Mexico D.F.: Confederación de Trabajadores Mexicanos, 1938).

53 The fact that World War II was looming, of course, put enormous pressure on everyone to find common ground.

Western civilization.[54] But they also appear in telling ways in the manifesto 'For An Independent Revolutionary Art'. As the original manuscript shows, the text for the manifesto was elaborated first by Breton, then augmented and edited by Trotsky.[55] In comparing the two versions side by side, it becomes apparent, for instance, that Breton was the one to introduce Freud into the text (paragraph 7). Trotsky, one of the orthodox Marxists most open to other theories of human behaviour such as Freudian psychoanalysis, did not object.[56] But he did suppress the opening paragraph in Breton's version, which originally read as follows:

> The analysis of ideological superstructures, which permits in the last instance one to see in certain cases (religion, morality) nothing but the pure and simple reflection of the economic conditions of life, allows to subsist as *partially* irreducible to [the economic conditions of life] three factors that contribute, through their partial autonomy, to the progressive modification of society. These are art, science and the pursuit of the social ideal in its most elevated form. Certainly these three domains can never pretend to escape the grip of dominant power that comes back, in the end, to economic development. But in them one finds translated distinct and fundamental aspirations, capable of reacting on the base of material necessity and of furnishing certain complementary elements of appraisal [*appréciation*]. All other conceptions of history will inevitably fall into fatalism.[57]

This paragraph critiqued, as Gérard Roche puts it, 'that caricature of Marxism that wants the ensemble of ideological superstructures [including art] to be a *direct* reflection of the economic and material conditions of existence'.[58] In 1938, the 'caricature' Roche describes was exceedingly strong, although under attack by Marxists such as Gramsci, Adorno, Benjamin and the Surrealists. In fact, Breton's suppressed paragraph reads very much like Adorno's concept of aesthetic autonomy, which describes a highly mediated relationship between art and the social sphere.[59] It can also be compared to Gramsci's theory of cultural

54 It should be remembered, however, that Breton was under the strict scrutiny of Albert Skira, *Minotaure*'s publisher. Skira, mindful of the wealthy and conservative readership of the magazine, refused to allow political discussions to be printed in it.

55 The original manuscript is located in the Trotsky Archives at Harvard University. Gérard Roche lays out beautifully the original Breton text alongside the final collaboration, making it easy to compare the two. Roche, 'Breton, Trotsky: une collaboration'.

56 Isaac Deutscher, *The Prophet Unarmed. Trotsky: 1923–1929* (London: Oxford University Press, 1963), p. 170.

57 Breton, quoted in Roche, 'Breton, Trotsky: une collaboration', p. 76. My translation.

58 Roche, 'Breton, Trotsky: Une collaboration', p. 85.

59 Adorno, however, was notoriously more pessimistic than Breton about the ability of art either to retain its autonomy or to provide an effective critique, i.e. one with real consequences. For an interesting analysis of this problem with regard to Adorno, see Thomas Crow, 'Modernism and Mass Culture in the Visual Arts', in Francis Frascina, ed., *Pollock and After: The Critical Debate* (New York: Harper and Row, 1985).

hegemony. Key here is Breton's argument that art (along with the other two categories he names) can provide a means of at least partially stepping outside our immersion in 'the economic conditions of life' so as to be capable of providing a critique of those conditions.[60] This, ultimately, is what Breton views art's political role to be.

Roche, oddly enough, does not view the suppression of this opening paragraph as a disagreement between Trotsky and Breton. But it is impossible to take it otherwise when viewed in the context of another significant argument inserted into the manifesto by Trotsky – he argues for centralized socialism in the realm of 'productive material forces', but for *anarchism* as a theory of cultural production:

> If, for the better development of the forces of material production, the revolution must build a socialist regime with centralized control, to develop intellectual creation an anarchist regime of individual liberty should from the first be established. No authority, no dictation, not the least trace of orders from above![61]

This addition to the manifesto's text makes it clear that Trotsky could not reconcile Marxism's commitment to collectivity with what he thought to be artistic production's individualist nature. Nor did he feel there was much room in Marxism for any notion of the relative autonomy of aesthetic configurations – those formal properties of a work of art or literature that produce its internal coherence.[62] When taken together, these two acts of textual revision suggest that Trotsky was wary of Breton's interest in foregrounding such a theory of culture in Marxism. Thus, whereas Breton (like Adorno and Gramsci) argues that social relations of power take an often distinctive form in culture, Trotsky dismisses the idea.

This difference of opinion caused – and causes – problems. The more amusing include Breton's anxiety over Trotsky's claim that after the proletarian revolution no one would paint any more.[63] The more serious appear embedded in the text of the manifesto itself, which advocates 'free' artistic expression but censors Socialist Realism along with 'pure art' and all 'reactionary' aesthetic motivations and forms. Then there is the added problem of what to do with someone like the muralist David Alfaro Siqueiros, a confirmed Stalinist

---

60 This also resonates strongly with Louis Althusser's famous notion of ideology, elucidated in his 'Ideology and Ideological State Apparatuses', in *Lenin and Philosophy*, trans. Ben Brewster (New York: Monthly Review Press, 1971).

61 Breton and Trotsky, 'For An Independent Revolutionary Art', in Breton, *What Is Surrealism?*, p. 185.

62 In this, Trotsky had not changed his 1924 opinion, expressed in *Literature and Revolution*. See note 47 above.

63 Mark Polizzotti, *Revolution of the Mind: The Life of André Breton* (New York: Farrar, Straus and Giroux, 1995), pp. 461–62.

(involved in the first assassination attempt on Trotsky) whose painting was far from being Socialist Realist. His mural in the Electricians' Union in Mexico City, *Portrait of the Bourgeoisie*, begun the year after Trotsky and Breton published their manifesto, is much more visually innovative than any of Rivera's murals in its use of perspective, narrative and new painting technologies.[64] Or what to do with the intractable Rivera himself, who could be either very politically astute or outrageously reactionary, depending on what day of the week one caught up with him.[65] Trotsky's essays on Rivera (the only Latin American artist he wrote about in any detail) concentrate purely on the content of the artist's murals, never on their form, and on the politics of the artist rather than the art.[66] This content, Trotsky argues, is revolutionary even when produced under the patronage of US capitalists such as Ford and Rockefeller (Rivera produced several murals in the United States, including the famous *Portrait of Industry* in Detroit, a 'portrait' of Ford's Rouge Plant).[67] Yet Trotsky never investigates the way in which form is essential, in relation to content, in distinguishing Rivera's work from the Socialist Realism that Trotsky detests.

Thus, while historian Alan Rose may have been correct in his conclusion – that, had Trotsky lived, he and Breton would have been forced to break – he arrives at it for all the wrong reasons. Rose claims that Trotsky's 'Marxist' view contrasted with Breton's view of humanity as basically 'anti-social'.[68] Instead of a Marxist view opposing a non-Marxist account as Rose argues, what we have are two different modes of conceptualizing Marxism itself. On the one hand, Trotsky

---

64 Siqueiros was one of the founders, along with Rivera and José Clemente Orozco, of the Mexican Mural Movement. On *Portrait of the Bourgeoisie* (1939), see Léonard Folgarait, *Mural Painting and Social Revolution in Mexico, 1920–1940* (Cambridge: Cambridge University Press, 1998).

65 On Rivera's political vagaries, see Anthony Lee, *Painting On the Left: Diego Rivera, Radical Politics and San Francisco's Public Murals* (Berkeley: University of California, 1998), and Raquel Tibol, prologue to Rivera, *Arte y Política* (Mexico D.F.: Editorial Grijalbo, 1979).

66 See Trotsky, 'La Ignorancia no es un Instrumento de la Revolución', *Clave*, no. 5 (1 February 1939), pp. 13–22, and 'El Arte y la Revolución', ibid., pp. 33–43.

67 Rivera's 1933 mural for the Rockefeller Center in New York was destroyed after he refused to remove the portrait of Lenin included in it.

68 Alan Rose, 'For an Independent Revolutionary Art', pp. 52–61. Rose is particularly pessimistic, arguing that Breton's work 'consistently presented man as a basically anti-social animal' in opposition to Trotsky's view of humanity in Marxist terms. Rose claims that Surrealism's artistic platform was too far from Trotsky's political platform to find a workable common ground, and that 'Trotsky would have been forced [had he not been assassinated] to oppose him [Breton]' (Rose, pp. 59–60). In this, Rose reiterates a long line of Marxist hostility towards Surrealism perhaps most interestingly exemplified by Sartre's scathing critiques. See Michel Beaujour, 'Sartre and Surrealism', *Yale French Studies*, no. 30 (1964). Rose's arguments, however, never come close to Sartre's sophistication, and say much more about his own inability to understand both Surrealism and Marxism than about the failures of those movements.

focused almost exclusively on the purportedly objective problem of economic exploitation, giving little thought to (among other things) exactly how culture or individual agency might actively be incorporated into Marxist theory. Breton and Surrealism, on the other hand, formed part of a Western Marxist tradition that saw true revolution as occurring on the level of culture as much as any other.

Nevertheless, Breton's efforts to harness Mexican culture for Surrealism's radical project proved difficult. Despite the inclusion of Rivera, Alvarez Bravo, Frida Kahlo and others in the 1940 International Surrealist Exhibition, held in Mexico City, and despite many other overtures to Mexican artists, on the whole they remained fundamentally sceptical of Surrealism's programme.[69] Rivera in particular, originally a key member of the Mexican sector of the FIARI, broke with Trotsky, Breton and the FIARI.[70] This collaborative failure between Mexicans and Surrealists occurred not because Surrealism did not conform to a Trotskyist programme, but more because Surrealism, despite its adamant anti-colonialist stance, slid too close to a Eurocentric attitude towards culture and social change with respect to Mexico. In this, it adhered to the general tendency in pre-World War II Western Marxism to view Europe, rather than elsewhere, as the seat of capitalist degeneration, and therefore as the site demarcated by Marx of potential revolution. The Surrealists therefore tended to treat Mexico as essentially unaffected by tensions of capitalism, as able to stand defiantly outside its tentacles and therefore closer to complete freedom.[71] While this view might lose some of its utopian character if it is understood in the context of Surrealism's rhetorical strategies of opposition to the deeply entrenched imperialism of both mainstream Western society and many elements of the Western Left, it is nevertheless the case that for most Mexicans – with the United States just to the north and the history of European domination an ever-present reality – it seemed a ludicrous argument.[72]

---

69 See Ida Rodríguez Prampolini, 'Antecedentes del surrealismo en México', in Ana Maria de Morales Beluzo, ed., *Modernidade: Vanguardes artisticas na América Latina* (São Paulo: Fundação Memorial de A.L., 1990), p. 151.

70 However, the break was due to political differences between Trotsky and Rivera, more than between the Mexican muralist and Breton. Rivera's differences with Trotsky are a complicated issue, and have yet to be well-investigated. See Trotsky's letters and essays on the subject in *Writings of Léon Trotsky,* and Raquel Tibol, prologue to Rivera, *Arte y Política*. By 1940, however, Rivera had overcome his differences with Breton enough to participate in the fourth International Surrealist Exhibition (importantly, the show was not organized by Breton himself, but by the Peruvian César Moro and by Wolfgang Paalen).

71 A particularly jarring example of this is Antonin Artaud's *Mexico and the Land of the Tarahumaras*, written after his visit in 1936. Olivier Debroise says of Artaud, 'he didn't visit Mexico; he visited a myth [created by Surrealism]'. Debroise, *Figuras en el trópico; plástica mexicana, 1920–1940* (Madrid: Océano, 1984), p. 158.

72 It is clear from Breton's later writing on Haiti, as well as from a long history of anti-colonialist interventions by other Surrealists, that Surrealism was very far from being naive as to the economic, ideological and political relations between Europe and its

This skewed sense of Mexico appears in 'Souvenir du Mexique', where Breton writes, for instance, of Emiliano Zapata having led the Indian peons and peasants to victory in the Mexican Revolution. While it is true that Zapata's agrarian army was the most revolutionary element of that historical moment, it is sadly not the case that they were the ultimate victors. After Zapata's assassination in 1917, his peasant army succumbed to the forces of a capitalist middle class that, despite the hopeful moment of Cardenismo, has ruled the country ever since. Thus, it is pure wishful thinking on Breton's part to view

---

(former) colonies. And it is also clear from the widespread Latin American and Caribbean interest in Surrealism that its vocal anti-colonialism was considered with great seriousness and enthusiasm. Nevertheless, it is important to separate the response of the Surrealists to Mexico from the Mexicans' response to Surrealism in the 1930s. For the Surrealists, Mexico in particular functioned as a fantasy 'other' to a Europe degenerating under the weight of capitalism and approaching war. In placing Mexico thus, the Surrealists were to a certain extent following a long tradition stemming back to the conquest of searching out sites of 'otherness' for regenerating European civilization in moments of crisis. In the specific case of Mexico, Surrealism's tendency on the one hand to emphasize the 'popular', the 'primitive' and the 'naive' in the work of artists such as Frida Kahlo, María Izquierdo, Alvarez Bravo and nineteenth-century printmaker José Guadalupe Posada, while on the other hand ignoring the sophisticated critique of modernism and avant-garde aesthetics offered by these same artists, led most of them to reject Surrealism out of hand. Unlike other Latin American countries such as Peru, Mexico never had an organized Surrealist movement, nor did its artists produce Surrealist manifestos. Although there was widespread interest in Surrealist aesthetics, much of this occurred in the 1940s and 1950s, after an influx of refugees after World War II. These refugees, including Paalen, Remedios Varo, Benjamin Péret, Leonora Carrington, themselves became more closely attuned to the particulars of Mexican culture in relation to its historical context, and therefore more able than prewar visitors like Breton to adjust their Surrealist views to it. And perhaps more than anything else, the stature of Mexican Muralism as an avant-garde, political and nationalist discourse in Mexico, Latin America and the world at large meant that Surrealism would find less fertile ground in Mexico than in other countries.

Diego Rivera, one of the few Mexican artists voluntarily to collaborate (he illustrated an issue of *Minotaure* and the 1938 printing of Breton's *Les Vases communicants*), was in a particularly awkward moment in his artistic career when he met Breton. His flamboyant politics, untimely criticism of Presidents Calles and Cárdenas, and open acceptance of commissions from US capitalists Ford and Rockefeller meant a dearth in public mural commissions in Mexico. Unable to count himself as an active part of the all-important cultural discourse on Mexican revolutionary nationalism during this period, he turned to Surrealism in the late 1930s as a means of regaining some of his lost stature. Significantly, by contrast, both Kahlo and Alvarez Bravo openly rejected the label 'Surrealist'. Izquierdo, like Rivera, for a short while also saw in Surrealism an opportunity for gaining a public reputation in international circles. Yet her work must be seen, not as responding to Antonin Artaud's characterization of it as the work of a 'primitive spirit' (the title of his essay on Izquierdo), but in terms of the sophisticated discourse on cultural nationalism of which she was part. See my essay, 'Painting Identities: Mexican Nationalism and Gender in the Work of María Izquierdo', *Oxford Art Journal* XXIII:1 (Spring 2000).

Mexico as defiantly free of capitalist influence in the late 1930s. And although his invocation for a French-speaking audience of Zapata as a revolutionary icon may have served to offer a poetic ray of revolutionary hope in an ever more desolate Europe, in Mexico it came far too close to the consistent mythification of Zapata that has shored up the ruling elite's ideology of 'revolutionary nationalism' at the expense of the peasantry and the indigenous from the 1920s until today.[73] Thus, despite the sense of agency concerning its own future that Breton imparts to Mexico, his utopian ideal is contradicted by the country's long and traumatic history of interaction with Europe, the US and capitalism, from the conquest and the Monroe Doctrine to NAFTA in our own time.

To return once again, therefore, to the photograph of Breton, Rivera and Trotsky with which I started is, finally, to think as much about what is left out of that picture as what is included. While we see an image of three of the most innovative thinkers of the twentieth century, engaged in jovial and excited conversation, what we do not see is the fragility of that moment.[74] Excluded from it are the theoretical discrepancies and fractures within Breton's and Trotsky's collaboration; absent too is any record of the external pressures that would drive all three men apart, all of which still resonate today.

73 The present revolt being led by the Zapatistas in Chiapas is arguably the only organized movement of any sort in Mexico's post-Revolution history that can claim to use the name of Zapata truly for the benefit of the indigenous and the peasantry.

74 I thank Anthony Lee for this descriptive term. On the fragility of the Fourth International, see Isaac Deutscher, *The Prophet Outcast. Trotsky: 1929–1940* (London: Oxford University Press, 1963), pp. 419–25.

Chapter 11

Aimé Césaire's Insurrectionary Poetics

E. San Juan, Jr.

> To win the energies of intoxication for the revolution – this is the project about which Surrealism circles in all its books and enterprises.
>
> Walter Benjamin

> Dialectical in essence, surrealism intends to sacrifice neither dreaming to action nor action to dreaming, but instead to foster their synthesis.
>
> René Crevel

> On the marvellous contact of the interior totality and exterior totality, perceived imaginatively and simultaneously by the poet, or more precisely within the poet, marvellous discoveries are made.
>
> Aimé Césaire

> Only through the objectively unfolded richness of man's essential being is the richness of subjective human sensibility (a musical ear, an eye for beauty of form – in short, senses capable of human gratifications, senses confirming themselves as essential powers of man) either cultivated or brought into being [...]. The forming of the five senses is a labor of the entire history of the world down to the present.
>
> Karl Marx

Aimé Césaire is easily the most important and well-known Caribbean intellectual who has utilized a singular interpretation of Surrealism in the interest of an anti-imperialist politics. The articles he wrote for *Tropiques* (circa 1941) criticized the colonial mentality bred by the 'obscurantism, sloth and jesuitism that is Martiniquan capitalism' ('Panorama') and, in the face of the fascist onslaught, affirmed civilization as 'that stamp of man's effigy on the universe' ('Presentation'). When he wrote his *Cahier d'un retour au pays natal* (hereafter *Notebook*), first published in 1939 and revised several times thereafter, Césaire's Eurocentric humanism had already been displaced by a historically oriented poetics of Negritude, not a systematic essentializing philosophy but an optic or sensibility to criticize imperialist ideology and actual practice.

Negritude acquired a more pronounced Marxist temper after World War II when Césaire joined the Communist Party and was elected deputy to the Constituent Assembly. His pamphlet *Discours sur colonialisme* (1950) remains one of the most eloquent 'third world' testimonies of a decolonizing vision and programme that anticipates Frantz Fanon, Amilcar Cabral and Che Guevara. Césaire subsequently resigned from the Party because of its failure to recognize the primacy of the colonial question, its denial of the integral and constitutive role of subaltern peoples of colour.

What is strange is that in spite of the discovery of Negritude in the 1930s, Césaire persisted in following a quasi-Hegelian approach to art whose idealism valorizes subjectivity at the expense of concrete determinations. This is evidenced by the propositions outlined in a 1945 essay, 'Poetry and Knowledge': the poet as a very complex and simple being who – within the lived confines of the dream and the real, day and night, between absence and presence – seeks and receives, in the sudden unleashing of internal cataclysms, the password of complicity and power'.[1] Instead of a consistent and rigorous espousal of a historical-materialist theory of socialist realism (exemplified by Georg Lukács or Antonio Gramsci), Césaire's aesthetics manifest a strong antinomian cast, a tendency to short-circuit the dialectical shifting of contraries, for example: 'Poetic knowledge is that in which man spatters the object with all of his mobilized riches'.[2] Against the charge of exoticism and mannerist obscurantism, Césaire responds by appealing to the demiurgic vocation of the poet: 'That's absurd. I am a West Indian. I want a poetry that is concrete, very West Indian, Martinican. I feel obliged to name the objects of Martinican reality, to call them by their name'.[3] Nationalitarian poetics is vindicated against the methodology of Surrealist 'derangement' and defamiliarization techniques.

One can say that Césaire has a fundamentally dialectical grasp of historical reality as a bundle of contradictions. The question is: does his Surrealist art succeed in critically apprehending the contradictory forces in experience in order to interpose a moment of revolutionary rupture when thought mutates into praxis, conscious action? Can a revolutionary politics be constructed on a mere juxtaposition of opposites – action/dream, reason/the unconscious, mind/history and so on – without any clear analysis of mediating processes? For classic Surrealism, the mediation is usually verbal, the shamanistic invocation of the 'marvellous'.[4] Can a revolutionary socialist strategy be founded on the gratuitous yoking of polarities that bypass the necessary mediations or transitional moments by thaumaturgic gestures of pure idealism, allowing the Peruvian poet Cesar Vallejo to condemn surrealist politics as anarchic, 'most abstract, mystical, cerebral', centred on the intellectuals' 'crisis of consciousness' instead

1 Aimé Césaire, in Michael Richardson, ed., *Refusal of the Shadow: Surrealism and the Caribbean* (New York: Verso, 1996), p. 146.

2 Ibid., p. 145.

3 Gregson Davis, 'Introduction', in *Non-Vicious Circle: Twenty Poems of Aimé Césaire* (Stanford: Stanford University Press, 1984), p. 10.

4 Cf. Alejo Carpentier's historicist idea of 'magic realism', *lo real maravilloso*.

of proletarian action?[5] I think a reading of some Surrealist texts by Césaire can discern a mode of political intervention (via a strategy of reappropriation and sublation) where dialectical mediations are contoured, where a socialist 'third world' aesthetic emerges from a Surrealist point of departure.

The antinomian predicament of Césaire's thinking derives in part from the origin of Surrealism as a blanket refusal of bourgeois society and a life dominated by instrumental or technological reason. Conflicts within bourgeois experience are displaced onto the level of contradictions between spheres of human activities (purposive conduct versus subliminal reflexes), between private and public domains. Rejecting normal life, the unconscious becomes the privileged site of freedom and self-fulfilment. Breton's 1924 *Manifesto* establishes the locus of psychoanalysis as the field of liberation. The key tenets of deploying 'pure psychic automatism' to exorcise the *diktat* of reason and of mobilizing the magic of art to evoke the dream-world are standard criteria in defining classic Surrealism. But if so, then Surrealism becomes a dogmatic if mystical logic ironically designed to liberate the unconscious from the stranglehold of reality. In an astute comment, Maynard Solomon locates the 'tragic flaw' of Surrealism in the theory of unconscious creativity. Quietism, not revolution, results from a political anarchism in art: 'The revolutionary-philosophical-Utopian-psychological superstructure erected above this theory [Breton's psychic automatism] (which denies both form and consciousness) can only serve to ward off the inevitable collapse of the entire synthesis'.[6]

Breton of course rectified the inadequacy according to the historical pressures of his milieu. In his *Second Surrealist Manifesto* (1930), historical materialism becomes the intellectual horizon for the revolutionary solution to human problems. In *Les Vases communicants* (1932), Breton conceives of poetry as the resolution to 'the irreparable divorce of action and dream' where 'Imagination is the queen of truth and the *possible* is one of the provinces of truth'. In his speech to the International Writers' Congress in 1935, Breton upheld the individual integrity of the work of art and the collective heritage of peoples against right and left political forces, using the revolutionary utopian slogan: ' "Transform the world," Marx said; "change life," Rimbaud said'. The rubric that encapsulates the cardinal Surrealist project is *hasard objetif*, objective chance (whose inspiration is Engels's famous aphorism that 'freedom is the recognition of necessity'), which Breton defined as 'the form of the manifestation of exterior necessity which finds its way to the unconscious', 'centre of conciliation and for natural necessity and human necessity – point of revelation, pivot of liberty'.[7]

---

5 Cesar Vallejo, *Autopsy on Surrealism*, trans. Richard Schaaf (Willimantic: Curbstone Press, 1982).

6 Maynard Solomon, *Marxism and Art* (New York: Knopf, 1973), p. 507.

7 André Breton, *What is Surrealism? Selected Writings*, ed. Franklin Rosemont (New York: Monad Press, 1978), pp. 245 and 203.

First explored in Breton's novel *Nadja* and later in *The Communicating Vessels* and *Mad Love*, 'objective chance' posits the persistence of a revolutionary situation in quotidian life where possibilities multiply, where (to quote the American Surrealist Franklin Rosemont) 'strategic intersections of internal necessity' beckon to us, signals of otherness or 'premonitory glimmers of *that which will be*, perceived darkly and hazardously through the cracks and fissures in the repressive structure of everyday life'.[8] 'Objective chance' subsumes the poetics of 'marronage' invented by Césaire as well as the metamorphic plotting of images in the *Notebook* where the poet fabricates a 'social phantasy', 'the physiological component of the social ego' in which human desires are socialized and invested with determinate significance.[9]

'Objective chance', however, suggests for many a forced amalgamation of dream and reality. It hypothesizes a premature marriage of Marx and Rimbaud which presumably spelled the end of the effective alliance of Surrealism and the Communists in Europe.[10] In attempting to fuse action and dream, reason and intuition, Breton tried to fashion a dialectical poetics committed to transforming both life and the world simultaneously:

> Borne by the current of his time, he will assume for the first time without distress the responsibility for the reception and transmission of signals which press upon him from the depth of souls. He will maintain at any price in each other's presence the two terms of the human relation, by whose destruction the most precious conquests would instantaneously become null and void: the objective awareness of realities, and their internal development in what, by virtue of a sentiment individual on one hand, universal on the other, is magical about it until proved otherwise. This relation can pass for magical in that it consists of an unconscious, immediate action of the internal on the external, so that there readily slips into the summary analysis of such a notion the idea of a transcendent mediation which would be, moreover, that of a demon more than of a god.[11]

Breton's pursuit of revolution via the magical transcendent mediation is symptomatic of a more profound predicament. Indeed he endeavoured to achieve 'the interpenetration of reason and unreason, a dialectical counterplay, a logical progression whose end is a transformed world, a land of fantasy [...] which is no longer fantastic: there is only the real'.[12] Part of the problem inheres

8 Franklin Rosemont, *André Breton and the First Principles of Surrealism* (London: Pluto Press, 1978), p. 62.

9 Christopher Caudwell, *Illusion and Reality* (New York: International Publishers, 1937), p. 321.

10 Robert Short, 'The Politics of Surrealism, 1920–36', *Journal of Contemporary History* I:2 (1966), pp. 3–25.

11 André Breton, *Les Vases Communicants*, in Maurice Nadeau, *The History of Surrealism*, trans. Richard Howard (New York: Macmillan, 1965), p. 304.

12 Herbert Read, *Art and Society* (New York: Schocken Books, 1966), pp. 123–24.

in conceiving of the dualism of internal and external realms of human action. Why not translate the outside and inside as manifestations of a larger historical process? What has become for Surrealism its irresistible aporia, the irreconcilable conflict between the oneiric, utopian-oriented imagination and the intractable limits of determinate historical reality, may be transcoded on another level so as to make it accessible to the impact of cultural praxis. One way of reconceptualizing the contradiction has been achieved by Césaire's method of critical dialectical transformation, a mode of reshaping one's view of the world that one can label 'marronage poetics'.

In a revealing interview with the Haitian poet René Depestre in 1967, Césaire traced the influence of the Surrealist movement on his own intellectual trajectory. Surrealism freed Césaire from servility to the French literary tradition: 'It was a weapon that exploded the French language. It shook up absolutely everything. This was very important because the traditional forms – burdensome, overused forms – were crushing me'.[13] Césaire wanted 'to create a new language, one capable of communicating the African heritage'. But it was not a total break since his object was 'to create an Antillean French, a black French that, while still being French, had a black character'. So he 'became a poet by renouncing poetry'[14] – a paradoxical mediation in which negativity is anatomized, divided and sublated. It was an escape from colonial subjugation, from alienation, via the weapons provided by the enemy. Given the thorough colonial assimilation of the Martinican middle stratum from which Césaire came, Surrealism produced not only disalienation but also 'a process of detoxification' in which 'deep and unconscious forces' were evoked. Césaire described the process of emancipating consciousness as 'A plunge into the depths [...] into Africa for me. [...] I felt that beneath the social being would be found a profound being, over whom all sorts of ancestral lawyers and alluviums had been deposited'.[15] Surrealism as a corrosive world-view destroyed the mystique of the colonial-racial superiority of Europe and released Césaire from the fetishism of French culture.

But that demystification was not enough. Conjoined with the geological metaphor is the grasp of historical specificities of the collective with which he then identified himself, in particular African singularity. That translated Césaire's existential situation into concrete consciousness: his identity as a black man. 'Negritude' is the philosophical mediation of negative Europe and positive Africa, a way out of the Manichean dilemma acutely diagnosed by Fanon in *The Wretched of the Earth*. The agenda of Negritude captures that process of 'conscientization', to use Paulo Freire's term. It was an affirmation of

---

13 Aimé Césaire, *Discourse on Colonialism*, trans. Joan Pinkham (New York: Monthly Review Press, 1972), p. 67.

14 Ibid., p. 66.

15 Ibid., p. 68.

pride in the African cultural heritage, and also in the revolutionary tradition of Negroes, for example, the revolutionary history of Haiti as 'Negritude in action'. Fully cognizant of the massive history of European racism epitomized in the treatment of Africa as the barbarian world and Europe as the civilized one, Césaire therefore could not accept a positivistic notion of Marxism, the dogmatic Soviet version hegemonic over the European left: 'I maintained that the political question could not do away with our condition as Negroes. We are Negroes, with a great number of historical peculiarities [...]. Marx is all right, but we need to complete Marx. I felt that the emancipation of the Negro consisted of more than just a political emancipation'.[16]

Césaire's identity evolved from a particularizing of Communism in the moment of Negritude. His conceptualization of Negritude sublated the inside and outside into a world-historical movement. But Negritude encompassed the solidarity of all black people in various parts of the world, not only in Africa; hence Césaire's belief that the Harlem renaissance, the insurrectionary past of Haiti, the revolutions in Algeria and Brazil and elsewhere, are all registered in his sensibility as part of a global 'Negro situation'. He also passionately affirmed that the Negro heritage has 'universalizing, living values' that could contribute to Europe in the same spirit as European artists (Picasso, Vlaminck, Braque) found inspiration in African art. Given this totalizing attitude, Césaire (with Senghor) 'refused to see the black question as simply a social question' or an economic problem. Césaire agreed with Depestre in the revolutionizing praxis that Marx first formulated in *Thesis on Feuerbach*: decolonization engages both consciousness and social reality at the same time. Alienation acquires more than a philosophical tenor in Césaire's concluding reflection: '[...] and I remember very well having said to the Martinican Communists, in those days, that black people, as you have pointed out, were doubly proletarianized and alienated: in the first place as workers, but also as blacks, because after all we are dealing with the only race which is denied even the notion of humanity'.[17]

Césaire's historically differentiated dialectic impelled him finally to reject a dogmatic Marxism embodied in the theory and practice of the French Communist Party. In 1956, he published his open *Letter to Maurice Thorez* in which he performed an act of self-determination, as it were, vis-à-vis the centralist norms of the party. But, as A. James Arnold correctly points out, it was the consciousness of his colonial status, his position as colonial subject, that motivated a dialectical surpassing of a brand of Eurocentric Marxism that ignored the historical reality of cultural and spiritual imperialism in the lived experience of millions of people of colour. Césaire inscribed in this public re-

16 Ibid., pp. 69–70.
17 Ibid., pp. 78–79.

enactment of his *Notebook* the first principles of his 'maronnage poetics' founded on a vision of singularity, a species of the 'concrete universal':[18]

> A fact of capital importance in my view is this: we people of color, in this precise moment of our historical evolution, have in our conscience taken possession of the entire area of our singularity. ...
> Singularity of our 'situation in the world', which can be mistaken for no other. Singularity of our problems, which can be subsumed under no other problem. Singularity of our history, interrupted by terrible transformations that belong to it alone. Singularity of our culture, which we intend to quicken in ever more real ways.[19]

This assertion of singularity, a fusion of the historically specific and the theoretically universal, becomes a controlling principle in Césaire's performance of a Surrealist art in dialogue with colonial reality. An exemplary illustration is Césaire's 'The Verb "Marroner"/for René Depestre, Haitian Poet'.[20] Reacting to the Communist Party spokesman and ex-Surrealist Louis Aragon's programmatic call for a return to conventional if more accessible literary forms, Césaire balks and instead invokes Boukman, the Haitian revolutionary, whose 'insane song' delivered Haiti 'with the forceps of the storm'. The poet addresses Depestre, his Haitian comrade, and urges him to become fugitives instead of slaves condemned to routine and mechanical labour:

> shall we escape like slaves Depestre like slaves?
> Depestre I indict the bad manners of our blood
> [...]
> Blood is truly a powerful vodun
>
> Is it true this season that they're polishing up sonnet
> for us to do so would remind me too much of the sugary
> juice drooled over there by the distilleries on the mornes
> when slow skinny oxen make their rounds to the whine
> of mosquitoes
>
> Bah! Depestre the poem is not a mill for
> grinding sugar cane absolutely not
> and if the rhymes are flies on ponds
>   without rhymes
>   for a whole season
> away from ponds

---

18 For a Marxist translation of the Hegelian concept of 'concrete universal' see Stefan Morawski, 'Introduction', in *Marx and Engels on Literature and Art*, eds, Lee Baxandall and Stefan Morawski (St Louis: Telos Press, 1973).

19 Césaire cited in A. James Arnold, *Modernism and Negritude: The Poetry and Poetics of Aimé Césaire* (Cambridge: Harvard University Press, 1981), pp. 171–72.

20 Aimé Césaire, *The Collected Poetry*, trans. Clayton Eshleman and Annette Smith (Berkeley, Los Angeles and London: University of California Press, 1983), pp. 368–70.

under my persuasion
let's laugh drink and escape like slaves
(Césaire, 1983, p. 369)[21]

Césaire summons images of Dessalines, the Haitian hero in combat, enacting a ritual of communication with the spirits. This encounter leads to a declaration of his aesthetics as one rooted in the dynamic vitality of natural life and its cycles, as well as in the solidarity of artists who resonate with their communities and the traditions that bind the past with the present and future. The poet envisages an organic and mutable poetics where form and content coalesce in the will to reconcile differences of geography and needs, preserving but also negating tradition in a selective and innovative search for new usable tools and skills. Césaire's drive to escape from what constricts deploys an astute maronnage strategy aimed at constructing a new time and space in the act of expressing the collective will toward liberation:

Comrade Depestre
It is undoubtedly a very serious problem
the relation between poetry and Revolution
the content determines the form

and what about keeping in mind as well the dialectical
backlash by which the form taking its revenge
chokes the poems like an accursed fig tree
but no
a report on this is none of my business
I'd rather look at the spring. Precisely,
it is the revolution
and the forms which linger
humming in our ears
[...]
bombaia bombaia
believe me as in the old days beat the good tom-tom for us
splashing their rancid night
with a succinct rutting of moudang stars.
(Césaire, 1983, p. 371)

Aside from the allusive use of Spanish, Portuguese and African terms in the last few lines, Césaire attempts here to recover the chronotope of the Haitian revolution against European imperialism in the use of 'bombaia', which refers to a Haitian rallying cry connected with Boukman's voodoo ceremonies at Bois Cayman on the eve of the 1791 revolts against the French. Boukman was a black slave who led the ferocious revolts in the various towns of Haiti at the start of the revolution.[22]

---

21 Ibid., p. 369.

22 On the Haiti slave revolt see the classic text of C.L.R. James, *The Black Jacobins: Toussaint L'Ouverture and the San Domingo Revolution*, 2nd edn (New York: Vintage, 1963).

The repetition of the status quo is interrupted, Hegel's dialectic of master and slave abrogated by the slave's refusal. The coining of the neologism '*maronner*' indexes Césaire's trope of 'blasting the continuum of history' to establish a new temporality, the 'Now-time' (to use Walter Benjamin's term) of epiphany and apocalypse. A *marron* (maroon) denoted a slave who has successfully escaped the plantation in order to live freely in the wilderness. A fugitive from legal and physical servitude, the *marron* symbolizes the artist's freedom from the bondage of European prosody and rhetoric. Césaire would like his art to pursue the path of the *marron* in disrupting the conservative mould of European discourse. According to Arnold, Césaire aligned himself with a basic Surrealist commitment: 'The poetry of Rimbaud is not his stylistics; it is his revolt [...]. The analogy with Surrealist practice is clear; Césaire's poetics [...] drew from Surrealism the means of expression required by the concrete realities of Martinican life'.[23] But the disruption is not just rhetorical nor polemical; it is also political and ethical in that it appeals to Depestre, and by extension all black revolutionary artists, to renew the forms in keeping with changes in the raw materials and substance of a constantly metamorphosing reality. Objective chance must reckon with subjective contingencies (the 'state of utter distraction' and arbitrariness that Breton [1962] values), with the decision to change what exists.

From a postmodernist optic, Césaire's poetics consorts with its Caribbean landscape of heteroglot and hybrid practices. The anthropologist James Clifford lauds the 'tropological landscape' of the *Notebook* where he finds syntactic, semantic and ideological transformations occurring incessantly. Clifford focuses on Césaire's neologistic and inventive stance as the matrix of 'radical indeterminacy'. We have already encountered Césaire's explanation of Negritude as a concrete, not an abstract, process of gaining consciousness. Clifford focuses on the historical and linguistic creation involved in Césaire's thinking, on the necessarily contingent and anti-essentialist operation of his knowledge of reality. Because of Césaire's rhetoric of ellipsis, antiphrasis and irony, the poet of *Notebook* (Clifford cites a Caribbean critic) 'holds himself at a distance from what he is and from what he says, in order to produce *the literary effect of derision*'.[24] Consequently, Césaire's Negritude is now interpreted to stand for a Caribbean form of modernity, a modernity concerned not with a naive concept of roots or blackness but with 'present process in a polyphonous reality'.[25]

Applied to '*marroner*' (to maroon, to abandon), the postmodernist ethnographer perceives in it images of shipwreck and desertion. '*Maroons*' designated fugitive slaves who resisted by escape, forming liberated enclaves within hostile

23 Arnold, *Modernism and Negritude*, pp. 184–85.

24 James Clifford, *The Predicament of Culture* (Cambridge: Harvard University Press, 1988), p. 178.

25 Ibid., p. 179.

territory. Although 'maronnage' has been adopted by scholars of maroon societies in the Guianas, Brazil and the Caribbean, Clifford argues that Césaire's neologism 'marroner' still has no translation. Affinities to the Spanish 'cimarron' (wild, runaway, from *cima* or mountain top, or from *cimarra* or thicket) cannot exhaust the connotations of Césaire's demiurgic verbal creation. Maroon societies grew out of a mixture of cultural elements, resilient and flexible combinations that transcend survivals of collective memory or tribal traditions. These slave cultures testify to a creolization process that amalgamated local experiences with a vast array of artifacts and practices from diverse sources.[26]

The poem to Depestre can be compared to the formation of such maroon habitats, chronotopes anticipated in the second part of *Notebook*. Originally titled 'Réponse à Depestre, poète haitien: Eléments d'un art poétique', Césaire opposed the French Communist Party's call to suppress 'formal individualism' in writing and return to traditional, simpler forms and messages. Césaire affirmed his will to experiment and break free from convention: 'Marronnons-les Depestre marronnons-les / comme jadis nous morronnions nos maîtres à fouet' [let's escape them Depestre let's escape them / as in the past we escaped our whip-wielding masters']. Clifford insightfully glosses the linguistic mutations that register the precise historical phenomena in which fugitive slaves in the Guianas, representing distinct African traditions, blended and altered each others' customs, languages and memories. He concludes that '*marronage* is no longer about simply escaping [them; the slave-owners]. It is also about reflexive possibility and poesis. Césaire makes rebellion and the remaking of culture – the historical maroon experience – into a *verb* [that] names the New World poetics of continuous transgression and cooperative cultural activity'.[27]

The postmodernist bias for pastiche, irony, parodic mimeticism, and ludic ambivalence illustrated in the preceding quotation animates Clifford's reading of Césaire's style, stressing its nuanced referencing of myriad elements. Maronnage indeed encapsulates the dialectical mediation, the social ordering of desires, that poetry generates.[28] But it distorts the political thrust of Césaire's opposition to a narrow, mechanical programme of social change. It blurs the essentially counter-hegemonic impulse of unifying the various strands in Afro-Caribbean and colonized people's histories in order to affirm their creativity and dignity. After all, Césaire jettisons the monadic Cartesian ego, the possessive/acquisitive 'I' for Negritude's 'we', the solidarity of the dispossessed and disinherited. While the emphasis on process, on the theme of 'freedom in

26 Eugene D. Genovese, *From Rebellion to Revolution* (New York: Vintage Books, 1979).

27 Clifford, *The Predicament of Culture*, p. 181.

28 Ernst Bloch, 'Marxism and Poetry', in *Literary Essays*, eds, Werner Hamacher and David Wellberg (Stanford: Stanford University Press, 1998), pp. 113–19.

passage' and cultural border-crossings, is important, it should not obscure the over-arching project of fashioning the occasion for exercising popular agency, the self-determining act of the poet (representing the colonized subalterns of colour) to destroy the bureaucratic/systemic impositions of imperial capitalism and its alienating ideological-cultural legacies. Otherwise, Césaire would remain an exhibitionist cosmopolitan, assimilating a multitude of voices but not forging any signature or singular voice of his own. In fact, he would be disavowing the quest for singularity that he announced in his unprecedented declaration of independence from the chauvinist/racist bureaucratic monolith. Against the complete assimilation of Césaire into a Eurocentric Surrealist leviathan, I would align myself with critics like Janis L. Pallister who valorizes the artist's quest for 'dominion over the word' as the sublime ideal of Césaire's poetic vocation.[29]

Before I examine Césaire's inflection of marronage poetics in the *Notebook*, let us reprise the original enunciation of the dilemma, the counterposing of dream (the unconscious) and what in Freudian terms has created it: a repressive bourgeois order. What frames this *problematique* is the goal of synchronizing two agendas, or two aspects of the same agenda: Breton's twin challenge of transforming the world and simultaneously changing life. For the way of conceptualizing the gap between the opposites often reflects not just the real process of reality but also its effect on the thinking subject.[30] This effect is an enigma in thought, an aporia. In Robert Short's formulation, the contradictions bedevilling Surrealism – between the spirit of revolt and revolutionary action, between an independent revolutionary art and the party's call for propaganda and didacticism, between ethical purity embodied in spiritual change and the practical necessities of political effectiveness – arise from the intransigent stance of Surrealist politics. Breton's 'will to total subversion' presupposes liberty as an absolute, an axiom of romanticism.[31] This obsession with purity and risk-laden *disponibilité*, observes Daniel Cottom, enabled the Surrealist inquiry into 'history as movement, collectivity, polemic, passion, and irrational form'.[32] But at the same time, the project of a 'systematic denunciation of bourgeois thought' announced in *La Révolution surréaliste* necessarily grounds such politics to concrete, earthbound practice. No compromise 'between the poetic image and the Absolute', between desires that were material for Marxists and desires that were subjective and spiritual for Surrealists.[33] No wonder the final break in 1935

29 Janis L. Pallister, *Aimé Césaire* (New York: Twayne Publishers, 1991), p. 114.

30 Fredric Jameson, 'Reflections in Conclusion', in *Aesthetics and Politics* (London: New Left Books, 1977).

31 Herbert Read, *The Philosophy of Modern Art* (Greenwich: Fawcett Publications, 1952).

32 Daniel Cottom, *Abyss of Reason* (New York: Oxford University Press, 1991), p. 245.

33 Short, 'The Politics of Surrealism', pp. 13 and 21.

with Stalinist Communism, the parting of ways with Aragon, Eluard and other comrades. The antithesis between dream and action, between the corrupt world and a visionary realm where needs and desires are fulfilled, can only sanction a pessimism in which failure at politics redeemed the revolutionary creator of new forms – a species of 'objective chance', as it were.

Surrealist chance, however, is premeditated if not demarcated by the social totality in motion. The reconciliation of opposites performed by revolutionary praxis (via *marronage* or Surrealist prefiguration of the marvellous) certainly depends on the nature of the historical conjuncture. The mediation of disparate experiences and values instanced by 'Response to Depestre' can only be carried out if the sense of historicity is preserved in some form of realist narrative. Given the reification sustained by the hegemonic order, psychic automatism needs to be replaced with a strategy of demystification: the decolonizing phase of satire implicit in a hermeneutics of suspicion. In addition, a method of synthesizing the reified fragments of a totality must be deployed so as to extrapolate a new or future space of enjoyment and release. Césaire's attempt to transform appearance into symbolic action, the phantasy of a 'social image'[34] where affects are mobilized to suture praxis and knowledge, is evidenced in the narrative design of *Cahier d'un retour au pays natal*.

Breton's appraisal of this poem in his 1943 essay may be interposed here. Celebrating the *Cahier* as 'the greatest lyrical monument of our times', Breton valued the conception of life that Césaire upheld. Stressing the 'singing' quality of the poem's 'abundant, all-permeating movement', its acts of refusal and revolt, its 'power of transmutation', Breton points to the dangers lurking behind nostalgia, the ideological aura shrouding the reality of colonial oppression: 'Behind this resplendence is the poverty of a colonial people, its shameless exploitation by a handful of parasites who defy even the laws which they themselves have erected and hardly feel any uneasiness about dishonouring'. The look backward opens the wound: 'It is reopened by all the grandeur of lost Africa, by the inherited memory of the abominable treatment suffered, by the consciousness of a monstrous and forever irreparable denial of justice of which an entire community was the victim'.[35] But this haemorrhage causes a transcendence of the event into a symbolic token or vehicle of some more universal significance which, for Breton, invests Césaire's poem with revolutionary import: its humanist message, 'the determined will to deliver the fatal blow to so-called 'common sense' which has impudently arrogated to itself the title of 'reason'; the imperative need to have done with this fatal dissociation of the human mind'.[36] Although cognizant of determinate forces in social life, Breton evinces again the typical Surrealist flaw of short-circuiting the dialectic by

34 Caudwell, *Illusion and Reality*.
35 Breton, *What is Surrealism?*, p. 234.
36 Ibid., p. 235.

writing out of the scene the contradictory manifold of 'common sense', which for a shrewd Marxist revolutionary like Gramsci offers precisely the room for political-ideological struggle.[37]

* * *

Materialist dialectics comprehends both the unity and the struggle of opposites, whereas the Surrealists tend to privilege the conflict and tension, given the exigencies of their historical milieu. The drive for reconciliation noted by Löwy[38] and other scholars obviously motivates Breton's, as well as Césaire's, concern with dissociation, the cleavage in the psyche induced by the social division of labour, in particular the split between manual and mental labour. This concern has also been noted by the philosopher Herbert Marcuse when he glosses Breton's notion of *hasard objetif*, objective chance. Marcuse appreciates the Surrealist project of transforming the world through the imagination which becomes productive of a new world that unifies reason and sensibility, that incorporates 'the human faculties and desires to such an extent that they appear as part of the objective determinism of nature – coincidence of causality through nature and causality through freedom'.[39] I think it is this dialectic of 'objective chance', an articulation of two kinds of causalities already anticipated in the neologistic poetics of 'maronnage', that informs the architectonics of Césaire's *Notebook*.

Many commentaries, among them Arnold's, have diagnosed the epic design of the *Notebook*, its deployment of the conventional artistic devices of satire, parody, apostrophe and so on. What has also been emphasized in the conventional literary analysis is the parabolic movement of the poem from the thesis describing colonial violence to a polemical antithesis leading to a synthesis of affirming Negritude as a site of reconciliation. Marronage is conveyed through the transition from metonymic realism (the description of Martinique, the urban landscape, etc.) to metaphoric devices and performatives conveying prophecy and expectations. The humanistic chord of the following passage has been praised by postcolonial critic Edward Said:[40]

---

37 Antonio Gramsci, *Selections from the Prison Notebooks* (New York: International Publishers, 1971).

38 Michael Löwy, 'Walter Benjamin and Surrealism', *Radical Philosophy*, no. 80 (November–December 1996), pp. 17–23.

39 Franklin Rosemont, 'Herbert Marcuse and the Surrealist Revolution', in *Arsenal: Surrealist Subversions*, eds, F. Rosemont et al. (Chicago: Black Swan Press, 1989), p. 32.

40 Edward Said, *Culture and Imperialism* (New York: Knopf, 1994), p. 280.

And we are standing now, my country and I, hair in the wind, my hand
puny in its enormous fist
and now the strength is not in us but above us, in a voice that drills the
night and the hearing like the
penetrance of an apocalyptic wasp. And the voice proclaims that for
centuries Europe has force-fed
us with lies and bloated us with pestilence,

for it is not true that the work of man is done
that we have no business being on earth
that we parasite the world
that it is enough for us to heel to the world
whereas the work has only begun

and man still must overcome all the interdictions wedged in the recesses
of his fervor and no race has
a monopoly on beauty, on intelligence, on strength

and there is room for everyone at the convocation of conquest and we
know now that the sun turns
around our earth lighting the parcel designated by our will alone and that
every star falls from sky to
earth at our omnipotent command.

(Césaire, 1983, p. 77)

Instead of recapitulating the findings of numerous structuralist analyses of the poem, I want to confine myself here to a gloss on the constellation of images linking certain nodal themes and motifs that articulate together objective chance, marronage and historical necessity.

The invocation of the 'apocalyptic wasp' culminating in the declaration of power over cosmic phenomena signals what Benjamin has called the revolutionary vocation of Surrealism: to organize pessimism, the milieu of resignation to the status quo, by expelling 'moral metaphor from politics [in order] to discover in political action a sphere reserved one hundred per cent for images'.[41] What Césaire has done is to dissolve the moralizing rhetoric of the early strophes where the unprodigal son returns 'the lonely ugliness' of his country's wounds – confronting the moment of becoming and passing in the look backward (which, for Brecht, constitutes the socialist-realist imperative[42]), the fugitive bridging past and future. In the same breath Césaire displaces the homage to Negritude in Haiti to an allegorizing of 'bodily innervations of the collective' to a revolutionary discharge, the 'profane illumination' of objective chance:

41 Benjamin, 'Surrealism', p. 191.

42 Bertolt Brecht, 'On Socialist Realism', in *Marxism and Art*, eds, Berel Lang and Forest Williams (New York: David McKay, 1969), pp. 226–27.

> I say right on! The old negritude
> progressively cadavers itself
> the horizon breaks, recoils and expands
> and through the shredding of clouds the flashing of a sign
> the slave-ship cracks everywhere [...] Its belly convulses and resounds
> [...] The ghastly tapeworm
> The cargo of this bastard suckling of the sea is
> of its cargo gnaws the fetid guts of the suckling sea!
>
> And neither the joy of sails filled like a pocket stuffed with doubloons, nor the tricks played on the dangerous stupidity of the frigates of order prevent it from hearing the threat of its intestinal rumblings
>
> in vain to ignore them the captain hangs the biggest loudmouth nigger from the main yard or throws him into the sea. Or feeds him to his mastiffs
>
> Reeking of fried onions the nigger scum rediscovers the bitter taste of freedom in its spilled blood
>
> And the nigger scum is on its feet
>
> (Césaire, 1983, pp. 79–81)

The fugitive slave is returning to the 'plantation' with a purpose: to disturb the peace of 'common sense' and rekindle creative forces pregnant within the body politic. Before this homecoming native addresses the elements, in particular the wind that earlier he called 'Reason', and seeks to drown himself in 'another moon' where he 'would fish for the night's evil tongue in its seized swirl', Césaire opens up what Benjamin calls 'the long-sought image sphere [...] in which political materialism and physical nature share the inner man, the psyche, the individual [...] with dialectical justice, so that no limb remains unrent'.[43] This field of images underscores a metamorphosis, or more precisely a transubstantiation, of 'the old negritude' which is a product of Orientalist essentialism. The trope of the slave ship, a surrogate for the carceral city described earlier, captures the historic 'middle passage' of the slave trade and its cruelties, but avoids moralizing by refiguring the sacrifices as birth-pangs of a new reality, a new life. The succeeding images evoke the scene of slaves in action, their dynamism seeming to propel 'the cleansed ship' which 'advances fearless upon the caving waters'. The allusion to a maternal vessel which breaks open to release the energies within reinscribes the journey of the native's return in a counter-memory of the early settling of Martinique, and the Caribbean, as an impregnation. What was planted in the beginning is now bearing fruit – a prophetic discovery of the collective body, which is the matrix of mystery in the everyday world.

---

43 Benjamin, 'Surrealism', p. 192.

Césaire's dialectic delineates mediations between opposites in a way analogous to the fugitive slave's act of tracing a path between closed and open spaces. The associative tropology of the *Notebook* incarnates the Surrealist optic in which everyday life becomes mysterious, and the mysterious becomes a quotidian affair. In the *Notebook*, the recognition of the 'marvellous' coincides with the perception of what seems inevitable in the unfolding of the past. The poet undergoing a spiritual metamorphosis finds himself exposed to the penetration of influences from the outside world. If poetry, according to Michel Beaujour, incarnates 'man's permanent aspiration as a speaking being to a beyond which only language, whose code is shaken by the poet, can offer him', then Césaire embodies this aspiration here.[44] Responding to the pressures of circumstances, the speaking subject intuits the mutations of a cacophony of sounds. Negativity modulates into intimations of alterity and metamorphosis:

> I hear coming up from the hold the enchained curses, the gasps of the dying, the noise of someone thrown into the sea [...] the baying of a woman in labor [...] the scrape of fingernails seeking throats [...] the flouts of the whip [...] the seething of vermin amid the weariness [...]
> (Césaire, 1983, pp. 61–63)

This approximates Breton's speculations on objective chance as the exploration of this 'almost forbidden word of sudden parallels, petrifying coincidences, and reflexes peculiar to each individual, of harmonies struck as though on a piano, flashes of light that would make you see, really *see*, if only they were not so much quicker than all the rest'.[45] What is being rendered in sensuous form is not circumstances or secular events, but the ideology from which the images spring, a network of practices and ideas subtending the position of the speaking subject.[46] Césaire pursues the risks the fugitive takes by mixing pain and pleasure in the hope of sparking a 'profane illumination' conducive to directed, conscienticized action (to use Paolo Freire's term).

Objective chance is often construed by Breton as 'the manifestation, more or less spontaneous, of necessity'.[47] In Césaire's signifying practice, this constellation of opposites is bound to precipitate a way to resolve the contradictions. The idea is dramatized in the immersion of the body, intellect and sensibility, in the flux of nature; knowledge and experience blend in the objective tendency of the poet's positioning of his presence (his embrace of the national or collective body

44 Michel Beaujour, 'Flight Out of Time: Poetic Language and the Revolution', *Yale French Studies*, no. 39 (1967), pp. 29–49.

45 Rosemont, 'Surrealism', p. 61.

46 Louis Althusser, 'Letter on Art in reply to Andre Daspere', *Lenin and Philosophy and Other Essays* (London: New Left Books, 1971), pp. 203–8.

47 Leon Trotsky, *On Literature and Art*, ed. Paul Siegel (New York: Pathfinder Press, 1970), p. 117.

evokes a mother-child liaison) in the historical vortex seized here in a tone of acceptance, not resignation:

> I accept, I accept it all
>
> and far from the palatial sea that foams beneath the suppurating syzygy of blisters, miraculously lying in the despair of my arms the body of my country, its bones shocked and, in its veins, the blood hesitating like a drop of vegetal milk at the injured point of the bulb [...]
>
> Suddenly now strength and life assail me like a bull and the water of life overwhelms the papilla of the morne, now all the veins and veinlets are bursting with new blood and the enormous breathing lung of cyclones and the fire hoarded in volcanoes and the gigantic seismic pulse which now beats the measure of a living body in my firm conflagration.
>
> (Césaire, 1983, p. 77)

This metamorphosis of the poet's consciousness dramatizes a combination of the secular and the natural worlds in a narrative invested with 'polysemic discursiveness',[48] the collective body materializing in an explosive discharge – a conjuring of the *physis* that Benjamin conceives of as 'produced in that image sphere to which profane illumination initiates us'.[49] Césaire has gone beyond soliloquy to a dialogic communication with his comrades in solidarity.

The *Notebook* thus epitomizes the revolutionary aspect of Surrealist art as 'profane illumination', a disclosure of the energies generating change in the body politic, in the social relations of production and reproduction. Césaire's text indeed calls into question 'symbolic and social finitudes' with a signifying practice, implicit not just in the *Notebook* but also in his earlier collection *Miraculous Weapons* as well as his later volumes of poems and plays,[50] that explodes the speaking subject in the site of contradictions, as I have shown. This site of what Julia Kristeva calls 'heterogeneous materiality' entails a textual performance that 'points toward the possibility – which is *jouissance* – of a subject who speaks his being put in process/on trial through action'.[51] This is enabled by Césaire paying careful attention not to elide the connections, linkages or stages of mediation that comprise the totality of the dialectic – in short, to plot the text around the axis of marronage, of fugitives in revolt.

From this perspective of stressing the historicity of contradictions, one conclusion can be proposed here. The fundamental reason why Césaire's Surrealism is more genuinely dialectical and therefore invested with more usable

48 Galvano Della Volpe, *Critique of Taste* (London: New Left Books, 1978), p. 138.

49 Benjamin, 'Surrealism', p. 192.

50 For instance, Caliban's challenge to Prospero in Césaire's version of Shakespeare's *The Tempest*, trans. Richard Miller (New York: Ubu Repertory Theater Publications, 1992).

51 Julia Kristeva, *Revolution in Poetic Language* (New York: Columbia University Press, 1984), p. 210.

revolutionary potential lies in its profound awareness of the reified totality of imperialism as a world-system. Césaire comprehends the notion of bourgeois hegemony together with its 'weak links', the colonized subjects. This grasp of the historical moment, the locus of typicality or singularity where the Marxist concept of *Verhältnis* is distilled,[52] transcends the mythopoeic transcendentalism that scholars like Arnold, Davis and Eshleman ascribe to Césaire, an idealistic and even liberal individualist aesthetic modified and sublated by the inscription of 'marronage' and its circumstantial determinations. Perhaps the most lucid proof of Césaire's historicizing imagination may be found in the *Discourse on Colonialism* in which he asserts that the key Surrealist text, *Chants de Maldoror* by Comte de Lautréamont, can be given 'a materialistic and historical interpretation' as an 'implacable denunciation of a very particular form of society'.[53]

In his eloquent prolegomenon to the Negritude movement, 'Black Orpheus', Jean-Paul Sartre points to the revolutionary negation of white European colonization which distinguishes the works of Léopold Senghor, Birago Diop and others. While 'white Surrealism' may offer a 'miraculous weapon' to refuse the status quo, its limitations remain because its method and purpose require a transcendence of race, class and other opposites, resulting in the crisis of 'impassiveness'. In contrast, Césaire's singular use of the 'objective' method avoids fabricating a 'calm unity of the opposites'. In fact Césaire exacerbates tensions and contradictions in which 'the throw of the dice', to use the Mallarmean idiom, enacts the practice of engaged, directed automatic writing. According to Sartre, 'What Césaire destroys is not *all* culture but rather white culture; what he brings to light is not desire for *everything* but rather the revolutionary aspirations of the oppressed negro; what he touches in his very depths is not the spirit but a certain specific, concrete form of humanity'.[54] In short, Césaire brings to a definitive fulfilment the Surrealist programme of creative nihilism in a revolutionary surpassing of itself: Negritude as love.

Before concluding, I want to illustrate Césaire's historicizing but also empirical and pragmatic imagination by focusing on two passages in the *Discourse*. Robin Kelley has cogently emphasized the theme of decolonizing Negritude that runs through this impassioned indictment of European barbarism, with motifs of a new insurgent or radical humanism and a 'model for dreaming a way out of our postcolonial predicament'.[55] But the *Discourse* is less a

52 Bertell Ollman, *Dialectical Investigations* (New York: Routledge, 1993).

53 Aimé Césaire, *Discourse on Colonialism*, trans. Joan Pinkham (New York: Monthly Review Press, 1972), p. 48.

54 Jean-Paul Sartre, 'Black Orpheus', in *Race*, ed. Robert Bernasconi (Oxford: Blackwell, 2001), p. 127

55 Robin D.G. Kelley, 'A Poetics of Anticolonialism', *Monthly Review* LI:6 (November 1999), pp. 1–21.

transcription of a dream than a performative event, indeed it rehearses the 'act of insurrection'. Whereas madness and delirium used to be located in the Otherness beyond the borders of bourgeois society, now Césaire finds it in the contemporary world, in the protagonists of colonialism, in the womb of the moribund hegemonic civil society. His identification of the negative phase in the form of the 'enemies', both the Western agents of the proverbial 'civilizing mission' and the local conduits in the neocolonial dependencies (Césaire thus belies the benign hybrid creatures of Western postcolonial theory), demonstrates again the grasp of the necessity of dialectical mediation, a pedagogical prerequisite if we want to burst asunder the totality of the oppressive but historically limited system. Listen to Césaire's epic-like catalogue delivered with Rabelaisian gusto:

> Therefore, comrade, you will hold as enemies – loftily, lucidly, consistently – not only sadistic governors and greedy bankers, not only prefects who torture and colonists who flog, not only corrupt, check-licking politicians and subservient judges, but likewise and for the same reason, venomous journalists, goitrous academicians, wreathed in dollars and stupidity, ethnographers who go in for metaphysics, presumptuous Belgian theologians, chattering intellectuals born stinking out of the thigh of Nietzsche, the paternalists, the embracers, the corrupters, the back-slappers, the lovers of exoticism, the dividers, the agrarian sociologists, the hoodwinkers, the hoaxers, the hot-air artists, the humbugs, and in general, all those who, performing their functions in the sordid division of labor for the defense of Western bourgeois society, try in divers ways and by infamous diversions to split up the forces of Progress – even if it means denying the very possibility of Progress – all of them tools of capitalism, all of them, openly or secretly, supporters of plundering colonialism, all of them responsible, all hateful, all slave-traders, all henceforth answerable for the violence of revolutionary action.
>
> And sweep out all the obscurers, all the inventors of subterfuges, the charlatans and tricksters, the dealers in gobbledygook. And do not seek to know whether personally these gentlemen are in good or bad faith, whether personally they have good or bad intentions. Whether personally – that is, in the private conscience of Peter or Paul – they are or are not colonialists, because the essential thing is that their highly problematical subjective good faith is entirely irrelevant to the objective social implications of the evil work they perform as watchdogs of colonialism.[56]

Here subjective and objective aspects are taken into account, evaluated and judged with all their nuances and ramifications, within the framework of a critical transformative project.

Césaire goes on to particularize the exemplars of bourgeois decadence, a modern barbarism embodied by 'the American hour' characterized by 'Violence, excess, waste, mercantilism, bluff, gregariousness, stupidity, vulgarity, disorder [...]. American domination – the only domination from

56 Césaire, *Discourse*, pp. 33–34.

which one never recovers. I mean from which one never recovers unscarred'.[57] What is striking, however, is the concluding statement in which Césaire warns Europe to undertake 'on its own initiative a policy of *nationalities*, a new policy founded on respect for peoples and cultures', an admonition which not only one-sidedly assigns responsibility to the residual if still dominant forces but also, and more crucially, brings to centre-stage the emergent force of popular resistance: the revolution of colonized peoples such as the Vietnamese and the Africans in the French colonies. Césaire redeems the emancipatory project of Surrealism by privileging national self-determination as the historic mission of the industrial proletariat. Objective chance exerts its efficacy through the intervention of Césaire's historicist understanding. I submit that while Césaire finally pays the customary tribute to the proletariat as the bearers of revolutionary tidings – Césaire is partly addressing the Communist Party of Martinique, he does not omit, elide or forget the catalyzing power of the subaltern peoples of colour without which revolution in the 'first world' is impossible. The maroons in its larger meaning are finally recognized as vanguard agents of socialist transformation. Césaire thus reaffirms the creative power of *marronage*, the revolt of slaves, that his practice of Surrealist Negritude first inaugurated and brought to the limelight especially in the *Notebook*, his dramatic works, and in his public life as a 'third world' intellectual. In effecting this convergence of Surrealism and Lenin's uncanny appreciation of the avant-garde role of anti-colonial revolutions, Césaire has resolved at a specific conjuncture the perennial ethical and political dilemma of European Surrealism.

57 Ibid., pp. 59–60.

Chapter 12

Hans Bellmer's Libidinal Politics

*Alyce Mahon**

> I tried to rearrange the sexual elements of a girl's body like a sort of plastic anagram. I remember describing it thus: the body is like a sentence that invites us to rearrange it, so that its real meaning becomes clear through a series of endless anagrams. I wanted to reveal what is usually kept hidden – it was no game – I tried to open people's eyes to new realities. [...] The anagram is the key to all my work.[1]
>
> Hans Bellmer, 1972

For Hans Bellmer the relation between the body and the text was critical. Inscribing the body and deconstructing the text were interdependent agendas throughout his career: the link between them lay in Surrealist discourse with which one could articulate the cultural polarities of the real and hyperreal, the concrete and the metaphysical.[2] Surrealist discourse operated as a type of *bavardage*, created out of juxtapositions of banal words, intimate experiences and chance encounters, liberating the emotions in a free-flow, unpremeditated manner.[3] In privileging certain concepts (the unconscious, play, humour, eroticism, excess) and subverting others (the unitary subject, logic, taboo and paternal/textual authority), Surrealist discourse was an avant-garde discourse of fragmentation, difference and multiplicity, underpinned by an insistence on the indefinable or the process of becoming.

As such, Surrealism might also be described as a feminine discourse, as in the *écriture automatique* initiated by André Breton and Philippe Soupault in *Les Champs magnétiques* (1919–20). It merged the lines of the *moi* and *toi*, the

---

* I wish to thank Ruth Henry and Dr Jean-François Rabain, for sharing their memories of Bellmer and Zürn with me. Thanks also to Adam J. Boxer, of the Ubu Gallery, New York, for his generous assistance, particularly in providing images. Some of the ideas in this essay were previously published in *Hans Bellmer, Katowice 1902–Paryz 1975* (Warsaw: wydawnictwo stowo/obraz terytoria and Fundacja Galerii Foksal, 1998), pp. 147–66, a publication that coincided with a retrospective exhibition of Bellmer's art in his home town of Katowice.

1 Hans Bellmer in interview with Peter Webb, Paris, 15 January 1972, in Peter Webb, *The Erotic Arts*, Appendix II (London: Secker and Warburg, 1975; 1983 edn), p. 370.

2 The relationship between the body and text was a key theme in much Surrealist art and literature and was explored, for example, in the 'Exquisite Corpse' parlour game.

3 See Jacqueline Chénieux-Gendron, 'Bavardage et merveille: Repenser le Surréalisme', *Nouvelle Revue de Psychanalyse*, no. 40 (1989), pp. 273–86.

subject and object, Self and Other, and insisted on an all-embracing confusion which led the reader to his or her own marvellous end. In de-possessing language, the reader was liberated from the rules and regulations of communal language and from Roland Barthes's 'sociolect' – normative language which ensures normative reading and normative thinking. Barthes described linguistic avant-gardism as the creation of 'texts of bliss' which 'impose a state of loss [...] that discomforts [...] unsettles the reader's historical, cultural, psychological assumptions, the consistency of his tastes, values, memories, [and so] brings to a crisis his relation with language'.[4] For Barthes, bliss could be achieved by textual 'cutting', the creation of two 'edges': the traditional, pleasurable obedient edge, and the avant-gardist, blissful, subversive edge. Their juxtaposition, which Barthes described in terms of 'the seam between them, the fault, the flaw', could become a source of erotic tension.[5] In the art of Hans Bellmer, we can recognize all three of these characteristics: a resolute avant-gardism; the feminine discourse of Surrealism; and a visual style akin to Barthes's 'cutting'. As such we can describe the fundamental preoccupation of Bellmer's work as a 'libidinal politics'.

As Jean-François Lyotard recognized in his 1974 book *Libidinal Economy* (*Economie libidinale*), libidinal economy is connected to political economy as representation (ideological, artistic, fantasmatic) and production (economic and material production). Representation and production are both part of a general process of libido-circulation, both bodily and economic systems being built upon desire. Lyotard's connection of representation and production allows us to appreciate images of the libidinal body as sources of both knowledge *and* resistance, with both passive and active potentials. It is this libidinal agency that allows the body under the Law to become a site of transgression. Lyotard, like Bellmer, was fascinated by the body, its surfaces, and what he termed its 'great ephemeral skin' (*la grande pellicule éphémère*). In *Libidinal Economy*, he identified Bellmer's art as exemplary of 'the organic body of political economy' in so far as it was based on a dismembering of the body, the 'displacement' of its parts and 'substitution' of others.[6] Lyotard describes Bellmer's art as transgressing the unified body. This transgression is evident in Bellmer's recurring motif of the 'little girl', drawn so that 'the fleshiness of the arm [is substituted] for that of the thighs and its faint fold for the vaginal slit'.[7] But for Lyotard, this transgressive displacement is not enough: 'there is no need to begin with transgression, we must go immediately to the very limits of cruelty,

4 Roland Barthes, *The Pleasure of the Text,* trans. Richard Miller (London: Hill and Wang, 1976), p. 14.

5 Ibid., pp. 6–7.

6 Jean-François Lyotard, *Libidinal Economy*, trans. Iain Hamilton Grant (London: Athlone Press, 1993), p. 2.

7 Ibid.

perform the dissection of polymorphous perversion, spread out the immense membrane of the libidinal 'body' which is quite different to the frame'.[8] Rather than transgression as such, Lyotard's libidinal economy is based on a development of the concept of *jouissance*.[9] He proposes that the position of the Other is 'an enjoyable [*jouissive*] position' and that its recognition is political.[10] But Lyotard goes further. In describing the 'libidinal journey', he alludes to Georges Bataille's review *Acéphale* (1936–39) and its celebration of the Nietzschean acephalic man who 'mythologically expresses sovereignty committed to destruction and the death of God'.[11] Lyotard's *Libidinal Economy* is central to this essay's examination of Bellmer, in that it offers a set of theoretical tools with which to interpret the perverse multiplications and metamorphoses of Bellmer's art.

While using Lyotard as theoretical frame, my examination of Hans Bellmer is structured on two premises: firstly, as Andreas Huyssen has suggested, that the feminine as a gendered trope was often used as a metaphorical threat to twentieth-century political, social and linguistic structures.[12] Secondly, that evidence of inscription, be it physical (constraint, pain, regimented) or psychic (ritual, adornment, habit), locates the body in a historically specifiable way, both for the inscription of the body and its reading by the viewer then and now.[13] I

---

8 Ibid.

9 *Jouissance* may be translated in the simplest terms as 'pleasure'; but as the verb *jouir* means to enjoy, to revel in, without fear of the cost, or to have an orgasm; it is best understood in psychoanalytic terms as a dispensing of pleasure without fear of the costs. It is the feminist connotation of *jouissance* that is used in this essay (in keeping with my analysis of Surrealism as a feminine discourse), one that is described by Elaine Marks and Isabelle de Courtivron as 'of a different order from the pleasure that is represented within the male libidinal economy often described in terms of the capitalist gain and profit motive. Women's *jouissance* carries with it the notion of fluidity, diffusion, duration. It is a kind of potlatch in the world of orgasms, a giving, expending, dispensing of pleasure without concern about ends or closure'. Elaine Marks and Isabelle de Courtivron, eds, *New French Feminisms: An Anthology* (Amherst: University of Massachusetts Press, 1980), p. 36, n. 8. Julia Kristeva's concept of *jouissance*, formulated in the same year as Lyotard's *Libidinal Economy*, is also centred on the pre-Oedipal, pre-symbolic, maternal realm of the Other and she describes it in Bataillean terms as Dionysian and orgiastic. See Julia Kristeva, *About Chinese Women*, trans. Anita Barrows (London: Marion Boyars, 1977).

10 Lyotard, *Libidinal Economy,* p. 5.

11 Georges Bataille, 'Propositions' in *Visions of Excess: Selected Writings 1927–1939,* ed. Allan Stoekl, trans. Allan Stoekl, Carl R. Lovitt and Donald M. Leslie, Jr. (Minneapolis: University of Minnesota Press, 1985), p. 199.

12 Andreas Huyssen, 'Mass Culture as Woman; Modernism's Other', in *After the Great Divide: Modernism, Mass Culture, Postmodernism* (London: Macmillan Press, 1986).

13 See Elizabeth Grosz, 'Inscriptions and Body-Maps: Representations and the Corporeal', in *Feminine/Masculine and Representation*, eds, T. Threadgold and A. Cranny-Francis (New Zealand: Allen and Unwin, 1990).

argue that Bellmer's creative use of the female body and exploration of libidinal *jouissance*, which even today provokes controversy or unease, must be understood within the historical context of its production and reception as a subversion of gender and national politics in the pre- and wartime Germany. Specifically, in this essay I will focus on three distinct phases of his career: firstly, his doll sculptures of 1933–36; secondly, his collaboration on a series of photographs and anagrams with poet Nora Mitrani from 1946–48; and thirdly, his photographic collaboration with writer Unica Zürn of 1958. Throughout, I will argue that Bellmer's libidinal politics is based on an 'anagrammatic' approach to the female form in both writing and the image (that is, the rearrangement of words/limbs or phrases/bodies into new words/limbs or phrases/bodies); and that Bellmer uses the anagram as a tool of provocation to demand an active, self-conscious role for the reader/viewer and, by extension, to deconstruct the totalitarian body politic of Nazi Germany – in which anyone that did not conform to or fit into a fascist Aryan ideal was made Other, objectified, repressed and ultimately destroyed.[14]

Bellmer admired the anagram for its paradoxical combination of rigid structure (a limited quota of letters with which to create a phrase) and illogicality. The anagram offered Bellmer a means to capture the rhythmical feminine fluidity of the acephalic unconscious, and a sense of conflict in its defiance of logic, linearity and traditional masculine tropes. The anagram created a space for overlap, confusion and play – a constantly shifting correspondence within which the verbal and the pictorial could exist in a perpetual state of metamorphosis between pleasure and pain, Eros and Thanatos. In its 'cutting' of linguistic and bodily units, it provided a suitable vehicle for avant-garde expression through textual slippage, instability and transgression. Bellmer's use of the female body in particular, as a site of violent or monstrous alterity, offered a subversion of

14 My critical reading of Bellmer differs from the readings of Xavière Gauthier, *Surréalisme et sexualité* (Paris: Gallimard, 1971), Rudolf Kuenzli, 'Surrealism and Misogyny', in *Dada/Surrealism*, no. 18 (1990), pp. 17–26, and Mary-Ann Caws, *The Surrealist Look: An Erotics of Encounter* (Cambridge: MIT Press, 1997), where Bellmer's representation of the female form is deemed misogynistic and effectively removed from social, political and historical consideration. It is also at variance with psychoanalytic readings of Bellmer such as Sue Taylor, *Hans Bellmer: The Anatomy of Anxiety* (Cambridge: MIT Press, 2000). Instead, it builds on such analyses of Bellmer's art as Hal Foster, *Compulsive Beauty* (Cambridge: MIT Press, 1993) and Therese Lichenstein, *Behind Closed Doors: The Art of Hans Bellmer* (Berkeley: University of California Press, 2001), both of whom analyze Bellmer in light of the psyche of fascism. But unlike Foster and Lichenstein, who confine themselves to the pre-World War II period, I believe that we must examine Bellmer's art beyond the *Poupée* and after World War II, specifically in light of his collaborations with women artists who were also addressing similar issues of sexual and national politics in their work, to ensure the highly complex psycho-sexual aspects of his work are adequately contextualized as socio-political works of resistance.

totalitarian corporeal knowledge-power, and was consistent with the Surrealists' faith in the economy of desire as political wherein the monstrous feminine threatened socio-political crisis in the established order.

From the Culture of Display in the Weimar Republic to *La Poupée*

Bellmer created his first *Püppe* sculpture in Berlin in 1933. Made of *papier-mâché* and plaster over an armature of wood and metal, the *Püppe* was about four feet in height and had moveable limbs. It was the subject of a series of ominous photographs by the artist published as *Die Püppe* (*The Doll*) in 1934. His second doll, *La Poupée* (*The Doll*, which is usually titled in French to distinguish it from the first), was created in 1935; made of glue and tissue paper, it was structured around a central ball joint and was more voluptuous in form and flesh-like in colour. This improved *Poupée* was again repeatedly photographed by Bellmer, often wearing ribbons in her hair and Mary Jane shoes and frilly ankle socks on her feet. Photographed indoors or out, with props, with several manipulated limbs, multiple orifices, and often headless and armless, the second doll presented – and still presents – the viewer with a disturbing display of erotic violence.

Bellmer's *Poupée* takes on new signification, however, if we recall Lyotard's understanding of libidinal economy: she becomes an embodiment of 'the very limits of cruelty [...] the dissection of polymorphous perversion', iconic of the libidinal body in all its heterogeneous glory.[15] If we historically contextualize Bellmer's *Poupée* with this understanding in mind we also find a socio-political signification to Bellmer's perverse manipulations of the mannequin-doll.

Just prior to the creation of the first *Püppe,* the Weimar Republic (1918–33) witnessed considerable social change. According to Maud Lavin, 'two key developments in the larger history of industry, rationalization and consumerism' took place: firstly, 'a rapid growth in the mass print media', and secondly, 'a dramatic redefinition of the social roles of women'.[16] These were interdependent developments, as the advertising and media industries promoted a 'New Woman' who – particularly in keeping with the 'New Objectivity' which dominated visual culture in the 1920s – was as sleek and efficient as a machine.[17] The ideal woman in Weimar society was often presented in the mass media in doll-like terms, notably through the fetishizing of her eyes and lips, so reducing woman to an infantile passivity. Ironically, women constituted the

---

15 Lyotard, *Libidinal Economy*, p. 3.

16 Maud Lavin, *Cut with the Kitchen Knife: The Weimar Photomontages of Hannah Höch* (London and New Haven: Yale University Press, 1993), p. 1.

17 See Janet Ward, *Weimar Surfaces: Urban Visual Culture in 1920s Germany* (California: University of California Press, 2001), pp. 9–13.

majority of the consumer market, seduced by this mechanization of their image as a mannequin-masquerade.[18] This commodity fetishism was also evident in the display windows of Berlin's department stores, and was exploited in the form of the female body – specifically, the wax mannequin. The mannequin, clothed and unclothed, again promoted the vision of modern woman-as-surface, encouraging visual pleasure but also the association between modernity and the feminine and the belief that the commodity characteristic of both was linked to the rise of prostitution and alienation in society. Walter Benjamin, for example, would write of the wax mannequin in terms of the superficial and monstrous in *The Arcades Project* (1927–40):

> The wax figure is in fact the scene where the appearance of humanity capsizes. That is to say, human surface, complexion and colour are expressed in her so completely and unsurpassably that this reproduction of its appearance outdoes itself, so that now the mannequin represents nothing but a dreadful, artful mediation between entrails and costume.[19]

This link between the Weimar New Woman and consumerism, on the one hand, and the wax mannequin as threatening masquerade, on the other, played a crucial role in Weimar art and film at the very time when Bellmer was a young student and commercial artist in Berlin. Bellmer attended the Berlin Technical College from 1923–24 befriending such Dada artists as George Grosz, Otto Dix and John Heartfield, and becoming familiar with the work of Kurt Schwitters. Grosz's art of this period anticipates Benjamin's association of the modern female with the monstrous as it is dominated by images of assault on the female body. In works like *John, der Frauenmörder* (*John, the Lady Killer*, 1918) or *Lustmord* (*Sexual Murder*, 1922), Grosz depicts Jack the Ripper characters engrossed in the mutilation of diseased and nameless whore-victims of the type whom contemporary advertising and window displays played off against the pure, 'white', cosmeticized female ideal of the new consumer society.

Hannah Höch, also one of this avant-garde circle, explored the same theme in focusing on the mannequin as a symbolic parody of the prevailing media construction of ideal, controlled femininity.[20] She would dress-up – or masquerade – as an avant-garde puppet, or photograph herself with her collection of Dada dolls. Her photomontages introduced a more violent take on woman-as-mannequin, as in her 1925 *Zerbrochen* (*Broken*; fig. 52) where she

---

18 See Lavin, *Cut with the Kitchen Knife,* ch. 4.

19 Walter Benjamin, 'Das Passagen-Werk', in *Gesammelte Schriften,* eds, Rolf Tiedmann and Hermann Schweppenhäuser, vol. 5 (Frankfurt A.M.: Suhrkamp, 1972) p. 516; in English as *The Arcades Project*, trans. Howard Eiland and Kevin McLaughlin (Cambridge: Belknap Press, 1999).

20 Lavin documents that the most popular doll sold in the Weimar Republic had 'a child's face and large, half-moon eyes – an expression filled with innocence, humour and wonderment'. Lavin, *Cut with the Kitchen Knife*, pp. 136–37.

cuts up identical images of a baby doll's face, layering them so that one ends up with a distorted, monstrous face with six eyes that parodies both the uniformity of the mannequin and the reductionism of mass reproduction. Here the construction of the ideal feminine was further subverted through the very procedure of photomontage – the cutting up, or mutilation, of ideal female types constituting an aggressive rejection of gendered cultural impositions.

Sexual violence and the depiction of the modern sexual woman as monstrous was also the subject of many Weimar films: beginning with Friedrich Murnau's blood-sucking, plague-carrying *Nosferatu* of 1922, and advancing to Josef von Sternberg's *The Blue Angel* of 1930, and, a year later, Fritz Lang's *M*.[21] The latter two films exemplify the intimate relationship between display and crime, sex and disease. In *The Blue Angel* (1930), starring *femme-fatale* Marlene Dietrich, we find a once-respected Professor Immanuel Rath losing his status, profession and sanity as he is seduced by Lola, a cabaret singer. When he proposes marriage to Lola, he asks her, ironically, if she realizes 'the gravity of this hour'. His moral downfall is signalled to the viewer in the form of a doll. At one point, when the Professor falls under Lola's spell as she sings on stage and gazes at him with her big eyes, the camera pans to a gargantuan naked mannequin posed beside the professor's viewing box. The following morning, when the Professor wakes up in Lola's bed, he is seen holding a baby doll. Though startled, he begins to play with the doll in a child-like stupor. Here, we see the effect of perverted femininity on society – where sex precedes culture, desire precedes responsibility – symbolized in a doll. In Lang's film *M*, Franz Beckert, a murderer of little girls, is depicted as a child-like (sucking sweets), feminized (sexually uncontrollable) victim of his own plague, of 'the evil thing inside me', the will to destroy. We find this compulsion visualized in a scene where display and consumption are literally juxtaposed: Beckert leads a potential victim, a little girl, to a toy store shop window and, as they stare at the goods on display, the viewer is witness to his sexual gaze and her innocent gaze simultaneously. His desire for her is like her desire for a toy – neither is in control and both are prey to consumer culture and its psychology.[22]

The exploration of sexual violence, masquerade and the use of montage by artists and filmmakers, undoubtedly influenced Bellmer at this formative stage of his career, especially as he would leave his engineering course at the Berlin Technical College in 1924 and earn a living illustrating books and designing advertisements for large industrial firms (e.g. Malik Verlag in Berlin), finally setting up his own advertising and design agency in Karlshort in 1927. His book covers and illustrations often consisted of violent depictions of women (appro-

21 See Maria M. Tatar, *Lustmord: Sexual Murder in Weimar Germany* (Princeton, New Jersey: Princeton University Press, 1995), ch. 7.

22 When National Socialism replaced Weimar democracy in 1933, *M*, like many other artistic explorations of sexual consumption and perversion, was banned by Goebbels.

priate to the narrative's melodramatic subject-matter), and his advertising designs often involved photomontage. In sum, his early work of the 1920s was implicated in the representation of the New Woman and was dependent on a culture of consumerism.[23]

Desiring Production, Female Criminality and *Les Jeux de la Poupée*

In 1933 National Socialism replaced Weimar democracy and Bellmer's father joined the National Socialist Party. Bellmer stopped his commercial work entirely in protest against Nazism, and created his first doll sculpture. Photographs of the doll were published privately as *Die Püppe* (*The Doll*) the following year.[24] In these photographs, the *Püppe* has stereotypical female accessories: ribbons, lace, stockings, high-heels and flowers. However, in many photographs she is also broken, battered, limbless and typically propped up against a bed, a door, or a studio wall. Woman as consumer and as object to be consumed is now represented in perverse, objectionable terms, defying any attempt at the scopophilia one could enjoy in a mannequin on display. The artist appears in one of the photographs, published as no. 3 in *Die Püppe*, as a semi-transparent, ghost-like Jack the Ripper, crouching beside a beret-clad, unfinished doll (fig. 53). It is an incestuous, bleak *mise en scène*, reminiscent of Lang's *M* in its uncanny coupling of an innocent girl and a troubled obsessive male.

Desiring-production was a key aspect of fascist control: the nurturing of fantasies which, when heightened, became murderous. In his study of 1920's *Freikorps* literature, Klaus Theweleit documents how the ideal fascist male 'became a rock amid the raging sea' – that sea, or quagmire, being a 'Red Flood' whose threat was propagandized in feminine terms as 'the whore of a republic; ravished Mother Germany; a gigantic menstruating vagina, teeming with every imaginable creature; internationalism'.[25] Here, a new body politic emerged with

23 The dolls of Lotte Pritzel were also an inspiration and had been the subject of a Dadaist article by Theodor Däubler in *Das Puppenbuch* in 1921, reproducing 21 of her dolls. See Peter Webb and Robert Short, *Hans Bellmer* (London: Quartet Books, 1985), p. 21. Max Reinhardt's production of Offenbach's 'The Tales of Hoffman' in 1932 was also a great influence: Hoffman's story of the 'Sandman' which features a lifeless doll-woman called Olympia was the main source of inspiration.

24 *Die Püppe* had ten photographs of the *Doll* (documenting her gradual construction) and a short introduction by Bellmer entitled 'Memories of the Doll Theme'. It was printed by a friend of Bellmer's, Thomas Eckstein, at Bellmer's own expense. A French edition of *Die Püppe* was published in 1936 as *La Poupée* by Guy Levis Mano in which Bellmer's essay was translated by Robert Valançay.

25 Klaus Theweleit, *Male Fantasies,* vol. 1, *Women, Floods, Bodies, History*, trans. Stephen Conway, Erica Carter and Chris Turner (Cambridge: Polity Press, 1987), pp. 362 and 404. The *Freikorps* was a voluntary army or militia. In the years between 1918 and 1923 it fought against Polish Communists and nationalists, the Russian Red

the rise of Fascism – but one that continued to use the female body as ideological metaphor. This Nazi iconography took the Weimar female ideal to an extreme and stressed the difference between maternal, moral, natural femininity (as symbolized by the *Kinder*, *Kirche*, *Küche* dictate) and perverse, weak, sexualized femininity.[26] By 1933, this distinction was made manifest in the form of social, political and cultural public spectacle. As Therese Lichenstein has documented in her recent study of Bellmer's dolls, a dramatic example of such public spectacle took place in Nuremberg on Sunday, 13 August 1933, when a young girl, with a shaved head, was paraded before the public by Storm Troopers, with a placard suspended from her shoulders bearing her shorn plaits and the words 'I have offered myself to a Jew'.[27] In sleeping with a Jew she had betrayed her country and her sex; she had to be symbolically castrated (through the cutting of her hair, a symbol of her sexuality) just as society had to be publicly purged of such treason.

Of course Berlin was not the only city at this time in which a peculiar obsession with modernity and its vices was articulated in gendered terms. In Paris in 1933, two much publicized cases involving murderesses seemed to prove the suspicion that modern woman was the bearer of modern vice. These were the cases of the Papin sisters and Violette Nozière. The Papin sisters were young maids who murdered the mother and daughter of the bourgeois household that employed them. Violette Nozière was an eighteen-year-old who robbed and poisoned her father.[28] Both cases seized the public imagination – as Elisabeth Roudinesco has documented:

> In the fall of 1933, all of France was obsessed with the Nozière affair. Street songs were being written on the subject, as for the celebrated criminals Vacher and Landru. The Satanic figure of the sorceress was being invoked, with calls for the stake, punishment, torture. ...[29]

The Surrealists in Paris were particularly intrigued by the cases of the Papin sisters and Violette Nozière, seeing both as acts of revolt against patriarchal

---

army, Latvian and Estonian nationalists in the Baltic region, and the German working class throughout Germany. It would become the core group of Hitler's SA.

26 See Wilfried Van der Will, 'The Body and the Body Politic as Symptom and Metaphor in the Transition of German Culture to National Socialism', in *The Nazification of Art: Art, Design, Music, Architecture and Film in the Third Reich*, eds, Brandon Taylor and Wilfried Van der Will (Winchester: Winchester School of Art Press, 1990).

27 Lichenstein, *Behind Closed Doors*, pp. 129–30.

28 Violette Nozière attempted to poison her mother too, but failed. She also claimed her father had been raping her for several years (though she retracted this four years later when she decided to become a nun). One of her reasons for robbing her parents was apparently so that she could provide her young lover, Jean Dabin, with money. See J.-M. Fitère, *Violette Nozière* (Paris: Presses de la Cité, 1975). André Breton interpreted this as an example of *amour fou*.

29 Elisabeth Roudinesco, *Jacques Lacan & Co.: A History of Psychoanalysis in France 1925–1985*, trans. J. Mehlman (London: Free Association Books, 1990), p. 18.

authority. As part of their defence of the Papin sisters, the Surrealists published 'before' and 'after' photographs of the sisters (once good, submissive girls, then demonic and wild-eyed) in *Le Surréalisme au service de la révolution* (fig. 15) and an account by Paul Eluard and Benjamin Péret of their case in which the sisters were presented as near-Sadean heroines – progressing from an education in a convent in Le Mans, to six years of domestic service for a bourgeois family, to a final act of rage which led them to gouge out the eyes and smash the heads of their employers. Eluard and Péret even ended their 'press report' with the poetic vision of the sisters triumphant after their act of revenge and 'fully armed from a song of Maldoror', thus aligning their act of violence to those of the Surrealist forefather, the Comte de Lautréamont and his novel *Les Chants de Maldoror* (1869).[30] The Surrealists also published an article by Jacques Lacan in their review *Minotaure* in 1933 in which he diagnosed the Papin sisters as suffering from paranoia (a state of delirium but also of immense creativity for Lacan and the Surrealists).[31]

In December of the same year, the Surrealists published a collection of poems and illustrations in support of Violette Nozière's parricide. They perceived Nozière's revolt against her parents as a revolt against bourgeois conformity and restrictions. Eluard hailed her as a girl dreaming for 'beautiful dresses of pure blood', free from the father-figure, while André Breton fantasized about the revolutionary prospects of her sexual deviance as a stance against social and moral hierarchy.[32] Thus the adolescent female as victim and heroine of society and subversion, respectively, was at the forefront of Surrealist thought in Paris at the same time as it emerged in the form of the *Püppe* in Berlin.[33] It is not surprising that in 1934 Bellmer would seek out Surrealists in Paris – asking his

30 Paul Eluard and Benjamin Péret, 'Revue de la presse', *Le Surréalisme au service de la révolution*, no. 5 (1933), pp. 27–28.

31 Jacques Lacan, 'Motifs du Crime Paranoïaque', *Minotaure*, nos 3–4, (1933), p. 28.

32 *Violette Nozières* (Brussels: Editions Nicolas Flamel, 1933), partially rpd in José Pierre, ed., *Tracts surréalistes et déclarations collectives*, vol. 1, 1922–1939 (Paris: Terrain Vague, 1980), pp. 247–62, 483–86; rpd with preface by José Pierre (Paris: Terrain Vague, 1991). Note that at the time the Surrealists spelt the name with a final 's', as in Nozières.

33 In terms of literature, Bellmer's obsession with the interior experience and projections of repressed desire was similar to those explorations articulated by Antonin Artaud and Henri Michaux. For example, in *L'Ombilic des Limbes* (Paris: Gallimard, 1925), Artaud wrote of the direct link between one's words and one's limbs; similarly, in his *Espace du Dedans* (Paris: Gallimard, 1944), Michaux presented an 'algebra of suffering', a decolonization of the self through bodily exploration. Both authors would greatly influence Bellmer's partner of 17 years: Unica Zürn. She was introduced to their work by the artist, and in his letters to her doctor Bellmer frequently compared her literary explorations and mental hallucinations to theirs. See Hans Bellmer and Unica Zürn, *Lettres au Docteur Ferdière* (Paris: Séguier, 1994).

young cousin Ursula, who was studying at the Sorbonne, to bring photographs of the *Püppe* from Berlin to André Breton – or that the Surrealists in turn would appreciate Bellmer's art as exemplary of their concept of 'convulsive beauty'.

Bellmer was soon embraced in Surrealist reviews and exhibitions. In December 1934, the Surrealists published 18 of Bellmer's photographs of the *Püppe* in *Minotaure* (no. 6) under the title 'Doll: Variations on the Assemblage of an Articulated Minor'.[34] The following year, Bellmer visited Paris and exhibited with the Surrealists in a group show at the Galerie des Quatre Chemins. Eluard was so inspired by Bellmer's doll that he wrote a short story, 'Appliquée', in *Minotaure* (no. 7) about the fantasies of a little girl which was illustrated by a couple of Bellmer's photographs.[35] In 1936, Bellmer's assemblage *Jointure de boules* (*Ball joint*) – two arms of his doll, joined at the shoulder by an eyeball and caught in black lace, was exhibited in the exhibition of Surrealist objects at the Charles Ratton Gallery in Paris; and in 1937 his photographs of his second *Poupée* were published in *Minotaure* (no. 10). In 1938 he moved to Paris for good.

Bellmer also collaborated with Eluard on a project of photographs and prose-poems, *Les Jeux de la Poupée* (*The Games of the Doll*).[36] This was a luxurious limited edition book collaboration with a frontispiece and 14 photographs by Bellmer, hand-coloured, often with startling pinks and greens which lend a psycho-sexual effect, each of which was accompanied by a short prose-poem by Eluard. Such collaborations between artists and writers were numerous amongst the Surrealists, and Eluard had collaborated with Max Ernst in 1922 on *Répétitions* and *Les Malheurs des Immortels*.[37] In her analysis of the collaboration between Eluard and Ernst, Eliane Formentelli offers a reading that is applicable to the collaboration between Eluard and Bellmer on *Les Jeux de la Poupée*:

> Between the 'representation of objects' and the 'representation of words' functions a system of exchange that is neither translation nor transposition but, rather, work, inscription, game, which, in both sectors,

---

34 It must be noted that *Minotaure* (1933–39) was not only a deluxe Surrealist review, it was a review that explored the potential of 'image-documents' and that promoted and indeed privileged photography as art. See *Focus on Minotaure,* exh. cat. (Geneva: Musée d'Art et d'Histoire, 1987).

35 Eluard's 'Appliquée' was also accompanied by an erotic postcard of nude girls from Bellmer's collection, and a photograph of one of Lotte Pritzel's dolls. See *Minotaure*, no. 7 (1935), pp. 15–16.

36 *Les Jeux de la Poupée* was intended for publication in 1939; due to the war, however, it was not published until 1949, by Editions Premières, Paris.

37 Max Ernst and Paul Eluard, *Répétitions* (Paris: Au Sans Pareil, 1922). This consisted of 35 poems and 11 collages, characterized by the repetition of certain images and refrains which were used to disrupt the reader's expectations. *Les Malheurs des Immortels* (Paris: Librairie Six, 1922) consisted of 20 poems and collages.

> involves the trace. The technique of the collage silences a garrulous rationalism by means of a bruise, a scratch, or the *violence of mute appearances*.[38]

This emphasis on the cutting technique of collage and the violence of mute appearance is pertinent to *Les Jeux de la Poupée* as it involves a visual cutting-fragmentation of the doll into body parts in its evocation of ominous, incestuous *mise en scènes* (fig. 54) and as Eluard's text specifically refers to the doll's 'mute mouth', a characteristic he finds tantalizing.[39] The *Poupée* as symbol of subversive eroticism, adolescent rebellion, mute violence and what Breton would describe in 1941 as an embodiment of 'human vertigo' would soon take on a horrific pertinence with the outbreak of World War II and with the 'moral summit', in Bataille's words, that would follow.[40]

Postwar Trauma and *La Croix gamahuchée*

The exploration of erotic 'vertigo' through the literal manipulation of the limbs of the *Poupée* and the metaphoric staging of the life and death drives in Bellmer's photographs, would find a different outlet in the aftermath of the war when Bellmer turned to the anagram as a mean of expression.[41] In 1947–48, he wrote a series of anagrams with his then lover, Nora Mitrani, a Jewish poet from Bulgaria.[42] Entitled

---

38 Eliane Formentelli, 'Max Ernst, Paul Eluard ou l'impatience du désir', *Revue des Sciences Humaines*, no. 164, (October–December 1976), p. 503, quoted in Renée Riese Hubert, *Surrealism and the Book* (Berkeley: University of California Press, 1988), p. 64. My italics.

39 Hans Bellmer, *Les Jeux de la Poupée* (Paris: Editions Premières, 1949). This text was also reproduced as a preface to an exhibition of Bellmer's work in Toulouse (Librairie Silvio Trentin) in 1944.

40 See André Breton, 'Genèse et Perspective Artistiques du Surréalisme' (1941) in *Le Surréalisme et la Peinture* (Paris: Gallimard, 1965), p. 81; and Georges Bataille, *On Nietzsche*, trans. Bruce Boone (London: Athlone Press, 1992), pp. 13–49.

41 Bellmer spent the war years in France: first in a refugee camp, Camp des Milles (September 1939–June 1940), then briefly with the other Surrealists at Air Bel in Marseilles, and lived in Castres from 1941 until the end of the war. As Pierre Dourthe documents in *Hans Bellmer: Le Principe de perversion* (Paris: Jean-Pierre Faur, 1999), p. 118, Bellmer was involved in the Resistance in Castres from 1941 to 1944. In May 1942 he married Marcelle Sutter and on 13 April 1943 his twin daughters, Doriane and Béatrice, were born. However, by Summer 1944 Bellmer and Sutter had separated and he would not see his daughters again for over 20 years.

42 The poet Joë Bousquet was also involved in this anagram project but only contributed to a few of the anagrammed variations on Nerval's phrase. Nora Mitrani (b. 1921, Sofia, Bulgaria–d. 1950, Paris), was raised in Paris. She studied philosophy at the Sorbonne during the Occupation and had to take a false identity as her mother was of Jewish extraction and had been shipped to Auschwitz when the Germans took the city. A self-proclaimed Trotskyite, Mitrani contributed highly incisive essays to many Surrealist

Rose au cœur violet, this series of anagrams is another example of the erotic 'cutting' of which Barthes wrote and the libidinal economy of Lyotard. Significantly, Bellmer viewed their collaboration in sexualized terms too, once telling Bernard Noël that 'Anagrams work better with two people, a man and a woman. A sort of competition or rather a liveliness which each encourages in the other'.[43] Taken from a line by Nerval – '*Rose au cœur violet*' [Rose with the Violet Heart] – they created a series of anagrammed variations of the phrase and through the rearranging of letters, explored the violation (*violé*) of the female sex (*rose*), the roles of love and violence, the Self and the Other, exposing the slippage between Eros and Thanatos in the process:

> Se vouer à toi ô cruel
> A toi, couleuvre rose
> [...]
> Couvre-toi, la rue ose
> Ouvre-toi, ô la sucrée
> [...]
> Curé, où Eros t'a violé – où l'écu osera te voir
> Où verte coloriée sua – cou ouvert sera loi
> O rire sous le couteau.[44]

A rose, a young woman's sex, is described as bewitching, enticing and sweet – but, in knowing this, has the potential to be cruel, daring and mocking.[45] The female sex laughs before the phallic knife – it is pillaged before the curate. In writing on *Rose au cœur violet*, Mitrani described this word play as an enactment of the 'mortal gravity of love', a gravity which causes vertigo, dizziness and madness.[46] She insisted that erotic art should evoke such fear – from which we might infer that with eroticism the body mediates freedom and with violent eroticism (e.g. Sadism), a determinate freedom.

Whether this is the love of cruelty or the cruelty of love between Bellmer and Mitrani is not our concern; rather, our concern is with their poetic insistence on

---

publications (including *La Révolution surréaliste; Néon*; *l'Almanach surréaliste du demi-siècle, Médium, Le Surréalisme, même*). In the 1950s she also worked at the CNRS participating in studies on 'The Sociology of Moral Life', amongst others. Her affair with Bellmer lasted from 1946 to 1948.

43 Bernard Noël, 'La Langue du Corps', *Obliques*, special number on Hans Bellmer, (Paris, 1975), p. 37, trans. in Webb and Short, *Hans Bellmer*, p. 200.

44 These are some of the anagrammed variations of the phrase as reproduced in Hans Bellmer, *Petite anatomie de l'inconscient physique ou l'Anatomie de l'image* (Paris: Terrain Vague, 1957), p. 44.

45 In his *Dictionnaire érotique* (Paris: Editions Payot and Rivages, 1978), Pierre Guiraud defines the rose as symbolic of the female sex, and notes the French saying 'perdu votre rose', to lose one's rose, as a poetic expression for the loss of virginity. That said, the anagram plays on further associations with *rose*, since a *rosette* signifies the anus, and *rosée* sperm.

46 Nora Mitrani, *Rose au cœur violet* (Losfeld: Terrain Vague, 1988), pp. 13–14. Mitrani planned to write a book on Bellmer with this title.

the inseparable nature of love and cruelty as interdependent permutations of the imagination and body. As a woman and an artist, it seems Mitrani found Bellmer's art liberating in its draughtsmanship which broke from traditional linearity, and, more importantly for our purposes, she saw his vision as liberating as she decried the restriction of woman to a utilitarian, patriarchal role.[47] She understood these anagrams as part of Bellmer's general artistic practice which she described as dedicated to the assassination of good consciences in its total liberation of the imagination:

> Bellmer looks forward to the time when the liberated imagination will rediscover its corporeal imaginations and destroy the contradiction between the interior and the exterior.[48]

In other words, Mitrani's perspective on the erotic, on Bellmer's permutations, on his feminine style and perverse subject-matter, suggests that she recognized his art as highly gender-political: the morphology of his representations of the fragmented female body was to be contextualized in terms of the need for woman to redefine and master her own image. It is worth noting that this was an opinion she held long after her relationship with Bellmer had ended, for a decade later, in the Surrealist review *Le Surréalisme, même,* she wrote of the need for women to 'cease to be slaves' in their own minds, and to become 'suffragettes of the whip'.[49] Mitrani and Bellmer seemed to share a particularly Bataillean notion of eroticism as the pursuit and transgression of erotic limits. This is not surprising, as Bellmer illustrated Bataille's erotic novel *Histoire de l'Œil* (*Story of the Eye*, 1928) in 1946 and as he later admitted that he agreed with Bataille that 'eroticism relates to a knowledge of evil and the inevitability of death, it is not simply an expression of joyful passion'.[50] *Rose au cœur violet* (and indeed Bellmer's photographs of his first and second dolls in general), shared with Bataille's novel the depiction of a series of shocking sexual exploits of an adolescent woman and her 'pink and dark' sex as it is described by the male narrator in Bataille's novel.[51] In *Histoire de l'Œil*, the female heroine, Simone, is not just sexually voracious, she is like Sade's Juliette, revelling in the sadistic abuse of a young friend Marcelle (leading to Marcelle's insanity and suicide) and of a priest (whom she effectively rapes to death).

Bellmer had also explored the subject of Bataillean perversion in a series of black and white photographs that he took of two models, one of whom was

47 Ibid., pp. 18–20.

48 Ibid., pp. 14–15; trans. in Webb and Short, *Hans Bellmer*, p. 204.

49 Nora Mitrani, 'Des esclaves, des suffragettes, du fouet' in *Le Surréalisme, même*, no. 3 (Autumn 1957).

50 Georges Bataille's *Histoire de l'Œil* was published under the pseudonym Lord Auch and illustrated by Bellmer with six etchings (Paris: K. Editeur, 1946); Bellmer in interview with Webb, *Erotic Art*, p. 369.

51 Georges Bataille, *Story of the Eye*, trans. Joachim Neugroschal (New York: Urizen, 1977; London: Penguin, 1982), p. 10.

Mitrani, in the summer of 1946.[52] In one photograph, we are confronted with a close-up image of a woman's vulva, dripping milk, beside a half-empty saucer, directly recalling Bataille's *Histoire de l'Œil* where Simone, on seeing a saucer of milk intended for a cat, proclaims 'Milk is for the pussy isn't it? / Do you dare me to sit in the saucer?'[53] In another photograph, we see two female torsos contorted in an aggressive sexual embrace in the corner of a room so that their bare legs are arranged into a cross-like form as one of the models inserts two fingers into the other's vulva. Here Bellmer may be seen to confound 'the masculine and the feminine, the Self and the You, sodomizing the Self in the You' – as he described it later in his 1957 publication *L'Anatomie de l'image* (*The Anatomy of the Image*).[54] But in twisting naked limbs so, in turning the photographic image on its head so that the limbs becomes swastika in form, and in giving it the title *La Croix 'gamahuchée'* (the cross of 'oral sex') which plays on the French word *la croix gammée*, the swastika, his exploration of libidinal politics clearly parodies the symbol of Nazi rule and the Nazi body politic (fig. 55).[55]

This photograph not only parodies Nazi symbolism, however. It may also be seen as confronting the aggression of postwar French society, as it called for political purges of collaborators in corporeal terms, especially in its newspapers. For example, an editorial in *Esprit* in December 1944 read 'Enough of this poison flowing through our veins [...] for this we must do whatever is necessary, however brutal'.[56] At the time of Bellmer's photographic studies, the *épuration* (the purging of collaborators) was under way in France as part of an attempt at postwar political and economic reconstruction. Women played a key material and symbolic role in this purge (which was comparable to the earlier Nazi public purges at Nuremberg) – those accused of being lovers of Nazis, so-called 'Horizontal Collaborators', were dragged out of their homes, stripped, shaved, mocked and paraded in public in a grotesque political carnival of which Paul Eluard wrote in his 1944 poem 'Comprenne qui voudra':

52 On Mitrani's role in these photographs see also Herbert Lust, 'For Women Are Endless Forms: Hans Bellmer's Dark Art', in *Hans Bellmer* (New York: Isidore Ducasse Fine Arts, 1999), p. 17, and Stephen S. Prokopoff and Martin Van de Guchte, 'New Realities, New Desires: The Photographs of Hans Bellmer', in *Hans Bellmer's Photographs* (Urbana-Champaign: University of Illinois, 1991), p. 34. Bellmer was also doing a series of drawings related to the Marquis de Sade's *Les 120 journées de Sodom* in 1946 and in 1961 he would publish a series of ten engravings entitled *A Sade* (Paris: Alain Mazo).

53 Bataille, *Story of the Eye*, p. 10.

54 Bellmer, *L'Anatomie de l'image*, p. 36.

55 Guiraud, *Dictionnaire érotique*, p. 359, defines 'gamahucher' as 'pratiquer le coït buccal, sur une femme ou sur un homme'. Marie-France Le Pennec, translates 'gamahucher' as 'pratiquer le cunilingue', its more common usage, in *Petit glossaire du langue érotique aux xvii et xviii siècles* (Paris: Editions Borderie, 1979), p. 62.

56 Editorial in *Esprit* (December 1944), quoted in Tony Judt, *Past Imperfect: French Intellectuals 1944–56* (Berkeley: University of California Press, 1992), p. 63.

La victime raisonnable
A la robe déchirée
Au regard d'enfant perdue
Découronnée défigurée
Celle qui resemble aux morts
Qui sont morts pour être aimés[57]

Bellmer could not but have been moved by this facet of the postwar French psyche in reaction to the trauma so many had suffered during the war. His own father (who had died in 1941) was part of that loathed Nazi machine. In addition, Mitrani's mother, who was of Jewish extraction, had been shipped to Auschwitz when the Germans took Paris. Bellmer's move from the plastic to the real in his Bataillean, anagrammatic photographs of Mitrani – especially as a swastika in the flesh – may be seen as a provocative exploration of the *jouissance* of sex and the *jouissance* of the torturer. While the *Poupée* could be sublimated as an embodiment of Nadja-esque 'convulsive beauty', a real woman photographed in a contorted, obscene pose that evoked sexual and political terror was a brutal assault on the eye of the beholder. Bellmer here captures Barthes's *punctum*: that aspect of the photograph which has the power of psychic expansion, causing a sense of anxiety and forcing the viewer to realize his 'gaze'.[58] In setting the scene for attraction and/or repulsion, he ruptures the traditional passive-active role of the viewer-artist, insisting on the complicity of both within the libidinal economics of representation itself.

"We Dote on Death": Bellmer and Unica Zürn

A decade later, Bellmer again returned to the anagram in collaborative ventures with German writer and artist Unica Zürn.[59] Bellmer met Zürn in Berlin at an exhibition at the Galerie Springer in 1953. From then until Zürn's suicide in 1970, they would live together in Paris as 'comrades in misery'.[60] Their relationship was complicated by Zürn's bouts of mental instability and is best

57 Paul Eluard, 'Comprenne qui voudra', from *Au Rendez-vous Allemand (1942–1945)*, in *Choix de Poèmes* (Paris: Gallimard, 1951), p. 301. See also Alain Brossat, *Les Tondues. Un Carnaval moche* (Levallois-Perret: Manya, 1992).

58 Roland Barthes, *Camera Lucida*, trans. Richard Howard (New York: Hill and Wang, 1981). Barthes contrasts this quality to photographs which do not alert the viewer to the 'gaze' – ones which only have 'studium': a mobilization of a 'half-desire'.

59 Unica Zürn (b. 1916, Berlin-Grunewald–d. 1970, Paris). For biographical information, see my entry on Zürn in *Dictionary of Women Artists*, vol. 2, edn, Delia Gaze (London: Fitzroy Dearborn, 1997).

60 This is how Unica Zürn described their relationship in her *Cahier 'Crécy'* (1970), reproduced in *Vacances à Maison Blanche: Derniers Ecrits et Autres Inédits*, trans. and ed. Ruth Henry (Paris: Editions Joelle Losfeld, 2000). See also my essay 'Twist the Body Red: The Art and Lifewriting of Unica Zürn', in *n.paradoxa, international feminist journal* III (1999), pp. 56–63.

described in Zürn's own diaries. Zürn was a schizophrenic – a diagnosis first made in 1957, based on her mental obsession with, and hallucinations of, a male figure she called alternatively 'L'Homme Jasmine', 'Monsieur M' and 'Monsieur ma Mort' – a father-lover figure of Electra proportions. Her mental state contributed to the stream-of-consciousness style of her writings and accompanying ink drawings and their schizophrenic perspectives. She kept notebooks and diaries on her illness in which she is haunted by Nazi imagery, Jewish victims, jack-booted doctors and insane women. She frequently turned to the anagram in her notebooks as a means of expressing her divided Self, and it was Bellmer who specifically introduced her to the anagram (as well as automatic drawing and decalcomania) as an artistic technique.

Zürn's anagrams might be described as both Surrealist and Sadean in their depiction of a world in which the banal becomes nightmarish and then terrifying, expressed through the subversion of common sayings and associations. For example, in one series of anagrams, death and desire overlap, and the body is twisted and manipulated through alliteration and repetition:

> Twist the body red / Twirl bread into dread / end the need, the hatchet, / hatches life. Your death looms / on the loom, your lead / will lead to loam. Wild harbingers, / we dote on death.[61]

Zürn's writing style involved that cutting and *jouissance* typical of Bellmer, twisting the normal meaning of words, cutting up phrases, and using alliteration for dramatic, violent effect. In *L'Homme Jasmine* (*The Man of Jasmine*), a text written from 1957 to 1967, Zürn used the anagram in a manner that allowed the reader to get a glimpse into her schizophrenic world of inner voices and faces. Zürn writes that she 'gains the impression that she is a medium', that there is 'a famous poet reciting a poem' in her belly, that she must kill herself just as a scorpion must 'stab this glory with her own sting'.[62] Her own body becomes her enemy from within, that which stifles and threatens her, and the anagram takes on an almost monstrous force in her life:

> The old, dangerous fever of the anagrams has her in its grip. She creates one after another. Dangerous for her because, once again, she shuts herself off completely from her surroundings.[63]

The anagram seems to be a compulsive catharsis for Zürn, pushing her to the edge of her insanity and leading to a paradoxical realization and loss of her Self at the same time.

---

61 This translation from German is given by Renée Riese Hubert, in *Magnifying Mirrors: Women Surrealists and Partnership* (Lincoln and London: University of Nebraska Press, 1994), p. 149.

62 Unica Zürn, *The Man of Jasmine, and Other Stories*, trans. M. Green (London: Atlas Press, 1994) pp. 41, 70, 98.

63 Ibid., p. 118.

Bellmer admired Zürn's work for its corporeal-textual instability – again, an instability similar to his own pictorial work. In an essay on her anagrams, published as a postscript to Zürn's *Hexentexte* (*Witchy Texts*) in 1954, he wrote of the 'anatomy of the image' and how the anagram, like the anatomy, invites us to dissect it into parts:

> We do not know much about the birth and anatomy of 'the image'. Truly, the human being knows his language even less than he knows his body: the sentence may be compared to a body, which invites us to disarticulate it, in order that its true contents may be recomposed through an endless series of anagrams. If one examines it closely, the anagram is born from a violent and paradoxical conflict [...] this feeling leads to an overpowering 'scent' and feverish readiness for discovery.[64]

This similarity between the cut-up body and the cut-up phrase is emphasized by Bellmer in one key example of the anagram that he explores in this postscript, namely the word 'Leib' (body) – which fascinates him as it could become 'Lieb' (love) or 'Beil' (hatchet/cleaver). The same letters, when alternated, become radically different, emphasizing the slippage between love and destruction and the ambivalent status of the body as cipher for either or both.

These ideas were explored by Bellmer in *L'Anatomie de l'image*. Here Bellmer continued to discuss his fascination with the feverish slippage between love and violence, describing of a photograph of a man and a woman he has bound with wire:

> We have a clear memory of a certain photograph of a man, who, in order to transform his victim, had tightly bound her thighs, shoulders and breasts with tight metal wire, criss-crossing in all directions, causing blisters, irregular spherical triangles running along the folds of the flesh, unsavoury lips, creating multiple breasts in unspeakable settings.[65]

The following year, in 1958, Bellmer took a series of photographs of Zürn which mimicked this image of cruelty and which seem to enact the anagrammatic example written of in *Hexentexte* where love (*Lieb*) or body (*Leib*) turns to a weapon for butchery, a cleaver (*Beil*). In a series of black and white photographs Bellmer binds Zürn in a manner similar to the 'victim' in *La Petite Anatomie*: manipulating her flesh to create 'multiple breasts' and binding her limbs to create very real traces of confinement on her body. The topography of these photographs is similar to those he made of his dolls: bleak close-ups of the objectified female, macabre in their intimacy and shocking in their domesticity.[66]

64 Hans Bellmer, postscript to Unica Zürn, *Hexentexte* (Berlin: Galerie Springer, 1954); trans. in Lichenstein, *Behind Closed Doors*, in Appendix, p. 175.

65 Bellmer, *L'Anatomie de l'image*, p. 40.

66 One might also compare Bellmer's tying up of the *Doll* and his 1958 photographs of Unica Zürn to Man Ray's *Vénus restaurée*, a headless plaster mannequin bound in rope of 1936 (object now lost, photograph only).

Like his earlier photographs, they are formally very beautiful: the texture of flesh is contrasted to that of wool and of cord and the body is framed in an unnatural way, the lens looming in like an anthropological explorer of physical abnormality. At the same time, the viewer becomes conscious of being the lens, of his or her role as voyeur within this corporeal manipulation.

One of these images of Zürn was reproduced on the cover of the Spring edition of *Le Surréalisme, même* in 1958. It is an image of her curled up on a bed, viewed from behind, and bound with twine so that the flesh of her back and thighs has turned into triangular, breast-like forms. Inside the cover of the review, the title of the photograph was given, 'Keep in a Cool Place', as indicated in Bellmer's mock-up (fig. 56). This title could be an attempt to remove the body from its real context, to keep it safely with the Surrealist discourse of 'mad love' or 'black humour'. Yet, if one remembers Bellmer's link between the body and cutting, his choice of title becomes much more disturbing and subversive: woman's body has been reduced to a joint of meat, fresh, bound and ready for consumption, playing with that *Leib-Beil* inversion or even the double meaning of the German word *Fleisch* as both 'flesh' and 'meat'.

However, a historical and political contextualization of Zürn's work leads us beyond the formal and into the inter-textual to view this collaboration, like her writing, as part of a life-writing. In Zürn's writings we are led into a violent world of black-booted soldiers, doctors and an ever-present 'fifth column' that spies on her – into the world of the hysteric, the paranoid woman, the monstrous. It is a world where she unremittingly seems to question herself about humanity itself as her nightmarish fantasies lead her from personal trauma to political trauma. For example, in *Notes concernant la dernière (?) crise* (*Notes on her Last (?) Crisis*, 1967), she sees the face of Charlie Chaplin turn to that of Hitler and then she writes that 'she sees the Jews who were tortured to death during the Nazi era. She looks at the clouds until dark falls, and she knows that today an elect community of people is standing on the roofs of buildings all over the world, and that like her they had been witnesses to the past'.[67] In Zürn's *Cahier 'Crécy'* (*Crécy Notebook*, 1970) another traumatic episode is documented where she describes smoking a cigarette and having a tremendous fear of suffocating herself and then all her fellow patients, then Paris and the entire world, so that she would 'resemble the Nazis who had killed millions of Jews'.[68]

As a woman who worked for Ufa (Universum-Film-AG) from 1933, and who collaborated with the Nazi political regime during the war – even if unwittingly – her writing seems frequently to return to one dreaded question – whether she is 'as terrible a murderer' as the Nazis.[69] Her exploration of the psychology of violence itself in her earlier anagrammatic work, in her notebooks written during

67 Zürn, *The Man of Jasmine*, p. 128.
68 Unica Zürn, *Cahier 'Crécy'* (1970), in *Vacances à Maison Blanche*, p. 98.
69 Ibid., p. 98.

hospitalization, coupled with her photographic collaboration with Bellmer, suggest that her obsessive exploration of fragmentation (physical and mental) is similar to Bellmer's need to explore the psychology of fascism and what she describes as 'these instincts, the most vile and the most repulsive, of the mass'.[70] Her fascination with the victimization of Jews by the Nazis seems to interplay with the disintegration of her identity, both being presented to the reader in a stream-of-consciousness writing style which transports the reader to the place of the Other.

Equally, Bellmer's photographs of Zürn may seem to take his exploration of the 'cutting' and *jouissance* of the Other to its logical aesthetic extreme. The emphasis on multiplicity and muteness in a bound, passive female form photographed so that her head is cropped from the picture frame, seems to anticipate Lyotard's call for 'the dissection of polymorphous perversion, spread out the immense membrane of the libidinal "body" which is quite different to the frame'.[71]

Libidinal Politics

To fully appreciate any work of art we must appreciate the complex political, ideological and psychological dynamics involved in its production. We must appreciate it as a 'text' that comes to us through many texts, or as Frederic Jameson words it, as a text that we apprehend 'through sedimented layers of previous interpretations'.[72]

To appreciate the subversive potential of Bellmer's work and the agenda behind his anagrammatic body-permutations one must locate him within his very particular socio-historical framework and in terms of contemporary gender and national politics. Viewing his photographs of the first and second dolls alongside those of two lovers, Mitrani and Zürn, respectively, allows us to appreciate the intertextual nature of his art and its consistent exploration of libidinal excess and libidinal politics. In his programme of 'cutting' or 'disarticulation' Bellmer presents images of sexual violence that are haunted by a will to evil. These images focus on the power of the Other to confront us with a heterogeneous monstrosity when appreciated against the backdrop of Germany under the Third Reich and the body politic it propagated.

In an interview in 1972 Bellmer stated 'If my work is found to scandalize, that is because for me the world is scandalous'.[73] His anagrammatic art and

70 Ibid., p. 41.

71 Lyotard, *Libidinal Economy*, p. 2.

72 Frederic Jameson, *The Political Unconscious: Narrative as a Socially Symbolic Act* (London: Routledge, 1981), p. 9.

73 Webb, *The Erotic Arts*, p. 370.

writing consistently conflate the flesh and the machine, desire and horror, so that lyricism is never free of abjection and we as viewers/readers are not sure whether we are being presented with a call for humanism or for terror. This, understandably, creates scandalous art – it make us uneasy, makes us 'suffer'. However, as Julia Kristeva has written, 'suffering is the place of the subject': we must face, and go through, the abject in all its libidinal *jouissance*.[74] Bellmer's art must be understood in light of his experience of a Nazi regime that despised the Other and operated a libidinal economy of horror, brutalization and suffering. To understand Bellmer is to understand his libidinal politics as the active and subversive transgressing and perverting of that Nazi psyche.

74 Julia Kristeva, *Powers of Horror: An Essay on Abjection,* trans. Leon S. Roudiez (New York: Columbia University Press, 1982), p. 140.

Chapter 13

Attacks of the Fantastic

Donald LaCoss

> Such fantastic pictures of future society, painted at a time when the proletariat is still in a very undeveloped state and had but a fantastic conception of its own position, correspond with the first instinctive yearnings of that class for a general reconstruction of society [...]. The significance of critical-utopian socialism and communism bears an inverse relation to historical development. In proportion as the modern class struggle develops and takes definite shape, this fantastic standing apart from the contest, these fantastic attacks on it, lose all practical value and all theoretical justification.
>
> Marx & Engels[1]

> In view of the solutions that are asked of us, routine completely upholstered in velvet is the most dangerous. Routine hatches more distress and death than any imaginary utopia.
>
> André Breton[2]

André Breton faced a hornet's nest of criticism when he returned to Paris from exile in the New World. Pro-Stalinist writers and publishers were promoting the notion that Surrealist political activity had been abandoned since 1940 and replaced with a fixation on mythological themes, magical thinking and utopian-socialist castles in the air. They supported their position by pointing to Breton's wartime projects: 'Prolégomènes à un troisième manifeste du surréalisme ou non' proposed the creation of a new 'social myths',[3] for instance, or 'Les Etats généraux' (1943), a poem that appeared to do nothing for the war effort since it called for 'the black race and the red race' to free themselves from white domination and for women to rise up against their male oppressors. The long and lyrical *Ode à Charles Fourier* struck many critics as equally irrelevant; composed by Breton on the road and rails between Chicago, Nevada and the Athapaskan and Zuñi reservations in the southwestern US, the poem was a

1 Karl Marx and Friedrich Engels, 'Manifesto of the Communist Party [1848]', translation from 1888 English edition, rpd in Robert C. Tucker, ed., *The Marx-Engels Reader* (New York: Norton, 1978), p. 498.

2 André Breton, *Arcane 17* (New York: Brentano's, 1944); English translation as *Arcanum 17*, trans. Zack Rogow (Los Angeles: Sun and Moon Press, 1994), p. 112. Translation modified.

3 André Breton, 'Prolégomènes à un troisième manifeste du surréalisme ou non', *VVV*, no. 1 (June 1942), pp. 18–26.

prismatic amalgam of automatic writing and hashed-together excerpts from the works of the eponymous eccentric pre-Marxist utopian writer.[4] And then there was *Arcane 17*, Breton's book-length text – although completed in Quebec during the anxious weeks following the D-Day invasion, the essay was more interested in the nineteenth-century occultist Eliphas Lévi, tarot cards, Romantic socialist anarchism and a folktale of the mermaid-fairy Melusina than in the war in Europe.[5] In their reading of these works, as well as the exhibitions of 1942 and 1947, Surrealism's foes claimed that they could find no progressive political content; some, in fact, decried Surrealism as reactionary or counter-revolutionary, since these works seemed to be encouraging fantasies rather than actually organizing people's dissatisfaction in a more 'practical' manner. Critics pounced on Surrealism for being obsolete and immaterial to the harsh conditions of the postwar world, saying that Surrealist activity succeeded only in doping the masses into quiescent states of subordination with their illusions, metaphysical evasions and reverie.

During a conversation published in the early spring of 1948, the interviewer, Aimé Patri, spurred Breton to respond to some of these charges. 'Since your return from the United States, a number of people have been claiming that Surrealism is dead', Patri proposed. 'Even some of your intimates have reproached you for abandoning the old Surrealist revolutionary spirit'.[6] Of particular confusion in this regard was the Surrealist insistence upon the 'poetic and historical function' of mythic and utopian thinking, investigations that seemed to 'entail an escape towards the past or outside of time' and an obvious affront to the doctrine of historical materialism that the French Stalinists proclaimed that they were exercising.[7] Breton responded by saying that his exposure to the daily functions of myth among the Hopi and the Haitians convinced him that the 'latent' content of waking life could be mobilized as a means of cultural resistance under adverse political and economic conditions. As for utopianism, Breton said that he was aware that there were many on the left who, 'with a shrug of the shoulders', saw it as 'the most poisonous' form of progressive thought. However, so long as people do not limit themselves to defining 'utopia' as 'dreams that, to all appearances,

---

4 André Breton, *Ode à Charles Fourier* (Paris: Editions de la Revue Fontaine, 1947).

5 *Arcane 17* was originally published in New York by Bretano's in 1944, and re-released in June 1947 by the Parisian publisher Sagittaire.

6 The turn toward Fourier sparked some internal problems for the movement in the years immediately following the war. Henri Pastoureau, *Ma Vie surréaliste* (Paris: Editions Maurice Nadeau, 1992), p. 207.

7 André Breton, interviewed by Aimé Patri, *Paru* (March 1948), rpd in Breton, *Entretiens 1913–1952* (Paris: Gallimard, 1952), English translation as *Conversations: The Autobiography of Surrealism*, trans. Mark Polizzotti (New York: Marlowe, 1991), pp. 213–20. Translation modified.

are impracticable',[8] then contemporary revolutionary militants should be free to comb through these social projects 'for anything viable'.

In the pages that follow, I take Breton at his word and explore how the Surrealist promotion of utopianism was not 'an escape towards the past or outside of time' (as Patri had put it), but was rather an integral part of the form and content of the movement's postwar radical politics.[9] Rather than see irresponsible flights of fancy, I read the Surrealists' research into utopianism after World War II as an effort to refine and deepen its commitments to social transformation, one that can be understood as part of the movement's political algorithm that lasts at least two decades to the wildcat uprisings and strike council occupations of 1968. While the paths of a dozen critical-utopian socialists and revolutionary Romanticists crisscross the magnetic fields of the postwar Surrealist political landscape, the single trail that I will follow in this essay is the one blazed by Charles Fourier. *Ode à Charles Fourier* (1944), the inclusion of five of Fourier's selections in Breton's *Anthologie de l'humour noir* (1950), and the Surrealist group's 1965 'L'Ecart absolu' international Surrealist exhibition at the Galerie L'Œil in Paris were just the most obvious of manifestations; from Breton's interest in Fourier in 1937 to the Franco-Czech 'Platform of Prague' Surrealist manifesto of 1968 ('Fourier, Marx, Engels, Lenin, Trotsky and Che Guevara have given revolutionary dynamism its greatest social impact'[10]), Fourier's visionary presence was at least as significant a centre of gravity for Surrealist theory and practice as Ann Radcliffe, Alfred Jarry and Lenin.

Of particular interest to my study of Surrealist politics and its thirst for utopian speculation is Fourier's baffling cosmogony of 1808, *Théorie des quatre mouvements et des destinées générales: Prospectus et annonce de la découverte* (hereafter *Theory of the Four Movements*)[11] and his equally manic *Le Fausse*

---

8 Breton's definition of a utopia may be an intentional reference to Lenin's view: 'Utopia is a wish that can never come true – neither now nor afterwards, a wish that is not based on social forces and not supported by the growth and development of political, class forces'. V.I. Lenin, *Collected Works*, vol. 18: April 1912–March 1913 (Moscow: Progress Publishers, 1963), p. 355. It is interesting to compare this statement to Lenin's defence of D.I. Pisarev's view of dreaming in *What is to be Done?*

9 An excellent turn of phrase here is that of Michel Löwy: 'For revolutionary romanticism, the aim is not a *return* to the past but a *detour* through it, toward a utopian future'. Löwy, 'Under the Star of Romanticism: Walter Benjamin and Herbert Marcuse', in Max Blechman, ed., *Revolutionary Romanticism: Drunken Boat Anthology*, no. 3 (San Francisco: City Lights, 1999), p. 198.

10 Collective declaration, 'The Platform of Prague' [April 1968], trans. in Michael Richardson and Krzysztof Fijalkowski, eds, *Surrealism Against the Current* (London: Pluto Press, 2001), p. 62.

11 Charles Fourier, *Théorie des quatre mouvements et des destinées générales. Prospectus et annonce de la découverte* (Leipzig: n.p., n.d. [Lyon: M. Rustand, 1808]). Unless otherwise noted, all quotations are taken from *The Theory of the Four Movements*, ed. Gareth Stedman Jones and Ian Patterson (New York: Cambridge University Press, 1996).

industrie (1835–36, hereafter *Incoherent Industry*).[12] What Surrealism's critics failed to recognize in the decades after 1945 is that the Surrealist fascination with experimental texts like *Theory of the Four Movements* and *Incoherent Industry* was not intended as an advocacy for a literal, instrumental application of Fourierism. *Theory of the Four Movements* and *Incoherent Industry* were not like those concoctions for bureaucratic authoritarianism peddled by Communist Party functionaries, nor were they the recipes for bourgeois-liberal capitalism publicized by the professional political scientists, lawyers and corporate executives who sat in parliament. Despite Breton's enthusiasm and erudition, neither *Ode à Charles Fourier* nor *Arcane 17* is in any way similar to the great number of 'serious' how-to manuals of applied Fourierism.[13] The handling afforded to *Theory of the Four Movements* and *Incoherent Industry* by the Surrealists is better understood if it can be compared to the psychical demolition practices of Nerval's 'El Desdichado' (1854) and F.W. Murnau's *Nosferatu: Eine Symphonie des Grauens* (1921–22) rather than the Earth Liberation Front's *Setting Fires with Electrical Timers* arson operations manual. Breton says as much:

> I can see no harm in throwing open a window onto the most grandiose of utopian landscapes. An epoch such as ours justifies all journeys taken for the sake of the journey itself (as were those of Bergerac and Gulliver),

---

12 Unless otherwise noted, all quotations attributed to *Incoherent Industry* are taken from the first volume of Charles Fourier, *La Fausse industrie morcelée, répugnante, mensongère, et l'antidote, l'industrie naturelle, combinée, attrayante, véridique, donnat quadruple produit. Mosaïque des faux progress, des ridicules et circles vicieux de civilization. Parallèlle des deux mondes industriels l'ordre morcelé et l'ordre combine* (Paris: Bossange, 1835–36).

13 Fourierism in France peaked with Victor Considérant before the June Days reaction. There were various attempts at Fourierist and quasi-Fourierist intentional communities in England, Germany, the US, Belgium, Sweden, Romania, Spain, Austria-Hungary, Switzerland, Italy, Poland, China, Venezuela and Argentina. In Russia in the late 1840s, there had been an anti-czarist organization (including a young Dostoevsky) committed to implementing Fourier's ideas. See Albert Brisbane, *Concise Exposition of the Doctrine of Association, or a plan for a re-organization of society, which will secure to the human race, individually and collectively, their happiness and elevation, based on Fourier's theory of domestic and industrial association* (New York: J.S. Redfield, 1843), and Mathieu Briancourt, *Visite au phalanstère* (Paris: Librairie phalanstérienne, 1848). There is also the vast body of work by Victor Considérant, such as *Considérations sociales sur l'architectonique* (Paris: Chez les libraires du Palais-Royal, 1834), and *Exposition abrégée du système phalanstérien de Fourier* (Paris: Librairie phalanstérienne, 1848); see also Jonathan Beecher, *Victor Considérant and the Rise and Fall of French Romantic Socialism* (Berkeley: University of California Press, 2001). Readers interested in this aspect of Fourier's work might wish to consult Carl Guarneri, *The Utopian Alternative: Fourierism in Nineteenth-Century America* (Ithaca: Cornell University Press, 1991); and Henri Desroche, *La Société festive: du fouriérisme écrit aux fouriérismes pratiqués* (Paris: Seuil, 1975).

> especially if these journeys make up a challenge to conventional modes of thinking whose failures are only too obvious to all.[14]

In other words, it was not Surrealists' belief in the practicality of the utopian mythologies of Fourier's peculiar socialism that led them to advance his schemes; rather, *Theory of the Four Movements* and *Incoherent Industry* were hailed by the Surrealists for their potentially liberating effect on the imagination, and their ability to do so in a way that far exceeded any other available remedies of the day which insisted on closed political systems. What is most important about this point is that this comparison does not make *Theory of Four Movements* and *Incoherent Industry* any less exemplary or instructional a subversive text from the Surrealists' perspective.

A Calculus of the Destinies

The boom of urban industrial-commercial enterprise that burst over Western Europe between 1760 and 1830 had done so at the expense of the individual's freedom, imagination, spontaneous creativity and sensibilities.[15] There had not been a progressive moral revolution to accompany the violent changes wrought by the Industrial Revolution, and the old, pre-industrial codes of virtue and ethics had become inextricably complicit in the soulless utilitarianism and egomaniacal materialism of *laissez-faire* bourgeois-liberal domination. This spiritual and mental poverty had inspired Romantics in France, Germany and England to innovate creative models of perception, behaviour and knowledge; in the works of pre-Marxist socialists like Fourier, Saint-Simon and Owens, this translated into the production of a communal ethos that opposed coercion and the selfishly competitive market with visions of just, cooperative, humanitarian solidarity.[16] Anarchists have always been convinced that beings will voluntarily work alongside others for the good of all if the distortions of capitalism, the Church, and State are dispelled; similarly, the Romantic socialists understood that the human capacities for altruism, progressive teamwork and shared passion

14 Breton, 'Prolégomènes à un troisième manifeste', pp. 18–26. Eighteenth- and nineteenth-century utopian thought has always informed Surrealist works; the alert reader can trace mention of such thinkers all the way back to an illustration from Nicolas Restif de la Bretonne, *La Découverte australe par un homme volant ou, le Dédale français* (1781) rpd in a collage included in an early issue of *Littérature*.

15 Surrealist Humphrey Jennings's *Pandaemonium: The Coming of the Machine as Seen by Contemporary Observers, 1660–1886* (New York: Free Press, 1985) is a brilliant compilation of evidence for this view.

16 See Henri Louvancour, *De Henri Saint-Simon à Charles Fourier: Etude sur le socialisme romantique français de 1830* (Chartres, 1913); and M. Friedberg, *L'Influence de Charles Fourier sur le mouvement contemporain en France* (Paris, 1926).

were pooled just below the hardened shellac of self-interest, self-estrangement and violence of all who lived in a capitalist society.

In the specific case of Fourier, his utopianism shared anarchism's distaste for authoritarian social organization and economic competition while respecting the value of individual differences, voluntary associations and the sanctity of desire; consequently, his inspired treatment for correcting the defects of modern Western civilization have long been recognized as foundational in the development of European socialism.[17] An embittered travelling textile salesman who had been imprisoned by the Jacobins and later spied on by the secret police apparatuses of Napoléon and the Bourbon Restoration, Fourier felt that he understood the ways that the Enlightenment's revolutionary ideals could be hijacked to serve tyrants and capitalists. The alienating tedium of work, the criminal waste of overproduction, and the ugly violence of destitution and class oppression seemed to multiply rather than diminish under this new world order. Fourier was disgusted by the degree to which people's lives could be ruined by an emerging class of professional profiteers and financial speculators and prophetically foretold of a coming age of inequity and misery built by the opaque mechanisms of a so-called 'free' market.[18]

Civilization was a monstrosity that had to be overcome; Fourier's solutions to the disease of civilization called for the creation of a commonwealth not unlike the ones floated by today's anarcho-primitivists who call for semi-rural, decentralized agricultural cooperatives founded upon principles of direct democracy and mutual aid.[19] This scheme for a revolutionary reorganization

---

17 E.S. Mason, 'Fourier and Anarchism', *Quarterly Journal of Economics* XLII:2 (February 1928), pp. 228–62.

18 Fourier's *L'Association domestique agricole* (1822) and *Nouveau monde industriel* (1829) look ahead to a world of increased 'fiscal trickery, systems of extortion, indirect bankruptcy, speculation on anticipated revenue, art of devouring the future [...] encouragement given to commercial plundering and rascality. Speculation given the power to scoff at law, to steal all the fruits of industry, to share in the authority of governments, and to spread everywhere the frenzy of gambling in public funds [...]. The progress of civilization is real enough, but it is progress in the art of legalizing and multiplying every conceivable disorder'. Trans. Jonathan Beecher and Richard Bienvenu in *The Utopian Vision of Charles Fourier: Selected Texts on Work, Love, and Passionate Attraction* (Boston: Beacon Press, 1971), pp. 196–98. This prediction has come true in our age of neo-liberal globalized capitalism, as illustrated by the practices of the World Trade Organization and the International Monetary Fund.

19 For more on contemporary anarcho-primitivism, deep ecology, and neo-Pleistocene critiques of civilization, readers may turn to John Zerzan's edited anthology *Against Civilization: Readings and Reflections* (London: Uncivilized Books, 1999), and *Future Primitive and Other Essays* (New York: Autonomedia/CAL Press, 1994); David Watson, *Against the Megamachine: Essays on Empire and its Enemies* (New York: Autonomedia, 1998); George Sessions, ed., *Deep Ecology for the Twenty-First Century* (Boston: Shambhala, 1994). Other commentators have pointed to the parallels between Fourier's thinking on pedagogy and some of the more libertarian theories of Western

of life on all planes of existence was the subject matter of his first book, *Theory of the Four Movements*; in its pages, Fourier folded vigorous condemnations of market competition, bureaucracy, the oppression of women,[20] and the moralistic suffocation of desire into a pioneering 'new field of thought' of his own invention that fell somewhere between philosophy, industrial psychology and prophecy. He proposed a minimum living standard, worker self-management, locally autonomous voluntary associations, and a restoration of existential meaning to the tasks of (mostly agrarian-artisanal) labour. But he made allowances for other changes to accompany these economic and social improvements, such as a near-hallucinatory state of sensual creation and gratification – a series of bold new notions on gastronomic (or to use his neologism, 'gastrophical') hygiene as the solution to starvation, malnutrition and gluttony – and wildly advanced forms of intimate, sincere sexual expression. He also countered capitalism's engineering of social space through urban planning with his own plans for building and maintaining a more progressive and socially just physical infrastructure.

Theory of the Four Movements (published the same year, coincidentally, as another Surrealist favourite, Hegel's *Phenomenology of the Spirit*) introduced Fourier's utopia under the disguise of proposals for commercial and agronomic reforms, and it served as the recyclable source for many of his later works. But what is most stunning about his treatise is the way that his reform package is bound to a wildly original understanding of natural history and cosmology that cuts deeply across the grain of conventional notions of 'civilization'. Because Fourier had been looking to create a profoundly revolutionary body of ideas, he avoided the usual approaches that sought 'social well-being through religious or governmental innovations', finding instead 'good only in functions which had no connection with priesthood or administration'. It was through the critical rejection of all existing political, social and moral codes that Fourier said he first caught a glimpse of the mechanisms of 'passionate attraction' – natural impulses and cadences that occur on a level below the threshold of thought processes and which persist regardless of civilization's attempt to repress them through the

---

educational reformers. As with all anarchists, the State, the military and religion were targets for Fourier; political systems and hierarchies of authority were inherently flawed and needed to be swept away in order for deep liberty to be achieved. Some might argue that the meticulous (if not obsessive) degree of detail and synchronization that went into Fourier's theories was indicative of an authoritarian streak (he was explicit in his formulae: statistics for the harvest of eggs and cherries, minute-by-minute work timetables, meal schedules and menus, furniture design for children, and specific colour patterns for the clothing), but his intention was to radically overhaul the structures of human life in order to set it on the road to harmony, at which point these structures will seemingly wither away since life will have become more intuitively natural.

20 'The extension of privileges to women is the general principle of all social progress'. Fourier, *The Theory of the Four Movements*, p. 195.

artificial constructs of moralization, rationalization, guilt, fear and intolerance. If one were to recalibrate his or her life to that unified rhythmic pulse buried under the noise and tumult of modern life, and work toward building social formations that were similarly fine-tuned to these rhythms, then human life would evolve into a new, more natural harmonious order of cooperative unity, free passion, profound fulfilment and ludic pleasure.

The cosmogony presented in *Theory of the Four Movements* is derived from the discovery of the Four Movements (social, animal, organic and material) that govern the 'General System of Nature', and the study of these movements that extends well beyond the physics of Newton and the metaphysics of Leibniz towards a previously unimagined hinterland of knowledge that Fourier calls a 'calculus of the destinies'. The paths of comets are predetermined by fluctuating gravitational fields, magnetic positions and planetary orbits; so too, the burning flames of human thought, action and emotion were guided by the quantum mechanics of 'impassioned gravitation' and 'passionate geometries'. It is only through reconciling life to these forces that human progress and joy could be achieved. As a result of this theorization, *Theory of the Four Movements* can be approached as an attempt to represent rehumanized and re-energized human beings derived from an ecological understanding of their universe rather then the isolated, alienated abstractions devised by the lawmakers, factory bosses, church ministers and judges who surround us today.

In Fourier's text, harmonies as unmistakable as those found in mathematics and music emerge that would be the codes for a new commonwealth whose ideal socioeconomic unit was the 'phalanx', a tightly-linked, intricately-interdependent and self-contained community that would no longer impinge upon the needs, desires and self-development of individuals through coercive laws, ethical discipline and economic exploitation. Properly erected, the phalanx would make all existing economic, moral and political theories obsolete: the fallout of modern industrial life (meaningless labour, poverty, pollution, alienation, boredom, misery and violence) would be eliminated, and the way is then prepared for 'the coming social metamorphosis' that promises to be 'the most astounding, and happiest, event possible on this or any other globe: *the transition from social chaos to universal harmony*'.

Theory of the Four Movements offers detailed accounts of life following this cataclysmic transmogrification. The auroras of the northern and southern circumpolar regions become more active and more frequent, eventually expanding to link together like the rings of Saturn and filling the earth's skies with rippling curtains of colour, light and heat. Over time, the outer edge of the earth's aurora-ring will extend to the corona of the sun, and the ensuing radiation will trigger a magical change in the natural world – animals will learn to play musical instruments, stars will copulate and spray us all with their sexual fluids, weather patterns will shift, new moons begin to revolve the earth, and the chemical composition of the world's oceans change to 'aigresel', a tart, potable liquid. Even the human body mutates under the rays of the 'northern crown' as human beings overcome the need for sleep and grow taller. Humans will also sprout an 'archibras' ('ancient arm'), a prehensile tail with a sensory organ at its tip that will act as a fifth limb and enable one 'to swim as fast as a fish', to 'reach a branch twelve feet high', to triple one's natural leaping velocity, and to form a revolving, conelike 'inverted parachute by means of which one can fall from a considerable height without risking more than a bruise'.[21]

It is obvious that *Theory of the Four Movements* was not a carefully crafted recipe for creating a Fourierist commune, nor did the Surrealists ever claim that organizing phalansteries would be the best solution to France's postwar political problems (as Jean Gaulmier points out, Fourier's critique of commerce would have relevance for anyone who had been forced to deal with the black market in France between 1940 and 1945).[22] Still, Stalinist anti-Surrealists (and more recent academics who have written on Surrealism) discarded the claims made by Breton and his circle to postwar political relevance that were based on an endorsement of an 'impossible' project such as Fourier's.[23] Utopianism was not political science, it was political science-fiction – since prehensile tails for

21 See Jonathan Beecher, 'L'Archibras de Fourier, un manuscrit censuré', *La Brèche: Action surréaliste*, no. 7 (December 1964), pp. 66–68; Charles Fourier, 'L'Archibras', ibid., pp. 69–71. Beecher happened upon the archibras text while doing research in the Archives Nationales between 1962–64 and realized that it had been expurgated from Fourier's work by Victor Considérant. Thinking that 'this was just the kind of thing that André Breton would be interested in', Beecher contacted the Surrealist group about his project and was subsequently invited by Vincent Bounoure to submit the piece for publication in *La Brèche*. According to Beecher, neither the archibras text nor his '*présentation de texte*' have ever been republished, but much of that material reappears in Beecher's *Victor Considérant*. Correspondence with author (16 March 2001). The story of the archibras adds a new dimension to Breton's statement in the *Second manifeste du surréalisme* that 'for our part, we say that we [Surrealists] are today willing to appear historically as the tail end of romanticism – but, if this be the case, then as an exceedingly prehensile tail'. André Breton, *Second manifeste du surréalisme* (Paris: Editions Kra, 1930).

22 See Gaulmier's annotations in Breton, *Ode à Charles Fourier. Edition présentée avec une introduction et des notes de Jean Gaulmier* (Paris: Klincksieck, 1961), p. 82, n. 12.

23 At the 1947 Galerie Maeght Surrealist exposition, the staircase entry into the space was made up to appear as a bookcase: each of the 21 steps was modified to appear as the spine of a book important to the Surrealists' formula for cultural revolution, including Rousseau's *Les Rêveries du promeneur solitaire* (1782); a volume of Friedrich Hölderlin's collected 'poems of madness' from the early 1800s; Kafka's *Der Prozess* (1925); Emmanuel Swedenborg's *Memorabilia, seu Diarium spirituale* (1766); and James G. Frazer's *The Golden Bough: A Study in Magic and Religion* (1900–23). Fourier's *Théorie des quatre mouvements* was prominently displayed in the installation, sandwiched between the notoriously difficult 'Second Part' of Goethe's (anti-)Romantic tragedy *Faust* (1831) and Xavier Forneret's wicked short story 'Et la lune donnait et la rosée tombait' (1836).

human beings were not the kind of realistic or practical solutions that parliamentary parties were pursuing between 1945 and 1950 in France in their efforts to resurrect the bourgeois republic and rebuild the French Empire, they should not be mentioned.

But what is truly radical in *Theory of the Four Movements* and *Incoherent Industry* is precisely that they are both wonderfully weird reads. It is their outrageously and unabashedly unfeasible criticism of capitalism, repressive family values and Western civilization – not their prescriptive acumen – that make these texts so revolutionary.[24] Practical policies like Five Year Plans, Monnet Plans, and Marshall Plans would never correct the most damaged and miserable features of human existence; that could only be addressed by redefining the very terms of the problem, by opening new avenues of alternatives, by contemplating the unthinkable and doing the unattainable. 'Poets and artists in particular would be inexcusable if they tried to guard against "utopias" ' solely on the basis of their supposed viability, Breton told Patri in the 1948 interview. Imagining the unimaginable is the responsibility of all creative people, often requiring them 'to draw, at least initially, from the vague realm where utopia reigns'.[25] This may be escapism, but as one underground

24 Fourier's exuberantly disjointed narrative make it even more so: chapters start, stop and are 'omitted' (though inexplicably included). A few years later, Fourier wrote an essay that said that his strange ramblings made him into a visionary holy fool who could get away with speaking the ugly truth to authority. He claimed that the 'studied bizarreness' of *Theory of the Four Movements* had been a ruse: he had concealed his very serious social critiques of contemporary civilization beneath and between eruptions of wild speculation in order to catch wary readers off guard and to draw critical fire, thereby anticipating possible objections to his theory while simultaneously playing a practical joke on the pretentious Parisian intellectual class that he despised. He was also concerned, it seems, that plagiarists would steal his ideas, but not if they were presented in such a loopy manner. This may have been his intent all along, or the later essay may have been an act of face-saving rationalization constructed after the fact by an embarrassed Fourier – the evidence is inconclusive and, for our purposes, beside the point, since it was the poetical impossibilities of *Theory of the Four Movements* that excited the Surrealists. See Fourier, 'Le Sphinx sans Oedipe, ou l'énigme des quatre mouvements', *La Phalange*, no. 9 (1849), p. 195. For more on this, compare the argument offered by Frank E. Manuel in *The Prophets of Paris* (Cambridge: Harvard University Press, 1962), pp. 243–48 to that of Jonathan Beecher, *Charles Fourier: The Visionary and His World* (Berkeley: University of California Press, 1986), p. 120. See also Frank E. Manuel and Fritzie P. Manuel, *Utopian Theory in the Western World* (Cambridge: Belknap, 1979), pp. 671–74. Fourier also claimed that the wild and woolly presentation of his theories in the *Theory of the Four Movements* was a way of avoiding the police censors that had been monitoring him since at least 1803; see '1818 Introduction', in Fourier, *Theory of the Four Movements*, p. 312.

25 André Breton, interviewed by Aimé Patri, *Paru* (March 1948), rpd in Breton, *Conversations*, p. 217. Translation modified.

newspaper of late has explained, those who most forcefully discourage escape often turn out to be prison wardens of one sort or another.[26]

Fragments for a Surrealist Utopia

Up until 1940, Breton's familiarity with Fourier's visionary writing had been culled from his reading of commentary by Engels and Marx on the traditions of critical-utopian socialism and extracts of Fourierism found in anthologies of social reformers.[27] He said that one morning in 1937 he noticed a bouquet of flowers anonymously left at the foot of Fourier's statue at rue Caulaincourt and boulevard de Clichy in the eighteenth *arrondissement*; at the time, he had been intrigued by this curious but passionate gesture honouring the one hundred-year anniversary of the half-forgotten socialist thinker's death (Fourier died on 10 October 1837), and it was only later, after his own serious study of Fourierism while living in the US during the war, that Breton understood the value of Fourier's ideas for Surrealism.

Before his trip West from New York City with the Chilean writer and photographer Elisa Latte Elena Bindoff Enet in 1945, Breton purchased the five-volume 1846 edition of Fourier's complete works in a used-book store to read along the way; he later claimed that they were the only books that he took with him on his trip westward.[28] He began work on his poetic ode to Fourier while on the road; in its final version, the poem makes allusions to the myths and the realities of the American West, including gold rushes and the Grand Canyon, as well as the ritual art and culture of the aboriginal peoples of Arizona and New Mexico. His love for Elisa, Fourier's revolutionary ardour, and the sensual drama of the southwestern deserts surge and snake through the stanzas of *Ode à Charles Fourier* like tributaries. There is also a steady stream of reminders of the grim struggles, philosophies and pleasures of Native Americans on the reservations, 'an oppressed people if there ever was one', says Breton.[29] A

26 'When we cannot stomach another hour of *this*, we side with those moments when we surprise ourselves, flashes in which anything feels possible, peak experiences that may last only instants. Call this escapist – perhaps it is; but what class of people is most disturbed by the idea of escape? *Jailers*. Right or wrong, selfless or selfish, possible or impossible, we're *getting out of here*'. CrimethInc. Secret Service, 'Until our most fantastic demands are met, fantasy will always be at war with reality', *Harbinger*, no. 4 (n.d. [November 2001]), p. 1.

27 Gérald Schaeffer, 'Un petit matin de 1937', in Marc Eigeldinger, ed., *André Breton: Essais et témoignages* (Neuchâtel: La Baconnière, 1950), pp. 83–110.

28 This according to an excerpt of a letter from Breton to Jean Gaulmier dated 21 January 1958 and rpd in *Ode à Charles Fourier* (1961).

29 Breton, quoted in an interview with Claudine Chonez for *Gazette des lettres* (31 July 1948), rpd in *Conversations*, p. 225. See also the Surrealist endorsement of the French edition of Don Talayesva, *Soleil hopi. L'Autobiographie d'un Indien hopi* (Paris: Plon, 1959).

rhythm of liberty and trust in the potential for radical change restlessly drive the work despite the haze of frustration, uncertainty, and confusion that must have surrounded Breton in his travels, and his free play with the a variety of myths of emancipation in the poem hint at a mind that sees more than just the human animal's ability to survive the morass of a six-year-old international crisis – more importantly and most urgently, he recognized a unique opportunity for the advancement of human progress.

Many critics in France and elsewhere found fault with Breton for *Ode à Charles Fourier*'s supposed apoliticism and its headlong flight into socially irresponsible fantasies of golden ages and New Jerusalems. But for those willing to read it against the dominant political exigencies of its day, the poem may arguably be Breton's most political in its uncompromising dedication to contemplating lives that did not return to normal after the war, but were motivated to demand more than ever before from one another and from their society. *Ode à Charles Fourier* does not sidestep the problems of post-bellum reconstruction in a post-fascist world, but instead refuses to surrender, revelling in fractured visions of long-lost alternatives and dreams of newfound possibilities. Perhaps Georges Bataille summed it up best in his review of the poem: 'Breton has given poetic expression to that hope that the great utopian [Fourier] has nurtured inside of him. But if it is possible to regret that more positive results have not come from it, then why not one recognize that it could be poetry itself that may mark its coming?'[30]

Another example of Breton's open enthusiasm for the hope promised in *Theory of the Four Movements* was a three-page fragment of an unfinished, undated and untitled draft for a Surrealist utopian text that, had it been completed, would have been more than two hundred pages in length with thirty illustrations.[31] Breton's brief notes for this unrealized effort are tantalizing, beginning where Fourier's aigresel, archibras and sidereal orgies left off in order to imagine a brave new world where encounters with 'personifications of oneiric forces' would be common. Breton's proposal also suggests that there will be discussions on ethics, a new declaration of human rights, an expansion of the dynamics of erotic love, and a 'new totemism', all of which would occur under clouds which take on stunning new shapes[32] and several new orbiting moons. Our planet would circle two suns (one of which is crescent-shaped) in Breton's

30 Georges Bataille's review of Breton's *Ode à Charles Fourier* in *Critique*, no. 18 (November 1947), p. 67.

31 André Breton, ['Projet d'écrit utopique'], rpd with a brief explanatory commentary by Philippe Bernier in Breton, *Œuvres complètes*, vol. 3 (Paris: Gallimard, 1988), pp. 343–45, 1243–44.

32 Incidentally, the 'Salle des superstitions' at the 1947 Surrealist exposition had a lowered ceiling from which hung bizarre clouds of gray organic forms designed by Yves Tanguy.

estimation, every 111 and 83 days, respectively. Nights last only one hour and only a few stars are visible, but their light would be more visible and the colours more intense. Breton's utopia also covered flora and fauna, particularly the increase in number of certain species of birds; ruminants would become extinct, but the number of star-nosed moles and Gila monster lizards would increase.[33] As in Fourier's work, Breton sees a situation where human physiology changes dramatically, and there would be a blurring of distinction between animals, vegetables and minerals – Breton refers to flint-ostriches, amethyst-trees, ferns of gold, pearl-moss, and dog-bottles inhabiting the ruins of lighthouses, churches, pyramids and petrified banyan trees.[34]

Had it seen publication in its day, there is little doubt that the imaginative extremism of Breton's utopian speculation would have been as controversial for the movement as had been their loud allegiances to Lenin, Luxemburg and Trotsky in the interwar era. But after ten years of seeing Europe crushed under the boots of fascist murderers and their self-serving political collaborators, the time had come for an even more revolutionary flavour of liberation that had exceeded the fantasies of Marx and Engels – there was a need for a set of ideas that would totally reorder the very fabric of the universe in the service of freedom, and the Surrealists saw this as the best reason for a renaissance of Romantic socialism and Fourierist poetics.[35] In a postwar political climate dominated by the viciously cynical Jesuit device of 'ends justify means',[36] talk

---

33 A room was constructed with 12 octagonal recesses where one viewed eerie altars dedicated to mythical beings or objects at the 1947 Galerie Maeght exposition, including characters from Jarry, Rimbaud and Lautréamont; magical objects by Duchamp and Victor Brauner; and totemic wild animals such as the predatory secretary bird (*Sagittarius serpentarius*), the star-nosed mole (*Condylura cristata*), and the Gila monster (*Heloderma suspectum*). Breton's mention of these animals in his utopian writing fragment helps to date it to this same period.

34 Mention of petrified banyan trees may help to date this document as well: in *Ode à Charles Fourier*, Breton writes: 'I salute you from the Petrified Forest of human culture/where nothing has been left standing', an allusion, perhaps, to his visit to the Painted Desert or Petrified Forest National Park in Arizona during the summer of 1945. Likewise the mention of Gila monsters, which Breton also records in his notebook during his trip and returns to in his utopian writing.

35 The centenary anniversary of the French revolutions of 1848 contributed to this atmosphere, surely; see Félix Armand, *Les fouriéristes et les luttes révolutionnaires de 1848 à 1851* (Paris: Presses universitaires de France, 1948). Breton is credited as being among the first to attempt to recover the work of Fourier. Beecher and Bienvenu, *The Utopian Vision of Charles Fourier*, pp. 416–17.

36 In May 1947, an eight-point questionnaire was circulated by Cause (the 'Bureau d'information et de liaison surréaliste') to members of the movement, and the answers were used to formulate the positions spelled out in *Rupture inaugurale*. According to Henri Pastoureau, Breton insisted on the inclusion of a question: 'In your estimation, does the end always justify the means on the political plane?' Henri Pastoureau, 'Le Fortune de surréalisme. Le Surréalisme de l'après guerre, 1946–1950', in

of Fourier introduced two things that were sorely lacking: a blackly humorous critical (and therefore revolutionary) spark[37] and an unwavering dedication to the complete emancipation of human beings. 'Action, even in the rigorous and unquestioned form it takes today for those who fight in the name of liberty, will only be valuable so long as our interpretation of the world [...] will not have the brakes slammed on it', Breton thundered.[38] The revolutionary poetry of Fourier's socialism was exactly the kind of critical extravagance that a truly free and freedom-respecting society should be able to tolerate and welcome.

The freedom of interpretation was seen by the Surrealists as a litmus test measuring a society's dedication to liberty. And, of course, for Surrealism, a substantial portion of this interpretive process included those critical and cognitive resources outside of instrumental reason, such as instinct and intuition. Fourierism had made provisions for these components of the human mind. What distinguishes some of the more interesting utopian writers from others in their field was their ability to incorporate the twilight territories of the human psyche into their social schema; in Fourier, it was his inclusion of behavioural motivation and deep creativity borne of the chaotic forces of emotion, perception and the sexual drives that made his theories so tantalizing. To their detriment, the public policy equations that constitute modern politics have long chosen to leave out the important emotional complexities in favour of a rationalized civil society and, in so doing, provide a narrowly inadequate set of instructions for the constitution of public affairs.

Utopianists like Fourier, on the other hand, do not shy away from even the most inexplicable of psychosocial factors and subsequently their writings veer into the poetical register. With the rapid narrowing of choices for expression and

---

Henri Jones, *Le Surréalisme ignoré* (Montréal: Centre éducatif et culturel, 1969), p. 128; see also Pastoureau, *Ma vie surréaliste*, p. 112. Although Pastoureau does not say as much, Breton's interest in this question can be traced back to a conversation he had with Camus in New York City about how 'the remaining free intellectuals must combat this particular precept as categorically and as actively as possible. I believe that the only truly effective affirmation of freedom today resides in such an unbridled rejection [of] that old Jesuit precept'. Breton, quoted in an interview with Jean Ruché for *Le Littéraire* (5 October 1946), rpd in Breton, *Conversations*, p. 205.

37 See the 'Surréalisme et fouriérisme' section of Gaulmier's introduction to Breton, *Ode à Charles Fourier* (1961), pp. 34–36; and André Breton, 'Charles Fourier, 1772–1837', in Breton, *Anthologie de l'humour noir* (Paris: Sagittaire, 1950), pp. 909–13. Breton's 1950 version of *Anthologie de l'humour noir* contains five selections from Fourier (including two from *Theory of the Four Movements,* 'Couronne boréale' and 'Méthode d'union des sexes en septième période [et non pas en huitième]'). Etienne-Alain Hubert discusses the evolution of the *Anthologie de l'humour noir* project from the 'Têtes d'orage' essay from *Minotaure*, no. 10 (Winter 1937) to the 1940, 1950, and 1966 editions of the *Anthologie* in Breton, *Œuvres complètes*, vol. 2 (Paris: Gallimard, 1988), pp. 1745–70.

38 Breton, *Arcanum 17*, p. 112.

living in postwar Europe, the Surrealists reacted by reclaiming some of the most radical notions of liberty available – notions of liberty so swollen with unlimited potential that life would seem magical and wholly unlike anything available to them. And it was this need for a language of unbounded imagination and emancipation that drew Breton to the critico-utopian socialists like Saint-Simon and Fourier (and Sade as well). One cannot underestimate the visionary power of the reformist writers of the first half of the nineteenth century, Breton wrote. What is so vibrant in their writing is not the viability of their social reform schemes, but rather their unrestricted power to dream with the same quality of 'extreme freshness' that one finds among non-European artisans of ritual objects and self-taught *art brut* creators.[39] 'We are particularly thirsty for this freshness today. In the social sphere as elsewhere, we can hope that [...] a considerable number of radical propositions formulated *outside the existing framework* will arise'. These proposals and the women and men who will advocate them will be brave enough to 'accept the risk of being branded as ingenuous and of gratuitous and inconsequential conjecture', and they will 'make language of the heart and the senses heard loud and clear' even though they are surrounded on all sides by 'the bankruptcy of the language of the mind'.[40]

In short, utopianism's attention to life's heteroclite elements is not a fatal flaw but is the secret to what makes these theories so compelling – it is the impossibilities at the centre of the utopian consciousness that give it the lasting exuberant allure that its more analytically hidebound counterparts lack and what will stimulate others to look beyond the handful of conventional solutions to social problems. 'I see Charles Fourier as a revolutionary only to the degree that he maintained and made sensible the idea that the whole cultural development of humanity has been affected in a sense which does not respond to any internal necessity, but only from pressures which might as well have been others and differently exerted', Breton pronounced in 1951.[41]

39 In October 1948, Breton, Jean Dubuffet, Michel Tapié, Charles Ratton, Jean Paulhan and Henri Pierre Roché formed the Compagnie de l'art brut with the intention of researching and promoting contemporary folk art, children's art, and the art of psychiatric patients. More research needs to be done on how the Compagnie de l'art brut was a reaction, on the one hand, against the established Parisian gallery industry and those owners and dealers who had catered to and collaborated with the Nazis, and on the other, the cultural imperialism of US State Department-supported abstract-expressionism. For details on the Paris gallery scene in the 1940s, see Michele C. Cone, *Artists Under Vichy: A Case of Prejudice and Persecution* (Princeton: Princeton University Press, 1992); on Cold War art and the Marshall Plan, see Frances Stonor Saunders, *Who Paid the Piper?: The CIA and the Cultural Cold War* (London: Granta, 1999).

40 Breton, *Arcanum 17*, p. 51. Translation modified.

41 André Breton, 'As in a Wood', originally published in *L'Age du cinéma*, nos 4–5 (August–November 1951), p. 30. English translation in Paul Hammond, ed., *The Shadow and Its Shadow: Surrealist Writings on the Cinema* (San Francisco: City Lights, 2000), p. 76.

Determinations of 'provisional unfeasibility' were not a good enough criterion for declaring utopian projects as impossible. Beyond the scientific laws of physics and biology, there should be no limits as to what can be proposed or imagined in a truly free society. Looking around him in the late 1940s, however, Breton saw immediately that freedom was far from guaranteed in Europe. Upon his return to Paris, Breton had found people who were satisfied in letting others liberate them from the Nazis but who were not prepared to liberate themselves from those very things that had made fascism into a reality. While he was still in exile in North America in 1944, Breton had been optimistic. 'Maybe the recent events have taught France and the world that liberty can only subsist in a dynamic state, that it becomes denatured and negates itself at the moment when one makes of it a museum piece', he wrote, recalling the implosion of the Third Republic, the rise of the Vichy police state, and the Nazi domination of Europe. 'Liberty can be quite well defined by contrast with all forms of servitude and constraint. The one weakness of this definition is that it generally represents liberty as a *state*, that is, as immobile, although all of human experience demonstrates that such immobility brings about its immediate ruin'.[42] But when *Arcane 17* was republished in France in June 1947, Breton's discussion of the stasis of 'liberation' in opposition to the dynamics of 'liberty' became even more prescient in the quickly-chilling climate of the Cold War where democratic principles were being retooled into synonyms for US-style social conservatism, anti-Soviet belligerence, and industrial-corporate capitalism.

> The effort of liberation only coincides in a partial and fortuitous manner with the struggle for liberty. A quite formal distinction between these two terms is imperative today when some are preparing to take advantage of this confusion to the detriment of liberty. The concept of liberation has the disadvantage of being a negative concept, of having only momentary value and only in relation to an actual and sharply-defined plundering that must be stopped [...] The concept of liberty, on the other hand, is a concept completely in control of its destiny, which reflects an unconditional view of what *denominates* a human being and it alone gives an appreciable meaning to human *growth*. Liberty is not, like liberation, a struggle against sickness, it is *health*. Liberation might make us believe that health has been recovered, though it only signifies a remission of the illness, the disappearance of its most obvious and alarming symptom. Liberty itself eludes all happenstance.[43]

In order to safeguard a living idea of liberty, possibilities need to be pushed further, and the political unconscious of postwar Europe needed to be accessed in order to accomplish this goal. The exercise of the imagination, no matter how wild, was not the escape from reality that Surrealism's Stalinist rivals condemned it as, but was instead a means for unveiling the hidden order that lies

42 Breton, *Arcanum 17*, p. 93.
43 Breton, *Arcanum 17*, p. 94.

beneath, that is the source of a revolutionary faith in the immense possibilities of social futures.[44] If people are not allowed to think freely, then they certainly will not be able to live freely. Utopian speculation was one practice that could serve this end.

Enduring Unfreedom

To best understand the political bearing of the Surrealists' adoption of Fourierist thought in the early Fourth Republic, one must re-examine the contextual field within which the Surrealists attempted to put Fourier's ideas to work for them. Likewise, one should be familiar with the breadth of the gap separating the postures and rhetorics of freedom enacted by French political officials from the actual experience of liberty that one would encounter on any given day.[45] Fourier had been explicit about what freedom was and what it wasn't in the political environment of his own day: he saw liberalism as a major obstacle in human emancipation for its failure to merge the forces of psychological liberation with its progressive social policies. Liberals defined liberty as freedom from tyranny, as the right to work in order to avoid starvation, and as being allowed to participate in a limited way through the channels of suffrage.[46]

44 'Surréalisme et fouriérisme', pp. 12–36, in Jean Gaulmier, 'Introduction', to André Breton, *Ode à Charles Fourier*, published in *Bibliothéque française et romane, série C: Etudes littéraires*, no. 2 (1960), pp. 7–60.

45 This is given a slightly different gloss in Carole Reynaud Paligot's chapter, 'L'Ethique libertaire du surréalisme', in her *Parcours politique des surréalistes, 1919–1969* (Paris: CNRS, 2001), pp. 210–26. Coincidentally, in the terminology of a Fourierist vocabulary, '*parcours*' is defined as 'a course of pleasure which increases in intensity'. While there is nothing to indicate that Reynaud-Paligot intended for this to be a subtext to her study, it certainly adds another dimension to the Surrealists' political history. See also Emile Lehouck, 'La Lecture surréaliste de Charles Fourier', *Australian Journal of French Studies* XX:1 (1983), pp. 26–36.

46 Take the example of French women's right to vote after the Second World War. An ordinance was passed in April 1944 by the Comité français de libération nationale (CFLN) that promised universal suffrage once the Nazis were finally expelled from France. This decision was hailed as a victory by many who had fought for the enfranchisement of women; after 1945, it was not unusual to hear it said that Charles de Gaulle had magnanimously given women the right to vote in return for their heroic sacrifices and patriotism during the Occupation (the General himself did little to set the historical record straight on the subject). The Surrealists' response was to continually remind women that issues of freedom and sexual independence far exceeded the privilege to participate in the liberal-bourgeois electoral system. Four or five months after the CFLN ordinance, Breton wrote in *Arcane 17* that the only meaningful postwar reconstruction must include 'the idea of the salvation of the earth by woman, of the transcendent vocation of woman, a vocation which has been systematically concealed, thwarted, or led astray to our day, but which nevertheless will be triumphantly affirmed one day'. Breton, *Arcanum 17*, pp. 51–62. In

To Fourier, this situation was far from satisfactory, as it still did not allow for the full exercise of human autonomy and the unleashing of those desires repressed by civilization. This was worsened to the point of travesty by the hypocrisies mouthed by professional politicians who claimed to be defending freedom and democracy but who, in actuality, 'have allowed their mania for simplification to confuse the debate about freedom. They have not been able to distinguish between the simple, compound, and bi-compound varieties of freedom'.

The concept of 'simple freedom (or physical) freedom' was Fourier's label for the person 'who has the barest necessities, a military ration' and lacks 'social freedom', thereby becoming a 'passive member of society' whose 'passions are completely unsatisfied'. Among non-European aboriginal peoples of the pre-contact era (in other words, those blissfully 'uncivilized'), Fourier recognizes a more advanced stage of liberty, the 'divergent compound freedom' that comes from actively participating in the public affairs of the community and doing pre-capitalist, pre-industrial labours which are less damaging to the body and less alienating to the psyche. The third stage – the 'destiny' of humans – is 'bi-compound freedom', which consists of 'active, physical freedom and active, social freedom in alliance with 'attractive productive work'. Bi-compound freedom 'presupposes unified adherence, the individual consent of every worker [...] and their impassioned collaboration in the performance of work and in the maintenance of the established order'.[47] A revolution in Fourierian terms meant

---

1948, Breton went further and denounced the Gaullists' cynical appropriation of the language and symbolism of female emancipation in a short text on the utopian 'Père' Barthélémy-Prosper Enfantin – any liberation of women must be made by women and not De Gaulle, adding that women's suffrage was not one of the 'conquests of feminism', but rather 'the absolute negation' of women's revolutionary struggle for basic human rights. *Da Costa Encyclopedia* (1948), trans. Iain White in Alaistair Brotchie, ed., *Encyclopaedia Acephalica*, Atlas Arkhive 3: Documents of the Avant-Garde (London: Atlas Press, 1995), p. 124. In the following years, the Surrealists criticized this short-sighted construction of political liberty for women and the democratic process by publishing articles on and by the nineteenth-century utopian socialist feminist Flora Tristan. See Breton's introduction to 'Flora Tristan: 7 lettres inédites', *Le Surréalisme, même*, no. 3 (Autumn 1957), pp. 4–5. For accounts of the debates over the role of French utopian socialism in the development of feminism, one can begin with Flora Tristan; see Dominique Desanti, *Flora Tristan, la femme révoltée* (Paris: Librairie Hachette, 1972); Máire Cross and Tim Gray, *The Feminism of Flora Tristan* (Providence: Berg, 1992); R. Rohrlich and E. H. Baruch, *Women in Search of Utopia: Mavericks and Mythmakers* (New York: Schocken, 1984); and Claire Goldberg Moses and Leslie Wahl Rabine, *Feminism, Socialism, and French Romanticism* (Bloomington: Indiana University Press, 1993). See also Sarane Alexandrian, *Le Socialisme romantique* (Paris: Seuil, 1972), pp. 116–18 and 365–407.

47 Charles Fourier, from *Traité de l'association domestique-agricole* [1841–43]. Trans. Beecher and Bienvenu in *The Uotpian Vision of Charles Fourier*, pp. 139–42. A different excerpt from *Traité de l'association domestique-agricole* appears following Henri Pastoureau's 'Pour une offensive de grand style contre la civilisation chrétienne', in André Breton and Marcel Duchamp, *Le Surréalisme en 1947* (Paris: Galerie Maeght, 1947), p. 83.

not only freedom from despotism, but freedom from the patterns of thought that made despotism possible; it was more than the right to work, it was also the right not to have to work in order to survive.[48]

One can see that Fourier's challenging notions on freedom influenced that passage in Breton's *Arcane 17* quoted above; Fourier had said that bi-compound liberty was 'the destiny of man [*sic*]'; Breton said that 'liberty [...] is a concept completely in control of its destiny, which reflects an unconditional view of what *denominates* a human being'. Breton's warning about maintaining the distinctions between 'the effort of liberation' and 'the struggle for liberty' in postwar Europe alludes to this. Breton cautions that 'some are preparing to take advantage of this confusion to the detriment of liberty', just as Fourier had warned of those bourgeois-liberals who thought that progressive politics meant only that one had the right to prevent abject poverty by toiling in a coal mine or textile mill and, if one were male and paid enough taxes, voting every few years. In 'Ajours', the short collection of generally anti-authoritarian essays that he had tacked on the end of the 1947 reissue of *Arcane 17*, Breton's saw a similar set of constraints that recently liberated people had decided to put on themselves and one another, and was discouraged by those who would consciously choose not to be free by enslaving themselves to noxious resurgent ideals like patriotism and militarism. Why would anyone settle for a liberation that is not free? This is what Breton saw happening among the French who were reluctant to de-realize the conventional categories of emancipation. The French Communists and Socialists who dominated the National Assembly shared the liberals' fear of freedom. 'Stalinism has *burnt the bridge* that, since the time of Saint-Simon, Fourier, Abbé Constant, Enfantin and Flora Tristan, has allowed those who strove toward the liberation of men and women, those who aimed at spiritual emancipation, to communicate freely', Breton explained.[49] Freedom from fascism was not enough, 'we must "remake human understanding"'. It was imperative that 'human life be *re-impassioned*, made valuable again' and do so by following the examples of 'Bacon, Condillac and Fourier', not De Gaulle,

48 Compare this to Paul Lafargue's notorious *Le Droit à la paresse* [1883], trans. as *The Right to Be Lazy* (Chicago: Charles H. Kerr, 1989): 'A strange delusion possesses the working classes of the nations where capitalist civilization holds sway. This delusion is the love of work, the furious passion for work'. Among the many reprints of this work by Marx's son-in-law was an edition put out in Paris in 1946 by Editions de la liberté, which found new readership among the strikers who paralyzed the presses, mass transit systems, the dockyards and the Renault plants. Roger Linet, *Renault 1947–1958. Les Années chaudes de la guerre froide* (Pantin: Le Temps des cerises, 1997); Robert Mencherini, *Guerre froide, grèves rouges. Parti communiste, stalinisme et luttes sociales en France: les grèves 'insurrectionnelles' de 1947–1948* (Paris: Syllepse, 1998).

49 André Breton interviewed by Francis Dumont, in Breton, *Conversations*, p. 230.

Truman and Stalin.[50] In support of his claim of the shallowness and hypocrisy of existing models of freedom, Breton pointed out that such thinking has lead to 'the lines that are always stretching around Parisian bakeries'[51] and 'the recent Indochina massacres'.

Breton's passing mention of the colonial war in southeast Asia refers to the brutal bombardment of Haiphong by the French navy in late November 1946, an attack that reportedly slaughtered hundreds, if not thousands, of men, women and children. This incident, though deliberately played down by the French press, marked the beginning of France's seven-year war to retain colonial possession of Indochina before being replaced in the field by the US. The French war in Vietnam illustrates the Surrealists' position that there was little respect for true democracy amid all the talk of liberty and liberation in Paris after 1945, especially among the Communists and the Socialists who saw no contradiction between their supposedly progressive politics and the bloody attempts to remake the prewar French Empire. The conquest of France by Germany and its subsequent humiliation had triggered a common desire to use imperialist prestige to renovate the nation and unite the fractured State. 'Without its Empire, France would be nothing other than a liberated country', one leading French politician gloated at the time. 'But thanks to her [sic] Empire, France is today a victorious country', an opinion that Communists saw no need to criticize.[52] The

50 Breton, *Arcanum 17*, pp. 102, 103 and 111. As translator Zack Rogow points out in his notes, it is not clear if Breton was referring to Francis Bacon or Roger Bacon here. Francis Bacon was the late sixteenth-century natural philosopher who constructed a means of inductive reasoning to challenge authority and pave the way for modern scientific experimentation. Roger Bacon was a famous astrologer, alchemist and magician from the early thirteenth century. (Rogow inexplicably gives the dates of Roger Bacon's life as 1510–1579 when in fact he lived from 1214 until about 1294.) Bacon's research into the philosopher's stone led to his persecution and censorship. Rogow supposes that Breton was referring to Francis Bacon – evidence he could have used to support his view should have included Bacon's hermetic-kabbalistic utopian work, *The New Atlantis* (1626).

51 Breton's reference to bakery lines came at a time when bread rations in Paris were worse than they had been during the Nazi Occupation, prompting some Parisians to openly suggest that life had been better under the Nazis and Vichy.

52 The statement was made by President of the Council of the Republic Gaston Monnerville, quoted in Raoul Giradet, *L'Idée coloniale en France, 1871–1962* (Paris: Table Ronde, 1972), p. 196. According to a national survey conducted in 1949, less than two per cent of those questioned thought that France should not pursue its imperialist ambitions. Jean Meyer, Jacques Thobie and Catherine Coquery-Vidrovitch, *Histoire de la France coloniale. Tome 2* (Paris: Armand Colin, 1990), p. 415. For an informed and in-depth discussion of the inability and unwillingness of French Communists and Socialists to oppose a return to colonialism after World War II, see Meyer et al., *Histoire de la France coloniale*, pp. 429–32. When Monnerville organized a government effort to increase the war budget to include the cost of waging war in southeast Asia, the Communists chose simply to abstain from voting rather than giving voice to their objection.

Surrealists, however, reacted immediately to the atrocities in Indochina and in a language that is impossible to interpret as 'apolitical'. And while there is no mention of copulating star systems or endlessly blazing Northern Lights, one can see the hand of Fourier's radical thinking between the lines of their blistering collective declaration, 'Liberté est un mot vietnamien'.[53]

'The press in so-called "free" France, subject to censorship now more than ever, remains silent' about the secret war in Asia,' the Surrealist tract began.[54] But make no mistake about it – such a battle was taking place, 'an imperialist war executed in the name of people who have only just been liberated themselves from five years of oppression against another people unified in common consent by their desire for liberty', one that had been nimbly engineered by a conniving 'admiral-monk' and his 'cruel capitalist tyranny of bureaucrats and priests'.[55] To cover up this shameful affair, 'not a word can be heard about the fierce repression being perpetuated [in Vietnam] in the name of democracy. Everything is being done to hide a scandal from the French people which upsets the entire world'. In 1946, 'as in 1919, capitalism has abused that noblest of key words – 'freedom' – in the name of patriotism and with the intent to secure total control, thereby preserving its traditional imperialist policies and reassembling the power of its bourgeois financiers, army and clergy'. The war in Vietnam also held a 'grave significance' for Communist officials, as it revealed their contempt for 'the anti-colonialist legacy that was once one of the most impelling forces of the workers' movement' and their 'flagrant disregard for the right of self-determination' of which they so often proclaim themselves the defenders. 'We call upon those who can still think clearly and with some modicum of honesty to remind [the Communists] that it is impossible to maintain freedom *here* while imposing slavery *there*'.[56]

The statement concludes that, in spite of all this and these supposedly new times, the Surrealists maintained that they have abandoned none of their long-standing demands, 'least of all the demand for a radical social transformation':

---

53 Collective Surrealist declaration, 'Liberté est un mot vietnamien', *Le Libertaire* (22 May 1947), p. 3.

54 There was also a colonial uprising that year against the French in Madagascar that lasted two years and left more than 89,000 Malagasy dead. For details, see Jacques Tronchon, *L'Insurrection malagache de 1947* (Paris: Maspero, 1974).

55 As High Commissioner for Indochina from 1945 to 1947, aristocrat, Carmelite monk and Gaullist Admiral Thierry d'Argenlieu repeatedly undermined ceasefire negotiations between Ho Chi Minh and the French government and hampered numerous attempts from Paris to defuse the start of a colonial war. Once war broke out in Vietnam, he retired to a monastery where he died in 1964. For details, refer to Jean Sainteny, *Histoire d'une paix manquée. Indochine, 1945–1947* (Paris: Amiot-Dumont 1953); and Jean Lacouture, *Hô Chi Minh* (Paris: Editions de Seuil, 1967).

56 Eventually, the Communists did take a stand against the war in Vietnam, but only after they were expelled from the government in May thanks to Cold War pressure from the US. The Socialists, however, remained pro-war.

> As always, we Surrealists still hold that our foremost objective be the liberation of humanity, and we cannot keep silent when confronted by a senseless and repugnant crime such as this. Surrealism only has meaning so long as it stands against a regime whose membership views this indignity as a joyous re-awakening, a regime that, from the moment of its inception, collapsed into a mire of compromise and extortion and that can only be a calculated prelude to the implementation of a new totalitarianism.

The language here resonated with a Fourierian appreciation for the state of awareness required for attaining a bi-compound freedom (Breton's *Ode à Fourier* had been published a few weeks before in February): antiwar appeals 'to conscience, to intelligence, or even to self-interest' only lead to 'lies, errors and inevitable internal divisions' in a world where those who had been liberated dare not ponder the true meaning of liberty. 'It is for this reason that surrealism has chosen a wider and more profound domain' for its argument, namely one that lies 'in proportion to a true human camaraderie. It is for this reason that [Surrealists] raise their voices in vigorous protest against imperialist aggression and address a comradely welcome to all of those who, in the present moment, personify the very coming into being of freedom'.[57]

The outbreak of war in southeast Asia was a moment of epiphany for those who were willing to interrogate the limits of emancipation following Europe's liberation from the despotism of Nazi rule.[58] By failing to move forward toward a more dynamic understanding and employment of liberty, the so-called civilized

57 Collective declaration, 'Liberté est un mot vietnamien', p. 3.

58 Much more research needs to be done on the topic of Surrealist involvement in resisting the war in Algeria (1954–62) to see how Fourier's radical ideals of freedom fit alongside the anarchists and Trotskyists whom the Surrealists had joined in a variety of demonstrations and action committees rallying in support of those who the French government had imprisoned as 'threats to the security of the nation'. Véra Hérold (*née* France Binard), editor of the Surrealist publication *NEON*, had presented a discussion on 'Fourier the Seer' to an anarchist cell in the fifteenth *arrondissement* in early May 1947; she was imprisoned in 1960 as a central figure in the 'Jeanson network', an underground of 40 anti-imperialists that helped hunted Algerian terrorists escape French security forces and smuggled more than ten billion francs to the Swiss bank accounts of the Algerian Front de libération nationale. For more on the Jeanson network's activities, see Marcel Péju, ed., *Le Procès du réseau Jeanson* (Paris: Maspero, 1961). Four months after Hérold's arrest, the Surrealists helped to write the notorious *Déclaration sur le droit à l'insoumission dans la guerre d'Algérie* (also known as 'Manifeste des 121'). Anarchosyndicalist Jehan Mayoux was one of the most politically explicit of the Surrealists; he had been sentenced to five years in prison in 1939 as a conscientious objector and was later fired from his teaching job for promoting draft-dodging among his students and for signing the Declaration of 121. Regarding the Declaration of 121 against the Algerian War, see 'Correspondance Jehan Mayoux-Louis Janover [17 October 1961]', *La Brèche: Action surréaliste*, no. 2 (May 1962), pp. 66–70. An excellent introduction to Surrealist involvement in the Algerian independence movement is provided by Paligot, *Parcours politique des surréalistes*, pp. 177–88.

world was repeating the same mistakes that had brought fascism to its apotheosis in the first place. This was certainly one of the themes underlying the activities of the para-Surrealist Da Costa group that surfaced in 1947.[59] The black humour of their gloss on the meaning of 'emancipation' (probably written by Marcel Duchamp) is worth repeating at length for its critique of the state of civil liberties in France after the Liberation in light of this discussion on Fourierism. The article refers to fictitious measures supposedly proposed in a decree of 23 May 1946 which called for a state-issued *Licence to Live*, a bureaucratic safeguard that the French National Constituent Assembly passed in order to prevent 'that unwholesome independence which goes hand in hand with the weakening of administrative vigilance', slated to go into effect on 14 July 1947.

> Postwar periods are generally characterized by a certain disorder. Once again, we have not failed to experience this. As soon as the Authorities relax their control, murky elements emerge from the shadows where war and the constraints that accompany it have temporarily kept them [...] We are aware that the efficacy measures are based on the creation, at short notice, of a new identity document, the veritable cornerstone of French security which our legislators have called a *Licence to Live*. Similar measures have been taken in a number of foreign countries [...] so that we may, as of now, foresee the definitive triumph of democracy upon the face of the earth [...] Contrary to the monstrous doctrines which totalitarian regimes have sought to make prevail [...] the *Licence to Live* bears the hallmark of a humanism at once generous and clear-sighted, the precious heritage of twenty centuries of Christian civilization.[60]

This arch statement was drolly illustrated by a seal of the French Republic featuring a fasces axe surmounted by a Phrygian cap and a copy of the supposed

---

59 The Da Costa circle consisted of once and future Surrealists Isabelle Waldberg, her husband Patrick, Breton, Robert Lebel, Marcel Duchamp, Georges Bataille, Georges Ambrosino, Jean Ferry, and others based around Adrienne Monnier's La Maison des amis des livres bookshop in the rue de l'Odéon. *Le Da Costa encyclopédique. Fascicule VII, volume II* was published without identification or date by Max Pol-Fourchet and meant to appear as a continuing installment of some unspecified previous work: it began in mid-word and mid-sentence with the title 'Fascicle VII, Volume II'. In 1948, two further fascicles appeared under the title *Le Memento universel Da Costa* (Paris: J. Aubier, n.d.). The name 'Da Costa' had been a running joke among the London Surrealists during the war, referring to a time when either Jacques-B. Brunius or E.L.T. Mesens (it is unclear which) entered a gathering, greeted the exiled Portuguese artist Antonio Pedro da Costa by name, and then proceeded to call everyone else in the room 'Da Costa' as well, and henceforth the name was used as a generic pseudonym for any of the Surrealists in exile (for instance, Breton was said to have done this in a Parisian café in 1947 upon meeting Candido and Antonio Pedro da Costa). See 'Da Costa Encyclopedia', in Alaistair Brotchie, ed., *Encyclopaedia Acephalica* (London: Atlas Press, 1995); Isabelle and Patrick Waldberg, *Un Amour Acéphale, Correspondence 1940–1949* (Paris: Editions de la Différence, 1992); and François Caradec and Noël Arnaud, *Encyclopédie des farces et attrapes et des mystifications* (Paris: Pauvert, 1964).

60 Trans. Iain White, in Brotchie, ed., *Encyclopaedia Acephalica*, p. 114.

'Licence to Live', which stated that the bearer of the permit had been granted the right to live for one year by 'the departments of health, censuses, and police' so long as the document is control-stamped every month. The form allowed spaces for cross-indexing with identification numbers from medical certificates, identity card, voter registration card, ration card, draft card, and Social Assurance references. In a direct reference to rising Cold War tensions, notes on the back of the form explained that Albanian, Bulgarian, Greek, Hungarian, Italian, Polish and Romanian nationals 'can obtain only a temporary *Licence to Live*, which they must have stamped daily'; the same restriction applies to the indigenous peoples of the French colonies 'as well as American citizens of colour (by virtue of the Franco-American convention of 28 October 1946)'. Parents were expected to present their children with a licence at birth: 'no infant aged more than one week can escape the sanctions provided for by law if found without a personal *Licence to Live*', the document warned. 'Domiciliary checks will be carried out at any hour of the day or night by Agents of the Authority' to be sure that licences are in order; those found not to be in compliance face 'capital punishment, to be carried out immediately at the expense of the interested party [. . .] foreign citizens will in addition be subject to deportation'.

Discussed in the context of the Da Costa encyclopedia's definition of 'emancipation', the *Licence to Live* gives voice to many of the same concerns already seen in *Arcane 17*'s passages on the difference between the 'struggle against sickness' that is liberation and the 'state of well-being' that is liberty; it also relates to the impossibility of maintaining 'freedom *here* while imposing slavery *there*' as elucidated in 'Liberté est un mot vietnamien'. Even when cloaked in 'humanism at once generous and clear-sighted, the precious heritage of twenty centuries of Christian civilization', a government-issued licence for living that had to be renewed every month under penalty of death (or death, followed by the deportation of the corpse, in the case of foreigners) in order to guard against 'disorder' would be greeted with ridicule in any self-identifying democracy or republic. But as the Surrealists saw it, people had become dangerously complacent about the limits that the State put on 'emancipation'. Nazi Germany and the Iron Curtain were not the only threats to freedom – from the French bureaucratic monoliths and colonial wars of the late 1940s to the *union sacrée* of the national security state in the US today, more and more people allow themselves to settle for less and less liberty, as Fourier had studied for himself and which the Surrealists had taken to heart. 'According to Fourier himself, a rising curve must be followed by a descending curve', Breton told Patri in the 1948 interview. 'We would have to take care not to desperately aggravate moral evil by stripping beings of the idea of freedom and by compromising the notion of justice'.[61]

61 Breton, quoted in an interview with Claudine Chonez for *Gazette des lettres* (31 July 1948), rpd in Breton, *Conversation*, pp. 224-25. See also Victor Crastre, 'André Breton et la liberté', in Marc Eigeldinger, ed., *André Breton*, pp. 213–27.

The internalization of boundaries that the State has put around freedom for a 'liberated' people – the cowed, passive acceptance of rising levels of domination, restriction and repressive policing – was a key factor in Fourier's disgust for Western civilization. Concomitant with the rise in repression in bourgeois-liberal European society, Fourier had also spotted sharp increases in the level of artifice that distracted and deluded the senses and the instincts. Anticipating the mid-twentieth-century research by Freudo-Marxists Wilhelm Reich and the Frankfurt School on the psychosexual origins and psychical costs of patriarchal State power, Fourier was alarmed by how unnatural, stifling conventions of thought and behaviour had been reified into civilized values of conformity and consent, and he deemed them to be ultimately toxic to the human animal. In their perpetually ungratified state (Fourier's calls them 'suffocated'), passions became twisted and poisonous, resulting in crime, malice, selfishness and war.

This puts Fourier's thinking on human liberty on a trajectory that takes us to Herbert Marcuse and beyond.[62] Fourier's criticisms of the consensual mentality and its pathologies of war, and the Surrealists' warnings about the inevitable ramifications of the hypocritical, lazy and compromised definitions of liberty allowed to circulate after 1945, lead us to Marcuse's thinking about 'unfreedom' in the lands of 'free' enterprise and 'free' elections. 'The modes of domination have changed: they have become increasingly technological, productive and even beneficial', Marcuse wrote. So much so, in fact, that 'people have been coordinated and reconciled with the system of domination to an unprecedented degree'. This has led new forms of totalitarianism to appear 'even where it has not produced totalitarian states [...] intensified progress seems to be bound up with intensified unfreedom'.[63] For the Surrealists of the postwar era, reading utopians like Fourier was a means of imagining a space where one could purge the poisons of civilization, of being able to define freedom as something other than just the absence of explicit tyrannies of Nazi occupiers. From the vantage point of the Romantic socialists, one could learn to become just as dissatisfied with the authoritarian strains of liberal civil society as one had been with the outright despotism of police states. In seeing a third term of unfreedom in the imperialist war in Vietnam and in the bureaucratic micromanagement of everyday life which was parodied by the Da Costa *Licence to Live*, the Surrealists were attempting to extend the expectations of free people, a fight that was not without political implications.

62 As explored in more detail in Jean Paul Thomas, *Liberation instinctuelle, liberation politique. Contribution fouriériste à Marcuse* (Paris: Le Sycomore, 1990).

63 Herbert Marcuse, *Eros and Civilization: A Philosophical Inquiry into Freud* (New York: Vintage, 1962), p. 4.

The Return of Charles Fourier

Just as expanded definitions of liberty like bi-compound freedom found their way into Surrealist tracts like 'Liberté est un mot vietnamien', Fourierian refusal can be found woven throughout *Rupture inaugurale*, a pamphlet put out a month after the declaration on Vietnam that spelled out the Surrealists' unwillingness to adhere unfalteringly to any formal political formula, no matter how apparently desirable to them. The theorists who were the 'successors of Marx' are 'directly responsible for out-of-date mores of our time and the persistent empire of the Christian doctrines on morality' because the Communists had 'never denounced current morals, except when they saw that doing it would serve an immediate political advantage'. Sade, Fourier and Freud, on the other hand, had 'opened the breach' to a new ethical order.[64] Surrealists continued to tout Fourierism as an alternative to the totalitarian excesses of Stalinism throughout the 1950s;[65] in the mid-1960s, while many of their contemporaries in Paris were dabbling with fashionably trendy forms of Maoism, Surrealists were agitating for an incredulous but unstoppable dialectical combination of Trotsky and Fourier: 'Trotsky, Fourier – the Invincible and the Unlimited, whose fusion clarifies in us the nature and the range of our revolutionary hope'.[66]

Shortly before Breton's death, an unmistakable tribute to one of Fourier's

64 In May, Cause had circulated an eight-point questionnaire to Surrealists in France, Belgium, England, Brazil, Canada, Chile, Denmark, Egypt, the US, Guatemala, Haiti, Hungary, Iraq, Japan, Mexico, Portugal, Romania, Sweden, Czechoslovakia and Turkey. The purpose of this exercise was not only to report on the Surrealist project at large but also to synchronize the movements' intentions and direction. Questions related to subjects such as Surrealism's objectives; Surrealists' position toward revolutionary action; the relationship between rationality, knowledge and reality; the role of love, literature and plastic arts in Surrealism; and whether or not religion improved the human condition at all were included. The data supplied by replies were synthesized into the *Rupture inaugurale* pamphlet. Cause, *Rupture inaugurale. Déclaration adoptée le 21 juin 1947 par le groupe en France pour définir son attitude préjudicielle a l'égard de toute politique partisane* (Paris: Editions surréalistes, 1947).

65 See especially André Breton and Benjamin Péret's response to the inquiry 'Les Intellectuels français devant le communisme', published in *Combat* (May 1950); collective response to the inquiry 'Ouvrez-vous? [Fourier]', *Médium. Communication surréaliste*, no. 1, n.s. (November 1953), p. 11; and André Breton, 'Schnorr & Cie', *Bief: Jonction surréaliste*, no. 1 (November 15, 1958), p. 3.

66 Jean-Claude Silbermann, 'Trotsky, Fourier', *La Brèche: Action surréaliste*, no. 7 (December 1964), p. 106. For further later writings on Fourier, see also Adrien Dax, 'A propos d'un talisman de Charles Fourier', ibid., no. 4 (February 1963), pp. 18–23; Emile Lehoucq, 'Un divertissement de Fourier, ibid., pp. 24–26; and Philippe Audoin, 'Le Talisman de Charles Fourier. Complément d'enquête', ibid., no. 8 (November 1965), pp. 70–77. To be accurate, however, one must also acknowledge that some Surrealists did fall prey to the flavours of the day, as there are some texts in *L'Archibras* that suggest a strong sympathy for Guevaraism.

most uncompromising notions was paid by the Surrealists. 'L'Ecart absolu', the 11th Exposition internationale du surréalisme of December 1965 at the Galerie L'Œil, explored that aspect of Fourierian thought that they saw as an obstinate commitment to permanent revolution in the service of total liberty.[67] In part, the exhibition sought to blast away the ideologies of technocracy and Cold War-inflected consumer culture that had been dominating French life and offered instead innumerable evocative possibilities for future dreams. '*Ecart absolu*' – 'Total Refusal' of all known theories – was an integral part of Fourier's social analysis first formulated in *Theory of the Four Movements* to explain his absolute disdain for civilization and his singular cosmogonic view of the world. 'The surest means of making useful discoveries was to deviate in every way from the paths followed by the dubious sciences [Fourier's term for politics, political economy, metaphysics and morality] which had never made the slightest discovery useful to society [...] I made it my business to remain in constant opposition to these sciences'. Fourier's *Incoherent Industry*, a text which began as an abolitionist's pamphlet before spiralling off into a beautifully frenzied textual collage, continued that line of inquiry and explicitly tied the Total Refusal method to an aggressive condemnation of the fundamental rot pervasive throughout Western civilization's most precious values.[68] The 'incoherent industry' of Fourier's title referred to the perverse, 'non-associative' (disjointed, exploitative, dangerous and inefficient in Fourier's terms) labours required to keep capitalist civilization alive – capitalism, of course, relies on an economic, industrial and financial base that is necessarily opaque, fractured, fragmented, and alienating for its workers. Fourier saw his method of complete disdain for all existing philosophical, scientific and epistemological systems as a means for clearing the slate and making way for innovative new discoveries, 'thus, *l'écart absolu* stemmed from the sense of the irrationality of moral restrictions and the vast possibilities of liberation implied in abolishing them'.[69]

In this respect, Fourier's '*écart absolu*' is akin to the Surrealists' own '*non conformisme absolu*' of the *Second Manifesto of Surrealism*;[70] it is also similar to Breton's 1942 dedication to always being the one who dares to say 'no':

> People must be absolutely convinced that once general consent has been reached on a given subject, individual resistance is the only key to the

---

67 Joyce Mansour and Suzy Embo, 'L'Ecart absolu, Exposition internationale du surréalisme 1965–66. Eléments mnémotechniques pour un rêve futur', *L'Archibras*, no. 1 (April 1967), 49–60.

68 Michel Butor memorably characterizes this strange work as 'an enormous message in a bottle thrown out into the sea in search of a recipient'. Butor, preface to Fourier's *Le Nouveau monde industriel* (Paris: Flammarion, 1973), pp. 20–21.

69 Mark Poster, introduction to *Harmonian Man: Selected Writings of Charles Fourier* (New York: Anchor, 1971), p. 7.

70 Gaulmier's annotations to Breton, *Ode à Charles Fourier* (1961), p. 93, n. 41.

> prison. But this resistance must be *informed* and subtle. By instinct I will contradict the *unanimous* vote of any assembly that does not take it upon itself to contradict the vote of a larger assembly. But by this same instinct I will give my vote to those who tend to *climb higher* to the greater emancipation of all beings with new programmes not yet tested by the facts. Given the historical process, wherein it is known that truth only shows itself in order to laugh up its sleeve and is never grasped, I declare myself on the side of this minority that is endlessly renewable and acts like a lever. My greatest ambition would be to guarantee that the theoretical importance of this minority continue to be transmissible after I am gone.[71]

It was with these perspectives in mind that the international Surrealist exhibition of 1965 was assembled.

Breton's short text on the show, 'Générique', cites *Incoherent Industry* as a decisive element in the ideological construction of the Surrealist exposition and he quotes a few of its more salient passages.

> Civilization raises only one thirtieth of its children with any well-being, and even they are still dissatisfied! When one sees this shameful fruit of so many sciences, shouldn't one doubt that this is what humans are really destined for, or is it, as Montesquieu thinks, a wasting disease, an interior vice, a secret and hidden venom, a level of transition to be crossed as fast as possible?

Breton's 'opening credits' thread Fourier's Total Refusal to the works of other rebellious 'inciters' that inform the *L'Ecart absolu* show, including the dialectics of sixth-century BCE natural philosopher Heraclitus the Obscure ('They do not comprehend how a thing can agree when at variance with itself. It is the harmony of turning back on itself, like that of a bow and a lyre', Breton quotes[72]); Picasso's ground-breaking cubism of pre-1914; and the stark, coloured-pencil drawings produced by Adolf Wölfli during his incarceration in a Swiss psychiatric facility from 1895 until his death in 1930.[73]

In his contribution to the catalogue, Philippe Audoin identified Total Refusal as the best means to undermine a specific outgrowth of capitalist civilization's consumer culture. By virtue of its role as a means of avoiding the standard contrivances of knowledge and emotion perpetuated throughout all facets of contemporary society, Total Refusal was a useful tool in stepping outside the bulwarks of insidious distraction and seductive mystification that isolate the individual from a satisfying connection with the world. Audoin argued that Total Refusal could bypass the miserable web of artificial desires which capitalist

---

71 André Breton, 'Prolégomènes à un troisiéme manifeste', pp. 18–26.

72 Breton also quoted this fragment in *Les Vases communicants* (Paris: Denoël et Steele, 1932), p. 134.

73 André Breton, 'Générique', in Breton, Jean-François Revel and Philippe Audoin, eds, *L'Ecart absolu* (Paris: Galerie L'Œil, 1965), n.p. [p. 1]. Rpd in *L'Œil*, no. 131 (November 1965), p. 36.

civilization has used to ensnare so many – the 'unintelligible babbling' of its advertisements, its penchant for 'delirious marketing', and the 'hypnotic effects of its audiovisual mechanisms' obscure the essences of human desire, substituting instead multiple worlds of shallow, flickering illusion. The sensations of direct experience have been usurped by a passive contemplation of images, fetishized objects and associated social activities, subordinating all beings to 'a conformism both numbing and cheerful' which is enforced by biased, distorted news coverage and the 'enormous mystification' that is continually being generated around meaningless events such as sports contests and 'cosmonautic competitions'.[74] In such a milieu, the Surrealists' cultivation of the Marvellous 'is not an evasion but a tendency toward that which will become real', a revolutionary position when one realizes how what appears at first to be an escape is actually a refusal of the narrow confines of the possible.[75]

Audoin quoted directly from *Incoherent Industry* in order to argue this view: 'In order to arrive at a continental New World, Columbus had to adopt a system of Total Refusal',[76] he recounts:

> One can appreciate the spirit in which the 11th *Exposition internationale du surréalisme* claims this sentence of Charles Fourier and the system of thought to which it is accredited. It is certainly about an outbreak of hostilities organized against a clearly-located form of social pressure [...] but if the objects or processes that are disputed there are necessarily evoked (the direction of the variation [*l'écart*] is given starting from the point where one deviates [*s'écarte*]), the emphasis is more accurately put on the distance to take from it and the new raised horizon. It is thus an operation of 're-orientation' which is proposed here, generally by means of the same devices that blaze or signpost the trails of enslavement.[77]

Audoin's explanation here of the value of Fourier's Total Refusal encourages the appropriation of given forms so long as they are turned against civilization through a process of simultaneous incorporation and negation. Such strategies

---

74 A reference to the propaganda war fought during the previous eight years around the Space Race between the US-Western Europe and the USSR. For more Surrealist discussion of the distractions of economico-military imperialism, see Gérard Legrand, 'Une Apparence de soupirail', in Breton, et al., eds, *L'Ecart absolu*, n.p. [p. 16].

75 'The act of "dropping out" is first an act of negation; whether it is carried out in reaction to the yoke of oppression, in response to the emptiness of alienation, or in the exhilaration of a newly kindled intellectual awareness'. Ron Sakolsky, preface to Sakolsky and James Koehnline, eds, *Gone to Croatan: Origins of North American Dropout Culture* (New York: Autonomedia/AK Press, 1993), p. 10. For more on this as it concerns utopianism in the US, see Sakolsky's introduction to Vachel Lindsay, *The Golden Book of Springfield* (Chicago: Charles H. Kerr, 1999).

76 Compare this to the statement that 'Christopher Columbus should have set out to discover America with a boatload of madmen'. André Breton, *Manifeste du surréalisme, poisson soluble* (Paris: Sagittaire, 1924), pp. 5–6.

77 Philippe Audoin, 'L'Air de fête', in Breton, et al., eds, *L'Ecart absolu*, n.p. [14].

are not unlike the process used by a sleeper's unconscious mind where the events and objects of the day's experience may erupt in mutated form as dreams, plucked from their typical place in reality and charged with a magical reverse polarity by the slumbering psyche into awesome new ideas and images (a process akin to the later developments of *détournement*, deconstruction and culture jamming). This can be seen most literally in graphic designer Pierre Facheux's 'Harmonic portraits' of Fourier shown at the exhibition. A portrait of Charles Fourier from the 1860s by an unknown painter from Breton's private collection was the basis for modification by Facheux and reproduced as the cover illustration of the catalogue and in an issue of the Surrealist journal *L'Archibras* (itself named after one of the more fantastic elements of Fourier's utopia). Facheux's alteration of the standard version of Fourier's image signals a preservation of just enough of the accepted codes of representation in order to cancel out and overcome them. The title refers to Fourier's imagined phase of 'Harmony', the social state of being that came to fruition when the community benefited fully from the passionate gratification of its individual members in the realms of work, play and love.

While the planning and execution of the *L'Ecart absolu* exposition at the Galerie L'Œil was afoot, an ambitious undertaking to gather and resurrect Fourier's writing was in the works, resulting in a twelve-volume project edited in part by a researcher close to Breton and the Surrealists, Simone Debout-Oleskiewicz.[78] Since the Soviets' brutal bulldozing of the Budapest uprising of 1956, many on the French ultra-left began a journey of politico-cultural experimentation and discovery similar to the one that the Surrealists had been on since the Spanish Civil War and Moscow Show Trials of the mid-1930s; by the time that Debout-Oleskiewicz's project had been completed, this discontent, political frustration and explosive social possibility had been boiling for a decade before spilling out with the strikers, protesters and street fighters in 1968. For some, the hunt for alternatives took shape in innumerable and ephemeral *groupuscules* of naive Maoist-Castro-Guevaraism;[79] the Surrealists of *L'Archibras* enthusiastically

78 *Œuvres complètes de Charles Fourier* (Paris: Editions Anthropos, 1966–68). Especially noteworthy is Debout-Oleskiewicz's admirable work on the seventh volume, a collection of long-lost material entitled *Le Nouveau monde amoureaux* (1967). Insight into Debout-Oleskiewicz's relationship with the Surrealist group was given to me by Jonathan Beecher in correspondence dated 16 March 2001.

79 For more on these currents, a recent but unfortunately uneven account can be found in Andrew Feenberg and Jim Freedman, *When Poetry Ruled the Streets: The French May Events of 1968* (Albany: University of New York Press, 2001). See also Alain Schnapp and Pierre Vidal-Naquet, *Journal de la commune étudiante. Textes et documents, novembre 1967–juin 1968* (Paris: Seuil, 1969); Rémi Hess, *Les Maoïstes français. Une dérive institutionnelle* (Paris: Anthropos, 1974); Marnix Dressen, *De l'amphi à l'établi. Les étudiants maoïstes à l'usine, 1967–1989* (Paris: Belin, 2000) and the classic Theodore Draper, *Castroism: Theory and Practice* (New York: Praeger, 1965).

rebuked those stodgy Stalinist bureaucrats of the PCF who had criticized the rebels' spirit of play, passion and desire as undisciplined and counter-revolutionary by invoking Fourier and his utopian socialism.[80]

Post-Surrealists Raoul Vaneigem, Guy Debord and their Situationist cohort were also among those who had spotted the ghost of Fourier haunting the anarchists, libertarian Marxists, council communists and assorted other dissidents in France in 1968. In Vaneigem's powerfully influential 1967 treatise on the revolution of everyday life, only Lautréamont and Marx are mentioned more often than Fourier;[81] he later explained that for this generation of insurgents, 'one of Fourier's great merits is to have shown the necessity to realize immediately – and for us this means from the inception of generalized insurrection – the objective conditions for individual emancipation. For everyone the beginning of the revolutionary moment must mark an *immediate rise in the pleasure of living*; the consciously experienced entry into the totality'.[82] The marvellously dialectical graffito of 'Be realistic; demand the impossible!' was scrawled throughout the streets of Paris with Romanticist (if not Surrealist) gusto. During a general strike on 10 March 1969, a 'commando' of *enragés* identified only as the 'Rue Gay-Lussac Barricaders' erected a bronze-coated plaster statue of Fourier on the long-empty pedestal in Place Clichy where Breton had seen it in 1937.[83] Within a day, however, it had been dismantled by the technical service of the Paris prefecture; like the Nazi security forces who had ordered the original Fourier statue pulled down during the Occupation, the Parisian police in 1969 regarded the presence of this utopian writer to be a distinct threat to public order.

For many, the uprisings that had almost brought down De Gaulle's government were hopelessly utopian. But there was no denying that the return

80 See the unattributed article 'Discordance = Harmonie [8 June]', in the special issue of *L'Archibras*, no. 4 (18 June 1968), pp. 14–15.

81 Raoul Vaneigem, *Traité de savoir-vivre à l'usage des jeunes générations* (Paris: Gallimard, 1967).

82 Raoul Vaneigem, 'Notice to the Civilized Concerning Generalized Self-Management', trans. Ken Knabb in *Situationist International Anthology* (Berkeley: Bureau of Public Secrets, 1989), p. 285, originally printed in *Internationale situationniste*, no. 12 (September 1969). 'Fourier had already remarked on how it would take workers several hours to put up a barricade that rioters could erect in just a few minutes. With the disappearance of forced labor, a free flow of creativity in all spheres simultaneously emerged', one situationist recounted of the uprisings. 'Everyone was able to effect reserves of creative energy subjugated during the time of survival, those days that had been condemned to manufacturing, shopping, television, and inert inactivity'. René Viénet, *Enragés et situationnistes dans le mouvement des occupations* (Paris: Gallimard, 1968), p. 15.

83 The incident was reported in an anonymous piece, 'Le Retour de Charles Fourier', *Internationale situationniste*, no. 12 (September 1969), p. 97. See also Beecher, *Charles Fourier*, p. 3.

of the repressed might pose a credible threat to business as usual; as Breton had told Patri, utopian visions often provide access to forgotten or ignored truths, meaning that a 'utopia might prove fruitful in reality, thereby revealing itself as having been not such a utopia after all'.[84]

Conclusion

A burning interest in the research work of Freud did not lead to the founding of a Surrealist psychoanalytic practice. Sade remained a resource for Surrealist theory and activity even though the group never literally built torture chambers or kidnapped young aristocrats – it was Sade's philosophical interrogation of societal norms through stories of ethico-sexual rebellion and crime that made him such a psychopolitical force for the Surrealists.[85] The impracticalities of Fourier's systems may have made them 'utopian', but the Surrealists refused to accept the disparaging insinuations of that term and saw nothing detrimental about political formations that encouraged daydreams or challenged impossibilities. What others deemed 'unrealistic' were defined by Surrealists as a condition where the imagination and intuition were in the process of breaking new ground, seeking unusual solutions to narrowly-defined situations.[86] Admittedly, in many

84 André Breton, interviewed by Aimé Patri, *Paru* (March 1948), rpd in Breton, *Conversations*, p. 217.

85 Explorations of this theme can be found in Svein Eirik Fauskevåg, *Sade dans le surréalisme* (Oslo: Solum Forlag A/S, 1982); and Tobia Bezzola et al., eds, *Sade surreal. Der Marquis de Sade und die erotische Fantasie des Surrealismus in Text und Bild* (Ostfildern-Ruit: Hatje Cantz, 2001).

86 Breton and his comrades embraced utopian thought because they believed that, in order to achieve the total transformation of life and society that revolutionaries like Lenin had originally proposed, the imagination had to be liberated and stretched into fabulous, new dimensions. In the early years of the Bolshevik Revolution, there had been poets, painters, architects and performance artists of the Soviet constructivist and Communist-futurist movements who fervently believed that a revolution could only succeed if people were shown how to think about what had previously been unthinkable. Following Lenin's death, the Soviet leadership fixated upon rigid and methodical enterprises of socioeconomic reorganization, thereby abandoning and ultimately purging the utopian elements that had been drawn to Bolshevism in the first place. See Lynn Mally, *Culture of the Future: The Proletkult Movement in Revolutionary Russia* (Berkeley: University of California Press, 1990); Richard Stites, *Revolutionary Dreams: Utopian Vision and Experimental Life in the Russian Revolution* (New York: Oxford University Press, 1989); Abbott Gleason, Peter Kenez and Richard Stites, *Bolshevik Culture: Experiment and Order in the Russian Revolution* (Bloomington: Indiana University Press, 1985). For those interested in the details of this thread in Surrealist thought, one could begin with Surrealist involvement in the controversies surrounding the suicide of Vladimir Mayakovsky, the Communist-futurist poet-laureate of the Red Army, in 1930; see André Breton, 'Lyubovnaya lodka razbilas o byt [July 1930]', in *Point du jour* (Paris: Gallimard, 1934).

of the instances where utopian speculation is evoked, the terms of engagement with the political sphere may come into question. However, if one were to allow the idea of political action to be dilated to include a vision of society organized on mutual aid and individual agreement; the desire to more closely calibrate human behaviour to an ethos of nature and instinct; a respect for individual differences which can operate in harmony without authoritarian control; the encouraging of the free self-fulfilment of one's personality; and the use of psychology to organize human energy and maximize satisfaction while safeguarding autonomy, then one might understand how Fourierism constituted an important plank in postwar Surrealism's political platform. The endorsement of all of Fourierism's idiosyncrasies was part of Surrealism's total and irrevocable endorsement of freedom. For the Surrealists, Fourier's adamant position on how and why the very definition of liberty needed to be reconsidered made him as political a figure as Peter Kropotkin or Messali Hadj.

One hundred years before the conversation between Breton and Aimé Patri that opened my essay, Marx and Engels said that critical-utopian schemes were admirable impulses that ultimately accomplished very little; while they served as a basis for critical understanding of class exploitation and were authentic manifestations of the proletariat's instinctual inclinations toward a world of social harmony, Marx and Engels concluded that they were just daydreams, 'fantastic attacks' on the bourgeois order. In his discussion with Patri, Breton referred to the traditional Marxist line, but went on to say that, prior to his murder, Trotsky had made a study of the Stalinist State that concluded that Marxism itself was ultimately a utopian system. Regardless, though, there was no mistaking the impact and importance of Marxist Communism and its Bolshevik students; even if Marxism was an 'impracticable' school of utopian thought, Breton asserted, it had immense value as a provider of 'precious tools of orientation' for modern human beings.[87] Likewise, then, the Surrealist reanimation of Fourier's Romantic socialism in the context of postwar Europe was a contribution to a similar sort of revolutionary orientation, one that might never be achieved, but one which would serve Surrealism's political ambitions to 'contribute to the social liberation of beings, work without rest toward a total renewal of behavioural customs, and reshape human understanding'.[88]

87 André Breton, interviewed by Aimé Patri, *Paru* (March 1948), rpd in Breton, *Conversations*, p. 217. Translation modified.

88 André Breton, 'Comète surréaliste [1947]', in Marc Eigeldinger, ed., *André Breton*, p. 22.

Chapter 14

Failure and Community: Preliminary Questions on the Political in the Culture of Surrealism

M. Stone-Richards

I

> Our ambition is to unite, through an indestructible knot – a knot of which we shall have passionately sought the secret as to its indestructibility – this activity of transformation to this activity of interpretation [...][1]

The facts of Surrealism's involvement with the politics of its day are only too well documented, if often neglected: the explicit and public politicization of Surrealism began with its denunciation of the French war against the native insurgents in Morocco in 1925, thus also making of this inaugural moment for Surrealism an intervention against European colonialism; to this we might add the internal dialogues from 1925 onwards on the nature of Surrealism as a movement: is Surrealism merely a movement in art or is it, indeed, a movement in culture, a movement that may properly be considered a social movement? In 1927 with the manifesto 'Au grand jour', five of the leading members committed themselves to the Parti communiste français (PCF), thereby beginning one of the most curious *pas de deux*-as-*danse macabre* in the history of the intersection of politics and culture.[2] The miserable and in many ways *pathetic* relationship between the Surrealists and the PCF not only bore out the accuracy of the radical anarchism of Antonin Artaud who, on the occasion of 'Au grand jour', without denying his inner relation to Surrealism, would take his distance from the movement in proclaiming the utter madness of Surrealism's involvement with any established political party, least of all the PCF. After the Aragon affair between 1931 and 1933, Surrealism

1 André Breton, 'Position politique de l'art aujourd'hui' (1935), *Œuvres complètes*, vol. 2, eds, Marguerite Bonnet et al. (Paris: Gallimard, 1992), p. 430.

2 Amongst the most important work on Surrealism and politics are Jean-Pierre Morel, *Le Roman insupportable: L'Internationale littéraire et la France, 1920–1932* (Paris: Gallimard, 1985), and the many incomparable essays of Robert Short, including 'The Politics of Surrealism, 1920–1936', *Journal of Contemporary History* I:2 (1966), 'Contre-Attaque', in *Entretiens sur le surréalisme*, ed. Ferdinand Alquié (Paris: La Haye, 1968), pp. 144–76.

would begin to take its distance from the Party, though in identifying itself with an independent radical left – the *ultra-gauche* – it would also be the beginning of that particularly French constellation that sought to unite organically the thought of Marx and Freud through Hegel. André Breton's *Les Vases communicants* (1932), following on from his especially close reading of Freud's *Traumdeutung* in Meyerson's translation as *La Science des rêves*, is amongst the most telling evidence of this cultural possibility of Freud, Hegel and Marx as the means for re-thinking what most mattered to this generation, namely, the modalities of individual and collective experience as a means of grasping the possibilities of community under industrial capitalism.[3] In *La Communauté inavouable*, his response to Jean-Luc Nancy's *La Communauté désœuvrée*, Maurice Blanchot outlines the context in which his generation, that is, the generation of the interwar years, came upon the unavoidability of the question of community:

> Why this appeal from or to 'community'? I'll outline in no particular order the elements of what was our history. The groups (of which the Surrealist group, loved or execrated, is the prototype); the many gatherings around ideas which did not yet exist and around dominant persons whose existence was larger than life: above all, the memory of the Soviets, the foreboding of what was already Fascism, but of which the sense, like the development, failed to fit the available concepts [4]

Les Vases communicants is in part a work of theoretical reflection in which Breton, responding to what escapes the texture and habits of concepts then available, seeks an internal rapprochement between Marxism and psycho-analysis through Hegelian thought by a profound thinking on desire in both personal and social dimensions – not the least significant aspect of Breton's thinking in this moving document is the manner in which he seeks to distinguish desire and pleasure – in a way that implicates his own sense of personal failure, the failure of desire to find its object from the personal disaster of his relations with Nadja in 1926 and apparently 'saved' from despair on that occasion by the encounter with X (Suzanne Muzard). The subsequent failure of X to fill the lack in the wake of Nadja – both the person and the récit *Nadja* – is as much the subject of *Les Vases communicants* as the relationship between politics and desire. Indeed, in the history of Surrealism between 1919 (from the composition of *Les Champs magnétiques* in the shadow of the Great War and the encounter with the tragedy of war trauma as captured in the proto-Surrealist récit 'Sujet' (1918), in the shadow of the death of Jacques Vaché to whom *Les Champs*

3 Thus Maurice Blanchot on Bataille and Surrealism: 'Communauté idéale de la communication littéraire. Les circonstances y aidèrent (importance de l'aléa, du hasard, du caprice historique ou de la rencontre; les surréalistes, André Breton avant tous les autres, l'avaient pressentie et même théorisée prématurément)'. Maurice Blanchot, *La Communauté inavouable* (Paris: Editions de Minuit, 1983), p. 40.

4 Ibid., pp. 14–15.

magnétiques is dedicated) and the outbreak of World War II, at each occasion of significant self-definition in relation to the political realm, there would be a crisis and concomitant sense of failure in the movement as it would reconceive its interiority and thereby its space of difference and thus some would leave (Philippe Soupault and Artaud) or be 'expelled' (André Masson and Michel Leiris). The eventual split between Breton and Louis Aragon in 1931–32 after the debacle of the Congress of Kharkov can, certainly, be represented as the choice between a Stalinist Communism or moral independence, but it could equally be understood as a rupture in the integrity of the group thereby foregrounding an important aspect of the importance of the group in Surrealist experience, namely, the narcissistic dimension of group cohesion.

After the rupture with the PCF as recorded in the still magnificent document 'Du temps que les surréalistes avaient raison' (1935), the Surrealists joined with Georges Bataille in 1935 to form a radical left non-party formation named Contre-Attaque: Union de luttes des intellectuels révolutionnaires, not only to challenge the Party but to explore 'the continuation of politics by other means' (Bataille). In so doing, both Bataille and Breton are clear that the creation of the Front Populaire in 1935 would not in itself be sufficient to bring about the kind of radical transformation of values that would alone suffice: it is not merely a rejection of capitalism and the bourgeoisie that would be required, but a fundamental change in the values and conceptions of reason that had informed Western and European self-understanding, the very values which, Nietzsche and Valéry had argued in a manner definitive for the Surrealist generation, that were also the basis of European nihilism. To this extent, though it might well be argued that the demands of working people for improvement in conditions and standards of work as embodied in the Popular Front government of Léon Blum could never be comprehensible to the emerging *ultra-gauche*, there is a certain methodological valence in the critique of the Popular Front as articulated by the ultra-left of Contre-Attaque. In the outline of a lecture 'Sur l'échec du front populaire', significantly on the return to power of Edouard Daladier in 1938 – the incumbent Prime Minister at the beginning of the Popular Front and so a powerful symbol of the failure of the Popular Front in France – Breton situates the failure of Blum and the whole Popular Front phenomenon in international terms: first, the Popular Front restricted itself to economic considerations narrowly conceived, and at the same time practised a politics of narrow national interest, thus failing to see how support of the vanguard forces in Spain would have been in its self-interests, when the 'dramatic European situation' demanded an international thinking.[5] For

5 Cf. André Breton, 'Sur l'échec du Front populaire [On the failure of the Popular Front]', in *Œuvres complètes*, vol. 2, pp. 1259–60. For an account of the way in which Breton reads the history of the vicissitudes of Surrealism through the history of its times, cf. M. Stone-Richards, 'A Type of Prière d'insérer: André Breton's *Le Verre d'eau dans la tempête*', *Art History* 16:2 (June 1993).

Bataille, it was above all imperative that politics be kept out of the hands of the PCF, away from the institutional practice of politics. It remains, though, that nothing offered by either Bataille or Breton could conceivably be understood as a plausible contribution to the practical solution of the everyday political problems of their day in terms of politics as understood in their time, and yet, in light of the crisis of European political culture, of which the dominant forms of totalitarianism, Stalinism and Nazism, were but the most dramatic symptoms, it might well be argued that Surrealism is internally linked to the larger failure of European political culture and that the development of their thought can only make sense if it is understood as an attempt, internal to this larger historical experience of failure and crisis, to reconceive the question of the political. Bataille and Breton can, very reasonably in this light, be seen to share a common terrain with Martin Heidegger, for example, if it is understood that what is at issue is not merely this or that stance in terms of the practice of institutional politics, but, instead, the re-thinking of the conditions of the political in an attempt to go beyond the politics and impasse of a European culture self-consciously nearing its end.[6] To this extent, it might be argued that what is required is a thinking of the meaning of *the political* in Surrealist discourse, and not the least surprising turn might be the recognition of the role and time of mourning in Surrealist thinking as recognition of the presence and role of failure in their disposition – to what extent, indeed, might it be said that mourning is linked to a politics of anger and failure? – no less than a confrontation with vexing questions as to the role of group transferential identification in the development of a new style of negation. The very title of one of the key works of transition to Surrealism proper from the period of the *mouvement flou*, the period, that is, of most intense group transferential dynamics in the formulation of Surrealism, Max Ernst's painting *Pietà, ou la Révolution la nuit* (1923), is an allusion to the complexities embodied in the relationship between imagining otherness, group dynamics and the question of what 'revolution' could mean since, in part, title and work make iconographical allusion to the failure of hysteria as captured in the pose – and photograph – of Blanche Wittman in a 'Sommeil hypnotique' from the *Iconographie de la Salpêtrière* of 1879–80 (vol. III, plate XXX). How to navigate this terrain of transition will be not only the abiding problem but the abiding contribution of Surrealism.

6 Cf. Karl Löwith, *Martin Heidegger and European Nihilism* (New York: Columbia University Press, 1995).

II

> A philosophy could not *succeed*. It is from the grandeur of its object that it derives its own grandeur; it conserves it in failure.[7]
>
> Aragon

> Consider a map of the world.
>
> Paul Valéry, 'The Crisis of the Mind', 1919

Fig. 57. *Le Monde au temps des surréalistes* (*The Surrealist Map of the World*), *Variété*, 1929

That Surrealism has always been informed by the experience – but never the celebration – of failure, negativity and a sense of radical incompleteness is something that its ablest contemporaries recognized, a generation which once emphasized the aspects of contingency and fragility intrinsic to the Surrealist liberation and the related attempt to construct 'a new ethics and a new aesthetics'.[8] Jules Monnerot, Bataille, Julien Gracq and Maurice Blanchot, when placed within the context of the best critical response to Surrealism – I think of André Rolland de Rénneville, the *Cahiers du Sud*, for example – can be seen as amongst the most fascinating of a very distinguished generation.[9] It is rarely observed that for Breton – no less than Lacan and Guy Debord – the French tradition of moral scepticism was determinant. From the beginning of the formulation in 1922 of the new ethos that would be Surrealism, there is an explicit acknowledgment of the import of the moralist tradition, most famously in 'La confession dédaigneuse' (1923):

> The moralists, I admire them all, particularly Vauvenargues and Sade. Ethics is the great conciliator. To attack it is still to render homage. It is there that I have always found my principal subjects of exaltation.[10]

---

7 Louis Aragon, 'Le songe du paysan', *Paysan de Paris* (Paris: Gallimard, 1926/1979), p. 237.

8 Georges Bourget, quoted in Yves Bridel, *Miroirs du surréalisme* (Lausanne: L'Age d'homme, 1988), p. 90.

9 On Monnerot in relation to Surrealism and the political in the context of the interwar period, cf. Jean-Michel Heimonet, *Jules Monnerot ou la démission critique, 1932–1990* (Paris: Editions Kimé, 1993); on Blanchot on the interpretation of Surrealism see the useful if rather coy study by Laurent Jenny, 'Mauvais rêve, Blanchot surréaliste', in *Critique*, nos 603–4 (August–September 1997).

10 André Breton, 'La confession dédaigneuse', *Les Pas perdus*, in *Œuvres complètes*, vol. 1 (Paris: Gallimard, 1988), p. 195. For an account of the role of the French moralist tradition in the diction of pessimism in Debord, cf. M. Stone-Richards, 'A Reflexion on the French and American Perception of Guy Debord', *Parachute*, no. 93 (January 1999); on the import of the moralist tradition in Lacan, cf. Serge Dubrovsky, 'Vingt Propositions sur l'amour-propre: de Lacan à La Rochefoucauld', *Parcours critique* (Paris: Galilée, 1980), pp. 203–34; and Malcolm Bowie, *Freud, Proust and Lacan: Theory as Fiction* (Cambridge: Cambridge University Press, 1987). On the relationship between revolutionary politics and melancholy, of which Blanqui would clearly be the

In this famous essay which, though published in 1923, is placed intentionally at the opening of *Les Pas perdus* in order to introduce to a larger public the thinking that had come to achieve coherence and form, the question of so many *enquêtes*, *Pourquoi écrivez-vous?*, is replaced by the question, in the shadow of the suicide of Jacques Vaché, *Pourquoi vivre*? (a question extended into the life of the group in the first two issues of *La Révolution surréaliste* with the *enquête*: *Le suicide, est-il une solution*?).[11] The register of moral scepticism, when linked, through the import of Pierre Reverdy's poetry of anguish and immobility, to the views of temporality, negativity and loss developed in the writers, Aragon, Vitrac, Desnos[12] as also the artists, Magritte and Ernst, along with the pursuit of the *insolite* in the city goes hand-in-hand with the experience of negativity (anguish): the suffocating boredom of the bourgeois interior that leads to the inflation of melodramatic violence in Ernst's *Une Semaine de Bonté* (fig. 58) explores the same structural terrain as Magritte's *The Threatened Assassin*, 1927 (fig. 59) or *The Lovers*, 1928 in the shared deployment of a sustained sense of the interplay of the psychic mechanisms governing anguish, pleasure and limit-experience.[13] Such a recognition of the role of negativity and limit-experiences leads to an evaluation of Surrealism from the viewpoint of an ethics of experience which enjoins a political dimension but for which practice there is no available model, not least because Surrealism from its inception can be seen as involved in a process of mourning in a manner that belongs to the nature of group activity as a form of exemplary validity, made all the more heightened by

---

type, cf. Michel Löwy and Robert Sayre, *Révolte et mélancholie: Le Romantisme à contre-courant de la modernité* (Paris: Payot, 1992).

11 That Vaché's letters are replete with the boredom and *désœuvrement* characteristic of soldiers at war – on which there is a very large literature in psychology and poetry, though the poetry of Wilfred Owen might suffice – is scarcely noted but would be far from negligible in the light of our study. On the question of tone of voice in the avant-garde, on the 'interiority' not permitted by the genre of the manifesto, see Breton's response to Claude Lévi-Strauss, in Breton, *Œuvres complètes*, vol. 3 (Paris: Gallimard, 1999), pp. 118–20.

12 Louis Aragon, *Le Paysan de Paris*, 1926; Roger Vitrac, *Connaissance de la mort*, 1926; Robert Desnos, *La Liberté ou l'amour*, 1927. The term *insolite* – a term taken from Symbolism – was the term which, for the Surrealists, translated *Unheimlich* before the accepted translation of *l'inquiétante étrangeté*. A fascinating account of negativity and the insolite is Jules Monnerot's phenomenologico-anthropological interpretation of Surrealism in his *La Poésie moderne et le sacré* (Paris: Gallimard, 1945), pp. 121–33; on Surrealist automatism and the experience of finitude, cf. Maurice Blanchot, 'Réflexions sur le surréalisme', *La Part du feu* (Paris: Gallimard, 1947), and 'L'inspiration, le manque d'inspiration', *L'Espace littéraire* (Paris: Gallimard, 1955).

13 For an extended interpretation of Magritte along such lines, cf. Marcel Paquet, *Magritte, ou l'éclipse de l'être* (Paris: Editions de la différence, 1982); for a comparable interpretation of Aragon's *Paysan de Paris* in terms of finitude and death, cf. Jacques Leenhardt, 'Le passage comme forme d'expérience: Benjamin face à Aragon', in *Walter Benjamin et Paris*, ed. Heinz Wismann (Paris: Cerf, 1986), pp. 163–71.

the role of *amitié* in the affective life of the group as an instance of the Kantian maxim of enlarged thought (*sensus communis*): think from the standpoint of everyone, the other.[14] It is within this light that the representation and comprehension of collective experience within Surrealism must be understood, for the group, as conceived within Surrealism – no less than in the Internationale situationniste and *Tel Quel* – is not a democratic collectivity, but an association based upon *solidarity*, and election, thus anything that would threaten the movement of the experience of solidarity could only hope to re-define the group at the risk of loss, a loss that would leave a difference within the group.[15] After many years of Breton bashing, no less than Sollers and Kristeva, and Debord too, would come to realize this lesson of Surrealism as setting a limit to the historical experience of the avant-garde: freedom, within the industrial complex of modernity, is realizable only within the affective bonds of collective experience. The ethical space constituted by such a mode of exemplarity is a possible movement toward a possible political realm. It can only be a possible movement toward a possible political realm as the group is a form of community with a difference, not least because, within the affective bonds of the group, the

14 It is thus, for Blanchot, in terms of the import of *amitié* to the group, that we might understand the significance of the violence in Surrealist exclusions, both the violence of the act of expulsion and the violence felt which is itself returned. 'Le surréalisme, tel qu'il faut en pressentir la destination, est et a toujours été une expérience collective. C'est le premier trait. Là, nous soupçonnons que le rôle de Breton fut différent de celui que, par admiration, affection ou rancune personnelle, on lui reconnaît. Il ne fut ni un maître, ni un guide, ni un président de parti, ni un chef religieux [...]. Peut-être, toutefois, eut-il ce pouvoir particulier, dans le surréalisme, non d'être plus l'un que ne le furent tous les autres, mais de faire du surréalisme l'Autre de chacun et, dans l'attrait de cet Autre tenu pour une présence-absence vivante (un *au-delà des jours* à l'horizon d'un espace inconnu sans un au-delà), de le vivre avec amitié au sens le plus rigoureux de ce terme exigeant, c'est-à-dire de faire de l'affirmation surréaliste une présence ou une œuvre d'amitié'. Maurice Blanchot, 'Le Demain joueur', in *L'Entretien infini* (Paris: Gallimard, 1969), pp. 598–99. Sartre's critique of the 1947 Exposition internationale du surréalisme at the Galerie Maeght, the first such exhibition after the war, was the occasion of the most public realignment of Breton and Bataille. Cf. the manifesto produced on this occasion, 'Rupture inaugurale', in *Tracts surréalistes et déclarations collectives* II: 1940–1969, ed. José Pierre (Paris: Eric Losfeld, 1982), pp. 30–36.

15 Commenting on the reception of the *Second Manifeste du surréalisme*, Bridel records the response of the Swiss poet Gustave Roud: 'Roud est frappé, dans ce second manifeste, par l'atmosphère d'incertitude et de terreur qui y règne. Le château où Breton situait les surréalistes dans le Premier Manifeste s'est transformé en tribunal et nous assistons à une série de condamnations, après un réquisitoire impitoyable. Roud touche ici un point très important de la vie du groupe surréaliste, tel qu'elle apparaît parfois à travers les textes polémiques, mais qui n'a été vraiment vu et traité avec tout le sérieux qu'il mérite que beaucoup plus tard, en particulier par Jules Monnerot dans *La Poésie moderne et le sacré*, en 1945. Cet aspect révèle bien d'ailleurs à quel point le surréalisme engage tout autre chose que la seule littérature'. Bridel, *Miroirs du surréalisme*, p. 142.

group permanently runs the danger of projecting its own narcissistic ideal as *the* ideal. Not only does this point to the manner in which Blanchot interpreted Bataille and Breton on the significance of community in the 1930s, it confirms the direction of Monnerot's great book *La Poésie moderne et le sacré* which, though published in 1945, goes back, in part, to 1933.[16] Indeed, from the occasion of his significant series of lectures in Haiti, Breton will frequently refer his readers to both Blanchot and Monnerot. Blanchot, declares Breton, author 'of two of the most remarkable works of recent times' – by which Breton must mean *Aminadab* (1942) and *Thomas l'Obscur* (1941) – whose interpretation of Surrealism, expressed through a review of Monnerot's *La Poésie moderne et le sacré*, concentrates on the experience of anguish and being painfully torn (*déchiré*) not only as a function of alienation under Capitalism but as an expression of 'the sense and value of this *nothing*, a proper object of poetry and liberty', in no way distinct from the demand for revolution. Thus Breton quotes Blanchot: 'How could poetry not interest itself in the social revolution?'[17] On many occasions Breton will mention Monnerot's still extraordinary *La Poésie moderne et le sacré* (1945) – the work which more than any other enabled Julien Gracq, Blanchot and Bataille to articulate the cultural significance of Surrealism to a post-World War II generation. In his interview, for example, with the great Haitian poet René Bélance, he refers his audience to the *absolutely convincing* study of *La Poésie moderne et le sacré* for further details on the specificites between Surrealist experience and the experience uncovered by ethnologists and anthropologists – at the level of the group, community, values, role of myth, etc.[18]

Monnerot was the first to reflect systematically upon the status of the group to the self-understanding of Surrealism. In doing so, he characterized the group in terms of a meeting of individuals based upon elective affinities. He terms it, using a term of English sociology, a *set*:

---

16 Cf. Jules Monnerot, *La Poésie moderne et le sacré*. Cf. also Jules Monnerot, 'Remarques sur le rapport de la poésie comme genre à la poésie comme fonction', *Inquisitions: Organe du groupe d'études pour la phénoménologie humaine* (June 1936), pp. 14–20. This unique issue of *Inquisitions* is available in facsimile with documentary material. Cf. Henri Béhar, *Du Surréalisme au front populaire: Inquisitions* (Paris: CNRS, 1990).

17 Maurice Blanchot, 'Réflexions sur le surréalisme' (1945), cited in André Breton, 'Le Surréalisme', lecture delivered in Port-au-Prince, Haiti, December 1945, published in *Conjonction* (Port-au-Prince), no. 1 (January 1946), rpd in André Breton, *Œuvres complètes*, vol. 3, pp. 166–67.

18 André Breton, 'Interview de René Bélance', in *Haiti-Journal* (Haiti; 12–13 December 1945), rpd in *Entretiens* (Paris: Gallimard, 1952/1969), p. 238. On the impact of Monnerot's book, especially its discussion of myth, cf. Antoine Compagnon, 'Evaluations du surréalisme: de l'"illisible" au "poncif" ', *André Breton: Cahier de l'Herne*, no. 72 (Paris: L'Herne, 1998).

> The Surrealist 'set' is but the unstable, missed, imperfect realization of an ideal Form, of a *Bund* (in the sense where *Bund* is opposed both to *Gesellschaft* (society of contract) and to *Gemeinschaft* (community)).[19]

In characterizing Surrealism as a *Bund* (a secret society or secondary community) in opposition to *Gesellschaft* and *Gemeinschaft*, Monnerot, like Bataille, understands Surrealism in terms of the more fundamental distinction between societies based upon affect (*Bund*) and societies based upon contract (which is implicitly a matter of representation) and thereby making of Surrealism a religious phenomenon as Bataille and Monnerot understand religion, that is, not as a necessarily theistic set of doctrines, but as a collective psychic phenomenon that is the necessary by-product of human affectively communal bonds. Monnerot and Bataille will identify the sacred and alterity (the heterogeneous) with the movement of affect against the homogeneous.[20] It is for this reason that Monnerot could identify the mobility of group dynamics in Surrealism as the elaboration of a project, yet a project drawing upon a mode of experience that could not permit achievement since from the opening chapter of *La Poésie moderne et le sacré* Monnerot identifies Surrealist experience with poetry understood as a function of affectivity and as such that which is not susceptible of and *works* against representation.[21] Moreover, in situating the development of Surrealism in terms of an economy of the crisis of expression, Monnerot articulates Surrealist experience in relation to the negativity of affectivity that opens onto the problem of the other: 'Being searching for itself and thinking to have seized itself seizes only the *other*'.[22] And yet, from beginning to end, though Monnerot spoke of Surrealism in terms of group dynamics and *sensibility*, was the first to conceptualize the importance of the collective dimension of the group and to understand the extent to which its accomplishment was a necessary function of group action, he consistently established an internal connection between the conditions of possibility of the group to failure and incompleteness which, for Monnerot – as with Blanchot later on in his account of automatic writing – becomes, in essence, identified with the work of a generation, which has defined what poetry is. Thus he could write that

> Authentic modern poetry [by which Monnerot meant art as experience], to the extent that it is completely independent of this *set* [= the Surrealist group in terms of the dynamics of inter-action characteristic of a *Bund*], or even precedes it chronologically, is Surrealist [... There are those whom one] can neither call Surrealists nor forget them when it is a

---

19 Monnerot, *La Poésie moderne et le sacré*, p. 73.

20 For Bataille's response to Monnerot, cf. Georges Bataille, 'The Surrealist Revolution' and 'The Moral Meaning of Sociology', in Georges Bataille, *The Absence of Myths: Writings on Surrealism*, ed. Michael Richardson (London & New York: Verso, 1994).

21 Cf. Monnerot, *La Poésie moderne et le sacré*, pp. 11 and 13.

22 Ibid., p. 31.

> question of Surrealism [...]. Others who were not Surrealists but who must nevertheless be evoked if one speaks of Surrealism: such as these two very different men: Georges Ribemont-Dessaignes and Georges Bataille.[23]

The common project elaborated by the interaction of these people characteristic of their generation, the kind of experience which preoccupied them required, argued Monnerot, a 'general phenomenology of the imagination'. In giving substance to this position, he said that 'The phenomenology of the feeling-of-other-presence [*sentiment-de-présence-autre*]' cannot fail to draw upon 'clinical descriptions produced by psychiatrists', for this is a kind of experience which empties, discharges [*debouchait*] *on the unlimited, the* informe *and the unknown*.[24] 'This poetry **gives onto** *madness* [*folie*], *but also onto dialectic-lyric, the elaboration of a problematic of existence, impossible possibility, possible impossibility. It gives onto the tragic*'.[25] For those who have lived the war (*la guerre 14–18*), says Monnerot, this sense of the tragic (and the final chapter of Monnerot's book, a chapter entitled 'La porte du tragique [The Gate of the Tragic]', contains a veritable lexicon of terms for failure, emptiness, the *informe*, incompleteness, the elsewhere) must not be reduced to an aesthetic conceived as a specialized activity separate from life, hence the ethical imperative to political action, however impossible of success this action may be, as a recognition that the struggle against a prevailing politicization of experience is not intended to replace this model by another politics *of* experience, but is intended to break the dangerous illusion that experience *is* political in the narrow sense of a particular prevailing nexus of power. Monnerot's articulation of a need for a general phenomenology of the imagination in Surrealism can here be explicated in terms of the Kantian formulation of *sensus communis*, for the communicability of sensation in the Kantian problematic makes recourse to imagination and aesthetic judgment in order to comprehend the possibility of a judgment having universal form which is not, however, a judgment of reason.

The question of judgment is at the heart of modernism and avant-garde experience, and inescapably so. Aesthetic judgment, says Kant, is autonomous, that is, free, and as such not rule-governed: aesthetic judgments are reflective judgments which 'derive' rules from the particular and not, as in judgments of reason, the particular from the universal. Though such judgments of taste are not rule-governed there is nevertheless a sense in which they are universal, and this must be so because the *ought* element in our judgments of taste point to and are presupposed by a common sense (*sensus communis*):

23 Ibid., pp. 190–91, n. 38.
24 Ibid., p. 37. My emphasis.
25 Ibid., pp. 175–76. My emphasis.

> [Judgments of taste] must have a subjective principle, which determines only by feeling rather than by concepts, though nonetheless with universal validity, what is liked or disliked. Such a principle, however, could only be regarded as a *common sense*. [...] Only under the presupposition, therefore, that there is a common sense (by which, however, we [also] do not mean an outer sense, but mean the effect arising from the free play of our cognitive powers) – only under the presupposition of such a common sense, I maintain, can judgments of taste be made.[26]

In section 39 of the *Critique of Judgment*, 'On the Communicability of Sensation', Kant emphasizes the precariousness of the type of pleasure pertinent to the beautiful as a judgment of taste: pleasure in the beautiful is not enjoyment, nor a law-governed activity, it is 'a pleasure of mere reflection. Without being guided by any purpose or principle whatever, this pleasure accompanies our ordinary apprehension of an object by means of the imagination, our power of intuition, in relation to the understanding, our power of concepts'.[27]

Our problem, that of embodiment, that is, of the status of the phantasmatic object and fragmentation in collective representation, is clearly implicated in these lines from Kant when we consider that he speaks of a pleasure which accompanies yet is distinct from our ordinary apprehension of an object – *yet*, this non-linguistic affective experience is communicable: in other words, a form of non-rule-governed, radically formless experience *necessarily* implies a community of comprehension. This is elaborated in section 40 of the third *Critique*, 'On Taste as a Kind of *Sensus Communis*' in which Kant enunciates the maxim requiring the individual 'to think from the standpoint of everyone else'. The problem of what Breton characterizes as the universal murmur, of the *écoute automatique* in relation to the collectivity is none other than this problem: how can any claim of judgment be made without the availability of a decision procedure? The answer can only be, as Hannah Arendt argued following Kant, through exemplary validity. If a judgment of reason is the subsumption of the particular under the general or universal – that is, under rule-governed activity – aesthetic judgment, on the other hand, is always a matter of the assessment of the particular. The problem that this poses to any account of the nature of thinking as an activity of universalization is that a particular cannot be assessed in terms of another particular.[28] In addressing Kant's account of this problematic, Arendt argues for the role of exemplarity in imagination. To take an example from Arendt, it is not that one can *demonstrate* any judgment that is non-cognitive, which is not, that is to say, a matter of reflection. How, then, might we understand courage? Courage is *like* Achilles; the beautiful is like this,

26 Immanuel Kant, *Critique of Judgment*, trans. Werner S. Pluhar (Indianapolis, 1987), section 20, p. 238.

27 Ibid., p. 189.

28 Cf. Hannah Arendt, *Lectures on Kant's Political Philosophy* (Chicago: University of Chicago Press, 1982), p. 76.

etc. No such 'judgment' can be of any value if it is not communicated or is not in principle communicable. The appeal of such a judgment is not *to* a *sensus communis* (a community of sense) but is, rather, an enactment of an implicit relatedness. It is almost like Wittgenstein saying, 'You don't understand? Then do this!' where the verb of action is always an invitation to comparative action. The mode of validity of any such perlocutionary exemplar derives from or is dependent upon its efficacy. To be courageous one must at least act like, be like .... In any case of exemplary validity there is clearly a question of identification. It is my argument that the transferential dynamic of group experience is the mechanism by which this mode of identification comes about and which cannot but be, in some sense, mimetic-affective and thus implicitly a question of the imaginary. Hence, in one sense, the language and tenor of appeal in much Surrealist writing, even when it is theoretical in nature, as it comes up against, time and again, the irreducible stratum of feeling. The appeal is to acknowledge, as though such acknowledgment would thereby open a path of action, indeed, a path to action. (Here we might consider the prevalence of the iconography of the pointed finger in Surrealist art from de Chirico onward.) Thus Breton in the mid-1930s in the Prague lectures on Surrealism and politics:

> Our ambition is to unite, through an indestructible knot – a knot of which we shall have passionately sought the secret as to its indestructibility – this activity of transformation to this activity of interpretation [...] We wish that this knot be made, and that it elicit the desire to unmake it, and that one does not succeed. [...] If one wishes to avoid that in the new society private life, with its opportunities [*chances*] and deceptions remain the great distributor as well as the great usurper [*privatrice*] of energies, then it is only right that subjective existence be prepared for a stunning revenge on the terrain of knowledge, of knowledge without weakness and without shame.[29]

Aragon, in the *Paysan de Paris*, not only cites Hegel, but also Kant on the nature of failure. There he had said that no philosophy could succeed, that, moreover, its grandeur is in relation to its failure and the object that mediated that failure, whether the object be conceived in Hegelian or Freudian terms, we might add. Here we might consider the role of the intersubjectively constituted object in the context of the group understood as a transferential phenomenon since, as is clear, the Surrealist object emerges in a context of internal crisis in the Surrealist group.

29 André Breton, 'Position politique de l'art aujourd'hui' (1935), in *Œuvres complètes*, vol. 2, p. 430. In this extract, Breton quotes from his earlier work *Les Vases communicants* (1932). On exemplary validity and *sensus communis*, cf. Hannah Arendt, *Lectures on Kant's Political Philosophy*.

The emergence and functioning of the Surrealist object in the collective

Though an exhibition of Surrealist objects was announced in *La Révolution surréaliste* in 1926 this was not to take place, and it would not be until 1931–32, in the midst of the internal rupture in the life of the group brought about by the concessions – betrayals? – made by Aragon and Sadoul on the occasion of the Congress of Kharkov in 1931, that there would begin a codification, which would also act as an impetus, of certain developments within Surrealism since the advent of Alberto Giacometti. The already anguishing problems entailed by the Surrealist attempt to join with the Parti communiste français were thus compounded by the Aragon affair and led to interminable internal discussions. Thus, as André Thirion, to whom most accounts of the origin of the Surrealist object in the specifically political dynamics internal to the group are indebted, comments that in relation to the *depression* caused by the Aragon affair the Surrealist group, in the Spring of 1931, subjected itself to critical examination. These discussions, reports Thirion, were endless – how could they be other than interminable? – and so in order to find a moment of conclusion as a means of exit, Breton delegated a commission, composed of Dalí and Thirion, whose responsibility was to 'present immediately realizable concrete proposals which took into account all that had been said'.[30] Where Thirion proposed anticlerical activity, 'Dalí proposed a program for the fabrication of objects with symbolic function "destined, wrote Breton in *Les Vases communicants*, to procure by indirect means a distinct sexual emotion" '.[31]

It is thus clear that not only was the rationale of the commission to formulate a plan of action which would involve the whole group in common activity, the accepted proposal would be one that would emphasize the affective dimension of collective experience. This aspect cannot be omitted from any comprehensive account of the origin and functioning of the Surrealist object, for as the Surrealists were being torn apart by the Aragon affair, Breton sought a means of communal, collective activity to re-enact the group transferential moment necessary to the identity of the group *qua* group. As is known, if not always fully appreciated, the *experience*, if not the fabrication, of Surrealist objects was a collective phenomenon and the concern with and codification of interest in the object without doubt came in response to a profound sense of internal *crisis* in the life of the group as a result of the Aragon affair. Dalí's proposal for the fabrication of objects with symbolic function destined to elicit by indirect means a distinct sexual movement became the means for this renewal of the ideal of the group. The elements of *crisis, movement* and *group* point to a discourse at once pathological (the source of the metaphoric usage of crisis) and phenomeno-

30 André Thirion, *Révolutionnaires sans révolution* (Paris: Robert Laffont, 1972), p. 315.

31 Ibid., p. 315.

logical-analytic: what is the nature of this movement, its source and what is its function in the economy of the group (the question of phantasmatic experience)? Our concern here is less with the theory of the object as formulated by Breton and Dalí than to make sense of the experience of the object and its functioning in the group.[32]

In 1933, there was published in *Le Surréalisme au service de la révolution*, a collection of five reports of 'Recherches expérimentales [Experimental researches]' on various modes of irrational knowledge of which the first concerned 'Sur la connaissance irrationnelle de l'objet *Boule de cristal des voyantes* (5 février 1933), [On the irrational knowledge of the object: *Clairvoyants' crystal ball*]', and, undertaken a week later, the second 'Sur la connaissance irrationnelle de l'objet *Un morceau de velours rose* (11 février 1933) [*A Piece of pink velvet*].'[33] The commentary for these two sessions was written by Arthur Harfaux and Maurice Henry. There is a clear methodology: concerning what type of objects are admissible and the manner of proceeding in the group:

> The method used to date consisted in this: an object, preferably simple, not too fabricated, was chosen, and posed on the table. [...] A list of questions was communally established, a list which afterwards served for experiences bearing on other objects. Then, one responded in writing to each of the questions: the responses were read, with summary comparison, before passing to the next question. [...] The responses will not be read and compared until the end of the game. They will be short, stripped down, and written immediately under the shock of a deep conviction.[34]

It is also made clear, that the response to the object by the members present can, and should, encompass the range of the senses 'for there is no reason that sight alone should be the generator of tactile, gustative, olfactive and auditive images'. Not only is the style of proceeding designed to enable the participants to respond 'under the shock of deep conviction' by taking only that 'amount of attention [...] necessary for contact with the object', it is recognized that certain images and association of ideas that may result from this experimental situation (encompassing the perceptual contact with the object) may be of a nature that is conducive to the construction of phantasmatically shared experiences: thus, in these 'Recherches expérimentales', there is considerable emphasis upon coincidences: 'formal coincidences, coincidences of atmosphere, symbolic coin-

32 For a detailed examination of Dalí's conception of the object along these lines, see M. Stone-Richards, 'Du mouvement, de l'objet et la question du lieu', in *Equinoxe: Revue internationale d'études françaises*, XX–XXI (Fall 2002), pp. 34–52.

33 *Le Surréalisme au service de la révolution*, no. 6 (1933), pp. 10–13 and 20–24.

34 Arthur Harfaux and Maurice Henry, 'A propos de l'expérience portant sur la connaissance irrationnelle des objets', ibid., p. 24.

cidences – two apparently different images being able to constitute two apparently different symbols of the same reality'. Harfaux and Henry, no less than Eluard in his summing up of the 'Possibilités irrationnelles de pénétration et d'orientation dans un tableau Georgio de Chirico: *L'Enigme d'une journée*', make of such coincidence a possible expressive mark of a perceptual condition susceptible to psychic contagion (that is, the mobility of cathexes at the level of the group):

> The lighting, the time, the temperature, the matter in contact with the object, the framework, the number of persons present and the network of their physical and mental states, etc., as many elements which tend to influence the thought of the experimenters, the phenomena of contagion, and, in consequence, the responses.

The resultant contagion being not only a function of the relations between the experimenters but, importantly, a function of 'the matter in contact with the object' – for which reason, the museum is not the place for a Surrealist object –

> It's a question of knowing the objects in their life, in their movement, to make the account of their possibilities. It is by placing them, through collective experience [experiment], in every situation possible, that one will obtain concrete and complete definitions from them, only valid, let it be understood, at a given moment, in a given place, and in given circumstances.

The repeated use of de Chirico's *L'Enigme d'une journée*, (fig. 60) formerly in Breton's collection along with de Chirico's *La Politique*, 1914 (fig. 61), attests both to the Surrealists attempt to think collectively in terms of the restructuring of a shared imaginary – with de Chirico's work functioning as an object of mediation – and to do so in terms of a re-thinking of the role of the city and the mapping of experience and the grid of traditional map-making (figs 57 and 61). In other words, the developing intersubjectively generated phantasms go hand-in-hand with a subjectively generated '*forme d'une ville*' (Baudelaire). That there is present a clear question of illusion and temporality cannot be avoided. Indeed, no considered reflection on the status of experience in Surrealist thought (with its frequent recourse to theatrical imagery) could avoid the recognition that it attested (i) to the presence of illusion (which is produced at the same time as the *instant* of disavowal in the scene of fetishism which thus becomes the 'source' or model of all subsequent experiences of illusion and the sensation of disaggregating spatial frames[35]), as also (ii) to temporality as constitutive of the human subject and experience as part of a metapsychology

35 Cf. Donald Winnicot for whom, whilst acknowledging that 'this matter of *illusion* is one which belongs inherently to human beings and which no individual finally solves for himself or herself', it is still necessary to distinguish the illusion due to fetishism (the delusion that is the denial of the maternal phallus) from the illusion due to

of movement, and, finally, (iii) to an understanding of the body as the form of a *transitional* conception of experience (here, not only Breton's automatism and *alea* in the city, but the paranoiac associations of Dalí become instances of the *béances de la représentation*). In this respect there is an implict, indeed, obvious connection between the theory of the experience of the Surrealist object, whether Dalinian or Bretonian, and the concern with illusion and double-images in the painting of Dalí, for the conception of the object adumbrated by Dalí is predicated upon the facticity of illusion which, for Dalí, in addition to its reference to the maternal realm,[36] is also asserted metaphysically as marking a lack inherent in reality from and through which 'simulacra can easily assume the form of reality and reality in its turn can adapt itself to the forces [*violences*] of simulacra'.

The style of evolution of the category and discourse of the Surrealist object, namely, that it was never the result of an individual but a collective effort, has important methodological as well as philosophical implications, aspects of which bear, not only on the status of the object in Surrealist thought, but on the interpretation of particular constructions such as *La Boule suspendue* (fig. 62). First, it means that the separation of individuals apart from the dynamics of the group could only be at the price of historical accuracy, and thus the tendency to set artists and thinkers against each other (Breton *contre* Dalí, say) ignores the sociological factor of the culture of Surrealism in terms of which a common set of concerns was forged through experimentation and dialogue. There is a vast body of material in the various Surrealist journals, but it fell to few to regard this situation as material for reflective thinking to be organized, either conceptually, or into a coherent position. On the matter of the Surrealist object, this task fell to Dalí and Breton. We shall come to see how telling was the response of each to the question as to whether the crystal ball was 'suited to metamorphoses': for Breton, 'It is the very place of metamorphoses (C'en est le lieu même,)' whilst for Dalí, 'it only reflects them'.[37]

---

transitional phenomena. D.W. Winnicott, 'Transitional Objects and Transitional Phenomena' (1951), *Collected Papers: Through Paediatrics to Psychoanalysis* (London: Institute of Psycho-Analysis and Karnac Books, 1992), p. 240.

36 In 'L'objet à travers l'expérimentation surréaliste', Dalí outlined four distinct phases in the development of the Surrealist object, the final stage of which is the 'tendance à la fusion avec l'objet, à l'unité avec l'objet (famine des objets, objets comestibles)' (Manuscript, Salvador Dalí Museum, St. Petersburg, Florida). Other than the presence of projective identification as a structuring function in this conception of the object, we should note that this reintegration is utterly of a piece with the pursuit of the maternal.

37 *LSASDLR*, no. 6 (1933), p. 20.

The question of place ('le lieu même') is here implicitly linked to the construction of a space of the imaginary that might be an intersubjectively posited spatiality. In 1916, the psychiatrist Georges Dwelshauvers, long admired by a post-Symbolist such as Tancrède de Visan, and who was amongst the first to recognize the potential of Bergson's philosophy of movement and *durée* for psychopathology, published *L'Inconscient*, much of which, in its early chapters, is devoted to the various registers of movement in human experience. In trying to distinguish the physiological from the psychological dimension of movement, Dwelshauvers considers the way in which the movement of a person is habitually in proportion to the anticipated task. In which case, observes Dwelshauvers, if one were confronted with a cardboard box so constructed as to appear like a metal box weighing five kilos, then in going to lift it the disproportion between one's mental and physical preparedness and the fact of what would be actually required to lift the box imitating metal would serve to bring to light the extent to which, ordinarily, movement 'is absolutely unconscious'.[38] This principle of disproportionality, which, moreover, is the phenomenological basis of the aesthetic effect of Duchamp's *Why not sneeze Rose Sélavy?* (1921), has long been known, of course; Dwelshauvers avails himself of the example as a way of showing how the failure of proportionality can make apparent what would otherwise lay hidden in habit, namely, the psychological dimension of movement.[39] (It is in this light that Dwelshauvers can point out that for the contemporaneous research in psychology the unconscious elements of movement are held to be indispensable to the recollection [*souvenir*] of objects.[40]) To show the degree to which the unconscious is implicated in movement, Dwelshauvers refers to a celebrated experiment carried out by Chevreul and reported by Chevreul in a letter to J.-J. Ampère in the *Revue des deux mondes* in 1833. The experiment concerned the holding in an outstretched hand of a pendulum with a weighted body on a flexible wire: does it move '*when one holds it in the hand above certain bodies, although the hand is immobile*'?[41] We do not need to describe the experiment at length, what is most relevant to our argument on the common object and movement in the shared structure of phantasmatic experience in Surrealism, is that, without in any way questioning the good faith of the participants, Chevreul, after acknowledging himself amazed at the movement of the pendulum whilst the arm seemed immobile, soon established that the movement of the pendulum occurred at the unconscious level where, indeed, there was a '*disposition or tendency to movement*, which, quite involuntary though it seemed to me, was thereby all the

38 Georges Dwelshauvers, *L'Inconscient* (Paris: Flammarion, 1916), p. 25.

39 Cf. ibid.

40 Cf. ibid., pp. 34–42.

41 E. Chevreul, 'Lettre à M. Ampère: Sur une classe particulière de mouvements musculaires', *Revue des deux mondes* II:1 (May 1833), p. 249.

more satisfying'.[42] Once the eyes of the experimental subjects were blindfolded, the movements ceased. The inference is then made that the disposition to movement is no longer a merely physiological phenomenon, but a psychic, unconscious phenomenon by which 'a thought is translated outside by movement'[43] (the pendulum being only a means for registering such movement), and so this research into the psychology of movement could propose that precisely what takes place in seances – the knocks and turning tables – is the transferral of thought through the disposition to movement since 'every mental image and every feeling [sentiment] are bound to movements'.[44] It is this psychic dimension of movement that is being exploited in many Surrealist objects such as Giacometti's *La Boule suspendue* and *L'heure des traces* in the context of a group experience (figs 62, 63 and 64): not mysticism, not spiritism, but the economy of affect in movement as passage and transition. The Surrealists do not simply replicate spiritists' seances – hence the importance of the questionnaires that, after the event, make the experience subject to the group in language, in other words, the re-introduction of the register of the symbolic into the experience of phantasy – they create a situation for experimentation for the communication of sensation. 'I count much more', wrote Breton in 1922, 'on the communication of these sensations than on the persuasive capacity of ideas'.[45] In the performative context of Breton's thought in the 1920s, this statement on the communication of sensations – the communicability of affect – entails first a reference to the rapport between hypnotist and subject in the *communauté de sensation*;[46] it entails, too, another dimension of the communicability of sensation in the paralogical dimension of thought for which, on the Kantian model, as with others, the aesthetic was the *exemplary* case, namely, *sensus communis*. As the many responses to the group experience of objects make only too clear, the shared movement of thought was not that concerning a spiritist *au-delà*, but the embodiment of an economy of affect as not infrequently typified by the archaic, anguish and desire.

42 Ibid., p. 251.

43 Ibid., p. 36.

44 Ibid., p. 38.

45 André Breton, 'Caractères de l'évolution moderne et ce qui en participe', *Œuvres complètes*, vol. 1, p. 292.

46 On this *communauté de sensations* in hypnotism and the study of telepathy, cf. Christine Moreau, 'Hypnose et télépathie', in Léon Chertok, ed., *Résurgence de l'hypnose: Une bataille de deux cents ans* (Paris: Desclée de Brouwer, 1984).

III

Surrealism and politics: exaltation, action and the space of power

> For in every action what is primarily intended by the doer, whether he acts from natural necessity or out of free will, is the disclosure of his own image. Hence it comes about that every doer, in so far as he does, takes delight in doing, and since in action the being of the doer is somehow intensified, delight necessarily follows [...]. Thus, nothing acts unless [by acting] it makes patent its latent self.[47]
>
> Dante

From the construction of a common object through transference in the group, I should now like to move to a structurally comparable phenomenon, the construction of shared affective bonds in the creation of a space of exaltation necessary to the appearance of a space of power without which there might be, on Arendt's analysis, no sustainable political space. In other words, to see the manner in which, through the category of exemplary validity, the faculty of *sensus communis* links the aesthetic and the political in Surrealist experience but does so in a manner that reveals the indeterminateness, incompleteness and insufficiency that Blanchot, Monnerot and Bataille held to be definitive of Surrealist experience.

After the debacle of its relations with the PCF, Surrealism gradually defined for itself a more ethically-based notion of protest, a notion of protest which opposed itself to institutionalized forms of politics. The political had, in some measure, to be distanced from politics, and the category of refusal can be seen to be a working model of a position from which a critique of politics might be achieved. This refusal is ethical, but not absolutely separate from the historical ground of the experience of the political. It will be articulated through a conception of exaltation, that is, an affective space in which a common object of accomplishment is sought, though permanently deferred. This way of thinking was to lead to a reformed, though temporary, alliance with Georges Bataille in the form of Contre-Attaque: Union de lutte des intellectuels révolutionnaires.[48]

Contre-Attaque was part of the Surrealists' response to 'le 6 février 1934', the right-wing demonstration at the Place de la Concorde which led to the resignation of the government of Edouard Daladier and which the left construed as a failed

47 The closing sentence of this epigraph, in the Latin, reads: *Nihil igitur agit nisi tale existens quale patiens fieri debet.* Quoted with translation from the Latin by Hannah Arendt, *The Human Condition* (Chicago: University of Chicago Press, 1958), p. 175

48 Cf. Georges Bataille, 'Front Populaire dans la rue', *Cahiers de Contre-Attaque*, no. 1 (May 1936); originally given as a speech on 24 November 1935; rpd in *Œuvres complètes*, vol. 1 (Paris: Gallimard, 1970), pp. 402–12. For an account of *Contre-Attaque*, cf. Robert Short, 'Contre-Attaque'. Elyette Guiol-Benassaya's *La Presse face au surréalisme de 1925 à 1938* (Paris: CNRS, 1982) provides a useful summary of the political reporting of the period.

fascist putsch. The left, rallying around a call by the CGT union, responded with a general strike on 12 February. The success of this counter-demonstration led eventually to the official formation of the Front Populaire on 14 July 1935 at a mass meeting in Montrouge, in the suburbs of Paris. From June 1936 to June 1937, a Front Populaire government, headed by Léon Blum, held power.

The achievements, crises and arguments of this period are well documented and continue to this day. Our concern here is not wholly with this documentation. The customary view of the Surrealists' involvement in the politics of this period (even of those sympathetic to the movement) is that this represented both the crisis and failure of Surrealism.[49] Such a view is too simple, for a number of reasons: first, it does not take into account Breton's and Bataille's understanding of the possibility of success for any change worthy to be considered revolutionary, not to mention their sanguine view of the Front Populaire;[50] second, and more importantly, it does not address the question of the meaning of *action* and thereby what the political could be in Surrealist discourse, a question implicit in the opening of *Nadja* – '*Qui suis-je*?' – which announces the tacit relations between '*Qui suis-je*?' and action through the collective, for if 'I' am that which I '*haunt*', the inadequacy of the word '*hante*' nevertheless

> gives me to understand that what I take to be the objective manifestations of my existence, manifestations more or less deliberated, is but that which crosses over, in the limits of this life, from an activity the true field of which is completely unknown to me.[51]

It is the nature of this field of activity in which the nature of the individual is fragmentarily revealed to itself that is at issue.

In 1937 Breton published 'Limites non frontières du surréalisme';[52] he made declarations against the Moscow trials in, for example, 'La vérité sur les Procès de Moscou' (3 September 1936), other agitatory material such as 'Camarades – les fascistes lynchent Léon Blum!' (February 1936) on the beating up of Léon

---

49 Cf. Robert Short, 'The Politics of Surrealism, 1920–1936', *Journal of Contemporary History* I:2 (1966), pp. 3–25; Henri Lefebvre, '1925', in *André Breton et le mouvement surréaliste*, special issue of *Nouvelle Revue française*, no. 172 (April 1967); Helena Lewis, *The Politics of Surrealism* (New York: Paragon House, 1988).

50 Resolution 5 of Contre-Attaque was unambiguous: 'Nous disons actuellement que le programme du Front Populaire, dont les dirigeants, dans le cadre des institutions bourgeoises, accéderont vraisemblablement au pouvoir, est voué à la faillite'. Declaration of Contre-Attaque: Union de lutte des intellectuels révolutionnaires, 7 October 1935; rpd in *Tracts surréalistes et déclarations collectives, 1922–1969*, vol. 1: 1922–1939, ed. José Pierre (Paris: Eric Losfeldt, 1980), p. 282.

51 André Breton, *Nadja* (Paris: Gallimard, 1928/1964), pp. 9–10.

52 Breton's article was first published in English at the time of the International Surrealist Exhibition in London. Cf. *Surrealism*, ed. Herbert Read (London: Faber, 1936), pp. 95–116 and subsequently in its French form in *Nouvelle Revue française*, no. 281 (February 1937), pp. 200–15.

Blum by Action française members; 'A ceux qui n'ont pas oublié la guerre du droit et de la liberté' (March 1936, written by Georges Bataille though issued under Breton's signature).[53] These political tracts by Breton were being published side by side with works considering artistic matters, as well as, most importantly, *L'Amour fou*,[54] excerpts of which had been published (in 1934) as 'La Beauté sera convulsive'[55] and 'Equation de l'objet trouvé.'[56]

Let us return to 'Limites non frontières du surréalisme', where the conception of political space which we are developing, following Arendt, is clearly in evidence. Breton writes of the spontaneity of the workers' strikes,

> inaugurating a totally unforeseen system of struggle on their part, proceeding to the forced occupation of the factories and, by the sole effect of the simultaneous adoption of such an attitude, came to realize triumphantly their leading demands. The spontaneity and the abruptness of this departure[57] (*for which, quite rightly, none of the existing political parties has taken responsibility*), *the peculiar quality of action undertaken to spread like oil*, the impression that it gave that nothing could stop it from achieving its immediate objectives [... these are such as] to make the most clairvoyant think that the French revolution has begun.[58]

Breton's emphasis on the spontaneous nature of the workers' strikes and insurrections was not idiosyncratic; he shared this with Bataille, and for similar reasons. For both Bataille and Breton, the success or failure of the Front Populaire was seen to depend on the extent to which it could remain *outside the institutional practice of politics*. Underlying this emphasis on a 'totally unforeseen system of struggle' on the part of the workers is the conviction held deeply by Breton and Bataille that the stage of capitalism reached in the form of bourgeois parliamentary democracy necessitated a new conception of political action. In the founding document of Contre-Attaque:

> We affirm that the current regime must be attacked with a renovated tactic. The traditional tactic of revolutionary movements has never been valid save when applied to the liquidation of autocracies. Applied to the struggle against democratic regimes, it has twice led the workers' movement to disaster. Our essential, urgent task, is the constitution of a doctrine *resulting from immediate experiences*.[59]

---

53 These works can be found conveniently collected in *Tracts surréalistes*, vol. 1.

54 In book-form, 2 February 1937.

55 *Minotaure*, no. 5 (1934), pp. 9–16.

56 *Intervention surréaliste*, special issue of *Documents 34* (Brussels, June 1934).

57 On the suddenness of the workers' manifestation most historians and commentators are agreed.

58 André Breton, 'Limites non frontières du surréalisme', *Œuvres complètes*, vol. 2, pp. 200–1. My emphases.

59 Resolution 3, Contre-attaque; rpd in *Tracts surréalistes*, vol. 1, p. 281.

Any such doctrine resulting from *des expériences immédiates* would be one which accorded a primacy of place to the affective bonds linking individuals in the moment of exaltation, in the moment of insurrection *in which a common object, a common goal was constituted* thereby instituting the conditions for a political space in which this commonality could be *accomplished*. This is what the political philosopher Hannah Arendt has termed the space of appearance:

> The space of appearance comes into being wherever men are together in the manner of speech and action, and therefore predates all formal constitution of the public realm and the various forms of government, that is, the various forms in which the public realm can be organized. *Its peculiarity is that, unlike the spaces which are the work of our hands, it does not survive the actuality of the movement which brought it into being,* but disappears not only with the dispersal of men [...] but with the disappearance or arrest of the activities themselves.[60]

Arendt's reference to the 'work of our hands' is crucial, here, for as Margaret Canovan points out, 'Wherever politics has been visualized in the image of making something – as in many revolutionary theories – the implications of the need for central direction, unified sovereignty, naturally follows'.[61] This need to eschew central control was not only motivated by a mistrust of the PCF but followed from Breton's theory of automatism and Bataille's conception of *informe* within a conception of accomplishment. But the reality of power, and particularly the power of the State, is something with which any theorist of the political domain within modernity has to reckon, for as Arendt observes, 'Power is what keeps the public realm, the potential space of appearance between acting and speaking men, in existence'.[62] It is such a conception of public space as a space of freedom and exaltation that linked Bataille and Breton in 1935 in their

---

60 Arendt, *The Human Condition*, p. 199. My emphasis.

61 Margaret Canovan, *The Political Thought of Hannah Arendt* (London: Methuen, 1974), pp. 69–70. Cf. Canovan's more recent *Hannah Arendt: A Reinterpretation of Her Political Thought* (Cambridge: Cambridge University Press, 1992). Arendt herself wrote: 'Since all acting contains an element of virtuosity, and because virtuosity is the excellence we ascribe to the performing arts, politics has often been defined as an art. This, of course, is not a definition but a metaphor, and the metaphor becomes completely false if one falls into the common error of regarding the state or government as a work of art, as a kind of collective masterpiece. In the sense of the creative arts, which bring forth something tangible and reify human thought to such an extent that the produced thing possesses an existence of its own, politics is the exact opposite of an art [...]. Political institutions, no matter how well or how badly designed, depend for continued existence upon acting men; their conservation is achieved by the same means that brought them into being. Independent existence marks the work of art as a product of making; utter dependence upon further acts to keep it in existence marks the state as a product of action'. Hannah Arendt, 'What is Freedom?', *Between Past and Future: Eight Exercises in Political Thought* (New York: Viking, 1961/1968), p. 153.

62 Arendt, *The Human Condition*, p. 200.

opposition to those concerned with seizing the power of the State. (Much later, in reflecting on May '68, Blanchot, no less than Foucault and Deleuze, would reject the very notion of the seizure of power as an implicitly totalitarian conception. Thus if there is question in Surrealist thought of utopia it is that of a negative utopia.) In 'Vers la révolution réelle', Bataille confronted this question directly:

> The question of Revolution, of the seizure of power, must be posed in positive and precise terms, in relation to an immediate reality. [...] All of revolutionary politics is dominated by the schema of the proletarian seizure of power [...]. Practically, considerations of this order result in no application, not even in a simple plan of action, and the only real objective has become party propaganda, electoral struggle.[63]

Instead, argues Bataille, it is necessary to recognize the transition from a capitalism of autocracies to a capitalism of democracy in which the conditions of struggle are entirely new '[and which] in no way hold out the possibility of movements analogous to the Paris Commune or the October revolution'.[64]

It is here, though, that the reality of power understood as that which maintains the public realm as *the potential space of appearance* between acting and speaking beings in the context of accomplishment, encounters what Paul Ricoeur has called *l'énigme du pouvoir*,[65] and thereby the aporias of Surrealist thought on the political in relation to desire, for 'a reflection on force leads directly to the enigma consituted by the phenomenon of power'.[66] In this light, the need to maintain the public realm as the potential space of appearance led Bataille to a conception of exaltation which attempted to turn the affective manipulation of the mass to left revolutionary ends and the form of the institutionalization of which would be nearer the model of the Terror than the Commune of 1871. As early as his 1925 review of Trotsky's *Lénine*, in the very midst of the internal debate on the nature and scope of the Surrealist revolution, Breton had touched on this problem, saying how unfortunate, regrettable it would be if as a group the Surrealists continued to refer to the Conventions and yet 'we should be able to relive with exaltation only the two years after which everything starts all over again'. Indeed, argues Breton, if the prestige of Marat and Robespierre is not to be without value (a useless prestige, he writes), a clear-sighted recognition of the implications of their *desire* is required:

---

63 Georges Bataille, 'Vers la révolution réelle: De la phraséolgie révolutionnaire au réalisme', *Les cahiers de Contre-attaque*, 1936; rpd in Bataille, *Œuvres complètes*, vol. 1 (Paris: Gallimard, 1970), p. 413.

64 Ibid., p. 414.

65 Cf. Paul Ricoeur, 'L'éthique et la politique', *Du texte à l'action: Essais d'hérméneutique* (Paris: Seuil, 1986).

66 Ibid.

> But if, as I think, we are above all in search of *insurrectional means* [my emphasis], I wonder, outside of the emotion that [Marat and Robespierre] have given us once and for all, I wonder practically what we are waiting for.[67]

To demand the ends is also to demand the means, thus Breton argued, linking the Front Populaire manifestations and the Spanish Civil War, that whilst for certain *temporary* forms of social exploitation passive resistance could be a legitimate response, it is nevertheless necessary to be prepared through violence for the return of 'exploitation under forms still infinitely more bold and sinister', not least because

> the entry onto the scene of the workers militia, to the horror of the government of the Popular Front, marks, as one has been able to say of the war, 'the continuation of politics by other means' [and which thereby brings forward] the time of the resolution of the social crisis in the *only place where it can take place* [my emphasis], which is to say, *in the street.*[68]

This 'automatism in the streets' is matched by Bataille who is equally clear, as we have shown, on the necessity of avoiding traditional politics:

> first we must protest against everything that is created in the empoisoned atmosphere of congresses and professional committees, at the mercy of lobbying manoeuvres.[69]

Bataille continues:

> If we speak of the Popular Front, what we wish to designate first in order to bind us strictly, in order to bind our origin to the emotion which composes it, is the existence of the Popular Front *in the street.*[70]

The question of violence, here, is intimately linked to the reality, the enigma of State power; it is, too, linked to the reality of failed revolutions.[71] In a sketch from *Les Cahiers de Contre-attaque* for a proposed study of 'L'autorité, les foules et les chefs', Bataille and Breton wrote:

> *Without any exception*, every revolution to date has been followed by an individualization of power. For revolutionaries, this fact poses an essential question, without doubt the capital question, even. We think that such a question must be elucidated in the most open manner, without

67 André Breton, 'Léon Trotsky: Lénine', *La Révolution surréaliste*, no. 5 (July 1925), p. 29.

68 Breton, 'Limites non frontières du surréalisme', pp. 201–2.

69 Bataille, 'Front populaire dans la rue', p. 404.

70 Ibid. My emphasis.

71 This question, namely, Why do revolutions fail?, motivated much of the work of Arendt and also the work of Walter Benjamin and the Frankfurt School. The status of the work of art as a site of imaginative possibility is intimately linked, for these thinkers, to the conditions for the success or failure of changes in the law.

> blind optimism or shrinking back. [. . .] Constraint and refusal in front of authority, can it, yes or no, be much more than the principle of individual isolation, the basis of human community?[72]

In order to protect the revolution, a model of community would be required which could maintain the form of exaltation resultant from the affective bonds realized in commonality, and in this respect, the role of exaltation in the creation of a space of appearance – whether in the role of common action by the Surrealists or in the practice of Acéphale by Monnerot, Bataille and others – is structurally comparable to the role of affective identification in Blanquist's group dynamics, with this singular difference, that the withdrawal (*le retrait*) by the Surrealists and Bataille from any engagement with the politics of parties goes hand-in-hand with an acute sense of incompleteness, failure and difference that prevents the narcissistic aspects of the group transferential ideal from being taken as a model of community to be imposed on others, as if, says Blanchot, 'to renounce failing [*échouer*] were more grave than to renounce succeeding'.[73] Likewise, Monnerot, in identifying before Sartre, the role of the instant in the temporality of Surrealist experience, could observe that in spite of the drive toward the absolute characteristic of Breton, Bataille and others within the culture of Surrealism, the specificity of the instant 'is that it offers no take to whomever would like to become fastened there. What is proper to time [. . .] is to be our death in action'.[74] The model of community thus slowly arrived at is one, then, unlike Communism or Fascism, which is based on a principle of incompleteness and insufficiency.[75] To speak of protecting the revolution, then, is not to speak of protecting the seizure of power, but of addressing how to leave open the modalities of encounter (*la rencontre*): chance and the movement of alterity in which, says Monnerot, 'The work's always uncompleted (it is at their peril and risk that they should become completed. The final trait risks to cross out everything that preceded) conceals a certain time of the powers of trial and shock'.[76] It is for this reason that Blanchot, from his 'Quelques réflexions sur le surréalisme' (1945) to *La Communauté inavouable*, (1983) refuses to place Bataille and Breton in opposition, even when one takes into account the very different role that Hegel plays in their thinking, *for nowhere is Bataille or Breton utopian* if by this one understands the presence, however heuristic, of a blueprint for the future. Thus could Blanchot quote Breton on the evident realization that the accomplishment of history could not possibly be taken to 'solve' the things that mattered:

---

72 Georges Bataille and André Breton, 'L'autorité, les foules et les chefs'; rpd in *Tracts surréalistes et déclarations collectives*, pp. 288–89.

73 Maurice Blanchot, *L'Espace littéraire* (Paris: Gallimard, 1955), p. 182.

74 Monnerot, *La Poésie moderne et le sacré*, p. 167.

75 Cf. Blanchot, *La Communauté inavouable*, pp. 15–17.

76 Monnerot, *La Poésie modern et le sacré*, p. 166.

> there are in us certain lacunae that all the hope that we place in the triumph of communism will not fill; has not man made himself irreducibly an enemy for man; and boredom, will it finish only with the world; every assurance as to life and honour, is it not vain, etc.[77]

It is thus significant that in *Les Vases communicants*, from which Blanchot's citation of Breton is taken, the *poète à venir* (the coming poet) as figure of the *communauté à venir* (the coming community) is a figure that remains within the power of the figure of night (Novalis), alongside *la fenêtre noire*.[78] No plan can be derived from its imagining. If this is a form of utopia, then it is an anarchist – or negative utopia – one without project, without design on the seizing of centralized power such as Blanchot holds was manifested in the events of May '68: *a community of lovers*:

> 'Without project': that was the mark, at one and the same time anguishing and fortunate, of a form of incomparable society which did not allow itself to be seized, which was not called upon to continue, to become installed, even if that would be through the multiple 'committees' through which there was stimulated a disordered-order, an imprecise specialization.[79]

In place of a traditional model of the revolutionary seizure of power, the negative utopia of May '68 – and here there is play upon utopia as *without place* – was instead characterized by a being-together (*d'être-ensemble*) in a time of the in-between (*entre-temps*) where the evidence of equality in fraternity was *explosive communication* and *the liberty of speech*.[80]

Bataille and Breton, during the Contre-Attaque phase, articulate a much under-appreciated aspect of a certain type of avant-garde thinking, that kind of non-technicist avant-garde thinking that is not bound to technology, namely, they begin to theorize *the failure of revolutions*, for all revolutions past have been betrayed, they argue, by the individualization of power arising from the 'need' to satisfy the mass (for example, through the redistribution of the goods of the ruling elite) which, need being in principle insatiable, has in its train necessitated a centralizing authority to control the mass. This centralized authority *is* the narcissistic ideal transposed to the realm of political sovereignty. Not surprisingly, Breton and Bataille's conception of political community alludes, but only in certain points, to a conciliar system of governance – the

---

77 André Breton, quoted in Maurice Blanchot, 'Réflexions sur le surréalisme', *La Part du feu* (Paris: Gallimard, 1949/1993), p. 100.

78 Cf. André Breton, *Les Vases communicants* (Paris: Gallimard 1932/1970), pp. 166–71.

79 Blanchot, *La Communauté inavouable*, p. 52. On the community of lovers and Blanchot's anarchist 'utopia', cf. the excellent study by Gerald Bruns, *Maurice Blanchot: The Refusal of Philosophy* (Baltimore and London: Johns Hopkins University Press, 1997), pp. 244–51.

80 Blanchot, *La Communauté inavouable*, p. 52.

nearest equivalent in modern times to the classical Greek conception of the *polis*. That such a system of governance would seem impracticable is not the criticism that some might think, for its impossibility points to the absence of any genuine political, that is, *public* space within the industrial complex of modernity in the form of the nation-state and the monopoly of power (that is, violence) which is part-and-parcel of its theory of sovereignty. We are instead given a *social* sphere, the sphere pre-eminently of violence and policing in the maintenance of normative practice. The conception of action and public space articulated by Breton and Bataille holds a paradigmatic significance in making clearer the nature of the reality of political power in modernity, not least by addressing the unacknowledged negativity of prevailing political power as also in addressing the question of the failure of revolutions of power and sensibility.

André Thirion, a former Surrealist and Communist who became a Gaullist in 1945, recognized the significance of Contre-Attaque[81] which he met with an intermingling of satisfaction and irritation, but nevertheless as 'one of the most significant texts of the period' precisely for its attempt to give a new and precise definition of revolution in a manner that freed the thinking of revolution from any relation to nationalism.[82] Quite rightly rejecting 'the myth of June 1936, that of the missed revolution',[83] Thirion points out that 'Nowhere did the workers on strike pass from the corporative to the political'.[84] An observation which cannot be gainsaid, but this same Thirion also pointed out that in 1939 these same workers had their gains significantly reduced under a new regime. Thus when he dismisses Trotsky's call *à l'époque* for the constitution of workers' councils as parody, he shows himself not to have grasped the significance of the conciliar system implied in Contre-Attaque, for at issue was a conception of the political which was first and foremost ethical. The conception of the political at issue is one which 'prolongs ethics [...] by giving it a sphere in which to operate. In addition, it prolongs the second constitutive requirement of ethical intention, the requirement of mutual recognition – the requirement that makes me say: your freedom is equal to my own. Indeed, the ethics of politics consists in nothing other than *the creation of spaces of freedom*'.[85] The absence of such spaces of freedom is part of the politics of melancholy.

There was never a capitulation on the part of the Surrealists to such conditions, for the integrity of the collective at the least secured itself in a state of grace, that state wherein the law of the social realm having been transcended,

81 'En octobre 1935, un tract publia la résolution *Contre-Attaque* scellant l'accord temporaire des deux écrivains français dont la pensée est la plus riche du XXe siècle, Bataille et Breton'. Thirion, *Révolutionnaire sans révolution*, p. 430.

82 Cf. ibid., p. 431.

83 Ibid., p. 427.

84 Ibid., p. 428.

85 Ricoeur, *Du texte à l'action*. My emphasis.

the group lives by its own contingency. In the manifesto published after the *Congrès pour la défense de la culture* in 1935, *Du temps que les surréalistes avaient raison*, the Surrealists recognized that

> Unhappily today opportunism tends to annihilate these two essential components of the revolutionary spirit such as it has hitherto manifested itself: the – dynamic and creative – refractory nature of certain beings, their concern in common action to fulfil, to the utmost possible, their obligations to themselves and others.[86]

Though there are differences in the positions of Bataille and Breton, they were absolutely agreed on one thing: that the possibilities of truly significant change (that is, changes in the forms and sensibilities of life which could alone be adduced revolutionary) could not be controlled or *predicted*, and thereby, at all costs, the tempestuous events of the mid-1930s had to remain in the streets, outside, that is, the normal practice of politics – and for both, this meant above all outside the control of the PCF. Thus for both Breton and Bataille, the subsequent failure of the Front Populaire, though deeply disappointing, was not a surprise.[87]

IV

Retracing beginnings

> ... in mourning time is needed ...[88]
>
> Sigmund Freud, *Mourning and Melancholia*, 1917

The refusal of the Party by the principal participants in the culture of Surrealism was but part of a larger refusal of European political culture; that they groped for an alternative conception of values is not something that anyone would deny. For many, the example of Surrealism, and not its theory, is what is commendable. What, after all, could a group of intellectuals possibly hope to achieve amidst such political and moral disaster? The example of Surrealism, however, resides as much in its theories as in its intransigence, and in this concluding section I shall consider some of the ways in which its implicit reflection on failure is part-and-parcel of the manner in which it both engages the power of the imaginary and yet avoids some of the pitfalls of the imaginary

86 André Breton, *Position politiques du surréalisme* (Paris: Sagittaire, 1935), pp. 109–10.

87 The degree to which Bataille anticipated and sought the rapprochement with Breton can now be more clearly appreciated with the publication of *Georges Bataille: Choix de lettres, 1917–1962*, ed. Michel Surya (Paris: Gallimard, 1997), pp. 109–10.

88 Sigmund Freud, 'Mourning and Melancholia', in *Standard Edition*, vol. 14 (London: Hogarth Press and the Institute of Psycho-Analysis, 1981), p. 252.

and the realization of the transferential dimension of the group ideal as a form of narcissism. Not only failure, but the sense that Surrealism is always confronted with its alterity is something that the generation of Monnerot, Rolland de Rénneville and Blanchot took for granted, hence Sartre, in his critique of Surrealism on the occasion of the 1947 *L'Exposition surréaliste*, could speak of its Hegelian anthropological dimension, its dimension of totality. As early as 1925, in 'Le bouquet sans fleurs', Breton declared that nothing would be beyond Surrealist commitment, and in so doing began that vertiginous openness to systems of knowledge whilst itself avoiding systematicity. This gives that distinctive tenor of *la connaissance surréaliste* (Breton's term) in which one encounters a plurality of voices. In his reflections on *Nadja*, Blanchot would go as far as to identify this plurality of voices as definitive of Surrealist experience – the necessary correlate of which is an incompleteness of experience – whereby through the affirmation of the collective dimension Surrealism is always experienced by its members as something always apart from them, as something always *in the third* (*en tiers*):

> The Surrealist affirmation affirms, thus, this multiple space which does not become unified, and which never coincides with the understanding that individuals, grouped around a faith, a work, can sustain in common.[89]

This plurality of voices and incompleteness is what distinguishes the Surrealist group from any other group as avant-garde, namely, 'to be several, not in order to realize something, but without any other reason (moreover hidden) than to bring plurality into existence in giving it a new sense'.[90] The understanding of Surrealism as an experience of alterity and negativity, of failure and limit-experience – and we note that not even a Thirion, still less a Monnerot or Blanchot, ever sets Bataille and Breton up as oppositions, however supposedly heuristically – should modify the way in which one might think the historical relationship between Surrealism and the PCF and by extension Surrealism and the political.

It has long been realized that the Surrealists' adherence to the PCF was less a mark of profound commitment to anti-capitalism as understood by traditional Communists than a mark of their profound *ethical* refusal of the world of the bourgeoisie, of the modern world as unremittingly bourgeois. To this extent, their anti-capitalism was contingent upon the perception that capitalism was the economic expression of the values of the bourgeois modern world, and parliamentary democracy its institutionalized political embodiment. Hence, Théodore Fraenkel, in the fascinating notes of a conversation with Léon Pierre-Quint in 1936, in the midst of the Front Populaire phenomenon, could dismiss the prevailing political options from a Surrealist point of view:

89 Blanchot, *L'Entretien infini*, p. 600.
90 Ibid., p. 601.

> We are living on completely outdated political ideas. The reactionaries depend on the Monarchists of the 17th century – and Maurras has brought no innovation – the liberals on the ideas of the 19th century: St. Simon etc – the Socialists: Proudhon, 1848, L. Blanc – the Communists on Marx, end of 19th century. But after 1918, the 20th century really started. The war made the breach [*coupure*] – which is an abyss. Every old ideology is outdated.[91]

For this reason Fraenkel, as recorded by Pierre-Quint, considered what a Surrealist group in politics might have been:

> For me, the autonomous group which needs to be created, would have for its essential aim less the overturning of capitalism – thus at least it would be Marxist – than the overturning of the bourgeoisie. Moreover it would be necessary to go deeper in order to see if capitalism and bourgeoisie are not indissolubly bound.

The refusal of the modern world as the symbolic representation of the values of the bourgeoisie was an ethical refusal entailing a political correlate, hence, too, Fraenkel's observation on the sense of political obligation which led the Surrealists to leave behind the '*anarchie Revue Blanche*' of their Symbolist filiations. The pathological term *crisis* that would seem so essential to any avant-garde's self-definition of itself *qua* avant-garde is a term that effects an intrinsic link to a contemporaneous world of political economy.[92] Thus at each stage of the self-definition which served to carry the Surrealists further into the relation between the ethical and the political, there is recourse to the language of crisis: 'Surrealist activity has just passed through a crisis which must come to an end',[93] it is said in 1927 in 'Au grand jour' as five Surrealists publicly declare themselves for the PCF. In 1925, as represented in 'Pourquoi je prends la direction de la Révolution surréaliste', there was an earlier definitional crisis as reported by Breton:

> We are in 1925. I speak for those who have seen the peace insinuate itself, and not a few governments failing; for those who have seen the inexpressible purpose to which they held begin to fade, some men and even some women weaken. Their eyes have the colour of time.[94]

---

91 Théodore Fraenkel, 'Notes in the hand of Léon Pierre-Quint, being the record of a conversation, November 1936', Naf 18360, Manuscript, Bibliothèque nationale, Paris. See Appendix I.

92 It is well known that the Surrealists' acceptance of the politics of the public domain began with supporting the Moroccan uprising against French colonial rule in 1925, the Riff incident as it is sometimes termed, but no less important is the state of the left in the Cartel des gauches, etc.

93 *Au grand jour* (Paris: Editions surréalistes, 1927); rpd in *Tracts surréalistes et déclarations collectives* I, p. 67.

94 André Breton, 'Pourquoi je prends la direction de la Révolution surréaliste', *La Révolution surréaliste*, no. 4 (July 1925), p. 1.

The essential question posed in this reflection by Breton: are we, Surrealists, are we artists, merely artists? What implication, implicit in Breton's language, would the response to this question have for the development of Surrealism, for Surrealism in its desire to pursue its *struggle*, a situation in which 'the conditions of struggle remain to be defined' and this in spite of 'the risk of absolute *désœuvrement* that we [Surrealists] were running'. Breton records the internal crisis as a mark of dialogue (*le débat*) centring around the problem of embodiment under the form of the passage to action, that is, in Breton's terms, the objectivation of ideas:

> From inside [our debate] it would be preferable to avoid the hardening of certain, more or less artificial opinions, which, in the nature of things, may one day paralyse us. [...] The problem of the objectivation of ideas which dominates the debate occupying us, is, naturally, that which has given occasion to the bitterest controversies amongst us.[95]

The struggle to be defined, at once linked to a *Guerre au travail! – C'est le parfait mannequin de Giorgio de Chirico, descendant l'escalier de la Bourse* (fig. 65) – is linked, too, in a serious if troubling way, to the problematic of violence as, in the next issue of *La Révolution surréaliste*, Breton, as we saw, in his review of Trotsky's *Lénine*, evokes the period of the Terror, demanding that the means be found for what we are waiting. The need to articulate the passage between that for which one waits (*ce que nous attendons*) and the means of its realization or embodiment compels Breton to reflect upon the meaning of 'Révolution surréaliste':

> If the words 'Révolution surréaliste' leave most people sceptical, at least, they do not deny us a certain ardour and the sense of certain possible devastations. It is for us not to misuse such a power.[96]

Whence the questions that would define the viability and exigencies of '*la cause surréaliste*'[97]:

> But Surrealism, is it a force of absolute opposition or an ensemble of purely theoretical propositions, or a system based upon the confusion of all plans, or the first cornerstone of a new social edifice? According to the response that each appears to elicit a comparable question, each will force himself to give *to Surrealism* all that he can: *the contradiction is not there to frighten us.*[98]

The recognition of this contradiction as intrinsic to, constitutive of what is distinctive to Surrealism, to *la cause surréaliste*, has long been noted. Hence Henri Ey, in 'La Psychiatrie devant le surréalisme', quotes Blanchot stating with

95 Ibid., p. 3.
96 Ibid.
97 Ibid.
98 Ibid. My emphasis.

characteristic simplicity: 'the characteristic [*le propre*] of Breton's school is to have always solidly maintained together irreconcilable tendencies'.[99]

It cannot, therefore, be a surprise to find Joë Bousquet, in a letter written to Breton after receiving the issue of *La Révolution surréaliste* containing Breton's review of Trotsky's *Lénine*, taking as evident the political implications of the ethical position of Surrealism:

> It's here that I have just read in *La Révolution surréaliste*, which I received some days ago, the article that you devoted to Lenin. I see that you consider the publication of [Trotsky's book] as an occasion to affirm that Surrealism as you have defined it [an ensemble of spiritual investigations, a state of mind, no longer an attitude of refusal, but, now, an attitude of combat] bears moreover its political application: which was obvious.[100]

Ce qui était évident. The question would remain, however, as to the mode, the *style* of this politics amidst 'irreconcilable tendencies', in the elaboration of a conception of experience as transitional, as passage, marked by radical contingency and fragility, and dissolutive modes such as anguish, *ennui*, the *informe*. Clearly, it could not be a question of a political party in the sense hypothesized by Fraenkel in his conversation with Léon Pierre-Quint, not least as Breton noted in 'Pourquoi je prends la direction de la Révolution surréaliste', because of '*le risque de désœuvrement absolu que nous courions*', but also because, as Blanchot observed in 'Le Demain joueur', 'Surrealism is always in third'. Breton does not speak of *la cause freudienne*, still less *la cause bretonienne*, he speaks of *la cause surréaliste* in terms of which it is demanded that 'each will make himself render *to* Surrealism all that he can'.[101] This presence of Surrealism as always in a relation of thirdness has implications also for the temporality of group experience as a model, a type, indeed, of avant-garde experience as a temporality of delay, of the provisional, a temporality that is in no way distinct from the temporality of mourning, in which mourning, Freud observed, time is needed.

The keen awareness of failure, incompleteness and the impossibility of adequation between an ideal and its possible instantiation in the political sphere constantly tempered the rhetoric of assertiveness that the Surrealists used in their manifestos: the writings beyond the manifestos never separate ethical reflection from the possibility of failure at the societal level. Hence the implicit importance and role of mourning in Surrealism: from the encounter with the traumatic

99 Maurice Blanchot, quoted in Henri Ey, 'La Psychiatrie devant le surréalisme', *Evolution psychiatrique* XIII:4 (1948), p. 44.

100 Joë Bousquet, letter to André Breton, 25 October 1925, in *Vers l'action politique: Juillet 1925–avril 1926*, ed. Marguerite Bonnet (Paris: Gallimard, 1988), p. 28.

101 Breton, 'Pourquoi je prends la direction de la Révolution surréaliste', p. 3. My emphasis.

neuroses in the Great War, from personal loss (Vaché, Nadja, Crevel) through the quest for purpose (the ruptures in deep friendship: Aragon, Eluard), there is a constant attempt to relate the movement of the group with the movement of the historical, but a historical defined in terms of the delayed recognition of personal, group and cultural loss: the time of Surrealism, from its inception, *à la veille d'une révolution*, is always *a time to come*: *il faut tout attendre de l'avenir* declares the frontispiece of *La Révolution surréaliste* in 1924; the poet evoked at the end of *Les Vases communicants* (1932) is the *poète à venir*, just as, in 'Rupture inaugurale' in 1947, marking the definitive break with Communism, now considered a form of moral extermination, '*Le surréalisme est ce qui SERA*'.[102] The temporality of Surrealism is inextricably linked to the movement of the loss of Europe (fig. 57), from the still-life collage letter that Breton made for Vaché, but which was never received by its addressee, to the still-life collage that he made to commemorate the death of Vaché at the end of the War in 1919 with the fragment 'Souvenez-vous de 1914 / Pas d'Allemands' creating in this circuitry a caesura of emptiness (fig. 66):

> Let it be well understood, however, that we do not wish to take any active part in the outrage that men perpetuate against man. That we have no civic attachment [*préjugé*]. That, in the current state of society in Europe, we remain attached to the principle of all revolutionary action, even indeed when it should take as its point of departure the class struggle, provided that it leads far enough.[103]

The moment of clear situating of the ethical in relation to the political in 1925 carries, internal to the imago of the group, the weights and contradictions in *the idea* of Europe become object of Surrealist critical agency. By 1933, Breton and most of the Surrealists, including Bataille at the time of the Contre-Attaque alliance in 1935, knew that revolutionary action in the Stalinist framework would not lead far enough, that Stalinism would be fundamentally incompatible with the ethical requirements of beauty, truth and justice:

> Let beauty, truth, justice incline their charming and spectral brows on our tomb, we are certain always to revive.[104]

---

102 Some of the most remarkable contemporaneous studies of Surrealism and politics are to be found in the *Cahiers du Sud*.

103 Breton, 'Pourquoi je prends la direction de la Révolution surréaliste', p. 3. The excellent issue of *Mélusine* on 'L'Europe surréaliste', contains some very fine studies on Europe in the imaginary of Surrealism. The account that I develop here, though continuous with this anthology, is markedly different in its emphasis on the temporality of delay and its link to the temporality of mourning as a means of encompassing the complex ambiguities of the Surrealists' attitudes to the idea/object of Europe. Of particular value is the bracingly written study by Jeanne-Marie Baude, 'L'image de l'Europe dans la Révolution surréaliste', in *Mélusine*, no. 14, *L'Europe surréaliste* (Lausanne: L'Age d'Homme, 1994), pp. 51–62.

104 Breton, 'Pourquoi je prends la direction de la Révolution surréaliste', p. 3.

The barbarism of Stalinism which led to the loss of faith in Communism on the part of the Surrealists – and the diction of faith is everywhere present in 'Pourquoi je prends la direction de la Révolution surréaliste' – still went hand-in-hand with a faith that, in Valéry's famous phrase as reported by T. S. Eliot, *L'Europe est finie*. It was finished by the Great War, which, in Fraenkel's words, opened up an abyss, and the only issue remaining for Valéry, in the still stunning reflections of 'La Crise de l'esprit européen', was the damning and telling question: 'Will Europe become *what it is in reality* – that is, a little promontory on the continent of Asia?'[105]

The Surrealists' response to this loss was not the register of superior nostalgia of a Valéry. Having broken with Valéry in 1927 upon his accession to the Académie, in 1928, Breton and Eluard made a series of *détournements* of Valéryan sententia, of which the most famous is the sententious declaration: 'A poem must be a debacle of the intellect. It cannot be anything else';[106] but as telling is the diction of *collective* exposure in another *détournement* of Valéry:

> Poetry, in a time of complication of the language, of conservation of forms, [...] of childishly meddling minds, is an exposed thing. We wish to say that one should invent verse today. And moreover the rites of all species.[107]

What in Eluard and Breton become the *débâcle de l'intellect*, the *chose exposée* – the articulation of which is *lyrisme* as 'the development of a protestation' – however ironic in relation to Valéry, are made part of an economy of traumatic penetration in a sleight *détournement* that makes the already proximal terms of Valéry's thought consistent with Surrealist thinking on passivity, whose origination cannot be held separate from the trauma of war:

> Lyricism is the genre of poetry which assumes the *inactive voice* – the voice indirectly returning to, or provoking – the things which one does not see and of which one experiences the absence.[108]

The ironic intention is to deflate the preciosity of Valéry. . . . Yet the language of penetration, inactivity and absence extends from the *impersonal* experience of 'the things which one does not see' to the level of 'Europe' as, also in 1929, the Surrealists produced *The World in the Time of the Surrealists / The Surrealist Map of the World* (fig. 57), a diminished Europe, which cannot but be seen as a

105 Paul Valéry, 'La Crise de l'esprit européen' (1919), was first published in English in two parts as 'The Crisis of the Mind' in *The Athenaeum* (11 April and 2 May 1919); rpd in new translation in *Paul Valéry: An Anthology*, ed. James R. Lawler (London: RKP, 1977), p. 102.

106 André Breton and Paul Eluard, 'Notes sur la poésie', *La Révolution surréaliste*, no. 11 (March 1928), p. 53.

107 Ibid.

108 Ibid.

response to Valéry's question, 'Will Europe become *what it is in reality* – that is, a little promontory on the continent of Asia?' *The World in the time of the Surrealists, the Surrealist map of the world* indicates an emphatic yes, whence the beginning of a dialogue between Surrealism in Paris and Eastern Europe, extending to Japan, and to the black world of Northern Africa, Haiti and Martinique. It cannot be lost sight of that much that is most creative in Surrealism after World War II will be due to the great women – such as Joyce Mansour – and black intellectuals present in the movement from the early 1930s – Monnerot's and the Martiniquan students' *Légitime défense*.

And yet. . . . The analysis of the loss of Europe of Valéry, whose nihilism was appreciated by Breton, is not so different from that of Breton. Valéry makes technology and a restricted rationalism incapable of recognizing otherness within itself the engine for the self-destruction of Europe. The symbol of this decline – that is, the declination – of the idea of Europe is a *bored* Hamlet – '*he broods on the taedium [l'ennui] of rehearsing the past and the folly of always trying to innovate*'[109] – coming upon the place of the skull of Yorick, and finding there many skulls:

> This one was *Lionardo*. He invented the flying man, but the flying man has not exactly served his inventor's purposes. [. . .] And that other skull was *Leibnitz*, who dreamed of universal peace. And this one was *Kant* . . . *and Kant begat Hegel, and Hegel begat Marx, and Marx begat.* . . .
>
> Hamlet hardly knows what to make of so many skulls. But suppose he forgets them! Will he still be himself? . . .[110]

The limit of this declination is reached in the automatic, because necessary, actions of a supremely rationally organized system of murderousness, an all-encompassing totalitarianism as the fate of Europe:

> By giving the name of progress to its own tendency to a fatal precision, the world is seeking to add to the benefits of life the advantages of death. A certain confusion still reigns; but in a little while all will be made clear, and we shall witness at last the miracle of an animal society, the perfect and ultimate anthill [une parfaite et définitive fourmilière].[111]

This is the ethically driven political imagination of European modernism in its acutest form that is common to a Valéry, Eliot through to Guy Debord. Valéry's 'définitive fourmilière' would become, in Debord's diction inflected through his appropriation of the French moralist tradition, 'this spoilt earth [*cette terre gâté*]' of the society of the spectacle. Since, unlike the Russian Constructivists or the Italian Futurists, there was never a celebration of technology, in no respect is this understanding of the critical thinking of European modernism an idea from

109 Valéry, 'The Crisis of the Mind', p. 100.

110 Ibid.

111 Ibid., p. 101.

which we have said, or indeed to which we can say, farewell as it constitutes the horizon of the critical experience of modernity. No European modernist outside the Russian Constructivists or the Futurists believed in the idea of progress, either in their art or their thought.

The questions concerning the qualitative and psychic dimension of movement and motility, particularly where those movements are, under certain conditions, confounded with the apparently quantitative or mechanical encompassing the possibility of any distinction between animal life and its mechanical simulacra, achieve their fullest significance in the midst of Breton's reflection on *l'humour noir* and the self-destruction of the idea of Europe. In the 1938 *Anthologie de l'humour noir*, Breton, after the *succès de scandale* of the *Exposition internationale du surréalisme*, takes up again the iconography of the mannequin in a way that returns it to 'Pourquoi je prends la direction de la Révolution surréaliste' and the cover of issue no. 4 of *La Révolution surréaliste* (fig. 65), commenting on the centuries' held curiosity of the difficulty of distinguishing, from a certain distance, authentic automata from pseudo-automata.[112] The form that this inescapable ambiguity has taken in our period, says Breton,

> is to have had it transposed by transferring the automata from the external world into the interior world. [...] Indeed, psychoanalysis has disclosed, in the depths of the mental attic, the presence of an anonymous mannequin 'without eyes, without nose and without ears', sufficiently akin to those that Giorgio de Chirico was painting towards 1916. This mannequin has revealed an extreme mobility [...] (it is from the need to give every licence to this mobility that Surrealism was born).[113]

And might we not say in the light of this passage, that *Europe*, *the idea* of Europe, had encountered the simulacra of its own unconscious wherein it found itself (like this anonymous being) 'driven by an engine of undoubted force which it obeys mathematically owing to an apparently cosmic movement which escapes it'?[114] The object of Europe. All the more so when Breton continues: 'The question which is posed, in relation to these automata as with others, is to know if there is a *conscious* being hidden in them – and to *what point conscious*?'

Given that at the metapsychological level of motility the coming into awareness of an ethical consciousness is inseparable from desire *in statu nascendi*, one could argue that the thinking of the limits of movement marks not only the limits of representation but the historical specificity and limits of

---

112 Cf. André Breton, 'Raymond Roussel', in *Anthologie de l'humour noir*; rpd in *Œuvres complètes*, vol. 2, p. 1067.

113 Ibid.

114 Ibid, p. 1068. On the idea of Europe in post-Heideggerian thinking, cf. Rodolphe Gasché, 'Alongside the Horizon', in Darren Sheppard, Simon Sparks and Colin Thomas, eds, *The Sense of Philosophy: On Jean-Luc Nancy* (London and New York: Routledge, 1997).

Surrealism whereby Surrealist experience, confronted with traumatic penetration and loss, becomes the fragmented configured body by means of which the tragic dimension of cultural experience is articulated through movement and immobility. Blanchot, in his interpretation of *Nadja*, understood the extent to which Surrealist experience enacted an understanding of negative infinity whereby its violence became intelligible in terms of its comprehension that it could not simply escape from the detested object by a simple act of negation, that, indeed, the object remains always present in some form, because the action of negation and object share the same medium, the imago, indeed. In the most Hegelian part of the *Paysan de Paris*, 'Le songe du paysan', Aragon goes so far as to establish a relation between failure and grandeur: 'A philosophy could not succeed. It is from the grandeur of its object that it derives its own grandeur; it conserves it in failure'. Blanchot long ago identified the nature of the movement of negation at work within the modes of Surrealist thinking that brings out the dimension of the imago no less than the relationship to (creative) violence:

> Surrealist *experience* aims for (it seems to me) the point of divergence from which all knowledge, as with any limited affirmation of life, escapes from itself in order to expose itself to the neutral force of dismantling [*désarrangement*]. Surrealist *experience* is experience of experience, whether this be found under a theoretical or practical form: an experience which dismantles and dismantles itself, to the extent that it develops and, developing, interrupts itself.[115]

The form of such tragic movement and immobility, of exposure and dismantling, in developing the phenomenology of experience and failure in Surrealism, in bringing out the texture of what Monnerot called *les parages*, or Blanchot *la mort enfin vécue*, is the form under which the ethical texture of Surrealist experience (*the experience of experience*) seeks, belongs to, the possibly reparative dimension *of* the work of beauty, truth and justice inseparable from *le travail du négatif à l'intérieur de la vue d'une idée de l'Europe finie* ... (fig. 67).

115 Blanchot, 'Le demain joueur', *L'Entretien infini*, p. 618.

Appendix I

Notes in the Hand of Léon Pierre-Quint Being the Record of a Conversation

Théodore Fraenkel

Source: Manuscript, Bibliothèque nationale, Paris, Nouvelle acquisition française 18360

Since this transcription was first made, the last twenty eight lines have been published in an edition of Théodore Fraenkel's *Carnets, 1916–1918* (ed. Marie-Claire Dumas with Michel Fraenkel & François Sullerot, pp. 149–150, Paris, 1990). Omissions due to illegibility are indicated by [. . .]. Italics correspond to the manuscript. This translation is published with the very kind permission of Monsieur Jacques Fraenkel.

Conversation with Théodore November 1936
Political attitude of the Surrealists

First, it had as a motto: the Revolution for the Revolution. Less a political theory than an expression of Romantic despair. Destruction of all that is. With what joy R[obert] D[esnos] will set fire to the apartments of these bourgeois masses where once he would have so liked to please and shine, where he experienced a contained rage from its vulgarity, that vulgarity of the petit bourgeois world [. . .] It's a kind of nihilist dream – not so far, it seems to me, from the Anarchism Revue Blanche of 1899. With this difference, that anarchism was a systematic theory, with an economic doctrine, consider Bakunin – a Communist doctrine for some – an individualist doctrine, for others, as one put it then – from all that nothing: certain terroristic bombings [. . .] and that *saying* of Laurent Thaillade.

The Surrealists wished to go further. Above all they sought to put their ideas into practice – Breton, tortured at once by the absolute and action, thought that Communism would be the party which would most quickly bring to the Surrealists the Revolution for which they longed. I imagine that if they thought that the Royalists were quite close to a revolution, they would have been disposed to support the Royalists . . . / a debatable idea – for the Surrealists were anti-traditionalists, to the Left, etc. . . . / It remains that the economic aspects of Communism were then a matter of indifference to them.

Soon, things changed. Marxism impassioned the Surrealists. They hated Capitalism; having maintained, from the fact of having operated in groups, a certain habit of collective discipline, at the same time they all adopt the ideas of the 'party'. Including the clichés of the party. Who desires the end desires the means. Dictatorship of the Proletariat – Lenin – The terror – The great and terrible destructions [*decimations*] – Russia. All these images attracted them and in their minds assumed a poetic color, still the same, that of their first despair: the Revolution. But at the same time they had the satisfaction of supporting their dreams through the most immediate reality of action: Communist politics.

Were they not victims of an illusion? The worker, the fate of the worker – basis of the party – was it not, in the end, a matter of complete indifference, *but for* the *hatred* of the bourgeoisie? Economic theories, instruments of work interested them only to the extent where they overturn what obtains – but not at all for what they make possible etc. . . . The Communists of the Party understood them well. They did not take the Surrealists seriously. Dissent – Polemics – an attempt at rapprochement by the Surrealist group and *Clarté* which was to end in the creation of a journal – *La Guerre Civile* – failed because the Surrealists had nothing to write on economic questions, which are the bread and butter of Communism.

Aragon indeed attempted, exceptionally, a study on the intellectual proletariat; an exception followed by some other exceptions – but which remained isolated – The *Philosophie* group, since become *L'Esprit*, was in alliance with two other groups for some weeks, but this could not be sustained and *Philosophie* was the first to withdraw. The idea which linked them all: Revolution for the sake of Revolution [*Révolution pour la Révolution*], too vague, too empty, was not able to prevail for each of these groups, considering too what was essential: Surrealism, economics, politics, mysticism [. . .] Its theory sought to sacrifice the idea of the group in favor of the revolutionary idea. Impossible for Surrealism: one cannot sacrifice everything for nothing. When the *Surrealists* then decided to *enter* the Communist Party (they did not all enter; disagreement amongst them; certain claimed that they would better aid the Party from the outside – pretext) – they were accepted with suspicion, as literary men, as bourgeois, as sons of privilege [and there was nothing that could lessen the misunderstandings]. If Breton began to attack the manner in which *L'Humanité* was directed: obviously the paper was not Surrealist since, in the end, the Surrealists wished Communism to become Surrealist.

What I regret, it's that the Surrealists had not created, in politics, an autonomous group. And if I agree with the details of their action, it is because I consider that no one better than they were undoubtedly *destined* to this action – and that having, all told, failed the present moment by attaching themselves to Communism, they still remain linked today to this action.

In Germany, there exists a workers' Communist Party, though extra-parliamentary – which groups many thousands of adherents – and which, in accepting as given Marxist theories, poses the moral and intellectual problems: what will the chief be? Who has the right to govern? etc. ...

In France, there is perhaps still much more to be done. We are living on completely outdated ideas. The reactionaries depend on the Monarchists of the 17th century – and Maurras has brought no innovation – the liberals on the ideas of the 19th century: St. Simon etc. ... – the socialists: Proudhon, 1848, L. Blanc – the Communists on Marx, etc., end 19th century. But after 1918, the 20th century really started. The war made the breach [*coupure*] – which is an abyss. Every old ideology is outdated.

Let's consider Communism for a moment. On the one hand, in Russia it is cut into two tendencies. The party in power [...] already so taken with power that it has rejected true Communism, and [on the other hand] the opposition which, in order to triumph, would like to reject the essential idea of Communism (which moreover it represents): the dictatorship and control of free discussion, democracy only for propaganda and victory. What irony!

In France, the Communists admit parliamentary democracy. Dictatorship is only therefore a means as long as Communism is not a majority in the country: if it is, no more dictatorship, no more revolution [...] the Republic becomes a Surrealist Soviet! Where, then, is your Revolution? For there is nothing unreasonable in thinking that some years hence, following an economic crisis, that the Communists may have a Parliamentary majority [...] which would be equally possible for the Socialists [...] since Socialists have really held power in England. [...] There would be no patriotism, Communists will bring about a Communist Republic.

Philosophy. Ph[ilippe] S[oupault] declares that the idea of Revolution for the sake of Revolution is an aesthetic point of view – and admits that there has been some evolution in the ideas of the *Surrealists*.

For me, the autonomous group which needs to be created, would have for its essential aim less the overturning of capitalism – thus at least it would be Marxist – than the overturning of the bourgeoisie. Moreover it would be necessary to go deeper in order to see if capitalism and bourgeoisie are not indissolubly bound.

Why? Because in the bourgeoisie everything is false, because it only allows for a disfigured life – narrow, painful, horrible. Because it is mean and heartless. Because it lacks intelligence; because it envisages nothing but what is given, the scientific. It has deformed Christianity into a Jesuistic Catholicism, into an infernal Puritanism.

Everything to rebegin: the idea of the family. The education of the child. The child *thing*, means in the mind of parents (read Jules Romain) – Children living between them. Freedom of travel etc. ... idem the sexual – idem the idea of *Patrie* and war. (This idea of war linked, it appears, to Capitalism.) Destroy as well *modern* colonialism.

I glimpse a new individualism. The individual being grouped, no longer in its family, not even by its country, but in a kind of association of young people from the age of 12 years and these diverse associations being every few years reunited *internationally* according to their intellectual and moral aptitudes or affinities.

It is only then that I should like to envisage an economic organization – based upon the associations.

I will tend much more freely toward Co-operatism – than towards the total seizure by the State of the whole of life.

For Co-operatism would organize itself quite naturally in line with the associations. ... If today I had to give a name to my Party, I should call it Individualism, Association, Cooperation.

Translated by M. Stone-Richards

Index